"In a world of resurgent inequality, a book on feminist perspectives – which prioritize issues of injustice, exclusion, and subjugation – on the current state of the knowledge and debates in marketing, communications, and consumption is most timely and welcome. The contributions deliberate and expose the gendered nature of institutional and social structures that implicate marketing practices as well as the overlooked female contributions to the production of marketing knowledge."

Guliz Ger, *Professor of Marketing, Bilkent University, Turkey*

"This invaluable and urgently needed volume will have pride of place on my bookshelves. The carefully curated chapters synthesise and foster interdisciplinary insight, debate and critique surrounding the relationships between marketing and feminism, applying rigorous scholarship in examining a rich array of gendered marketplace practices, ideologies and activism. The collection addresses intersections of gender, class, age and race from the perspectives of an international, multi-generational group of feminist scholars drawing on a range of disciplines."

Stephanie O'Donohoe, *Professor of Advertising and Consumer Culture, University of Edinburgh Business School, UK*

"This tour de force volume provides a comprehensive and innovative study of the intersections among marketing, gender, and feminist theory. These collected works deftly trace out the marginalized voices, socio-cultural complexities, historical relations, and politics-of-identity conflicts that have shaped the marketing of gender and the gendering of marketing theory and practice. *The Routledge Companion to Marketing and Feminism* is a must read for anyone seeking to understand marketing's gendered past, present and future."

Craig Thompson, *Churchill-Bascom Professor of Marketing, University of Wisconsin-Madison, USA*

The Routledge Companion to Marketing and Feminism

This comprehensive and authoritative sourcebook offers academics, researchers and students an introduction to and overview of current scholarship at the intersection of marketing and feminism.

In the last five years there has been a resurrection of feminist voices in marketing and consumer research. This mirrors a wider public interest in feminism – particularly in the media as well as the academy – with younger women discovering that patriarchal structures and strictures still limit women's development and life opportunities. The "F" word is back on the agenda – made high profile by campaigns such as #MeToo and #TimesUp. There is a noticeably renewed interest in feminist scholarship, especially amongst younger scholars, and significantly insightful interdisciplinary critiques of this new brand of feminism, including the identification of a neoliberal feminism that urges professional women to achieve a work/family balance on the back of other women's exploitation.

Consolidating existing scholarship while exploring emerging theories and ideas which will generate further feminist research, this volume will be of interest to researchers, academics and students in marketing and consumption studies, especially those studying or researching the complex inter-relationship of feminism and marketing.

Pauline Maclaran is Professor of Marketing and Consumer Research at Royal Holloway, University of London, UK.

Lorna Stevens is Associate Professor of Marketing at the University of Bath, UK.

Olga Kravets is Senior Lecturer at Royal Holloway, University of London, UK.

Routledge Companions in Business, Management and Marketing

Routledge Companions are prestige volumes which provide an overview of a research field or topic. Surveying the business disciplines, the books in this series incorporate both established and emerging research themes. Compiled and edited by an array of highly regarded scholars, these volumes also benefit from global teams of contributors reflecting disciplinary diversity.

Individually, *Routledge Companions in Business, Management and Marketing* provide impactful one-stop-shop publications. Collectively, they represent a comprehensive learning and research resource for researchers, postgraduate students and practitioners.

The Routledge Handbook of Financial Geography
Edited by Janelle Knox-Hayes and Dariusz Wójcik

The Routledge Companion to Asian Family Business
Governance, Succession, and Challenges in the Age of Digital Disruption
Edited by Ho-Don Yan and Fu-Lai Tony Yu

The Routledge Companion to Marketing Research
Edited by Len Tiu Wright, Luiz Moutinho, Merlin Stone and Richard P. Bagozzi

The Routledge Companion to Talent Management
Edited by Ibraiz Tarique

The Routledge Companion to Corporate Social Responsibility
Edited by Thomas Maak, Nicola M. Pless, Sukhbir Sandhu and Marc Olitzky

The Routledge Companion to Global Value Chains
Reinterpreting and Reimagining Megatrends in the World Economy
Edited by Renu Agarwal, Christopher Bajada, Roy Green and Katrina Skellern

The Routledge Companion to Marketing and Feminism
Edited by Pauline Maclaran, Lorna Stevens and Olga Kravets

For more information about this series, please visit: www.routledge.com/Routledge-Companions-in-Business-Management-and-Marketing/book-series/RCBUS

The Routledge Companion to Marketing and Feminism

Edited by
Pauline Maclaran, Lorna Stevens
and Olga Kravets

LONDON AND NEW YORK

First published 2022
by Routledge
2 Park Square, Milton Park, Abingdon, Oxon OX14 4RN

and by Routledge
605 Third Avenue, New York, NY 10158

Routledge is an imprint of the Taylor & Francis Group, an informa business

© 2022 selection and editorial matter, Pauline Maclaran, Lorna Stevens and Olga Kravets; individual chapters, the contributors

The right of Pauline Maclaran, Lorna Stevens and Olga Kravets to be identified as the authors of the editorial material, and of the authors for their individual chapters, has been asserted in accordance with sections 77 and 78 of the Copyright, Designs and Patents Act 1988.

All rights reserved. No part of this book may be reprinted or reproduced or utilised in any form or by any electronic, mechanical, or other means, now known or hereafter invented, including photocopying and recording, or in any information storage or retrieval system, without permission in writing from the publishers.

Trademark notice: Product or corporate names may be trademarks or registered trademarks, and are used only for identification and explanation without intent to infringe.

British Library Cataloguing-in-Publication Data
A catalogue record for this book is available from the British Library

Library of Congress Cataloging-in-Publication Data
Names: Maclaran, Pauline, editor. | Stevens, Lorna, editor. | Kravets, Olga, editor.
Title: The Routledge companion to marketing and feminism / edited by Pauline Maclaran, Lorna Stevens and Olga Kravets.
Description: 1 Edition. | New York, NY: Routledge, 2022. |
Series: Routledge companions in business, management and marketing | Originally published under title: Marketing and feminism, 2000. | Includes bibliographical references and index.
Identifiers: LCCN 2021036460 (print) | LCCN 2021036461 (ebook) | ISBN 9780367477578 (hardback) | ISBN 9781032187563 (paperback) | ISBN 9781003042587 (ebook)
Subjects: LCSH: Marketing. | Feminism. | Women consumers.
Classification: LCC HF5415 .R6426 2022 (print) | LCC HF5415 (ebook) | DDC 658.8—dc23
LC record available at https://lccn.loc.gov/2021036460
LC ebook record available at https://lccn.loc.gov/2021036461

ISBN: 978-0-367-47757-8 (hbk)
ISBN: 978-1-032-18756-3 (pbk)
ISBN: 978-1-003-04258-7 (ebk)

DOI: 10.4324/9781003042587

Typeset in Bembo
by codeMantra

Contents

List of figures   xi
List of tables   xiii
About the contributors   xiv

1 Editors' Introduction to the Companion   1
PAULINE MACLARAN, LORNA STEVENS AND OLGA KRAVETS

SECTION 1
Women in the history of marketing   15

2 Goddesses of the household: Martha Van Rensselaer and the role of home economics in marketing theory   17
MARY ELLEN ZUCKERMAN

3 Creating the critical consumer: Helen Woodward and Hazel Kyrk on self-determination and the good life   31
MARK TADAJEWSKI

4 Marketing's hidden figures: black women leaders in advertising   45
JUDY FOSTER DAVIS

5 Marketing education and patriarchal acculturation: the rhetorical work of women's advertising clubs, 1926–1940   59
JEANIE WILLS

SECTION 2
Gender representations in the marketplace   73

6 Feminist brands: what are they, and what's the matter with them?   75
CELE C. OTNES AND EILEEN M. FISCHER

7 "One, two, three, four, what are we fighting for?": deconstructing climate crisis war messaging metaphors using ecofeminism 90
SUSAN DOBSCHA AND ANDREA PROTHERO

8 Menstruation in marketing: stigma, #femvertising, and transmedia messaging 102
CATHERINE A. COLEMAN AND KATHERINE C. SREDL

9 In search of the female gaze: querying the Maidenform archive 120
ASTRID VAN DEN BOSSCHE

10 From identity politics to the politics of power: men, masculinities and transnational patriarchies in marketing and consumer research 138
WENDY HEIN AND JEFF HEARN

SECTION 3
Feminist perspectives on the body in marketing 157

11 Materializing the body: a feminist perspective 159
ANU VALTONEN AND ELINA NÄRVÄNEN

12 Transformations: is there a role for feminist activism in women's sport? 171
JAN BRACE-GOVAN

13 Women's sexual practices: the B-spot of marketing and consumer research 189
LUCIANA WALTHER

14 Taking off the blindfold: the perils of pornification and sexual abjectification 206
ALEXANDRA S. ROME

15 The quest for masculine to-be-looked-at-ness? Exploring consumption-based self-objectification among heterosexual men 222
JACOB OSTBERG

SECTION 4
Difference, diversity, and intersectionality 239

16 Are all bodies knitworthy? Interrogating race and
   intersecting axes of marginalization in knitting spaces 241
   ALEV PINAR KURUOĞLU

17 Marketing and the missing feminisms: decolonial
   feminism, and the Arab Spring 257
   NACIMA OURAHMOUNE AND HOUNAIDA EL JURDI

18 Unfolding climate change inequities through
   intersectionality, Barad's new materialism, and
   post/de-colonial Indigenous perspectives 268
   LAUREL STEINFIELD

19 Consumption beyond the binary: feminism in transgender lives 296
   SOPHIE DUNCAN SHEPHERD AND KATHY HAMILTON

20 Ageism, sexism, and women in power 308
   MINTA SANGHVI AND PHILLIP FRANK

21 Our aging bodies, ourselves 323
   LISA PEÑALOZA

SECTION 5
Gendering digital technologies in marketing 339

22 Black women's digital media and marketplace
   experiences: between buying, branding, and Black Lives Matter 341
   FRANCESCA SOBANDE

23 The symbolic violence of digital (anti-)feminist activism 351
   ALIETTE LAMBERT AND ANA-ISABEL NÖLKE

24 Big Brother is monitoring: feminist surveillance
   studies and digital consumer culture 368
   LAUREN GURRIERI AND JENNA DRENTEN

25 Seeking safety and solidarity through self-documentation: debating the power of the self(ie) in contemporary feminist culture 388
MARGARET MATICH, RACHEL ASHMAN AND ELIZABETH PARSONS

SECTION 6
Feminist futures: problems, priorities, and predictions 401

26 How the economic sex/gender system excludes women from international markets 403
LINDA SCOTT

27 The politics of epistemic marginality: testimonies-in-opposition 420
BENEDETTA CAPPELLINI AND MARTINA HUTTON

28 Women who work: the limits of the neoliberal feminist paradigm 434
CATHERINE ROTTENBERG

29 Putting pornography on the marketing agenda: a radical feminist centring of harm for women's marketplace inequality 445
LAURA MCVEY, MEAGAN TYLER AND LAUREN GURRIERI

30 Manifesting feminist marketing futures: undertaking a 'visionary' inventory
Feminist Collective 460
ELIZABETH PARSONS, DANIELA PIRANI, RACHEL ASHMAN, ATHANASIA DASKALOPOULOU, KATY KERRANE AND CATHY MCGOURAN

Index 477

Figures

9.1 "I dreamed I was bewitching in my Maidenform bra," October 1950, *Maidenform Mirror*, Maidenform Collection, Archives Center, National Museum of American History, Smithsonian Institution (NMAH.AC.0585 Box 19 Folder 0)   121

9.2 Maidenform executives and advertisers Norman, Craig & Kummel at work on the Dream contest of 1956, *Maiden-forum*, Maidenform Collection, Archives Center, National Museum of American History, Smithsonian Institution (NMAH.AC.0585 Box 21 Folder 0). Pictures are credited to *Women's Wear Daily Staff Photo*. Left: Joseph and Beatrice Coleman (on the right) meet with Florence St George and Richard C. Bouton. Right: Kay Daly and staff at NC&K (fourth from the left)   127

9.3 Stills from the 'Cocktail Promenade' party footage by Allan H. Mogensen, February 1939, Maidenform Collection, Archives Center, National Museum of American History, Smithsonian Institution (NMAH.AC.0585 OV 585)   128

9.4 Photograph of William Rosenthal, President of Maidenform (left), and Ernest Silvani, Executive Head of the Designing Department (right). *Maiden-forum*, May-June 1954, Maidenform Collection, Archives Center, National Museum of American History, Smithsonian Institution (NMAH.AC.0585 Box 22 Folder 10).   129

9.5 Left: Two golfers pose in their 'Twins' costumes, *Maidenform Mirror*, October-November 1956, Maidenform Collection, Archives Center, National Museum of American History, Smithsonian Institution (NMAH.AC.0585 Box 20 Folder 0). Right: Eileen J. Boecklen at an archaeological dig, *Maidenform Mirror*, February 1952, Maidenform Collection, Archives Center, National Museum of American History, Smithsonian Institution (NMAH.AC.0585 Box 19 Folder 0)   132

9.6 Drawing by ten-year-old Robert Baruch, son of Ann Baruch who was a Maidenform employee in Bayonne's manufacturing plant, *Maiden-forum*, November 1953, Maidenform Collection, Archives Center, National Museum of American History, Smithsonian Institution (NMAH.AC.0585 Box 22 Folder 8)   133

21.1 Women's march for the right to choose. Austin, Texas, January 2018   330

xii *Figures*

26.1. This scatterplot illustrates the vast gap between male and female ownership of land in a regionally balanced sample of about half the countries in the world. The black dots show that 70 to 90% of landholders in most countries, rich and poor, are men. Countries are shown alphabetically, starting with Algeria and ending with Zambia   412

26.2 Here the same data that appeared as a scatterplot of an alphabetical list of countries in the previous figure has been re-graphed to show instead the distribution curve. We can thus see more easily that the handful of outliers fade in importance compared to the greater bulk of the distribution between 5 and 15%. The bigger picture that women have been excluded from land ownership should therefore not be subordinated by over-emphasizing the exceptions in analysis   413

Tables

8.1	Sample Instagram Post Data	110
12.1	Summary of Participants	175
12.2	Summary of Activists' Key Points and Implications for Research	183
13.1	Scholarly Literature at the Intersection of Sex and Consumption (Sex in Advertising Excluded)	193
18.1	A Comparison and Merger of Feminisms—Intersectionality Theory + Barad's New Materialism	276
22.1	Black Women's Concerns about Corporate Co-Optation and Their Digital Content	348
23.1	Theoretical Concepts Underpinning the Theory of Symbolic Power	355

About the contributors

Rachel Ashman is a Senior Lecturer in Marketing at the University of Liverpool, UK. Her research interests lie at the interface between digital modes of communication and consumers, specifically looking at contexts such as food and entrepreneurship. Rachel is a BAM Peer Review College Member. In addition to other outlets, her work has been published in the *Journal of Consumer Research*, the *Journal of Business Research*, *Computers in Human Behavior* and *European Journal of Marketing*.

Jan Brace-Govan is an independent scholar recently retired from Monash University's Department of Marketing. Drawing on critical marketing analyses her research focuses on social justice, gender, physical activity and embodiment. Her research has appeared in leading journals and book chapters.

Benedetta Cappellini is a Professor of Marketing at the University of Durham. She is interested in food studies, consumer culture, critical marketing and sociology of consumption. Topics she has recently studied include food cultures, meal practices, austerity, intensive mothering and domestic violence.

Catherine A. Coleman (PhD, University of Illinois, Urbana-Champaign) is a Professor of Strategic Communication at Texas Christian University. Her research focuses on transformative consumer research and consumer culture, particularly issues of gender and consumer vulnerabilities. Her research has used institutional theory to understand advertising professionals' development of gendered representations and on issues of gender justice, self and happiness, brand histories, and representation in advertising. Her scholarly work has been published in the *Journal of Advertising*; *Journal of Public Policy & Marketing*; *Journal of Business Research*; *Journal of Marketing Management*; and *Consumption, Markets & Culture*, among other scholarly outlets.

Athanasia Daskalopoulou is a Senior Lecturer in Marketing at University of Liverpool Management School. Athanasia's interpretive research programme focuses on market dynamics, consumer culture theory, gender and arts marketing. Athanasia's work has been published at international peer-reviewed journals such as *Sociology*; *European Journal of Marketing*; *New Technology, Work and Employment*; *Journal of Services Marketing*; *Advances in Consumer Research*.

Susan Dobscha is a Professor of Marketing at Bentley University in Waltham, MA. Her research has appeared in such publications as *Harvard Business Review*, *Journal of Business Ethics*, *Journal of Retailing*, *Journal of Public Policy & Marketing* and *Journal of Marketing Management*. She edited two books: *Death in A Consumer Culture*, and

Handbook of Research in Gender and Marketing. Her research focuses on sustainability, gender, death and transformative leadership. She has been interviewed by the *New York Times, The Washington Post, The Philadelphia Inquirer, Fast Company* Magazine, *Quartz* Magazine, and has created podcasts for Business Insider, Better Business Bureau, Amplify and NPR Online. She is also a mother to two children, age 19 and 16, and lives in Marblehead, MA.

Jenna Drenten is Associate Professor of Marketing in the Quinlan School of Business at Loyola University Chicago. Her research explores how digital technologies and social media platforms present new opportunities for consumers to express their identities and navigate life transitions.

Sophie Duncan Shepherd is a PhD candidate at the University of Strathclyde. Their doctoral research explores transgender consumers' experiences of vulnerability and empowerment through feminist methods and analysis.

Hounaida El Jurdi an Assistant Professor of Marketing at the Olayan School of Business, AUB. Her research interests are focused on consumer culture in non-western contexts, with a specific focus on consumer identity, the body and the politics of representation. In terms of methodology, her approach is mainly interpretive and encompasses ethnographic research, historical research, hermeneutic analysis and action research. Her research is interdisciplinary in terms of theoretical grounding with a strong emphasis on transformative approaches focusing on ethical implications of marketplace practices and topics with social impact. Her work has appeared in the *Journal of Macromarketing; Journal of Consumer Marketing; Consumption, Markets & Culture;* and *Journal of Marketing Management.*

Eileen M. Fischer is a Professor of Marketing, and the Tanenbaum Chair of Entrepreneurship and Family Enterprise, in the Schulich School of Business at Toronto's York University. Her research spans the fields of marketing and entrepreneurship, and she has published in premiere journals in both fields. She is a former co-editor of the *Journal of Consumer Research* and serves on the editorial review boards of many leading marketing and entrepreneurship journals. She has a long-standing interest in feminism as it matters in marketplaces.

Judy Foster Davis, PhD, is a Professor of Marketing and Integrated Marketing Communications at Eastern Michigan University, USA. A graduate of Howard and Michigan State universities, she is a member of the Race in the Marketplace Research Network and the Editorial Advisory Board of *Advertising & Society Quarterly.* She served as a co-editor of the *Journal of Marketing Management*'s Special Issue on marketplace racial dynamics and received the journal's 2019 "Best Paper" award for "Selling whiteness? A critical review of literature on marketing and racism". She published *Pioneering African-American Women in the Advertising Business: Biographies of MAD Black WOMEN* (Routledge 2017).

Phillip Frank is an Associate Professor at Missouri Western State University. He teaches marketing research, strategic marketing, digital marketing and international marketing and trade. His research revolves around prosocial behavior and international youth culture. His articles have appeared in journals including the *Journal for Product & Brand Management,* the *Journal of Business Ethics Education* and the *Journal of*

Social Media in Society. He lives in Saint Joseph, Missouri, and spends his time when not teaching and outdoors with friends and family.

Lauren Gurrieri is a Senior Lecturer in Marketing at RMIT University, Melbourne, Australia. Her research examines gender, consumption and the marketplace, with a focus on gender-based inequalities in consumer and digital cultures.

Kathy Hamilton is a Professor of Consumption, Markets and Society at the University of Strathclyde, Glasgow, Scotland. She is an interpretive consumer researcher and has a long-standing interest in consumer vulnerability research and how various contexts, such as poverty, transform market interactions. She is currently leading an interdisciplinary project funded by the Leverhulme Trust on the ways in which community service spaces can ameliorate vulnerability. Kathy is also interested in therapeutic consumption. Her work has been published in journals such as *Journal of Consumer Research, European Journal of Marketing, Sociology, Annals of Tourism Research* and *Journal of Marketing Management*.

Jeff Hearn is a Professor Emeritus at the Hanken School of Economics, Finland; Professor of Sociology at the University of Huddersfield, UK; Senior Professor of Gender Studies at Örebro University, Sweden; and Fellow at the UK Academy of Social Science. He is a co-managing editor of *Routledge Advances in Feminist Studies and Intersectionality* book series; and was (Co-)Chair of RINGS: International Research Association of Institutions of Advanced Gender Studies 2014–2020. Recent books include: *Men of the World: Genders, Globalizations, Transnational Times*, Sage, 2015; *Revenge Pornography*, with Matthew Hall, Routledge, 2017; *Engaging Youth in Activism, Research and Pedagogical Praxis: Transnational and Intersectional Perspectives on Gender, Sex, and Race*, co-ed. with Tamara Shefer, Kopano Ratele, Floretta Boonzaier, Routledge, 2018; *Unsustainable Institutions of Men: Transnational Dispersed Centres, Gender Power, Contradictions*, co-ed. with Ernesto Vasquez del Aguila, Marina Hughson, Routledge, 2019; and *Age at Work*, with Wendy Parkin, Sage, 2021.

Wendy Hein is a Senior Lecturer in Marketing at Birkbeck, University of London. Her interest in gender stems from her PhD at the University of Edinburgh, which focused on men's consumption practices. Wendy has been a co-ordinator of marketing as a subject discipline of the UN PRME gender equality working group since 2011, is a board member of the Macromarketing Society and is a co-founding and advisory board member of GENMAC (Gender Markets Consumers). She has presented on gender issues in markets, marketing and consumption at major international conferences, and published in various edited books and journals such as the *Journal of Public Policy & Marketing* and the *Journal of Business Research*.

Martina Hutton is a Senior Lecturer in Marketing at Royal Holloway University of London. Her research focuses on economic inequality, consumer poverty and marketplace stress and exclusion. With a PhD from the internationally renowned UCD School of Social Justice, she is an experienced qualitative PEFT (Participatory, Emancipatory, Feminist, Transformative) researcher, engaging with diverse groups of people experiencing poverty/deprivation and the stakeholders who represent their interests. Her work appears in the *Journal of Business Research*; *Journal of Public Policy & Marketing*; *European Journal of Marketing*; *Consumption, Markets & Culture*; *Qualitative Market Research*; and the *Journal of Marketing Management*.

About the contributors xvii

Katy Kerrane is a Lecturer in Marketing at the University of Liverpool Management School, UK. Her research interests revolve around family consumption, motherhood, gender and ethnicity. She has presented her research to a range of academic audiences (e.g. British Sociological Association, European Advances in Consumer Research) and has published in the *European Journal of Marketing* and *Sociology*.

Olga Kravets is a Senior Lecturer at Royal Holloway, University of London and holds a PhD in Economics from the University of Sydney, Australia. Her research interests are in politics of consumer culture, with the focus on studying inequalities from critical theory, feminist and decolonial perspectives. She has been a co-organiser of *Consumption, Markets, and Culture* Doctoral Seminar since 2007 and she co-edited The SAGE *Handbook of Consumer Culture*. Her research has been published in the *Journal of Marketing, Business History Review, Journal of Material Culture, Marketing Theory, Journal of Macromarketing, Journal of Marketing Management*, among others and edited books.

Alev Pınar Kuruoğlu is an Assistant Professor with the Consumption, Culture and Commerce research unit at the University of Southern Denmark. Her main research and teaching interests lie within the political, spatial and affective dimensions of markets and consumer cultures. Her current research projects attend to the intersections of social class, ethnicity and centre-periphery dynamics in market-mediated contexts such as gyms, music scenes, food spaces and online craft communities. Her work has been published in *Consumption, Markets and Culture* and the *Journal of Sociology* as well as in edited peer-reviewed books. She co-hosts the *Tales of Consumption* podcast.

Aliette Lambert is a Lecturer of Marketing, Business and Society at the University of Bath. Her research focuses on identity and subjectivity in relation to digital and consumer culture, as well as issues related to sustainability, which she studies from critical, feminist perspectives. Her work has been published in journals such as *Academy of Management Journal, Marketing Theory, Journal of Travel Research, Psychology & Marketing* and *Journal of Business Ethics*. Aliette's teaching revolves around critical perspectives on digital (marketing) culture; she is inspired by her students who illuminate important issues around digital life and practice, such as those addressed in this book.

Pauline Maclaran is a Professor of Marketing and Consumer Research at Royal Holloway, University of London. Her research interests focus on cultural aspects of contemporary consumption, and she adopts a critical perspective to analyse the ideological assumptions that underpin many marketing activities, particularly in relation to gender issues. Her work includes co-editing *Marketing and Feminism: Current Issues and Research* (2000).

Margaret Matich is a feminist activist, writer and curator. Their research centres on the contemporary feminist movement, contemporary art, visual culture and consumption. More specifically, her recent work examines zine culture, digital protest, the aesthetics of resistance and feminist theorisations and representations of the body.

Cathy McGouran is a Lecturer in Marketing at the University of Liverpool Management School. Her interpretive research program primarily focuses on sustainability and marketing ethics. Cathy's work has been published in journals such as the *European Journal of Marketing* and the *Journal of Strategic Marketing*, and she has presented her research at several international conferences.

Laura McVey is a doctoral student in Marketing at RMIT University, Melbourne, Australia. Her research examines the intersection of markets and violence against women, specifically through the context of the online pornography industry.

Elina Närvänen is an Associate Professor of Services and Retailing at Tampere University. She also leads the research group "Wastebusters" which focuses on issues of waste and circular economy. Her research interests are in interpretive consumer research, sustainability and qualitative research methods. She has published her work in several international journals and books, including *European Journal of Marketing*; *Journal of Public Policy & Marketing*; and *Consumption, Markets & Culture*.

Ana-Isabel Nölke's research revolves around the sociology of consumption, with particular focus on diversity marketing in terms of the representation of marginalised groups in the media. As a researcher, she assures the impact of her work through consulting and seminars for advertising agencies, companies and the wider public. She is part of the editorial board for LGBTQI$^+$ diversity of the Spanish publishing house *Editorial Comares*.

Jacob Ostberg is a Professor of Advertising and PR at Stockholm Business School at Stockholm University, Sweden. He earned his PhD in 2003 at Lund University, Sweden. His research interests revolve around how meaning is created in the intersection of marketing, popular culture and consumers' lived lives. In particular, Ostberg has been interested in questions around gender and masculinity in a Nordic setting, and how the influence of a particular state-sponsored gender ideology has shaped consumer culture.

Cele C. Otnes is a Professor of Marketing and the Anthony J. Petullo Chair of Business Administration in the Gies College of Business at the University of Illinois at Urbana-Champaign. Her research interests explore the intersection of rituals and consumer behaviour. She is the co-author with Pauline Maclaran of *Royal Fever: The British Monarchy in Consumer Culture*, of *Cinderella Dreams: The Allure of the Lavish Wedding* with Elizabeth Pleck, and of articles on gift-giving and ritualistic consumption in journals rooted in the disciplines of marketing, anthropology and advertising.

Nacima Ourahmoune is an Associate Professor at Kedge Business School, France. Her research tackles critical and socio-cultural approaches of branding and consumption. One of her research areas examines gender justice issues in established and emerging markets. Her work has appeared in the *Journal of Public Policy & Marketing, Marketing Theory; Journal of Business Research; Journal of Macromarketing; Consumption, Markets & Culture; and Journal of Marketing Management*. Nacima is a board member at GENMAC (Gender Markets Consumers), an academic and advocacy group.

Elizabeth Parsons is a Professor of Marketing at the University of Liverpool Management School. Her research falls broadly into the areas of Consumer Culture, Critical Marketing and Organisation Studies. Recent topics include marketplace exclusion, gender and identity at work and mealtime and food cultures. She is a co-editor in Chief of *Marketing Theory*, a journal that promotes critical and alternative approaches to marketing scholarship.

Lisa Peñaloza is a Professor of Marketing at KEDGE Business School, Bordeaux, France, where she teaches cultural branding strategy, qualitative research and consumer culture in the marketing MS, Executive DBA and PhD programs. Her ethnographic research explores how people collectively produce identity and community, with attention to intersectionalities of gender, race/ethnicity and class as such identities and communities converge and diverge in consumption and markets.

Daniela Pirani is a Lecturer in Marketing at the University of Liverpool. Her research interests include gender performances in the marketplace, cultural branding, food practices and visual consumption. She has published on the commodification of veganism, on family in advertising and on the creation of brand practices.

Andrea Prothero is a Professor of Business and Society at University College Dublin, Ireland, and Co-Director of the UCD Centre for Business and Society (CeBaS). Her research broadly explores the area of marketing in society with a key focus on sustainability and gender issues.

Alexandra S. Rome is an Assistant Professor of Marketing at ICN Business School. Her research focuses broadly on consumer culture with a focus on gender, sexuality and the market mediation of social life. Her current research agenda includes several projects exploring the pornification of culture and the role of digital technologies in consumption. Her work has been published in journals including *Marketing Theory*, the *Journal of Macromarketing* and *Psychology & Marketing*.

Catherine Rottenberg is an Associate Professor in the Department of American and Canadian Studies at the University of Nottingham. Her most recent books include the co-authored *The Care Manifesto* (Verso, 2020) and the monograph *The Rise of Neoliberal Feminism* (Oxford University Press, 2018).

Minta Sanghvi is an Associate Professor in the Management and Business Department at Skidmore College, where she teaches business and marketing, and a seminar on gender and political marketing in the United States. Her research centres around gender and intersectionality in marketing and consumption. Her book *Gender and Political Marketing in the United States and the 2016 Presidential Election: An Analysis of Why She Lost* was published by Palgrave MacMillan in 2019. She has published articles in the *Journal of Marketing Management* and *Journal of Business Research*. Taking her research beyond words, Dr. Sanghvi co-curated an art exhibit titled: Never done: 100 years of women in politics and beyond at Frances Young Tang Teaching Museum.

Linda Scott is an Emeritus DP World Professor of Entrepreneurship and Innovation at the University of Oxford, and the author of *The Double X Economy: The Epic Potential of Women's Empowerment*, a book shortlisted for the Royal Society Prize for Best Science Book of 2020, as well as recognised by the *Financial Times*/McKinsey Best Business Book of 2020. Professor Scott has been a Senior Consulting Fellow to Chatham House, the Royal Institute for International Affairs. She founded the Global Business Coalition for Women's Economic Empowerment and currently consults for both USAID and the World Bank on gender and economics. Scott works with multinational corporations, international agencies, national governments and global NGOs designing and testing programs to better include women in the world economy.

Francesca Sobande is a Lecturer in Digital Media Studies and the Director of the BA Media, Journalism and Culture programme at JOMEC at Cardiff University.

Francesca's work focuses on the media experiences of Black women in Britain, digital remix culture, creative work and the politics of popular culture and power. She is the author of *The Digital Lives of Black Women in Britain* (Palgrave Macmillan, 2020), and her research has been published in international journals including *European Journal of Cultural Studies*; *European Journal of Marketing*; *Marketing Theory*; *Television & New Media*; *Consumption, Markets & Culture*; and *Communication, Culture & Critique*.

Katherine C. Sredl (PhD at the University of Illinois, Urbana-Champaign) is a Clinical Professor at Loyola University Chicago https://orcid.org/0000-0001-7426-9836. Dr. Sredl's research broadly addresses the sociology of consumption in two interrelated domains of marketing: consumer behaviour and media. She applies theories of social hierarchies to understand globalisation as an intersectional phenomenon in post-socialist, post-conflict and post-colonial contexts, developing theory on ideology, vulnerability, privilege and gender justice, and has focused on issues of media and gender to study representation of changing gender norms in media. Sredl's scholarly work has been published in the *Journal of Macromarketing*; *Consumption Markets & Culture*; and numerous edited volumes, among other academic outlets.

Laurel Steinfield (DPhil, University of Oxford) is an Assistant Professor of Marketing at Bentley University. Her research focuses on social stratifications, including gender, racial, class and global North-South hierarchies. As a sociologist, transformative consumer researcher and marketing professor, she studies how social stratifications interact with marketplace dynamics and how resulting injustices may be transformed through public- or private-enterprise interventions, social innovations and/or entrepreneurial endeavours. She has published in numerous journals and various edited books. She is on the advisory board of GENMAC (Gender Markets Consumers) and Transformative Consumer Research, is a member of RIM (Race in the Marketplace) and works with organisations in their empowerment endeavours.

Lorna Stevens is an Associate Professor of Marketing at the University of Bath. Her research is primarily in the domains of media consumption, experiential consumption, advertising, branding and popular culture. Much of her work applies a feminist lens to critique cultural texts and explore their underlying gendered ideologies. She co-edited *Marketing and Feminism: Current Issues and Research* (2000) and has published in a range of journals including *Sociology, European Journal of Marketing, Journal of Retailing* and *Journal of Macromarketing*.

Mark Tadajewski is currently a Visiting Honorary Professor of Marketing at the University of York and Royal Holloway, University of London. He has a long-standing interest in the development of marketing theory. He has published extensively, edits the *Journal of Marketing Management*, acts as an Associate Editor for the *Journal of Historical Research in Marketing* and functions as a co-editor of two book series for Routledge.

Meagan Tyler is a Senior Lecturer in the School of Management and a research theme leader in the Centre for People, Organisation and Work (CPOW) at RMIT University, Melbourne, Australia. Her research interests are based around feminist theory and gender inequality in a range of contexts.

Anu Valtonen is a Professor of Cultural Economy at the University of Lapland, Faculty of Social Sciences. Her research interests relate to critical and feminist theories, feminist new materialism, qualitative methodologies, bodies, senses, sleep and more-than-human issues. Her work has been published, for instance, in *Human Relations*; *Management Learning*; *Organization*; *Annals of Tourism Research*; *Journal of Material Culture*; *Journal of Marketing Management*; and *Consumption, Markets & Culture*.

Astrid Van den Bossche is a Lecturer in Digital Marketing and Communications at the Department of Digital Humanities at King's College London. Prior to joining King's College, she was a Lecturer in Marketing at Goldsmiths, University of London, and she completed her DPhil at the Saïd Business School at the University of Oxford. Her research interests span across marketing history and theory, economic socialisation through fiction and computational methods in the study of consumer culture.

Luciana Walther, DSc, is an Associate Professor at the Federal University of São João Del Rei, Brazil. Her research examines the intersections of marketing, consumption, gender, sexuality and sustainability, drawing on qualitative methods, namely, depth interviews, projective techniques, ethnography, videography and art-based research. In 2017, she earned the honourable mention of the Sidney Levy Award, for the second-best Consumer Culture Theory dissertation-based article published in the previous year. She is currently the Latin America Representative on the Board of the Consumer Culture Theory Consortium. Her recent work can be found in the *Journal of Business Research*, *Journal of Marketing Management*, *Marketing Theory* and *Handbook of Research on Gender and Marketing*.

Jeanie Wills is an Associate Professor and DK Seaman Chair in Technical and Professional Communication in the Ron and Jane Graham School of Professional Development in the College of Engineering at the University of Saskatchewan. While not a "pioneer" of advertising as most of her research subjects are, Jeanie was the Creative Director of a midmarket Canadian radio station for most of the 1980s. From there, she studied Rhetoric and Popular Culture, earning an Interdisciplinary PhD and writing a dissertation that examined religious metaphors in the memoirs of the early American advertising men like Claude Hopkins and George Rowells. Wondering where all the women in advertising were, Jeanie began archival research in 2013 and found them in the archives with the help and financial assistance of Schlesinger Library, Radcliffe. She is also grateful for the funding support of the Social Sciences and Humanities Research Council of Canada.

Mary Ellen Zuckerman is a Distinguished Service Professor and Dean of the School of Business at SUNY Geneseo. She has served as Dean of the School of Business at Ithaca College and Provost at SUNY Brockport. She holds a PhD in History and an MBA in Finance from Columbia University in NYC. She has published three books and numerous articles focused on the history of advertising, the magazine industry, women's magazines, the market research field and gender and advertising. She is currently working on a biography of home economist and education leader Martha Van Rensselaer.

1 Editors' Introduction to the Companion

Pauline Maclaran, Lorna Stevens and Olga Kravets

Against the backdrop of a formidable feminist resurgence, this collection aims to provide a leading sourcebook on marketing and feminism that offers academics, researchers and students an overview of contemporary scholarship. Fast growing online grassroots activism, as well as silence-breaking movements such as #MeToo and #TimesUp, have fuelled a renewed interest in feminism. Socio-political demonstrations against gendered violence have become both prominent and global. For instance, a song composed by a feminist collective in Santiago, Chile, to mark the International Day for the Elimination of Violence Against Women (2019) went viral, sparking mass protests in over two dozens of countries and hundreds of cities across the world. The song titled 'The Rapist Is You' resonated powerfully with millions of women globally as it foregrounded the systemic nature of rape culture and violence, thus articulating and bringing feminist theories to the masses (*BBC News*, 2019). Similarly, a local protest, the Aurat March in Pakistan (2018), has now become an annual protest around the world to mark International Women's Day, with many voices uniting to demand fundamental human rights for women and protest against continued abuses and experiences of violence. Within the academy, greater diversity in relation to conceptions of feminist subjectivities has arisen, to acknowledge and make more visible the many constituencies that have historically been excluded in feminist theorising, namely queer, lesbian, gay, bisexual and trans women as well as Black and ethnic minority women (Dean and Aune, 2015). In relation to the marketing discipline, the need is as great as ever for scholarly research in this area, research that questions the ongoing gendered nature of institutional and social structures that implicate marketing practices and activities.

Feminist scholarship has long played a major role in revealing how the gendered nature of much theorising often masks taken-for-granted assumptions that embed heteronormative ideologies about the roles of men and women in society. Thus, initial critiques of marketing came from outside the marketing discipline, led by second-wave feminists in the 1960s and 70s. Activists such as Betty Friedan (1963) saw marketers as being complicit in a patriarchal system that sought to manipulate and control women through domesticity. They targeted advertising in particular where negative female stereotypes abounded, stereotypes that served to reinforce passive, decorative models of compliant femininity.

As regards marketing and consumer research scholarship, feminist perspectives first arrived during the 1990s, undertaken by feminists who worked in marketing departments within universities and who could elaborate more deeply on the gendered nature of marketing activities and the markets they underpinned. Delving into the feminised position of the consumer, such research exposed the masculinist biases of much

DOI: 10.4324/9781003042587-1

marketing discourse that reinforced gender norms, privileging masculine attributes and values (Costa, 1991; Bristor and Fischer 1993; Hirschman, 1993; Fischer and Bristor, 1994). Feminist scholars within marketing were better placed to understand the intricate workings of the marketer/consumer dyad together with the nuanced transfers of meaning involved in exchange processes. For example, Linda Scott (2005) used her marketing knowledge to critique feminist reductions of fashion to sexual objectification. She argued that this over-emphasis on appearance worked to exclude many women and impeded the movement's progress to achieve its true aims of equality for all women around the globe (Scott, 2005).

This initial work stimulated further research in the area addressing itself to the ideological biases of much marketing and consumer research and culminating in the various studies that contributed to an edited collection on *Marketing and Feminism* (2000) undertaken by two of the editors for this present volume. Subsequent work on feminism and marketing remained a steady trickle through the early 2000s but seemed to be somewhat subsumed into wider identity politics debates within interpretivist consumer research or consumer culture theory, as the former has come to be more commonly known (Cova, Maclaran and Bradshaw, 2012).

In the last decade, however, there has been a resurrection of feminist voices in marketing and consumer research, a resurrection that mirrors the wider public interest in feminism to which we have just referred. As young women around the world discover that patriarchal ideologies, structures and strictures still limit women's development and life opportunities, they harness the power of the internet to reposition the 'F' word, making it mainstream, high profile and ubiquitous. This renewed feminist activism has also manifested itself on the streets, most recently – at the time of writing this introduction – in the Reclaim These Streets campaign in the UK, and the widespread vigils to raise concerns about women's safety at night following the murder of a young woman as she walked home through a main London thoroughfare at 9 pm in March 2021. These vigils recall the Reclaim the Night movement, founded in the UK in 1977, which continues to be active. Nowhere has this type of movement been more prominent than in India where the horrors of an ongoing rape culture have been well-documented (Varman, Goswami and Vijay, 2018). One of India's leading feminist movements, the #IWillGoOut campaign began in 2016 and has organised nationwide marches to protest against sexual harassment on the streets and demand safer public spaces for women and the LGBTQI communities.

Returning to academia, there are insightful interdisciplinary critiques of new brands of feminism, particularly the identification of a neoliberal feminism (Rottenberg, 2018) that urges professional women to achieve a work/family balance at the expense of other women's exploitation. Within marketing, the focus on the role of the market in gender (in)justice has intensified with studies revealing insights about the marketisation of women's empowerment and the global gender asymmetries in marketing and consumer behaviour (Hein et al., 2016). Even marketing initiatives designed to do good – i.e. social marketing campaigns or fair trade schemes – may be misaligned with the embodied realities of producers and consumers in developing economies. Such studies have prompted renewed calls to make gender visible and to identify gender power in market systems.

Amidst this resurgence of interest in feminist issues, we are pleased to note the recent flurry of special issues in the marketing journals that shine the spotlight on gender. The *Journal of Macromarketing* published a special issue in September 2020 on gender issues

(Gurrieri, Previte and Prothero, 2020). The co-editors identify key themes in gender scholarship: identity in the marketplace, representation, gender roles, vulnerability and quality of life; binary differences; and the relationship between gender, markets, marketing and society. They also discuss the gendered structural and systemic inequalities within the marketing academy itself. Drawing on the Queen chess-piece analogy they argue that macromarketing topics need to be similarly mobile, fluid and adaptable. The overlapping issues of class, race and age co-exist with gender, and they advocate for more feminist theorisations and tools to dismantle deep-seated biases in how we acquire knowledge, paying greater attention to issues of emancipation and social change.

The Spring of 2021 saw three special issues on gender. Coleman, Fischer and Tuncay-Zayer co-edited a special issue on Gender, Markets and Consumers in the *Journal of the Association for Consumer Research* (published online 19 March 2021). In their editorial they consider the gendered inequalities that have been brought into sharp focus in the past year. In response to this they propose a research agenda that addresses gender issues in relation to intersecting strands of socio-economic and racial inequities, healthcare, food and housing poverty; the 'invisible labour' of housework, caregiving and home-schooling; and the alarming rise of domestic violence in lockdown.

The *Journal of Marketing Management* also featured two special issues in quick succession on gender, the first published online March 2021 and the second in April 2021. In the first, Andy Prothero and Mark Tadajewski address inequalities and injustices in marketing practice and academia and discuss the growing impetus amongst feminist activists to protest and seek social transformation and consciousness raising. In a memorable turn of phrase they refer to the 'hydras of neoliberalism, the patriarchy and its enablers', and critique the rise of hyper-individual and performance-based subjectification. The second special issue by Susan Dobscha and Jacob Ostberg (2021) directs attention back to consumption, markets and marketing organisations. In a prophetic note they emphasise the pressing need to build the gender-marketing corpus in the face of increasing resistance to gender ideology from conservative majorities around the globe.

All of these special issues are testament to the relevance of feminist perspectives in marketing, and all of them identify new areas for research at this interface. In order to maximise this renewed interest, our volume consolidates existing scholarship and serves as a springboard to further generative research. The collection – comprising 30 chapters across 6 separate sections – includes a mix of international feminist researchers, and we have tried to include early career scholars alongside more established scholars. We thus hope this volume will provide academics and students with convenient access to feminist perspectives in marketing and consumer behaviour, offering as it does, a single repository on the current state of knowledge, contemporary debates and relevant literature. We believe it will also serve as a resource for researchers not only in marketing and consumer studies, but also those in media and cultural studies, communications and women's studies.

The proposed structure of six thematic sections is intended to reflect the increasing interdisciplinary diversity of contemporary research at the intersection of marketing and feminism. The first section foregrounds some of the female contributions to marketing theory and practice that have hitherto been overlooked, the 'silent voices' in marketing. This is in keeping with the feminist project to reinstate women's voices – omitted in most historical accounts because of prevailing patriarchal contexts and value systems – across the social and physical sciences. The four subsequent sections feature topics in marketing and consumer research most impacted by feminist approaches and theory, namely, representation, the body, intersectionality and digital technology. The final section on feminist futures highlights current limitations whilst mapping directions for the future.

Section 1: Women in the history of marketing

A pressing priority for feminist scholars is to investigate how women's voices are missing from historical accounts and to reinstate women in the production of disciplinary knowledge. When it comes to the history of marketing thought, women do not usually feature in the long list of male marketing scholars noted for their contributions to the discipline (see, for example, the Sage Publications series, *Legends in Marketing,* which is all male).

To counter this historic exclusion our first section showcases some of the important contributions to both theory and practice made by women. We are particularly pleased to have Mary Ellen Zuckerman commence the section with her chapter on 'Goddesses of the Household', a term applied to home economists whose expertise guided women in household management and the use of new, more efficient technologies. Zuckerman initially drew attention to the overlooked role of home economists and their many intersections with marketing in her pioneering paper on the topic with Mary Carsky (Zuckerman and Carsky, 1990). Now, for our volume, she documents the contributions of home economist and educator Martha Van Rensselaer, named by the National League of Women Voters in 1923 as one of the 12 most influential women in the US. Van Rensselaer played a key role in the developing field of home economics, a discipline intersecting with marketing in these years. Whilst maintaining a strong focus on educating consumers, especially rural dwellers, about new products and technology, she created and grew the home economics department at Cornell University.

The home economics theme continues in Chapter 3 as Mark Tadajewski explicates the foundational role played by home economist Hazel Kyrk in critical marketing studies through her early critiques of capitalist market relations. Challenging conventional economic theory, Kyrk's work emphasised the importance of understanding the role of context in shaping consumer decisions, a role that we tend to take for granted now. She also highlighted the ways purchasers can be active participants who influence producers rather than passively succumbing to marketplace logics. As such Kyrk was an early pioneer of the co-creation of value theory widely acknowledged in contemporary marketing and consumer research. In the same chapter, Tadajewski features a second major analyst of marketing and consumption behaviours, Helen Woodward, another female in marketing history whose work has also been under-appreciated to date. This time the focus is on the advertising industry where Woodward used her skills not only to develop highly successful campaigns for clients but also to critique the manipulative lifestyle visions that proliferated in women's magazine advertising, visions that failed to tell the full story about their products. In this respect, Woodward joined various activist projects and lobbying groups to foreground consumer rights and encourage more critically reflexive consumption.

The advertising industry remains under scrutiny in Chapter 4, but now the spotlight is on the intersection of race and gender. Calling our attention to Black women leaders in advertising, Judy Foster Davis paints a rich picture of the many obstacles these women – Barbara Gardner Proctor, Caroline R. Jones, Joel P. Martin, Valerie Graves and Carol H. Williams – had to overcome to forge a successful career in advertising. She exposes the power matrix of domination within the advertising industry that manifested at structural, disciplinary, hegemonic and interpersonal levels for these women and limited their professional opportunities. Yet, despite the many barriers they encountered, the women featured here persevered, using pragmatic forms of resistance and activism, to ultimately achieve success in this industry. Importantly, in her conclusion, Foster Davis follows a tradition in the Black community to 'Say Their Names' and acknowledges other Black women in the advertising industry who faced similar hurdles but whose contributions are still largely invisible in our discipline's history.

Women's advertising clubs were set up in the early part of the 20th century to champion women's employment in the industry and to sell an ideology about women's 'fitness' for the profession. In the final chapter on historical aspects, Jeanie Wills details how, even though these clubs perpetuated sexist stereotypes of the new businesswoman, they also created space for women in business by publishing in trade magazines and networking nationally and internationally.

Section 2: Gender representations in the marketplace

In the section on representation it is fitting that we acknowledge the foundational work done by the late, great Barbara B. Stern who brought feminist literary theory into the study of advertising texts and their narratives, drawing our attention to the gender codes embedded in them and the gender issues involved in our interpretation of them. She did the groundwork that showed us how a feminist literary lens can enable us to deconstruct texts to reveal their underlying gendered ideologies and constructs. The five chapters below all shine a light on gendered narratives in the contemporary marketplace, addressing the evolving issues, conflicts and contestations of gender representation and indeed feminism itself within them.

We begin with a discussion of the nature of feminist brands, some driven by genuine commitment and others somewhat more cynical in their intentions. In Chapter 6, Cele Otnes and Eileen Fischer assess those aspects of feminism most prone to co-option for branding purposes, and the brands that proudly proclaim their feminist credentials. Their analysis shows the polyvocality of these marketplace manifestations, reflecting the multiplicity of feminist perspectives and principles on which they draw. Framing their discussion in relation to product, person and movement, they consider the challenges and contentions of feminist branding: the dominance of neoliberal feminist perspectives, the lack of intersectionality and inclusiveness and the insistence on individual rather than collective action, to name but a few. They also address the perils and pitfalls of nailing one's feminist colours to the mast, namely the stigmatism and exclusion that may result. Nevertheless, their chapter concludes that feminism and branding may be comfortable bedfellows if the latter comes from a genuine place, namely commitment to feminist principles of equality and emancipation, and they conclude by proposing an agenda for future research at this fascinating intersection.

Susan Dobscha and Andrea Prothero, Chapter 7, consider gendered representation in a very different sphere: that of the eco-system and the climate crisis. They critique the enduring and persistent use of the military metaphor in the marketing discipline, showing how this narrative is also the preferred one in climate crisis movements. Offering an eco-feminist perspective, they counteract this masculinist narrative in how the climate crisis is represented. To demonstrate the dominance of the military metaphor they analyse the rhetoric of the World War Zero movement and contrast this with that of the Extinction Rebellion movement. The latter, they suggest, primarily draws on metaphors aligned with eco-feminist principles, such as collective responsibility, non-violence and the inter-connectedness and interdependence of nature and society. Ultimately, they argue that the climate crisis privileges a masculine, 'conflict' narrative over a feminine, 'connect' one. Their chapter is a rallying cry for an eco-feminist perspective in how the climate crisis is framed, represented and communicated.

The next study, Chapter 8, considers femvertising and how sanitary product brands use feminist discourses and social movements to position their brands. Catherine Coleman and Katherine Sredl chart the difficulties brands have as they navigate the stigmatised waters surrounding menstruation, and the narratives of care, protection, concealment and freedom that predominate in their messaging. Offering a review of the menstruation stigma literature, they show how women are positioned as morally and physically inferior, cursed by their bodies' menstrual cycles. To illustrate their points they use examples of femvertising from Dove's 'Campaign for Real Beauty' in 2004 to current examples such as Always' #Like a Girl campaign. Negative framing persists, they argue, with Always emphasising what women can do despite menstruation, thus continuing to shy away from the reality of menstruation as a natural process and reinforcing a shame and stigma narrative. In terms of challenging the stigma, young feminists on Instagram are leading the vanguard to change how menstruation (and being a woman) is represented. Through their shared lived experiences they are building a 'confidence culture' that may go some way to de-stigmatise menstruation, challenge brands and healthcare economics and perhaps reframe how the female body and its natural cycles are represented by such brands in the marketplace.

Astrid Van den Bossche in Chapter 9 also focuses on the relationship between advertising and feminism, taking us back in time to an advertising campaign for Maidenform that ran from 1949 to 1969. The campaign was based on an 'I Dreamed …' narrative and caused both widespread amusement and condemnation throughout the 20 years it ran. The ads drew on tropes associated with allure and bewitchment to show the powerful effect of women displaying themselves in their bras in everyday settings, using humour and sexual innuendo that reflected the prevailing attitudes and norms of the time. Rather than discussing the ads from a Freudian perspective, Van den Bossche reframes the campaign from a feminist perspective, showing that whilst the campaign can be interpreted from a critical, male gaze perspective, it can also be viewed from a female gaze one. In doing so she argues that a more nuanced and emancipatory narrative emerges, one of female agency and power. Her chapter suggests that in gender representation analyses we also need to consider the audience(s) of those texts as well as the historical, social and cultural context from which they spring.

The final chapter in our section, Chapter 10, turns the spotlight on men, masculinity and transpatriarchies. Wendy Hein and Jeff Hearn consider existing work on masculinity in marketing and consumer research, which has typically focused on representation and men's identity projects in the marketplace. They argue that we need to go beyond this to consider the wider political, systemic and structural forces that shape us as gendered subjects. Masculinity research in our field has not typically grappled with issues of gender power structures and patriarchy, and nor has it problematised the category of men. However, there is a broader critical stream that theorises hegemonic masculinity, men and patriarchal relations, and the authors call for more work on the hegemony of men that is de-naturalised, deconstructed and transnationalised. The apolitical and un-feminist emphasis needs to change, they argue, so that we critically interrogate the global practices and systems that support and reinforce continued gender inequalities. They conclude that the personal continues to be political and transcends the private sphere and national borders. It is therefore time that researchers on men and masculinity grasp the nettle of transpatriarchies and the myriad forms of 'disaster patriarchy' spawned by it across the world.

Section 3: Feminist perspectives on the body in marketing

Reclaiming the female body has been central to feminist scholarship for a considerable period of time, and this section reflects its continued importance in feminist research in our domain. The works of embodied or corporeal feminists and of French feminist writers have contributed much to our understanding of how we can research the body beyond the Cartesian thinking that has served women so badly in the past. More recently, feminist researchers have turned to embodied theory as a means of understanding the connections and negotiations that all bodies engage in and seek to reconcile the mind and body (gendered) thinking that persists. The five chapters in this section continue this debate, with contributions that explore embodied experiences in the marketplace; women's bodies as sources of physical prowess and potential power, female sexuality and sexual practices; and gender issues in relation to objectification, subjectification and abjectification in the marketplace.

We are pleased to begin this section with Chapter 11 from Anu Valtonen and Elina Närvänen whose work has made an important contribution to our understanding of the body, embodied experiences and material practices, and the gender issues embedded therein. They critique how much work in consumer research has framed the body as an object of display or as a self-identity construction project that is subordinate to and separate from the mind, thus reinforcing dualistic thinking. Pointing to the new materialist turn in research on the body, they emphasise that bodies are not just discursive, performative entities but are also lived in. Materialist feminists emphasise the 'fleshy, biological, material body' and its interactions with its socio-material surroundings, including the natural world and non-human others. The authors demonstrate this theoretical lens in relation to two case studies – on sleep and food waste – showing the entanglement of the body with social and discursive constructions. Overall, they challenge us to embrace a materialist feminist perspective as a means to dismantle the patriarchal, social dominance of much research in our field.

Jan Brace-Govan continues to explore the dominance of masculinist perspectives in Chapter 12 on women's sport and the potential for feminist activism within it. She shows how binary thinking positions women as having weak bodies and unstable minds and discusses the socio-cultural conditioning that impacts on women's sport, including the valorising of masculine codes in competitive sports management and indeed in management generally. Whilst she shows how women's sports are beginning to be taken seriously, she also notes that women continue to be under-represented in leadership roles within it. Findings from a study conducted with activists show how feminists can collectively challenge the patriarchal framing of competitive sports. The chapter concludes that collectivity and connection, mentoring, intersectional thinking and

8 Pauline Maclaran et al.

decolonialisation theories may bring about opportunities for transformation in women's sports and for feminist activism within them.

Chapter 13 turns to female sexuality and sexual practices. Luciana Walther notes the reluctance of marketing researchers to engage in these topics and seeks to address that in her overview of research on sexuality, erotic consumption and feminist perspectives and issues pertaining to it. Acknowledging the problematics of women's erotic consumption, she draws on a poststructuralist, feminism lens to discuss the inherent tensions between subjects' perception of themselves as free agents whilst simultaneously engaging in practices that affect their sense of themselves as equal partners. Revealing how the power of the virgin/whore binary persists in Brazil, she argues that postfeminist perspectives have thwarted alternative envisionings of women's sexuality and their sexual practices. She concludes with a call for more research to challenge the 'blind spot' of this seemingly taboo topic.

Alexandra Rome also explores female sexuality and sexual practices in Chapter 14, but her target is the pornification of culture and women's sexual abjectification within it. After discussing porn tropes and narratives in contemporary consumer culture, she identifies two competing discourses in the feminist literature on pornography. Her findings from a longitudinal study of young American women's sexual practices are framed within a corporeal and 'gross-out' feminist perspective. Rome uses these to discuss the shift from objectification to subjectification in the postfeminist 1990s and 2000s, a period that served to reinforce a neoliberal perspective of women as simultaneously agentic and compliant to patriarchal norms. In response to this shift, she addresses sexual abjectification and a return to corporeal feminist activism, which positions female bodies as subversive, untamed and unruly. Abjectification goes further, to embrace physical, psychic and sexual shortcomings, and may be seen as a step in the right direction. However, she offers a cautionary warning that these new subject positions may merely serve to reinforce neoliberal norms and controls within patriarchy.

Our final chapter on the body, Chapter 15, returns to issues of objectification, however the focus shifts to men's experiences. Jacob Ostberg offers an overview of the literature on gender representation in the marketplace, specifically on self-objectification, self-sexualisation, the male and female gaze and masculinity. Drawing on research conducted with heterosexual men in the Swedish fashion industry, his findings reveal men's reluctance to self-objectify or self-sexualise themselves for fear of ridicule and condemnation by other heterosexual men. As such, Ostberg suggests that social capital is more important to them than 'erotic capital', as the former reinforces their position as dominant, active subjects. Although male/female, subject/object dichotomies persist, he notes the 'crack in the phallocentric order', which has led to a growing objectification of men in popular culture and which may yet disrupt such dichotomies.

Section 4: Difference, diversity and intersectionality

The increasing recognition of gender diversity and its many different expressions beyond the male/female binary is surely one of the defining features of the 21st century. *Facebook* (UK) now has over 70 definitions of gender, and the popular dating app *Tinder* allows users to choose from 37 options (Maclaran and Kravets, 2018). Alongside stronger acknowledgement of difference and diversity is the principle of intersectionality, a guiding tenet of much feminist thought since bell hooks theorised the intersection of race, class and gender in her most famous book, *Ain't I a Woman? Black Women and Feminism* (hooks, 1981). For hooks and other Black feminists, each additional dimension of inequality makes an individual increasingly vulnerable and subordinate, and she made forceful critiques of the domination of feminism by middle-class white women, critiques that still very much resonate today.

Indeed, the commencing chapter to this section, Chapter 16, poignantly illustrates these points as Alev Kuruoglu interrogates race and the intersecting axes of marginalisation in knitting spaces that have become popularised as a way to revalidate feminine labour. Drawing on the work of hooks and other non-white feminist theorists – Audre Lorde, Gloria Anzaldua, Sara Ahmed, Nirmal Puwar and Patricia Hill Collins – along with other intersectional, decolonial and critical feminist scholars, Kuruoglu questions assumptions of collective identity and political unity within such spaces. Coupling her own personal experiences with testimonies of racialised experiences, Kuruoglu reconceptualises knitting spaces as spaces of exclusion for some whose bodies do not 'fit'.

Nacima Ourahmoune and Hounaida El Jurdi provide a further decolonising perspective in the chapter that follows. Chapter 17 introduces the MENA region as a missing and misrepresented gendered space within the marketing and gender literature. Reiterating that most feminist accounts in marketing and consumer research come from a Western theoretical perspective, they highlight the need for more local feminisms to be acknowledged in relation to the 'Global South'. To this end, Ourahmoune and El Jurdi foreground decolonial feminism and its relationship with Arab feminisms. In so doing, they show how women living in the Arab world are not passive victims succumbing to patriarchy, but rather they are active in resisting and at the forefront of digitally led revolutions.

In a change of focus, Chapter 18 by Laurel Steinfield melds together an intersectionality analysis with Karen Barad's feminist new materialism of agential realism to broaden debates to include the non-human. She shows how inequities are produced through ever-evolving intra-actions not only between humans and the structures, practices and norms they (re)produce, but also (non)human elements and discourse. These intra-actions create marks on bodies or differences that matter, which unfold into (dis) advantages. To appreciate this dynamism that underscores inequities, Steinfield outlines how scholars can combine various feminist and post-/decolonial queer and indigenous perspectives to produce what she terms a 'holistic agential praxis'.

Moving to yet another critical intersection, in Chapter 19 Sophie Duncan Shepherd and Kathy Hamilton look at the conflict experienced by those who cannot identify with the traditional assumptions underpinning the male/female gender binary. Underlining the importance of these non-normative experiences of consuming gender as vital for marketing academics and practitioners, Duncan Shepherd and Hamilton position transgender and gender non-conforming consumers within a broader overview of gender in consumer and marketing research. As part of their critique, they overview the key tenets of queer and transgender theorising to show how these perspectives can help challenge and question normative gender assumptions.

To finish this section we turn to the intersection of age and gender with two chapters that look at the paradoxical place ageing women occupy in Western society as well as how it impacts on their careers. Chapter 20 by Minita Sanghvi and Phillip Frank paint a vivid picture of the ageism that affects women politicians in the US and the difficult position they find themselves in because they are judged more negatively and at an earlier age than men. She applies a feminist critical discourse analysis to deconstruct ageist media narratives around Nancy Pelosi, using this case study to illustrate how older women in power are impacted by such discrimination. From demeaning characterisations about their appearance, their age and their mental faculties, they have to face a continual barrage of comments that devalue and diminish their authority and power. Ultimately such negativity attempts to displace them from positions of power and to desecrate their work.

Chapter 21 brings fresh insights on this intersection with Lisa Peñaloza's reflections on women and ageing in the marketing and consumer research discipline. She gives a deeply personalised account of her own scholarly experiences as befits her long-standing engagement with both the marketing discipline and feminist perspectives. Her engrossing introspection merges an overview of theoretical approaches and topics regarding ageing women in marketing and consumer research that include history, demographics, abilities, subjectivities and institutions, with consideration of intersectionalities of race/ethnicity and class. After putting forward her plans for consciousness-raising in sprinkling academic work with insights drawn from creative writing, media, film and market practice, she discusses trends and future opportunities for research and practice concerning ageing women.

Section 5: Gendering digital technologies in marketing

The relationship between technology, gender and social reproduction is a long-standing concern of feminist scholarship. Conceiving of technology broadly beyond tools and in terms of technical artefacts, cultures and practices that are not exterior to humans and society, feminist scholars have probed into socio-political qualities of technology and its role in organising social relations and constituting subjectivities (Wajcman 2009). The four chapters in this section pick this line of inquiry to discuss and critique the heralded transformative potential of the new, digital technology with its unique capacities for both connectivity and atomisation of society. The authors explore how the questions of injustice and inequality, subjugation and oppression, morality and ethics, which are central to the feminist project, are bound up with digital technology. Building on the understanding that technology is always already socio-politically structured and inextricable from the existing power relations, the chapters explore digital technology as a site of capitalist-patriarchal governance and outline the possibilities and limits of feminist praxis through digital media, tools and spaces.

Opening the section, Francesca Sobande undertakes an examination of the racist and sexist dynamics that structure Black women's contemporary digital experiences, highlighting the intersectional nature of oppression and how digital media intensify white supremacist, anti-Black and misogynistic abuse online. She urges us to critically interrogate the popular use and co-optation of Black women's digital media in marketing and branding, particularly as a response to the Black Lives Matter (BLM) movement. The chapter methodically unpacks the marketers' interest in Black digital experience in recent years and shows how industry engagement undermines communal potentials of Black women's creative work, whilst amplifying extractive and unequal power relations. Drawing on her own empirical work in Britain, Sobande details key concerns related to corporate co-optation of Black women's digital content and its connection to racial capitalism. The author argues for the need to systematically attend to racial capitalism in all feminist efforts to challenge neoliberal feminism in the marketplace and the commodification of feminist work in digital spaces.

Aliette Lambert and Ana-Isabel Nölke set out Chapter 23 with the question of 'what drives people to act seemingly against their own interests' to interrogate why some women reject feminism and the role social media plays in conjuring up and validating such a stance. Through a feminist reading of Bourdieu's theory of symbolic power, the authors demonstrate that online feminist activism is heavily shaped and circumscribed by the digital platforms that systemically centre individual experience. Lambert and Nölke then argue that such integral privileging of the individual, her choice and agency, implicates digital feminist activism in a backlash against ideas and ideals of feminism. The authors disentangle a complex web of discourses within the notion of 'tradition' and the imagined 'feminist' subjectivity in order to show how personal agency is employed to embrace traditional gender roles and to bracket structural influences in constructing an anti-feminist position. The chapter concludes with a call to beware of the social media-imposed focus on personal stories in feminist activism, instead actively seeking ways to highlight macro-practices of oppression and solutions for collective actions to challenge structural inequality and hegemonic power.

Continuing the theme of oppression, Lauren Gurrieri and Jenna Drenten explore the new surveillance possibilities of digital technologies. Building on the feminist studies of technology, the chapter identifies three focal points for investigating surveillance and its implications for the construction of subjectivities. The authors detail the surveillance regimes embedded in and enacted through each point, namely that of self-tracking practices, technologically mediated relationships and digital data-driven categorisations of consumers. Gurrieri and Drenten point out the persistence of a deeply problematic common conception of technology as 'neutral', instead of as already profoundly gendered and steeped in relations of power. They argue that with the proliferation of digital technologies and their integration across marketing and consumer culture, the capacities for surveillance intensify. Such development necessitates a distinct feminist approach that exposes how privilege and oppression operate through new digital technologies, thus reproducing extant inequalities.

In 'Seeking Safety and Solidarity', Margaret Matich, Rachel Ashman and Elizabeth Parsons methodically unpick the affordances and hindrances embedded within digital technology to reveal ideological blind spots common to 'selfie', self-documentation and representation online, as a novel mode of feminist activism. The authors highlight the need to take heed of the materiality of technology and the hierarchies of power therein, and the ways these are implicated in reframing or even inverting the resistive forms of self-representation and identity. The chapter examines how selfies are used to reclaim the female body, emancipating it from the dominant 'systems of looking', and to make certain bodies, individuals and stories visible, thus resisting their historical marginalisation. The authors then call attention to the negative impact at play when the increased visibility translates into the increased ways the marginalised bodies are objectified and othered. In the main, the authors argue for a critical approach to digital feminism that is reflexive of the ways digital technology fosters opportunities for self-imaging, validation and solidarities, whilst also reconfiguring their forms and meanings to align with neoliberal patriarchal schemas of looking.

Section 6: Feminist futures: problems, priorities, and predictions

The final section covers a range of important feminist issues to provide us with action points and high-priority avenues for further research. To this end, Linda Scott, one of the most high-profile and long-standing researchers at the intersection of marketing and feminism, focuses Chapter 26 on what she terms *The Double X Economy,* the title of her new book on women's disempowerment (Scott, 2020). Opening with the shocking statistic that 99% of international trade is controlled by men, she explores the numerous economic constraints on women that include barriers to capital and networks as well as access to materials, labour and even market information. Impoverished women in agricultural economies often suffer the most from the severe constraints they experience in accessing larger markets and trying to move from a subsistence economy. In her detailed discussions, Scott challenges neoclassical economic thought for denying global inequality as well as much feminist critique of capitalism that, in her view, detracts from defeat of the patriarchy. Notably, the chapter finishes by calling for more creative research approaches to understanding the gendered dimensions of global economic inequalities.

Continuing the theme of marginality but, on this occasion, from within the academy, Benedetta Cappellini and Martina Hutton in Chapter 27 reflect on the 'politics of epistemic marginality' and how to use this as a way forward in disrupting the gendered nature of the academic status quo. They conceptualise this type of knowledge politics as the relationships between the 'subjects/objects' of inquiry, the 'knowers' and their experiences of theorising and disseminating within their disciplinary boundaries. Interrogating these relationships more closely through accounts from feminist-orientated marketing scholars or others who do research at the margins, Cappellini and Hutton reveal the processes whereby multiple marginalities emerge from various oppositional moments. Overall the chapter argues that being at the margins can be a form of epistemic privilege, providing critical resources to dislodge structural disciplinary hierarchies and anchors in knowledge (re)production.

Chapter 28 by Catherine Rottenberg moves from academic subjectivities to a dominant Western feminist subjectivity, one that is described more fully in her book entitled *The Rise of Neoliberal Feminism* (Rottenberg, 2018). Homing in on Ivanka Trump's *Women Who Work* text, Rottenberg elaborates how *Trump* construes the ideal female subject as one who capitalises constantly on all her activities, be they hobbies, friendships or professional. This strand of feminism has increasingly become 'common sensical', proliferating through popular media forms that ensure its place in the wider cultural landscape. Rottenberg's key argument, however, is that the conversion of women into generic rather than gendered human capital remains incomplete. Her chapter illustrates how the ideal of a happy work-family balance continues to perpetuate traditional notions of sexual difference. In conclusion, she considers how neoliberal feminism is erasing other long-standing divisions and political differences that have powerful implications for feminist futures.

The study that follows by Laura McVey, Meagan Tyler and Lauren Gurrieri in Chapter 29 continues discussions on how the marketplace produces and reproduces power relations that foster inequality. This time the focus is on pornography as a site where markets perpetuate women's sexualised inequality. Adopting a radical feminist approach, these authors explore the harm caused to women in terms of the commercialised, racialised and sexualised violence that is engendered through pornography. In so doing, their analysis makes visible the material and cultural marketplace dynamics that foster gender inequality and challenges the tacit, yet widespread acceptance of the pornification of culture.

The final chapter of both this section and the volume fittingly proposes a future research agenda. Written by the Feminist Collective – consisting of six scholars at the University of Liverpool – Chapter 30 revisits three areas of particular lacunae in marketing feminist scholarship: intersectionality and identity, the pornification of culture and the feminisation of poverty. Exploring work in these areas over the last five years, the collective identifies key studies that have progressed our knowledge, whilst also pinpointing significant gaps. We hope this volume will help address some of these gaps, and many of the chapters develop these themes more fully. The Liverpool Collective's conclusion aptly returns us to where we began – the silences in marketing's history – as the authors note the pressing need to return to structures of knowledge production within the marketing academy. In so doing, they remind us of Prothero and McDonagh's (2018) study revealing the continued absence of female voices in marketing and consumer research journals: a clarion call, indeed, to all of us feminist scholars that there is much more work to be done!

References

BBC News (2019). "Las Tesis feminist protest song of Chile goes global." 19 December https://www.bbc.co.uk/news/av/world-50751736 (accessed 10 June 2021).

Bristor, J. M. and Fischer, E. (1993). Feminist thought: Implications for consumer research. *Journal of Consumer Research*, 19(4), 518–536.

Coleman, C., Fischer, E. and Tuncay-Zayer, L. (2021). A research agenda for (gender) troubled times: Striving for a better tomorrow. *Journal of the Association for Consumer Research*, 6(2), 205–210.

Costa, J. A. (ed.) (1991). *Proceedings of the First Conference on Gender, Marketing and Consumer Behaviour*. Salt Lake City: University of Utah Printing Service.

Cova, B., Maclaran, P. and Bradshaw, A. (2012). From postmodernism to the communist horizon. *Marketing Theory*, 13(2), 213–225.

Dean, J. and Aune, K. (2015). Feminism resurgent? Mapping contemporary feminist activisms in Europe. *Social Movement Studies*, 14(4), 375–395.

Dobscha, S. and Ostberg, J. (2021). Introduction to the special issue on gender impacts: Consumption, markets, marketing, and marketing organisations. *Journal of Marketing Management*, 37(3–4), 181–187.

Fischer, E. and Bristor, J. (1994). A feminist poststructuralist analysis of the rhetoric of marketing relationships. *International Journal of Research in Marketing*, 11, 317–331.

Friedan, B. (1963). *The Feminine Mystique*. New York: W. Norton & Co.

Gurrieri L., Previte J. and Prothero, A. (2020). Hidden in plain sight: Building visibility for critical gender perspectives exploring markets, marketing and society. *Journal of Macromarketing*, 40(4), 437–444.

Hein, W., Steinfield, L., Ourahmoune, N., Coleman, C., Zayer, L. T. and Littlefield, J. (2016). Gender justice and the market: A transformative consumer research perspective. *Journal of Public Policy & Marketing*, 35(2), 223–236.

Hirschman, E.C. (1993). Ideology in consumer research 1980 and 1990: A Marxist and feminist critique. *Journal of Consumer Research*, 19(4), 537–555.

hooks, b. (1981) *Ain't I a Woman? Black Women and Feminism*. Boston, MA: Southend Press.

Maclaran, P. and Kravets, O. (2018). Feminist Perspectives in Marketing: Past, Present and Future, in Tadajewski, M., Denigri-Knott, J., Dholakia, N. (eds) *The Routledge Companion to Critical Marketing*. Abingdon: Routledge, pp. 64–82.

Prothero, A. and McDonagh, P. (2018). 'Death by a Million Cuts': Gender (In)Equality in the Marketing Academy. In *14th ACR Gender, Marketing and Consumer Behavior Conference*, Dallas, TX.

Prothero, A. and Tadajewski, M. (2021). #MeToo and beyond: Inequality and injustice in marketing practice and academia. *Journal of Marketing Management*, 37(1–2), 1–20.

Rottenberg, C. (2018). *The Rise of Neoliberal Feminism*. Oxford: Oxford University Press.

Scott, L. (2005). *Fresh Lipstick: Redressing Fashion and Feminism*. New York: Palgrave.

Scott, L. (2020). *The Double X Economy: The Epic Potential of Empowering Women*. New York: Farrar, Straus and Giroux.

Varman, R., Goswami, P. and Vijay, D. (2018). The precarity of respectable consumption: Normalising sexual violence against women. *Journal of Marketing Management*, 34(11–12), 932–964.

Wajcman, J. (2009). Feminist Theories of Technology. *Cambridge Journal of Economics* 34, 143–152.

Zuckerman, M. E. and Carsky, M. L. (1990). Contribution of Women to U.S. Marketing Thought: The Consumers Perspective, 1900-1940. *Journal of the Academy of Marketing Science*, 18(4), 313–318.

Section 1
Women in the history of marketing

2 Goddesses of the household
Martha Van Rensselaer and the role of home economics in marketing theory*

Mary Ellen Zuckerman

Introduction

In 1923, the National League of Women Voters named home economist and educator Martha Van Rensselaer one of the 12 most influential women in the United States, alongside such notables as suffragist Carrie Chapman Catt, educator M. Carey Thomas, and reformer Jane Addams. Earlier in her career, Van Rensselaer had been given a different label by a regional newspaper reporting on lectures by homemaking experts, terming them "Goddesses of the Household." Taken together, these titles reflect the esteem and position that experts on the home held in a society looking for guidance on how to learn about the new products and equipment appearing in the consumer marketplace.

Born in 1864 in western New York, Martha Van Rensselaer compiled an impressive record of accomplishments before her death in 1932. She served as one of the state's first female County School Commissioners, holding the position for six years, successfully supervising the largest school district in the state. She co-founded a home economics department at Cornell University that grew from several courses into today's College of Human Ecology. She oversaw the expansion of extension homemaking services reaching out to rural farmwomen, then transitioning that operation into federally funded New York State Home Bureaus, providing information and advice about the home and ways to improve the efficiency and quality of housework. Van Rensselaer and her professional and personal partner Flora Rose were the first two women awarded the title of professor at Cornell University. Van Rensselaer took on the Presidency of the young American Home Economics Association from 1914 to 1916. During World War One Van Rensselaer served as first the state, then the national director of Food Conservation under U.S. Food Administration director (and later U.S. President) Herbert Hoover. In the early 1920s, Hoover asked her to travel to post-war Belgium to report on food needs there, work for which she received the Belgian "Chevalier Order of the Crown." Van Rensselaer edited the Home-making Department of mass circulation magazine *Delineator* for the first half of the 1920s, reaching millions with her practical household advice and information about product usage.

Van Rensselaer's dedication and desire to help the rural farmwomen of New York State propelled her dissemination of practical homemaking information across the state

---

* Cited in Zuckerman (2017); portions of this chapter appeared in Zuckerman (2013, 2017).

and beyond. The work she and partner Rose undertook in the residential student home economics program at Cornell, and the extension outreach illuminates one strand of messages sent by home economists to homemakers, that of educating them about scientific methods and products they could purchase to improve housework quality and efficiency, and how to be educated consumers. However, as public employees of the state, Van Rensselaer and Rose were prohibited from endorsing particular product brands, so they stayed off a path taken by other home economists who worked more closely with manufacturers and touted consumption more aggressively.

Van Rensselaer played a key role in the developing field of home economics, a discipline intersecting with marketing in these years. Her career parallels and deviates from that of some other home economists as they navigated their role in understanding and directing consumer behavior, influencing manufacturers' practices, and contributing to marketing thought. Two examples from Van Rensselaer's work illustrate her approach in developing consumer awareness of new products emerging in the U.S. marketplace in the 20th century: (1) Van Rensselaer's communications through her work at Cornell School of Home Economics, Farm Institutes, and lecture demonstrations; and (2) her writings as Editor of the Home-making Department of mass circulation magazine *Delineator* in the 1920s.

Home economists, home economics, and marketing

The field of home economics began gaining momentum as a coherent discipline in the last decade of the 19th century, culminating in the Lake Placid (NY) meetings begun in 1899. In that year Melville Dewey, a politically connected New York State librarian, and his wife Anna brought together the most prominent individuals in the home economics field. The group shaped and defined the new field, focusing on domestic science; ultimately giving it a name (Home Economics); and, after meeting for several years, birthing a national association, the American Home Economics Association, in 1909. In the early years, these home economists emphasized educating women in their role as housewives, which included informed consumption (Craig, 1944; Goldstein, 2012). However, much of the early emphasis in the field focused on sanitation (bacteriology), nutrition (chemistry), and rational home management skills (drawing on scientific management work) to lessen physical effort expended (Tomes, 1998).

Eventually, as the industrialized economy of the U.S.-made products increasingly available nationally, with a concomitant need for consumers, home economists became concerned with such questions as consumer choice, the household's interaction with the marketplace, and consumer purchasing power. Home economists taught women to be knowledgeable about uses, quality, ingredients, and prices of the products now manufactured outside the home. The plethora of new goods being produced presented problems of consumer choice, and, even before that, a lack of awareness about the best ways to improve the quality of life through the use of new "devices." How would these products improve sanitation, nutrition, and efficiency in housework (Hunt, 1908; Frederick, 1923; Andrews et al., 1940; BPCP, n.d.,)? Home economists initially took a scientific stance toward consumption, as they had toward other domestic issues such as sanitation, nutrition, and home management. Demonstrations of new products, write-ups about usage and features, information on efficiency all led to increased awareness and product use, particularly among rural consumers (Nystrom, 1929, pp. 15, 69–70; Craig, 1944; McGovern, 2006).

Home economists themselves took varied paths in the disciplines early years, before professionalization occurred. Some joined universities, educating new cohorts of home economists. Others, such as Hazel Kyrk and Elizabeth Hoyt, produced pioneering works investigating consumption behavior (Zuckerman and Carsky, 1990; Tadajewski, 2013). Still others focused on the practicalities of educating consumers and turned toward assisting product manufacturers. Some joined the government when the federal Bureau of Home Economics was created in 1923 with Dr. Louise Stanley as the Director.

Professionals in this developing field became entwined with and mirrored trends in the nascent field of marketing in several ways. Home economists had a clear focus on the consumer and the consumers' needs, an emphasis that became increasingly important in marketing. Some home economists underwent the transition from providing information about products and new technologies to telling consumers about which goods to purchase, a trajectory reflected in the shift from informational to persuasive advertising. Home economists found places in universities, where they fought for recognition, as did marketing educators; often the two disciplines were housed in the same academic unit (Bartels, 1988; Goldstein, 1994; Rutherford, 2003). Home economists also intersected with the field of marketing in practical ways, moving to careers in the business world where companies sought their expertise to better market to consumers. Home economists engaged in and influenced marketing areas such as creating consumer awareness, product development and quality, product standardization, effective distribution, retailing public relations, improved labeling, product and consumer research, and effective communication and advertising to consumers. Some home economists necessarily took on the multiple roles of representative of the consumer and partner of the manufacturer or business; Goldstein has termed this role "mediators" (Goldstein, 2012, p.10).

Perhaps the best example of a home economist who carried on the twin missions of educating the consumer and assisting the marketer is Christine Frederick. Like Van Rensselaer, Frederick became well known in the field of home economics. She was the first woman to address Congressional hearings on distribution and home buying problems, a frequent speaker before advertising and sales conventions, and the author of a comprehensive book on female consumers. Her initial work (before 1920) centered on testing products and scientific homemaking ideas, writing about these in women's magazines and, eventually, in manufacturers' promotional pamphlets (Frederick Papers). Frederick's major contribution to marketing thought came through her 1929 book, *Selling Mrs. Consumer*, targeted to marketers and marketing educators. It informed them of the importance of meeting the consumer's needs and provided guidelines on methods of reaching her (Frederick, 1929; Zuckerman, 1994). However, Martha Van Rensselaer took a different direction when educating consumers and marketers.

Martha Van Rensselaer

Martha Van Rensselaer was born and raised in western New York, a rural area she came to know well. In her position there as School Commissioner of Cattaraugus County, NY, she traveled her district (the largest in New York State) by horse to visit every school. This often necessitated staying overnight in a local farmhouse where she spent time questioning, observing, and gaining a keen understanding of the homemaking problems and priorities of farm wives. She drew on this information throughout her career, remaining close to the rural housewives who sought to improve the quality of their lives with the new technology and products coming on to the market.

After losing a third term as school commissioner in a politically charged election, Van Rensselaer had drawn on her contacts to join Cornell University in 1900, as part of its Extension Service (Scholl, 2008; Zuckerman, 2019). Here she began publishing bulletins containing practical information for housewives (Rose et al., 1969). In 1904, Van Rensselaer, with home economist Flora Rose, established the Department of Home Economics at Cornell. As Co-Chair of the department she developed expertise in the products created for the home, their distribution, and the needs of the consumers using them.

As a home and consumer economist, journalist, and academic administrator, Van Rensselaer embodied several of the traits noted above about early home economists. She maintained a strong focus on consumers, on raising their awareness and educating them about new products and technology. She worked in an institution of higher education, creating and growing the home economics department at Cornell University. She made a foray into the commercial world and ultimately moved back into the world of academia. She provided clear and detailed information to consumers, but did not try to persuade them to use one brand over another. However, throughout her career she had a practitioner orientation in that she consistently went out to meet with consumers, talking with them, visiting with them in their homes, discovering their needs and habits. Extension service work of the kind Van Rensselaer was responsible for at Cornell played a significant role in in raising consumer awareness among rural farm women. The extension services offered by Cornell's home economics department reached thousands of rural farm women in New York State and exposed them to new products and processes for homemaking. This raised awareness in their minds of the emerging goods being marketed nationally.

Educating the rural consumers

In the late 19th- and early 20th-century United States, rural families, often living in isolated locations, had limited knowledge about the new products and conveniences starting to appear in national markets. State and federal governments, universities experts, and manufacturers all sought to reach these rural consumers. Telephone, radio, Rural Free Delivery, and better roads all promised an end to the isolation on farms as well as providing access to more information about products pledging efficiency and less work (Holt, 1995).

While manufacturers attempted to advertise to consumers, much information farm families gained about new products came from their local universities, a trusted source. Schools of Agriculture, many created in the United States under the provisions of the 1862 federal Morrill Act, identified ways they could reach farmers to aid them in increasing output, improving quality, and more reliably producing food. Agricultural Schools ran winter courses, created informational bulletins, sent representatives out to talk with farmers' groups, and held Farmers' Institutes. All these activities ultimately fell under the title of "extension services," which played an important role in developing the rural consumer market. Initiatives to improve farm methods eventually broadened to include a focus on farm families and farm life. Agriculture Schools began communicating with farm wives about ways to improve housework efficiency and quality of home life (True, 1928).

These outreach efforts coincided with the establishment of home economics courses and departments in Agricultural Schools. Paralleling the work focused on the mostly male farmers, activities targeted at the home exposed farm wives to new equipment, products, and ways of conducting housework and other farm chores. Experts developed the farm wife consumer market through informational activities such as educational bulletins, short winter courses, women's meetings at Farmers' Weeks and Institutes, and demonstration agents and lecturers fanning out from the Colleges. These efforts expanded the farm wives' horizons, creating in them a willingness to seek out new products and processes. The abundant information cultivated a fertile field for advertisers who began reaching rural housewives through women's and farm journals (Prawl et al., 1984).

Van Rensselaer penned such bulletins and circulars emanating from Cornell's Home Economics department, reaching thousands of women across the state in the early 1900s. She regularly encouraged farm wives to respond with problems they wished to see discussed in her bulletins and courses. Van Rensselaer started informational reading clubs (eventually numbering over 300 throughout New York State), lectured at regional institutes (where the local newspaper termed the speakers the aforementioned "Goddesses of the Household"), and visited women in their homes to determine topics of interest. She strongly considered consumer opinions and preferences, modifying and adding subjects as needed, "trying to satisfy through talks the growing demands of an awakening public for information on the subjects related to home and family life..." (Rose, 1969, p.27). Clearly a market existed for the information, a pent-up need, which marketers could capitalize on.

The programs run by Van Rensselaer communicated about and demonstrated the latest methods and equipment for rural housekeeping. She educated women about changing their household routines and prepared them for the next step of purchasing new products. Van Rensselaer's professional experiences as a County School Commissioner in western New York and as Director of the Farmer's Wife Reading program and home extension work at Cornell gave her rich insight into the needs of farm women. As an educator she believed it to be her mission to understand these requirements and provide information to meet them, in what would become a tenet of marketers as well.

Van Rensselaer also offered on-site opportunities at Cornell for rural women to learn about housekeeping methods and the products that might help them achieve efficiency. The Short Winter course paralleled instruction offered to male farmers since the mid-1890s. Van Rensselaer created a curriculum centered on topics of interest to farm women and launched it in 1906. In the first year luminaries of the home economics world including Anna Barrows, Isabel Bevier, Maria Elliott, Ellen Richards, Marion Talbot, and Mary Schenck Woolman took time to lecture the farm women, who eagerly put aside their daily round of work to learn scientific ways of keeping their homes clean and attractive, of feeding their families, and of raising their children.

Another program targeted at farm wives, created by Van Rensselaer and her colleagues, initially called the Homemakers' Conference and held during Cornell's Farmers' Week, continued this development of the rural women's market. Farmer's Week had taken place at Cornell University since the late 1890s. The first Homemakers' Conference, aimed at women, was added in 1909. This combined event proved successful and lasted at least through the 1940s. In its early years this week of demonstrations, lectures, and socializing showed farmer and farmers' wives the most up-to-date ways to perform farm work. Farm families saw in action new products, services, and the latest conveniences. Being shown and given information about these new pieces of equipment by the credible experts from the School of Agriculture, including the home economists, undoubtedly caused the farm families to think more favorably about possibly investing in these unfamiliar products. The demonstrations and lectures prepared this market of consumers, providing them with data in this initial information gathering stage. For Van Rensselaer and her colleagues, their educational focus on improving the quality of life for farm families through the introduction of better agricultural and domestic science principles included showing products and goods that might help.

Participants saw demonstrations of how the equipment worked. Expert instructors would "provide instruction in cooking, furnishing, general housekeeping, home sanitation…" (Rose, 1969, p. 32). After learning new techniques and ways to improve housekeeping, these women would turn to purchasing items. The extension efforts educated women and men about possibilities beyond their own farm, communities, and knowledge, preparing them to step into the world of consumption.

The School's public funding by the New York State legislature precluded staff from identifying or indicating preferences for any particular brand of goods. Van Rensselaer and others in the School adhered to the "no recommendations" policy. This meant that the Cornell Home Economics division maintained its focus on educating homemakers as producers and conservers of quality home and family, albeit with a consumer role, and spent less time emphasizing particular products or developing relations with businesses. But outreach work in extension services as well as the demonstrations at the Household Conference primed the farm wives market for consumption.

Over the years, thousands attended the short Winter Course and the Household conference. Holding these events at Cornell where appliances and products could be easily demonstrated in the new Home Economics building continued to expose rural homemakers to the advantages of modern home goods through the teens, 20s, and 30s. They saw the new conveniences, equipment, and ways of preparing nutritious food and efficiently cleaning up. Home Economics staff and faculty from the School of Agriculture dominated the program with a sprinkling of local experts, hands-on demonstration agents, and state officials, inducing trust in the attendees. More nationally known names appeared occasionally, adding to the Institute's credibility and attesting to its influence. In 1918, with the war effort on, social activist Jane Addams and Julia Lathrop of the Children's Bureau of the Department of the Interior both attended (Conference Program, February 11–16, 1918, Boxes 16, 23, MVRP). In the 1920s, then Governor Franklin D. Roosevelt came; Eleanor Roosevelt appeared in the early 1930s (*New York Herald Tribune*, February 17, 1929, n.p.; and "Program of 21st Farm and Home Week Announced", n.d., n.p. both in Box 16, MVRP). Large numbers flocked to hear experts, and well-known figures provide useful information and ideas.

By the 1920s, book exhibits could be seen. Here evidence exists that seeing products at the Farm and Home conference led to purchases, even though attendees couldn't buy the volumes there. Cornell librarian Dorothy Riddle reassured a publisher,

> Although we are unable to make sales at the Book Fair owing to this being a state college, we do have very definite proof that a large number of sales are made as a result of the books being seen here. If you could have seen the hundreds of people who sat at the tables taking notes of authors, publishers and prices for the sole purpose of buying books either individually or for their clubs, or for recommendations to their local libraries, I think you would feel repaid for the effort you put into sending these books to us.
> (Dorothy Riddle to Robert F. Evans, 3/2/1930, Folder 12, Box 16, MVRP)

Demonstrating equipment usage, ways of preparing foods, cleaning and decorating the home, making clothes, and efficiently carrying out the homemaker duties transmitted a persuasive message. The setting felt personal, and the speakers had expert credibility in the eyes of their audiences, as well as a sense of familiarity, as many of the product demonstrators had, like Van Rensselaer, experienced rural life. The need to buy appropriate utensils, equipment, storage containers, and cleaning supplies for the most efficient and hygienic home was a message communicated powerfully to the audiences, creating an appetite and developing a market for goods, equipment, and conveniences on the farm (Holt, 1995, p. 48; Tomes, 1998, p. 197).

Van Rensselaer and her staff kept up with the latest appliances and equipment for the home so they could appropriately train their students. For example, in 1910, when planning for the new Home Economics building, Van Rensselaer and Rose traveled out west to visit other institutions, taking particular note of kitchens, as they wanted the best possible equipment in their new demonstration kitchen. Gaining knowledge of possible items available commercially was essential for a professional home economist (MVR to Mrs. Dewey, 8/11/1910, Box 12, MVRP).

Throughout the years, Van Rensselaer and her colleagues adhered to the policy of no brand recommendations. Van Rensselaer settled on *educational value* as her criterion. She described the tricky road the state-supported Agriculture School trod in getting out the best information to incipient consumers:

> We have found, however, that household conveniences interest people greatly. Manufacturers are generally very glad to put their wares on exhibition. We take the ground that we cannot enter into it from a commercial standpoint, but we can show what we think is good from an educational standpoint and speak a good work (sic) for labor saving devices.
> (MVR to Mrs. Trowbridge, 2/20/1912, Box 16, MVRP)

Van Rensselaer would show the new conveniences, but only after she and her staff were convinced of the utility and soundness of products and without specifically endorsing a particular brand. The trust bond she and the home economics staff built up with their constituency remained unblurred by advertising pressure.[1]

This pattern of including products and demonstrating them without naming brands continued over the years. A 1919 program notes exhibits for economical household furnishings, clothing and millinery, equipment for stain removal, the economical kitchen, and fireless and steam pressure cookers and their meal possibilities (Program for 1911 Home-maker's Conference, February 11–14, p. 8, Box 63, MVRP). They showed these equipment and goods but carefully refrained from endorsing or giving detailed explanations on how to use items.

Despite the restrained amount of specific product information that could be gleaned from this Home Conference week, the visual presence of these labor-saving devices and home enhancements helped develop consumer desires, if not preferences. Certainly, it motivated some individuals to seek out additional information from manufacturers and sales people. Gaining the initial information from this reliable source may in fact have increased farm women's belief that these products would be valuable. These relatively isolated and rural individuals trusted friends and family, but many also placed confidence in the home economics department at Cornell, where the staff, led by Van Rensselaer, had expended so much energy reaching out to them.

At Farmers' Week Van Rensselaer also recognized the increasingly popular topic of how the housewife could be an educated and savvy consumer. She lectured and provided an opportunity for shared discussion on the subject of how women keeping house for their families should think about spending their money.

Educating female consumers nationwide

Van Rensselaer was also one of a number of home economists (including Christine Frederick, Sarah Splint, Lita Bane, and Katherine Fisher) who published in mass circulation women's journals. Many simultaneously engaged with the newly developing advertising industry, straddling the two roles of informing women about new household techniques and appliances and advising advertisers on how to persuade women to buy. Van Rensselaer's editorship at the *Delineator* illuminates another aspect of the historical relationship between home economics and the marketing fields of advertising and consumer behavior (Shapiro, 1986; Strasser, 1989; Berlage, 1998; Stage and Vincenti, 1997).

Van Rensselaer saw mass magazines as an appropriate outlet to continue her mission of educating consumers, albeit often a more urban and affluent consumer than those she worked with through Cornell. She had published a number of journal articles about rural homemakers in the tens and teens. Van Rensselaer took over as Editor of the Home-making Department at the *Delineator* in spring 1921, hired by new Editor Marie Mattingly Meloney. Van Rensselaer's appearance in Meloney's magazine was announced with great fanfare (*Delineator*, April, 1921, p. 2). Butterick wanted the best "experts" they could find for all aspects of their publications, and Van Rensselaer qualified, being a well-known home economist. Melony believed that the credibility Van Rensselaer held with rural housewives would translate over to her middle-class readers. Promotional materials touted Van Rensselaer and the great household work she was doing at Cornell. The magazine routinely featured photographs of product testing in the workrooms at the University (Butterick Publishing Company (Story) 1925, p. 11).

Delineator created the new household department to compete with those at other top journals, and as a logical content companion in a venture dependent on advertising targeted at women. For Van Rensselaer this offered a way to keep her eye on the needs of the female consumer. In taking the position, she also garnered assurances about not being required to name particular manufacturers in her columns, and permission to use her colleagues from Cornell as contributors to the department.

Van Rensselaer's first column sounded the themes, which she would cover in the following years. She called for putting housework on a rational, scientific, businesslike basis. And, she noted, consumers have power:

> The efficiency of the world's workers depends on diet, good housing, comfortable clothing and adequate recreation, and the housekeeper more often than not holds the key to the situation. What can she do about it? **Her standards create the demand**.
>
> (emphasis added, *Delineator*, April, 1921, p. 26)

Van Rensselaer reflected progressive, social housekeeping themes, but also emphasized consumer purchasing power, a developing movement in the 1920s. Topics covered in the monthly *Delineator* Home-making Department under Van Rensselaer included detailed information about household cleaning and cooking, care of floors and furniture, nutrition, and proper use and design of numerous pieces of household equipment. In early years, Van Rensselaer always included an editorial section that often stressed the need for consumer education. The technical articles focused on food, recipes, household cleaning, care of floors and furniture, and proper use of household equipment provided practical consumer information. The tone of her pieces was scientific, advocating rational housekeeping and educated, intelligent consumption. This stood in contrast to the advertising, some of which pitched the idea that buying their product would easily solve a plethora of the purchaser's problems, rather than the information driven and rational consumption advocated by Van Rensselaer. Mouthwash, medicines to improve digestion, even arch supports could save marriages, income, the entire family… at least according to the ads. Van Rensselaer and her staff offered a different, more focused route to solving these issues, reflecting diverging perspectives of the home economist as consumer educator and the marketer.

Delineator's Meloney desired that products and equipment be tested at Cornell University, so the connection could be highlighted. Staff there could not test or recommend products by particular manufacturers on request, due to their state funding. Whether or not to provide specific product names was a dilemma faced by other women's journals as well in these earlier years of advertising, reflecting some uncertainty about the shape of the new consumer culture (Rutherford, 2003, p. 78; Zuckerman, 1998). At *Delineator* articles provided information about food products, equipment, household cleaning, and furnishing items, but specific branding was absent. Instead, a notice appeared telling readers that they could write in for the names of featured products. For example, an entire article appeared on what to look for when purchasing a washing machine, containing a great deal of technical information, with no specific manufacturers mentioned. Similar articles appeared evaluating refrigerators and kitchen implements, again with no particular brand named. In a page authored by Van Rensselaer, featuring items one should never go camping without, no brands or stores were mentioned; rather, readers were told to write in, including a self-addressed stamped envelope, if they could not locate an item (*Delineator*, August, Van Rensselaer, July 1922, pp. 44, 46, January 1924, p. 55, 1926, pp. 21, 65). An article on the eleventh hour Christmas gifts afforded inexpensive gift ideas, but no details on where to buy them or name of brands (*Delineator*, January 1923, p. 50).

This meant information given to consumers was not influenced by manufacturers or advertising. However, readers might be justified in feeling that some useful consumer information was missing. However, consumers, their appetites whetted, could seek the specific brand information elsewhere, often right in the pages of women's journals.

Home economists were finding their way in this evolving marketplace. Some, who like Van Rensselaer affiliated with magazines or other publications, allowed their names to be used in ads. For example, "Learn Raisin Cookery from these Famous cooks," a two-page ad for Sun-Maid raisins appearing in *Delineator*, featured six well-known cooks and home economists, with pictures and recipes by each of them, preceded by their names. The biographies provided make it clear that all were associated with a women's magazine or a newspaper.

Christine Frederick again provides another useful comparison to Van Rensselaer; Frederick's journey from journalist and household management expert to advisor to manufacturers was one taken by some home economists. Frederick, like Van Rensselaer, was well known in the women's magazine and home economics world. Like other home economists such as Katherine Fisher, Lita Bane, and Lillian Gilbreth, her publications and public lectures provided her with credibility in the eyes of housewives. Unlike some of the newer home economists but like Van Rensselaer in her early years, Frederick had not trained academically; rather she had schooled herself in the science of home management at her Applecroft Home Experiment Station in her Long Island home, where she tested new products and systems, as Van Rensselaer did at Cornell. By the 1920s, Frederick was testing 1,800 products in her home lab (Butterick Publishing Company (Story), 1925, p. 16; Frederick, 1929, p. 167). Frederick, like Van Rensselaer and peer home economists, believed strongly that part of the modern housekeeper's job lay in learning to be an educated consumer (Strasser, 1982, p. 249).

In the 1920s, Frederick held the job of household editor at *Designer* magazine. Simultaneously she wrote promotional booklets for manufacturers, demonstrating how to use products and offering recipes. Frederick possessed a keen understanding of the value of promotion (helped by a course she took with pioneering advertising psychologist Walter Dill Scott while at Northwestern University). Yet Frederick remained careful to show consumers how products would help them meet their needs (CMFP, 1931). For example, in 1931 Frederick wrote *Frankfurters as You Like Them*, a booklet of recipes for Stahl-Meyer Imported Style frankfurters. She promised that these would save homemakers time and energy, important attributes for housewives. This was both good marketing strategy (showing how the product met the need of the consumer) but also, Frederick could argue, genuinely helpful to interested homemakers.

Frederick's business-oriented transformation from consumer guide to business advisor occurred in the 1920s, and was one echoed by other home economists who also counseled both female consumers and advertisers. Formally, trained home economists entering the business world hoped their consumer and scientific orientation would influence marketing practices. Home economists took jobs in banks, hotels, and land companies, as well as in firms manufacturing foods, textiles, and appliances. Despite the consumer orientation many had been trained with, they were not wholly consumer proponents. For example, in 1918, banks employed home economists in home service departments. The home economists educated consumers on the use of saving accounts and bank services, and taught them financial management. Their primary responsibility, however, was to generate consumer accounts for the bank. Scholar Glenna Matthews argues that the evolution of the home economics discipline, which came to stress efficiency and business-like procedures in the home, made it easier for the experts advising about the home to step into the business marketplace and accept money for advice to advertisers, endorsements, etc. (Soliday, September 1921; Harrison, October 1923; Sellars, June 1923; Keown, June 1924; Fisher, October 1927; Rowe, October 1927; Gerber, January 1934; Matthews, 1987; Goldstein, 2012).

Van Rensselaer, however, never made this transition in part because of her association with Cornell University, and she never expressed a desire to do so or regret that she had not. Readers of Van Rensselaer's columns would look in vain for direction to particular brands. She did at times liken the home to a small business and the housewife to a business manager, tapping into efforts to increase the status of homemaking.

Van Rensselaer and her staffers at Cornell prepared pamphlets made available to *Delineator*'s readers, similar to the material they created for their rural extension work at the College as part of their consumer education mission. These informational brochures reflected Van Rensselaer's commitment to education; they also mimicked the practice of many manufacturers who offered consumers pamphlets, filled with product usage information, often written by home economists such as Frederick (*Delineator*, 1922–1923; Strasser, 1989).

Van Rensselaer's editorial venture ended in the mid-1920s, when Meloney left *Delineator* in a dispute with new owners (*Delineator*, September 1926, November 1931; MMMP, 1926). The higher class, urban readers, and associated advertisers the new management wished to attract made a poor fit for the wide-ranging product and equipment testing Van Rensselaer undertook at Cornell's academic test facilities, particularly as this activity targeted rural women. While new management wished to increase circulation, they desired urban rather than rural readers.

Management also sought to bolster *Delineator*'s own Home Service Institute in New York City, close to the advertisers so crucial to the magazine's profitability rather than using the test kitchens in the academic environment of Cornell University; as the advertising industry grew in size and sophistication, the prestige and credibility offered by the University became less important (BPCP, 1931). Another home economist, Mildred Maddocks Bentley, took over the magazine's own institute, allowing the new editorial team to take more control over content (*Delineator*, October 1926, p. 1; Tucker, n.d., p. 38). Within months, specific manufacturers' names and brands appeared in articles, something that had never happened under Van Rensselaer's editorship (e.g. Delineator, December 1926, pp. 22–23).

Conclusion

Martha Van Rensselaer was one of a group of home economists who influenced and interacted with the marketing field in the United States in the early 20th century. They sought to put consumer (usually female) awareness and education about new household techniques, products, and appliances at the forefront of their efforts. A number of these home economists pursued their educational mission in academia and through mass circulation publications. Some eventually worked for manufacturers, advertisers, and the government.

Van Rensselaer chose to inform women through mass media, the classroom, lecture circuit, and demonstrations, never working directly with advertisers. Through her work in the Home Economics division at Cornell University, in bulletins and magazine articles, and finally as Home-making Department editor at *Delineator*, Van Rensselaer educated consumers about the most recent household techniques and appliances. She gave guidance to homemakers on the best ways to incorporate modern products and techniques into their homes. She also helped shape and train students who came to Cornell University to study home economics.

Two specific initiatives illustrate Van Rensselaer's method of educating consumers. Through Cornell University's extension services, she provided information to farm wives about new, scientific methods for keeping healthy, sanitary, and efficient homes. Programs in Cornell's home economics extension service such as home reading and study clubs for farm wives, short winter courses, and, most importantly, the Homemakers' Conference during the Farmers' Week conveyed factual information, but more importantly, different ways of thinking about farm problems. As a Cornell brochure put it: "Education consists largely in broadening one's sympathies and in giving him (the student) new means of attacking any problem" (Cornell Winter Course, 1909–1910, p. 1, Box 20, MVRP).

These new ways of reasoning included expanding the mind to include the idea of purchasing. Using new conveniences logically resulted from the scientific housekeeping and efficiency propounded by Van Rensselaer and other home economists. When appliances and utensils could in fact make housekeeping easier, farm wives needed to be exposed to and informed about these pieces of equipment, just like the male farmers, which could improve output and reduce labor in the fields and barns. Home economists like Van Rensselaer presented these tools in their role as experts in social science. While Cornell University did not explicitly link its information and demonstration to consumerism, rather laying claim to informational education, they did in fact help develop the consumer market. After this exposure to the newest pieces of equipment and products, it is difficult to imagine that interested farmers' wives would not seek out additional information for purchasing products, if not immediately, then in the future. They would fail to receive much brand-specific data from the College of Agriculture's Home Economics department but their newly whetted consumer appetites could seek information from other venues. Fruitful sources could be local newspapers, magazines, family members, or neighbors, or commercial outlets such as storekeepers, salesmen, or paid advertisers. Raising of consumer awareness, employing multiple modes of providing information, and using credible sources in communications are all tenets which would be used by marketers.

Van Rensselaer expanded her audience of female consumers when she became the editorial of the Homemaking section of mass circulation women's magazine, *Delineator*, from 1921 to 1926. Her expertise as a home economist again gave her enormous credibility. The extent to which Van Rensselaer succeeded in influencing women about product awareness for their benefit was captured by a phrase in a Butterick Company promotional brochure where they talked about Van Rensselaer being "a great influence still further multiplied" (Butterick Publishing Company (Story), 1925, p. 11). Through her monthly *Delineator* columns, Van Rensselaer contributed both knowledge and information to millions of homemakers. Van Rensselaer's stint as Editor of the Home-making Department at the *Delineator* highlights the continuum of job possibilities set before home economists in this early phase of their professionalization as they struggled to reconcile their mission of helping female homemakers with the requests from manufacturers for assistance, the government for information, and the constraints of the commercially supported media.

As Van Rensselaer's career demonstrates, the breadth and depth of the activities of home economists in the first decades of the 20th century influenced and intersected with those of marketers.

Note

1 The federal National Bureau of Standards faced the same issue when disseminating information on testing and standardization for home items; see McGovern (2006), p. 165.

References

Andrews, B., et al. (1940), *Sharing home life*. J.B. Lippincott Company, New York, NY.
Bartels, R. (1988), *The History of Marketing Thought*, Publishing Horizons, Columbus, OH.
Berlage, N.K. (1998), "The establishment of an applied social science: home economists, science and reform at Cornell University, 1870–1930", in Silverberg, H. (Ed.), *Gender and American Social Science: The Formative Years*, Princeton University Press, Princeton, NY, pp. 185–231.

BPCP (n.d.), *Various, Butterick Archives and Library, Archival Papers*, Butterick Archives and Library, New York.

Butterick Publishing Company (Story) (1925), *The Story of a Pantry Shelf, an Outline History of Grocery Specialties*, Butterick Publishing Company, New York.

CMFP (1931), *Frederick, C.I.M. (1883–1970), Archival Papers*, The Schlesinger Library on the History of Women in America, Cambridge MA.

Craig, H.T. (1944), *The History of Home Economics*, Pennsylvania State University Press, University Park.

Delineator (1921–1926), Butterick Publishing Company, New York.

Fisher, K. (1927), "Home economics in business roundtable", *Journal of Home Economics*, Vol. 19, pp. 598–600.

Frederick, C. (1923), *Household Engineering: Scientific Management in the Home*, American School of Home Economics, Chicago, IL.

Frederick, C. (1929), *Selling Mrs. Customer*, The Business Bourse, New York.

Gerber, D. (1934), "The home economist in business", *Journal of Home Economics*, Vol. 26, pp. 22–23.

Goldstein, C. (2012), *Creating Consumers: Home Economists in Twentieth-Century America*, UNC Press, Chapel Hill.

Harrison, M.E. (1923), "How and why the business world needs home economics", *Journal of Home Economics*, Vol. 15, pp. 553–554.

Holt, M.I. (1995), *Linoleum, Better Babies & The Modern Farm Woman, 1890–1930*. University of New Mexico Press, Albuquerque.

Keown, M.E. (1924), "Home economists in business," *Journal of Home Economics*, Vol. 16, pp. 457–458.

Matthews, G. (1987), *Just a Housewife: The Rise and Fall of Domesticity in America*, Oxford University Press, New York.

McGovern, C. (2006), *Sold American*, UNC Press, Chapel Hill.

MMMP (1926), *Meloney, M.M. (1883), Marie Mattingly Meloney Papers, 1891–1943, Archival Papers, MS#0864*, Rare Book & Manuscript Library, Columbia University, New York.

Nystrom, P. (1929, 1976 reprint), *Economic Principles of Consumption*, Arno Press, New York.

Prawl, W., Medlin, R. and Gross, J. (1984), *Adult and Continuing Education Through the Cooperative Extension Service*, University of Missouri Press, Columbia.

Rose, F., Stocks, E. and Whittier, M. (1969), *"A Growing College, Home Economics at Cornell University*, Cornell University, Ithaca NY.

Rowe, B.M. (1927), "Progress in home economics in business", *Journal of Home Economics*, Vol. 19, pp. 576–578.

Rutherford, J.W. (2003), *Selling Mrs. Consumer*, University of Georgia, Athens.

Scholl, J.R. (2008), "Early FCS extension specialist: Martha Van Rensselaer," *Family and Consumer Sciences Research Journal*, Vol. 37, No. 2, pp. 149–156.

Sellars, M. (1923), "Home economics women in business", *Journal of Home Economics*, Vol. 15, pp. 297–300.

Shapiro, L. (1986), *Perfection Salad: Women and Cooking at the Turn of the Century*, Henry Holt and Company, New York.

Soliday, J.H. (1921), "The home service department from the bankers' point of view", *Journal of Home Economics*, Vol. 13, pp. 439–440.

Stage, S. and Vincenti, V. (Eds) (1997), *Rethinking Home Economics: Women and the History of a Profession*, Cornell University Press, Ithaca, NY.

Strasser, S. (1982), *Never Done, a History of American Housework*, Martha Van Rensselaer 383, Henry Holt and Company LLC, New York, NY.

Strasser, S. (1989), *Satisfaction Guaranteed: The Making of the American Mass Market*, Pantheon Books, New York.

Tadajewski, M. (2013), "Helen Woodward and Hazel Kyrk: Economics Radicalism, consumption symbolism and female contributions to marketing theory and advertising practice", *Journal of Historical Research in Marketing*, Vol. 5, No. 3.

Tomes, N. (1998), *The Gospel of Germs*, Harvard University Press, Cambridge, MA.

True, A.C. (1928), *A History of Agricultural Extension Work in the United States, 1785–1923*, US GPO, Washington, DC.

Tucker, J. (n.d.), *Recollections of My Forty Years with Butterick, Butterick Archives and Library (BPCP)*, Butterick Publishing Company, New York.

Van Rensselaer, M., *(n.d.) Papers (MVRP), A Guide to the New York State College of Home Economics Records, 1875-1979, archival papers, (23-2-749)*, Division of Rare and Manuscript Collections, Cornell University Library, Ithaca, NY.

Zuckerman, M.E. (1994), "Creating Mrs. Consumer: the career of Christine Frederick," presented at the Organization of American Historians, April, Seattle, Washington.

Zuckerman, M.E. (1998), *A History of Popular Women's Magazines in the United States, 1792–1995*, Greenwood Press, Westport, CT.

Zuckerman, M.E. (2013), "Martha Van Rensselaer and the *Delineator* homemaking department," *Journal of Historical Research in Marketing*, Vol. 5, No. 3, pp. 370–384.

Zuckerman, M.E. (2017), "Creating a market of rural homemakers," in *Proceedings of the Conference on Historical Analysis and Research in Marketing*, June, Liverpool, England.

Zuckerman, M.E. (2019), "Many females will vote: campaigning, politics and newspaper marketing," in *Proceedings of the Conference on Historical Analysis and Research in Marketing*, June, Ottawa, Canada.

Zuckerman, M.E. and Carsky, M. (1990), "Contributions of women to U.S. marketing thought: the consumers' perspective," *JAMS*, Vol. 18, No. 4, pp. 313–318.

3 Creating the critical consumer
Helen Woodward and Hazel Kyrk on self-determination and the good life

Mark Tadajewski

Introduction

We know relatively little about the early female pioneers who produced path-breaking contributions in our field (Zuckerman and Carsky, 1990). To be sure, there have been autobiographical accounts (e.g. Fitz-Gibbon, 1951; Maas, 2012; Wells Lawrence, 2003) and important studies of practitioner-consultants including Dorothy Liebes (Blaszczyk, 2008), Madam C.J. Walker and A'Lelia Walker (Dossett, 2009), Katherine Blackford (Tadajewski, 2012), Lillian Gilbreth (Graham, 2013), Pauline Arnold (Jones, 2013), Barbara Gardner Proctor (Davis, 2017), Caroline Robinson Jones (Davis, 2013), Christine Frederick (Zuckerman and Carsky, 1990) published. We continue this endeavour.

The two individuals we examine in this chapter were major analysts of marketing and consumption behaviour. Helen Woodward (1882–1960) was a successful copywriter in the advertising industry. Unusually, when her role failed to generate the creative inspiration and excitement she craved, at age 42 she moved in a different direction, engaging in reflection on her career and life, taking on the role of a critical commentator on marketing and advertising practice. She also turned a lifelong interest in fiction into writing multiple novels.

We should note that Woodward does not self-associate with feminism. This might be due to a slight misinterpretation of what this entailed. Her work does draw on the assumptions undergirding liberal feminism and sometimes takes on a Marxist feminist patina (Bristor and Fischer, 1993). She did not see men and women as fundamentally different. Her associates, by contrast, viewed things otherwise. Some of the men she interacted with did consider themselves as superior. Reflecting this bias, Woodward was sometimes treated as if she should be grateful for her role and remuneration. But sedimented beliefs about what women could and could not do had no place in her worldview. She recognised that men had access to different opportunities, and these advantages were often naturalised.

Nonetheless, self-belief, hard work and innate talent propelled her to success. Throughout her life, she was tireless in ensuring her own financial security and provided advice to other women seeking success – a trait consistent with other female pioneers in the advertising industry (Wills and Raven, 2020). Woodward's desire for autonomy and security links her with feminist values traceable back to 1640 (Wills and Raven, 2020). Beyond these similarities with feminist thought, her stance in relation to the business system is commensurable with critical marketing studies. She used her

DOI: 10.4324/9781003042587-4

skills to highlight the problems accompanying consumption decisions – particularly when they are shaped by the lifestyle visions paraded in women's magazines, revealing where advertisements and marketing communications failed to tell the full story about their products.

In undertaking this project, Woodward manifests socialist values, spotlighting the shaping of the discursive domain by powerful interests – notably government, manufacturers, advertisers and lobbying groups – whose actions, largely, buttressed the status quo (e.g. Hirschman, 1993: 547). In her efforts to stimulate consumer criticality, Woodward shone a searchlight on the practices of mendacious social actors. As we shall see, her recommendations straddle the lines between encouraging critical (i.e. more informed deliberation within the context of consumer culture) and critically reflexive consumption (i.e. challenging cultural codes and economic arrangements, often moving outside of mainstream consumption patterns) (Ozanne and Murray, 1995).

Our second female pioneer, Hazel Kyrk (1886–1957), can likewise be viewed as an early contributor to critical marketing studies. She undertook domestic work and later multiple teaching positions to support her career aspirations (Lobdell, 2000; van Velzen, 2003). As we shall unpack in detail, Kyrk was a highly knowledgeable, theoretically informed academic. Her major contribution, *A Theory of Consumption*, is our primary focus and deserves far more attention than it has received to date (Mason, 1998, 2000). It still has considerable potential to invigorate thinking and connect with contemporary developments in marketing thought on the contextual shaping of consumer practice.

Conditions of possibility

The late 19th century saw extensive industrial growth. While women had long been employed in various ways (e.g. via the putting out system of finishing garments for factories and in 'service'), the early 20th century witnessed a massive increase in the numbers of women working in retailing at low wages, for long hours and in sometimes unpleasant conditions (Bondfield, 1899). Women were often involved in other marketing-related industries. They pasted street advertising and functioned as mystery shoppers crisscrossing the railroads as inconspicuous judges of service quality (Pope, 2004).

At around the same time, social and ideological pressures were notable. Engaging in work was their second role. It did not usually mean a reduction in household labour. Furthermore, self-advancement required educational opportunities as well as an employment context amenable to workforce change, neither of which came easily. Problematic biological arguments were proffered for limiting educational advancement. Women were inferior, so the argument went. They would not be able to cope with the intellectual strains of the university environment. Academic institutions were less than enthusiastic in welcoming them, unless they had specialised women's colleges. These locations, in turn, offered a career path. Irrespective of talent, women generally occupied lower levels of the scholarly hierarchy, taught more and received less remuneration than their equivalent male peers (Goodsell, 1929).

Of course, there were other options available. For many the advertising industry held out the promise of intellectual stimulation and financial self-sufficiency (Davis, 2013). Helen Woodward's fascinating life keys into this set of expectations.

Helen Woodward: on feminism and socialism

The life narrative of Helen Rosen Woodward underlines the difficulties faced by those without financial resources to support their career desires. Lacking wealth, Woodward was fortunate to possess high levels of motivation, a voracious reading habit and dedication to self-development (Woodward, 1935). Reflexively, she registered that her personal background and epistemological-political commitments were likely to make life tricky. When she calls attention to the difficulties wrought by perceptions of her gender, religious orientation (Jewish), radicalism and pacifism, it is hard not to marvel at her success (Woodward, 1926, 1935).

Woodward's fiscal situation prevented her from taking up a place at Radcliffe College. Unable to secure a part-time job and lacking the connections necessary to negotiate the scholarship process, the barriers to entry appeared insurmountable (Woodward, 1935). Life intervened, so she headed into the advertising industry. This provided a practically based education that substituted for the missed university experience:

> MOST young copywriters consider an advertising agency a sort of college for learning advertising...The training is good. It is to the advertising writer what the clinic is to a physician. An advertising agency is a lively place. You pass so abruptly from non-skid tyres to safety pins, from silk stockings to glass doorknobs. You write one hour about a tree surgeon and the next about cogwheels. It is a place of swift movement – of constant shifts – of things finished at the last possible gasp – of seconds grabbed from eternity – of hurrying and joshing and smoking and swearing...all is colored by the fury of creation.
> (Woodward, 1926: 200–201; emphasis in original)

She enjoyed the work, became a proficient writer and used multiple strategies to engage her reader (e.g. obtaining celebrity endorsement, using country of origin appeals).

Like Hazel Kyrk, Woodward's knowledge was informed by the critically oriented literature. Both were profoundly influenced by political economy. Woodward was conversant with international events, absorbed fiction and possessed a vivid imagination honed by literary immersion – an interest that paid dividends for employers who called on her to produce circulars and leaflets that promoted their book distribution business. Woodward's imagination was her toolkit. She had little problem conjuring ideas for clients.

The fact she was a successful woman caused some friction, leading her to cultivate an interpersonal skillset that included handling patronising men. These interactions did not, however, lead her to feminism which she appears to have viewed as a response to male bias against women. Rather, she understood gender-related problems as more systemic and economically oriented than a reflection of personal animus. Initially, she devoted her energy to traversing the existing system.

She underlines her ambition, knowledge, skills and 'stupendous intellect' (Woodward, 1935: 207) as drivers of career success. Even so, she reminds the reader that these attributes and skills come with a cost. The exceptionally talented or highly intelligent, she submits, is likely to pay a penalty for their acuity. Undermining the social ideology that maintained women were biologically and socially unfit for certain forms of education or work, she indexes social and behavioural similarities across genders:

> We women are not so easy to work with as men. When you see a woman who is doing well in business, you nearly always see one who is neurotic or weary or tempestuous. Seldom do you see one who is calm and serene. It is this way. Women who are much abler than others are not normal, and men who are abler than others are not normal either. Both such men and women have some things in them which are stronger than in other people. They are not made up evenly of ingredients like a well-made bread, but have too much of one thing, like a soufflé, and have to be handled with care.
>
> (Woodward, 1926: 231–232)

In this explication of her views, there are shades of liberal and Marxist values. As she further explains,

> I was too often reminded that I was merely a woman. One thought kept me from becoming a feminist – the thought that the trouble did not come from any innate antagonism on the part of men, but from a basic economic situation. It was evident enough from what I saw that as soon as enough women was [sic] needed outside of the home the discrimination against them would disappear. It seemed foolish to feel resentment against men as men for the difficulties that came to me as a woman. It wasn't their fault or mine; we were both living in a changing civilization and were equally victims of a general condition.
>
> (Woodward, 1926: 222–223)

Woodward shared a similar trajectory to other high-flying and deeply motivated people (Davis, 2013, 2017). She identified opportunities with rapidity, looking for roles that were better paid, whose employment conditions were more conducive to productivity and happiness. This led her to work for various organisations including the Hampton Advertising Agency, J.A. Hill Company, *Review of Reviews*, *Woman's Home Companion*, among others. Interestingly, she conceptualised the consumer in a variety of ways, modifying this over the course of her career.

Conceptualising the consumer

At the start of her career, she was exposed to unethical conduct and this initially made her contemptuous of the consumer (Woodward, 1926). Slightly later, she makes the case that people were malleable beings, who were relatively easy to manipulate. In sentiment that forms a condition of possibility for her later shift towards acting as an advocate for the customer, she points out that many individuals were all too willing to trust their senses, believe what they are told and follow the often spurious logic provided by marketers. It is this credulity that advertisers manipulated. By contrast to other professionals, Woodward avoids depicting the audience as an active reader, critically engaging with the claims of marketers (cf. Jones, 2013; Scanlon, 2013). This did not mean the consumer lacked agency. Woodward diagnosed rising cynicism among some groups.

As she started to feel disenchanted with the advertising business, her orientation to the buyer was mollified by her growing concern for public welfare – a perspective fostered by engagement with the consumer movement, including the League of Women Shoppers (LWS). Nor were Woodward's critiques limited to armchair theorising. She was a member of the Women's Trade Union League, protested with strikers and joined a cooperative enterprise (a restaurant) (Woodward, 1926).

In wanting to help other people navigate the marketplace, she put her intelligence and training to work in the interests of the ultimate user. This shift is less surprising when we appreciate Woodward's politics. In her autobiographies, she repeatedly stresses her interest in socialism, highlighting the commitment of family members to socialism and radicalism. Since Woodward was an avid reader, she delved into Edward Bellamy's (1888/1996) classic, *Looking Backward*. When we read Bellamy, it is not difficult to determine his book's appeal to Woodward, since it connects with some of the values she held (and which link her with liberal and Marxist feminism, even if she never adopted the terms).

Bellamy describes a world which has undergone massive structural change. The profoundly unequal marketplace – an issue that Woodward touches upon – has disappeared. A version of state socialism replaces capitalist relations. State management of production is the norm. The excessive costs of manufacturing and distribution are controlled. Marketing and sales activities are radically transformed. They are not needed in this rationalised world. The consumer is in control, determining their own needs, and wants without the influence of masters of persuasion. If information is sought, the government provides it. Furthermore, the kind of concern Woodward had for her financial security is no longer an issue in Bellamy's socialist utopia. Inequalities of income are absent. Everyone receives the same wage. Similarly, the relations between men and women are equalised.

In some respects, Woodward's turn towards helping the purchaser make better decisions can be interpreted as an attempt to help increase rationality over emotionality, working against the machinations of marketers at the same time. She was returning to her roots: 'I always came back to Socialism. Socialism was heaven' (Woodward, 1935: 165). This concern for others manifested in Woodward's popular writings for *The Nation*.

Creating a critical consumer

It is certainly true that Woodward's politics oscillated during her lifetime, starting out more radical, moving towards a greater level of conservatism as her success grew and eventually recalibrating back to activism. Nevertheless, she did intervene actively in the business and marketing system in more critical directions. Her practice differentiates her from commentators who had extensive links to the business community and promoted their products in 'ethically questionable' ways such as Christine Frederick (Scanlon, 1995: 69). Not only did Woodward try to change perceptions about the role of women in advertising, she turned her practical knowledge against those peddling their problematic wares to the public. In her interrogations of capitalism, marketing and the publishing system, she occupies a liminal space, operating on the borderland between a critical and critically reflexive mindset (Ozanne and Murray, 1995). Certain consumption habits are questioned, less market-focused tactics are applauded and more informed decision-making is valorised.

Her publications in *The Nation* gave Woodward the space to 'say something that will be of direct use when the consumer starts to spend money' (Woodward, 1939e: 360). Clearly, in trying to motivate people to think critically about their purchasing strategies, Woodward is aware that most of us are not logical machines, weighing up our choices in a neoclassical sense of seeking maximum utility (something Kyrk concurred with). Because we are all too human, we are invariably swayed by our emotions (Woodward, 1926).

In her later writing, advertising is often positioned as a powerful force (Woodward, 1939c). It is the vehicle for selling products that are rarely distinguishable in terms of product quality and satisfaction. Nor is the marketplace a domain of mutual benefit and satisfaction for all. For those with limited funds, they will be bypassed as targets for marketer attention by and large. Low-income consumers and those on the relief rolls scarcely merit a glance: 'they don't live in the clean, nice advertising world at all' (Woodward, 1938c: 476).

Woodward often makes arguments against raw empiricism, that is, against people trusting their own senses or, more indirectly, the advice of service operators in product selection (Woodward, 1939c). Securing information about the items we buy can be difficult, and considerable knowledge, training and energy were needed to avoid making bad decisions (Woodward, 1938a). This was made more challenging courtesy of efforts to 'bewitch the customer' (Woodward, 1939c: 620). Pseudo-scientific claims, long lists of indecipherable and chemically derived ingredients, misleading labels and oversized packaging, all hampered evaluation processes (Woodward, 1939c). Illuminating the issues confronting the unwary, she writes,

> Take candy and the big-looking 50-cent package that holds no more than a 10-cent package. The actual weight is put in mighty small type. There's a rum toffee without either rum or toffee; "wild cherry" drops whose label is marked in tiny type, "added acid, artificial flavor, certified food color" – you need a magnifying glass to learn that only the sugar is genuine. It seems beyond belief that a manufacturer will try to sell Easter eggs poisoned with lead and zinc dyes. But apparently a penny is a penny, and a hundred children's pennies make a dollar.
> (Woodward, 1938b: 17)

The complexity of the marketplace, the rise of me-too products and the promotion of adulterated and dangerous items (Woodward, 1939a, 1939b, 1939c) meant that 'There are many products in which it is hard for the consumer to find out what's good and what's not' (Woodward, 1937: 718). Manufacturers and retailers did not always act with the customers' interests in mind. Consistent with socialist narratives, Woodward understood how the profit motive skewed business policies (Woodward, 1939a, 1939e). Vigilance in the marketplace was a necessity and increasingly assisted by multiple groups. Such political activism was a definite concern for those seeking to influence the consumer:

> A CUSTOMER used to be just a person you sold something to – "the fall guy." But in these large days of public relations, the customer has become the consumer, and everybody's worried about him. The manufacturer and the ad-man are losing sleep because maybe the consumer isn't being treated right…What causes all this sudden furore…Quite simply the customer has shown symptoms of lassitude…Young people especially no longer believe advertising with their old abandon. Advertisers' first reaction, of course, was indignation…Then the good ladies swung into line and

we found anti-advertising propaganda running through such powerful women's groups as the American Home Economics Association, the Association of University Women, Parent-Teachers Association, American Federation of Women's Clubs, and the American League of Women Voters. And through the teachers who are members of these organizations, anti-advertising doctrine went into schools and colleges.

(Woodward, 1938d: 388–389; emphasis in original)

Woodward regularly reminded her readers about the information provided by these groups and others, including The General Federation of Women's Clubs and Consumers' Union. She cited appropriate publications (e.g. *The Consumers' Guide*) and accentuated the importance of monitoring cases progressing through the court system (Woodward, 1939b, 1939c). In cases like those associated with foods, drugs and cosmetics, people had to counterpoint the lobbying efforts of manufacturers and marketers (e.g. Woodward, 1939a) and carefully scrutinise lists of harmful products (Woodward, 1939c). Woodward puts this in vivid terms,

> The new Food, Drugs, and Cosmetics Act was passed not quite a year ago, and only part of it – that dealing with new or dangerous drugs and devices and poisonous cosmetics – went into effect at once…But it did not altogether stop the interstate shipping of dangerous eyelash dyes, and the Food and Drug Administration had to seize *Lash-Lure*, the most notorious of them. It has seized seventy-nine shipments of poisonous cosmetics and started five criminal prosecutions, and has seized forty-two shipments of dangerous drugs and fifty-one shipments of dangerous devices. In all those cases legal action was taken, but thousands of other products were withdrawn from the market the moment the act was passed.
>
> (Woodward, 1939d: 671)

Notably, she warned shoppers about highly marketed and expensively packaged cosmetics that were poor value. In place of purchasing habits that redistributed hard-earned income to the deep pockets of avaricious merchants, she provided 'some practical dollar-saving suggestions' with respect to face cleansing (Woodward, 1939b: 614). At other times, Woodward questioned patterns of consumption that were rapidly becoming cultural conventions consistent with the Diderot effect (McCracken, 1988). Products became successful in the marketplace, she argued, for various reasons. Government policy, advertising creativity and repetition, combined with a degree of credulity, performed various roles in different product categories:

> SHAVING cream is the perfect example of a business that is non-essential and has been created entirely by advertising. It costs more than a cake of shaving soap and it does not work so well. Now don't say that you know all about shaving and I don't. Before you speak, read a little farther. How did this fantastic business grow up? Just before the war it seemed to men that everything about shaving must be modern to go with the safety razor. A modern razor demanded a modern kind of soap. Away with the old-fashioned shaving mug! Colgate's Rapid Shaving Cream, which appeared in 1914–15, was the first nationally successful cream. It was followed by a number of others. They were sold by a dramatization of the idea of speed. You saved

time by using them and time was money. So you actually saved money by spending a little extra for the cream. But even to this day it surprises the ad men to find that men believe them when they say it takes less time to use a tube of cream than a glass with a cake in it.

(Woodward, 1939c: 430; emphasis in original)

In short, Helen Woodward certainly left her mark. She received the praise of the advertising industry and critically minded figures associated with the consumer movement.

Hazel Kyrk

Kyrk started her academic career at Wellesley College as an instructor (1911–1912), before moving to the University of Chicago to pursue Ph.D. research (1913–1914). The latter project continued while she worked at Oberlin College (Lobdell, 2000). At Oberlin, Kyrk was an instructor, then Assistant Professor of Economics, before helping with the war effort. Following the armistice, she joined the Food Research Institute at Stanford, afterwards relocating to Iowa State College, ultimately returning to the University of Chicago (1925), obtaining the position of full professor in the early 1940s and retiring in 1952 (Lobdell, 2000).

As a contributor to 'consumption economics' her books, the seminal *A Theory of Consumption* (Kyrk, 1923) and the *Economic Problems of the Family* (Kyrk, 1933), connect with debates in marketing theory. She places consumer behaviour within its socio-historic context. Although the issue of 'why' people consume was of interest, normative considerations feature prominently in her writing (i.e. 'how' they should act).

Kyrk's account of the economy chimes with present discussions about the importance of registering the contingency of exchange relations; the role of context in shaping consumer decisions; the fact that purchasers are sometimes active participants who influence producers and not merely passive recipients of marketplace logics; as well as the need for defatalism regarding social change (Tadajewski, 2010a, 2010b). What the latter means is that the present ordering of the economy can be modified if it no longer serves appropriate purposes. This is not to say that she encouraged a shift from capitalism to socialism.

On socialism and power relations

In her 1923 text, Kyrk was attentive to the issue of socialism, examined some of the core assumptions in the literature, highlighted the benefits of centralised control of production and distribution (e.g. delimiting the production and circulation of 'undesirable lines') and appreciated the potential for expert guidance of the economy to result in social benefit. Even so, she makes the case that expert-led production and distribution would run into considerable problems due to the contextual, temporal and individual relativity of consumption choices. The type of 'authoritative control' she associates with socialism would not be 'easily secured'. Her reasoning is acute: it would be difficult for us to come to agreement on which items were necessary and desirable.

So, at the back of her reflections, someone – above and beyond the actual consumer – was going to make the ultimate decision about what constituted the good life. By contrast to other groups writing about socialism at this juncture such as the League for

Industrial Democracy, Kyrk's analysis took her down a similar path to that later shared by Wroe Alderson and colleagues who visited Russia in the 1950s (Tadajewski, 2009). Having someone else's interpretation of the 'good life' forced upon us can reduce agency and self-expression. In Kyrk's framing,

> The "good life" is imposed on the individual from without. He wants to live in a Chicago or a Gopher Prairie. Shall he be forced to live in an Athens? There is no individuality, in choosing the instruments of material life. There is an odious suggestion of a method analogous to the feeding, clothing, and amusing of the children of a household, of the soldiers of an army, or the inmates of a reformatory. But the situation is vastly different when the needs of the general public are to be met. The goods furnished, unless they reflect the felt needs and the inclinations of consumers, will not be chosen and paid for. Articles may not be taken from the public warehouse, or not taken in the quantities provided; the public theatres and art galleries may not be patronized. All that we know of the irrationality of human conduct, the variability of human wants, the dynamic nature of standards, the multiplicity of human interests, throws serious doubts upon the workability of a system of authoritative control.
>
> (Kyrk, 1923: 40)

In posing the questions that guide her work, Kyrk tackles complex power relations. As she indicates, the 1920s witnessed extensive questioning of the economic system. Within marketing scholarly inquiry sometimes took critical directions due to the impact of the German Historical School on our teaching and research (Jones and Tadajewski, 2018). In a manner which resonates with much contemporary reflection about the use of Gross Domestic Product to serve as our orientation device in evaluating the direction of society, Kyrk ruminates,

> New questions in regard to human welfare, and its relation to industrial organization, are now coming up, and there is pressure upon economic theory to show in all respects how the present order works, for good or ill. It is no longer felt that the sole question to be raised in regard to the operation of the economic order is how much wealth can it turn out. Another question is, What are the costs? And still another, Are the results worth the effort? But what are the results? Who fixes the ends and purposes toward which effort is directed, and how is organization for the purpose effected?…What is the place of the consumer in the industrial scheme? What scope in the guidance of economic activity is allowed to him [sic], for whom, nominally, it exists? Through what agencies can he make his interests felt?…How are consumers' purposes and desires formed?
>
> (Kyrk, 1923: 8)

In this quote, she is starting to problematise economic theory by asking questions about the lived reality of the consumer. Her work, then, wants to examine 'the world beyond the demand curve' (Kyrk, 1923: 19). We must explore the buyer, their consumption decisions, the power flowing between different actors (e.g. the 'monopolist, profiteer, speculator and middleman') neither clinging to academic theory nor the 'popular view' (Kyrk, 1923: 19).

Consumer decision-making

Kyrk identifies many limits to human decision-making and choice. For starters, there are various social influences which impact upon our actions. Financially, we are hemmed in by access to capital. Individual choices are circumscribed by purchasing power. This is compounded by producer sovereignty. Manufacturers do not produce everything desired, since 'dollar votes' are not equally distributed. People are consequently treated differently by virtue of their pocketbook. As part of their efforts to canalise demand, producers' marketing and advertising campaigns influence consideration sets in conjunction with wider social pressures. Even when Kyrk talks about the 'choices' available to the individual, they are often starkly delimited:

> Absolute freedom of choice is almost inconceivable even without the stern economic limitations mentioned. The consumer's standards and values, which he [sic] attempts to realize upon the market, are social products; he does not make them for himself, nor can he change them lightly or at will. What are the "means of life and culture" which he is to choose? They are the product of strong social forces: custom, convention, fashion, opinion. The result is that no sooner does one say that under the present organization consumers have freedom of choice, then one must begin to explain and qualify the statement. It must be shown that the consumer's power is not per capita, but per dollar; that producer's take the initiative, that they seek to direct and control demand, and even at times to deceive and defraud the purchaser. It must be further acknowledged that, from the standpoint of the individual consumer, his choices are bound by the limits of his income, by the producing possibilities of his time, made manifest to him by existing stocks of goods and their prices, and by the adequacy of the market facilities with which he is in touch.
> (Kyrk, 1923: 45)

Not only does she register that our buying and using habits are cultural constructions, Kyrk calls upon us to think about the structuring of consumption in communal terms. Are our consumption strategies efficient, wasteful or useful to us and others? Why do we value the goods and services we consume? Are there other ways of life that might be more beneficial? How do we arrive at our interpretation of a good life, rather than perform unthinking adherence to social convention?

In Kyrk's eyes, critical reflection on the good life is an ongoing process that should continually merit attention as we progress through our life-course. We will invariably make poor decisions along the way, learn from them, change our views and modify our habits (although this activity will be difficult). In this process, we need to reorient our self-perception. Leaving behind economic theory that hinges on assumptions of utility maximisation and logical choice, the characters who appear in the pages of Kyrk's publications are emotional, fallible and sociable, often steered by others who are equally imperfect, hence the need for self-surveillance regarding our decisions.

Still, most people do not exhibit a high need for cognition. Kyrk refers to the unthinking nature of human existence. We are too reliant on social cues; we look at the consumption patterns enacted by others and often follow them. After having evaluated Veblen's variant of trickle-down theory, Kyrk largely concurs, stressing the 'inequality in the distribution of wealth' and its redirection 'of the productive powers of society to meet the desires of the few' (Kyrk, 1923: 53). This, in turn, influences the 'standards of consumption' that people deem appropriate, with them buying 'symbols of success' to compete in games of status distinction:

> Certainly there is no doubt that the canons of the necessary, the decent, the desirable which are incorporated in current standards of consumption and expenditure are moulded in no small degree by the conspicuous spenders and wasters, by influences peculiar to a regime of pecuniary emulation.
> (Kyrk, 1923: 54)

This can have negative consequences. Our thoughtlessness is fundamentally wasteful and harmed those who had limited access to resources. Rather than axiologically ground our lives on ephemeral status competition, Kyrk held that consumption should be used to maximise family welfare.

Beyond the frailties of individual decision-making, it was apparent that the production and marketing systems were not optimal. Looking at the overall organisation of society, the externalities – the noise, dirt and crowded cities – came in for attention. Kyrk sums up our social nexus in the following way:

> For the sake of gains as consumers, individuals consent to more hazardous and less interesting work as workers…And upon the whole, the current methods of production seem to meet with approval. True, modern production has its peculiar hazards; it is monotonous, deadening, fatiguing. But even the most radical critics of the present order, who are most alive to its defects, would be unwilling to throw overboard the productive powers of modern industrial methods. They regard this power for productivity as, at least, a potential blessing. The defects lie, it is said, in our preoccupation with industry as an achievement, in our neglect of all interests but the pleasures of seeing the wheels go around, and in the pecuniary organization which distributes the benefits unequally, diverts production to socially undesirable purposes, and fails to protect against adverse working conditions.
> (Kyrk, 1923: 68; see also Plotkin, 2014)

On the other hand, as Woodward's activism reminds us, there were groups like the League of Women Shoppers (LWS) who did attempt to engage with questions of distributive justice using their purchasing power. One of the problems these groups ran into were allegations of communist influence. Woodward, for example, was a 'director' of the LWS (Woodward, 1939e: 360), and many other prominent figures, including Eleanor Roosevelt, were linked to it:

> Virtually every well-known woman radical and liberal of the 1930s seems to have been on its letterheads, and many of them participated actively. Founded in 1935 and claiming 25,000 members in thirteen chapters by 1939, the LWS mobilized middle- and upper-class women to "use their buying power for social justice, so that the fair price they pay as consumers will also include an American standard of living for those who make and market the goods they buy".
> (Storrs, 2006: 47)

The targeting of the consumer movement by politically aggressive, right-wing conservative constituencies was notable for various reasons including their focus on groups who were 'predominantly female' and seeking to redress the balance of power in the marketplace and public policy circles (Storrs, 2006: 41). Helping to increase the power, influence and knowledge of the consumer was a quite dangerous commitment. Challenging the advertising industry potentially led to accusations of communist sympathy. It propelled capitalism, and any moves to curtail its power were easily framed as anti-American.

Focusing on advertising, expressing concerns about the living standards of less affluent groups, highlighting the prevalence of white supremacy in the retailing environment (in both hiring policies and treatment of customers) and promulgating these issues via 'savvy legislative digests, letters to editors, and press releases' served to gain the attention of those wanting to maintain the status quo (Storrs, 2006: 50).

Many of those attacked in ostensible anti-communist action were 'left-feminists' (Storrs, 2006), and the ramifications of the attempts to discredit their redistributionist agenda were widespread, diluting the potential for substantive social change in relation to public welfare. These 'left-feminists':

> ...pursued a vision of women's emancipation that insisted on class and racial justice as well as "pure" gender equality...the anti-communist attack on consumer advocates had antifeminist effects. It not only marginalized important left-feminists, it discredited their proposals on issues from housing to health-care, which they correctly understood to be of particular concern to poor and working-class women... The Right also used the fear of communism to taint liberal policies. When the consumer movement revived in the 1960s, its objectives were less redistributive, and they were expressed in terms of the entitlement of specific categories of consumers rather than in terms of promoting the general public welfare.
>
> (Storrs, 2006: 43)

The actions taken against groups committed to public policy change and consumer education meant that the vision for social change they incubated and advanced was sometimes undermined. Capitalistic market relations require, as Woodward and Kyrk averred, constant vigilance. This remains true today.

Conclusion

In this chapter we have explored the contributions of two female pioneers. Helen Woodward had an impressive career, shifting gears in her early 40s from working as an advertising practitioner to focus her energies on various endeavours, including functioning as a critical commentator on the marketing and advertising industries. Always a keen observer, well informed by political and social theory, she wanted to help the buyer make the most of their income and avoid dangerous products. As part of groups like the LWS she was swept up in the anti-communist movement of the 1930s to 1950s. While the attack on the consumer movement did not appear to have serious ramifications for her, it did set back the progressive agenda of this community, rendering it less redistributive in orientation when it reappeared in the 1960s.

As an early pioneer in consumer economics, Hazel Kyrk deserves far more attention than she has received in our discipline. She wrote an extremely sophisticated text in the 1920s, *A Theory of Consumption*, which initially attracted some limited attention, yet soon disappeared off the radar of marketing thinkers. Mason attributes the comparative neglect of Kyrk's book to gender politics and 'the male-dominated academic and business environment of the 1920s and 1930s' (Mason, 2000: 177). By 1938, marketing academics did think that consumption required more attention and the infusion of 'new approaches to the subject' (Mason, 1998: 149). This was comparatively slow to occur, with assumptions of consumer rationality – something that both Woodward and Kyrk questioned – continuing to exert academic power (cf. Tadajewski, 2006) until the consumer, their lived experience and cultural perspectives gained greater traction in the second half of the 20th century (Mason, 1998).

References

Bellamy, E. 1888/1996. *Looking backward*. New York: Dover Publications.
Blaszczyk, R.L. 2008. Designing synthetics, promoting brands: Dorothy Liebes, DuPont fibres and post-war American interiors. *Journal of Design History* 21(1): 75–99.
Bondfield, M.G. 1899. Conditions under which shop assistants work. *The Economic Journal* 9(34): 277–286.
Bristor, J.M. and E. Fischer. 1993. Feminist thought: Implications for consumer research. *Journal of Consumer Research* 19(March): 518–536.
Davis, J.F. 2013. Beyond "caste-typing?": Caroline Robinson Jones, advertising pioneer and trailblazer. *Journal of Historical Research in Marketing* 5(3): 308–333.
Davis, J.F. 2017. *Pioneering African-American women in the advertising business: Biographies of MAD black women*. Abingdon: Routledge.
Dossett, K. 2009. "I try to live somewhat in keeping with my reputation as a wealthy woman": A'Lelia Walker and the Madam C.J. Walker manufacturing company. *Journal of Women's History* 21(2): 90–114.
Fitz-Gibbon, B. 1951. *Macy's, Gimbels, and me*. New York: Simon and Schuster.
Goodsell, W. 1929. The educational opportunities of American women – Theoretical and actual. *The Annals of the American Academy of Political and Social Science* 143(1): 1–13.
Graham, L. 2013. Lillian Gilbreth's psychologically enriched scientific management of women consumers. *Journal of Historical Research in Marketing* 5(3): 351–369.
Hirschman, E.C. 1993. Ideology in consumer research, 1980 and 1990: A Marxist and feminist critique. *Journal of Consumer Research* 19(March): 537–555.
Jones, D.G.B. 2013. Pauline Arnold (1894–1974): Pioneer in market research. *Journal of Historical Research in Marketing* 5(3): 291–307.
Jones, D.G.B. and M. Tadajewski. 2018. *Foundations of marketing thought: The influence of the German Historical School*. London: Routledge.
Kyrk, H. 1923. *A theory of consumption*. Boston, MA: Houghton Mifflin.
Kyrk, H. 1933. *Economic problems of the family*. New York: Harper & Bros.
Lobdell, R.A. 2000. Hazel Kyrk. In *A biographical dictionary of women economists*, eds. R.W. Dimand, M.A. Dimand, and E.L. Forget, 251–253. Cheltenham: Edward Elgar.
Maas, J. 2012. *Mad women: The other side of life on Madison Avenue in the 60s and beyond*. London: Bantam Books.
Mason, R.S. 1998. Breakfast in Detroit: Economics, marketing, and consumer theory, 1930–1950. *Journal of Macromarketing* 18(2): 145–152.
Mason, R.S. 2000. A pathfinding study of consumption. *Journal of Macromarketing* 20(2): 174–177.
McCracken, G. 1988. *Culture and consumption: New approaches to the symbolic character of consumer goods and activities*. Bloomington: Indiana University Press.
Ozanne, J.L. and J.B. Murray. 1995. Uniting critical theory and public policy to create the reflexively defiant consumer. *American Behavioral Scientist* 38(4): 516–525.

Plotkin, S. 2014. Misdirected effort: Thorstein Veblen's critique of advertising. *Journal of Historical Research in Marketing* 6(4): 501–522.

Pope, D. 2004. Birth of a salesman: The transformation of selling in America by Walter A. Friedman. *Business History Review* 78(3): 562–564.

Scanlon, J. 1995. *Inarticulate longings: The Ladies' Home Journal, gender, and the promises of consumer culture*. New York: Routledge.

Scanlon, J. 2013. "A dozen ideas to the minute": Advertising women, advertising to women. *Journal of Historical Research in Marketing* 5(3): 273–290.

Storrs, L.R.Y. 2006. Left-feminism, the consumer movement, and red scare politics in the United States, 1935–1960. *Journal of Women's History* 18(3): 40–67.

Tadajewski, M. 2006. Remembering motivation research: Toward an alternative genealogy of interpretive consumer research. *Marketing Theory* 6(4): 429–466.

Tadajewski, M. 2009. Quaker travels, fellow traveller? Wroe Alderson's visit to Russia during the cold war. *Journal of Macromarketing* 29(3): 303–324.

Tadajewski, M. 2010a. Toward a history of critical marketing studies. *Journal of Marketing Management* 26(9–10): 773–824.

Tadajewski, M. 2010b. Critical marketing studies: Logical empiricism, 'critical performativity' and marketing practice. *Marketing Theory* 10(2): 210–222.

Tadajewski, M. 2012. Character analysis and racism in marketing theory and practice. *Marketing Theory* 12(4): 485–508.

Van Velzen, S. 2003. Hazel Kyrk and the ethics of consumption. In *Toward a feminist philosophy of economics*, eds. D.K. Barker and E. Kuiper, 38–55. London: Routledge.

Wells Lawrence, M. 2003. *A big life (in advertising)*. New York: Touchstone.

Wills, J. and K. Raven. 2020. The founding five: Transformational leadership in the New York League of Advertising Women's Clubs, 1912–1926. *Journal of Historical Research in Marketing* 12(3): 377–399.

Woodward, H. 1926. *Through many windows*. New York: Harper & Brothers.

Woodward, H. 1935. *Three flights up*. New York: Dodd, Mead and Company.

Woodward, H. 1937. About coffee. *The Nation*, December 25: 717–718.

Woodward, H. 1938a. Pocket guide: Virgin wool. *The Nation*, November 12: 509–510.

Woodward, H. 1938b. Young shoppers. *The Nation*, December 31: 17–18.

Woodward, H. 1938c. Republican in sheep's clothing. *The Nation*, 147(19): 475–477.

Woodward, H. 1938d. *It's an art*. New York: Harcourt, Brace and Company.

Woodward, H. 1939a. Pocket guide. *The Nation*, April 1: 376–377.

Woodward, H. 1939b. Pocket guide: Is grade a milk richer?. *The Nation*, May 27: 614–615.

Woodward, H. 1939c. Pocket guide: Shaving the soap. *The Nation* April, 15: 430–431.

Woodward, H. 1939d. Pocket guide. *The Nation*, June 10: 671–672.

Woodward, H. 1939e. Letters to the editors. *The Nation*, March 25: 360.

Zuckerman, M.E. and M.L. Carsky. 1990. Contribution of women to U.S. marketing thought: The consumers' perspective, 1900–1940. *Journal of the Academy of Marketing Science* 18(4): 313–317.

4 Marketing's hidden figures

Black women leaders in advertising

Judy Foster Davis

In late 2016, the motion picture *Hidden Figures* debuted in theaters, drawing widespread acclaim and earning an Academy Award nomination. Based on the book of the same title, it introduced to the public sphere the history of several unknown real-life black women whose mathematical and engineering acumen helped to successfully launch American astronauts into space in the 1960s (Shetterly 2016). Until recently, the stories of important black women advertising leaders were similarly obscured from the historical record (Davis 2016). What these hidden figures have in common is that most also started their careers in the 1960s, confronted significant oppressions in their professional lives based on gender and race – yet overcame these challenges to produce significant accomplishments. This chapter examines prominent African-American advertising women and their careers through the lens of black feminism.

Black feminism: intersectionality and the matrix of domination

Black feminist thought leaders understand that feminist theory must reflect the "lived experiences" of black women in order to be perceived as relevant and credible. This outlook is necessary since it is well documented that traditional feminist frameworks, which typically relate to the interests, concerns, and lifestyles of middle-class white women, often do not align with the values, experiences, and realities comprising black women's lives. Traditional feminist approaches tend to downplay the privilege that whiteness affords to white women, or serve to denigrate or misrepresent aspects that are important to black women – such as motherhood, family roles, relationships with men, faith, and activist communities – which are often vital sources of identity, support, and kinship among black women (Collins 2013; McFadden 2011; Roth 2017). The discord between black and white women's perspectives on feminism is so stark that some rejected the term "feminist" in favor of "womanist" to center black women's existences and leadership styles (Roth 2017). Therefore, the work of black women thought leaders Kimberle Crenshaw and Patricia Hill Collins provides the foundation for this examination, given that they focus on the unique positionality of black women. A fundamental idea undergirding this analysis is intersectionality, a concept introduced by Crenshaw (1991) to demonstrate how social inequities operate in coextensive, overlapping, and interlocking manners to create unique patterns of oppression for black women based on identity. Initially introduced to illustrate how concurrent identities uniquely compound legal discriminations against black women, the intersectionality concept became so popular that it was adapted to analyze multiple interrelating identities involving race, gender, social class, sexual orientation, etc., in a variety of contexts (Gopaldas

DOI: 10.4324/9781003042587-5

and DeRoy 2015; Thomas 2013). A 2016 Ted Talk on intersectionality by Crenshaw garnered more than 4.3 million views by mid-2021, underscoring the concept's broad appeal (Ted.com 2016). However, critics contend that the intersectionality concept has been co-opted by privileged white women, who – for example – became the most compelling faces of the 2017 #MeToo movement, which denounced sexual exploitation of women, although it originated with Tarana Burke, a black woman activist (Villeseche, Muhr and Sliwa 2018; Sobande 2019). This observation underscores complaints that issues concerning black women often fail to attract the levels of attention or sympathy as those associated with black men or white women, rendering black women somewhat invisible at the same time that they are vulnerable on multiple dimensions (Collins 2000; Ted.com 2016).

Delving more deeply into the lived experiences of black women, Collins extended Crenshaw's work by providing a detailed and nuanced model of intersectionality: the Matrix of Domination which is characterized by experiences of intersecting oppressions (Collins 2000, 23). This model identifies four essential domains of power and oppression:

1. The *Structural domain* which organizes power and oppression at the broad institutional level. This domain consists of practices and policies utilized by the government, legal systems, educational systems, housing and financial markets, labor markets, media industries; health care systems; and corporate/industrial systems such that resources are unequally distributed. Power at the structural level operates through laws and regulations of social institutions and often works to disadvantage black women and other marginalized groups.
2. The *Disciplinary domain* which manages power and oppression at the organizational level, often relying on bureaucratic hierarchies and methods of surveillance. Such oppression occurs in settings such as courts, banks, schools, hospitals, media outlets, business settings, and so on. In this domain, rules and policies are established within organizations in order to control behaviors through cultural norms, standards, and values in the organizations.
3. The *Hegemonic domain* which justifies and legitimizes oppression based on ideas and ideologies within societal cultures and social systems. Examples include philosophies and teachings conveyed in religious and educational settings; in family, community, and kinship groups; in social organizations and through media images. Dominant groups create and maintain a popular system of "commonsense" ideas that support their right to rule (Collins 2000, 284). Members within organizational groups may police one another and suppress each other's dissent (Collins, 2000, 299).
4. The *Interpersonal domain* which normalizes oppression that takes place in the form of everyday practices among people. Here, discriminations are a routine aspect of daily lives such that they go unnoticed, unidentified, and often unchallenged. In this domain, the manipulation of ideas, images, symbols, and ideologies by the dominant group has potent ability to shape consciousness.

Against the potentially devastating effects of the intersecting domains of oppression and power exerted against black women, black feminist theorists recognize that many black women are not only concerned with oppression, but are equally engaged with resistance and activism as methods of empowerment (Alina 2015; Collins 2000). Black women's acts of resistance may manifest through music, art, literature, scholarship, social and political activism, and other forms of leadership. Later in this chapter, I discuss ways that black women advertising leaders have engaged in a myriad of acts of resistance and activism.

Black women, the advertising business, and the power matrix

The Matrix of Domination model has particular relevance to understanding the advertising industry and the experiences of black women professionals from structural, disciplinary, hegemonic, and interpersonal perspectives. Before discussing pioneering black adwomen, let's begin with a look at the broad structural dimensions of the industry's interdependent institutions: large holding companies, agencies, trade associations, corporate advertisers, media organizations, and vendors. At the institutional level, advertising is different from many white-collar professions, in that it generally requires no particular licenses, exams, or certifications in order to practice, unlike fields like medicine, law, and public accounting. The industry also operates with little regulatory oversight or union participation which often influences employment practices. Instead, the industry is heavily driven by personal relationships and networks which tend to include and exclude certain types of people (Bendick and Egan 2019). Boulton (2016, 139) notes, "Structural impediments and barriers of unpaid internships, nepotism, and homosocial reproduction that favor those already in power" establish the pathway into advertising workplaces. Within this context, the cultures of advertising firms are shaped by the beliefs, attitudes, preferences, personalities, and behaviors of those in positions of power and authority. As noted by sociologist Anthony Cortese (2008, 100), in advertising organizations, "Cultural beliefs favor whites over people of color, males over females and the privileged over the disadvantaged." Therefore, over much of its 150-year history, the advertising industry has been characterized by a poor reputation regarding equitable treatment with respect to employment, compensation, and advancement opportunities for women and ethnic minorities despite decades of calls to action on these issues and the deployment of dedicated diversity officers and programs (Bendick and Egan 2019; Boulton 2016; Broyles and Grow 2008; Chambers 2008; Davis 2016; Monllos 2019; Thomas 2017).

In recent years, however, the fortunes of white women and ethnic minorities in advertising seemed to diverge. For example, work by Maclaran, Stevens, and Catterall (1997) found that female marketing managers often encountered a "Glasshouse Effect" in their career progression, whereby they were concurrently bound by gender-based barriers which limited their advancement to certain levels within the company and were simultaneously pigeonholed into areas like Creative or Research, while lacking access to client-facing and managerial roles. Similarly, in 2012, an advocacy group named the 3% Conference was established to address the low numbers of adwomen in creative management positions – hence the name of the organization. By 2015, the numbers of women creative managers increased from 3% to 11% – nearly a four-fold increase (Batthany 2015). This statistic and other data revealed an interesting phenomenon: the increased feminization of marketing practice. By 2008, women accounted for 66% of all advertising jobs across all service areas in advertising agencies (Broyles and Grow 2008). Moreover, between 1980 and 2018, the percentage of women managers in advertising and marketing increased from 14% to 44% (Sherman 2018). Even more striking was a 2020 report indicating that – for the first time – pay levels for senior-level marketing women outpaced those of men, indicating progress towards gender parity (Pasquarelli 2020). Therefore, white women appeared to have made excellent progress in the advertising business.

Despite women's advancements in advertising, opportunities for people of color, especially African-Americans, seemed to stagnate over the same period. Prior to civil rights legislation in the U.S. in the 1960s, overt forms of discrimination were pervasive in advertising and other white-collar industries. In advertising, women were hired mainly in clerical roles and black people often could not get hired at all – although several black men served as salesmen and consultants to white corporations after World War II when it became apparent that the black consumer market was lucrative (Davis 2013). Passage of the Civil Rights Act of 1964 outlawed employment discrimination on the basis of race, national origin, religion, and gender; and created the EEOC (Equal Employment Opportunity Commission), which holds the power to pursue lawsuits against victimized workers. Even then, employment growth for racial minorities was slow and torturous. By 2009, black employment was 5.3% of the total industry (Bendick and Egan 2009.) In 2019, the black employment rate was still about 5% of the total advertising workforce of 629,000 (Rahaman 2019), and 7% among the member companies of the Association of National Advertisers (ANA) trade group (ANA-AIMM 2019, 10). Moreover, the ANA data showed the proportion of black employees was the lowest among all non-white minority groups in the industry and had greater concentrations in clerical and entry-level jobs. Noting that blacks comprised only 3% of Chief Marketing Officer roles among its member companies, the ANA (2019, 7) concluded, "…representation of ethnic marketers among the ANA overall memberships, as well as among CMOs, remains too low." Additional empirical data and research reveal discriminatory treatments and microaggressions experienced by black advertising professionals (Boulton 2016; Center for Talent Innovation 2019; Rittenhouse 2020). A 2019 study by the Center for Talent Innovation (CTI), sponsored by the advertising holding company IPG and other marketing organizations, found that black corporate professionals were four times as likely to say they had experienced racial prejudice in the workplace compared to white professionals (58% vs. 15%); 43% of black executives had heard racially insensitive remarks in their presence; and only 19% of black corporate employees believed that someone of their background could attain a top job within their company. These findings, consistent with Combs' (2003) study, indicated that blacks are treated differently in corporate workplaces; are often excluded and isolated from professional networking groups; and are not provided advancement opportunities commensurate with their knowledge, talents, and skills. Interestingly, only 40% of the total workforce believed that their company's diversity and inclusion efforts were effective (Center for Talent Innovation 2019). A very compelling finding was that black professionals were more than twice as likely as whites to say that white women were the main beneficiaries of diversity and inclusion efforts (29% vs. 13%); but that white women were seen by only 12% of black *and* white employees as using their influence to advocate for other underrepresented parties (Center for Talent Innovation 2019; Sherman 2018). Speaking to the racialization and inequities that exist within advertising institutions (Ray 2019), grievances among blacks working in advertising came to a boiling point in 2020, as the world was reeling from widespread social unrest in response to police brutality, perceived racist treatment of black people, and elevation of the #Black Lives Matter movement. More than 600 black advertising professionals formed a non-profit coalition, backed by the 4A's (American Association of Advertising Agencies) trade group, and wrote an open letter to ad industry leaders, calling for an end to systemic racism in the industry and providing a list of 12 demands seeking improvements (Diaz 2020a, 2020b). Among other things, they asked for transparency with respect to reporting workforce diversity data on an annual basis; commitment to increased black representation at all staffing levels – especially senior and leadership positions; bias training among all human resource and management personnel; a wage equity plan for black men and women; and the establishment of a diversity review panel to impede the spread of racially offensive and culturally insensitive marketing portrayals (Zorrilla 2020).

Where does this situation leave black women? Despite the advancement of white women, they have not enjoyed similar benefit. In fact, a 2017 EEOC study found a total of only 93 black female executives in all advertising, public relations, and related agencies in the U.S. among 8,734 total executives, which included 3,037 white women (*Advertising Age* 2017). Hence, black women represented only about 1% of the total number of executive positions, prompting the EEOC to conclude:

> …black women have the lowest upward mobility among other major demographic groups in advertising, PR and related fields, while black women in other professional services industries, such as legal, accounting and management consulting, have higher executive representation in leadership roles.
> (Advertising Age 2017)

Advertising Age, the industry's leading trade publication, also addressed the unique discriminations towards black adwomen, who reported experiencing consistent microaggressions in the workplace, social exclusion from interpersonal networks, being subjected to racial stereotyping, and being labeled as "overly ambitious or too aggressive" by leadership (Rittenhouse 2020). One black ad woman commented anonymously, "We are pushed to accept racism because we're always just trying to take care of our jobs and not get fired and not look like the angry Black woman" (Rittenhouse 2020). These reports mirrored experiences for black women in corporate settings from other studies, where they reported less access to support advocacy and networking resources compared with white women, less progress, and diminished satisfaction with their employment situations (Center for Talent Innovation 2019; Combs 2003). The lack of support by white female colleagues was seen as particularly vexing, with the Center for Talent Innovation (2019, 8) concluding,

> We've heard many times from D&I [Diversity and Inclusion] leaders that their company must 'solve for women's challenges first' because there are more established solutions there, and it is easier to gain C-suite buy-in. Yet there is consensus across race and gender that White women do not pay these gains forward.

Putting this background in context, the situation for black women in the advertising industry – especially in managerial roles – appears particularly precarious given their dual oppression status. The Matrix of Domination manifests in the advertising industry in ways which significantly constrain black women's collective progress. Therefore, if change is to occur at the structural level, top leadership in the industry must understand their role in establishing and organizing the power hierarchies which allow racial inequities and white privilege to flourish in advertising institutions and actively commit to transforming these structures.

Pragmatic feminists: black women advertising leaders

Despite the presence of significant challenges for black women, a number entered the advertising profession in the 1960s and 1970s and made significant accomplishments, often serving in historic managerial and entrepreneurial roles. Yet, these women and their experiences are not generally well known. Therefore, their careers are examined here, based on five black women advertising leaders whose lives have been chronicled in full-length biographies or memoir (Davis 2016; Graves 2016). Short profiles of each are provided, followed by discussion of their collective experiences in light of the disciplinary/organizational, hegemonic, and interpersonal domains of Collins' Matrix of Domination model, with examples. I argue that these women likely did not view themselves as "feminists" in the popular sense of the term, but mainly as pragmatists – i.e. realists and doers. As such, this examination also highlights how these women engaged in various forms of pragmatic resistance and activism as means to cope with their circumstances.

Barbara Gardner Proctor (1932–2018)

Born during the Great Depression and raised by her grandmother in poverty in Black Mountain, North Carolina, Proctor was the first black woman in the world to establish an advertising agency: Proctor and Gardner in Chicago in 1970. After attending Talledega College on scholarship, she ended up in Chicago by happenstance in the mid-1950s and worked a variety of jobs, including as a music critic and record company executive. Married briefly and divorced with a young son by the early 1960s, she became the first black woman hired in a general market agency – Post-Keys-Gardner (no relation) in 1963. Later, as an entrepreneur, a hallmark of Proctor's advertising work was the avoidance of any assignment which she deemed as denigrating to the image, dignity, or economic circumstances of women or black people. Therefore, she shunned liquor and tobacco accounts in favor of family-oriented brands like Jewel Food Stores, Kraft Foods, Sears and American Family Insurance. Cited by U.S. President Ronald Reagan during his 1984 State of the Union Address, and featured on the national news program *60 Minutes* in early 1984, Proctor was heavily engaged in business and civic leadership. The recipient of many industry and civic awards, she served as the first African-American chair of Chicago's Cosmopolitan Chamber of Commerce in 1976, and was invited by Governor Thompson of Illinois to co-chair the Gannon-Proctor Commission – a bipartisan group convened in 1983 to develop solutions to alleviate the legal, social, and economic discriminations experienced by women in Illinois.

Caroline R. Jones (1942–2001)

Jones entered advertising in 1963 as a secretary at the J. Walter Thompson agency in New York City after graduating from the University of Michigan. After successfully competing for a spot in Thompson's annual women's Copywriter's Workshop trainee program, she became the first black person trained as a copywriter in the history of the agency. In 1975, the Benton Harbor, Michigan native became the first black woman appointed to an executive position at a major mainstream advertising agency – BBD&O in New York City. She was also a major figure in several significant entrepreneurial ventures established by black advertising professionals including Zebra Associates in 1969, Mingo-Jones Advertising in 1977, and eventually her own independent shop – Caroline Jones Advertising/Caroline Jones, Inc. in 1987. She did creative work for major brands including American Express, Anheuser-Busch, Prudential, Toys R Us; the U.S. Postal Service, Greyhound, Western Union, and several non-profits garnered her top recognitions and awards from the Advertising Women of New York, the *Wall Street Journal*, and other industry organizations. Divorced with one son, she was active in youth mentoring and published a book concerning careers in advertising. However, battling business and health problems in the late 1990s, she succumbed to a difficult battle with breast cancer by 2001. She was named posthumously by *Advertising Age* as one of the "100 Most Influential Women" in the history of advertising.

Joel P. Martin (1944–)

An artist and entrepreneur, Martin was one of the first black female Art Directors in the advertising industry and the first black woman to open a full-service advertising agency in New York City. Raised in Ohio by her divorced mother, she graduated from Ohio State University with an art degree in the mid-1960s at a time when many American companies were actively seeking black employees following passage of the 1964 Civil Rights Act. After a few years in corporate America, she was hired at the McCafffrey & McCall advertising agency in New York, whose principals were actively involved in liberal political causes. In this progressive environment, Martin did creative work for Dr. Martin Luther King, Jr's Poor People's Campaign and other agency clients until she was promoted to Art Director. Leaving the agency to become a wife and mother, she did freelance work while her daughter was a preschooler. Seeking a professional life that was compatible with her home life and creative interests, she launched J.P. Martin and Associates in 1974 with her husband Bob, who handled the managerial aspects of the agency. During this so-called "Golden" era of black-oriented advertising, targeting the black consumer market was in high demand among mainstream marketers such as Anheuser-Busch, Carnation, Revlon, and other agency clients. Some of the agency's most compelling and award-winning work involved raising black consciousness and enhancing self-esteem among black children. However, by the late 1980s, Martin lost her passion for running the agency, along with a major client, and decided to shutter the firm and pursue other ventures. She later earned a Ph.D., and became a successful international executive coach, motivational speaker, author, and breast cancer survivor.

Valerie Graves (1950–)

From modest beginnings, teen motherhood, and a few years at Wayne State University in Detroit, Graves responded to a call for "more Afro-Americans" by a local advertising executive near her hometown of Pontiac, Michigan, and began her career in 1974 at the Darcy, MacManus & Masius agency in Michigan as a traffic coordinator/junior copywriter. Spending the first ten years of her career at general marketing agencies such as BBD&O, J. Walter Thompson, and Kenyon & Eckhardt in a variety of creative roles, she was often the only black person in her department or company. Gaining managerial experience at the Ross Roy agency in Michigan in the mid-1980s, she eventually joined Uniworld, a black-owned agency founded by advertising pioneer Byron Lewis in New York City, where she served for 14 years as its Chief Creative Officer. Later, from 2005–2010, she was the Chief Creative Officer for Vigilante, the urban market subsidiary of the general market Leo Burnett agency. Doing work for brands such as Ford, General Motors, AT&T, Burger King, Pepsi, and Bill Clinton's presidential campaign, she was recipient of ADCOLOR's "Legend" Award and the ANA's Multicultural Excellence

Award, and was recognized as one of the "100 Best and Brightest" by *Advertising Age*, among other industry honors and recognitions. Graves spent much of her career doing multicultural work, which she regarded as her "calling" (Deighton 2020). One of the most respected black creative professionals in the industry, she published her memoir in 2016.

Carol H. Williams (1950–)

After attending Northwestern University near her hometown of Chicago, Williams rose from advertising intern to creative executive at the Leo Burnett agency. She was the first African-American woman to be appointed as Vice President and Creative Director at two major agencies: Leo Burnett in Chicago in 1976; and Foote, Cone & Belding – San Francisco in 1980, thus becoming the highest-ranking black woman in advertising at the time. Her work for Pillsbury – "Say hello to Poppin' Fresh Dough" and Secret antiperspirant – "Strong enough for a man, but made for a woman" – are among the most memorable lines in advertising history. Yet, she left advertising briefly in the early 1980s, married orthopedic surgeon Dr. Tipkins Hood, and had a daughter. Doing occasional freelance projects and realizing that corporate America was still profiting from her ideas, she launched the Carol H. Williams Agency in 1986 out of her family's home. Her agency attracted some of the leading national advertisers including Procter & Gamble, General Motors, Nissan North America, Coca-Cola, Allstate, Coors, Marriott, the U.S. Army, and many others. Most of her firm's advertising was aimed at the black consumer market, but a 2007 commercial for Disney titled "Signs" – featuring a black boy lovingly communicating with his deaf grandfather through sign language – was the top-rated commercial among all audiences. Winning nearly every industry award available, in 2017 Williams was the first and only black woman creative professional inducted into the prestigious AAF Advertising Hall of Fame (Maheshwari 2017). Outspoken with respect to equity issues in the industry, she continues to serve as CEO of her company which is the largest independent advertising agency in the world that is both 100% black and woman-owned.

Pragmatic navigation of oppressions in advertising organizations

A confluence of hegemonic and interpersonal oppressions shaped these women's roles and opportunities at the organizational level where these women were employed. In these settings, power dynamics are critical as the dominant group manages the workforce by deploying resources, meting out rewards and punishments, and setting the rules and standards that guide daily activities. All of the women entered the advertising business via general market advertising agencies where they were often one of the few, the first, and/or the only black woman. Several prevailing ideologies and norms constricted the appropriate roles of women in these organizations. For example, at J. Walter Thompson, where Jones started in the early 1960s, the only way women were hired in was as secretaries, regardless of background, education, or experience. During this era, advancement for small numbers of women into areas such as Research or Creative/copywriting often provided the only escape from clerical positions. At these general market agencies, women's assignments often concerned "women's products" like beauty, personal care, food, and cleaning brands, which was the norm for most adwomen. The Creative Department was also deemed suitable for women's careers, and all of the subjects of this examination worked primarily in the Creative area. Account work, however, which involved working directly with clients, money, and deals, was a male province handled by "account men," Martin acknowledged (Davis 2016, 188). These practices put these women at an experiential disadvantage when it came to eventually running their own departments or businesses, since they had limited exposure concerning how to negotiate contracts, and engage in selling and other aspects of business management. Martin admitted struggling with this dimension of running her agency, explaining: "I came from an Episcopalian background and nice women didn't sell" (Davis 2016, 135). Conversely, admen were hired in at any level with greater salaries, and often enjoyed a "boy's club" or "locker room" atmosphere, where male-oriented entertainment was common and women were often excluded from private clubs, golf outings, meetings, and similar settings (Davis 2016, 189). Their biographies show that Proctor and Jones found themselves in environments which were decidedly more conservative compared to the more liberal and progressive cultures where Martin, Graves, and Williams were initially employed.

The background suggests that the shift towards feminization of the profession had limited impact on black women's opportunities in general market firms. However, traits typically associated with females – such as creativity, intuition, social interaction, nurturance, helpfulness, cooperation, collaboration, teamwork, high integrity, and relationship-building skills – were recognized as valuable assets in a service profession like advertising (Alvesson 1998; Madaran and Catterall 2000). The black adwomen profiles were noted for their excellent social and relationship-building skills, which would help them as their careers evolved (Davis 2016, 189). They also found inventive ways to overcome their "otherness" in their respective companies. Jones found support at Thompson by mimicking the dress styles of senior women at the agency – including hats and white gloves – in order to fit in (Davis 2016, 103). Graves attributed her early success to her ability to "think, write and joke like a white guy" (*Behind the Scenes* 2017). Martin and Williams displayed exceptional creative talent early on, attracting the attention of influential men who mentored them at McCafffey & McCall and Leo Burnett, respectively. Later, when Proctor decided to launch her own firm, she was so attuned to the idea that men were best suited to run advertising firms, and that she named her agency "Proctor & Gardner" to give the illusion of a male partner, which "soothes the male chauvinists" who preferred a more "businesslike" male in the background, she explained (Davis 2016, 80). However, despite women's increasing numerical presence in advertising firms, male authority in top level positions was the norm – globally – well into the 2000s (Arnberg and Svanlund 2017; Liesse 2013).

Another ideology shaping their opportunities in advertising was the assumption that advertising professionals of color had an affinity for multicultural work. Black professionals were barred from the advertising industry for so long; hence, the only way many could get a foothold in the business was by helping corporate advertisers address black consumers (Davis 2002; 2013). Civil Rights gains, a prosperous post-World War II economy, and other factors revealed the viability of the black consumer market to mainstream marketers (Davis 2013). Therefore, starting in the mid-1940s and accelerating into the 1970s and 1980s, a noticeable number of black professionals entered the advertising business as counselors and specialists helping mainstream brands court black consumers. Most were black men, but several were women, and Proctor, Jones, Martin, and Williams all launched black-owned agencies in the 1960s, 1970s, and 1980s. And although Graves was not an entrepreneur, she served as the Creative Head at a black-owned agency and at a subsidiary of a white agency focused on urban and multicultural consumers. There was some controversy among black business leaders about the specialty orientation, saying that restricting black professionals to black-oriented assignments amounted to "segregated integration" (Chambers 2008, 128) and an Economic Detour which would marginalize and limit long-term business prospects (Davis 2002). Although they had all been trained on general-market assignments, Proctor, Martin, and Graves preferred and thrived doing specialty work; but Jones wanted to work beyond those confines and complained: "When I walk in the door to pitch an account, people automatically think 'black advertising'" (Davis 2016, 121). Similarly, Williams, who had earned a stellar reputation reviving brands for general market consumers, recalls that she was approached by the Pacific Bell telephone company in the mid-1980s, asking if she did "targeted advertising" – i.e. code words for the black consumer market. Although she had never specialized, the prospect assumed her expertise in this area (Davis 2016, 163). Saying "yes" in order to get the assignment, Williams did substantial research in order to learn how to craft successful specialty advertising. Regardless of the disputes concerning ethnic targeting by marketing professionals of color, the practice became endemic in the industry to the present, growing to include Latinx, Asian, and other ethnic specialists under the "multicultural marketing" banner.

Resistance, activism, and empowerment

Recognizing their positionality in the advertising business and their roles as black women, these leaders engaged in acts of resistance, activism, and empowerment-seeking throughout their careers. Prime examples were quitting jobs when working conditions became unsatisfactory; changing companies when opportunities for better pay and advancement were available elsewhere; and gaining control over their personal work lives by becoming entrepreneurs. For example, when Proctor was fired from Chicago's North advertising in 1969 for refusing to participate on an advertising campaign she considered offensive to women, black people, and the Civil Rights movement, and she decided to launch her own firm, rationalizing, " I learned you really don't make decisions…unless you are the boss" (Davis 2016, 79). During her career, Jones often had problems with pay equity and changed employment situations as a result. In fact, after partnering with Frank Mingo, a black man, to build the Mingo-Jones company into a top performing minority agency, she had a bitter dispute with him over compensation and managerial issues and left abruptly in 1986 to start her own firm. In these circumstances, entrepreneurship served as a manifestation of resistance and activism whereby these women could claim the autonomy to shape their lives on their own terms. Martin and Williams were similarly motivated by the independence offered by entrepreneurship.

In addition to their career pursuits, all five of the women were mothers and therefore had to negotiate and navigate satisfactory child-rearing and care situations in line with their personal circumstances. Martin and Williams, who were both married, took some time off from the industry when their children were very young to care for their families. However, Proctor, Jones, and Graves, who were single due to divorce and other circumstances, had to make arrangements with family members or other caregivers in order to work and raise their children. It was not uncommon for their children to accompany them to their offices. Proctor, for example, made it a practice to arrange her daily work schedule so that she could spend time with her son every morning or evening each day – even as a business owner with demanding client meeting schedules.

These women were also activists through their creative work and art direction, committed to providing imagery and messaging that was respectful and empowering towards women, children, and people of all backgrounds. Their presence also added value to the industry in significant ways. For example, in the 1990s, Jones successfully intervened to dissuade the Aunt Jemima brand from using a proposed advertising theme "Aunt Jemima is alive and cookin'" in a commercial with a popular black actress, which would have inflicted significant damage to the brand's reputation had it been executed (Davis 2007). They were also heavily involved in public service, civic, and political engagement; youth mentoring, public speaking, and other acts intended to foster uplift among their respective communities. Readers are encouraged to take a closer look at the full-length biographies of these pioneering black advertising women as their stories are intriguing, triumphant, bittersweet, and sometimes tragic. They experienced concurrent and sometimes extreme forms of gender and race-based oppressions in their careers, yet applied coping strategies in pragmatic ways which allowed them to persevere in their endeavors and serve as important leaders models in the industry.

Say her name: other black women advertising leaders

In the context of this chapter, it is not possible to discuss all black women leaders in advertising – past and present – and I acknowledge that the stories of these pioneers, trailblazers, and innovators have yet to be fully old. However, a tradition in the black community is to "Say Their Names" – that is, to give acknowledgment to those who are often unrecognized, marginalized, or rendered invisible in society, in order to give them their due respect. Therefore, in the spirit of those who have confronted intersectional inequities in the advertising industry, the names of other black women who have made significant contributions to the advertising profession are provided here.

Kirsten Atkinson	Faye Ferguson	Alma Hopkins
Danielle Austen	Esther Franklin	Dani Jackson-Smith
Shante Bacon-Cius	Ann Fudge	Linda Jefferson
Nadja Bellan-White	Heide Gardner	Tracey Jennings
Karyn Blackett	Terri Gardner	Verdia Johnson
Kimberly Blackwell	Deborah Gray-Young	Shirley Barnes Kalunda
Ayiko Broyard	Amber Guild	Kendra Hatcher King
Sarah Burroughs	G. Joyce Hamer	Adele Lassere
Gina Christie	Cheryl Harps	Kai Deveraux Lawson
Tricia Clark-Stone	Joya Harris	Renetta McCann
Vida Cornelius	Vita Harris	Lisa McConnell
Marian Cullers	Barbara Delfyette Hester	Faith Morris
Traci Dinkins	Donna Hodge	Marissa Nance
Robyn Ennis	Nakesha Holley	Monique L. Nelson
Nunu Ntshingila-Njeke	Erika Riggs	Teneshia Jackson-Warner
McGee Williams Osse	Barbara Simmons	Tiffany Warren
Candace D. Queen	Deidre Smalls-Landau	Leslie Wingo
Deadra Rahaman	Shanteka Sigers	Emma Young

#SayHerName

References

Advertising Age. 2017. "There are Fewer Than 100 Black Women Execs in Adland." *AdAge.com*, 24 March, viewed 25 June 2020, https://adage.com/article/agency-news/ad-club-ny-ipg-host-summit-black-women-execs/308420.

Alina, M. 2015. "On *Black Feminist Thought*: Thinking Oppression and Resistance Through Intersectional Paradigm." *Ethnic and Racial Studies*, vol. 38, no. 13, pp. 2334–2340.

Alvesson, M. 1998. "Gender Relations and Identity at Work: A Case Study of Masculinities and Femininities in an Advertising Agency." *Human Relations*, vol. 51, no. 8, pp. 969–1005.

ANA-AIMM. 2019. *A Diversity Report for the Adverting/Marketing Industry*, November. Association of National Advertisers Alliance for Inclusive and Multicultural Marketing: New York.

Arnberg, K. & Svanlund, J. 2017. "Mad Women: Gendered Divisions in the Swedish Advertising Industry, 1930–2012." *Business History*, vol 52, no. 2, pp. 268–291.

Batthany, J. 2015. "Why This Advertising Mother of the Year Hopes We Won't Need to Celebrate Working Mothers in Advertising Much Longer." *The Drum*, viewed 1 July 2020, https://www.thedrum.com/opinion/2015/03/31/why-advertising-mother-year-hopes-we-won-t-need-celebrate-working-mothers.

Behind the Scenes. 2017. "Valerie Graves – Valerie Graves Creative." *YouTube*, 2 May, viewed 24 June 2020, https://www.youtube.com/watch?v=g-cc9joHA-g&t=26s.

Bendick, M. & Egan, M. 2009. *Research Perspectives on Race and Employment in the Advertising Industry*. Bendick and Egan Economic Consultants, Inc.: Washington, DC.

Bendick, M. & Egan, M. 2019. "The Global Advertising Workforce: Who Is Excluded and Why It Matters." *Proceedings of the Race in the Marketplace Research Forum*, June 25–27, Paper Session 10.2: Marketing Professionals, Organizations and Society, Universite Paris-Dauphine, Paris, France.

Boulton, C. 2016. "Black Identities Inside Advertising: Race Inequality, Code Switching, and Stereotype Threat." *Howard Journal of Communications*, vol. 27, no. 2, pp. 130–144.

Broyles, S. & Grow, J. 2008. "Creative Women in Advertising Agencies: Why So Few 'Babes in Boyland?'" *Journal of Consumer Marketing*, vol. 25, no. 1, pp. 4–6.

Center for Talent Innovation. 2019. *Being Black in Corporate America: An Intersectional Exploration*. Center for Talent Innovation: New York.

Chambers, J. 2008. *Madison Avenue and the Color Line: African-Americans in the Advertising Industry*. University of Pennsylvania Press: Philadelphia.

Collins, P.H. 2000. *Black Feminist Thought: Knowledge, Consciousness and the Politics of Empowerment*, 2nd ed. Routledge: New York.

Collins, P.H. 2013. *Black Feminism'*, in *On Intellectual Activism*. Temple University Press: Philadelphia, pp. 3–16.

Crenshaw, K. 1991. "Mapping the Margins: Intersectionality, Identity Politics, and Violence Against Women of Color." *Stanford Law Review*, vol. 43, no. 6, pp. 1241–1299.

Combs, G. 2003. "The Duality of Race and Gender for Managerial African American Women: Implications of Social Networks on Career Advancement." *Human Resource Development Review*, vol. 2, no. 4, pp. 385–405.

Cortese, A. 2008. *Provocateur: Images of Women and Minorities in Advertising*. Rowman and Littlefield: New York.

Davis, J.F. 2002. "Enterprise Development under an Economic Detour? Black-Owned Advertising Agencies, 1940–2000." *Journal of Macromarketing*, vol. 22, no. 1, pp. 75–85.

Davis, J.F. 2007. "Aunt Jemima Is Alive and Cookin'?: An Advertiser's Dilemma of Competing Collective Memories." *Journal of Macromarketing*, vol. 27, no. 1, pp. 25–37.

Davis, J.F. 2013. "Realizing Marketplace Opportunity: How Research on the Black Consumer Market Influenced Mainstream Marketers, 1920–1970." *Journal of Historical Research in Marketing*, vol. 5, no. 4, pp. 471–493.

Davis, J.F. 2016. *Pioneering African-American Women in the Advertising Business: Biographies of MAD Black WOMEN*. Routledge: New York.

Deighton, K. 2020. "This Line Is for Employees Only: Stories of Being Black in Advertising, 1969–2020." *The Drum*, 26 February, viewed 25 June 2020, https://www.thedrum.com/news/2020/02/26/line-employees-only-stories-being-black-advertising-1969-2020.

Diaz, A. 2020a. "Black Execs Form Nonprofit 600 & Rising, Backed by the 4As, to Hold Ad Industry Accountable for Racial Equity." *Advertising Age*, 17 June, viewed 20 June 2020, https://adage.com/article/agency-news/black-execs-form-nonprofit-600-rising-backed-4as-hold-ad-industry-accountable-racial-equity/2262476.

Diaz, A. 2020b. "More Than 600 Black Agency Professionals Call for End to Systemic Racism in Open Letter to Industry Leaders." *Advertising Age*, 9 June, viewed 20 June 2020, https://adage.com/article/agency-news/more-600-black-agency-professionals-call-end-systemic-racism-open-letter-industry-leaders/2261381.

Gopaldas, A. & DeRoy, G. 2015. "An Intersectional Approach to Diversity Research." *Consumption Markets & Culture*, vol. 18, no. 4, pp. 333–364.

Graves, V. 2016. *Pressure Makes Diamonds: Becoming the Woman I Pretended to Be*. Akashic Books: New York.

Liesse, J. 2013. "Women in Advertising: the Agency Challenge." *Advertising Age*, 22 July, pp. 10–11.

Maclaran, P., Stevens, L., & Catterall, M. 1997. "The 'Glasshouse Effect': Women in Marketing Management." *Marketing Intelligence and Planning*, vol. 15, no. 7, pp. 309–317.

Madaran, P. & Catterall, M. 2000. "Bridging the Knowledge Divide: Issues on the Feminisation of Marketing Practice." *Journal of Marketing Management*, vol. 16, no. 6, pp. 635–646.

Maheshwari, S. 2017. "An Ad Woman at the Top of an Industry That She Thinks Still Has Far to Go." *New York Times*, 24 April, viewed 24 April 2017, https://www.nytimes.com/2017/04/24/business/carol-williams-advertising-hall-of-fame.html.

McFadden, C. 2011. "Critical White Feminism: Interrogating Privilege, Whiteness and Anti-racism in Feminist Theory." Thesis, University of Central Florida, viewed 15 May 2020, https://stars.library.ucf.edu/honorstheses1990-2015/1159.

Monllos, K. 2019. "Clients Need a Cultural Sensitivity Workshop": Confessions of a Black Woman in Advertising." *Digiday*, 5 November, viewed 25 June 2020, https://digiday.com/marketing/clients-need-cultural-sensitivity-workshop-confessions-agency-producer-racist-ads-happen/.

Pasquarelli, A. 2020. "Female Marketers Saw Pay Rise above Male Counterparts in 2019, Study Finds." *Advertising Age*, 17 June, viewed 20 June 2020, https://adage.com/article/cmo-strategy/female-marketers-saw-pay-rise-above-male-counterparts-2019-study-finds/2262631.

Ray, V. 2019. "A Theory of Racialized Organizations." *American Sociological Review*, vol. 84, no. 1, pp. 1–28.

Rittenhouse, L. 2020. "Black Professionals Describe Agencies as Hotbeds for Racism and Microaggression." *Advertising Age*, 19 June, viewed 20 June 2020, https://adage.com/article/agency-news/black-professionals-describe-agencies-hotbeds-racism-and-microaggression/2262246.

Rahaman, D. 2019. "Missing the Mark: Non-Diverse Agencies and Brand Marketers." *LinkedIn.com*, 13 September, viewed 20 June 25, 2020, https://www.linkedin.com/pulse/missing-mark-non-diverse-agencies-brand-marketers-deadra-rahaman/.

Roth, B. 2017. "The Reception of Black Feminist Intellectuals and Black Feminist Theory in Modern America" in *Black Intellectual Thought in Modern America*, edited by B. Behnken, G. Smithers & S. Wendt, 138–169. University Press of Mississippi: Jackson.

Sherman, E. 2018. "More Women Managers Than Ever Before, but There's a Big Downside." *Inc.*, 23 February, viewed 25 June 2020, https://www.inc.com/erik-sherman/more-women-are-managers-than-ever-before-but-theres-a-big-downside.html.

Shetterly, M. L. 2016. *Hidden Figures: The Story of the African-American Women Who Helped Win the Space Race*. HarperCollins: New York.

Sobande, F. 2019. "Woke-Washing: 'Intersectional' Femvertising and Branding 'Woke' Bravery." *European Journal of Marketing*, https://doi-org.ezproxy.auckland.ac.nz/10.1108/EJM-02-2019-0134.

Ted.com. 2016. "The Urgency of Intersectionality." *Ted Talk by Kimberle Crenshaw*, viewed 6 April 2021, https://www.ted.com/talks/kimberle_crenshaw_the_urgency_of_intersectionality.

Thomas, K.D. 2013. "Deconstructing Hegemonic Masculinity: Understanding Representations of Black and White Manhood in Print Advertising." *Advertising and Society Review,* vol. 14, no. 2.

Thomas, K.D. 2017. "Privilege: The Neglected Obstacle in Attaining Equity in the Ad Industry." *Journal of Advertising Education,* vol. 21, no. 2, pp. 10–14.

Villeseche, F., Muhr, S. & Sliwa, M. 2018. "From Radical Black Feminism to Postfeminist Hashtags: Re-Claiming Intersectionality." *Ephmera: Theory & Politics in Organization*, vol. 18, no.1, pp. 1–16.

Zorrilla, M. 2020. "600 Black Advertising Professionals Demand Meaningful Action from Leadership in Open Letter." *Adweek*, 9 June, viewed 20 June 2020, https://www.adweek.com/agencies/600-black-advertising-professionals-demand-meaningful-action-from-leadership-in-open-letter/.

Suggested Reading:

Davis, J. F. 2016. Pioneering African-American Women in the Advertising Business: Biographies of MAD Black WOMEN. Routledge: New York.

Graves, V. 2016. Pressure Makes Diamonds: Becoming the Woman I Pretended to Be. Akashic Books: New York.

Maheshwari, S. 2017. "An Ad Woman at the Top of an Industry That She Thinks Still has Far to Go." New York Times, 24 April, viewed 24 April 2017 <https://www.nytimes.com/2017/04/24/business/carol-williams-advertising-hall-of-fame.html>.

5 Marketing education and patriarchal acculturation

The rhetorical work of women's advertising clubs, 1926–1940

Jeanie Wills

This chapter constructs a narrative that inserts early 20th-century American women's advertising clubs into discussions about histories of marketing and advertising education. Scholars such as Tadajewski (2011) and Witkowski (2012) find marketing education occurring outside of the privileged space of academic research. Tadajewski offers insight into the education offered by correspondence schools such as the Arthur Sheldon/Felton School. Witkowski, noting that the study of marketing education would benefit from examining venues other than academic institutions, analyses two Polish-language "how to" books, the first books on sales published in America. The Women's Advertising League of New York (formed 1912) and the Philadelphia Club of Advertising Women (PCAW, formed 1916) are two such venues offering marketing education to women and operating outside the academic world.

While the women's club movement in America always participated, broadly, in community education, suffrage, and social reform (Blair, 1980, 1994; Gere, 1997; Giddings, 1984; Knupfer & Woyshner, 2013; Martin, 1987; Rogow,1993; Scott, 1993; Sharer, 2004) women's advertising clubs focused specifically on the *professional* development of women who worked in advertising and on the education of women who wanted to work in advertising.[1] Focusing on women's professional development and education meant coaching women's rhetorical or communication behaviors to construct a professional ethos suitable for work in the industry. The two forerunners in providing educational opportunities for young women were the New York League of Advertising Women (NYLAW), which later became Advertising Women of New York in 1934, and the PCAW.

These clubs, like other educational associations and jurisdictions, served a larger social agenda. Witkowski (2012, 110) notes that the Polish language books, in addition to educating their audiences about sales and marketing, may have served as an agent for acculturating those audiences into the "American economic mainstream" and normalizing "the character and behavior of salesmen and market exchange within the framework of American business norms." Likewise, the courses the women's advertising clubs offered acculturated women into American business norms and taught women how their male peers and colleagues would tend to see them; however, they also implicitly taught women rhetorical strategies with which to navigate the social, historical, and economic constraints of the corporate and professional world. Thus, while the overt pedagogical objectives of the PCAW may have been to give "complete information on women's work in Advertising in the many fields in which they are successful and told 'how to' enter and advance in those fields" (Clair & Dignam, 1939, 9), a symbolic objective was to accustom their students to business culture. Thus, the adwomen also implicitly prompted their students to develop a professional ethos that would enable

DOI: 10.4324/9781003042587-6

them to grow and thrive in advertising and marketing positions within the social and cultural constraints of their business communities.

The PCAW's advertising courses, and subsequent textbook that was an outgrowth of its course, introduced students to advertising and marketing and the various careers one could have, as a woman, in the industry. They linked marketing and advertising with caretaking, teaching, and ethics and morality, thus rhetorically linking their advertising and marketing work with gendered expectations of behavior. In effect, the textbook is a site of struggle to view competence through a gendered lens. While this group of privileged white women absorbed, recreated, reimagined, and repackaged stereotypes of a monolithic white middle-class womanhood, they also inserted women advertising and marketing professionals into a narrative of American advertising success. Along with an introduction to a technical education, club education prepared women for the social and cultural experience of corporate America in ways that a formal education simply could not, primarily because a formal business and marketing education did not serve women the same way it served men. The teaching and training offered by the women's advertising clubs countered both the educational and social prejudices that women faced.

This chapter offers a brief history of the PCAW's foray into advertising and marketing pedagogy; outlines the symbolic functions of the club's pedagogical strategies; and demonstrates how the club's pedagogical practices obliquely countered the prejudice against women in business and armed students with rhetorical strategies to combat it. At the same time, the instructional philosophy coached students to position themselves in conventional ways that would be palatable and non-threatening to their male peers, as subordinate, helpful, and supportive.

The PCAW began their incursion into women's education in 1926, with the Advertising League of New York Women following in 1928. Both clubs produced "textbooks" as a result of courses that were designed and taught by their members. These textbooks were used by high school guidance counsellors to help them recommend careers for students, by women taking courses with PCAW, and by a general audience who might be interested in the subject matter. Because PCAW's textbook appeared first, in 1939, before the New York Club's 1942 publication, this chapter focusses primarily on it.

According to an informational pamphlet about PCAW, the club's work in educating young women started in 1926 when they began awarding two-year scholarships in the Charles Morris Price School of Advertising and Journalism for the young women whose essays most effectively addressed "Better English in Business (PCAW, History-Informational Pamphlet, ND, 6).[2] This pamphlet claims that "the value of elementary instruction in advertising largely influenced the decision to establish a course of our own;" The PCAW's first annual free class in advertising, developed and taught by club women who worked in these areas of specialization, started in 1927. By a decade later, the "eighth class has just been completed with 37 graduates. Over five hundred women thus far have studied this course" (PCAW, nd, 6. History-Information Pamphlet). By 1938, PCAW had developed an "Advanced Lecture Course" called "Advertising Beckons Women" and by the following year, it had produced a textbook with 22 chapters written by 22 different women who were experts in various fields of advertising and marketing. The book *Advertising Careers for Women* surveys opportunities for women in advertising and marketing, and offers practical advice on pursuing work in the industry. It was the first textbook of its kind directed to women for women and by women. However, as others have noted, the definition of "woman" focused narrowly on white, middle-class, and married (Scanlon,1995; Westkaemper, 2017). People of color were actively excluded from the advertising profession (Chambers, 2008; Davis, 2017), and women of color were actively excluded from women's advertising club memberships (Westkaemper, 2017). The adwomen reified stereotypes of the "typical" *white* middle-class housewife in their pedagogical approaches to teaching advertising.[3]

These adwomen exploited cultural stereotypes using quantitative knowledge about women's economic influence to qualitatively assert their "natural" role in this industry. Because empirical evidence showed that women were primary consumers of household goods, including vehicles, adwomen claimed sales, advertising, and marketing expertise *because* they were women, as is evidenced in an article by Dorothy Dignam (1936) entitled "Women Know Women" (Dignam Collection, Schlesinger Library) which tautologically expresses this essentialist philosophy as it obscures diversity. Likewise, the textbook pairs thematic clusters of assertions about the adwoman's "natural" fit for the business with a paradoxical "rhetoric of expectations." In this latter cluster, the instructor adwomen identify and affirm sexist stereotypes, but they also coach their students in what constitutes "professional behavior" for women. Their work outlines expectations of women's professional behavior, which often means identifying appropriate behavior and juxtaposing it with inappropriate behavior. For example, "'*Is being friendly necessary*'? Yes! And this is one of the most difficult lessons for a shy novice. Clams, exhibitionists, and society queens do not impress Business" (Kidd, 1939, 90). Most of the authors in the textbook advocate skill in gender presentation as well as in technical areas, thus emphasizing the message that women belonged in advertising and marketing *because* of their gender.

These messages countered the ones that women might receive from other venues that offered advertising and marketing courses. Because education stabilizes and perpetuates the ideologies of the dominant culture, it also excludes those who are marginalized. Education and business historians Antler (1977), Gordon (1990), and Strom (1992) each chronicles the struggles women faced in the pursuit of post-secondary education. Gordon notes protests from male students and faculty alike at the "feminization" of higher education. Strom (1992, 68) observes that "Business professionals … did not see womanly benevolence (or womanliness in general) as positive qualities… Promoters of the new professionalism … emphasized its inherent manliness." Thus, for many women, an academic education "function[ed] as yet another mode of exclusion" (Enoch, 2008, 6). Education primarily serves three symbolic functions: it stabilizes and perpetuates the values of the dominant culture, and it includes and acculturates as it simultaneously excludes and disenfranchises.

Educational agendas not only teach skills, but they also acculturate students with both an explicit and implicit rhetoric of expectations for appropriate behavior. As the drive for professionalization changed how people entered the workforce, universities, and colleges adapted by developing business courses and offering credentials. In the U.S., the first post-secondary level marketing class, called distribution, was taught in 1902/1903 at the University of Michigan (Ross, 2008, 7). Other business courses followed soon after. The new business courses taught students the technical and economic mysteries of marketing and distribution as they simultaneously modeled and shaped the ideal ethos of the successful business and marketing professional. In this way, business education stabilized and perpetuated the values of the dominant culture. Those traits and habits were cast as exclusively male according to Hilkey (1997, 143–144):

> 'manhood' became an indispensable aspect of the American ideology of success … [with] far-reaching implications for how men might see themselves [and] how womanhood and the feminine would be defined. Indeed, the equation of manhood and success was built in part on the equation of the feminine with failure.

According to Strom (1992, 69), the newly developing world of business professionals was, in fact, hostile to the presence of women and other demographics of "outsiders":

> intellectuals of the Progressive period, including the founders of the business professions, sought to link their academic training and intellectual values to a masculine American tradition of heroism rooted in pragmatism, experimentation, and exploration, while rejecting pure idealism as inherently feminine and merely sentimental. Casting activities of the new professionals in the heroic mold was critical to making them manly.

While American women did have access to higher education, they did not have *equal* access to all disciplines, especially those concerned with business. When they did have access to such educations, they would not have seen in themselves the characteristics of the "successful businessman" or, especially, of the successful "adman" whose portraits are drawn in books such as those authored by American advertising pioneers such as Claude Hopkin or Ernest Elmo Calkins.[4]

When women wanted a business education and sought the training, prestige, and networking opportunities that a professional education from a college or university business program might give them, they were often funneled into program streams that prepared them for secretarial and support work. Scanlon (1995, 173) states,

> When an adult extension program in business at Columbia University attracted as many women as it did men, the university decided to segregate the women in secretarial training, limiting the business training only to men. The Harvard Graduate School of Business Administration kept its doors closed to women until 1963.

While universities and colleges educated women for the so-called caring and nurturing professions (social work, nursing, and teaching), they were less welcoming when women attempted business studies. Antler (1977, 59) notes that while there was a great influx of women students into colleges and universities in the 1890s and 1900s, administrators and trustees at various institutions began to set arbitrary limits on the amount, kind, and quality of education that women could receive. The result of these educational limits meant that when women applied to these programs, they might be streamed into clerical and administrative courses, while men learned the business of business. When women were streamed into "appropriately feminine" areas of study, women like pioneer adwoman Helen Woodward (1926, 6) may have lamented that their "natural aptitude was hidden by the wrong training."

When educated women did succeed in entering the business world, "most" according to Antler (1977, 333) "experienced conflict between the ideals they learned in college and the values of the business and professional world." Woodward (1926, 7) scoffs at the values of "Honor, Courage, Justice, and Steadfastness" that her public-school education advocated. When Woodward notes, cynically, one might argue, that business is the pursuit of money above all else, she acknowledges the competitive nature of business. Woodward's recognition of the dissonance in values suggests that she underwent an acculturation process in her early career in business and advertising. Other authors pointed to the potential conflict a lack of acculturation causes: a 1920 article, "Women in Business" in *The Office Economist* written by Katherine Chamberlain, claims that girls do not receive the same "training" in childhood that boys do because boys are always aware of the expectation that they will have to earn their living (Dignam Scrapbook, nd, WHS). Antler (1977, 335) asserts that because educational institutions did not encourage women to earn their livings or compete with men, few women were prepared to do so. She also observes that women who were interested in careers that were considered "ill-suited" to stereotypical feminine virtues found it difficult to legitimize their aspirations. However, when the adwomen identified themselves with their audience, they symbolically paired advertising and marketing to those stereotypical virtues, thus creating an associative link between the audience's imagined characteristics and the adwomen's professional roles.

The rhetorical education the PCAW stabilized and perpetuated patriarchal hierarchies and attitudes, including and acculturating the "right" kind of adwoman, while excluding the "wrong" kind. That the club women sought male approval for their endeavors is evident from a 1939 note to "Our Lecture Course Committee" from one of the book's editors, Blanche Clair; she apprises stakeholders of the steps remaining before the club-sponsored publication, *Advertising Careers for Women*, will be available for retail sale. Along with bubbling enthusiasm, the note expresses anxiety about bringing the book to the attention of their male colleagues. Clair asks the committee members, "Can we afford to take a booth at the Advertising Convention…? It's the only way the men members of advertising clubs will know about the book." Underpinning the PCAW's textbook is a commitment to developing an experiential and gendered heuristic which serves a dual persuasive purpose. First, by claiming that women's socially proscribed gender roles gave them a special advantage in advertising and marketing, adwoman built a topos that legitimized and familiarized, to both businessmen and wider society, their ambitions to work in sales, marketing, and advertising; second, this trope functioned as a device of (limited) inclusion because it countered the cultural perception of business as exclusively male territory. Women were cued to see their domestic experiences and aspirations as a significant prerequisite to working in advertising, thus demonstrating the substantial benefit of housewifery and mothering, but this was a convenient fiction since many adwomen seemed to prefer their careers to the lives they imagined their audience had. Likewise, adwomen routinely claimed that the influence of feminine virtues benefitted the profession of advertising, an argument that, again, addressed both male and female advertising professionals and students, as well as the wider community.

However, the adwomen did not leave their students to flounder around trying to mobilize gendered domestic experience into advertising and marketing experience, but instead they gave students the gift of a disciplinary vocabulary. This very practical gift meant that the students from the Advertising Beckons Woman course had access to an "insider's knowledge" and specialized understanding which is crucial to joining a professional community: one must develop competency using the vocabulary of the community to participate in it (Blyler & Thralls, 1993). This training would also give them an advantage should they choose to advance their advertising training or to work in the business. Lastly, the PCAW's textbook also taught a "rhetoric of professional expectations" to women, inviting them to see themselves the way their male peers and other members of society would and then coaching them to behave in ways that would both counter and affirm stereotypes of women.

The pedagogical strategies of the ad club educators relied on a heuristic of personal experience combined with reflective practice. For example, a PCAW newsletter *Adland* (1936, 12) notes that "Club members give lectures on the various phases of advertising, merchandising, writing and selling, based on present successful practice and valuable personal experience;" one chapter's author insists that an advertising career begins in a girl's home: "It may be a bore to 'help mother,' but putting three well-balanced meals on the table 365 days a year gives you an understanding of home problems you'll need all through your business career" (Ebbot, 1939, 115), and thus, the logic goes, domesticity itself can be leveraged into a kind of professional activity, perhaps to make it less of a bore. Similarly, Dorothy Dignam (1939), in "Ideas and Copy," advises young women to shop mindfully with an eye to writing an advertisement about their experience, for example, of fabrics that would answer questions about value and economy, durability, and fashion. In essence, the adwomen are instructing their students in the art of becoming, in the words of Donald Schoen, a reflective practitioner. Schoen explores how professional practitioners from a variety of disciplines develop what he describes as intuitive or artistic professional knowledge as they "think in action." The adwomen instructors attempted to train their students' judgments about significant questions to ask of a product on behalf of the consumer so that they could craft an effective and convincing campaign or marketing strategy. However, the ad club's heuristic of personal experience was predicated upon the supposition that all women would have access to the same (middle-class, gendered) experiences, and these suppositions led to an unspoken assumption that there was a way to extrude an essence "natural" to women.

For example, a "Fashion Coordinator" for department store window displays, Mary Northrup, says, "Naturally, a woman is better equipped by *instinct*, background, and common interests to understand what will appeal to other women" (48) [my emphasis]. Northrup offers advice about art training, but notes, "Primarily, a woman is hired for her understanding of fashion, color, and the feminine viewpoint" (56). The direct article "the" that proceeds "feminine point of view" emphasizes that there is only one and it is, of course, white, middle class, heterosexual, and obedient to the social order.

This monolithic point of view enables the adwomen to claim that women in advertising and marketing elevate the industry from sheer commercialism to the nurture of the nation. Ida Wells held a rare position for a woman, as a space buyer, and, according to Dignam, was renowned for being ethical in a branch of the marketing and advertising business that lent itself to financial abuse and conflicts of interest (Dignam, ND, Scrapbook).Thus, Wells' ethical reputation becomes a warrant that explains why a woman could, and should, do this job. In a similar fashion, home economics expert and one of the founders of the NYLAW, Christine Frederick (1939, xix), pens the "Historical Introduction" to the textbook, saying,

> It is my belief that women have always been more vigorous than men in their denunciations of unrefined, and sometimes misleading, copy. And advertising women today have a double responsibility, to the profession and to the purchaser, in maintaining a standard of good taste, honesty, and sincerity in every word of advertising.

Continuing with a rhetorical tradition of American women claiming the right to speak in public because of their role in raising its future citizens, Frederick affirms women's roles as moral conscience, not for the nation, but for the advertising and marketing industry. Likewise, she links the adwoman's purpose to the consumer movement, and thus gains rhetorical legitimacy for the claim that a woman's knowledge is more authoritative than a man's. For example, Frederick (1939, xxi) claims the consumer movement presents "a peerless opportunity for women in advertising" because

> it offers a medium for thorough discussion and consumer testing of products before any advertising is written, and it backs up the woman copywriter when she and the manufacturer differ as to what women actually want in advertising information.

Of course, Frederick presumes the manufacturer is male; however, she positions female advertising copywriters as advocates for the consumer, rather than as sales agents for products. Thus, Frederick performs a symbolic merger wherein "consumer" and "advertiser" are consubstantial, and the characteristics associated with the consumers' movement accrue to the adwomen. For example, Frederick (1939, xxi) describes a

> consumer movement of the helpful and cooperative sort during the war when women willingly curtailed the use of certain foods and experimented with substitutes. And after the war there was a consumer movement 'out of the kitchen' which was met by new housekeeping aids and all the beauty and efficiency of the modern kitchen.

Here Frederick symbolically links the consumer movement's advocacy for better quality, cooperation, and liberation with the role of the adwoman and her obligation to be the interlocuter between the consumer movement and the manufacturers. The adwomen themselves helped to stabilize women's roles in advertising while simultaneously perpetuating stereotypes about women's nature and "natural talents."

If the pedagogical strategies of PCAW and other women's clubs sought to balance competing understandings about women's roles in advertising, they also worked to exclude those women who were not "suitable" for the adwoman club. Many of the textbooks chapters pinpoint the kind of "female" behaviors and traits that adwomen deemed "inappropriate" to the marketing and advertising industry. Women are variously accused of being emotional, petty, mentally unstable, and lacking ambition. The authors lavishly illustrate the behaviors that women are "known for" but must work to overcome. For example, Elizabeth Hale Lally's (1939, 35) "The Advertising Manager's Job" notes:

> The opportunities are increasing, therefore, and it is only difficult to figure out why women haven't moved up faster. The retail advertising professional would seem a "natural" for feminine temperaments ... But let me be frank and tell you that women are likely to become emotionally involved in inner store politics and handicapped by their own short, and sometimes petty rather than long-range, views of the situation. This, of course, does not lessen the prejudice against them.

This author (1939, 36) goes on to say,

> Then, too, the long store hours, ... play havoc with feminine nerves. A retail advertising job demands a sensitive, alert, penetrating, and volatile intelligence, but it takes a pretty thick-skinned individual to stand the pressure of long hours and the constant drive to push up the store's sales figures.

Dorothy Reid Daub's chapter (1939, 58–59) "Fashion Copywriting" outlines some of the skills students should acquire to succeed in this branch of advertising, but notes, "Too many copywriters stay in a rut because they are content to do their daily job as it is handed to them: they do not have the ambition nor the gogetiveness to keep pushing ahead." Ann Schlorer Smith (1939, 132) identified as the Treasurer and Advertising Director of "Mrs. Schlorer's, Inc." tells her audience, "The job you finally acquire depends on you ... especially on the driving force within you." According to these adwomen, those without ambition need not apply, and adwomen alone bear responsibility for not being successful.

The adwomen's textbook is filled with negative examples of "feminine behavior" juxtaposed with ideals for gendered professional behavior. For example, the authors caution their students about being over-confident, unavailable, or insubordinate. Martina Gilchrist (1939, 79) advising on "Buying and Producing Fashion Artwork" says, "Don't alienate the art director's interest by being unintentionally bumptious" and proclaiming you can do " 'as well as *that*' – pointing to the work of his head artist in a current ad;" Women are advised to eschew any sort of social networking when she says,

> Don't come in via the president's office, even if your father does play golf with him. The head of an advertising department intends to hire on ability alone [and] ... Don't show the slightest hesitancy to start in any capacity.

Once one has work, so another author advises she must "be willing to give up dinner and theatre because a fashion copywriter has responsibilities to too many people" (Daub, 1939, 59). The PCAW instructors seek to exclude what they deem as inappropriate or unprofessional behaviors, thus creating their own hierarchy of what it took to be a successful.

The club's advertising and marketing curriculum prepared students what to expect on the job which not only included being technically competent but also becoming cognizant of how to "manage" professional relationships with male colleagues. Edith Ellsworth (1939, 14) in "Plans, Media, and Management" notes that "a woman taking full responsibility as production manager" is rare, while observing the duties of the production chief. She follows the list of duties with, "And most of those you deal with in engraving houses and printing establishment will be men who are used to dealing with men." Because it is the last sentence of the paragraph, it is not immediately clear how this statement links to the early part of the paragraph which introduces this branch of advertising. However, it becomes clear in the topic sentence of the next paragraph: "Two *other* factors that make this field difficult for women are time pressure and nerves" (14) [my emphasis].

The women who taught advertising courses through their clubs were not only offering their students vocational training but preparing women to participate in the industry, which meant outperforming men while managing socially constructed work conventions and masculine expectations; for example, in a June 1927 *Adland News* issue, the editor reports that

> Dr. Reinhardt, also a fellow-member of PCAW gave an interesting talk] on the ... subject of efficient businesswomen. It was rather disturbing to hear that we must be 400% fit mentally and physically. Pretty soft for a man to make the 100% mark.

The club members also prepare women to accept less money for the same work. Hale Lally (1939, 36) claims women advertising managers are on the rise for two reasons:

> the first is economic. Women have worked under men for so long, learning the details and demands of an advertising job, that they are frequently able to 'take over the desk' at less salary, of course, when a man is moved to another position.

Predictably, the second is because of the eternally needed feminine point of view.

In addition to teaching their students about managing and relating to denizens of industry and business, each adwoman instructor also introduced the students to a professional vocabulary. Each profession and each branch of each profession requires a specialized vocabulary, and another important aspect of the club's pedagogical philosophy was to give the students the power of "discipline specific speech" by teaching them both skills and the vocabulary of the profession.

The PCAW's courses introduced students to "the advertiser's parlance – layout, copy, media, color, engraving, typography, direct mail – all come to have significance to these ambitious young women" (*Adland News*, 1930). Edith Ellsworth (1939, 2) writes about the opportunities for women, asking her audience to consider what kind of "mind" they have and linking agency jobs to particular strengths – this strategy introduces students to a common language when she describes the various areas of specialty that are housed within agency work, such as "space buying," "merchandising," and "electrotypes." She starts the body of her piece, "Plans, Media, Management," with a definition of the term "account executive":

> The account is a collective term meaning the advertising and [the] product. The advertiser is your client, and together with his products and his problems you have an account. The account executive 'controls' certain accounts; contacts the client, advises with him, gets plans and copy okayed, and is the representative of the agency in general… It is a top agency position, in responsibility and remuneration; but women have already proved that they are equal to the task.

One of the keys ways of fitting in is understanding the hierarchy of an organization, as well as understanding the specialized jargon of a discipline. Gilchrist (1939, 75–76), discussing the process of creating art layouts, introduces some of the technical aspects of the process that includes telling her readers that artists will have to be able to talk about the persuasive intentions that occur through light, dark, dominance, unity, and vitality. Each of the authors introduces some specialized aspect of vocabulary which gives their students a semantic framework within which to understand the hierarchies and disciplinary jargon of the industry. Ellsworth (1939, 14) notes the significance of learning the technical vocabulary of a discipline when she says,

> a secretarial or clerical position in a busy mechanical department is excellent training for any girl who is going to make advertising her career. She will learn terms and processes that are … necessary to an advertising manager. Also, this knowledge will give her opinions an authority that raises her in the estimation of masculine coworkers and employers.

The PCAW's education made clear that the most conventional way into an advertising and marketing career for a woman was to become a secretary and provide performative evidence of competence to gain masculine approval. Alongside this advice, the adwomen smuggled in unspoken advice: be a helper and be humble and give credit to others more than to yourself. Ellsworth (1939, 11) says, "Take a business course and sell yourself to the head to the research department as a superintelligent stenographer, who can also assist in compiling figures and analysing questionnaires." Her point is to advise students to be seen to "work their way up" by rhetorically linking their professional capabilities to a traditional and normalized career stream for women. Another author (Roché, 1939, 181) suggests that women cannot be attached to their creative work:

> Women are well-fitted for promotion work. But you cannot be possessive with your ideas. You must find your satisfaction in evolving workable ideas; then relinquish them freely to the agents. And never assume more credit than is due you; rather, assume less.

The club's pedagogical materials suggest the various ways that women in advertising and marketing could be rejected and dismissed. That everyday sexism was routine is evident in the cautions they share with their students. Dorothy Dignam (1939, 23) most directly expresses that expectations are gendered when she warns students about how to accept criticism of their ads:

> "Even if good copy is 'killed' (that is, put aside entirely), it isn't cricket for you, *as a woman*, to cry or sulk or bang doors or show other signs of defeatism." [my emphasis] Dignam also notes, "The advertising agency is, and probably always will be, a masculine stronghold."

Adwomen positioned themselves in advertising and marketing as irreplaceable and inevitable because of their gender. They built this identity on a foundation of misogynistic beliefs that they perpetuated but from which they also benefitted. They sold this narrative to themselves, to students, and to the men with whom they competed for jobs. They made their arguments based on essentialist stereotypes of women and affirmed "the rightness" of women's place in the home from their vantage place in business; however, they also made successful careers for themselves and made advertising education more democratic for the "right kind" of women, first, by providing access to education through scholarships and then by developing and teaching a curriculum that they sold as gender specific.

Like their suffragette sisters justifying the right to speak in public (Campbell, 1989) the advertising women developed a rhetorical justification for their place in business, and particularly in advertising and marketing. The women defended their fitness for advertising and marketing and in doing so reveal the kinds of backlash that many may have faced in their careers. Reading the textbook generated and sponsored by the PCAW reveals an implicit rhetorical agenda that sought to prepare their students to engage productively which meant teaching students how to reason and construct arguments; how to analyse audiences and develop appropriate persuasive appeals; and, perhaps, most importantly, how to construct a public *ethos*, most simply defined as "character as it emerges in language" (Baumlin, 1994, 263). To be heard, speakers had to be *accepted* by an audience. Thus, a "student" who received this rhetorical education learned that speakers or authors must build common ground with an audience so that their messages will be given a hearing. That a rhetor's public character is fashioned by her but only completed upon the audience's acceptance of that ethos demonstrates a key element of *all* rhetorical transactions: "rhetorical structures work best when they 'fit into' or 'work on' psychological structures already in place" (Alcorn, 1994, 15). That the advertising woman's pedagogical strategies may have worked against them to exclude them from executive and leadership positions may be true, but it is also true that women's clubs and especially business and professional clubs like the Philadelphia club and the NYLAW were leaders in educating women. The PCAW and NYLAW taught marketing and advertising, but also rhetorical strategies, like language practices and social behaviors that made possible their success in advertising.

Notes

1 The Associated Advertising Clubs of America, formed 1906, started offering these kinds of courses for their members in 1910 (Schultz, 1982, 22); however, in the eastern USA at least, women were not allowed to join men's clubs, so it is likely these courses would not have accepted female students
2 The Advertising Federation of America (AFA) originated the essay topic and the women's clubs promoted the contest, but invited only women to enter the essay contest, which changed yearly. For example, in 1927, the topic invited contestants to explain what constituted a "good advertisement" and provide a clipping of an ad that exemplified the qualities discussed. This was not an egalitarian contest open to any young woman: contestants had to submit a letter of recommendation with the "head of the contestant's firm" (PCAW Adland, 1927).
3 Laird (1989, 286–287) traces the historical progression of the logic of women writing to women and the associated targeting of the female consumer of "'comfortable income.'"
4 On the other hand, the J.Walter Thompson agency's "Women's Editorial Department" (1920s–1930s), under the authority of Helen Resor-Stanley, was populated by mostly university and college educated women, some with PhDs. These women had degrees from prestigious women's universities such as Vassar and Radcliffe, but Resor-Stanley provided opportunities to women that were rare in other advertising agencies (Applegate, 2012; Fox, 1984; Scanlon, 1995, Scott, 2005; Sutton, 2009). According to Jennifer Scanlon (1995, 179–180), it was not uncommon for American women who worked in advertising to hold degrees and even PhDs; However, these same highly educated and skilled women most often ended up in clerical work with little chance for advancement because they were not, usually, trained and practiced in the business culture.

References

Alcorn, Marshall W. (1994). "Self-Structure as a Rhetorical Device: Modern Ethos and the Divisiveness of Self." In Tita French Baumlin & James S Baumlin (eds.), *Ethos: New Essays in Rhetorical and Critical Theory*, 3–6. Dallas, TX: Southern Methodist University Press.
Antler, Joyce. (1977). *Educated Women and Professionalization: The Struggle for a New Feminine Identity, 1890–1920*. New York: Garland.
Applegate, Edd, ed. (1994). *The Ad Men and Women: A Biographical Dictionary of Advertising*. Westport, CT: Greenwood Press.
Baumlin, James S. (1994). *Ethos: New Essays in Rhetorical and Critical Theory*. Edited by Tita French Baumlin. Dallas, TX: Southern Methodist University Press, 1994.
Blair, Karen J. (1980). *Clubwoman As Feminist: True Womanhood Redefined, 1868–1914*. New edition. New York: Holmes & Meier Publishers.
Blair, Karen J. (1994). *The Torchbearers: Women and Their Amateur Arts Associations in America, 1890–1930*. Philanthropic Studies. Bloomington: Indiana University Press.

Bledstein, Burton J. (1978). *Culture of Professionalism: The Middle Class and the Development of Higher Education in America.* 6th edition. New York: W W Norton & Co Inc.
Blyler, Nancy Roundy, and Charlotte Thralls, eds. (1993). *Professional Communication: The Social Perspective.* Newbury Park, CA: Sage.
Campbell, Karlyn Kohrs. (1989). *Man Cannot Speak for Her.* New York: Praeger.
Chambers, Jason. (2008). *Madison Avenue and the Color Line: African Americans in the Advertising Industry.* Philadelphia: University of Pennsylvania Press.
Clair, Blanche, and Dorothy Dignam, eds. (1939). *Advertising Careers for Women.* New York: Harper & Brothers.
Daub, Dorothy Reid. (1939). "Fashion Copywriting." In Blanche Clair and Dorothy Dignam (eds.), *Advertising Careers for Women*, 58–68. New York: Harper & Brothers.
Davis, Judy Foster. (2017). *Pioneering African-American Women in the Advertising Business: Biographies of MAD Black WOMEN.* New York: Routledge, Taylor & Francis Group.
Dickenson, Jackie. (2016). *Australian Women in Advertising in the Twentieth Century by Jackie Dickenson.* London: Palgrave Pivot.
Dignam, Dorothy. (nd). *Scrapbook. Dignam Collection.* Madison: Wisconsin State Historical Society.
Dignam, Dorothy. (1936). "Women Know Women." *The Wharton Review*, 9,18,20.
Dignam, Dorothy. (1939). "Ideas and Copy." In Blanche Clair and Dorothy Dignam (eds.), *Advertising Careers for Women*, 17–33. New York: Harper & Brothers.
Ebbott, Dorothy. (1939). "The Home Economist in the Advetising Department." In Blanche Clair and Dorothy Dignam (eds.), *Advertising Careers for Women*, 107–119. New York: Harper & Brothers.
Ellsworth, Edith. (1939). "Plans, Media, Managment." In Blanche Clair and Dorothy Dignam (eds.), *Advertising Careers for Women*, 1–16. New York: Harper & Brothers.
Enoch, Jessica. (2008). *Refiguring Rhetorical Education: Women Teaching African American, Native American, and Chicano/a Students, 1865–1911.* Carbondale: Southern Illinois University Press.
Fox, Stephen. (1997). *The Mirror Makers: A History of American Advertising and Its Creators.* Chicago: University of Illinois Press.
Frederick, Christine. (1939). "Historical Introduction." In Blanche Clair and Dorothy Dignam (eds.), *Advertising Careers for Women*, xiii–xxi. New York: Harper & Brothers.
Gere, Ann. (1997). *Intimate Practices: Literacy and Cultural Work in U.S. Women's Clubs, 1880–1920.* Urbana: University of Illinois Press.
Giddings, Paula J. (1984). *When and Where I Enter: The Impact of Black Women on Race and Sex in America.* New York: Bantam Books.
Gilchrist, Martina. (1939). "Buying and Producing Fashion Artwork." In Blanche Clair and Dorothy Dignam (eds.), *Advertising Careers for Women*, 1–16. New York: Harper & Brothers.
Gordon, Lynn D. *Gender and Higher Education in the Progressive Era.* New Haven: Yale University Press, 1990.
Hilkey, Judy Arlene. (1997). *Character Is Capital: Success Manuals and Manhood in Gilded Age America.* Chapel Hill: University of North Carolina Press.
Kidd, Elizabeth. (1939). "How to Advertise Cosmetics and Toiletries." In Blanche Clair and Dorothy Dignam (eds.), *Advertising Careers for Women*, 84–96. New York: Harper & Brothers.
Knupfer, Anne Meis, and Christine A Woyshner. (2013). *Educational Work of Women's Organizations, 1890–1960.* London: Palgrave Macmillan.
Kwolek-Folland, Angel. (1994). *Engendering Business: Men and Women in the Coporate Office, 1870–1930.* Baltimore, MD: Johns Hopkins University Press.
Laird, Pamela Walker. (1989). *Advertising Progress: American Business and the Rise of Consumer Marketing.* Baltimore, MD: The Johns Hopkins University Press.
Laird, Pamela Walker. (2007). *Pull: Networking and Success since Benjamin Franklin.* Cambridge, MA; London: Harvard University Press.
Lally, Elizabeth Hale. (1939). "The Advertising Manager ." In Blanche Clair and Dorothy Dignam (eds.), *Advertising Careers for Women*, 34–46. New York: Harper & Brothers.

Lears, Jackson. (1995). *Fables of Abundance: A Cultural History of Advertising in America.* New York: Basic Books.
Martin, Theodora Penny. (1987). *The Sound of Our Own Voices: Women's Study Clubs 1860–1910.* Boston, MA: Beacon Press.
Northrup, Mary. (1939). "The Display Woman's Job." In Blanche Clair and Dorothy Dignam (eds.), *Advertising Careers for Women*, 47–57. New York: Harper & Brother.
PCAW, (nd). History-Informational Pamphlet, Bryn Mawr. Philadelphia Club of Advertising Women Archives. Collection.
PCAW. "Adland," 1936. Bryn Mawr. Philadelphia Club of Advertising Women Archives.
PCAW. "Adland News," 1927. Bryn Mawr Philadelphia Club of Advertising Women Archives.
Roché, Alice. (1939). "How to Advertise Insurance." In Blanche Clair and Dorothy Dignam (eds.), *Advertising Careers for Women*, 176–185. New York: Harper & Brothers.
Rogow, Faith. (1993). *Gone to Another Meeting: The National Council of Jewish Women, 1893–1993.* Judaic Studies Series. Tuscaloosa: University of Alabama Press.
Ross, Billy I. (2008). *A Century of Advertising Education.* St. Petersburg, FL: American Academy of Advertising.
Rutherford, Janice. (2003). *Selling Mrs. Consumer: Christine Frederick and the Rise of Household Efficiency.* Athens: University of Georgia Press.
Scanlon, Jennifer. (1995). *Inarticulate Longings: The Ladies' Home Journal, Gender and the Promise of Consumer Culture by Jennifer Scanlon.* New York: Routledge.
Schön, Donald A. (1983). *The Reflective Practitioner: How Professionals Think in Action.* New York: Basic Books.
Schultz, Quentin J. (1982). "An Honorable: The Quest for Professional Advertising Education: 1900–1917." *Business History Review* 56(1): 16–32.
Scott, Anne Firor. (1993). *Natural Allies: Women's Associations in American History.* Urbana: University of Illinois Press.
Scott, Linda. (2010). *Fresh Lipstick: Redressing Fashion and Femininism.* New York: Palgrave MacMillan.
Sharer, Wendy B. (2004). *Vote and Voice: Women's Organizations and Political Literacy, 1915–1930.* Studies in Rhetorics and Feminisms. Carbondale: Southern Illinois University Press.
Smith, Ann Schlorer. (1939). "From Manufacturer to Grocer to Pantry Shelf." In Blanche Clair and Dorothy Dignam (eds.), *Advertising Careers for Women*, 47–57. New York: Harper & Brother.
Strom, Sharon Hartman. (1992). *Beyond the Typewriter: Gender, Class, and the Origins of Modern American Office Work, 1900–1930.* Women in American History. Urbana: University of Illinois Press.
Sutton, Denise H. (2009). *Globalizing Ideal Beauty: How Female Copywriters of the J. Walter Thompson Advertising Agency Redefined Beauty for the Twentieth Century.* Basingstoke: Palgrave Macmillan.
Tadajewski, Mark. (2011). "Correspondence Sales Education in the Early Twentieth Century: The Case of The Sheldon School (1902–39)." *Business History* 53(7): 1130–1151. https://doi.org/10.1080/00076791.2011.590935.
Westkaemper, Emily. (2017). *Selling Women's History: Packaging Feminism in Twentieth-Century American Popular Culture.* New Brunswick, NJ ; London: Rutgers University Press.
Witkowski, Terrence H. (2012). "Marketing Education and Acculturation in the Early Twentieth Century: Evidence from Polish Language Texts on Selling and Salesmanship." Edited by Ben Wooliscroft. *Journal of Historical Research in Marketing* 4:(1): 97–128. https://doi.org/10.1108/17557501211195082.
Woodward, Helen. (1926). *Through Many Windows.* New York: Garland Publishing.

Section 2

Gender representations in the marketplace

6 Feminist brands

What are they, and what's the matter with them?

Cele C. Otnes and Eileen M. Fischer

Always, a brand of feminine sanitary products, launched its worldwide program "Always Keeping Girls in School" in 2006. Its purpose was to empower girls entering puberty to manage the stigma of menstruation "safely, hygienically, with confidence, and without shame…." (Always.com 2020, online) Yet in 2019, when Always removed the iconic "Venus" female symbol from its packaging to be more inclusive of transgender and nonbinary customers, some feminists lashed out at the brand for "basically denying the existence of women" (Haddad 2019, online).

The death of U.S. Supreme Court Justice Ruth Bader Ginsburg on September 18, 2020 spurred an outpouring of gratitude for her decades of work supporting equal legal rights for women, and for serving as a role model "of female influence, authenticity, dignity, and voice…[and an] embodiment of hope for an empowered future" (Lithwick 2019 online). However, others criticized "Notorious RBG" for not doing enough to advance equality—specifically, by representing "middle-class white women's feminism," and not incorporating race, class, and/or intersectional dimensions in her advocacy (Schueller, 2020, online).

The Women's March movement that mobilized in the wake of the election of Donald Trump in 2016 garnered widespread media attention and global protest events aimed at increasing social justice. But within months, a splinter group had formed. Organizers believed the New York leadership team of the Women's March was out of touch with the interests of women living in central regions of the U.S., and that its leadership was not sufficiently racially diverse. A separate social movement organization, March On, soon formed, leading to confusion and perceptions of competition between the two organizations.

What do Always, Ruth Bader Ginsburg, and the Women's March have in common? We aver that although one is a product, one a person, and one a social movement, each can be regarded as representing a type of feminist brand. Perhaps surprisingly, however, the term feminist brand typically only appears as an undefined label in media headlines—e.g., "Justin Trudeau's Feminist Brand is Imploding" (Laidlaw 2019, online). In short, no body of marketing research illuminates the scope or implications of feminist branding practices.

The paucity of research on feminist brands by marketing scholars is particularly striking, given that brands of various kinds increasingly co-opt one or more core

DOI: 10.4324/9781003042587-8

tenets of feminism—such as advocating women's empowerment or emphasizing gender equality—to market products, services, or experiences (Banet-Weiser, Gill, and Rottenberg 2020). Furthermore, even brands historically associated with the masculine sphere (e.g., in financial planning and technology) are incorporating feminist tenets in their brand narratives (Mahmudovah 2017; Martin, Loudenback, and Pipia 2016). At the same time, increasing numbers of "person brands" (Parmentier, Fischer, and Reuber 2013) also seek to benefit in the marketplace by positioning themselves as feminist (Pruchniewska 2018; Salzman 2015). Moreover, an ever-expanding array of branded feminist movements are emerging across the globe (Mendes 2015). To address the gap in the marketing literature, our chapter examines the nature and implications of feminist brands. We deliberately pluralize the term, because as our initial examples above demonstrate, different types of feminist brands manifest themselves in the marketplace to different stakeholders, and in different ways.

We organize this chapter as follows. First, we review contemporary conceptualizations of feminism that appear particularly prone to being co-opted for branding purposes. We then examine how researchers explicitly explore linkages between feminism, brands, and branding. Next, we offer a definition of feminist brands that acknowledges both variability in the entities that may wear the feminist moniker, and the variants of feminist precepts that may inform them. We explore how the three types of brands we identify above—product, person, and movement—illuminate variants of this definition, and are informed by contemporary strands of feminism. We discuss the contentions that might arise for these types of brands, as they incorporate various approaches to feminist branding. Finally, we offer insights and suggestions for academics and practitioners to further their understanding of the construct of feminist brand in general, and of its variants.

Contemporary strands of feminist thought

Marketers and consumer researchers have long recognized there is no such thing as a single version of feminist thinking (e.g., Catterall, Maclaran, and Stevens 1997, 2000; Dobscha 1993; Hirschman 1993; Maclaran 2012; Scott 2006; Stern 1993). As Joy and Venkatesh (1994, 345) aver, feminist thought ascribes to "no central texts, no definitive techniques. [Feminism] is multidisciplinary in its explanations and offers insights without privileging any one." Because our purpose here is to highlight strands of feminist thought implicated in feminist branding practices, we begin by singling out two categories that marketing scholars have discussed at length (e.g., Bristor and Fischer 1993; Maclaran and Stevens 2019). These are: "liberal feminism" (roughly corresponding to what elsewhere is referred to as first- and second-wave feminism; e.g., Maclaran 2015) and "intersectional feminism" (roughly equivalent to fourth-wave feminism; e.g., Maclaran and Stevens 2019). We then highlight more recent development in variants of feminism, including "neoliberal feminism" and "popular feminism" (Banet-Wieser, Gill, and Rottenberg 2019). Recently, these two strains have provided considerable grist to the mill for marketers engaged in feminist branding.

Bristor and Fischer (1993) note liberal feminism is anchored in the liberal philosophy that believes a just society is one that allows individuals to exercise autonomy and to be fulfilled; as such, this philosophy entails a belief in the equality of all people. While liberal feminism acknowledges that men and women may differ due to socialization experiences or access to opportunities, this strand downplays sex differences as meaningful.

Its main concern is that all people, regardless of sex, should enjoy equal rights and protections. Liberal feminists rely upon legislation to ensure that women receive equitable access to opportunities and equal protection of their basic human rights. Liberal feminism has been criticized for primarily benefiting the interests of white, middle-class, heterosexual women, and for downplaying meaningful differences between and within genders.

In contrast to liberal feminism, intersectional versions of feminism are attuned to intersections between gender, sexuality, race, ethnicity, class, and ability. Fourth-wave intersectional feminism emerged as a critique of liberal feminism, and is grounded in the thinking of prominent Black feminist scholars such as bell hooks (1981, 1984) who incisively analyzed how racism and sexism intersect to oppress Black women in North America. Intersectional feminism, coupled with the rise of online tools for organizing social movements, has galvanized the activism of new generation (Maclaran and Stevens 2019). At the same time, intersectional feminism has been criticized for directing attention toward identities and experiences, and away from institutional remedies for systemic inequalities entrenched by capitalism (e.g., Rottenberg 2014).

A third feminist perspective, dubbed neoliberal feminism, was "spawned from the husk of liberalism" (Rottenberg 2014, 418–419). Unlike classic liberal feminism—the raison d'être of which is to reveal the limited extent to which women enjoy equality, and to seek regulative remedies that collectively benefit women—the neoliberal version is disinterested in deploying collective action to achieve equality. Rather, it concerns itself with how individual women can and should assume responsibility for their own well-being and self-care. Sheryl Sandberg's *Lean In* (2013) epitomizes this version, which suggests that acting individually, women should be entrepreneurial in optimizing their resources, taking personal initiatives, and innovating to achieve their personal and professional objectives (Rottenberg 2018, 422). Neoliberal feminism is critiqued both for serving the interests of already-privileged women and for deterring collective action; indeed, some consider neoliberal feminism a contradiction in terms (Rottenberg 2014, 2018).

Leading thinkers refer to a related but distinct contemporary variant of feminism as popular feminism (e.g., Gill 2016)—a "safely affirmative" variant that is visible, accessible, and for those who fear being tainted as radical, non-threatening. Compared to many strands of feminism that overtly criticize institutions and individuals perceived as obstructionist, popular feminism is understood as a "happy" feminism that is "corporate friendly" (Banet-Weiser, Gill, and Rottenberg 2019, 9). Its premise is that the increased presence of women in cultural, political, and economic realms will solve all gender-related inequities. Scott (1991) refers to this strain as an "add women and stir" kind of feminism, where the mere presence of women is thought sufficient to call a feminist agenda into being. Yet as Banet-Wieser, Gill, and Rottenberg (2019) observe, popular feminism tends to obscure critiques of patriarchal structure and systems of racism and violence, and to oversimplify the solutions to gender inequities.

We offer two main observations stemming from this selective overview of feminist perspectives. First, each version (even those associated with feminism's early waves) continues to be present in and inform contemporary debates. Indeed, newer versions often co-exist with those that arose earlier. Second, no version of feminism is immune to critique, an observation that foreshadows our discussion of feminist brands. Before turning to that discussion, however, we review the limited (and mainly tangential) research that interrogates linkages between feminism and branding.

Marketing scholarship on feminism, brands, and branding

Catterall, Maclaran, and Stevens (1997) provide an overview of the topics scholars explore that reside at the intersection of marketing and feminism. Their review demonstrates that most of this research originates in disciplines besides marketing, and that a clear agenda for exploring issues pertaining to marketing and feminism is lacking. Over 20 years later, this comment unfortunately still rings true. Relative to the importance of feminism in social and political discourse, a mere smattering of literature in marketing-oriented journals adopts or articulates any feminist lens. Unsurprisingly, then, academic literature that specifically explores the construct of feminist brands or branding—conceptually or empirically—is essentially absent from the marketing canon (or from the canon of any discipline, for that matter).

Most of the extant literature that does delve into linkages between feminism and marketing resides in one of two main research streams. The first examines or critiques the broad ethical issues pertaining to the intersection of these domains. Maclaran (2012, 462) notes research of this type "goes to the heart of debates between feminism and marketing: is it exploitation or empowerment?" Joy and Venkatesh (1994) provide a thorough discussion of both sides of this question. They cite Bordo's (1993) enumeration of the three problematic ways the marketing industry exploits women and the female body: by promoting "the notion of the slender body as a cultural icon, the plasticity of the female body as postmodern paradigm, and the dieting body and its ideological imagery created by and through advertising" (Joy and Venkatesh 1994, 351). Related to the issue of idealization of the female form, the authors specifically call for study of the ethical issues inherent in the promotion of plastic/cosmetic surgery by the medical industry—a call several scholars subsequently answer, by exploring whether this practice is exploitative, emancipatory, or both (e.g., Braun 2010; Davis 1995, 1997; Heyes 2016; Tait 2007; Tiefer 2008). Other issues spurring ethical debates at the intersection of marketing and feminism include the still-popular topic, first explored in the 1970s, of women's role portrayals in the media (e.g., Ferguson, Kreshel, and Tinkham 1990; Lundstrom and Sciglimpaglia 1977; Vezich, Gunter, and Lieberman 2017), and the linkages between feminism, marketing, and motherhood (e.g., O'Donohue et al. 2013; Rothman 2000).

A second robust research stream that explores the interplay of marketing and feminism appears across several disciplines—such as women's studies, marketing, advertising, English, and history. This work coalesces around exploring the specific construct of "fem-vertising" (see Coleman's [2021] chapter in this volume for a thorough review of this literature). The social media company *SheKnowsMedia* coined the term, defining it as advertising that challenges "gender norms by building stereotype-busting, pro-female messages and images into ads that target women" (*SheKnowsMedia*, 2017). Researchers typically tackle one of two types of problems in this relatively new area of study. The first is whether fem-vertising appeals shape consumers' perceptions of brands, that is, whether they influence awareness, liking, and purchase intentions (e.g., Abitbol and Sternadori 2016; Akestam, Rosengren, and Dahlen 2017; Drake 2017). Most of this research, conducted by scholars in advertising and marketing, is experimental. The second, more recent fem-vertising-related topic adopts a more explicit practitioner focus, exploring both the strategic benefits of leveraging fem-vertising, and how to maximize the effectiveness and efficiency of this appeal (Abitbol and Sternadori 2020; Feng, Chen, and He 2019; Hsu 2018).

Neither of these broad streams of literature offer an explicit definition of the term feminist brand(s), much less a meaningful or thorough discussion of their dimensions. To address this ambiguity, we offer a definition of the construct that we believe: (1) integrates the intersecting feminist discourses that influence and inform branding efforts; (2) captures the descriptive and normative dimensions of the definition, and (3) can be useful in propelling future research.

Feminist brands: a definition

Our understanding of the term brand resonates with the definition Parmentier (2011, 219) offers—that it is "a repository of meanings fueled by a combination of marketers' intentions, consumers' interpretations, and numerous sociocultural networks' associations." Informed by our review of the contemporary feminist literature, and the ways its core tenets can intersect with and influence the commercial sphere, we offer the following definition:

> A feminist brand is a polyvocal entity affiliated with and co-constructed by key stakeholders, whose meaning is rooted in one or more precepts from potentially conflicting versions of feminism. These precepts range from promoting equality between men and women in all spheres of life through collective action, to recognizing diversity owing to intersections of gender with race, sexuality, age, economic status, and so on, to empowering and self-actualizing individual women, to advocating women's increased representation in cultural, political, and economic realms.

Implicit in this definition is that feminist brands can align with different feminist values or subsets of these values, and that doing so may in fact generate or reveal inherent tensions between the various strains of feminism that can impinge upon, or be impinged upon, brand meanings. As such, feminist brands need not embrace all the tenets our definition articulates. Indeed, firms or other entities that try and align themselves with multiple variants of feminism might find themselves generating a brand message that is not only too complex for commercial purposes, but that is also likely to be inherently contradictory. Our definition also acknowledges that feminism is dynamic, and that as new versions of feminism unfold, additional precepts can shape the ways marketers and other stakeholders leverage feminism in their strategic branding efforts.

In addition, we assert that feminist branding is a much broader strategy than the research on "fem-vertising" would imply—namely, that the core function of branding is to drive advertising and social media messaging. As firms' strategic marketing actions have become increasingly transparent to consumers, an organization committed to authentically embracing feminism is more likely to infuse all touchpoints of the brand—from the firm's ethics and management policies, to its choice of supply-chain partners, promotional strategies, and customer-engagement practices and policies. In fact, many brands now tout their feminist practices in these historically less visible facets of marketing as core aspects of their brand messaging. For example, a key strategic initiative by the global investment firm Goldman Sachs is "Goldman Sachs 10,000 Women," an initiative that "fosters economic growth by providing women entrepreneurs around the world with a business and management education, mentoring and networking, and access to capital" (Goldman Sachs 10,000 Women, 2020, online).

Three categories of feminist brands

To illustrate our insights with reference to contemporary cases, we discuss three common categories of brands described as "feminist" to varying degrees in the academic and popular literature (see our introductory vignettes for this chapter). We describe how each category typically adheres to the tenets of some variant of feminism, by discussing exemplars and explicating some of the unique challenges stakeholders face in each category. By focusing on these three categories, we do not imply that these are the only types of brands that can be "feminist." For example, we also could have considered feminist media brands (e.g., Schau 2012; Stevens and Maclaran 2012) or nation brands [Jezierska and Towns; 2018; Sundström and Egström, 2020]). We simply assert that these three types contain a diversity of brands within and across categories, and that they are pervasive and pragmatic representations of feminist brands.

Feminist product brands

We define "product brands" as all goods, services, or experiences consumers can purchase or use to achieve various goals, and that do not have at their core a human being or a group of people. We deliberately distinguish between product and person brands because as we will demonstrate, these can leverage different strains of feminism, and face different challenges when crafting their branding strategies. Until the rise of social media, the most visible marketing element leveraged for local, national, or global product brands was advertising. As Williamson (1978) observes, the role of ads is to communicate narratives about commodities to increase their desirability for consumers. Goldman, Heath, and Smith (1991, 334) observe that traditionally, advertising campaigns aimed at women have spun brand stories "most often about the desire for self-identity, whether it is the desire to be a good mom or the desire for flawless golden hair or the desire for respect…." However, product brands that incorporate feminist tenets in their promotional strategies may eschew appeals that fuel "the fire of desire" (Belk, Ger, and Askegaard 2003), to promote more of a collective conscience about the importance of understanding and supporting feminist issues.

One example of a product brand that explicitly embraces both a liberal feminist stance and that of intersectional feminism is Littlefeminist.com, a subscription-based children's bookseller, who asserts that its target audience is children from birth to age 9. The opening statement on its website declares, "Our feminism is *intersectional*, which means it's anti-racist, body-positive, trans & gender non-conforming inclusive, and challenges ableism & classism" ("About Us," 2020). Consistent with the pillars of liberal feminism—and strategically extending its target audience beyond most feminist product brands—the company explains its books are appropriate and important for both young boys and girls, and that its core values are equality, empathy, and "everyone." The explanation provided in the "everyone" category reads as if it could be lifted directly from the liberal feminist playbook: "Feminism is the belief that all genders should have equal rights, which is why we should all be feminists" ("About Us," 2020).

A second example of a global product brand that literally wears its neoliberal feminist positioning on its sleeve is the Swedish fashion brand Gudrun Sjödén, bearing the name of its 79-year-old founder, CEO, and design director. The brand's origin story is steeped in neoliberal feminism, as it traces Sjödén's journey after graduating from college in 1963, through apprenticeships at other design firms, to registering her brand in 1974, to opening her first store in Stockholm in 1976 (Bornold and Engström, 2017). The tenets of entrepreneurialism, innovation, individualism, and sustainability (or ecofeminism; Dobscha and Prothero, 2012) are the key drivers of the brand; Sjödén was "one of the first ever fully eco-friendly labels, and she proudly carries that ethic… still today" (DiBoscio, 2017). Sjödén's employees—including all executives—are almost exclusively women. While the brand does quietly support communal feminist causes through monetary gifts, it channels most of its overt messaging to supporting its customers' (known as "Gudrun Girls'") creativity. Specifically, it rewards customers for the creative ways they combine Gudrun's designs in unique, often quirky ways. The company's website lauds photo contest winners and brand ambassadors for their ability to express their individuality, and celebrates their accomplishments. The story of brand ambassador Rachel Awes succinctly illustrates the neoliberal voice of the brand:

> There is no holding back in the way Rachel styles her Gudrun outfits, each one a greater explosion of color, pattern and fun than the previous. 'What I found in Gudrun is that she captured all this [creativity] in me, and raised up my wardrobe… Being an ambassador for her is life changing, it's saying yes to my own authentic evolution and revolution of being me.'
> ("Coloring Outside the Lines" 2020)

Yet what can appear as innovative and entrepreneurial to one group also can be perceived as disrespectful to another. Consistent with one of her most common design strategies, in 2013 Sjödén launched a collection inspired by artifacts and customs from a specific subculture—this time, the Nordic-based Sámi. Sjödén used the word "Lapp" to refer to the Sámi in her catalog, and was strongly criticized for not understanding that the word not only had gone out of favor, but is now considered offensive. In addition, she co-opted specific sacred pieces of the gákti, the Sámi traditional costume, in ways that diluted their symbolism as signifiers of social status and connections (Kramvig and Flemmen 2019). Thus, Gudrun Sjödén's neoliberal embrace can also serve as a cautionary tale for other marketers who may wish to consider adopting this variant of feminism.

Feminist person brands

Marketing researchers have demonstrated a growing interest in the phenomenon of person branding (e.g., Parmentier, Fischer, and Reuber 2013; Rein et al. 1997; Fournier and Eckhardt 2019). While early interest centered on celebrities as person brands (e.g., Thomson 2006), attention has increasingly turned to person branding as an activity through which "ordinary" people build their professional success (e.g., Parmentier and Fischer 2020) and compete for attention online (e.g., Smith and Fischer 2020). It is therefore unsurprising that both people who fit the definition of celebrities and those who do not might strive to imbue their person brands with one or more strands of feminism.

Prominent within the category of celebrity feminist person brands is Ruth Bader Ginsburg, mentioned in one of our opening vignettes. Arguably, the "Notorious RBG" brand is virtually synonymous with the precepts of liberal feminism: Bader Ginsburg came to fame through her work appealing a U.S. Internal Revenue Service decision that an unmarried man could not deduct the salary he paid a nurse to care for his mother, since he was a son, not a daughter. She contended this policy violated the equal-protection clause of the U.S. Constitution, selecting to argue for equal rights based on a case that entailed sex-based discrimination against a male, to make the broader point that many such laws discriminated against women. Ginsburg's successful legal outcome thus established that the principle of sex-based discrimination should entail equal protection for men or women. This appeal created the template for the constitutional revolution that demolished hundreds of laws systematically discriminating against women, and became the cause that defined her career (Lithwick, 2019). Yet as we note earlier, critics operating from the logic of intersectional feminism fault Ginsburg for having done too little to serve the interests of women beyond those in privileged middle-class positions (Schueller 2020). In other words, Ginsburg was criticized for representing the epitome of "white feminism," or the ability of white women to exercise "personalized autonomy, individual wealth, perpetual self-optimization, and supremacy" (Beck 2020), and for casting a blind eye to the inability of women of color to leverage these assets.

Within the category of "ordinary" people who leverage feminism to build their professional brands are many who rely on social media platforms to gain attention (Pruchniewska 2018). One compelling example in this category is Leandra Medine Cohen, who launched a fashion blog in 2010 with the appellation of *Man Repeller*. Indicative of Medine Cohen's alignment with a neoliberal version of feminism, she noted, "I feel very much like the Man Repeller ethos isn't about fashion…It's much more about a woman feeling comfortable in her own skin, and we're using fashion as the vehicle to discuss this sense of self-confidence" (Wallace 2014). Yet while some praise Medine Cohen as a feminist icon (e.g., Aleksander 2010), others who are more committed to liberal and intersectional feminism fault her for being insufficiently active in her support of feminist causes, and of women of color in particular. Ultimately, criticism of both her lukewarm commitment to feminism and to racial equality contributed to the demise of her once-popular blog in 2020 (Tashjian 2020).

While these are but two examples of feminist person branding, many more exist (for example, Chidgey [2020] lists Emma Watson, Jennifer Lawrence, Lena Dunham, Miley Cyrus, Taylor Swift, and Beyoncé among others). Our observation is that virtually all examples of feminist person brands that come to mind are at some point criticized for failing to adhere sufficiently to some feminist precepts, and even to have betrayed feminist principles, Thus, even the most successful feminist person brands seem susceptible to developing doppelgänger brand images (Thompson, Rindfleisch, and Arsel, 2006) as flawed feminists. Perhaps this should not be surprising, given that many noted feminist scholars claim that the very notion of "'self-branding' and 'self-promotion' serve to shatter any sense of cohesive community and commitment" associated with collective feminist goals (Banet-Weiser and Juhasz 2011, 1769). Notwithstanding legitimate criticisms, however, feminist person brands may advance some feminist causes, even while leaving other less successfully addressed.

Feminist branded movements

The final feminist-branded entity we consider is social movements. While some may argue that feminism as a whole represents a movement of sorts, there are many feminist-branded causes that speak to distinct issues and concerns. One that has attracted considerable scholarly attention is "SlutWalks," an ongoing series of protest marches that originated at York University in Toronto, following a police officer advising a group of students at a campus safety event that women who wanted to avoid being victimized should avoid dressing like "sluts." Responding to the voicing of an implicit rape myth (i.e., clothing invites or even justifies rape; Tanenbaum 2015), local activists organized a march on police headquarters, demanding accountability for this "slut-shaming" by a law enforcement official. The protest swiftly attracted global attention of both participants and scholars (e.g., Nguyen 2013; Reger 2015; Ringrose and Renold 2012). Over the course of a few short years, activists in over 50 countries organized independent SlutWalk marches. Although each adopted its own aim and form, they shared the goals of ending rape culture and victim-blaming attitudes. Critical responses to the marches vacillated between a celebration of their transnational organization and vibrant constellation of tactics, to a critique of pandering to pornification through its protest aesthetic and for lacking a race and class analysis (Chidgey 2020; Mendes 2015). Yet again, we see a feminist brand that aligns itself with liberal feminist precepts of the right to gender equality, while falling afoul of intersectional feminist sensibilities.

Another more recent feminist-branded social movement also attracting widespread attention is the one we mention in our opening vignette, the #March4Women. Compared with SlutWalks, the goals of the #March4Women were arguably more aligned with popular feminism, given their focus on increasing women's representation in elected offices. However, this movement's objectives were diffuse enough to also embrace objectives of recognizing and redressing inequalities faced by women, consistent with liberal feminism. Unsurprisingly, the tensions that led to splinter organizations distancing themselves from the original #March4Women organization reflect critiques of the movement based on intersectional feminist precepts.

In general, research on leveraging branding tactics to support feminist movements contributes to identifying both the pros and cons of such endeavors. On the plus side, branding practices may help attract economic and human resources that movements can deploy to successfully pursue their objectives. Conversely, branding typically results in the mainstreaming of movements, a process that tends to privilege certain women (white, cis-feminists) over others (poor, BAME, migrants, LGBTQ+, disabled, old). Moreover, receiving awards and grants may result in feminist organisations having to be accountable to patrons rather than the constituents they intend to serve, leading to a normalization of neoliberal values (Mendes 2017).

Future research

This chapter demonstrates that feminist branding practices are alive, well, and proliferating in the marketplace, despite the lag in marketers' scholarly efforts to define, dimensionalize, or interrogate the construct. To initiate more systematic research on feminist brands, our chapter contributes a definition and numerous examples of various kinds of feminist brands. Below, we offer thoughts on where attention is required from both academics and practitioners.

Directions for academic research

We believe scholarly efforts shouldbe devoted to gaining a more rigorous and robust understanding of what can be perceived as successful feminist brands. Without dismissing critical feminist arguments that there is a fundamental tension between feminism and branding (e.g., Banet-Weiser and Juhaz 2011), we can conjecture that some brands are actually beneficial. Thus, questions for scholars to consider can include: under what conditions can a feminist brand benefit a wide(r) range of stakeholders, including those at the often-overlooked intersections formed by race, age, ability, and so on? We encourage research on specific brands that stakeholders perceive as authentically dedicated to feminist causes, and that resonate as sincere in their commitment and messaging. Even if we accept that few if any feminist brands are exempt from critique, we believe it is important to better understand those feminist brands that do, on balance, further feminist agendas.

We also encourage research on how people are affected by their involvement in or relationships with feminist brands. For example, how does immersion in a branded feminist movement affect an individuals' goals, priorities, and sense of purpose? How are the leaders of feminist movements affected by their experiences relative to those who become active after a movement gains momentum? Likewise, how does building a feminist person brand affect individuals who pursue that course of action? And how do feminist person brands manage when faced with critiques of their feminist positioning?

We also observe that it is somewhat ironic that much of the prior work related to feminist branding (especially the work on "fem-vertising") relies heavily on experimental methods, given that feminist research in particular advocates qualitative approaches, because of the emphasis on empowering and empathizing with informants, and in advocacy research, on leading change (McHugh 2014). Indeed, it seems that foundational qualitative work into what diverse categories of women (and men) think and feel about feminist branding practices, and how these perceptions impact their integration of brands into their lives is in order. Given that some feminist brands (including, but not limited to, feminist movement brands such as the Women's March) involve not consumers' financial, emotional, and physical commitment, these could serve to be transformational in consumers' lives, providing them with purpose and meaning. Indeed, we note that feminist product, person, and movement brands often face criticism for inconsistent practices. Yet what remains less understood is whether customers/participants actually reap the promised benefits of equality and emancipation that these brands proffer.

This question is particularly important to understand when, for example, feminist movement brands challenge deep-rooted social norms and beliefs. Consider the new initiative titled "#NoMarriage" in South Korea, which advocates that women forego marriage and childbirth to pursue their own career goals and not be held back by the domestic drudgery valorized as "women's work" by a society steeped in patriarchy. The economic and demographic impact of this movement is already understood (Lee 2019). Yet what deserves research attention is whether and how such movements help women feel supported and empowered as they engage in controversial collective protests that advocate real cultural change.

Directions for practitioner-oriented research

Given space limitations, in this section we will focus primarily on research that could benefit practitioners charged with creating or managing feminist product brands, and who face the challenge of creating value for their firms and their customers. As our chapter makes clear, most feminist brands are likely to be targets of criticism; that being the case, it is important that future research identify the trade-offs firms could face if they strive to pursue a feminist agenda in the commercial sphere, and the short- and long-term consequences incurred when doing so. Such research must be attuned to the differences that exist for firms attempting to build both a feminist organizational culture and identity internally, and to market feminist offerings (see, for example, D'Enbeau and Buzzanell 2013), versus those only touting feminist brands in the marketplace.

Dobscha and Prothero (2012) assert feminist brands may face stigmatization in the marketplace, especially if they align with more assertive forms of feminism (meaning they are not merely invested with neoliberal or popular versions of feminism that prove unthreatening to the status quo). Research is required, however, to understand whether these stigmas can effectively be combatted without withdrawing brands from the market, or having to strategically reposition them to drop any alignment with a specific variant (or variants) of feminism.

Relatedly, existing research sheds limited light on brands that adopt a more intersectional feminist positioning, and we lack systematic study of whether aligning with few versus many strands of feminism can be beneficial to firms and brands. Again, we believe case studies of firms that adopt (and perhaps reshape or relinquish) visible feminist brand positionings—and that illuminate the impact doing so has had on the firms' attainment of goals—would be invaluable.

Conclusion

Just as variants of feminism proliferate and evolve, so do the ways brands can be perceived and positioned. We hope this chapter provides coherence with respect to the meaning of feminist brands, proves useful to academics and practitioners who wish to better understand the interrelationship between marketing and feminism, and offers a roadmap for productive study of the construct.

The authors contributed equally to this chapter.

References

Abitbol, Alan, and Miglena M. Sternadori. 2016. "You Act like a Girl: An Examination of Consumer Perceptions of 'Femvertising'." *Quarterly Review of Business Disciplines* 3 (2): 117–128.

Abitbol, Alan, and Miglena M. Sternadori. 2020. "Consumer Location and Ad Type Preferences as Predictors of Attitude Toward Femvertising." *Journal of Social Marketing* 10 (2): 179–195, advance publication.

"About Us." https://littlefeminist.com/about-us/, accessed January 5, 2021.

Åkestam, Nina, Sara Rosengren, and Micael Dahlen. 2017. "Advertising 'Like a Girl': Toward a Better Understanding of 'Femvertising' and Its Effects." *Psychology & Marketing* 34 (8): 795–806.

Aleksander, Irina. 2010. "Fashion Triumph: Deflecting the Male Gaze." *New York Times*, October 12. https://www.nytimes.com/2010/12/16/fashion/16MANREPELLER.html.

Banet-Weiser, Sarah, and Alexandra Juhasz. 2011. "Feminist Labor in Media Studies/Communication: Is Self-Branding Feminist Practice?" *International Journal of Communication* 5: 1768–1775.

Banet-Weiser, Sarah, Rosalind Gill, and Catherine Rottenberg. 2020. "Postfeminism, Popular Feminism and Neoliberal Feminism? Sarah Banet-Weiser, Rosalind Gill and Catherine Rottenberg in Conversation." *Feminist Theory* 21 (1): 3–24.

Beck, Koa. 2020. *White Feminism: From the Suffragettes to Influencers and Who They Leave Behind*. New York: Simon & Schuster.

Belk, Russell W., Güliz Ger, and Søren Askegaard. 2003. "The Fire of Desire: A Multisited Inquiry into Consumer Passion." *Journal of Consumer Research* 30 (3): 326–351.

Bordo, Susan. 1993. "Feminism, Foucault and the Politics of the Body." *Up Against Foucault: Explorations of Some Tensions Between Foucault and Feminism*, edited by Caroline Ramazanoglu, 179. London: Routledge.

Bornold, Salka H., and Patrik Engström. 2017. "The House That Gudrun Built," *Form* 5: 37–45.

Braun, Virginia. 2010. "Female Genital Cosmetic Surgery: A Critical Review of Current Knowledge and Contemporary Debates." *Journal of Women's Health* 19 (7): 1393–1407.

Bristor, Julia M., and Eileen Fischer. 1993. "Feminist Thought: Implications for Consumer Research." *Journal of Consumer Research*, 19 (4), 518-536.

Catterall, Miriam, Pauline Maclaran, and Lorna Stevens. 1997. "Marketing and Feminism: A Bibliography and Suggestions for Further Research." *Marketing Intelligence & Planning* 15 (7): 369–376.

Catterall, Miriam, Pauline Maclaran, and Lorna Stevens. 2000. *Marketing and Feminism*. London: Routledge.

Chidgey, Red. 2020. "Postfeminism™: Celebrity Feminism, Branding and the Performance of Activist Capital." *Feminist Media Studies*, published online August 12.

"Coloring Outside the Lines." 2020. https://gsw.gudrunsjoden.com/us/gudruns-world/empowerment.

Davis, Kathy. 1995. *Reshaping the Female Body. The Dilemma of Cosmetic Surgery*. New York: Routledge.

Davis, Kathy. 1997. "Cosmetic Surgery as Feminist Utopia?" *European Journal of Women's Studies* 4 (1): 23–37.

D'Enbeau, Suzy, and Patrice Buzzanell. 2013. "Constructing a Feminist Organization's Identity in a Competitive Marketplace: The Intersection of Ideology, Image, and Culture." *Human Relations* 66 (11): 1447–1470.

DiBoscio, Chere. 2017. "Granny Cool: A Rare Interview with Gudrun Sjoden." http://elux-magazine.com/fashion/interview-with-gudrun-sjoden/.

Dobscha, Susan. 1993. "Woman and the Environment: Applying Ecofeminism to Environmentally-Related Consumption." *Advances in Consumer Research* 20 (1): 36–40.

Dobscha, Susan, and Andrea Prothero. 2012. "(Re)Igniting Sustainable Consumption and Production Research Through Feminist Connections," *Gender, Culture, and Consumer Behavior*, edited by Cele C. Otnes and Linda T. Zayer, 371–392. New York: Routledge.

Drake, Victoria E. 2017. "The Impact of Female Empowerment in Advertising (Femvertising)." *Journal of Research in Marketing* 7 (3): 593–599.

Feng, Yang, Huan Chen, and Li He. 2019. "Consumer Responses to Femvertising: A Data-Mining Case of Dove's 'Campaign for Real Beauty' on YouTube." *Journal of Advertising* 48 (3): 292–301.

Ferguson, Jill Hicks, Peggy J. Kreshel, and Spencer F. Tinkham. 1990. "In the Pages of *Ms.*: Sex Role Portrayals of Women in Advertising." *Journal of Advertising* 19 (1): 40–51.

Fournier, Susan, and Giana Eckhardt. 2019. "Putting the Person Back in Person-Brands: Understanding and Managing the Two-Bodied Brand." *Journal of Marketing Research* 56 (4): 602–619.

Gill, Rosalind. 2016. "Post-Postfeminism?: New Feminist Visibilities in Postfeminist Times." *Feminist Media Studies* 16 (4): 610–630.

Goldman, Robert, Deborah Heath, and Sharon L. Smith. 1991. "Commodity Feminism." *Critical Studies in Media Communication* 8 (3): 333–351.

"Goldman Sachs 10,000 Women." https://www.goldmansachs.com/citizenship/10000women/#.

Haddad, Tareq. 2019. "Always Sanitary Products Accused of Erasing Biology after Venus Symbol Removed from Packaging," *Newsweek*, October 21. https://www.newsweek.com/always-sanitary-products-accused-erasing-biology-venus-symbol-removed-packaging-1466677.

Heyes, Cressida J. 2016. *Cosmetic Surgery: A Feminist Primer*. London: Routledge.

Hirschman, Elizabeth C. 1993. "Ideology in Consumer Research 1980 and 1990: A Marxist and Feminist Critique." *Journal of Consumer Research* 19 (4): 537–555.

hooks, b. (1981). *Ain't I a Woman: Black Women and Feminism*. Boston, MA: South End Press.
hooks, b. (1984). *Feminist Theory: From Margin to Center*. Cambridge, MA: South End Press.
Hsu, Chung-Kue Jennifer. 2018. "Femvertising: State of the Art." *Journal of Brand Strategy* 7 (1): 28–47.
Jezierska, Katarzyna, and Ann Towns. 2018. "Taming Feminism? The Place of Gender Equality in the 'Progressive Sweden' Brand." *Place Branding and Public Diplomacy* 14 (1): 55–63.
Joy, Annamma, and Alladi Venkatesh. 1994. "Postmodernism, Feminism, and the Body: The Visible and the Invisible in Consumer Research." *International Journal of Research in Marketing* 11(4): 333–357.
Kramvig, Britt, and Anne Britt Flemmen. 2019. "Turbulent Indigenous Objects: Controversies around Cultural Appropriation and Recognition of Difference." *Journal of Material Culture* 24 (1): 64–82.
Laidlaw, Katherine. 2019. "Justin Trudeau's Feminist Brand Is Imploding," *Atlantic*, March 12. https://www.theatlantic.com/international/archive/2019/03/canada-trudeau-feminism-wilson-raybauld/584677/.
Lee, Jihye. 2019. "The #NoMarriage Movement is Adding to Korea's Economic Woes." *Bloomberg.com*, July 23. https://www.bloomberg.com/news/articles/2019-07-23/the-nomarriage-movement-is-adding-to-korea-s-economic-woes.
Lithwick, Dahlia. 2019. "The Irony of Modern Feminism's Obsession with Ruth Bader Ginsburg," *Atlantic*, January–February. https://www.theatlantic.com/magazine/archive/2019/01/ruth-bader-ginsburg-feminist-hero/576403/.
Lundstrom, William J., and Donald Sciglimpaglia. 1977. "Sex Role Portrayals in Advertising." *Journal of Marketing* 41 (3): 72–79.
Maclaran, Pauline. 2012. "Marketing and Feminism in Historic Perspective," *Journal of Historical Research in Marketing* 4 (3): 462–469.
Maclaran, Pauline. 2015. "Feminism's Fourth Wave: A Research Agenda for Marketing and Consumer Research." *Journal of Marketing Management* 31 (15–16): 1732–1738.
Maclaran, Pauline, and Lorna Stevens. 2019. "Thinking Through Feminist Theorising: Poststructuralist Feminism, Ecofeminism and Intersectionality." *Handbook of Research on Gender and Marketing*, edited by Susan Dobscha, 229–251. Cheltenham, UK: Edward Elgar Publishing.
Mahmudovah, Anora (2017). "Sallie Krawcheck: Get Ready for 'Financial Feminism,'" January 17. https://www.marketwatch.com/story/sallie-krawcheck-get-ready-for-financial-feminism-2017-01-19.
Martin, Emmie, Tanza Loudenback, and Alexa Pipia. 2016, "22 Successful Women-Led Companies That Prove There's Much More to Business Than Profits." *Business Insider*, June 29. https://www.businessinsider.com/bi-100-the-creators-women-2016-6.
McHugh, Maureen C. 2014. "Feminist Qualitative Research: Toward Transformation of Science and Society." *Oxford Handbook of Qualitative Research*, edited by Patricia Leavy, 137–164. Oxford: Oxford University Press.
Mendes, Kaitlynn. 2015. *SlutWalk: Feminism, Activism and Media*. Basingstoke: Palgrave Macmillan.
Mendes, Kaitlynn. 2017. "Brand Feminism: Promotional Culture and Contemporary Feminist Activism." Paper presented at *Media, Public Spheres and Gender Annual Conference*.
Nguyen, Tram. 2013. "From SlutWalks to SuicideGirls: Feminist Resistance in the Third Wave and Postfeminist Era." *Women's Studies Quarterly* 41 (3/4): 157–172.
O'Donohoe, Stephanie, Margaret Hogg, Pauline Maclaran, Lydia Martens, and Lorna Stevens, eds. 2013. *Motherhoods, Markets and Consumption: The Making of Mothers in Contemporary Western Cultures*. London: Routledge.
Parmentier, Marie-Agnès. 2011. "When David Met Victoria: Forging a Strong Family Brand." *Family Business Review* 24 (3): 217–232.
Parmentier, Marie-Agnès, Eileen Fischer and A. Rebecca Reuber. 2013. "Positioning Person Brands in Established Organizational Fields." *Journal of the Academy of Marketing Science* 41 (3): 373–387.

Parmentier, Marie-Agnès and Eileen Fischer. 2020. "Working It: Managing Professional Brands in Prestigious Posts." *Journal of Marketing*, forthcoming. https://doi.org/10.1177/0022242920953818.

Pruchniewska, Urszula M. 2018. "Branding the Self as an "Authentic Feminist": Negotiating Feminist Values in Post-Feminist Digital Cultural Production." *Feminist Media Studies* 18 (5): 810–824.

Reger, Jo. 2015. "The Story of a Slut Walk: Sexuality, Race, and Generational Divisions in Contemporary Feminist Activism." *Journal of Contemporary Ethnography* 44 (1): 84–112.

Rein, Irving, Philip Kotler, and Martin Stoller. 1997. *High Visibility: The Making and Marketing of Professionals and Celebrities*. Columbus, OH: McGraw-Hill.

Ringrose, Jessica, and Emma Renold. 2012. "Slut-Shaming, Girl Power and 'Sexualisation': Thinking through the Politics of the International SlutWalks with Teen Girls." *Gender and Education* 24 (3): 333–343.

Rosén Sundström, Malena, and Ole Elgström. 2020. "Praise or Critique? Sweden's Feminist Foreign Policy in the Eyes of Its Fellow EU members." *European Politics and Society* 21 (4): 418–433.

Rothman, Barbara Katz. 2000. *Recreating Motherhood*. Piscataway, NJ: Rutgers University Press.

Rottenberg, Catherine. 2014. "The Rise of Neoliberal Feminism." *Cultural Studies* 28 (3): 418–437.

Rottenberg, Catherine. 2018. *The Rise of Neoliberal Feminism*. Oxford: Oxford University Press.

Salzman, Marian. 2015. "10 Women Power Brands," *Forbes*, September 8. https://www.forbes.com/sites/mariansalzman/2015/09/08/10-power-women-brands/?sh=5b4d6fd57c44.

Sandberg, Sheryl. 2013. *Lean In: Women, Work, and the Will to Lead*. New York: Random House.

Schau, Hope. 2012."'The Creation of Inspired Lives:' Female Fan Engagement with the *Twilight Saga*," *Gender, Culture, and Consumer Behavior*, edited by Cele C. Otnes and Linda Tuncay Zayer, 33–60. New York: Routledge.

Schueller, Jennifer. 2020. "Amid the Outpouring for Ginsburg, a Hint of FF," *New York Times*, September 21. https://www.nytimes.com/2020/09/21/arts/ginsburg-feminist-backlash.html.

Scott, Joan W. 1991. "The Evidence of Experience." *Critical Inquiry* 17(4): 773–797.

Scott, Linda M. 2006. *Fresh Lipstick: Redressing Fashion and Feminism*. Basingstoke: Palgrave Macmillan.

SheKnowsMedia. 2017. "The 2017 Femvertising Awards Winners." https://skmfemvertisingawards.splashthat.com/.

Smith, Andrew and Eileen Fischer. 2020. "Pay Attention, Please! Person Brand Building in Organized Online Attention Economies." *Journal of the Academy of Marketing Science*. https://doi.org/10.1007/s11747-020-00736-0.

Stern, Barbara. 1993. "Feminist Literary Criticism and the Deconstruction of Ads: A Postmodern View of Advertising and Consumer Responses." *Journal of Consumer Research* 19(4): 556–566.

Stevens, Lorna and Pauline Maclaran. 2012. "The Carnal Feminine: Consuming Representations of Womanhood in a Contemporary Media Text." *Gender, Culture, and Consumer Behavior*, edited by Cele C. Otnes and Linda Tuncay Zayer, 63–86. New York: Routledge.

Tait, Sue. 2007. "Television and the Domestication of Cosmetic Surgery." *Feminist Media Studies* 7 (2): 119–135.

Tanenbaum, Lorena. 2015. *I am Not a Slut: Slut-Shaming in the Age of the Internet*. New York: Harper Perennial.

Tashjian, Sarah. 2020. "What Happened to Man Repeller?" https://www.gq.com/story/what-happened-to-man-repeller.

Thomson, Matthew. 2020. "Human Brands: Investigating Antecedents to Consumers' Strong Attachments to Celebrities." *Journal of Marketing* 70 (3): 104–119.

Tiefer, Leonore. 2008. "Female Genital Cosmetic Surgery: Freakish or Inevitable? Analysis from Medical Marketing, Bioethics, and Feminist Theory." *Feminism & Psychology* 18 (4): 466–479.

Thompson, Craig J., Aric P. Rindfleisch, and Zeynep Arsel. 2006. "Emotional Branding and the Strategic Value of the Doppelgänger Brand Image." *Journal of Marketing* 70 (1): 50–64.

Vezich, I. Stephanie, Benjamin C. Gunter, and Matthew D. Lieberman. 2017. "Women's Responses to Stereotypical Media Portrayals: An fMRI study of Sexualized and Domestic Images of Women." *Journal of Consumer Behaviour* 16 (4): 322–331.

Wallace, Benjamin. 2014. "What's So Alluring About a Woman Known as Man Repeller?" https://www.thecut.com/2014/02/man-repeller-leandra-medine-profile.html.

Williamson, Judith. 1978. *Decoding Advertisements: Ideology and Meaning in Advertising*. London: Marion Boyers.

7 "One, two, three, four, what are we fighting for?"

Deconstructing climate crisis war messaging metaphors using ecofeminism

Susan Dobscha and Andrea Prothero

Introduction – the climate crisis

Climate experts are frantically trying to get the planet's attention: "The climate crisis is the defining issue of our lifetimes (Mulholland, 2019)," and "Our collective failure on global warming has as much to do with the ways that scientists and environmentalists have approached and presented the problem as with how their opponents have resisted possible solutions (Howe, 2014, 6)." In our capacity as sustainability researchers in marketing we share their feelings of panic. In this chapter we review the use of a war metaphor as a popular messaging tool of choice in addressing the climate crisis. We examine war as metaphor through an analysis of what we label the war strategies of the environmental group *WorldWarZero* and compare this to the ecofeminist principles utilized by *Extinction Rebellion (ER)*. We argue that the utilization of ecofeminist strategies revolving around inter-connected strategies and collaboration, alongside co-operative and conciliatory actions, will more likely to lead to much needed societal change in addressing the climate crisis. Below, we briefly introduce the reader to a history of global warming before exploring the use of war metaphors within marketing, and as a messaging tool for solving the climate crisis. Next we consider the core principles of ecofeminism, before providing arguments as to how utilizing ecofeminist principles as an alternative messaging tool is better equipped to tackle the climate crisis.

Global warming was first raised as a theoretical concept by the Swedish scientist, Svante Arrhenius in 1896 (Weart, 2008), and greenhouse gases themselves were highlighted by Irish physicist John Tyndall in 1861 (Howe, 2014). Since 1957 other terms have emerged to describe this phenomenon. The term "global warming" dominated the discourse in the 1980s but this proved confusing to many – as more extreme weather events directly attributed to CO_2 changes, including hurricanes and snow blizzards, were not viewed in the same way as the term "global warming" suggested. In the 1990s "climate change" became popular as a means through which to more accurately reflect the erratic weather changes a rise in atmospheric CO_2 brings about. This term was preferred by climate-deniers as it sounded more passive than previous terms (Howarth and Sharman, 2015). As the authors stated, the descriptive language used to describe this crisis does indeed shift public opinion. As a result, *The Guardian* and other newspapers have advocated for their journalists to use "climate emergency" or "climate crisis" as this "more accurately describes the environmental crises facing the world" (Zeldin-O'Neill, 2019).

Revelle and Suess (1957) first brought the warming of our planet through human use of fossil fuels to our attention, although it was Bolin and Eriksson (1959) a few years later

DOI: 10.4324/9781003042587-9

who emphasized the potential dangers of the warming of atmospheric CO_2. Over 70 years later we have witnessed this rise in temperatures through what is known in scientific circles as the Keeling Curve. The Keeling Curve highlights the consistent increases in CO_2 within our atmosphere, while also demonstrating the problem is continuing to worsen (Howe, 2014). We now know that the world is warming at an unprecedented rate (Weart, 2008), and it is human activity that is the cause of this warming. In 2006, Former USA Vice President Al Gore participated in a documentary *An Inconvenient Truth* that was meant to bring the concept of global warming to a worldwide stage. At that time, he presented his compelling evidence over 1,500 times to audiences of all ages. He noted that this moment in time should be viewed as not just a crisis but also as an opportunity. We build on this idea by suggesting in order to recognize potential opportunities to affect change, we must use messaging that is based on interconnectedness, collaboration, and compassion, alongside co-operative and conciliatory actions, and not that which relies on the use of a war metaphor.

No matter what it is called (we are using climate crisis hereafter), clearly the planet is getting hotter, and human consumption and production are at fault (Prothero et al., 2011). And the Intergovernmental Panel on Climate Change (IPCC) stated in 2018 that the planet has 10 years (at the time of writing – November, 2020) to turn around this continuous warming trend. In the hard hitting report the IPCC (2018) very clearly lay out what lies ahead if we do not make serious inroads in tackling the problems our reliance on fossil fuels has created. Major global cities, from Boston to Shanghai, will be permanently flooded by 2050, and the climate crisis will see rises in temperatures and sea levels accompanied by unprecedented heatwaves, which, in turn, will lead to famine, poverty, and significant global population displacement (Kulp and Strauss, 2019).

In order to tackle the recommendations made by the IPCC other scientists require us to reduce our greenhouse gas emissions by 50% by 2030 and we will need this to reach zero per cent by 2050 (Falk et al. 2020). This is not, by any means, an easy task. It is monumental. It requires collaborative efforts from governments, the science communities, business, civil society organizations, and society generally. And, it requires these efforts now. The climate crisis is not a future problem, but it is a very real current one.

As stated earlier, labels matter. And labels bring with them other linguistic devices, such as metaphors. Below we discuss the use of metaphors in marketing with particular emphasis on war metaphors. War metaphors have had a long history in business and marketing and now have seeped into sustainability discourse.

War metaphor

Perhaps no other metaphor in marketing has had more endurance than the war metaphor. While other metaphors, including relationships, communities, exchange, and service-dominant logic have also found a home in our discipline (Vargo and Lusch 2004), war as a metaphor has certainly endured through many academic eras. Used as a metaphor in marketing though is perplexing to us given the commonly accepted definition ("a state of usually open and declared armed hostile conflict between states or nations"), coupled with the fact that marketing as a discipline was borne out of economics and psychology, neither of which used it in their ontological underpinnings. Furthermore, the war metaphor seems at odds with the perceived function of marketing espoused by the American Marketing Association and other governing bodies:

"Marketing is the activity, set of institutions, and process for creating, communicating, delivering and exchanging offerings that have value for customers, clients, partners, and society at large (Definition of Marketing-AMA website)." However, "people in power get to impose their metaphors (Lakoff and Johnson, 1980, 157)," and in marketing a war metaphor is commonplace.

The use of the war metaphor in marketing, and in indeed business more generally, was prevalent in the latter half of the twentieth century. Indeed, in the 1980s marketing as warfare was de rigueur. This proliferation is evidenced in the best-selling book of Ries and Trout in 1986 (with a more recent updated 20th anniversary issue published in 2005), which, as the quote above demonstrated, focused on battlefields, attacks, and tactics. And, this was perpetuated in other books (Davidson, 1972; Durö and Sandström, 1987; Durö, 1989; Garsombke, 1987; Levinson, 1998; Martin, 2006; Ries and Trout, 1981) around the same time. Indeed, we even witnessed the development of a "war field manual" for marketers (Michaelson, 1987). Academic journal articles also built further on the metaphor (Kotler and Singh, 1981; Parks, Pharr and Lockeman, 1994; Ho and Choi, 1997). Whether it was adopting offensive or defensive marketing strategies, guerrilla strategies, engaging in price wars, or targeting consumers, the overall emphasis was on 'beating' the competition and 'winning' consumers. This was to be achieved through marketing strategies, which very often adopted military terminology. Indeed, as Ries and Trout (1986, 1) emphasized in their introduction "The true nature of marketing today is not serving the customer; it is outwitting, outflanking, outfighting your competitors." And the chapters' headings read like a war manual – with headings such as "The principle of force", "The superiority of the defense", "The nature of the battleground" alongside four chapters on the principles of – defensive, offensive, flanking and guerrilla warfare. These war strategies were not only required in the development and implementation of marketing strategies, but also of the marketing managers implementing them, with the final chapter of Ries and Trout's bestselling book talking of "The marketing general" who needs to be a field marshal. As Rindfleisch (1996, 8) in his criticism of the war metaphor in marketing proffered – markets were seen as "strategic battlegrounds" and market actors were imbued with "competitive motivation" to achieve "strategic competitive advantage." Indeed, they emphasized the war analogy in the marketing materials of their own book. From the back cover:

> You've got your hands on one of the greatest marketing manuals ever written – the classic that defines the strategies, plans, and campaigns of today's marketing battlefield. Marketing is war. To triumph over the competition, it's not enough to target customers. Marketers must take aim at their competitors – and be prepared to defend their own turf from would-be attackers at all times. This indispensable guide gives smart fighters the best tactics – defensive, offensive, flanking, and guerrilla. It's the book that wrote the new rules!
>
> (Ries and Trout, 1986, back cover)

As Koller (2008) stated metaphors are "constitutive of social relations, one of the clearest manifestations of power is the possibility to control discourse and hence cognition (Koller 2008, 104)." She also found in her study of marketing metaphors that war metaphors outpaced relationship metaphors two to one with words such as "campaign," "launch," and "target" being the most commonly used. Disturbingly, she found terms like "blood on the spear" and "jihad" also used frequently. As Tadajewski (2006, 165) stresses:

> what is more problematic is the lack of interest in connecting the production of marketing knowledge to wider societal relations of power/knowledge which influence how knowledge regimes gain legitimacy and institutional support within a particular socio-temporal context. Commensurate with this emphasis on the non-discursive, it seems advisable that marketing scholars should periodically revisit the development of marketing history in order to establish how forms of knowledge become institutionalized, rethinking – where necessary – the ordering of marketing discourse.

While the use of the war metaphor in marketing has been widely critiqued (e.g., Catley 2016; Cespedes 2014; Desmond, 1997; Reindfleisch, 1996; Rosenberg and van West, 1984;), as Koller's article demonstrates, marketing has not moved fully on from the war metaphor, particularly in business practice. Indeed, recent articles still discuss the metaphor with examples including "*thinking like a warrior*" (Bekoglu and Ergen, 2014) and "*the bright side of having an enemy*" (Harutyunyan and Jiang, 2019). In order to engage in critical analysis with the war metaphor in marketing, in particular how it is being co-opted and applied as a messaging tool by current climate crisis leaders globally, we apply ecofeminism. Ecofeminist theory is not new to marketing, and yet has not quite captured the discipline as an informative critical framework as much as others have.

Ecofeminism

Ecofeminism has roots in feminist and Marxist theory as well as in early environmental studies, and was introduced into the lexicon in 1974 by François d'Eaubonne. It is that branch of feminist theory that claims women and nature have been simultaneously damaged and suppressed by patriarchy (d'Eaubonne, 1974; Mies and Shiva, 1993). Its basic tenets attempt to examine oppressive dualisms such as nature/culture, mind/body, and, particular to this paper, war/peace that leave women out of positions of power and decision-making when it comes to manifesting policies related to damage to the environment, including the climate crisis. Dualisms are linguistic pairs that are often thought of as separate but equal categories (nature/culture or mind/body, for example) but in reality maintain and perpetuate hierarchies that overvalue men's contributions and undervalue those of women. Language used, for example, in corporate social responsibility initiatives or sustainable development programs, "has power implications that render thought and action about what is feasible or infeasible, legitimate or illegitimate, as it creates a particular view of the world and orders people, nonhumans, nature and so on (Irving and Helin 20, 3)." As Maclaran and Stevens (2019, 239) state:

> ecofeminism ultimately seeks to question binary systems that are socially constructed to devalue women and the environment, offering economic, spiritual and political reasons as to why patriarchal values are harmful and destructive, calling for an ethic of care and a transformational philosophy of a connected, human, ecological self, rather than an individualistic, androcentric, and anthropocentric self.

Ecofeminist theory is present in several published studies in marketing. Beginning with Dobscha (1993), an ecofeminist research agenda was established to guide future scholars to critically evaluate sustainable marketing and consumer practices with a different lens. Critical in this agenda was the emphasis on connecting the feminist agenda with sustainability (Dobscha and Ozanne 2001; Lozada and Mintu-Wimsatt 1995). This emphasis attempted to shift conventional thinking away from marketing's contribution to anti-ecological practices (McDonagh and Prothero, 1997) and toward a more egalitarian, communal view of nature that would lead to a better relationship between marketing and the environment. Shifting emphasis away from individual consumption choices (which inevitably fall on women's shoulders to uphold) toward the patriarchal structures such as international commerce conglomerates (big agra, big pharma, big oil) that are the largest contributors to the climate crisis could lead to a more impactful response to reversing the effects of climate variability (Vinz 2009). Unfortunately, save for a few exceptions, marketing academic work continues to focus on sustainability at the individual consumption level (McDonagh and Prothero, 2014). Stalwart researchers such as Lorna Stevens and Pauline Maclaran have continued through their scholarly output to push for an ecofeminist agenda as a means to affect global change when it comes to climate issues, and the role marketing plays in contributing to this crisis. In addition, Littlefield (2010) used ecofeminist theory to illuminate the relationship between men and hunting. This important study showed that men also have intimate connections to nature, albeit in a hierarchal, dominating way, thus highlighting the importance of breaking down dualisms so that all consumers could improve their connections to nature (McDonagh and Prothero, 1997; Dobscha and Prothero, 2012). Recently, Stevens, Kearney, and Maclaran (2013) and Stevens, Maclaran, and Kearney (2014) adopted an ecofeminist perspective in a study of how cows are used as metaphors in advertising. Their reading of these ads, a technique adopted from Hirschman (1998), found that cows were place-holders in ads for such themes as male domination, the animal as "other," and the "monstrous feminine." Their use of metaphor analysis found that cows are imbued with cultural meaning that they labeled "benevolent mastery." They concluded that these metaphors represent and maintain patriarchal structures that limit our capacity to confront critical environmental issues Maclaran and Stevens (2019, 243) conclude that "ecofeminist thinking exemplifies how feminist approaches can contribute to unmasking the unquestioned and taken for granted 'norms'…to offer a more problematic interpretation of cultural texts and discourses that may lead to our re-evaluation of those texts and discourses." Other ecofeminist work in marketing includes Paddock (2017) who studied Caribbean women's "unhealthy" relationships with food, Ballard (2016) who examined PETA advertisements, and Yudina and Fennell (2013) who critiqued the use and treatment of animals in tourism marketing.

Thus, application of ecofeminist theory to modern social problems relies heavily on an intersectional reading of gender and nature and the dismantling of patriarchal dualisms that maintain patriarchy and reinforce women's inferior place in modern organizational and relational structures (Irving and Helin, 2018), while also aiming to protect the natural environment from detrimental human activities.

From a sustainability perspective, as previous works have pointed out (Dobscha and Prothero, 2012), marketing journals continue to publish sustainability research that provides "an excellent window into the weaknesses inherent in the discipline's core coverage of the topic of sustainability (Dobscha and Prothero, 2012)." Most sustainability research in marketing lacks a critical perspective and continues to use "established" but highly problematic research frameworks and theories, such as resource theory, market orientation, cause-related marketing, corporate social responsibility, and consumer judgment and decision-making (McDonagh and Prothero, 2014). None of these studies confront the core assumptions undergirding the way we conceive of sustainability and the limited way in which we study it. As Dobscha and Prothero (2012, 387) stated:

> Researchers in marketing and consumer behaviour must begin to explore the overconsumption patterns of the north that then fuels environmentally devastating manufacturing and distribution practices…marketing could work in tandem [with feminist economists] to educate consumers about the full consumption cycle and the negative health effects of not just consuming but also producing toxic products.

So far, their recommendations appear to have the same effect as a tree falling in a forest with no one there to hear it.

War metaphors and the climate crisis

Ecofeminist theory allows us to interpret war metaphors being used in climate crisis messaging to illuminate that neoliberalism itself is built on an overarching ideology which focuses on competitive battlegrounds. And, this has implications for governments, business, society, and most importantly our planet and its survival. These findings support and extend Irving and Helin's (2018) ecofeminist analysis of the World Business Council for Sustainable Development report where they found three themes: (1) categorizing women as "separate," (2) making women's labor invisible, and (3) maintaining oppressive dualisms that have long been used to maintain patriarchal structures. Indeed, most sustainable development documents (especially those written for African nations) have a separate section for women, that often describes "micro-financing," "empowerment," and "inclusion." By demarcating women as separate from the overall goals ("radical exclusion"), it bolsters the narrative that women need saving; are dependent on help from large, mostly, male organizational and commercial institutions; and are economically inferior until "relief" is administered. Second, it also ignores the invisible and unpaid labor still performed mainly by women: "the historical record reveals a distinct pattern of restrictions on women's choices in order to ensure a generous and inexpensive supply of domestic labour (Folbre and Bittman (2004, 20)." Again, large governing bodies such as the British and US Census Bureaus essentially erased women's domestic labor from the record in the 1800s. In essence, oppressive gender narratives MUST continue to exist in modern-day initiatives, even those as well-intentioned as "the green new deal," in order to maintain this "cooperation constraint (Folbre, 1994, 207)." Folbre goes on to explain: "Current forms of gender inequality are not simply a by-product of different class arrangements, but the outcome of more complex strategic interactions." Third, their findings highlight how dualistic language seeps into the most well-meaning of initiatives and that power structures continue to dominate the sustainability narrative.

Critical analysis of WorldWarZero and Extinction Rebellion

When John Kerry, a well-known American diplomat, presidential candidate, senator, and now the chief "Czar" of Climate in the new Biden administration in the USA, launched his WorldWarZero website in 2019 (https://worldwarzero.com), many saw this as a movement in the right direction, with the USA finally righting its ship away from climate-denial back into the reality of a true, global climate crisis (Friedman, 2019). His initiative, labeled "star-studded" by the *New York Times*, pointed out that the name was purposeful in its use of a war metaphor:

> The name, World War Zero, is supposed to evoke both the national security threat posed by the earth's warming and the type of wartime mobilization that Mr. Kerry argued would be needed to stop the rise in carbon emissions before 2050.
> (Friedman, 2019, n.p.)

The organization applies the war metaphor quite explicitly: "Vote For Earth and help us create a powerful army of activists and influencers that forces the world to confront the climate crisis. We can win this war to create a better, healthier world, but only with your support." Labeling it a "national security threat" is merely a subtler version of the war metaphor: "America will soon have a government that treats the climate crisis as the urgent national security threat it is." And by using leftover metaphors from World Wwar II, the organization states that "defeating climate change isn't something to fight over – it's something to fight *for*." And those activists who choose to buy into this war metaphor are labeled a "powerful army" that will "force" the world to "confront the climate crisis" with the ultimate goal being to "win this war."

In comparing WorldWarZero with another group whose focus is the climate crisis – Extinction Rebellion (ER) we notice some stark differences (https://rebellion.global). ER arose following a protest against the British government and its environmental policies in 2018. Since then it has developed into a global movement aiming to "halt mass extinction and minimise the risk of social collapse" (Extinction Rebellion, 2020). While ER uses some warlike metaphors such as "our demands," "rebels," "civil disobedience," overall, they are espousing ecofeminist ideals. They describe themselves as "a decentralised, international and politically non-partisan movement using non-violent direct action and civil disobedience to persuade governments to act justly on the Climate and Ecological Emergency" (Extinction Rebellion, 2020). Ecofeminist ideals within their overall values include, for example, a focus on shared vision through a regenerative culture which avoids blaming and shaming; and within an organization which is "leaderless and truly global, each new group makes the movement stronger, bringing in new perspectives, wisdom, expertise, energy and inspiration" (https://rebellion.global/about-us/).

This very brief comparison of two types of climate crisis messaging demonstrates how an ecofeminist approach can help in tackling the climate crisis. As non-profits and philanthropists continue to use war metaphors (combating the climate crisis, WorldWarZero), the damages of the climate crisis continue to march on. We witness, for example, the marginalization of women's already robust participation in the climate crisis. For example, The Chipko movement in India in 1973 (which later became known as the treehugger movement) was organized and fortified by women. Ironically, the term "treehugger" was later co-opted by climate-deniers and used as a euphemism for climate activists. Second, war has always excluded women from participating in combat roles, yet, war has nothing but a substantial deleterious effect on women's lives through loss of life, caring for wounded veterans, and caring for family members with PTSD. Relatedly, women provide the invisible backbone for war to exist. Their domestic and emotional labor begins with birthing and raising male children who then populate volunteer armies; in many cases women are not compensated for the losses they endure, and are expected to perform the extra duties required once a war is over, i.e., raise children alone, be widowed, lose house and other resources.

Another facet that ecofeminism helps us highlight is the addition of war/peace dualism that should be added to the hierarchal dualisms that are central to ecofeminism. War oppresses both women and nature and thus even metaphorically should not be used to sell citizens on the idea of climate solutions. When the climate crisis is framed as war, it perpetuates a patriarchal and neoliberal perspective. War language such as fight, might, strategy, offenses, diplomacy, and accords avoid the real scrutiny that needs to be placed on capitalism and the neoliberal agenda which are ultimately responsible for the crisis.

Utilizing an ecofeminist messaging dialogue

Moving forward, there will be various organizations attempting to address the climate crisis, from governments at supra, national, and local levels, to businesses and civil society organizations. As the *WorldWarZero* webpage demonstrates many of these have been and, we expect, will continue to use a war metaphor in their messaging attempts. However, we argue that a focus on war metaphors is built around a patriarchal system which undermines both women and nature, and will ultimately fail in bringing about the systemic change required to address the crisis. We thus argue for the use of an ecofeminist messaging approach.

A war metaphor does not work because ultimately we are at war with ourselves, or more specifically with a neoliberal philosophy. It is this focus on competition and the free market that has caused the climate crisis, and ultimately addressing the very significant and real problem requires a change to this neoliberal agenda. Thus, instead of "confronting" the climate crisis we "connect" with it; we do not see it as a "national security threat," this is an anthropocentric perspective. Instead, an ecofeminist approach that focuses on the threat to the future survival of our planet and our species, we argue, will be more productive in bringing about change. In economics there has been a call for an ecofeminist perspective relying on (re)productivity (Kesting, 2011, 2), whereby the "economic system is embedded in the social and natural system(s)." Using messaging which recognizes this is, we argue, more likely to lead to the systemic changes we need moving forward.

To this end a number of salient ecofeminist principles must be recognized before an ecofeminist messaging approach can endure. These include:

- Recognizing that nature and society are inseparable, and thus, the needs of society cannot be valued over those of nature;
- Acknowledging domination over nature is equally inappropriate;
- Emphasizing inter-connectedness is key, and an ecofeminist approach will embrace "complexity, irreversibility and uncertainty" (Kennet and Heinemann, 2006);
- Introducing a communal approach which talks of respecting the planet while simultaneously developing a messaging strategy that does not focus on assaulting the climate crisis and fighting it head on.

While messaging alone is not enough to address the climate crisis, it can play a fundamental role in getting on board all stakeholders to (a) recognize there is a catastrophic problem in the first place; (b) commit to playing a role in addressing the issue and; (c) provide guidance as to what are the most effective ways in which to bring about change.

Building on these ecofeminist principles, with an overall focus on communal approaches to change which revolve around inter-connectedness, collaboration, co-operation, and conciliatory activities what then would new messaging look like? Marketing strategies, aimed at addressing the climate crisis, need to focus on messaging which centers around how we can collaborate to eliminate the climate crisis not go to war with it. In this way we connect feminist ideals with sustainability, tackle the ecofeminist problems which dualisms perpetuate, and at the same time challenge taken-for-granted norms. This is something that needs to be applied across business/society/CSO/government and policy makers. Below we offer possible recommendations for consideration.

Messaging efforts should create and raise awareness about the real causes of the climate crisis. Capitalism, neoliberalism, materialism, and overconsumption are bigger contributors to the planet's warming than individual consumption choices. It is critical to move messaging away from responsibilizing consumers (Eckhardt and Dobscha, 2019) to engage in individual consumption actions and focus instead on the production process that contributing to rising global temperatures. This shift in focus will remove the burden from women who still globally account for 90% of all household purchasing. For example, instead of making the consumers who are purchasing non-recyclable packaging the enemy, we must instead hold the producers of the packaging accountable.

We also recommend messaging efforts to avoid war metaphors and instead use alternative metaphors of communitas, inclusivity, representation, and heterogeneity. Instead of war-mongering, re-label goals of creating climate solutions using peace and planet stability. By recommending a peace message, there is a natural path between climate solutions and the flourishing of important, universal social structures such as family, local communities, and friendship networks.

Messaging strategies should incorporate ecofeminist principles that show the crucial connection between nature and society. Eradicating this hierarchal dualism allows citizens to experience that their societal stability is heavily reliant on the health of natural surroundings. The wildfires in California or the floods in Iowa are both the result of climate change, and yet they are extremely specific and localized and require specific and localized solutions. These messages need not devalue nature or women. The presence of dualistic thinking in climate crisis communication frames women as "the other" and excludes their often invisible labor related to nature. All stakeholders, not just companies, should contribute to this repositioning of their messaging strategies.

Conclusion

Overall, we argue there are a number of problems with a reliance on the war metaphor both in marketing and in the use of the metaphor as a guiding strategy in addressing the climate crisis. First, it is important to remember that we are not at war with the planet, which many of these strategies imply, even if that is not their intention. We cannot "beat" the climate crisis, by fighting the planet – it is our own behaviors and actions which need to change. In that sense, we are at war with ourselves! And, whether we attempt to tackle the issue through technological, social, economic, or cultural solutions – they all share one thing in common – to succeed we need inter-connectedness and collaboration, alongside co-operative and conciliatory actions. An ecofeminist messaging approach we believe will bear more fruit in changing society and addressing the climate crisis before it is too late.

References

Ballard, M. S. 2016. "The upholding of heteropatriarchy: An ecofeminism critique of PETA advertisements." *ENV 434 Environmental Justice*. Retrieved from: https://digitalcommons.salve.edu/env434_justice/3/. Accessed: 20/04/2021.

Bekoglu, F. B. and Ergen, A. 2014. "Art of war and its implications on marketing strategies: Thinking like a warrior." *International Journal of Research in Business and Social Science (2147-4478)*, 3 (3): 37–47.

Bolin, B. and Eriksson E. 1959. "Changes in the carbon dioxide content of the atmosphere and sea due to fossil fuel combustion." In *The Atmosphere and the Sea in Motion*, edited by Bert Bolin, pp. 130–142. New York: Rockefeller Institute Press.

Catley, C. 2016. "Why war metaphors no longer cut it in business strategy." *Minute Hack*. Retrieved from: https://minutehack.com/guides/why-war-metaphors-no-longer-cut-it-in-business-strategy. Accessed: 30/11/2020.

Cespedes, F. V. 2014. "Stop using battle metaphors in your company strategy." *Harvard Business Review*. Retrieved from: https://hbr.org/2014/12/stop-using-battle-metaphors-in-your-company-strategy. Accessed: 30/11/2020.

d'Eaubonne, F. 1974. *Le Féminisme ou La Mort*. Paris: Pierre Horay.

Davidson, H. J. 1972. *Offensive Marketing: Or How to Make Your Competitors Followers*. Harmondsworth: Penguin.

Delbaere, M. and Slobodzian, A. D. 2019. "Marketing's metaphors have expired: An argument for a new dominant metaphor." *Marketing Theory* 19 (3): 391–401.

Desmond, J. 1997. "Marketing and the war machine." *Marketing Intelligence & Planning* 17 (7): 338–351.

Dobscha, S. 1993. "Women and the environment: Applying ecofeminism to environmentally-related consumption." *Advances in Consumer Research* 20: 36–40.

Dobscha, S. and Ozanne J. 2001. "An ecofeminist analysis of environmentally sensitive women: Qualitative findings on the emancipatory potential of an ecological life." *Journal of Public Policy and Marketing* 20 (2): 201–214.

Dobscha, S., and Prothero, A. 2012. "(Re) Igniting sustainable consumption and production research through feminist connections." In *Gender, Culture, and Consumer Behavior*, edited by C. Otnes and L. Tuncay Zayer, pp. 403–424. London: Routledge.

Durö, R. 1989. *Winning the Marketing War: A Practical Guide to Competitive Advantage*. Chichester: Wiley & Son Ltd.

Durö, R. and Sandström, B. (1987). *The Basic Principles of Marketing Warfare*. Chichester: John Wiley & Son Ltd.

Eckhardt, G. M. and Dobscha, S. 2019. "The consumer experience of responsibilization: The case of Panera Cares." *Journal of Business Ethics* 159 (3): 651–663.

Extinction Rebellion (2020). Extinction Rebellion. Available at: https://rebellion.global/about-us/. Accessed: 14/12/2020.

Falk, J., Gaffney, O., Bhowmik, A.K., Bergmark, P., Galaz, V., Gaskell, N., Henningsson, S., Höjer, M., Jacobson, L., Jónás, K., Kåberger, T., Klingenfeld, D., Lenhart, J., Loken, B., Lundén, D., Malmodin, J., Malmqvist, T., Olausson, V., Otto, I., Pearce, A., Pihl, E., and Shalit, T. 2020. *Exponential Roadmap: Future Earth*. Retrieved from: https://exponentialroadmap.org/wp-content/uploads/2020/03/ExponentialRoadmap_1.5.1_216x279_08_AW_Download_Singles_Small.pdf. Accessed: 18/12/2020.

Folbre, N. 1994. *Who Pays for the Kids? Gender and the Structures of Constraint*. London and New York: Routledge.

Folbre, N. and Bittman, M. (Eds.). 2004. *Family Time: The Social Organization of Care* (Vol. 2). London: Psychology Press.

Friedman, L. 2019. "John Kerry launches star-studded climate coalition." *The New York Times*, November 30. Retrieved from: https://www.nytimes.com/2019/11/30/climate/john-kerry-climate-change.html.

Garsombke, T. W. 1987. "Military marketing warfare: A comparative review of the use of combative philosophies and terminology." *Journal of Marketing* 51 (1): 135–138.

Harutyunyan, M. and Jiang, B. 2019. "The bright side of having an enemy." *Journal of Marketing Research* 56 (4): 679–690.

Hirschman, E. C. 1998. "When expert consumers interpret textual products: Applying reader response theory to television programs." *Consumption, Markets, and Culture* 2 (2): 259–309.

Ho, S. K. and Choi, A. S. 1997. "Achieving marketing success through Sun Tze's art of warfare." *Marketing Intelligence & Planning* 15 (1): 38–47.

Howarth, C. C. and Sharman, A. G. 2015. "Labeling opinions in the climate debate: A critical review." *Wiley Interdisciplinary Reviews: Climate Change* 6 (2): 239–254.

Howe, J. P. 2014. *Behind the curve: Science and the politics of global warming*. Seattle: University of Washington Press.

Intergovernmental Panel on Climate Change. 2018. Global warming of 1.5°C. Retrieved from: https://www.ipcc.ch/sr15/. Accessed: 30/11/20.

Irving, S. and Helin, J. 2018. "A world for sale? An ecofeminist reading of sustainable development discourse." *Gender, Work & Organization* 25 (3): 264–278.

Kennet, M. and Heinemann, V. 2006. "Green economics: Setting the scene. Aims, context, and philosophical underpinning of the distinctive new solutions offered by Green economics." *International Journal of Green Economics* 1 (1–2): 68–102.

Kesting, S. 2011. "What is 'green' in the green new deal–criteria from ecofeminist and post-Keynesian economics." *International Journal of Green Economics* 5 (1): 49–64.

Koller, V. 2008. Contradictory metaphors in contemporary marketing discourse. *Confronting Metaphor in Use: An Applied Linguistic Approach* 103: 126.

Kotler, P. and Singh, R. 1981. "Marketing warfare in the 1980s." *The Journal of Business Strategy* 1 (3): 30.

Kulp, S. A. and Strauss, B. H. 2019. "New elevation data triple estimates of global vulnerability to sea-level rise and coastal flooding." *Nature communications* 10 (1): 1–12.

Lakoff, G. and Johnson, M. 1980. "The metaphorical structure of the human conceptual system." *Cognitive Science* 4 (2): 195–208.

Levinson, J. C. 1998. *Guerrilla Marketing: Secrets for Making Big Profits from Your Small Business*. Boston, MA: Houghton Mifflin Harcourt.

Littlefield, J. 2010. "Men on the hunt: Ecofeminist insights into masculinity." *Marketing Theory* 10 (1): 97–117.

Lozada, H. and Mintu-Wimsatt, A. 1995. *Ecofeminism and Green Marketing: Reconciling Nature and Hu(Man)kind*. Washington, DC: American Marketing Association.

Maclaran, P. and Stevens, L. 2019. "Thinking through feminist theorising: Poststructuralist feminism, ecofeminism and intersectionality." In *Handbook of Research on Gender and Marketing*, edited by Susan Dobscha, pp. 229–251.Cheltenham: Edward Elgar Publishing.

Martin, S. W. 2006. *Heavy Hitter Sales Wisdom: Proven Sales Warfare Strategies, Secrets of Persuasion, and Common-sense Tips for Success*. Chichester: John Wiley & Sons.

McDonagh, P. and Prothero, A. 1997. "Leap-frog marketing: The contribution of ecofeminist thought to the world of patriarchal marketing." *Marketing Intelligence & Planning* 15 (7): 361–388.

McDonagh, P. and Prothero, A. 2014. "Sustainability marketing research: Past, present and future." *Journal of Marketing Management* 30 (11–12): 1186–1219.

Michaelson, G.A. (1987). *Winning the Marketing War. A Field Manual for Business Leaders*. Lanham, MD: Madison.

Mies, M. and Shiva, V. (1993). *Ecofeminism*. London: Zed Books.

Mulholland, J. 2019. "Why the climate crisis is the most crucial story we cover in America." *The Guardian*. Retrived from: https://www.theguardian.com/environment/2019/oct/16/climate-crisis-america-guardian-editor-john-mulholland. Accessed: 30/11/2020.

Paddock, J. R. 2017. "Changing consumption, changing tastes? Exploring consumer narratives for food secure, sustainable and healthy diets." *Journal of Rural Studies* 53: 102–110.

Parks, B., Pharr, S. W., and Lockeman, B. D. 1994. "A marketer's guide to Clausewitz: Lessons for winning market share." *Business Horizons* 37 (4): 68–74.

Prothero, A., Dobscha, S., Freund, J., Kilbourne, W. E., Luchs, M. G., Ozanne, L. K., and Thøgersen, J. 2011. "Sustainable consumption: Opportunities for consumer research and public policy." *Journal of Public Policy & Marketing* 30 (1): 31–38.

Revelle, R. and Suess, H. E. 1957. "Carbon dioxide exchange between atmosphere and ocean and the question of an increase of atmospheric CO_2 during the past decades." *Tellus* 9: 18–27.

Ries, A. and Trout, J. 1981. *Positioning: The Battle for Your Mind*. New York: McGraw-Hill.

Ries, A. and Trout, J. 1986. *Marketing Warfare*. New York: McGraw-Hill.

Rindfleisch, A. 1996. "Marketing as warfare: Reassessing a dominant metaphor." *Business Horizons* 39 (5): 3–10.

Rosenberg, L. J. and Van West, J. H. 1984. "The collaborative approach to marketing." *Business Horizons*, November–December, 29–35.

Stevens, L., Kearney, M., and Maclaran, P. 2013. "Uddering the other: Androcentrism, ecofeminism, and the dark side of anthropomorphic marketing." *Journal of Marketing Management* 29 (1–2): 158–174.

Stevens, L., Maclaran, P., and Kearney, M. 2014. "Boudoirs, cowdillacs and rotolactors." In *Brand Mascots: And Other Marketing Animals*, edited by S. Brown and S. Ponsonby-McCabe, pp. 110–122. Milton Park: Routledge.

Tadajewski, M. 2006. "The ordering of marketing theory: The influence of McCarthyism and the Cold War." *Marketing Theory* 6 (2): 163–199.

Vargo, S. L. and Lusch, R. F. 2004. "Evolving to a new dominant logic for marketing." *Journal of Marketing* 68 (1): 1–17.

Vinz, D. 2009. "Gender and sustainable consumption: A German environmental perspective." *European Journal of Women's Studies* 16 (2): 159–179.

Weart, S. R. 2008. *The Discovery of Global Warming*. Cambridge, MA: Harvard University Press.

Yudina, O. and Fennell, D. 2013. "Ecofeminism in the tourism context: A discussion of the use of other-than-human animals as food in tourism." *Tourism Recreation Research* 38 (1): 55–69.

Zeldin-O'Neill, S. 2019. "'It's a crisis, not a change': The six Guardian language changes on climate matters." *The Guardian*. Retrieved from: https://www.theguardian.com/environment/2019/oct/16/guardian-language-changes-climate-environment. Accessed: 30/11/2020.

8 Menstruation in marketing

Stigma, #femvertising, and transmedia messaging

Catherine A. Coleman and Katherine C. Sredl

In a 2020 collaboration with Swedish feminine care brand Intimina, the Pantone Color Institute created the custom "Period" red to de-stigmatize and normalize menstruation (Jardine 2020). This campaign is among others in recent years from brands such as Queen V, Lola, Thinx, and Libresse that have been testing the boundaries, amidst broader feminist discourses and social trends such as the #MeToo movement, of long-standing taboos surrounding menstruation. Their strategies address various historically problematic physical, cultural, and embodied representations of menstruation, such as making #BloodNormal (Libresse), imagining what it would be like if men had periods (Thinx's MENstruation campaign), and telling gripping "Womb Stories" (Libresse). But these efforts remain controversial. For example, Plan International UK's #periodemoji design, leveraging emoji language to overcome period shame, was rejected until their partnership with NHS Blood and Transplant yielded a blood drop emoji (Plan International UK 2020). A recent "New Way to Period" campaign from Modibodi, a brand that sells leak-proof underwear, was initially removed by Facebook for violating guidelines with "shocking, sensational, disrespectful or excessively violent" content–red period blood (Smiley 2020). Ultimately, in the wake of social media backlash and upon review, Facebook retracted its decision. These examples suggest both the inveterate stigma of menstruation and the shifting discourses in the digital era, in which new avenues for activism have opened conversations and offered opportunities to challenge stigmas.

This chapter arises out of a shared interest between its authors of the ways that gender stigmas are reproduced and challenged in online contexts by brands and consumers. We build on two prior research projects. The first examined ways in which stigmas of feminism have been used to (de)legitimize feminists and underlying tenets of feminism, drawing from almost 8,000 tweets using Always #likeagirl and the backlash #likeaboy, as well as hashtags reflecting broader cultural conversations about gender (Coleman and Zayer 2015). The second examined lived, embodied experiences of menstruation as visually depicted on Instagram (Sredl and Robertson 2018). Building on these two projects and, as with Maclaran and Kravetz (2018), finding inspiration from recent feminist fourth-wave use of internet as an area for further theorizing, we explore ways by which stigmas are challenged and reproduced in brand-driven femvertising discourses for menstrual products (e.g., Always) and Millennial and Gen Z consumer discourses of menstruation using transmedia (i.e., hashtags, visual, text) content.

Contemporary discourse around stigmatized representations of women's bodies reflects new interest in feminism among Gen Z and Millennial consumers, producing a form of activism focused on the restructuring of social institutions in ways that support

DOI: 10.4324/9781003042587-10

and are supported by neoliberalism (Keller 2019). Questions of agency are highlighted in neoliberal contexts, with (young) women "often presented as autonomous, agentic, and empowered subjects" (Gill and Scharff 2011, p. 9). Indeed, this is how various scholars have interpreted femvertising campaigns including Always #LikeAGirl (e.g., Varghese and Kumar 2020; Windels et al. 2020); thus, we consider Prügl's (2015) work on governmentality and the neoliberalization of feminism. As advertisers have become more attuned to problematic representations of gender, perhaps due to years of sustained critique (Zayer and Coleman 2015) and likely due to "the social media jury… challenging cultural norms and notions about how we talk about – and to – women" (Zmuda and Diaz 2014), they increasingly have employed empowerment marketing, go-girl marketing, and femvertising (Davidson 2015). Nonetheless, "marketers are being careful not to label themselves or their messages as feminist" (Zmuda and Diaz 2014), highlighting the ongoing stigmatization and regulation of feminism and feminist goals in the marketplace. Scholars have examined ways in which such stigmatizations, as those surrounding menstruation, reinforce advertisers' perceptions of women's vulnerabilities and reiterate discourses about protection of women and women's bodies (Malefyt and McCabe 2016). These tensions suggest that while scholars have begun to answer calls for further examination of femvertising discourses, the politics of gender, and their implications for gender relations in business and society (Zayer, Coleman, and Orjuela 2018), there is still much to learn.

To achieve our aim, we begin with a brief discussion on stigma and stigmatization of menstruation. Much of the academic, including feminist, literature on menstruation relies on Goffman's (1963) stigma theory (MacLean, Hearle, and Ruwanpura 2020). In fact, according to Johnston-Robledo and Chrisler (2013), menstruation is stigmatized through all three of Goffman's (1963) categories: body, character, and identity. Feminist scholars understand menstruation to be a biological event experienced within contexts of sociocultural and political meanings and practices, both personal and collective: it is "complex, subjective, interactive, varied, and politized" (see also Bobel 2010; Johnston-Robledo and Stubbs 2013, p. 1). Menstruation is a particularly established way by which gendered bodies are ascribed meaning, and protection/hiding is a common theme of coping responses to the stigmas of menstruation, making menstruation discourses an intriguing context. Next, we review scholarship on representations of menstruation in consumer culture, which leads to a discussion of more recent "empowerment" efforts through femvertising and, specifically, Always #LikeAGirl. These concepts frame our ultimate aim of incorporating consumer-generated online techno and visual discourse on periods into the conversations of stigma and gender. Noting prior research on online activism and social movements, we consider the iterative engagement with menstruation between brands and consumers to understand how stigmas of menstruation and menstruating bodies are reproduced or challenged.

Stigma and menstruation

In the decades since Goffman's (1963) seminal sociological work on stigma, scholars across a range of disciplines from medicine, psychology, health sciences, and, of course, marketing and consumer research have examined and utilized the concept of stigma to understand social interaction and identities. The term stigma is handed down from the Greek practice of burning or cutting physical marks into those deemed tainted or immoral and to be avoided, though, today, stigma is an attribute that yields a discrediting or "spoiled social identity," and, thus, a matter of social context (Bos et al. 2013; Goffman 1963). Stigma can be overt or subtle, and often relates to power and exploitation, norm enforcement, and disease avoidance (Bos et al. 2013).

Drawing from previous theories, Pryor and Reeder (2011) developed a conceptual model comprising four related manifestations of stigma – self-stigma, stigma by association, structural stigma, and public stigma, the latter of which they argue is the foundation of the other three. Public stigma is defined as "the consensual understanding that a social attribute is devalued," and structural stigma relates to ideologies and institutions that are "perpetuated by the hegemony and the exercise of social, economic, and political power" (Bos et al. 2013, p. 4). Thus, as Sandikci and Ger (2010) argue, while any difference theoretically could be stigmatized, stigmatization ultimately reflects power and dominant group interests, suggesting that the choice to engage with stigmatized practices demonstrates struggles for power. More recent developments towards identifying social processes that incorporate structural discrimination further open opportunity to examine the influence of power in determining the distribution of stigma and even the moral processes underlying stigma (Link and Phelan 2001). This is important because menstruation has been found in various ways across cultures to both maintain women's disempowered social positions and to mark them as less pure, physically and morally – for example, in preventing girls and women from obtaining a full education (Steinfield et al. 2019) or accessing places of worship (MacLean, Hearle, and Ruwanpura 2020), and through shame. The latter is particularly apparent in dominant representations, such as "the curse" of menstruation (Luke 1997) or the double entendre of the menstrual stain–the stain of blood and the stain of character when one fails to contain evidence of menses (Johnston-Robledo and Chrisler 2013). These discourses may result in isolation and/or purification practices (e.g., Johnston-Robledo and Chrisler 2013; Steinfield et al. 2019), thereby maintaining control over women's bodies and leading women to seek various ways to control periods (MacLean, Hearle, and Ruwanpura 2019; Merskin 1999), often turning to market-based solutions. Thus, we turn briefly to literature in consumer research on stigma and stigma management to frame further discussion of menstrual stigma management.

Stigma management and menstruation

Extant literature in marketing and consumer research has examined ways in which marketplace stakeholders (re)create or resist stigma within broader sociocultural contexts (Mirabito et al. 2016). Stigmas are not static, but rather relying on cultural institutions that support and enforce stigma, "the rendering of stigma is an active, continually evolving process" (Mirabito et al. 2016, p. 172). As such, importantly, stigmas are subject to management and change. Consumer research on stigma management reveals a variety of contexts of focus on the self or institutions for reform (Adkins and Ozanne 2005; Crockett 2017; Sandikci and Ger 2010; Scaraboto and Fischer 2013; Ustuner and Holt 2007). This scholarship, found primarily in consumer culture and transformative consumer research literatures, demonstrates ways by which consumers utilize various coping strategies and marketplace resources to accept, negotiate, or challenge stigmas (Adkins and Ozanne 2005; Kozinets 2001) through individual and collective identity work (Thompson 2014), for example, by embracing (Sandikci and Ger 2010), reappropriating (Scaraboto and Fischer 2013), and/or counternarrating (Crockett 2017) stigmatizing terminology and practices.

Similarly, research on menstrual stigma management demonstrates various ways, often through great effort, by which women the world over have worked to manage menstruation and stigmas associated with it, including through marketplace solutions, such as the use of oral contraceptives to regulate or eliminate periods and menstrual hygiene or sanitary products. Various projects have been dedicated to examining discourses of menstruation in what Kane (1990, p. 82) considered "powerful weapons in an ideological battle for control of women's sexuality" – advertisements (e.g., Erchull 2013; Mandziuk 2010; Merskin 1999; Park 1996).

Menstruation marketing and femvertising

As menstruation is invested with historical and cultural stigmatizing myths, it is not surprising that modern advertising reflects myths and taboos associated with women's bodies, particularly in "feminine hygiene" advertising (Merskin 1999). Scholars have outlined a history of representations relying on stigmas that paradoxically focus on sanitizing and protecting the female body to provide freedom and secrecy, concealment, and discretion to protect the female character (e.g., Erchull 2013; Johnston-Robledo and Chrisler 2013; Mandziuk 2010; Merskin 1999; Park 1996). Messages promoting cleanliness and purity coincide with 20th-century modernity projects, in which the social, medical, and commercial intersect. In her examination of the 1920s Kotex ads, for example, Mandziuk (2010) argues that advertisers were navigating an ideological space between the "hygienic crisis" of menstruation, accompanied by its prohibitive embarrassments, and newfound freedoms of the modern world (see also Erchull 2013; Merskin 1999; Johnston-Robledo and Chrisler 2013). Malefyt and McCabe (2016) demonstrate that these conflicts have persisted into the 21st century, as advertisers approach menstruation as something women should hide, a vulnerability, something from which commercial products can protect women. Through content analysis of sanitary product ads and interviews with female informants, the authors argue that brands place and characterize women in dichotomous states of "on or off" their periods and offer agency in a box of tampons, while women understand their menstruation as natural, agentic, and powerful. The authors conclude that as long as advertisers continue to focus on the functional protection aspects of sanitary products, their appeals will always frame periods and, by extension, women's bodies as problematic; women will continue to embody the paradox of periods as social stigma that they need help hiding with the use of sanitary products, even as they understand their periods as natural embodiments of their womanhood.

For younger generations of consumers, claims of protection and freedom from periods are proving insufficient. Millennial and Gen Z consumers increasingly expect transparency, "healthy and sustainable" products, safe alternatives (Abrams 2015; McNeil 2003), and for brands to enact values. Recently, entrepreneurial brands have promoted alternatives to the disposable pads and tampons long promoted as women's ticket to freedom. In addition to newer products such as period underwear and liquid-catching disks, consumption of menstruation cups such as DivaCup has also increased. While period product alternatives such as these only make up a fraction of the $19 billion global market for menstruation products (Wertheim 2015), they are contributing, along with birth control that limits or eliminates flow and decreases demand, to declining or stagnating sales of traditional feminine hygiene products (Gilbert 2016). Additionally, women are starting to "normalize" periods by posting about them on social media and by using period tracker apps (Rabin 2015). To respond to these challenges and with the realization that they were losing relevance, particularly among emergent consumers 16–24 years, Always created the #LikeAGirl campaign to connect with girls and young women on social media and reconnect with them emotionally (Campaign 2015). Thus, a femvertising campaign was born.

Femvertising context

Many date the rise of femvertising back to Dove's 2004 "Campaign for Real Beauty," which was hailed as a groundbreaking shift in discourses of and about women, calling out the beauty industry of which they are a part for its unrealistic and often harmful representations. But the term "femvertising" wasn't introduced for another decade, when SheKnows (2014) documented "a shift in marketing where companies realized that women didn't need to be pandered to or objectified, and ads that inspired women or empowered them were much more likely to create positive buzz around a product." Dove and other brands that employ femvertising may seek to challenge norms, but they do so within the parameters of commercially viable messages of female empowerment (Lambiase, Bronstein, and Coleman 2017). Even industry trade press, which celebrated the ways in which femvertising was challenging gender norms, at the same time, warned of pinkwashing and noted ways in which advertisers were simultaneously distancing themselves from feminism (Zmuda and Diaz 2014).

Histories of feminism and marketing tell of a sorted and complex relationship, punctuated by "longstanding, and largely irresolvable, arguments about the role of the market in opposing or assisting the feminist cause" (Maclaran 2012, p. 462). Certainly, marketers have long deployed mixed messages of empowerment and repression to sell, with advertising representations often serving as a site of critique by feminist scholars (Lambiase, Bronstein, and Coleman 2017). Thus, while not an entirely new phenomenon (Maclaran 2012), the rise of "femvertising" in recent years resonates with the tensions of this relationship.

Femvertising is defined by SHE Media as "advertising that employs pro-female talent, messages and imagery to empower women and girls." Scholars have defined it as "advertising that challenges traditional female advertising stereotypes," and have distinguished it from prior advertising themes of female liberation for challenging social norms through more explicit acknowledgment that advertising has been at least partially responsible for those stereotypes (Åkestam, Rosengren, and Dahlen 2020, p. 795; see also Eisend 2019). In welcoming this phenomenon in 2014, SheKnows highlighted ten ads that "got femvertising right." At the top of that list was the Always "Like A Girl" campaign.

Always, the Procter & Gamble-owned feminine product brand launched the "Like A Girl" campaign video on the Always YouTube channel on June 26, 2014. In alignment with much of the historical discourse surrounding menstruation, Always claims a long-standing brand purpose "to empower women and safeguard girls' confidence." Building on brand research indicating a strong decline in girls' confidence as they go through puberty and responding to stagnant sales, the brand determined it time to make their brand purpose explicit (Zmuda and Diaz 2014). A "reading" of the ad suggests the aims of the campaign are to catalyze a social movement "to keep girls' confidence high during puberty and beyond," to counteract negative impacts of stereotypes. The brand closes its message by directing viewers to the brand's social media pages to carry out the call-to-action, which is, "So tell us... what do YOU do #LikeAGirl?" When the Leo Burnett advertising agency placed the commercial on February 1, 2015, during Super Bowl 50, the campaign garnered significant attention from media and consumers alike, which is reflected in ongoing engagement with the hashtag #LikeAGirl.

Social media has been touted as a democratizing force (Kozinets 2001); stigmatization involves power and (dis)empowerment (Sandikci and Ger 2010). Social media may offer a platform for women to challenge the ideologies of advertising, its normative view of women as vulnerable, and the context in which advertising exists: the neoliberal marketplace in which young women are the ideal, self-transforming consumers (Sredl 2018). As young women seek self-definition through participating in social media, they may be opposing who or what is normalized through gendered representations and discourses in ads (Murray 2015). As Keller (2019) notes, recent years have been marked by an increased interest among feminist scholars and the public in the ways that women and girls use social media for feminist activism, including using hashtags and crowdsourced content. For example, Xiong, Cho, and Boatright (2019) demonstrate the interaction between mobilizing forces such as social movement organizations and online spread of the #MeToo movement, a form of hashtag activism. Thus, Always #LikeAGirl is particularly intriguing because femvertising, which is driven by commercial organizations with a platform, is positioned as empowering; but periods have long been stigmatized. We draw from brand- and consumer-generated content on Instagram surrounding the "femvertising" campaign #LikeAGirl and period-related hashtags (e.g., #period, #menstruationmatters, #periodmemes) to understand how stigmas about women's bodies and lives, specifically menstruation, are challenged and reproduced through brand- and consumer-generated hashtag and visual online content.

Sites of analysis

While the "Like A Girl" campaign's YouTube debut may make YouTube seem like an ideal site for data collection, the platform is more inclined toward entertainment than toward engagement around topics of menstrual stigma (Arthurs et al. 2018; Lobato 2016). The Always #likeagirl hashtag is a call-to-action for women and girls to share their experiences on Instagram and other social media sites that function on a hashtag economy.

Hashtags and Instagram

Hashtags are a form of user-generated content (UGC), a "cultural genre" (Daer et al. 2014; Drenten and Gurrieri 2018, p. 52), and a means of categorizing and searching content, as well as organizing community on the internet. Hashtags include a phrase that categorizes posts, such as #period, and provide a metacomment about the post, such as #periodpain. While both Twitter and Instagram utilize hashtags and much of Always' early focus for #likeagirl was on Twitter, social media scholars note that hashtags are both functionally different by design across these platforms and that users employ them to different ends: "on Twitter they serve mainly to aggregate conversations; on Instagram they specify the content of pictures as well as connect to ad hoc communities" (Caliandro and Graham 2020, p. 2). Thus, we focused on Instagram as our site of analysis for two reasons. First, social media scholars recently have argued that Instagram's visual focus opens new ways of "exploring sociocultural processes… through the eyes of social actors, to glimpse into their everyday micro-rituals and private moments" (Caliandro and Graham 2020, p. 2) and call for a native focus on Instagram. Second, as we discuss in the next paragraph, posting on Instagram about one's menstruation might be part of menstruation for Millennial and Gen Z women.

Research on consumer practices around menstruation suggests that most users who post about menstruation are Millennials and Gen Z (Rosenberg 2018). Second, with 1 billion monthly active users, and making up 70% of the 75.2 billion likes, reactions, shares, and comments on brand-owned content on social media in 2020, Instagram is particularly popular among teenagers, young Millennials, and Gen Z adults (18–34 years old) (AudienceProject 2020; Cooper 2020). Thus, we conceptualize the data we collected to represent voices of these generations. Historically, the visual focus of menstrual product advertising yielded various inorganic and euphemistic visual metaphors for menstruation and bodies controlled by institutional forces; the visual focus of Instagram allows Gen Z and Millennial consumers and brands to iteratively re-image menstruation and stigma. In this way, we answer calls to move beyond discussions of representation and textual analysis (Gill and Scharff 2011; Mitchell 2013) toward the discursive contributions of transmedia UGC in navigating stigma and (em)power(ment).

Instagram, started in October 2010, supports images, video (under 15 seconds), and text, in the forms of captions and hashtags. Instagram's algorithm creates an interdependence between users, algorithms, and the platform that structure user behavior such that consumers may use popular hashtags to gain visibility and followers (Cotter 2018). Prior feminist media studies scholarship demonstrates, "Femvertising themes are accentuated by social media and online conversation, especially the hashtag" (Rodrigues 2016 as cited by Varghese and Kumar 2020, p. 6).

Method of analysis

We reviewed hashtags from 2017 through 2020 and captured Instagram data (captions, comments, images, likes) on menstruation-related hashtags and on #LikeAGirl. We captured data for 96 hours surrounding both November 28, 2017, and September 23, 2018 (192 hours total), and on all brand posts on the @always_brand account as of December 28, 2020 (454 total posts). We focused analysis on hashtag data collected prior to late 2018, when algorithmic changes created accessibility changes, decreasing the value of hashtags and prioritizing "top posts" selected by the algorithm (Morales n.d.).

For #LikeAGirl, we entered the term in the Instagram search bar, and then screenshot Instagram-generated results that show the top and recent posts. We then opened the top and recent posts and the images, captions, and comments. Next, we reviewed all posts from the @always_brand account (they did not appear in the top and recent #LikeAGirl results). We determined period-related hashtags by first searching 27 US English terms for menstruation. We screenshot the top and recent report to archive that information. For the 10 posts under the most recent and popular hashtags, we used screenshots to record captions, images, top comments, and likes. Not all posts for each hashtag relate to periods or gender, as #LikeAGirl is often used to access the algorithm and get likes, but the majority do.

To begin analysis, we found a place of distance from the data and our assumptions by reading posts with questions of what "surprised, intrigued, and disturbed us" about the data to guide the distancing process (Chiseri-Strater and Sunstein 1997). We discussed our reactions and noted them. Next, we followed an iterative process of reading posts to look for patterns and meanings, and to develop themes within hashtags (Thompson 1997). Then, we compared themes between groups. Finally, we sought areas for theory development by comparing themes with relevant scholarly literature on stigma, gender representation, femvertising, and (fourth-wave) feminism. We then returned to our notes about what "surprised, intrigued, and disturbed us," and explored how our theoretical insights answered our reactions.

Analysis

We identify three ways that content negotiates feminist goals of collective struggle against oppressive power relations (Prügl 2015) and reproduces and/or challenges stigma. Drawing from Pryor and Reeder's (2011) taxonomy of stigma, we find that transmedia content (1) signals public and self-stigma through images and hashtags to other users who may engage in similar individual work surrounding empowerment, (2) reappropriates stigmatized bodies with tactics such as humorous and/or transgressive posts of menstruation and menstrual stigma, which we argue may include forms of de-stigmatization by association, and (3) engages with structural stigma by using hashtags and images that signal women's health issues related to reproduction and menstruation. Through each of these themes, we consider brand and consumer content as reproducing and/or challenging stigma and examine iteration as consumers and brand (re)generate content.

Signal public and self-stigma

Data show that most #LikeAGirl posts are user-generated, as opposed to brand-generated, content. Content often relates to empowerment through sports, including by professional, able-bodied female athletes (not sponsored content), and especially through traditionally male-dominated sports. This sport orientation aligns with the commercial framing of the original #likeagirl ad, which focuses on physical abilities such as throwing, running, and fighting. The hashtag also includes reflection about female empowerment in general (see Table 8.1).

In Post 1 (see Table 8.1), Top #LikeAGirl posts [date September 23, 2018] notably, of the nine top and recent posts, four are about the body – weightlifting (2), gymnastics (1), exercise or weight loss (1) – two are about inspiration, one is about women doing something in a traditionally male domain (the band), and one is about girls.

For example, Post 2a and 2b (See Table 8.1) is a post and caption showing a professional mountain bike athlete talking about individual athletic success in a male-dominated sport, as in Post 1. In the caption, the author reflects on her journey of individual physical and emotional strength. We suggest that, in many ways, the brand-introduced hashtag captures or at least rides a feminist movement online related to women's rights to excel in sports and to have individual agency as expressed through self-improvement and achieving goals. We base our suggestion on the majority of posts with this message.

The text image in Post 3 (see Table 8.1), an @always_brand #LikeAGirl post, signals recovering from shame. As a whole, the text seeks to engage the brand in a movement to create new understandings of tenacity and will as valued female attributes. By signaling shame (failed test, something devalued) and re-framing it as success (Keep Going), Always challenges and reappropriates public and self-stigma (Pryor and Reeder 2011; Scaraboto and Fischer 2013). Through "Tell us about a time," users and brand engage

110 *Catherine A. Coleman and Katherine C. Sredl*

Table 8.1 Sample Instagram Post Data

Instagram Post Content	Date	Title	Description
1	September 23, 2018	Top and recent #likeagirl posts	Top posts reflecting focus on body (4), inspiration (2), and girls (1)
2a	September 19, 2018	Athletic journeys of individual physical and emotional strength	Image: photograph by photographer Mauricio Ramos of woman in bike helmet and gear for Revista Bike MX in Mexico City
2b	September 19, 2018	Athletic journeys of individual physical and emotional strength	Copy accompanying post image 2a: "Hoy, desde que me desperté hasta ahorititita, ha sido uno de esos días incre´ibles llenos de buenas noticias y nuevas oportunidades. Por días como hoy se que voy por el camino indicado tomando decisiones difíciles pero acertadas. Cada día me convenzo más de que lo correcto es seguir a tu propio corazón y hacer lo que te apasiona! Me encantaría poderles pasar literalmente este sentimiento de certeza que tengo para que se dieran cuenta de que si creen en ustedes mismos -todo va a estar bien- pero como es imposible transferirles el sentimiento solo van a tener que confiar en mi cuando les digo que... VAN A ESTAR BIEN, confien en ustedes, en sus talentos y en sus pasiones y trabajen duro. Todo va a salir bien!" [algo cursi, se los advertí] Accompanied by a photograph by photographer Mauricio Ramos for a BMX Bike company, Revista Bike MX, in Mexico City
3	November 28, 2017	always_brand post using #likeagirl to reframe failure as tenacity	Image: blue background Copy: Failure can be part of success. Learn and try again with a new plan. Tell us about a time when you failed a test. How did you keep going #LikeAGirl? KEEP GOING #LikeAGirl Always (logo)
4	September 23, 2018	Top user-generated posts using #period and #periodproblems reappropriate stigma using visuals and hashtags	Posts use humor in videos and images to discuss period leaks and period symptoms Ex. video: "of my crisp white bermuda shorts" and "me on my period"
5	September 23, 2018	Top user-generated posts using #period and #periodproblems reappropriate stigma using visuals and hashtags	Posts reappropriate stigma using visuals and hashtags. Examples: "every girl has felt this at least once. She got her first period and thought she was going to die," with image of girl sitting on floor; three posts include "me on my period," with humorous pictures of various period-related faces and gestures; two posts speak of crying or lashing out right before period in humorous reference to hormones

Instagram Post Content	Date	Title	Description
6	September 23, 2018	Top user-generated post using #period and #periodproblems reappropriate stigma using visuals and hashtags	Image: toilet bowl with menstrual blood and toilet paper Caption copy: I'm a woman now
Post 7	September 19, 2018	Metonymy for pain	*Image: computer keyboard covered with individual packets labeled Asprin, Aleve, and Bayer* *Caption copy: "I'm exhausted and on day TEN of my first period since IUD removal (you're welcome). I forgot I used the past of my purse Ibuprofen and was dying at work – until the Dinosaur left work to bring me this glorious stockpile."*
Post 8	September 18, 2018	Women challenge structural stigma in visual and text	Video by EndoTalk, an RMIT media student collective focused on conversations about endometriosis. Various people holding sign reading, "what is endometriosis?" while answering the question Caption copy: "What is endometriosis? We asked around campus at RMIT. Under-researched and under-discussed. Let's talk about it!"

#likeagirl content, images, and captions in a movement to reform social and individual understandings about shame and women's bodies that underlie and prevent women's access to public spaces where society recognizes personal success and power, such as sports and school.

In spite of always_brand #LikeAGirl posts challenging stigma around the female body, they are silent on the topic of menstruation. Likewise, #LikeAGirl brand and consumer-generated content situates feminism amidst neoliberal individualism and its gendered subjectivity of individual body and self-work required to succeed in market institutions (Windels et al. 2020). A criticism of this campaign might be that by not talking about menstruation and by focusing on girls who are premenstrual, it enabled user discourse on Instagram to remain silent on that, too. In fact, very few #LikeAGirl posts also mention menstruation in images or captions. Thus, the hashtag, while reappropriating the stigma of a woman's body in a male dominated space, avoids engagement with the moral processes that ascribe taboo meanings of uncleanliness to the stigmatized body.

Reappropriate stigmatized bodies

While the #LikeAGirl content reappropriates the stigma of a woman's body in a male-dominated space, yet neglects menstruation, #periodproblems and #period posts images and captions address menstruation directly (see Table 8.1. Posts 4 and 5). Accounts in #period and #periodproblems use humor as a strategy (Pryor and Reeder 2011; Scaraboto and Fischer 2013) to reappropriate transmedia discourse about protection by challenging menstruation as unclean and women's bodies as devalued. Humor works as a vehicle for managing the fear of uncleanliness. As we see in the top post on #period (Post 4), leaks are a topic of humor instead of fear. The bottom right post in Post 5 (see Table 8.1) humorously discusses management of menstruation-induced hormonal mood swings. Post 6 (see Table 8.1) offers an unapologetic image of blood that Always does not mention. These visual depictions of pain and of blood offer reflections of embodied experiences of menstruation which, through the visual, are a strategy for challenging bloodless, inorganic (i.e., blue liquid) representations of menstruation in ads (Malefyt and McCabe 2016).

Engage with structural stigma

In Post 7 (see Table 8.1), pain depicted visually through medicine is a shared experience with the audience and point of reflection. Our interpretation of the image and caption is that they engage with women's health issues related to reproduction and menstruation at the level of structure. The caption describes a woman's struggle with hormonal and/or barrier contraception (IUD), removing the device, and type 1 diabetes; the image and text convey a large quantity of medicine needed to manage menstruation after removal of the IUD. The reflection includes discussion of support from partners, such as the partner who brought in the medicine. Marketplace actors are implied for the unjust consequences of their actions on women's health. In this case, the injustice is the pain during extended menstruation after IUD removal.

In Post 8 (see Table 8.1), the text in the image and the caption @endotalk tells a similar association between women's health and marketplace actors involved in providing care. The image and the caption call the viewer's attention to endometriosis, a difficult to diagnose disease. Many observers have noted that young women's – most cases present in teenage years – pain in menstruation is often not approached as a diagnosable problem by many gynecologists. Instead, medical professionals may see the pain as a patient's failure to manage menstruation according to social and moral norms of being "solely and invisibly responsible for their menstruation" (Johnson 2019, p. 1). We suggest that this post frames endometriosis as an intersectional (age and gender) site of menstrual injustice.

Based on our findings about period-related hashtags that engage with structural stigma, we suggest that women trying to manage their menstrual flow, including pain and pregnancy or no pregnancy, when they meet the marketplace, may experience menstrual injustice: "the oppression of menstruators, women, girls, transgender men and boys, and nonbinary persons, simply because they menstruate" (Johnson 2019, p. 1; Johnston, Lobreto, and Christler 2013) that creates marketplace vulnerabilities, as women are temporarily vulnerable when they face a marketplace that seems to stigmatize them for the very need that drives them to the market (Baker et al. 2005).

Comparing #LikeAGirl and user-generated content

The #likeagirl call-to-action uses the conventions of online social movement (e.g., Xiong, Cho, and Boatright 2019) and, as of the end of 2020, more than 1.7 million posts (1,712,793 as of 12.30.2020) have taken up that charge. Analysis of the original commercial suggests that the brand does challenge stigmas of girls' – and by extension women's, as girls grow up – bodies and their capabilities. This is, indeed, an important message regarding girls' and women's capabilities and esteem. While we recognize that no one ad or campaign can combat all oppressive stereotypes, we are particularly interested in what is markedly absent or hidden. The brand is a menstrual hygiene brand; while the brand markings may alert consumers to this, the campaign resolves any discomfort before it arises by silencing menstruation. In fact, the campaign is created on the belief that content that makes periods explicit will not go viral: "'Nobody will ever share anything that has the Always logo on it.' Who would want to be associated with periods?" (Campaign 2015). In this way, the commercial perpetuates the notion that menstruation is something to be hidden.

#likeagirl, as used over time by Always and by consumers, focuses on girls' and women's empowerment through physical abilities (e.g., running, fighting). Therefore, it is not surprising that the hashtag picked up momentum among users in posts about sports. In its role as cultural producer of meaning, #likeagirl messages offer a shared voice online, through a hashtag language, to challenge stigmas about bodies and highlight a particular point of social change. Some critics of femvertising argue that it focuses on individual change and overlooks feminist calls for a movement of equity and institutional change (Varghese and Kumar 2020). While stereotypes solidify meaning as they move reflexively through social institutions such as advertising and in individual lives (Zayer and Coleman 2015), many posts find the answer in "confidence culture" (Windels et al. 2020). That is, the messages call for individual activism, and self-work around the issue of confidence and stigmatized bodies. In this way, we suggest the campaign and engagement surrounding it as representing the marketplace maturity of the Fourth Wave of feminism and similar liberal and neoliberal feminist perspectives, with their focus on self-responsibility. Yet, the use of social media engagement with branded messaging, such as #likeagirl, within the Fourth Wave of feminism may also be viewed as a form of activism; for example, women (including anyone identifying as menstruating) come together collectively and share individual experience. Through their numbers, Gen Z and young Millennial women may find agency and the power to bring about a change: in attitudes about women and stigmas about their bodies.

As #likeagirl gained traction in the Instagram algorithm, users began hashtagging it for content seemingly unrelated to the original campaign. For example, our data included men posting images of themselves with #likeagirl and #likeforlike. The goal of using the hashtag this way may be to increase reach and followers as the hashtag gained views. always_brand posted its first #EndPeriodPoverty Instagram image and caption on August 7, 2018. We suggest that the brand may have been reacting to users posting unrelated content and a potential loss of control of their campaign. Perhaps the brand was also taking an offensive position in light of the mounting successes of feminist political action to end period poverty by making period products free or at least tax-free. In Scotland, for example, Labour MSP Monica Lennon initiated an effort to make period products free in 2016 and succeeded to do so in 2020 with the Period Products (Free Provision) (Scotland) Bill (Diamond 2020). Another motivation for Always to use the word period in its corporate social responsibility hashtag and campaign might be to connect with the ideas of other online Fourth Wave feminist movements that used social media to reclaim meanings of the female body as natural, such as the #freethenipple campaign (Matich, Ashman, and Parsons 2019; Stevens and Houston 2016), as opposed to framed by the male gaze. #EndPeriodPoverty introduced fresh ideas to Always' corporate social responsibility campaign and maintains or gains interest among consumers (Varghese and Kumar 2020). While change to generate interest is not unusual, we think that #EndPeriodPoverty may have also provided Always with intersectionality that is missing in #LikeAGirl and is valued by Gen Z and Millennial consumers (Rosenberg 2018).

In contrast to the #likeagirl brand and user focus on girl empowerment and fighting stereotypes of girls' bodies, UGC around period hashtags such as #periodsbelike re-materializes menstruation with images of blood and brings to the forefront the shame associated with menstruation. This content signals the morality of a system that seems to judge women as having a broken character if their bodies and menstruation are anything other than private and controlled. Institutionalized menstrual injustice in the healthcare system's approach to women who want to experience agency through their menstruation, either through disease management or reproductive management, seems to leave them stigmatized. We suggest that period-related hashtags challenge the balance of power in the context of healthcare and women's health.

In summary, our analysis suggests that hashtags and visuals on Instagram in the context of a feminine hygiene marketing campaign challenge public and self-stigma through empowerment themes, while UGC surrounding non-branded period-related hashtags challenge stigma through association by reappropriating stigma through humor and transgression and challenge structural stigma through awareness in the context of women's health (Pryor and Reeder 2011). Through our analysis, we "embrace partial explanations and unresolved contradictions, looking for more horizontal connections" (Maclaran and Kravetz 2018, p. 71), which helps us to identify modest contributions from our data and, importantly, identifies areas that warrant further research to understand intersections of feminism and marketing. We seek more questions than answers, and it is to these that we turn next.

Answers and questions

In this research, we address iterative engagement with menstruation between brands and consumers on Instagram to understand how stigmas of menstruation and menstruating bodies are reproduced or challenged on this social medium. We demonstrate that reappropriation of stigmatized bodies extends from body size to menstruation (Scaraboto and Fisher 2013). Likewise, we argue that @always_brand captures or rides a feminist sports movement in Instagram. Based on our analysis, we suggest that further research is needed on the intersection of menstrual justice and consumer vulnerability (Baker et al. 2006; Johnson 2019; Johnston, Lobreto and Chrisler 2013).

Several themes that emerge from our analysis are notable for future research. We identify the ways that hashtags, captions, and visuals signal shared goals among users as they challenge public and self-stigma in the context of women's bodies as less than and therefore excluded from spaces where groups who are not stigmatized by gender (men) are allowed, such as individual sports. We think these posts, like the use of visuals of blood when consumers reappropriate stigmatized bodies, suggest that further research is warranted about the ways in which stigmas can be challenged via visuals on social media. We suggest further research on the ways that algorithms and visuals embolden participants in online feminist movements in general, picking up some hashtags and not others. The common thread of sports in the posts suggests avenues of exploration in the domain of consumer culture theory on transmedia, and the meaning of gendered sports in the marketplace might illuminate understandings of gender and the marketplace.

We further demonstrate that visual depictions of pain and blood are a powerful strategy for de-stigmatizing menstruation, perhaps because visuals discuss menstruation in ways that feminine hygiene brands do not. Social media may offer a transmedia context for revisiting the work of Malefyt and McCabe (2016) on the ways that women discuss and visually represent their experiences of menstruation in comparison with brand representations of their product's benefits.

Another avenue for discussing insights and further inquiry comes in comparing the first findings section – #LikeAGirl, Signal Public and Self-stigma – with the third – Engage with Structural Stigma and menstruation-related hashtags. In both sets of findings, consumers and Always frame the object of agency as the body and the self. While #LikeAGirl posts seem to imply "the sky's the limit" for female weightlifters and those who practice manifestation, our analysis suggests that agency is perhaps more complicated and often limited when it is socially situated in other institutional structures, such as the medical establishment, which are similarly invested with stigmatized meanings. A criticism of femvertising is that it echoes neoliberal ideology by focusing on the individual over structural change (Prügl 2015). Comparing transmedia gendered corporate social responsibility content with consumer-generated content on gendered themes might reveal similar patterns.

While not developed in this chapter, we found that niche brands tend to have the same tone as #period posts, which may provide an avenue for further research with a focus on the managerial implications of gendered segmenting, stigma, and niche positioning strategies. Some niche brands, we think, may communicate their position through framing mainstream brands as stigmatized and themselves as challenging stigma.

Our last comment on further avenues of research looks at #EndPeriodPoverty and #periodpain. Always starts its corporate social responsibility campaign with #LikeAGirl and moves to #EndPeriodPoverty, a nod to menstrual justice. The new hashtag openly uses the word period, and we suggest that move addresses stigma. Likewise, Always explains #EndPeriodPoverty in post captions as a financial and sociocultural problem of not having enough money for the required products and as shame at asking for help. This framing shifts the focus of the problem from Always to consumers. Yet we argue that menstrual justice comes from both de-stigmatizing menstruation and removing consumer vulnerabilities such as price. In neoliberal style, #EndPeriodPoverty individualizes the problem and looks to corporate social responsibility for a solution to a problem it helped create. In contrast, as we see with #periodpain, when engaging with structural stigma, consumers ask other consumers to come together to challenge structures that create vulnerability and menstrual injustice. While not fully developed in this chapter, we find this new hashtag and the issue of moral obligations to consumers (to access products and to equitable healthcare) to be an interesting context for further research on the relationship between corporate social responsibility, the marketplace, vulnerability, and feminism.

As a final thought of the chapter, we reflect on the initial phases of the project, how it evolved, and where we hope it develops. When we started this project, we expected we would criticize #LikeAGirl as another form of the neoliberal marketplace using women for its own needs through empowerment ideologies while telling them it is invested in women's causes. However, as we analyzed the data, especially UGC, women's empowerment via sports emerged as a potentially desirable outcome for women and for the brand. In future research, we hope to explore #LikeAGirl as a means of shedding light on gendered hashtag communities on Instagram and embodied power in the form of sport. In the case of period-related hashtags, we were delighted from the beginning to see representations of our lived experiences and feminist views. We were intrigued by the ways in which technology, especially algorithms, visuals, and hashtags, frames fourth-wave feminism and how many Gen Z and Millennial women perform feminism on Instagram. Having viewed many #period posts, we consider future research avenues that explore posting on social media as part of the ritual of menstruation. We remain curious about the relationship between social media, feminist goals of collective social movement, and challenging oppressive structures in a neoliberal state full of tropes about entrepreneurism, individual achievement, and manifesting goals (Prügl 2015).

References

Abrams, R. 2015. Under Pressure, Feminine Product Makers Disclose Ingredients. *The New York Times,* October 26. https://www.nytimes.com/2015/10/27/business/under-pressure-feminine-product-makers-disclose-ingredients.html.

Adkins, N. R., and J. L. Ozanne. 2005. "The Low Literature Consumer." *Journal of Consumer Research* 32: 93–105.

Åkestam, N., S. Rosengren, and M. Dahlen. 2020. "Advertising 'Like a Girl': Toward a Better Understanding of 'Femvertising' and Its Effects." *Psychology & Marketing* 34: 795–806.

Always, Procter & Gamble, and Leo Burnett. 2015. "#LikeAGirl." *Campaign*, October 12. https://www.campaignlive.co.uk/article/case-study-always-likeagirl/1366870.

Arthurs, J., S. Drakopoulou, and A. Gandini. 2018. "Researching YouTube." *Convergence: The International Journal of Research into New Media Technologies* 24(1): 3–15. https://doi.org/10.1177/1354856517737222

AudienceProject. 2020. "Percentage of U.S. Internet Users Who Use Instagram as of 3rd Quarter 2020, by Age Group." Chart. September 17, 2020. *Statista*. Accessed April 30, 2021.

Baker, S. M., J. W. Gentry, and T.L. Rittenburg. 2005. "Building Understanding of the Domain of Consumer Vulnerability." *Journal of Macromarketing* 25(2): 128–139. https://doi.org/10.1177/0276146705280622.

Bobel, C. 2010. *New Blood: Third-Wave Feminism and the Politics of Menstruation*. New Brunswick, NJ: Rutgers University Press.

Bos, A. E. R., J. B. Pryor, G. D. Reeder, and S.E. Stutterheim. 2013. "Stigma: Advances in Theory and Research." *Basic and Applied Social Psychology* 35 (1): 1–9.

Caliandro, A., and J. Graham. 2020. "Studying Instagram Beyond Selfies." *Social Media + Society* 6(2): 2056305120924779.

Chiseri-Strater, E. and B. S. Sunstein. 1997. *Fieldworking: Reading and Writing Research*. Upper Saddle River, NJ: Prentice Hall.

Coleman, C. A., and L. T. Zayer. 2015. "Ban the Word Feminist? Control and Subversion of Stigma in Social Movements and Consumer Culture." In *NA – Advances in Consumer Research Volume 43*, edited by Kristin Diehl and Carolyn Yoon, 254–259. Duluth, MN: Association for Consumer Research.

Cooper, P. 2020. "140+ Social Media Statistics that Matter to Marketers in 2020," *Hootsuite*. Accessed 20 February 2020. https://blog.hootsuite.com/social-media-statistics-for-social-media-managers/#instagram.

Cotter, K. 2018. "Playing the Visibility Game: How Digital Influencers and Algorithms Negotiate Influence on Instagram." *New Media & Society* 21(4): 895–913. https://doi.org/10.1177/1461444818815684.

Crockett, D. 2017. "Paths to Respectability: Consumption and Stigma Management in the Contemporary Black Middle Class." *Journal of Consumer Research* 44: 554–581.

Daer, A.R., Hoffman, R. & Goodman, S. (2014). Rhetorical Functions of hashtag forms across social media applications. In *Proceedings of the 32nd ACM International Conference on the Design of Communication CD-ROM*, 1–3.

Davidson, L. 2015. "Femvertising: Advertisers Cash in on #feminism." *The Telegraph*, January 12. http://www.telegraph.co.uk/women/womens-life/11312629/Femvertising-Advertisers-cash-in-on-feminism.html.

Diamond, C. 2020. "Period Poverty: Scotland First in World to Make Period Products Free." *BBC Scotland News*, 24 November. https://www.bbc.com/news/uk-scotland-scotland-politics-51629880.

Drenten, J., and L. Gurrieri. 2018. "Crossing the #bikinibridge: Exploring the Role of Social Media in Propagating Body Image Trends." In *The Dark Side of Social Media: A Consumer Psychology Perspective*, edited by A.C. Scheinbaum, 49–70. New York: Routledge.

Eisend, M. 2019. "Gender Roles." *Journal of Advertising* 48 (1): 72–80.

Erchull, M. J. 2013. "Distancing through Objectification? Depictions of Women's Bodies in Menstrual Product Advertisements." *Sex Roles* 68: 32–40.

Gilbert, M. "Executive Summary, Feminine Hygiene and Sanitary Protection Products." *Mintel*, March 2016. Accessed April 30, 2021. http://academic.mintel.com/display/747679/.

Gill, R., and C. Scharff. 2011. "Introduction." In *New Femininities: Postfeminism, Neoliberalism and Subjectivity*, edited by Rosalind Gill and Christina Scharff, 1–17. New York: Palgrave.

Goffman, E. 1963. *Stigma: Notes on the Management of Spoiled Identity*. Englewood Cliffs, NJ: Prentice Hall.

Jardine, A. 2020. "Pantone Has Created a Shade of Red Called 'Period,'" *Advertising Age*, September 29. Accessed July 11, 2020. https://adage.com/creativity/work/pantone-has-created-shade-red-called-period/2283911.

Johnson, M. E. 2019. "Menstrual Justice." *UC Davis Law Review* 53 (1): 1–79.

Johnston-Robledo, I. and J. C. Chrisler. 2013. "The Menstrual Mark: Menstruation as Social Stigma." *Sex Roles* 68: 9–18.

Johnston-Robledo, I. and M. L. Stubbs. 2013. "Positioning Periods: Menstruation in Social Context: An Introduction to a Special Issue." *Sex Roles* 68: 1–8.

Kane, K. 1990. "The Ideology of Freshness in Feminine Hygiene Commercials." *Journal of Communication Inquiry* 14: 83–92.

Keller, J. 2019."'Oh, She's a Tumblr Feminist': Exploring the Platform Vernacular of Grils' Social Media Feminisms." *Social Media + Society* 5 (3): 2056305119867442.

Kozinets, R. V. 2001. "Utopian Enterprise: Articulating the Meanings of Star Trek's Culture of Consumption." *Journal of Consumer Research* 28: 67–88.

Lambiase, J., C. Bronstein, and C. A. Coleman. 2017. "Women versus Brands: Sexist Advertising and Gender Stereotypes Motivate Transgenerational Feminist Critique." In *Feminists, Feminisms, and Advertising: Some Restrictions Apply*, edited by Kim Golombisky and Peggy J. Kreshel, 29–60. Lanham, MD: Lexington Books.

Link, B. G. and J. C. Phelan. 2001. "Conceptualizing Stigma." *Annual Review of Sociology* 27: 363–385.

Lobato, R. 2016. "The Cultural Logic of Digital Intermediaries: YouTube Multichannel Networks." *Convergence* 22 (4): 348–360. https://doi.org/10.1177/1354856516641628.

Luke, H. 1997. "The Gendered Discourses of Menstruation." *Social Alternatives* 16 (1): 28–30.

Maclaran, P. 2012. "Marketing and Feminism in Historic Perspective." *Journal of Historical Research in Marketing* 4 (3): 462–469.

Maclaran, P. and O. Kravetz. 2018. "Feminist Perspectives in Marketing: Past, Present and Future," in *The Routledge Companion to Critical Marketing*, edited by Mark Tadajewski, Matthew Higgins, Jancie Denegri-Knott, and Rohit Varman, 64–82. Abingdon: Routledge.

MacLean, K., C. Hearle, and K. N. Ruwanpura. 2020. "Stigma of Staining? Negotiating Menstrual Taboos amongst Young Women in Kenya." *Women's Studies International Forum* 78: 1–10.

Malefyt, T. de Wall and M. McCabe. 2016. "Women's Bodies, Menstruation and Marketing 'Protection:' Interpreting a Paradox of Gendered Discourses in Consumer Practices and Advertising Campaigns." *Consumption Markets & Culture* 19 (6): 555–575.

Mandziuk, R. M. 2010. "'Ending Women's Greatest Hygienic Mistake': Modernity and Mortification of Menstruation in Kotex Advertising, 1921–1926." *Women's Studies Quarterly* 38 (3&4): 42–62.

Matich, M., R. Ashman and E. Parsons. 2019. "#freethenipple – digital activism and embodiment in the contemporary feminist movement." *Consumption Markets & Culture*, 22 (4): 337–362. doi: 10.1080/10253866.2018.1512240.

McNeil, D., Jr. 2003. Menstrual Cups, at Age 66, Begin to Make Up for Lost Time. *The New York Times*. February 4. Retrieved from http://www.nytimes.com/2003/02/04/health/menstrual-cups-at-age-66-begin-to-make-up-for-lost-time.html.

Merskin, D. 1999. "Adolescence, Advertising, and the Ideology of Menstruation." *Sex Roles* 40 (11/12): 941–957.

Mirabito, A. M., C. C. Otnes, E. Crosby, D. B. Wooten, J. E. Machin, C. Pullig, N. R. Adkins, et al. (2016), "The Stigma Turbine: A Theoretical Framework for Conceptualizing and Contextualizing Marketplace Stigma." *Journal of Public Policy & Marketing* 35 (2): 170–184.

Mitchell, K. 2013. Review of *New Femininities: Postfeminism, neoliberalism and subjectivity*, edited by Rosalind Gill and Christina Scharff. *Feminist Theory* 14 (3): 361–371.

Morales, E. n.d. "Instagram Hashtags in 2020 – Everything You Need to Know." *Medium*. Retrieved from https://medium.com/swlh/instagram-hashtags-everything-you-need-to-know-3761a825a268.

Murray, D. C. 2015. "Notes to Self: The Visual Culture of Selfies in the Age of Social Media." *Consumption Markets & Culture* 18 (6): 490–516.

Park, S. M. 1996. "From Sanitation to Liberation?: The Modern and Postmodern Marketing of Menstrual Products." *Journal of Popular Culture* 30 (2): 149–168.

Prügl, E. 2015. "Neoliberalising Feminism." *New Political Economy* 20 (4): 614–631.

Pryor, J. B. and G. D. Reeder. 2011. "HIV-related Stigma." In *HIV/AIDS in the Post-HAART Era: Manifestations, Treatment, and Epidemiology*, edited by John C. Hall, Brian J. Hall, and Clay J. Cockerell, 790–806. Shelton, CT: PMPH-USA.

Rabin, R. C. 2015. "How Period Trackers Have Changed Girl Culture." *The New York Times*, November 12. https://well.blogs.nytimes.com/2015/11/12/how-period-trackers-have-changed-girl-culture/.

Rodrigues, R. A. 2016. "Femvertising: Empowering Women Through The Hashtag? A Comparative Analysis of Consumers' Reaction to Feminist Advertising on Twitter." Master's Thesis, Lisbon School of Economics and Management, University of Lisbon, Lisbon.

Rosenberg, J. 2018. "Feminine Hygiene and Sanitary Protection Products US." *Mintel*, April 2018. Accessed April 30, 2021. https://reports-mintel-com.flagship.luc.edu/display/860303/.

Sandikci, Ö. and G. Ger. 2010. "Veiling in Style: How Does a Stigmatized Practice Become Fashionable?" *Journal of Consumer Research* 37 (1): 15–36.

Scaraboto, D. and E. Fischer. 2010. "From Individual Coping to Collective Action: Stigma Management in Online Communities." In *Advances in Consumer Research*, 37, edited by Margaret C. Campbell, Jeff Inman, and Rik Pieters, 28–31. Duluth, MN: Association for Consumer Research.

Scaraboto, D. and E. Fischer. 2013. "Frustrated Fatshionistas: An Institutional Theory Perspective on Consumer Quests for Greater Choice in Mainstream Markets." *Journal of Consumer Research* 39 (April): 1234–1257.

SheKnows. 2014. "The 10 Most Inspirational Ads of 2014." *Self*, December 28. https://www.self.com/story/10-womens-inspirational-ads.

Smiley, M. 2020. "Facebook Bans Ads for Period Underwear Because It Shows Red Menstrual Blood." *Adweek.com*, October 1, 2020. https://www.adweek.com/agencies/facebook-bans-ad-for-period-underwear-because-it-shows-red-menstrual-blood/

Sredl, K. C. 2018. "Gendered Market Subjectivity: Autonomy, Privilege, and Emotional Subjectivity in Normalizing Post-Socialist Neoliberal Ideology." *Consumption, Markets and Culture* 21 (6): 532–553. https://doi.org/10.1080/10253866.2017.1374950.

Sredl, K. C., and E. Robertson. 2018. "Breaking Menstruation Taboos Online: Self-Disclosure and Period-Related Hashtags." Paper presented at *GENMAC2018: 14th Conference on Gender, Marketing, and Consumer Behavior*, Dallas, TX, October 9–11.

Steinfield, L. A., C. A. Coleman, L. T. Zayer, N. Ourahmoune, and W. Hein. 2019. "Power Logics of Consumers' Gendered (In)justices: Reading Reproductive Health Interventions through the Transformative Gender Justice Framework." *Consumption Markets & Culture* 22 (4): 406–429.

Stevens, L. and S. Houston. 2016. "Dazed Magazine, Fourth Wave Feminism, and the Return of the Politicised Female Body." Paper presented at the *13th Conference on Gender, Marketing and Consumer Behaviour*, Paris, July 4–6.

Thompson, C. J. 1997. "Interpreting Consumers: A Hermeneutical Framework for Deriving Marketing Insights from the Texts of Consumers' Consumption Stories." *Journal of Marketing Research* 34 (4): 438–455. https://doi.org/10.1177/002224379703400403.

Thompson, C. J. 2014. "The Politics of Consumer Identity Work." *Journal of Consumer Research* 40: iii–v.

Ustuner, T., and D. B. Holt. 2007. "Dominated Consumer Acculturation: The Social Construction of Poor Migrant Women's Consumer Identity Projects in a Turkish Squatter." *Journal of Consumer Research* 34 (1): 41–56.

Varghese, N. and N. Kumar. 2020. "Feminism in Advertising: Irony or Revolution? A Critical Review of Femvertising." *Feminist Media Studies*, Advance online publication. https://doi.org/10.1080/14680777.2020.1825510.

Wertheim, B. 2015. "Options for Periods Include Cups and Special Underwear." *The New York Times*, November 15. https://www.nytimes.com/2016/11/15/well/live/options-for-periods-include-cups-and-special-underwear.html.

Windels, K., S. Champlin, S. Shelton, Y. Sterbenk, and M. Poteet. 2020. "Selling Feminism: How Female Empowerment Campaigns Employ Postfeminist Discourses." *Journal of Advertising* 49 (1): 18–33.

Xiong, Y., M. Cho, and B. Boatwright. 2019. "Hashtag Activism and Message Frames Among Social Movement Organizations: Semantic Network Analysis and Thematic Analysis of Twitter During the #MeToo Movement." *Public Relations Review* 45: 10–23.

Zayer, L. T., and C. A. Coleman. 2015. "Advertising Professionals' Perceptions of the Impact of Gender Portrayals on Men and Women: A Question of Ethics?" *Journal of Advertising* 44 (3): 1–12.

Zayer, L. T., C. A. Coleman, and J. Orjuela. 2018. "Femvertising Discourses and Online Consumer Engagement: A Case Analysis of Under Armour's #IWillWhatIWant Brand Campaign." In *The Routledge Handbook of Positive Communication*, edited by José Antonio Muñiz-Velázquez and Cristina Pulido, 203–212. New York: Routledge.

Zmuda, N. and A. C. Diaz. 2014. "Female Empowerment in Ads: Soft Feminism or Soft Soap." *Advertising Age*, September 2. http://adage.com/article/cmostrategy/marketers-soft-feminism/294740/.

9 In search of the female gaze
Querying the Maidenform archive

Astrid Van den Bossche

When Maidenform's "I Dreamed…" ads appeared in the United States in 1949, the public's response—a mixture of amusement and disapproval—propelled the campaign into iconicity. Depicting a confident model wearing only a bra from the waist up but otherwise neatly clothed in the latest fashion (e.g., Figure 9.1), the tagline suggested that the model found herself dreaming of performing a wide variety of activities in her celebrated undergarments. The ads, which were concisely described by the contemporaneous Institute for Motivational Research as "Maidenform's dreamwalk in the semi-nude […that associated] the bra with 'wishful dreams' of passion" (1958a, 88), multiplied their diversions across popular media until the campaign was retired in 1969. They drew extensively on current themes, tropes and events that gave the ads a sense of timeliness and underwrote their seriality. The ad above, for example, was one of three variations on the "I dreamed I was bewitching" tagline published in time for Halloween. Sporting a conical hat and armed with a broom, the model peers into the distance, perhaps scoping out a costume party: "This dream goes out at night! Was there ever such artful magic? Me… marvelously moulded, abra-ca-da-bra-ed to beauty by my Maidenform bra." The trope of the witch lends a rebellious quality to the image: her womanhood is abject and persecuted on the one hand, but self-determined and admired on the other (Greene 2018)—in the cult of domesticity of the 1950s, her ability to ridicule the patriarchal order made her particularly unsettling (Blécourt 2017). This was the Maidenform dreamer: she was beautiful, she was wilful and therefore she was dangerous; armoured in her magical undergarment, she played the game but threatened to upset the rules.

Today, it is tempting to regard the Maidenform ads (henceforth referred to as the 'Dreams') as texts that either broke away from 1950s gender norms by depicting women absorbed in their occupations, or as one that reinforced them by emphasising its objectifying beauty culture. Either way, the depiction of the female body is at the epicentre of these divergent readings: Were the Dreams a celebration of poise and joy, or were they mirages for a misguided sense of liberty? From the press attention it received at its launch, to scholarship produced long after its end, the Dreams have commonly been interpreted through the 'male gaze.' For example, commentators at the time argued that, for better or for worse, the campaign was exemplar of the psychoanalytic levers that advertisers could pull to entice manipulable (read female) customers to purchase their goods. While insightful in its own right, this explanation bypasses the experiences of the undergarments' consumers. Did these women conform to the cognitive and behavioural patterns assumed by the (primarily male) pundits who drew the ads into public debate? Do these descriptions sufficiently capture

In search of the female gaze 121

Figure 9.1 "I dreamed I was bewitching in my Maidenform bra," October 1950, *Maidenform Mirror*, Maidenform Collection, Archives Center, National Museum of American History, Smithsonian Institution (NMAH.AC.0585 Box 19 Folder 0).

their experiences? Were there feminist ways of experiencing the ads and can these be recovered?

In this piece, I explore what a feminist historian can do to recover vestiges of the female gazes that lingered on the ads, and thereby restore their significance (cf. Scott 2015, 2006). I focus on the first decade of the Dreams—roughly between 1949 and 1958, when the ads circulated like wildfire and before they took on more explicit sexual innuendos. I do not provide an in-depth reading or history of the campaign, which I have done elsewhere (Van den Bossche 2014, 2019), and more contextualisation would be needed to articulate a new history of the campaign's reception. Instead, the purpose of this chapter is to reconstruct the possibility of a female gaze by revisiting the archive and reflecting on select historical records and ephemera.

The gaze and the historical record

Looking is not a neutral activity. It takes place in a context imbued with the pre-existing knowledge that the spectator brings to it. It may be mediated through technology (be it a pair of glasses or a smart phone); it may be intertwined with other senses, such as touch and smell. Looking is therefore cultural as much as it feels mundane because it uses one's seemingly straightforward physiological capacity for vision. The gaze is a special case of looking: it is directed, intent and sustained (Sturken and Cartwright 2018); it is aware of itself, and of itself in relation to others. Because it is dependent on the context, knowledge and predisposition of the viewer (who may be the creator, a subject or the audience), cultural and visual theorists argue that it defines a power relation between those doing the gazing and those who are being gazed upon (cf. Berger 1972; Olin 2003). Feminist approaches to visual culture have leveraged the concept of the gaze to highlight how subjects and readers are gendered in the very act of pictorial address, often reinforcing patriarchal constructs. In these studies, the gaze has been used as a way to dissect narrative or pictorial point of view (Warhol and Herndl 1997) and as a way to theorise the experiences of female viewers (Doane 1982; Gamman and Marshment 1988). Oscillating between representation and reception, the gaze is often theorised as constituted by both.

Film critic Laura Mulvey's theorisation of the gaze is of particular interest here, not only because it is seminal, but because it is especially concerned with Classical Hollywood, which produced the culturally dominant visual register of the feminine when the Dreams were first published. Using psychoanalytic theory, Mulvey showed how scopophilia (used in the Freudian sense as the pleasure in looking) is predicated on a patriarchal order that structures the relationship between audiences and actresses. Women on screen are neither the "bearer, nor maker, of meaning" (Mulvey 1975, 7) because they are scripted, shot and edited in such ways that render the absence of a penis unthreatening to a male audience. As audiences identify with the male protagonist, we are invited to either ascertain the woman's guilt (of not having a penis) and subsequently forgive, save or fetishise her. Either way, her depiction is both a trigger and a remedy for castration anxiety. Female audiences internalise the male gaze as their own and are thus 'masculinised,' though subsequent scholarship sought to complexify this position and probe its "unstable, oscillating [sexual] difference" (Mulvey 1989, 29).

Mulvey's critique was foundational to subsequent gender analyses in visual culture and became a backdrop against which scholars urgently asked whether gazes that did not conform to the assumed white, heterosexual and patriarchal audiences of the Hollywood film could exist, and what kind of identification, resistance and pleasure these could afford (e.g., Gamman and Marshment 1988; Sassatelli 2011). Together, however, these perspectives articulated a theorisation of how women's to-be-looked-at-ness in visual culture (Mulvey 1975) structured their understanding and experience of themselves, and culminated in studies of the internalised panoptic gaze (Friedberg 1994), where the "essential attribute of [the] dominant system is the matching of male subjectivity with the agency of the look" (Doane 1982, 77). In his BBC documentary and eponymous book *Ways of Seeing* (1972), John Berger summarised the argument as:

> ... *men act* and *women appear*. Men look at women. Women watch themselves being looked at. This determines not only most relations between men and women but also the relation of women to themselves. The surveyor of woman in herself is male:

the surveyed female. Thus she turns herself into an object – and most particularly an object of vision: a sight.

(1972, 47)

Advertising has been a particularly well-discussed site of visual production and consumption, and although there has been no shortage of writing about women in relation thereof, the female gaze in promotional culture remains more of a mystery (Friedberg 1994). Where the male gaze has been identified (Barthes 1972; Williamson 1978), inverted (Patterson and Elliott 2002) or expanded (Schroeder and Zwick 2004), it has also remained the analytical default. As identified by feminist critics, the difficulty lies in the construction of a gaze that is not entangled in a patriarchal hegemony (Warhol and Herndl 1997): is it enough for a woman to be the creator, or for gender roles and stereotypes to be reversed? Even where men are found to be depicted for the viewing pleasure of women, these representations can be critiqued as emerging from a patriarchal logic of submission, objectification and possession. Most recently, studies on the postfeminist gaze reveal a viewer who is struggling between identifying herself as the subject and as the object of the gaze, a scrutinising dynamic that has the potential of dulling or even nullifying feminist critique (Rome, O'Donohoe, and Dunnett 2020).

This varied deployment of the gaze is subject to historical context, and receptive to studies where sex is understood "as a category of [social] thought" (Kelly-Gadol 2015, 8). Rather than seeing womanhood as a category decontextualised from history, or formulating a history where male and female sexes are perpetually pitted against each other, feminist historians have argued for a continuous appraisal of gender as constructed, structural and situational (Scott 1986). In the case of the gaze, the trick lies in articulating the multiplicity of potential spectator positions and their implied powers. As Mulvey reflected, textual analysis should be accompanied by its historicisation, thus acknowledging that there are "multiple audiences and spectator positions, multiple ways in which different kinds of social groups are distanced, or entranced" (in interview with Sassatelli 2011, 129). One practical difficulty is therefore that a reappraisal of these texts must sit between the analysis of the image and traces of its reception.

To start such a contextualisation of the Dreams, take, for example, a round-table discussion on the question, "Do Americans commercialize sex?" published in the *Ladies Home Journal* in October 1956. The participants ('two mothers and five young people') widely condemned the depiction of women and romance in popular media as promoting a picture of desirability that is too focused on physical attractiveness and sexual pleasure:

MRS. MARCH: [On watching TV with her daughters on a Sunday afternoon] But when the program came on we couldn't [enjoy it]. As my husband said, "That is the type of thing that twenty-five years ago was burlesque, for men only." [...]

MISS GARNER: You say you saw on TV what would have been for men only some years back. I think that here is, maybe, one of the roots of the problem: that men and women have ideally a different viewpoint. I think with men the physical aspects are a good deal sharper and that with women sex is more a matter of affection. So that one of the problems is that women and children are being presented with what some shortsighted businessmen have decided is family entertainment because it is momentarily commercially profitable.

MR. SCHULTZ: Women have asked for such treatment. One of the basic problems, I think, is that in the last 20 or 30 years women have forced themselves into a much more prominent place, and in doing this they have cast away a lot of the virtues of true womanliness.

While the panellists seem to be in general agreement, they are debating the gaze and who is responsible for it. Popular entertainment and commercial ventures had turned images ('burlesque') that had been 'for men only' into the standard for mass media. A panellist cites sexual difference as the cause, and in response one of the men diverts the blame from 'shortsighted businessmen' to women: *they* have forgotten their 'true' womanliness. Advertisements such as Revlon's 'Cherries in the Snow' were seen as particularly seditious, as well as some bra advertisements: "I think slogans like 'You will be more lovable in a lovable brassiere' are—well, they make a false connection between love and sex and that is something I think is bad" (Hickey 1956). In an example of such a Lovable ad,[1] a cartoon depicts a woman observing a solar eclipse while a man observes her through a telescope; "tha-a-a-t's LOVABLE!" is scrawled at his feet in red, while a red dotted line connects the lens to her breasts to drive the point home. Other undergarment ads such as the Playtex Leap[2] were seen as less suggestive, and were therefore "less guilty [... because they] just show what to wear when." The question was therefore not necessarily how much the ads showed, but what they implied.

The Dreams as psychoanalytic trips

Although the model's state of undress was key to the Dreams' message, the dominant interpretation of the campaign focused primarily on the image's association with the Freudian naked dream. For example, two months after the first Dream appeared, the ads were discussed in this light by WOR breakfast radio show hosts Dorothy and Dick. As transcribed in the *Maidenform Mirror*:

DICK: Isn't that an old nightmare, in the middle of Times Square with no clothes on?
DOT: Yes. That's a familiar nightmare. But most people consider it embarrassing.
DICK: Not this girl.
DOT: No, she's happy as a clam.
DICK: Of course, she's wearing her Maiden Form.
DOT: I must investigate those… (laughs) … before I go shopping for broccoli.
(*Maidenform Mirror* 1949b)

To the broader public, the reference to the naked dream was novel and fun (or, to those who disapproved, novel and in bad taste). But to advertising professionals who were conversant in psychoanalytic theory, the image showed a woman who had given into her libidinal, exhibitionistic impulses. Some believed that audiences were drawn to it because it allowed them to undergo a similar form of catharsis (or neurotic release, depending on how alarmed the commentator was at the prospect) just by identifying with her. The image therefore contained a specific threat to the patriarchal order: joyful self-possession had no place in a culture where the image of the female body was reserved for male consumption.

Some vocal pundits, notably including Vance Packard, author of the scathing but influential *The Hidden Persuaders* (1957), felt that the ads threatened the integrity of the mind and of society (Nelson 2008). Speaking at the 1957 Visual Communications Conference held in New York, Packard reportedly dampened the mood of the 450 art directors in the audience by specifically questioning "the morality of exploiting sexual attitudes for commercial purposes" (*Broadcasting* 1957, 31), of which, as he wrote in his book, the Maidenform Dreams were "the most controversial of the eye stoppers of this sort" (1957, 76). To Packard, the lines between women's bodies and sexual pleasure on the one hand, and visual pleasure and moral integrity on the other, were very short indeed: taking issue with motivation research in particular, he found suggestive advertising morally reprehensible because he feared that libidinal consumption (which it would invariably promote) would lead to the regress of human rationality (Tadajewski 2010). What bothered Packard most about the Maidenform ads was that because the model was dreaming, her "undressed state was [deemed] permissible" (1957, 76). To him, the sexual connotations of the image were amplified because of their oneiric setting; it gave expression to a freedom of mind that did not square with the scopophilic pleasures of the 'girlie,' who could be fetishised, punished or saved. To give his interpretation more weight, he unwittingly (but tellingly) mischaracterised the ads by noting that the model was "wandering about among normally dressed people" (1957, 76), even though these supposed audiences were certainly implied, but rarely portrayed. The gaze, then, is the true problem here: the presence of diegetic gazers denied that the model could have a mental space that was entirely her own.

It would be a mistake to suggest that the psychoanalytical interpretation did not play a role in women's experiences of the ads: it did, because as illustrated above, it was an important reason why the ads featured in the popular press. Claims that the ads had roots in psychoanalytic insights, which were encouraged by Maidenform's advertising agency Norman, Craig & Kummel, were reinforced by commissioning Dichter's Institute for Motivational Research for a short report on Maidenform's television advertising in 1958. We can get a glimpse of what respondents conveyed to the researchers in the write-up (Schwarzkopf 2015), but their voices are heavily parsed through the motivation research lens, which assumed that consumption satisfied deep-seated and often repressed desires. As such, in a fairly typical assessment, the Institute advised that:

> The Maidenform commercials tend to successfully emphasize an identification approach based on vicarious realization of some common feminine aspirations. Many of these desires are barely conscious. The identification process itself in these instances is almost completely unconscious. Direct questions, or questions which attempt to measure feelings of relatedness to the commercial generally encounter resistance [sic].
>
> (1958b, 38)

Were the women who were interviewed so prude that they could not admit to identifying with the ad's "sex symbolism" (p. 39), or did they not recognise themselves in that line of questioning? When *Life* magazine initially refused to run the Clairol 'Does she… or doesn't she?' ads because they thought the tagline too suggestive, the women who were subsequently polled failed to see the innuendo (Fox 1984).

Besides providing a titillating backstory to the ads, psychoanalytic theory does not explain why the ads were successful, even though subsequent feminist analyses suggested that they spoke to the reader's false consciousness (Coleman 1995; Lyons 2005).

Regarding a 1951 Dream that showed a female editor at work, for example, Coleman describes the model's pointy hat as taking on "the aggressive suggestion of male penetration," and deems that this phallic symbol would have been recognised as such by contemporaneous audiences (1995, 14). But hats would also have been recognised as part of this woman's professional attire. As ridiculous as some designs might have been, conspicuous hats were "a badge of membership in the sisterhood of the empowered: fashion commentators and editors, poker-faced mannequins, salesgirls, brisk *premières*, designers, and knowing customers" all sported them (Marling 1994, 21). Placing greater importance on arcane symbolism than on commonplace dressing practices is an example of how women's histories can be overshadowed by theory which may very well illuminate certain inequalities, but also run the risk of obscuring what still remains to be explained (Scott 1986). The psychanalytic discourse has a way of bypassing voices that rejected the universalising interpretation of bawdiness by declaring them delusional. It is an effective silencing strategy predicated on a dubious theory that did little to examine the everyday experiences of Maidenform's female audiences.

Querying the archive

To recover these experiences, I began by posing a series of 'what if...' questions (Mordhorst 2008): what if the primary thing that one sees is not exhibitionism, but what the model is doing? What if the primary concern of a reader was the product, not the representation? Or the body, not the semi-nude? Armed with these reminders to shed the prevailing narrative of the Dreams, I reflected on whether the historical record could support alternate understandings. As liminal spaces between memory and forgetting (Zeitlyn 2012), archives transform their contents from once holding specific functions and meanings for specific groups of people, to now holding the potential of remembrance for only part of those who lived it. Where they conserve traces of experience, they also reveal silences: in the making of sources, in their selection for inclusion, in what is of interest to the perusing historian. Reading against the grain of the archive—actively looking for what one might expect to be absent, actively questioning authorial power—is a strategy that can help formulate answers to our what-ifs.

The main repository that I will consider here is what is left of Maidenform's corporate archive, which was donated to the Smithsonian's National Museum of American History's Archives Center in the 1990s. Out of the documents and ephemera preserved in this collection, the company's magazines, the *Maidenform Mirror* (for trade) and the *Maiden-forum* (for employees), proved the most bountiful, as they are both primary and secondary sources of the meaning-making that occurred within Maidenform and with their trade relationships. The layers that are present here—the forces that have shaped these vestiges of the company's memory, intentional and accidental alike—are manifold. Working backwards, we have the curators at the Archives Center who mind the collection, and we have the family, grandchildren of the Maidenform founders and once senior management of the company, who chose to donate this collection to the Museum. Then, we have the corporate archivists who preserved copies of the magazines and a seemingly random array of letters, photographs, display materials, prints, research reports, memos, a handkerchief and desiccated balloons. We have the magazines' editors and reporters, mostly women, who were otherwise regular employees seeking out stories of interest. Finally, we have the everyday life of the Maidenform employees, including their work experiences, their values, their lives outside of work and their own undergarment stories. Remembering these layers is helpful because it starts to clarify where selections, omissions and reconfigurations may have taken place.

One persistent line of investigation when discussing the female gaze is whether the text in question was produced by women. With Maidenform, this question needs to contend with the gendered power dynamics of workers within the company and their agencies (Figure 9.2). That the Dreams were in many ways a female creation is incontestable: successful executives such as Kitty d'Alessio, Kay Daly and very likely Mary Fillius played a critical role in the advertising's artistic direction, though contemporaneous documentation of their activities is sparse. Fillius, for example, is often credited as the copywriter responsible for the Dreams, but the only surviving account of her involvement is both vague and dissatisfying. In his retelling for *Ad Age*, which was kept as a press clipping in the Maidenform archive, adman Joe Sacco explains how the dream idea was originally presented to Seamprufe by art director Herman Davis, who enlisted Fillius for the copy. Seamprufe turned it down. A few months later, Fillius had moved agencies and was tasked with producing a breakthrough campaign for Maidenform. According to Sacco, she struggled and he suggested that she take Davis's idea. Sacco's account has been questioned as usurping the credit due to Fillius (Synycia 2016), and he indeed summarises the Dream's origin story as starring "the man who 'dreamed' it, the client who rejected it, the girl who 'borrowed' it [...] and my own stunned complicity in this comic but colossal saga" (1977, 63). He is full of occasionally patronising praise for Fillius, who had died by the time this article was published. Yet his account is also vocal on one important detail, and silent on another. The former is that the Seamprufe dreamer was "wearing an anxious smile and not much else besides a frilly slip" (1977, 63), thus suggesting a measure of self-consciousness; and the latter is that between the Seamprufe and the Maidenform pitches, this anxious smile disappeared, and the ad was adapted so that it worked with a bra. The account's implication is that Maidenform (and specifically, their newly minted Advertising Director, Joseph Coleman) was visionary,

Figure 9.2 Maidenform executives and advertisers Norman, Craig & Kummel at work on the Dream contest of 1956, *Maiden-forum*, Maidenform Collection, Archives Center, National Museum of American History, Smithsonian Institution (NMAH.AC.0585 Box 21 Folder 0). Pictures are credited to *Women's Wear Daily Staff Photo*. Left: Joseph and Beatrice Coleman (on the right) meet with Florence St George and Richard C. Bouton. Right: Kay Daly and staff at NC&K (fourth from the left).

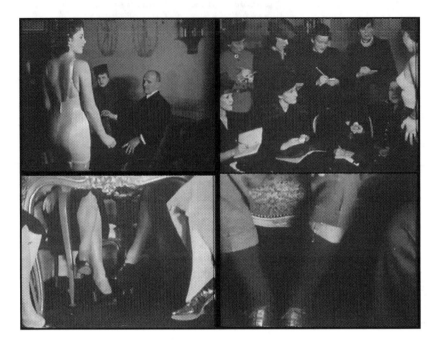

Figure 9.3 Stills from the 'Cocktail Promenade' party footage by Allan H. Mogensen, February 1939, Maidenform Collection, Archives Center, National Museum of American History, Smithsonian Institution (NMAH.AC.0585 OV 585).

whereas Seamprufe was not; but the ideas that were presented were unlikely to have been identical. The role that Fillius played in creating or modifying the pitch will remain unknown, but given that she was later credited for the work by the head of her agency (Synycia 2016), we can surmise that her intervention was critical.

The very company, having been founded by seamstress Ida Rosenthal and shopkeeper Enid Bissett, is an example of the entrepreneurial acumen of women in the industry (Peiss 2001); negotiating femininity from its founding, it adopted a 'Woman-to-Woman' marketing strategy (Synycia 2016) and fostered beauty culture as a corporate glue (Howard 2001). But this came with a continuous mediation between gender roles and standards even within Maidenform's four walls. Women who were not part of the founding family typically occupied jobs in manufacturing; the company's middling-ranks of managers, salespeople and designers were overwhelmingly male.[3] By necessity, there was a frankness in the display and discussion of the undergarments—but also a self-consciousness that this was the case.

Film footage of a new product line's 'coming out party' in 1939 gives a small glimpse into what promotional life at the company might have felt like (Figure 9.3). Professionally attired men and women are seen drinking cocktails in a smallish reception room in a high-rise building, posing, cheering and smiling for the camera, sometimes goofing around. Rather incongruously, models in a variety of bras and girdles walk among the merry party. As the event progresses, they converse with the attendees, presumably buyers, and often turn around to show their bodies from different angles. There are stolen glances, intent, surveying, appraising looks, averted or uninterested looks. One young man, conspicuous in the crowd for chewing gum, seems more interested in the models' girdled behinds than their breasts. The footage feels dominated by suited men, though one shot shows seven hatted women taking notes as Ida Rosenthal presents a model. Then, something odd: the cameraman decides to focus on the stockinged legs of a group of seated female attendees. He pans up; one woman uncrosses her legs, quickly rearranges her skirt and squeezes her legs closer together. The next shot is a close-up of a pair of male legs; the owner tugs at his trousers to cover his sock suspenders. The shot swiftly pans up to reveal his face: he is laughing and says something to the camera. There is humour at play here, a joke about the mediated gaze and its gendered implications, a momentary juxtaposition that is papered over with a tug and a chuckle but nevertheless exposes the absurdity of the camera eye's obsession with female limbs.

Though the footage predates the Dreams, they provide a genealogy to the 'dreamatic' fashion shows and cocktail parties that characterised early efforts to enchant trade partners, as well as the playful, sometimes roguish, tone used in its internal communications. Humour was clearly the company's strategy for operating in a domain where dominance over the product, the image and the gaze was contested. In a 1954 *Maiden-forum* article, for example, the bra has come to life under the care of William Rosenthal and Ernest Silvani: they sit at a table looking down at the illustration of a bra that has been propped up. An eye framed by long eyelashes sits on each cup and a pair of contoured lips animate the centre front gore (Figure 9.4). The bra's look is sultry, and her lips are slightly parted; the straps undulate downwards in an echo of the waist. Thus anthropomorphised, this hyper-feminine creature lures the gaze of the observer and seems to respond to Rosenthal and Silvani's pensive looks: a reminder that the gazed-upon can stare back. Granting her consciousness, the story details that she 'happily anticipates' being added to the product line.

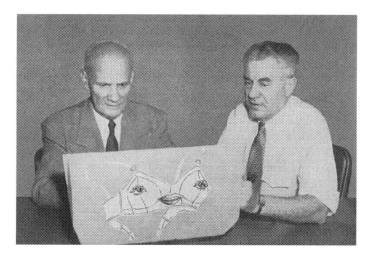

Figure 9.4 Photograph of William Rosenthal, President of Maidenform (left), and Ernest Silvani, Executive Head of the Designing Department (right). *Maiden-forum*, May-June 1954, Maidenform Collection, Archives Center, National Museum of American History, Smithsonian Institution (NMAH.AC.0585 Box 22 Folder 10).

Thus prone to celebrating the whimsical, the *Maidenform Mirror* and *Maiden-forum* are replete with examples of how the Dreams appealed to the imagination of its audiences. These include parodies and spoofs, photographs, drawings, fan letters, jokes, poems and reprints, but also retail efforts such as fanciful window displays and fashion shows. What can these ephemeral instantiations tell us? The window displays, in which the models materialised into fantastical three-dimensional scenes with mannequins or cardboard illustrations, suggest that the Dreams would not have been so offensive to the public so as to ban them from the streets, and that shoppers were ready to be amused and enchanted. Window dressing practices were developed during the 19th-century creation of the *flâneuse*, the female consumer whose gaze needed to be catered to and mobilised in the new public arenas of consumption, the department store, shopping centres and eventually the shopping mall (Friedberg 1994). Based on the participants in the frequent display contests held by Maidenform, those who seemed most successful in these arts were women.[4]

Far from mindless entertainment seekers, however, Maidenform assumed its audiences to be educated and informed. At the launch of the Dreams, Maidenform sponsored CBS's *Vanity Fair,* which was directed by Frances Buss, hosted by Dorothy Doan and invited varied guests including (the real) Maria von Trapp, Salvador Dalí and the first female commissioner of the FCC, Frieda B. Hennock (CBS 1948, 1949; Buss Buch 2005). In the episode singled out by the *Maidenform Mirror* to announce its sponsorship of the program, Doan "interviews Mrs. Eleanor Roosevelt, Madam Hasam Meta and Miss Marguerite Cowie, all three delegates to the United Nations" (*Maidenform Mirror* 1949a). The four women are depicted looking intently at each other, in earnest conversation. This show, although later described as "a magazine-style program of interviews, beauty tips and advice, and other topics of interest to housewives" (Terrace 2009, 1605), was more ambitious than this. In Buss's own description, there were "many intellectual kinds of guests on the program. Dorothy was bright enough to conduct good interviews with bright people" (2005). These interviews were bookended by product demonstrations that seemed to match their attention for detail, where Doane promoted the bra herself, "show[ing] it as though it were the finest Irish lace" (Buss in McMahon and Fisher 2007, 144) and "indicat[ing] stitching, darts, insets or any other distinctive feature, doing just what an expert salesgirl would do but doing it in the home" (*Maiden-Forum* 1949).

One set of ephemera that stands out for its communicative qualities are the photographs, drawings, paintings and anecdotes that consumers shared with Maidenform. One artefact came from Mrs. Sara Rigney, who engaged in a 'lively correspondence' with Joseph Coleman following her expression of unhappiness at the Dreams. Ending in conciliation, she sent him a picture of the abstract expressionist painting that their correspondence had inspired (*Maidenform Mirror* 1950). Although the print is small and the colouring is lost, we can just about make out an entangled female figure glancing backwards, possibly fleeing the scene. She is wearing a witch's hat, which in its pointy end transforms into a hand that is poised to grab a moon-like shape. Though the accompanying article is brief and does not describe the painting itself, it does give away a curious detail about the artist: Rigney seems to have first written to Maidenform as 'Miss Topsy Smith.' It is difficult to determine whether there was any intended meaning in her pseudonym, but passing as unmarried was a deliberate choice. Critiquing the Dreams may have come with a host of associations that she wished to escape. Did her position in society, as a married woman, change the way she and her objections would be perceived? Might she have feared, as Nochlin highlighted on the position of women critiquing the portrayal of women in the arts, "to invite derision, to reveal herself as one who does not understand the sophisticated strategies of high culture and takes art 'too literally'?" (1989, 29). Making her points as a single woman could, perhaps, have shielded her from some facile dismissals, such as being out-of-touch. Though the *Maidenform Mirror* suggests there was an amicable conclusion of Coleman and Rigney's debate, the painting could be read as an expression of the trappings of the undergarment.

Some women used the tagline as a way to subvert the power dynamic in being subjected to the public gaze. Mona Grove, a performer, wrote a letter to Maidenform to tell them that "I dreamed I danced the hula in my Maidenform bra. It was no dream! I really did!" To the apparent amusement of the audience, her sarong had slipped down to reveal her bra during a Hawaiian solo (*Maidenform Mirror* 1952). She made light of the mishap by associating it with the unruffled Dreamer who is exposed by intent. Intent was key to the subversiveness of the Dreamer in a landscape that sought to keep the female body and its undergarments hidden—asserting the tagline as one that could apply to themselves was a way to reject intimations of indecency. Thus embracing this image of self-possession, the *Maidenform Mirror* documents various women who appeared as Dreamers at fancy dress parties (usually in pairs), such as Mrs. Hugh Oldenburg and Mrs. Edward Wirka in their "I dreamed I was twins" costumes for the Blackhawk Country Club "dress-up day for golfers" (Figure 9.5, left). Oldenburg and Wirka gaze (proudly? haughtily?) into the distance as they pose for the camera, which is positioned at a low angle—a technique that aggrandises the subject. They are hatted, gloved and accessorised, but their costumes are not exact replicas of the ads. They omitted the capes, for example, that draped over the models' shoulders, and they both opted for strapped, lacy long-line bras that covered the entirety of their torsos, suspender hooks left visible. (The models, on the other hand, are wearing the strapless Pre-Lude Six-Way, one of them in the long-line version neatly tucked into her skirt.) These slight modifications, which took some wardrobe coordination, show how the costumes were put together to toe the line between recognition and comfort: although they stopped short at completely bare shoulders or midriffs, they are demonstrably wearing underwear. One might imagine the amusement in ideating, procuring and enjoying the costumes enough to send a picture to Maidenform HQ.

Apart from fancy dress occasions, the Dreams also lent other situations levity and flair, and women seemed to weave Maidenform bras into stories about their daily lives quite deliberately. In the case of archaeologist Eileen J. Boecklen, my favourite, the Dream cheekily gave expression to a practice that blurred the line between the pursuit of a profession and the pursuit of beauty. Boecklen's letter to Maidenform describes how she and her team members at an archaeological field school would take off their shirts to tan better while digging: "I went digging in my Maidenform Bra," she writes (Figure 9.5, right). The photograph enclosed shows Boecklen posing at a dig holding a pickaxe in both hands, supposedly taking a break in her arduous work. She is wearing a bra, her underpants stick out from her work trousers and she is smiling at the camera. She is the picture of confidence. Women were using the image of the Dreamer to own the image of their own publicly exposed bodies.

These anecdotes reveal a variety of attitudes towards work, play and the female body—and some are indicative of how pervasive Maidenform's figure-shaping credentials were.

Figure 9.5 Left: Two golfers pose in their 'Twins' costumes, *Maidenform Mirror*, October-November 1956, Maidenform Collection, Archives Center, National Museum of American History, Smithsonian Institution (NMAH.AC.0585 Box 20 Folder 0). Right: Eileen J. Boecklen at an archaeological dig, *Maidenform Mirror*, February 1952, Maidenform Collection, Archives Center, National Museum of American History, Smithsonian Institution (NMAH.AC.0585 Box 19 Folder 0).

Mrs. Floyd D. Strong, head of a church youth choir in Topeka, wrote in to tell of a 'cute' story that unfurled while her choir awaited an important dress shipment:

> Time was aflyin', and one of our large stores was wild with anxiety over the failure of the last shipment of the lovely blue material for 10 dresses to arrive. To make a laugh and to erase the nervousness on the part of the 10 girls (and myself) and their mothers – I clipped the full page with the caption "I dreamed I was a social butterfly" etc., and I waived it gayly at choir practices – saying to them – "We can sing for Mr. Stassen [the governor] in our Maidenform bras!" One doll of a little 13 year old piped up with "Even a Maidenform bra could do me no good!" We all roared.
> (*Maidenform Mirror* 1956)

Not only does Strong indicate that she knew the cut-out would be recognised and understood as a joke, but also that it was deemed suitable for a church-going teenage audience. The girl's quip shifted Strong's attempt from easing the team's tensions to unpicking female body ideals, which was very much focused on the breast at the time (Matelski 2017)—and they all 'roared.' Laughter, here, both affirms and dispels the pressures placed on women, the gazes that constructed their figures and the accoutrements that shaped them. Contrast this to the roundtable reprinted above, where a respondent worried whether equating sex appeal and physical appearance in bra advertising was socialising children into questionable morals. Children, then, were likely aware of the campaign and would have constructed their own meanings—some of which have survived and been related to me as vestiges of memories concerning their mothers' undergarments or their own surreptitious viewings of the ads. One mother, at least, thought her son's reimagining of the Dream was innocent enough to share with the *Maiden-forum* (Figure 9.6).

Figure 9.6 Drawing by ten-year-old Robert Baruch, son of Ann Baruch who was a Maidenform employee in Bayonne's manufacturing plant, *Maiden-forum*, November 1953, Maidenform Collection, Archives Center, National Museum of American History, Smithsonian Institution (NMAH.AC.0585 Box 22 Folder 8).

Conclusion

Emancipation and oppression tend to be constructed as binary opposites, thus providing little room in the analysis for the nuances of situational power and structural constraints, which are the levels at which cultural texts such as the Dreams operated. In this chapter, I queried whether a female gaze—one that does not automatically fall in one camp or the other—could be reconstructed by looking beyond the texts themselves and grappling with the constitutive levels of the archive, reading against the grain of its records and broadening the focus to what the campaign spawned. What this search reveals is a history that is far more complex than suggested by the common imagination of mid-century undergarment advertising as bawdy and sexist. Even the industry itself, featuring some high-profile women with celebrated careers and complex relationships to sex and gender, requires further unpacking. In 1957, model Jean Desmond, flanked by two designers, addressed the male-dominated Goodfellowship Corset Club to reject in no uncertain terms their invitation to membership, which had been extended to discourage the founding of a women's club. Daring the men to try on a girdle, she made her experiences plain: "You men don't appreciate the importance of women to this industry" (*Women's Wear Daily*, September 1957, p. 18). She was certainly not a mindless participant in the patriarchal hoax.

I contend that it is not possible to understand Maidenform's success without attempting to recover how it engaged the female gaze. The way in which Maidenform may have influenced what has been identified as the erotisation of advertising (e.g., Levine 2007; Rutherford 2007; Reichert and Lambiase 2014) hung on a living and shifting construal of gender that requires investment in a more complex theory of change (Kelly-Gadol 2015): it is not a simple trajectory from one form of oppression to another. After the Dreams, Maidenform continued to experiment widely with the gaze: first in the "Keep your eye on Maidenform" campaign, of which the television ads zoomed in on a woman's eye to concretise her gaze, then in the late 1980s ads where male celebrities spoke 'candidly' about their romantic partner's lingerie, thus explicitly bringing in the male gaze. Although they challenged the stereotype of the insipid lingerie model in the 1990s, failing to hit the mark meant that Maidenform was sometimes cast as the figurehead of an oppressive, sexualised advertising landscape. A parody published in the feminist magazine *Heresies* makes fun of Maidenform's feminist aspirations by showing a bathroom door slightly ajar, headed by "Men used to masturbate to our ads" (Van den Bossche 2014). To understand this trajectory, we must "ask more often how things happened in order to find out why they happened" (Scott 1986, 1067), and thus articulate the fields construed by the female gaze. This is to enable a history that divulges how social power is both structural and dispersed, but also where…

> …there is room for a concept of human agency as the attempt (at least partially rational) to construct an identity, a life, a set of relationships, a society with certain limits and with language—conceptual language that at once sets boundaries and contains the possibility for negation, resistance, reinterpretation, the play of metaphoric invention and imagination.
>
> (Scott 1986, 1067)

Actively seeking out the female gaze is an epistemic commitment that forces us to recognise the structural impositions, inequities and injustices that constrained the lives of women, without condemning their mental and material lives to a unilateral experience of subjugation. Agency under these conditions, and what one decided to do with it, becomes the historical quest. Reading ads by acknowledging the gendered perspectives of commentators reveals which angles we risk missing, while parodies, photographs, letters and other ephemera become repositories of the female mind. Seen through this lens, Maidenform's Dreams become more capacious: sites for setting new cultural standards as well as resisting, subverting and negotiating constraints.

Notes

1. See *Modern Screen*, November 1952, p. 85 (https://archive.org/details/modernscreen4445unse/page/n1155/)
2. An example can be seen in *Photoplay*, July 1955, p. 21 (https://archive.org/details/photoplayjuldec100macf_10/page/n26/). This is unlikely the ad that the panellist was referring to—earlier versions depicted the image in the bottom left more prominently—but the ad is notable for its voyeuristic interpellation.
3. Interestingly, several letters of correspondence between Maidenform and female designers negotiating the sale of a bra or girdle design have survived. These were bought, patent-rights included, at a fixed price ($25 to $100)—freelancers did not retain royalty rights.
4. Alternatively, there may be a selection bias at play here: women display designers celebrated their creations and sent them in to the contests, where male designers might not. Either way, it is indicative of a form of engagement and potentially pride in their work.

References

Barthes, Roland. 1972. *Mythologies*. New York: Moonday Press; Farrar, Straus & Giroux.
Berger, John. 1972. *Ways of Seeing-*. London: BBC and Penguin Books.

Blécourt, Willem de. 2017. "Witches on Screen." In *The Oxford Illustrated History of Witchcraft and Magic*, edited by Owen Davies, 253–280. Oxford: Oxford University Press.
Broadcasting. 1957. "Art Directors Study Visual Ads," June 3, 1957.
Buss Buch, Frances. 2005. *Talking about Dorothy Doan Interview by Karen Herman. Moving Image*. Television Academy Foundation. https://interviews.televisionacademy.com/people/dorothy-doan.
CBS. 1948. *Vanity Fair, a CBS Television Interview Show. From Left to Right, Gil Fates, Dorothy Doan and Frieda B. Hennock*. Photograph. Getty Images. https://www.gettyimages.com.au/detail/news-photo/vanity-fair-a-cbs-television-interview-show-from-left-to-news-photo/1189663836.
CBS. 1949. *Dorothy Doan with Salvador Dali for "Vanity Fair" Television Program*. Photograph. News Photo – Getty Images. https://www.gettyimages.com.au/detail/news-photo/dorothy-doan-with-salvador-dali-for-vanity-fair-television-news-photo/107783779.
Coleman, Barbara J. 1995. "Maidenform(Ed): Images of American Women in the 1950s." *Genders* 21: 3.
Doane, Mary Ann. 1982. "Film and the Masquerade: Theorising the Female Spectator." *Screen* 23 (3–4): 74–88. https://doi.org/10.1093/screen/23.3-4.74.
Fox, Stephen R. 1984. *The Mirror Makers: A History of American Advertising and Its Creators*. 1st ed. New York: Morrow.
Friedberg, Anne. 1994. *Window Shopping: Cinema and the Postmodern*. University of California Press. https://www-fulcrum-org.gold.idm.oclc.org/concern/monographs/rv042t566.
Gamman, Lorraine, and Margaret Marshment. 1988. *The Female Gaze: Women as Viewers of Popular Culture*. London: Women's Press.
Greene, Heather. 2018. *Bell, Book and Camera: A Critical History of Witches in American Film and Television*. Jefferson, NC: McFarland.
Hickey, Margaret. 1956. "Do Americans Commercialize Sex?" *Ladies Home Journal* 73 (10), October 1956. ProQuest Vogue Archive.
Howard, Vicki. 2001. "'At the Curve Exchange': Postwar Beauty Culture and Working Women at Maidenform." In *Beauty and Business: Commerce, Gender, and Culture in Modern America*, edited by Philip Scranton, 195–216. Hagley Perspectives on Business and Culture. New York ; London: Routledge.
Institute for Motivational Research. 1958a. *The Motivations of Word-of-Mouth Advertising/How Advertising and Word-of-Mouth Influence Each Other*. Marlborough: Adam Matthew Digital.
Institute for Motivational Research. 1958b. *The Motivating Response Patterns to Two Maidenform and One [Playtex] Commercials*. Marlborough: Adam Matthew Digital. http://www.consumer-culture.amdigital.co.uk/Documents/Details/Hagley_Dichter_BX042_959TV.
Kelly-Gadol, Joan. 2015. "The Social Relation of the Sexes: Methodological Implications of Women's History." In *Just Methods : An Interdisciplinary Feminist Reader*, edited by Alison M. Jaggar, 6–13. Routledge. https://www.taylorfrancis.com/books/9781315636344.
Levine, Elana. 2007. *Wallowing in Sex: The New Sexual Culture of 1970s American Television*. Durham, NC: Duke University Press.
Lyons, Nancy. 2005. "Interpretive Reading of Two Maidenform Bra Advertising Campaigns." *Clothing and Textiles Research Journal* 23 (4): 322–332.
Maidenform Mirror. 1949a. "Maiden Form Adds TV to New Advertising Schedule," October 1949. NMAH.AC.0585 Box 19, Folder 0. Maidenform Collection, 1922–1997, Archives Center, National Museum of American History.
Maidenform Mirror. 1949b. "Maiden Form's 'Dream Series' Hits the Airways on WOR," October 1949. NMAH.AC.0585 Box 19, Folder 0. Maidenform Collection, 1922–1997, Archives Center, National Museum of American History.
Maidenform Mirror. 1950. "Maiden Form's Dream Ads Provoke Artist's 'Nightmare,'" August 1950. NMAH.AC.0585 Box 19, Folder 0. Maidenform Collection, 1922–1997, Archives Center, National Museum of American History.

Maidenform Mirror. 1952. "Nice People," February 1952. NMAH.AC.0585 Box 19, Folder 0. Maidenform Collection, 1922–1997, Archives Center, National Museum of American History.

Maidenform Mirror. 1956. "Harold Stassen Almost 'Feted' by Topeka Church Choir 'in Their Maidenform Bras,'" March 1956. NMAH.AC.0585 Box 20, Folder 0. Maidenform Collection, 1922–1997, Archives Center, National Museum of American History.

Maiden-Forum. 1949. "Maiden Form Makes Bow over TV," December 1949. NMAH.AC.0585 Box 22, Folder 5. Maidenform Collection, 1922–1997, Archives Center, National Museum of American History.

Marling, Karal Ann. 1994. *As Seen on TV: The Visual Culture of Everyday Life in the 1950s.* Cambridge, MA; London: Harvard University Press.

Matelski, Elizabeth. 2017. *Reducing Bodies: Mass Culture and the Female Figure in Postwar America.* London: Routledge.

McMahon, Ed, and David C. Fisher. 2007. *When Television Was Young: The Inside Story with Memories by Legends of the Small Screen.* Nashville, TN: Thomas Nelson.

Mordhorst, Mads. 2008. "From Counterfactual History to Counternarrative History." *Management & Organizational History* 3 (1): 5–26. https://doi.org/10.1177/1744935908090995.

Mulvey, Laura. 1975. "Visual Pleasure and Narrative Cinema." *Screen* 16 (3): 6–18.

Mulvey, Laura. 1989. "Afterthroughts on 'Visual Pleasure and Narrative Cinema' Inspired by King Vidor's *Duel in the Sun* (1946)." In *Visual and Other Pleasures*, edited by Laura Mulvey, 29–38. London: Palgrave Macmillan.

Nelson, Michelle R. 2008. "The Hidden Persuaders." *Journal of Advertising* 37 (1): 113–126. https://doi.org/10.2753/JOA0091-3367370109.

Nochlin, Linda. 1989. *Women, Art, and Power and Other Essays.* New York: Westview Press.

Olin, Margaret. 2003. "Gaze." In *Critical Terms for Art History, Second Edition*, edited by Robert S. Nelson and Richard Shiff, 318–329. Chicago, IL: University of Chicago Press.

Packard, Vance. 1957. *The Hidden Persuaders.* London: Penguin Books.

Patterson, Maurice, and Richard Elliott. 2002. "Negotiating Masculinities: Advertising and the Inversion of the Male Gaze." *Consumption Markets & Culture* 5 (3): 231–249. https://doi.org/10.1080/10253860290031631.

Peiss, Kathy. 2001. "On Beauty… and the History of Business." In *Beauty and Business: Commerce, Gender, and Culture in Modern America*, edited by Philip Scranton, pp. 7–22. Hagley Perspectives on Business and Culture. New York; London: Routledge.

Reichert, Tom, and Jacqueline Lambiase. 2014. *Sex in Advertising: Perspectives on the Erotic Appeal.* New York: Routledge.

Rome, Alexandra Serra, Stephanie O'Donohoe, and Susan Dunnett. 2020. "Problematizing the Postfeminist Gaze: A Critical Exploration of Young Women's Readings of Gendered Power Relations in Advertising." *Journal of Macromarketing* 40 (4): 546–562. https://doi.org/10.1177/0276146720950765.

Rutherford, Paul. 2007. *A World Made Sexy: Freud to Madonna.* Toronto: University of Toronto Press.

Sassatelli, Roberta. 2011. "Interview with Laura Mulvey: Gender, Gaze and Technology in Film Culture." *Theory, Culture & Society* 28 (5): 123–143. https://doi.org/10.1177/0263276411398278.

Schroeder, Jonathan E., and Detlev Zwick. 2004. "Mirrors of Masculinity: Representation and Identity in Advertising Images." *Consumption Markets & Culture* 7 (1): 21–52. https://doi.org/10.1080/1025386042000212383.

Schwarzkopf, Stefan. 2015. "Marketing History from Below: Towards a Paradigm Shift in Marketing Historical Research." Edited by Stefan Schwarzkopf. *Journal of Historical Research in Marketing; Bingley* 7 (3): 295–309.

Scott, Joan W. 1986. "Gender: A Useful Category of Historical Analysis." *The American Historical Review* 91 (5): 1053–1075. https://doi.org/10.2307/1864376.

Scott, Linda M. 2006. *Fresh Lipstick: Redressing Fashion and Feminism.* Reprint edition. New York: Palgrave Macmillan.

Scott, Linda M. 2015. "Woodbury Soap: Classic Sexual Sell or Just Good Marketing?" *Advertising & Society Review* 16 (1). https://doi.org/10.1353/asr.2015.0008.
Sturken, Marita, and Lisa Cartwright. 2018. *Practices of Looking: An Introduction to Visual Culture*. Third edition. New York: Oxford University Press.
Synycia, Natasha. 2016. "Ida Rosenthal and Her Maidenformidable Empire: Booming Business and Dreamy Advertising in Postwar United States." Ph.D., United States, University of California, Irvine.
Tadajewski, Mark. 2010. "Enest Dichter, Motivation Research and the 'Century of the Consumer.'" In *Ernest Dichter and Motivation Research: New Perspectives on the Making of Post-War Consumer Culture*, edited by Stefan Schwarzkopf and Rainer Gries, 91–106. London: Palgrave Macmillan. http://www.palgrave.com/us/book/9780230537996.
Terrace, Vincent. 2009. *Encyclopedia of Television Shows, 1925 Through 2007*. Jefferson, NC: McFarland.
Van den Bossche, Astrid. 2014. "The Id Goes Shopping in Its Maidenform Bra: Navigating Gender Spheres in the Postwar 'Dreams' Campaign." *Advertising & Society Review* 15 (2). https://doi.org/ 10.1353/asr.2014.0012.
Van den Bossche, Astrid. 2019. "Paper I – Dreamatic Undergarments: Recovering the Material Orchestrations of the Maidenform 'I Dreamed…' Campaign." Advertising as Orchestration: Papers on Attuning Cognition and History in the Study of Persuasion (Doctoral Dissertation), University of Oxford, Oxford.
Warhol, Robyn R., and Diane Price Herndl. 1997. *Feminisms: An Anthology of Literary Theory and Criticism*. Second edition. New Brunswick, NJ: Rutgers University Press.
Williamson, Judith. 1978. *Decoding Advertisements: Ideology and Meaning in Advertising*. Ideas in Progress. London: Boyars.
Zeitlyn, David. 2012. "Anthropology in and of the Archives: Possible Futures and Contingent Pasts. Archives as Anthropological Surrogates." *Annual Review of Anthropology* 41 (1): 461–480. https://doi.org/10.1146/annurev-anthro-092611-145721.

10 From identity politics to the politics of power
Men, masculinities and transnational patriarchies in marketing and consumer research

Wendy Hein and Jeff Hearn

As with the feminist mantra 'the personal is political', men, masculinities and transnational patriarchies have deeply shaped all facets of life, including our own. As this chapter has been written during the time of Covid-19, how can we begin a chapter on transpatriarchies, as a shorthand, in marketing and consumer research (MCR)? How can we begin any chapter these days without looking at our personal lives first? In many ways, we all live in tight 'bubbles' these days and are confronted with our unique histories. So, how can we not look at our personal lives to understand transpatriarchies and their impact on us? Both authors have had different journeys, yet both share a deep connection to transnational movements and developments, which, we believe, help us illustrate the importance of why and how critical perspectives of men, masculinities and transpatriarchies matter, with a particular focus on the context of representations.

We therefore begin this chapter by providing some background to our childhood and how we have come to live our mobile lives, followed by a more mainstream review of how the study of men and masculinities emerged in MCR. Subsequently, we offer fundamental theories linked to feminist, critical studies of men and masculinities (CSMM), including transpatriarchies, seeking to maintain and to add to the momentum gained by collective research efforts which have started to change MCR towards greater considerations of power and transnational gender relations. Flash forward to our contemporary lives, we highlight how MCR needs to play a greater role in raising the gender equality agenda by offering insights into how transpatriarchies and the hegemony of men affect all our lives via continued systemic and structural, unequal gender power relations.

Biographical notes from the authors

There are always many ways of telling biographical stories. For me, Jeff, one way is to talk of growing up in London with my mother, sister, nearby grandmothers and a somewhat distant father, all making their way and trying to 'do their best' after the traumas of the Second World War. Another is the experience of infant school from five to seven, where my best friends were three girls – Gillian, Judith and Mavis – never to be seen again with the totally 'normal' move at seven to all-boys junior school, followed by all-boys grammar school – and then a men-only college at university in the 1960s, even while Women's Liberation begun to flourish. I liked music from Melanie, Bob Dylan and Neil Young, and then a little later, John Prine and the Roche Sisters – all, apart from Young, from the US (see Hearn and Melechi 1992). In the late 1970s, I became heavily involved in men's broadly anti-sexist consciousness-raising groups and activities, and under-fives campaigning for better provisions for pre-school children and

DOI: 10.4324/9781003042587-12

their carers, in practice mainly mothers, and after a while realised that personal-political agendas merged with those in academia and research. I didn't feel comfortable in how I was expected to behave 'as a man'. Patriarchy was pretty much everywhere and pretty obvious, and was heavily inflected with class, race and racism, and much more. And again, moving to Finland in the late 1990s meant learning all about gender and patriarchy in a different way. The world still is immensely patriarchal, even if its forms have shifted and elaborated, not least through the spread of information and communication technologies (ICTs) and intensifying ecological damage.

Wendy's journey begins in Berlin in the 1980s, born into a home where my mother had been the 'breadwinner' and my father a mature student. This would change as I grew up and moved across different parts of Germany, as my father's career slowly took precedence and my mother, a kindergarten teacher, moved on to work as a main carer for my sister and me. Germany, especially Berlin, in the 1980s was thriving culturally within its national borders, as I vividly remember Peter Schilling's 'Major Tom – Völlig losgelöst' competing for the number one chart spot with Nena's '99 Luftballons', adding their voices to the immensely influential 'New German Wave' (or Neue Deutsche Welle). German language music dominated and touched a cultural nerve by tackling politics and technology, often via a post-punk sarcasm. Women and men appeared in the media – at least in my childhood memories – as equals. Certainly not in equal numbers, but women were allowed to be fierce, loud and visible. I was a tomboy, immensely active, never able to sit still. My experiences of patriarchy linked to expectations of behaving like a 'good', quiet girl, which increased as I grew older and moved to more conservative areas in Germany. Upon finishing school, I benefitted from the freedoms brought along by further European integration, which allowed me to live and study in various countries – Ireland and Spain in particular – and which eventually led me to start career and family in the UK in the 2000s. Patriarchy continues to shape my life and the life of those around me, across countries, places and spaces, which makes me think how things could be different.

Contextualising the authors' narratives within broader cultural representations of their time, the 1970s and 1980s saw their share of resistance and rebellion, even within the mainstream as, for example, seen in the case of David Bowie (Lindridge and Eagar 2015). The UK produced its own 'New Wave' music in the 1980s, with groups such as Duran Duran featuring heavily in the charts. It was this time where men often had longer hair than women, women wore leather jackets, arm and headbands; despite its temporary resonance, the effeminate, gender-fluid male look would soon find its demise in the backlash era of the 1990s (Mort 1996; Nixon 1996). Music and representations are equally nested within the politics and socioeconomics of their time. Germany, along with France and the Nordic region, represented powerful counter movements to the drastically liberal politics of the US and the UK. Instead of privatising markets, their post-war politics were based on state-provisions with greater investments, in their respective ways, in social and care infrastructures. These political directions continue their impact within those countries to this day.[1] On the other hand, the Reagan/Thatcher politics that triumphed in the 1980s set the scene for the neoliberal politics that shape all our lives today, particularly within the Western world.

How does all this link to men, masculinities, transpatriarchies and feminism? Ultimately, experiences, identities and representations cannot be removed from the systemic values, ideologies and structures that produce them. It also shows how we engage in and co-produce these structures, and appropriate values from a very young age, highlighting the importance of care in early years in particular. Patriarchy or transpatriarchies emerge as much in and as the macro forces that build our global politics, relations and institutions, including markets and consumption, as in the micro forces reflected in the whirl of everyday life. This chapter then aims to contribute to a surge of feminist writing in MCR that seeks to call out the more systematic gender power relations within marketing and consumption within the previously depoliticised research on men and masculinities with its heavy focus on representation and identity.

Men, masculinities and gender representations in MCR

Men have often been the protagonists within MCR, yet, until relatively recently, remained notably ungendered in this research (see Belk and Costa 1998; Schouten and McAlexander 1995; Wooten 2006). The initial and explicit gendering of men and masculinities can be mainly attributed to influences from other disciplines whose research focused on images and representations. Research from Cultural Studies, including work from Frank Mort and his 1980s effeminate 'New Man' imagery (1988, 1996), followed by the 1990s 'New Lad' backlash discourse (Nixon 1992, 1996, 1997), heavily shaped initial studies on this topic in MCR. Examples include research on representations and the inversion of the gaze, or 'mirrors of masculinity' (Patterson and Elliott 2002; Schroeder and Zwick 2004),[2] which sparked an interest in men's real-life engagements with ads (Elliott and Elliott 2005) and self-presentations as negotiated through popular and normative discourses (Östberg 2010). This extended to research about the rise of the metrosexual male in the 2000s (Tuncay 2006; Tuncay and Otnes 2008a, 2008b) closely followed by the übersexual (Rinallo 2007) or retrosexual (Östberg 2013). This surge of research on men and masculinities in MCR led to an increasing awareness that men too were gendered (Östberg 2012a, 2012b).

Parallel and linked to research on representations, men's lived identities emerged in MCR. As before, this research benefitted from discussions in other disciplines, particularly drawing on debates surrounding masculinity in crisis (Horrocks 1994; Pleck 1995). For example, consumption became a resource for the construction of heroic (Holt and Thompson 2004), phallic (Thompson and Holt 2004) and productive (Moisio et al. 2013) men and masculinities. Playing and (re)inventing masculine norms has been central to this research, as, for example, linked to negotiations of 'safe' and 'dangerous zones' (Rinallo 2007). The explicit gendering of men and masculinities linked to increasing vulnerabilities and potential crises within men, alongside their continued ambivalence, was central to studies on men's consumption traditionally associated with women's practices, with implications for shopping and retail spaces (Otnes and McGrath 2001; Tuncay and Otnes 2008a, 2008b). Despite a focus on men as gendered, once again, the gendering aspects were still neglected. Studies of men and masculinities were largely directed by the Consumer Culture Theory (CCT) tradition (Arnould and Thompson 2005), where research on the commodified male addressed issues of lifestyle, fashion, body consumption and 'new forms' of masculinities (see Edwards 1997; Simpson 1994; Osgerby 2001). MCR followed the lure of the text and the visual, which led to research on identity politics. However, rather than addressing 'the political' within identities, this research remained void of challenges or critiques of existing gender power structures (based on feminist theorisations of men and masculinities, for example).

Research has since then expanded the boundaries of men and masculinities in MCR, for example, linking to discussions of men in domestic roles and the gendering of 'the private' (see Gentry and Harrison 2010; Coskuner-Balli and Thompson 2013), men's gender relations and socialisations (Littlefield and Ozanne 2011) or humour in gender and gendering practices (Hein and O'Donohoe 2014), all of which mainly focus on identity constructions. As we can see from recent research, the gendering of men and masculinities through MCR has had their impact of men's consumption, arguably leading to greater inclusivity in some areas (Petrylaite and Hart 2021). Nevertheless, further and wider issues such as patriarchy and patriarchal relations remain widely neglected. While this body of work has significantly added to our understandings and theorisations of gender within MCR, research on men and masculinities still has to address deeper issues of gender power relations (Hearn and Hein 2015). In response to this, we now come to examine the growing research area of critical studies on men and masculinities and the theorising of transpatriarchies.

What is the critical study of men, masculinities and transpatriarchies?

From a critical and feminist perspective, gender is shorthand for a complex set of embodied, institutionalised structures, practices and processes, and one of the most fundamental and powerful structuring principles of most societies. Gender is not equivalent to either sex or sexuality, nor indeed is it to women and femininity; rather, it equally concerns men, masculinities and LGBT*IQA+ people and social movements. Gender is a matter of relations constructed with local and broader gender orders. Global and transnational gender relations are (still) characterised by various forms of male dominance, although of course with huge variations in the form and extent of that dominance, and the myriad complexities and complications in gender regimes – and thereby how this various forms of dominance relate to and impact on MCR.

Similar to some of the trends we have seen in MCR, studying men, and indeed policy development on men and boys, have become more popular in recent years across many parts of the world, perhaps most notably through the work of MenEngage Alliance and its members networks. Yet studying men is not anything special and not anything new. In fact, men, and women, have studied men for centuries, but often as an 'absent presence'. Academia, academic canons and academic disciplines, including MCR, are all full of books and articles by men, on men, for men (Prothero and McDonagh 2021)! And studying men is not necessarily in itself linked to progressive social change; it all depends on how it is done and can easily even be retrogressive.

Critical studies on men and masculinities

It is contradictory that Critical Studies on Men and Masculinities (CSMM), as a series of attempts to study men and masculinities differently from the malestream, has developed. CSMM has expanded considerably over the last 40 years or more (see Kimmel et al. 2004; Gottzén et al. 2019). CSMM refers to critical, explicitly gendered studies of men and masculinities that engage with feminist and other critical gender scholarship, as opposed to non-gendered, non-feminist or anti-feminist scholarship. They comprise *historical, cultural, relational, materialist, deconstructive, anti-essentialist* studies on men (Hearn and Pringle 2006). The idea that the gendering of men derives from a fixed, inner trait or core is antagonistic to CSMM; men are not essentialised or reified. Studies range from masculine psychology to ethnographies of certain men's and boys' activities; to investigations of masculinities in specific discourses; and then onto broader societal, collective and more global analyses of men. Many studies have been local, personal, bodily, immediate, interpersonal, as in the so-called 'ethnographic moment' (see Connell 2000), but increasingly there is the turn to the place of men and masculinities in the 'big (historico-spatial-socio-political) picture' (Connell 1993).

The broad critical approach to men and masculinities in CSMM can be characterised in recognising men and masculinities as *explicitly gendered*, emphasising men's and boys' differential relations to *gendered power*. Accordingly, men and masculinities are seen: as *socially constructed, produced and reproduced*, rather than as 'naturally' one way or another; as *variable and changing* across time (history) and space (culture), within societies and through life courses and biographies; and spanning the *material, the discursive* and the *intersections of gendering with other social divisions*.

Beginning from the critique of sex role theory, the most developed and well-cited approach in CSMM is that in which masculinities – hegemonic, complicit, subordinated and marginalised masculinities – are differentially framed in relation to theorising of patriarchy and patriarchal relations, that is, including men's unequal relations to men, as well as men's relations to women (for example, Connell 1987, 1995; Carrigan et al. 1985). The concept of hegemonic masculinity has been a central pillar, while other masculinities, in particular complicit masculinity, have been taken up far less in critical analysis. Hegemonic masculinity has been defined variously, most notably as "… the configuration of gender practice which embodies the currently accepted answer to the problem of legitimacy of patriarchy, which guarantees (or is taken to guarantee) the dominant position of men and the subordination of women" (Connell 1995: 77). These gendered processes operate at institutional, interpersonal and intrapsychic (psychodynamics) levels, along with contradictions, contestations and long-term historical gender transformations. Masculinities theory has been extremely important and influential, with many applications and many different interpretations, and hegemonic masculinity in particular, in theoretical, empirical and policy studies (see Connell and Messerschmidt 2005; Hearn et al. 2012; Morrell et al. 2012), along with a range of critiques of masculinities theory and the concept of hegemonic masculinity (see Hearn 2004, 2012).

From masculinities to the gender hegemony of men

We now turn to two key challenges for masculinities theory, for CSMM more generally and for MCR. Specifically, in focusing primarily on and so de-naturalising multiple masculinities, men as a social category may be re-naturalised in assuming it is the variation in masculinities that is at issue, with less attention to the given social category of men. The primary focus on the diversity of masculinities may inadvertently divert attention from interrogation of the social category of men, and even naturalise men. In this sense, hegemony has often been applied in a relatively restricted way in some applications of hegemonic masculinity. On the other hand, we may ask: what is more hegemonic than the social category of men? This is fertile ground for critical analyses in MCR. Indeed, many contemporary forms of marketing research has pointed to greater variations in masculinities yet solidified the category of men.

Thus, we are more concerned here with *the hegemony of men* and gender hegemony. Thus, when speaking of 'men', we do not refer to any essence or given-ness. Rather, men are best understood as both a *social category* formed by the gender system, and *collective and individual agents*, often dominant, though not necessarily so, together constituting the hegemony of men (Hearn 2004, 2017) or, more widely, gender hegemony. While there is much literature and politics problematising 'women' as a category, 'men' is much less problematised as a social category, typically *not* so problematised even within CSMM.

Dominant uses of the social category of men are contested and contingent in many ways. First, the assumption that men are based in the biological is typically seen as foundational, even though it is difficult to give a foundational definition of what male is: chromosomal, hormonal, genital, somatic and so on. Second, the notion of men is variable historically across time and cultures – as is clear in the multifarious gender patterns, including transgender, non-binary and third sexes/genders across societies. Third, the category of men is used differentially, as individuals, groups of men, all men, the gender of men, in state, military, educational, medical and religious discourses, and in discursive, rhetorical and other ploys. Fourth, there are the shifting relations of identity, physiological variation, embodiments and social movements, as in LGBT★IQA+, gender ambiguous, gender plural (Monro 2005) and gender diverse politics and practice. Fifth, the differential definitions of age and generation, in terms of the social definitions of boys, young men, old men, disabled men, dying men, as well as men cast as insane or outcast in other ways, problematise a clear concept of men. Sixth, the diffusion of ICTs and other bio- and socio-technologies facilitates the creation of, for example, virtual men and non-binary categories. Seventh, the social category of men is (re)created in interplay with other social categories, such as class, ethnicity and sexuality. Finally, there are human-animal relations. To analyse the hegemony of men, men need to be thoroughly de-naturalised and deconstructed, as postcolonial theory deconstructs the white subject or queer theory the sexual subject.

From the ethnographic moment to trans(national)patriarchies

A second challenge for CSMM, and thereby for MCR, concerns moves from the local ethnographic moment(s) in studying masculinities to global, postcolonial and transnational approaches (Varman and Belk 2012; Hearn 2017). Interestingly here, formulations of both hegemony and patriarchy have characteristically been based on a single society or nation (Bocock 1986). Thus, in the cited definition of hegemonic masculinity, "… the configuration of gender practice which embodies the currently accepted answer to the problem of legitimacy of *patriarchy*, which guarantees (or is taken to guarantee) the dominant position of men and the subordination of women" (Connell 1995: 77) (our emphasis), it is this reference to patriarchy that needs to be *transnationalised*. The contextualisation of much, probably most, research on men and masculinities, even within and while recognising patriarchy, has been framed at the national or societal, 'methodologically nationalist', level, rather than transnational.

Despite insights on the relations of men, masculinities, nation and nationalism, gendering men has often remained primarily within confines of the nation-state or supra-nation-state, as in the case of the EU. This leads to reconsiderations of changing forms of neopatriarchy, neoliberal patriarchy and 'neoliberal neopatriarchy' (Campbell 2014), and transnational patriarchies in making sense of contemporary neoliberalism and globalisation. Indeed, in simultaneously affirming and deconstructing the nation, transnationalisation(s) is perhaps a more useful term than globalisation.

For example, while local patterns of work, or its lack, are still the major context for much labour market activity, globalisation challenges gendered work divisions, for example, through economic restructurings and migrations. The impacts of gendered global relations of production and reproduction are very uneven (Scott et al. 2011), often contradictory, as we can also see in markets such as sex tourism (Hein et al. 2016). Globalisation, seemingly paradoxically, creates, even liberates and constrains, even oppresses – even at the same time for the same people and groups. In many global processes, physical and virtual, particular groups of men are the main purveyors of power (Connell 1993; Hearn 2015). Intensification of gender inequalities proceeds by extending the means for accumulation and concentration of resources around those already with more resources – through increased mobility of labour, technologies, industry, production and reproduction. Gendered globalisation is severely complicated by financial crisis, that is, gendered financial crises (Walby 2015; Maclean 2016). This applies in the gendered structuring of moves to the financialisation of capitalism, and the consequent very uneven growth and development, and intensifying financial linkages, all gendered. Economic crisis highlights gendered aspects and biases in policy development (Young et al. 2011).

Concentrations of capital are increasing, and inequalities growing in China and much of Europe and North America, though not in all of Latin America. In the early 2010s, it was reported how the richest "1% are getting richer and the 99% are getting poorer. The wealth of the world's 475 billionaires is now worth the combined income of the bottom half of humanity" (Nixon 2012; also Fuentes-Nieva and Galasso 2014; Hardoon et al. 2016). By 2020, the situation has escalated. The Oxfam report, *Time to Care* (Coffey et al. 2020), reported "The world's 2,153 billionaires have more wealth than the 4.6 billion people who make up 60 percent of the planet's population". This is not only an issue of wealth inequality but is deeply gendered and raced, with wealthy elites accumulating "vast fortunes at the expense of ordinary people and particularly poor women and girls:

- The 22 richest men in the world have more wealth than all the women in Africa.
- Women and girls put in 12.5 billion hours of unpaid care work each and every day—a contribution to the global economy of at least $10.8 trillion a year, more than three times the size of the global tech industry.
- Getting the richest one percent to pay just 0.5 percent extra tax on their wealth over the next 10 years would equal the investment needed to create 117 million jobs in sectors such as elderly and childcare, education and health" (Oxfam 2020).

If this does not provide evidence for the impact of gender on the systematic, globally unequal distribution of wealth, a recent briefing by US Aid (2021) explained how and that gender inequality is causing poverty, not the other way around. This means that any effort to reduce inequities requires the tackling of transnational gender inequality first. Related to tackling these inequities, global and transnational corporate managerial elites remain highly gendered. The 'transnational capitalist class' (Sklair 2001) is in practice very much a male transnational capitalist class. Men's domination continues at the highest corporate levels, with relatively little gender change at high levels over time, even with greater numbers of women in some arenas of middle management and the established professions. Gender divisions of managerial control are also maintained partly through men's domination of engineering and ICT industries, even with greater dispersal away from Western centres to India, for example (Poster 2013). Global restructuring has led to the movement of capital, finance and industrial production, and facilitated large-scale, often precarious, employment, predominantly for women as cheap *labour*.

Movements of women into the labour market have involved both rural-urban migration and cross-national migration, and disruption of local gender orders and their relations of production and reproduction. Childcare and other reproductive care work, as also studied in recent transformative consumer research (Steinfield et al. 2019a), are restructured to become the everyday responsibility of relatives and others in local communities, mirroring patterns long established in some regions, for example, Southern Africa. Gendered labour migrations based on shifts in reproductive labour include global care chains, for example, beyond Eastern Europe and global nurse care chains, for example, from the Philippines. These care chains are deeply embedded, normalised and frequently invisibilised within dispersed private worlds, and now possibly exposed during Covid-19, as research on global au pair work highlights (Cox 1997, 2014). Furthermore, global shifts affect men and women unevenly, with the loss of assumption of life-long employment for many, including those in the global North formerly reliant on manufacturing or extractive industries.

Gendered and contradictory global change also concerns consumption flows (Kravets and Sandikci 2014), online image manufacture (Gurrieri and Drenten 2019) and transnational branding as essential aspects of MCR (Cayla and Eckhardt 2008). With growing inequalities, what may be a routine purchase of, say, trainers, in one part of the world may become a reason to mug or kill in another (Ratele 2014). Transnational commercialisation of sex, sexuality and sexual violence is another aspect of globalisation (Hein et al. 2016), with expansions of relatively new configurations of flesh/online sex industry. Virtualisation processes, the new normal of marketing in at least many parts of the world, present sites for both reinforcements and contestations of hegemony in terms of bodily presence/absence of men. ICTs bring contradictory effects for men's and women's gendering, sexuality and violences, as men act as producers and consumers of virtuality, represent women in virtual media and are themselves represented.

To make sense of all this means moving beyond limiting patriarchy, like hegemony, to a particular society or nation. In the contemporary world, the concept of patriarchy is now even more useful in looking at gender relations beyond the personal and interpersonal, and towards the global and the transnational. Gender hegemony can be seen in terms of not just patriarchy but as transnational patriarchies, or transpatriarchies, combining patriarchies, intersectionalities and transnationalisations. Transpatriarchies speak of the structural tendency and individualised propensity for men's transnational gender domination – focusing on non-determined structures, forces and processes, not totalising unity or fixity. Within transnational patriarchal processes, the transnational carries overlapping meanings, both reaffirming and deconstructing the nation, as in:

- *moving across* something or *between* two and more national boundaries;
- *metamorphosing*, problematising, blurring, transgressing, even dissolving national boundaries;
- *creating new configurations*, intensified transnational, supranational, deterritorialised, dematerialised or virtual entities (Hearn and Blagojević 2013).

Transnationalisations, as noted, take many forms and have many implications for men and gender relations. They comprise acutely contradictory processes, with multiple forms of difference, presence and absence for men in power (Haase et al. 2016) and men dispossessed (El Jurdi and Ourahmoune 2021), with the latter receiving rarely attention in MCR. Movements from the national to the transnational can be more voluntary or more involuntary (Sharifonnasabi et al. 2020); structural, institutional, organisational or individual; or through complex webs and networks (Djedidi et al. 2017). Structured patriarchal gender domination shifts from being limited to domestic, national or societal contexts towards transnational contexts. These are historico-geographical processes, moving from the domestic and the individual to nation-state to the transnational: new forms of trans(national)patriarchies.

Within transpatriarchies, gendered distribution of wealth and well-being, presence/absence of sustainable gender egalitarian social and political arrangements and long-term environmental (un)sustainability are strongly interconnected. Men's practices are heavily embedded in social, economic and cultural relations so that men's transnational dominant or complicit practices are easily equated with that seen as normal. In contrast to the call for "equality, liberty and fraternity [or responsible solidarity]", economic exploitation and inequalities are both anti-democratic in themselves and facilitated by anti-democratic movements, and these social forces together facilitate ecological damage, all dominated by certain groups of men – against the interests of the mass of people.

Transnational processes and transpatriarchies entail intersections of gender relations with *inter alia* citizenship, ethnicity, location, migration, movement, nationality, racialisation, religion, space (Steinfield et al. 2019b). Multiple transnational patriarchal arenas range from transnational business and global finance corporations and governmental organisations, and the persistence of the hegemony of men in dominating global value chains (McCarthy et al. 2020), to military institutions and the arms trade, international sports industries, and bio-medical industries and transfers, through to arenas of migration, religion, virtualisation, environmental change, knowledge production – and marketing and consumption (Hearn 2015: 20–21). Transnationalisations involve a variety of transnational spaces: physical, social, virtual. Changing relations of national and transnational space have different implications for power, prestige and wealth – raising different connections between men, transnationalisation and social stratification. Different groups of men move transnationally, between nations, more or less situated in and between different national and transnational realms, with variable consequences depending on their political-economic power and prestige.

Importantly, transpatriarchies operate partly in the flesh, partly virtually, creating new forms of extended power for certain groupings of men. Apart from extensions of transnational patriarchal power, as through new technologies, corporate concentrations or ecological damage, they facilitate processes of transnational individual and collective *non-responsibility* of men; problems created are held to be the business of others elsewhere, as part of a long history of patriarchal imperialism and colonialism. Such changes bring processes of loss of entitlement and privilege for some men. Such losses, or perceived losses, of power among certain groupings of men interplay with processes of sustaining and recouping of patriarchal power. In such ways local men and local masculinities increasingly need to be understood within the contexts of *trans(national) patriarchal hegemony of men*.

How do men, masculinities and transpatriarchies matter in marketing?

Contrasting these conceptualisations with dominant research on men and masculinities in MCR, we can recognise how men's power and the politics of gender relations have remained largely invisible and arguably even silent. Paying due credit to this research, it introduced men and masculinities as gendered to marketing scholarship to a point where men realised they were actively marketed to, and not just producers of marketing discourses (Nixon and Crewe 2004). Men became targets, segments, not dissimilar to women. Their role as consumers was thus firmly established, and along with it, the multiple masculinities of a man, both in individual and in relational terms. It seemed men were suddenly made conscious that they too are consumers who depend on commercial discourses for the construction of their identities, linked to a marketing dependency to display power and compensate for their insecurities (Witkowski 2020). Remember the Gillette ads in the 1980s. Was this really "The Best a Man Can Get"?

While this scholarship thus drew attention to men and masculinities as a topic of study, there was little talk of men's links to patriarchy. This does not mean that patriarchy has not been raised in MCR, but predominantly so in connection to how it affects women (McVey et al. 2020), in the context of developing countries (Venugopal and Viswanathan 2020), or women's empowerment (Scott 2000). The notion that patriarchy has the purpose of naming the systematic power of men with the aim of *dis*empowerment has been rarely acknowledged, similar to research on how patriarchy is produced, how, by what or whom.

An example of this can be seen in research on gender violence in MCR, which has only recently seen much-needed attention (i.e. Joy et al. 2015). Gurrieri et al. (2016) examined the taboo of gender-based violence in advertising and raised concern regarding the normalisation of violent images of women. Varman et al. (2018) led conversations on violence in marketing, including sexual violence (Varman et al. 2018). Similar to normalised violence as featured in gendered advertising, this study used Butler (2004) to address the 'respectability' of women in the context of sexual violence. While this research makes reference to patriarchy and describes it as a source of power inequalities, it still often lacks more explicit conceptualisation. New research continues to advance debates on patriarchy within MCR, clearly recognising the void that has been left by a continued invisibility and 'normalised violence' within MCR to this point (Martin et al. 2020; Gurrieri 2021). Men and masculinities and gendered power relations have been equally central within transformative consumer research (TCR, Zayer et al. 2017; Steinfield et al. 2019c). Given the momentum of research on these topics, it is important to add to these conversations by extending this transdisciplinary scholarship.

Maintaining momentum on men, masculinities and transpatriarchies in MCR

As we find ourselves within this specific point in history, we link back to our biographical narratives and wonder how the above theorisations help us make sense of some of the contemporary realities of markets, marketing and consumption as they intersect across socio-political, cultural, economic realms and drip into everyday life, instilling in us continued systems and structures based on neoliberal capitalist transpatriarchies. These days, I – Wendy – regularly get up at 5 am and work well into the night. Yet, despite these long, at times interrupted, working hours, I still do not manage to clear the backlog left behind by months of caring duties alongside an increased, normalised and legitimated workload during the global pandemic. Even worse, I know I am not alone. Decades of feminist efforts that have led to marginal progress to reduce unequal labour distributions, as for example articulated in the 'second shift' (Hochschild and Machung 2012), have been undone, almost overnight. MCR has its role to play in addressing these issues that require much-needed, urgent attention, and not just at the margins, but across all levels of scholarship, policy and most importantly at a transnational level.

In its Global Gender Report, the World Economic Forum (WEF) recently calculated that the impact of Covid-19 has set gender parity (as per their measurements) back by another generation, from a previous 99.5 to 135.6 years (WEF 2021). While millions of people across the globe continue to suffer and die from Covid-19, it thus emerges that and how women bear the brunt of this pandemic disproportionately. Without much-needed joint efforts, women and girls face a greater, lasting impact than their male counterparts. This is arguably due to the distinctive systems of transnational work, care and consumption chains that have, as stated above, liberated and at the same time oppressed us. The pandemic has exposed that advances on gender equality have remained at surface level, as clearly indicated by the massive breakdowns, revealing the deeply embedded, continued stranglehold of transpatriarchies and their distinctive impact on all our lives. MCR needs to continue its research efforts into transnational private and public, working and consuming lives with a focus on gender power relations.

As we said in the opening, if ever the private was political, it is now – but the personal is political now at a level well beyond nations. Isolation and restrictions of freedoms have led to extreme levels of (not just) domestic violence that are, once again, hidden and invisible, this time quite literally within the supposed 'safe spaces' of our homes (Kofman and Garfin 2020). Importantly, rather than focusing on the impact on women, research is required that exposes the structural and systemic issues – or 'disaster patriarchy' (V 2021) – contributing to this 'double pandemic'. Research areas such as medicine, law and psychology have reported on issues of violence, oppression and abuse, yet MCR has remained silent. One example: the *Journal of Public Policy and Marketing* established research agendas in response to changing dynamics of Covid-19. The editors selected important research areas that require urgent attention. While all these are valid and often intersect with topics we raise above, such as race in the marketplace and the 'essential workforce' during the pandemic, gender (in)equities and the transnational structuring of patriarchies and patriarchal relations were not among the chosen agenda topics (Scott et al. 2020).

If anything, the pandemic has also exposed the lasting impact and possibly dangerous trajectories of incapable and irresponsible male leaders, contextualised in the rise of transnational populist movements, all of which are deeply linked to the hegemony of men and MCR. Men's continued power becomes apparent via Trump's (and his different kinds of associates') politics and his lasting legacy in the US, Johnson's (and his different kinds of associates') politics in the UK and the increasing boundaries – as in both socio-cultural boundary-making and the strengthening of nationalism and national boundaries –which deeply affect the lives of many, including both Wendy's and Jeff's. Paradoxically, transpatriarchies exist alongside nationalisms and increasingly rigid national boundaries. Brexit in the UK has arguably created unnecessary expenses and diverted attention away from important areas, which legitimated cuts in social care, healthcare, a severe neglect of childcare, particularly during the early years (Guardian Editorial 2021), all underpinned by deeply neoliberal capitalist values which are contributing to increasingly unequal wealth distributions – all of which are once again linked to transnational markets and dynamics.

We often associate poverty with developing countries, yet, despite growing, unprecedented levels of wealth, the US leads in poverty rankings within the developed world (Rank 2004). The pandemic has worsened these rates once again (Tanzi and Saraiva 2021) and threatens to destroy the many advances to address these issues. Remember that gender inequality creates poverty (US Aid 2021) not the other way around? This emphasises yet again the urgency to raise the gender equality research agenda, and along with it, research on systems and structures of transpatriarchies and the hegemony of men. MCR research plays a vital role in maintaining and adding to this collective research agenda.

Examples of Trump and Johnson, alongside other leaders of their time, also draw attention back to the importance of extending the research agenda on men, masculinities and transpatriarchies in the context of representations and power displays (Collinson and Hearn 2020). The normalised narcissism, controversial jibes by both leaders and at times seemingly expected transgressions are exemplary of celebrity, PR (Summers and Morgan 2008) and corporate culture (Cragun et al. 2020) rather than responsible governmental leadership, especially during times of crisis. Alongside critical investigations of power constructions in their representations, research is required on the propaganda machine afforded by some groups of men's privileged access to media which sustains transpatriarchies. MCR has a role to play in extending the research agenda by adding much-needed critical perspectives on the structures that have led to and sustain the power of these 'opinion leaders'. Given the authors' shared biographies – one raised by post-war parents in Germany, the other directly impacted by post-war UK – it is important to raise consciousness regarding the pervasiveness of social class, imperialist, militaristic and downright nastiness within everyday cultural and often normalised representations. A transpatriarchal lens can equally advance understandings on the increase in nationalism predominantly, but not exclusively, by men and masculinities in power, which have arguably led to the legitimising of political activities such as Brexit and the need to control national borders. Paradoxically, much of this upsurge in nationalism arises through transnational nationalistic collaborations.

Lastly and importantly, MCR has made vast strides in its research on consumer movements on the one hand (Chatzidakis et al. 2021), while unpacking the politics and exploitations of social justice marketing on the other (Sobande 2020). Critical gender and feminist perspectives have emerged in this research stream in the context of sexualised labour in digital cultures (Drenten et al. 2020). Conceptualisations of transpatriarchies and the politics of ICTs could provide potential for adding and extending this research further and thus maintaining its momentum in addressing structures and systems that liberate at the same time as creating new forms of violence and oppressions. Movements such as #MeToo (Chandra and Erlingsdóttir 2021) or Black Lives Matter (Crockett and Grier 2021) lend themselves to further interrogations, and link to intersectionality research in MCR (Steinfield et al. 2019b) and new materialist configurations (Steinfield 2019). These are just a few examples to highlight how men and masculinities can be approached differently via a wider lens of transpatriarchal MCR.

Conclusion

Despite increasing interest in critical work on men and masculinities in MCR, significant gaps remain to address the systemic and structural issues linked to transnational patriarchies and the hegemony of men. Recent research has shown that there is a place for this scholarship in MCR and related disciplines (Varman et al. 2018; Zayer et al. 2020; Gurrieri 2021). Yet, deep issues continue with research on men and masculinities that is unfeminist and apolitical. Speaking of the political: some disciplines where gender, feminism and patriarchy are well established have argued for a need to move away from politicising research due to its potential to limit change (Halberstam 2019). However, if the political is a problem in some feminist research, MCR sits somewhere near the other end of the spectrum in that it has hardly begun political interrogations to understand the deeply concerning practices, systems and structures that maintain existing power relations. While the wider subject discipline of MCR thus needs to address its own issues, it is equally important for feminist scholars in MCR to engage in transdisciplinary research and contribute to the many debates on the issues we raise above that are dominant and recognised in other fields. Ultimately, given the challenges we face at this point, it is our collective responsibility to maintain this research agenda, and MCR, at this point, is not doing its fair share!

The research area on men, masculinities and transpatriarchies as it links to MCR cannot be easily reduced to a 4 × 4 matrix. Given that transpatriarchies are deeply intertwined with neoliberal capitalism, and link in their own ways to political, economic, socio-cultural and technological arenas – which include representations and identity politics – this research is complex and at times uncomfortable. Yet, it is these broader macro structures and power relations that also impact our everyday lives and are instilled in us from a very early age. Addressing these complexities is aided by multiple voices and perspectives, again benefitting from transdisciplinary engagement. It is these complexities that link to broader issues, such as transnational poverty, ecological sustainability (Steinfield and Hein 2018), violence and global inequities based on gender power relations as potentially a source, not a product or consequence of these issues (US Aid 2021). Given these insights, we require a research agenda in MCR that can contribute to these challenges. If, even by conservative measures (WEF 2021), Covid and other dynamics have set us back by yet another generation before we reach gender equality – more than 100 years – it is these complexities that need to be collectively and urgently tackled.

The personal continues to be political. Although this message may still not have reached mainstream MCR, it is our responsibility to change it.

Notes

1. If you ask Wendy, Germany still has the best public swimming pools, sports centres, unbelievably good healthcare and some regions even have good childcare! No comparison to the Nordic region of course (Molander et al. 2019; Molander 2021)!
2. see also Mulvey (1989), Goffman (1979), Williamson (1978), Neale (1992), Cohan and Hark (2012) as notable influences.

References

Arnould, E. J. and C. J. Thompson. 2005. "Consumer culture theory (CCT): Twenty years of research." *Journal of Consumer Research* 31 (4): 868–882. https://doi.org/10.1086/426626

Belk, R. W. and J. A. Costa. 1998. "The mountain man myth: A contemporary consuming fantasy." *Journal of Consumer Research* 25 (3): 218–240. https://doi.org/10.1086/209536

Bocock, R. 1986. *Hegemony*. London: Tavistock.

Butler, J. 2004. *Precarious Life: The Powers of Mourning and Violence.* London: Verso.
Campbell, B. 2014. *End of equality.* London: Seagull.
Carrigan, T., B. Connell, and J. Lee. 1985. "Toward a new sociology of masculinity." *Theory and Society* 14 (5): 551–604. https://doi.org/10.1007/BF00160017
Cayla, J. and G. M. Eckhardt. 2008. "Asian brands and the shaping of a transnational imagined community." *Journal of Consumer Research* 35 (2): 216–230. https://doi.org/10.1086/587629
Chandra, G. and I. Erlingsdóttir, eds. 2021. *The Routledge Handbook of the Politics of the #MeToo Movement.* London: Routledge.
Chatzidakis, A., P. Maclaran, and R. Varman. 2021. "The Regeneration of Consumer Movement Solidarity." *Journal of Consumer Research.* https://doi.org/10.1093/jcr/ucab007
Coffey, C., P. Espinoza Revollo, R. Harvey, M. Lawson, A. Parvez Butt, K. Piaget, D. Sarosi, and J. Thekkudan. 2020. *Time to Care: Unpaid and Underpaid Care Work and the Global Inequality Crisis.* Oxford: Oxfam International.
Cohan, S. and I. R. Hark, eds. 2012. *Screening the Male: Exploring Masculinities in the Hollywood Cinema.* London: Routledge.
Collinson, D. and J. Hearn. 2020. "Trump v Biden: A duel of contrasting masculinities." *The Conversation*, October 23, Accessed 31 May 2021. https://theconversation.com/trump-v-biden-a-duel-of-contrasting-masculinities-148300
Connell, R. W. 1987. *Gender and Power.* Oxford: Basil Blackwell.
Connell, R. W. 1993. "The big picture: Masculinities in recent world history." *Theory and Society* (22): 597–623. https://doi.org/10.1007/BF00993538
Connell, R. W. 1995. *Masculinities.* Cambridge, MA: Polity.
Connell, R. W. 2000. *The Men and the Boys.* Berkeley, CA: University of California Press.
Connell, R. W. and J. W. Messerschmidt. 2005. "Hegemonic masculinity: Rethinking the concept." *Gender & Society* 19 (6): 829–859. https://doi.org/10.1177/0891243205278639
Coskuner-Balli, G. and C. J. Thompson. 2013."The status costs of subordinate cultural capital: At-home fathers' collective pursuit of cultural legitimacy through capitalizing consumption practices." *Journal of Consumer Research* 40 (1): 19–41. https://doi.org/10.1086/668640
Cox, R. 1997. "Invisible labour: Perceptions of paid domestic work in London." *Journal of Occupational Science*, 4 (2): 62–67. https://doi.org/10.1080/14427591.1997.9686422
Cox, R., ed. 2014. *Au Pairs' Lives in Global Context: Sisters or Servants?.* Hamburg: Springer.
Cragun, O. R., K. J. Olsen, and P. M. Wright. 2020. "Making CEO narcissism research great: A review and meta-analysis of CEO narcissism." *Journal of Management*, 46 (6): 908–936. https://doi.org/10.1177/0149206319892678
Crockett, D. and S. A. Grier. 2021. "Race in the marketplace and COVID-19." *Journal of Public Policy & Marketing*, 40(1): 89–91. https://doi.org/10.1177/0743915620931448
Djedidi, A., N. Ourahmoune, and D. Dalli. 2017. "Global local dialectical relationship in a Mediterranean context." In *NA – Advances in Consumer Research*, Vol. 45, edited by A. Gneezy, V. Griskevicius, and P. Williams, 406–409. Duluth, MN: Association for Consumer Research.
Edwards, T. 1997. *Men in the Mirror: Fashion, Masculinity and Consumer Society.* London: Cassel.
El Jurdi, H. A. and N. Ourahmoune. 2021. "'Revolution is a woman' – The feminisation of the Arab spring." *Journal of Marketing Management* 37 (3–4): 360–363. https://doi.org/10.1080/0267257X.2021.1880162
Elliott, R. and C. Elliott. 2005. "Idealized images of the male body in advertising: A reader-response exploration." *Journal of Marketing Communications*, 11 (1): 3–19. https://doi.org/10.1080/1352726042000263566
Feuntes-Nieva, R and N. Galasso. 2014. *Working for the Few: Political Capture and Economic Inequality.* Oxford: Oxfam International.
Gentry, J., and R. Harrison. 2010. "Is advertising a barrier to male movement toward gender change?." *Marketing Theory* 10 (1): 74–96. https://doi.org/10.1177/1470593109355246
Goffman, E. 1979. *Gender Advertisements.* London: Macmillan International Higher Education.
Gottzén, L., U. Mellström, and T. Shefer, eds. 2019. *Routledge International Handbook of Masculinity Studies.* London: Routledge.

Guardian Editorial. 2021. "The Guardian view on early years education: England's toddlers need attention." *The Guardian*, May 10, Accessed May 31. https://www.theguardian.com/commentisfree/2021/may/10/the-guardian-view-on-early-years-education-englands-toddlers-need-attention?CMP=Share_AndroidApp_Other

Gurrieri, L. 2021. "Patriarchal marketing and the symbolic annihilation of women." *Journal of Marketing Management* 37 (3–4): 364–370. https://doi.org/10.1080/0267257X.2020.1826179

Gurrieri, L. and J. Drenten. 2019. "Visual storytelling and vulnerable health care consumers: Normalising practices and social support through Instagram". *Journal of Services Marketing*, 33 (6): 702–720. https://doi.org/10.1108/JSM-09-2018-0262

Gurrieri, L., J. Brace-Govan, and H. Cherrier. 2016. "Controversial advertising: Transgressing the taboo of gender-based violence." *European Journal of Marketing* 50 (7/8), 1448–1469. https://doi.org/10.1108/EJM-09-2014-0597

Haase, M., I. Becker, A. Nill, C. J. Shultz, and J. W. Gentry. 2016. "Male breadwinner ideology and the inclination to establish market relationships: Model development using data from Germany and a mixed-methods research strategy." *Journal of Macromarketing* 36 (2): 149–167. https://doi.org/10.1177/0276146715576202

Halberstam, J. 2019. "After feminism, after politics". Keynote at *Radical Democracy Conference*, April 26–27. New York: New School for Social Research. https://www.radicaldemocracy.org/2019/04/21/radical-democracy-2019-schedule-is-now-online/

Hardoon, D., S. Ayele, and R. Fuentes-Nieva. 2016. *"An Economy for the 1%."* Oxfam Briefing Paper, January 18. Oxford: Oxfam International, Accessed 31 May 2021. https://www.oxfam.org/sites/www.oxfam.org/files/file_attachments/bp210-economy-one-percent-tax-havens-180116-en_0.pdf

Hearn, J. 2004. "From hegemonic masculinity to the hegemony of men." *Feminist Theory* 5 (1): 49–72. https://doi.org/10.1177/1464700104040813

Hearn, J. 2012. "A multi-faceted power analysis of men's violence to known women: From hegemonic masculinity to the hegemony of men." *Sociological Review* 60 (4): 589–610. https://doi.org/10.1111/j.1467-954X.2012.02125.x

Hearn, J. 2015. *Men of the World: Globalizations, Genders, Transnational Times*. London: Sage.

Hearn, J. 2017. "Two challenges for critical studies on men and masculinities: The hegemony of men, and trans(national)patriarchies." *Časopis za kritiko znanosti, domišljijo in novo antropologijo [Journal of Critique of Science, Imagination and New Anthropology]*, 45 (267): 23–34.

Hearn, J. and W. Hein. 2015. "Reframing gender and feminist knowledge construction in marketing and consumer research: Missing feminisms and the case of men and masculinities." *Journal of Marketing Management* 31 (15–16): 1626–1651. https://doi.org/10.1080/0267257X.2015.1068835

Hearn, J. and A. Melechi. 1992. "The Transatlantic gaze: Masculinities, youth and the American imaginary." In *Men, Masculinity and the Media*, edited by S. Craig, 215–232. Sage, Newbury Park, CA.

Hearn, J. and K. Pringle. 2006. *European perspectives on men and masculinities*. London: Palgrave Macmillan.

Hearn, J., M. Nordberg, K. Andersson, D. Balkmar, L. Gottzén, R. Klinth, K. Pringle, and L. Sandberg. 2012. "Hegemonic masculinity and beyond: 40 Years of research in Sweden." *Men and Masculinities* 15 (1): 31–55. https://doi.org/10.1177/1097184X11432113

Hein, W. and S. O'Donohoe. 2014. "Practising gender: The role of banter in young men's improvisations of masculine consumer identities." *Journal of Marketing Management* 30 (13–14): 1293–1319. https://doi.org/10.1080/0267257X.2013.852608

Hein, W., L. Steinfield, N. Ourahmoune, C. A. Coleman, L. T. Zayer, and J. Littlefield. 2016. "Gender justice and the market: A transformative consumer research perspective." *Journal of Public Policy & Marketing* 35 (2): 223–236. https://doi.org/10.1509/jppm.15.146

Hochschild, A. and A. Machung. 2012. *The Second Shift: Working Families and the Revolution at Home*. London: Penguin.

Holt, D. B. and C. J. Thompson. 2004. "Man-of-action heroes: The pursuit of heroic masculinity in everyday consumption." *Journal of Consumer Research* 31 (2): 425–440. https://doi.org/10.1086/422120

Horrocks, R. 1994. "Masculinity in crisis." *Self & Society* 22 (4): 25–29. https://doi.org/10.1080/03060497.1994.11085458

Joy, A., R. W. Belk, and R. Bhardwaj. 2015. "Judith Butler on performativity and precarity: Exploratory thoughts on gender and violence in India." *Journal of Marketing Management* 31 (15–16): 1739–1745. https://doi.org/10.1080/0267257X.2015.1076873

Kimmel, M. S., J. Hearn, and R. W. Connell, eds. 2004. *Handbook of Studies on Men and Masculinities.* London: Sage Publications.

Kofman, Y. B. and D. R. Garfin. 2020. "Home is not always a haven: The domestic violence crisis amid the COVID-19 pandemic." *Psychological Trauma: Theory, Research, Practice, and Policy* 12 (1): 199–201. http://dx.doi.org/10.1037/tra0000866

Kravets, O. and O. Sandikci. 2014. "Competently ordinary: New middle class consumers in the emerging markets." *Journal of Marketing* 78 (4): 125–140. https://doi.org/10.1509/jm.12.0190

Lindridge, A. and T. Eagar. 2015. "'And Ziggy played guitar': Bowie, the market, and the emancipation and resurrection of Ziggy Stardust." *Journal of Marketing Management* 3 (5–6): 546–576. https://doi.org/10.1080/0267257X.2015.1014395

Littlefield, J. and J. L. Ozanne. 2011. "Socialization into consumer culture: Hunters learning to be men." *Consumption Markets & Culture* 14 (4): 333–360. https://doi.org/10.1080/10253866.2011.604494

Maclean, K. 2016. "Gender, risk and the Wall Street alpha male." *Journal of Gender Studies* 25 (4): 427–444. https://doi.org/10.1080/09589236.2014.990425

Martin, D. M., S. Ferguson, J. Hoek, and C. Hinder (2020). "Gender violence: Marketplace violence and symbolic violence in social movements." *Journal of Marketing Management*, 1–16. https://doi.org/10.1080/0267257X.2020.1854330

McCarthy, L., Soundararajan, V., and Taylor, S. (2020). "The hegemony of men in global value chains: Why it matters for labour governance." *Human Relations.* https://doi.org/10.1177/0018726720950816

McVey L., L. Gurrieri, L., and M. Tyler. 2020. "The structural oppression of women by markets: The continuum of sexual violence and the online pornography market." *Journal of Marketing Management*, 1–28.doi: https://doi.org/10.1080/0267257X.2020.1798714

Moisio, R., E. J. Arnould, and J. W. Gentry. 2013. "Productive consumption in the class-mediated construction of domestic masculinity: Do-it-yourself (DIY) home improvement in men's identity work." *Journal of Consumer Research* 40 (2): 298–316. https://doi.org/10.1086/670238

Molander, S. 2021. "A gendered agency of good enough: Swedish single fathers navigating conflicting state and marketplace ideologies". *Consumption Markets & Culture* 24 (2): 194–216. https://doi.org/10.1080/10253866.2019.1696316

Molander, S., I. A. Kleppe, and J. Ostberg. 2019. "Hero shots: Involved fathers conquering new discursive territory in consumer culture". *Consumption Markets & Culture* 22 (4): 430–453. https://doi.org/10.1080/10253866.2018.1512252

Monro, S. 2005. *Gender Politics: Activism, Citizenship and Sexual Diversity.* London: Pluto.

Morrell, R., R. Jewkes, and G. Lindegger. 2012. "Hegemonic masculinity/masculinities in South Africa: Culture, power, and gender politics." *Men and Masculinities* 15 (1): 11–30. https://doi.org/10.1177/1097184X12438001

Mort, F. 1988. "Boy's own? Masculinity, style and popular culture". In *Male Order: Unwrapping Masculinity*, edited by R. Chapman and J. Rutherford, 193–224. London: Lawrence & Wishart.

Mort, F. 1996. *Culture of Consumption: Masculinities and Social Space in Late Twentieth-Century Britain.* London: Routledge.

Mulvey, L. (1989). *Visual and Other Pleasures.* Basingstoke: Palgrave.

Neale, S. (1992). "Masculinity as spectacle." In *The sexual subject: A Screen reader in Sexuality*, edited by S. Neale, 277–87. London: Routledge.

Nixon, B. 2012. "The biggest challenge in human history." *Global Teach-In*, April 25, Accessed 31 May 2021. http://www.brucenixon.com/pdf/GlobalTeachIn-25April.pdf

Nixon, S. 1992. "Have you got the Look? Masculinities and the Shopping Spectacle". In *Lifestyle Shopping: The Subject of Consumption*, edited by R. Shields, 149–169. London: Routledge.

Nixon, S. 1996. *Hard Looks: Masculinities, Spectatorship and Contemporary Consumption*. London: UCL & St. Martin's Press.

Nixon, S. 1997. "Exhibiting masculinity". In *Representation: Cultural Representations and Signifying Practices*, edited by S. Hall, 291–330. London: Sage.

Nixon, S. and B. Crewe. 2004. "Pleasure at work? Gender, consumption and work-based identities in the creative industries." *Consumption Markets & Culture* 7 (2): 129–147. https://doi.org/10.1080/1025386042000246197

Osgerby, B. 2001. *Playboys in Paradise: Masculinity, Youth and Leisure Style in Modern America*. Oxford: Berg.

Östberg, J. 2010. "Thou shalt sport a banana in thy pocket: Gendered body size ideals in advertising and popular culture." *Marketing Theory* 10 (1): 45–73. https://doi.org/10.1177/1470593109355255

Östberg, J. 2012a. "The challenge of the 'new masculinity': Conservative reactions to a new consumption ethos." In *Nordic Fashion Studies*, edited by P. McNeil and L. Wallenberg, 37–56. Stockholm: Axl Books.

Östberg, J. 2012b. "Masculinity and fashion." In *Gender, Culture, and Consumer Behavior*, edited by C. Otnes, C. and L. T. Zayer, 253–281. London: Routledge.

Östberg, J. 2013. "Masculine self-presentation. In *The Routledge Companion to Identity and Consumption*, edited by A. A. Ruvio and R. W. Belk, 129–136. Abingdon: Routledge.

Otnes, C. and M. A. McGrath. 2001. "Perceptions and realities of male shopping behavior." *Journal of Retailing* 77 (1): 111–137. https://doi.org/10.1016/S0022-4359(00)00047-6

Oxfam. 2020. "World's billionaires have more wealth than 4.6 billion people." *Oxfam*, January 20, Accessed 31 May 2021. https://www.oxfam.org/en/press-releases/worlds-billionaires-have-more-wealth-46-billion-people

Patterson, M. and R. Elliott. 2002. "Negotiating masculinities: Advertising and the inversion of the male gaze." *Consumption, Markets and Culture* 5 (3): 231–249. https://doi.org/10.1080/10253860290031631

Petrylaite, E. and D. Hart. 2021. "Men's consumer identities and their consumption norms in the perceived, conceived and lived spaces of spas." *Journal of Marketing Management* 37 (3–4): 266–293. https://doi.org/10.1080/0267257X.2019.1707266

Pleck, J. H. 1995. "The gender role strain paradigm: An update." In *A New Psychology of Men*, edited by R. Levant and W. S. Pollack, 11–32. New York: Basic.

Poster, W. 2013. "Subversions of techno-masculinity: Indian ICT professionals in the global economy." In *Rethinking Transnational Men: Beyond, Between and Within Nations*, edited by J. Hearn, M. Blagojević, and K. Harrison, 113–133. New York: Routledge.

Prothero, A. and P. McDonagh. 2021. "'It's hard to be what you can't see' – Gender representation in marketing's academic journals." *Journal of Marketing Management* 37 (1–2): 28–39. https://doi.org/10.1080/0267257X.2020.1862984

Rank, M. R. (2004). *One Nation, Underprivileged: Why American Poverty Affects Us All*. Oxford: Oxford University Press.

Rinallo, D. 2007. "Metro/fashion/tribes of men: Negotiating the boundaries of men's legitimate consumption." In *Consumer Tribes*, edited by B. Cova, R. V. Kozinets, and A. Shankar, 76–92. Oxford: Butterworth-Heinemann.

Schouten, J. W. and J. H. McAlexander. 1995. "Subcultures of consumption: An ethnography of the new bikers." *Journal of Consumer Research* 22 (1): 43–61. https://doi.org/10.1086/209434

Schroeder, J. E. and D. Zwick. 2004. "Mirrors of masculinity: Representation and identity in advertising images." *Consumption Markets & Culture* 7 (1): 21–52. https://doi.org/10.1080/1025386042000212383

Scott, L. M. 2000. "Market feminism: The case for a paradigm shift." In *Marketing and Feminism: Current Issues and Research*, edited by M. Catteral, P. MacLaran, and L. Stevens, 16–38. London: Routledge.
Scott, L., J. D. Williams, S. M. Baker, J. Brace-Govan, H. Downey, A. M. Hakstian, G. R. Henderson, P. S. Loroz, and D. Webb. 2011. "Beyond poverty: Social justice in a global marketplace." *Journal of Public Policy & Marketing* 30 (1): 39–46. https://doi.org/10.1509/jppm.30.1.39
Scott, M. L., K. D Martin, J. L. Wiener, P. S. Ellen, and S. Burton. 2020. *The COVID-19 Pandemic at the Intersection of Marketing and Public Policy.* https://doi.org/10.1177/0743915620932151
Sharifonnasabi, Z., F. Bardhi, and M. K. Luedicke. 2020. "How globalization affects consumers: Insights from 30 years of CCT globalization research." *Marketing Theory* 20 (3): 273–298. https://doi.org/10.1177/1470593119887469
Simpson, M. 1994. *Male Impersonators: Men Performing Masculinity.* New York: Routledge.
Sklair, L. 2001. *The Transnational Capitalist Class.* Oxford: Blackwell.
Sobande, F. 2020. "Woke-washing: 'intersectional' femvertising and branding 'woke' bravery." *European Journal of Marketing* 54 (11): 2723–2745. https://doi.org/10.1108/EJM-02-2019-0134
Steinfield, L. A. 2019. "1, 2, 3, 4. I declare… empowerment? A material-discursive analysis of the marketisation, measurement and marketing of women's economic empowerment." *Journal of Marketing Management*, 1–37. https://doi.org/10.1080/0267257X.2019.1699850
Steinfield, L. A. and W. Hein. 2018. "Women-led partnerships and the achievement of the sustainable development goals." In *Partnerships for the Goals. Encyclopedia of the UN Sustainable Development Goals*, edited by W. L. Filho, A. M. Azul, L. Brandli, P. G. Özuyar, and T. Wall. Cham: Springer. https://doi.org/10.1007/978-3-319-95963-4_20
Steinfield, L. A., C. A Coleman, L. T. Zayer, N. Ourahmoune, and W. Hein. 2019a. "Power logics of consumers' gendered (in)justices: Reading reproductive health interventions through the transformative gender justice framework." *Consumption Markets & Culture* 22 (4): 406–429. https://doi.org/10.1080/10253866.2018.1512250
Steinfield, L. A., J. Littlefield, W. Hein, C.A. Coleman, and L.T. Zayer. 2019b. "The TCR perspective of gender: Moving from critical theory to an Activism-Praxis Orientation." In *Handbook of research on gender and marketing*, edited by S. Dobscha, 186–210. Cheltenham: Edward Elgar Publishing.
Steinfield, L. A., M. Sanghvi, L. T. Zayer, C. A. Coleman, N. Ourahmoune, R. L. Harrison, W. Hein, and J. Brace-Govan. 2019c. "Transformative intersectionality: Moving business towards a critical praxis." *Journal of Business Research* 100: 366–375. doi: https://doi.org/10.1016/j.jbusres.2018.12.031
Summers, J. and M. J. Morgan. 2008. "More than just the media: Considering the role of public relations in the creation of sporting celebrity and the management of fan expectations." *Public Relations Review* 34 (2): 176–182. https://doi.org/10.1016/j.pubrev.2008.03.014
Tanzi, A. and C. Saraiva. 2021. "U.S. suffers sharpest rise in poverty rate in more than 50 years." *Bloomberg*, January 25, Accessed 31 May 2021. https://www.bloomberg.com/news/articles/2021-01-25/u-s-suffers-sharpest-rise-in-poverty-rate-in-more-than-50-years
Thompson, C. J. and D. B. Holt. 2004. "How do men grab the phallus? Gender tourism in everyday consumption." *Journal of Consumer Culture* 4 (3): 313–338. https://doi.org/10.1177/1469540504046518
Tuncay, L. (2006). "Conceptualizations of masculinity among a 'new' breed of male consumers." In *Proceedings of 8th Conference on Gender and Consumer Behaviour*, edited by L. Stevens and J. Borgerson, 312–327. Edinburgh: Association for Consumer Research.
Tuncay, L. and C. C. Otnes. 2008a. "Exploring the link between masculinity and consumption." In *Brick & Mortar Shopping in the 21st Century*, edited by T. M. Lowrey, 153–170. New York: Taylor and Francis.
Tuncay, L. and C.C. Otnes. 2008b. "The use of persuasion management strategies by identity-vulnerable consumers: The case of urban heterosexual male shoppers." *Journal of Retailing* 84 (4): 487–499. https://doi.org/10.1016/j.jretai.2008.09.004

US Aid. 2021. "A briefer: Gender inequality causes poverty." *US Aid*, Accessed 31 May 2021. https://banyanglobal.com/wp-content/uploads/2021/03/Gender-Inequality-Causes-Poverty-Briefer.pdf

V (formerly Eve Ensler). 2021. "Disaster patriarchy: How the pandemic has unleashed a war on women." *The Guardian*, June 1, Accessed 1 June 2021. https://www.theguardian.com/lifeandstyle/2021/jun/01/disaster-patriarchy-how-the-pandemic-has-unleashed-a-war-on-women

Varman, R. and R. W. Belk. 2012. "Consuming postcolonial shopping malls." *Journal of Marketing Management* 28 (1–2): 62–84. https://doi.org/10.1080/0267257X.2011.617706

Varman, R., P. Goswami, and D. Vijay. 2018. "The precarity of respectable consumption: Normalising sexual violence against women." *Journal of Marketing Management* 34 (11–12): 932–964. https://doi.org/10.1080/0267257X.2018.1527387

Venugopal, S. and Viswanathan, M. 2020 "Negotiated agency in the face of consumption constraints: A study of women entrepreneurs in subsistence contexts." *Journal of Public Policy & Marketing*. https://doi.org/10.1177/0743915620953821

Walby, S. 2015. *Crisis*. Cambridge, MA: Polity.

WEF. 2021. *Global Gender Gap Report 2021*. https://www.weforum.org/reports/global-gender-gap-report-2021

Williamson, J. 1978. *Decoding advertisements: Ideology and meaning in advertising*. London: Marion Boyers.

Witkowski, T. H. 2020. "Male compensatory consumption in American history." *Journal of Macromarketing*, 40 (4): 528–545. https://doi.org/10.1177/0276146719897107

Wooten, D. B. 2006. "From labeling possessions to possessing labels: Ridicule and socialization among adolescents." *Journal of Consumer Research*, 33 (2): 188–198. https://doi.org/10.1086/506300

Young, B., I. Bakker, and D. Elson, eds. 2011. *Questioning Financial Governance from a Feminist Perspective*. London: Routledge.

Zayer, L. T., C. A. Coleman, W. Hein, J. Littlefield, J., and L. Steinfield. 2017. "Gender and the self: Traversing feminisms, masculinities, and intersectionality toward transformative perspectives." In *The Routledge companion to consumer behavior*, edited by M. R. Solomon and T. M. Lowrey, 147–161. London: Routledge.

Zayer, L. T., W. Hein, J. Brace-Govan, C. A. Coleman, R. L. Harrison, N. Ourahmoune, M. Sanghvi, and L. Steinfield. 2020. "The renaissance of gender equality research and sustainable development in the academic context of marketing: Championing paths forward." In *Struggles and Successes in the Pursuit of Sustainable Development*, edited by T. K. Tan, M. Gudić, P. M. Flynn, 139–150. London: Routledge.

Section 3

Feminist perspectives on the body in marketing

11 Materializing the body
A feminist perspective

Anu Valtonen and Elina Närvänen

Introduction

In this chapter, we set out to materialize the body with the help of feminist literature. While the body has invited considerable attention in marketing and consumer research, many authors have focused on analyzing discursive or social aspects of the body. We continue these valuable contributions by drawing theoretical inspiration from recent feminist new materialist literature (Alaimo and Hekman 2008) and theories of affect (Blackmann and Venn 2010). These theoretical sources enable us to grasp the way pre-linguistic, visceral, material, and biological aspects entangle with discursive ones. We employ two case studies to illustrate the way this approach enables us to theorize the body. The first case deals with sleeping bodies, and it highlights the intertwined relations of sexed bodies, affects, and material culture. The second case is about reducing food waste as an embodied activity and as care for more-than-human worlds.

We begin with a literature review of the body in marketing and consumer research, with an emphasis on studies informed by feminist research. Then, we outline basic ideas of feminist new materialism and theories of affect and the way they theorize the body. The two case studies that follow illustrate each in their own way how the feminist materialist approach enables researchers to advance existing debates on embodiment. To conclude, we discuss the potential benefits of a feminist new material approach to marketing and consumer research and outline ideas for future research.

Previous feminist consumer research on the body

The intricate relationship between body, gender, and consumption has interested several consumer culture researchers for the past decades. The first of them published their work at the beginning of the 1990s and positioned it, alongside the postmodern turn, to critique mainstream consumer behavior research. The mainstream represented the psychological and cognitive paradigm rooted in mind-centered and rational philosophy. Drawing from poststructuralism, interpretive consumer researchers questioned the separation between mind and body, rational and irrational, or male and female – in both marketing and consumers' experiences, revealing these as socially constructed categories (Joy and Venkatesh 1994; Thompson and Hirschman 1995). For instance, Joy and Venkatesh (1994) argued for the importance of studying the body as a site of cultural representation and social power. They emphasized consumers as more than rational information processors – as minds or machines – but as embodied beings whose wants and desires are not only mental but embodied. Early on interpretive researchers recognized that consumer culture is proliferating with marketing that links consumer products to (especially female) bodies, but the issue of the body is continuously skated over in consumer and marketing research.

Joy and Venkatesh (1994) drew theoretically from postmodernism (especially French poststructuralism) and feminism and reflected upon female body rituals including diet and make-up, and the need for feminist writing of the body within consumer research. Relying on Foucault among others, Thompson and Hirschman's (1995) study revealed how consuming bodies are objectified in consumer culture through processes of normalization, problematization, and the operation of the disciplinary gaze. Consumption is hence portrayed as the means through which bodies are disciplined according to cultural norms, especially related to bodily appearance. The embodied self was discussed as part of consumers' identity construction where consumption was used to "gain better control of their bodies and over the historical trajectory of their lives and identities" (Thompson and Hirschman 1998, 408). Also, other related studies focused on contexts where bodies are at a display, or their appearance is worked upon as part of consumers' identity projects, such as plastic surgery (Askegaard, Gertsen, and Langer 2002; Sayre 1999; Schouten 1991).

A stream using visual analysis to study images of female and male bodies in advertising emerged in the late 1990s – showing the stereotypical and gendered ideals implemented in the marketing practice and how they impact consumers' identity construction (e.g. Patterson and Elliott 2002; Schroeder and Borgerson 1998; Schroeder and Zwick 2004). For instance, studies focused on idealized male bodies in advertising and consumer culture causing ambivalence for consumers (Östberg 2010) and how representations of the human body were used in marketing technology products (Buchanan-Oliver et al. 2010). Many of the researchers in the first streams utilized the work of the philosopher Susan Bordo (1993) to link the concepts of body, feminism, and consumption together. The body was in several studies presented as "a central site of representation, heavily invested with multiple, shifting layers of cultural meaning" (Buchanan-Oliver et al. 2010).

While the first streams of research focused largely on images and discourses of the body as well as its representations in social situations and its interrelationship with consumer identities, later the focus moved toward spatial and kinetic dimensions of bodies moving in space such as in retail stores, museums, or gyms (Joy and Sherry 2003; Pekkanen et al. 2017; Peñaloza 1998; Sassatelli 2010). Through movement, bodies become linked with emotions and affects, as shown in the context of salsa dancing where the movement of the body creates emotional experiences (Hewer and Hamilton 2010; see also Kuuru and Närvänen 2019). Other studies (Joy and Sherry 2003; Venkatesh et al. 2010) linked together body, experience, art, and fashion, arguing that aesthetic experiences are thoroughly embodied. Women's experiences and representations of the physically active female body were studied also by Brace-Govan (2010) who traced feminist and political discussions of women's physical activity from first-wave feminism to third-wave activists and postfeminists. This study revealed physically active female bodies as increasingly role models for desirable femininity, health, and well-being as well as illuminated the ritualized visibility of male sports (see also Johansson et al. 2017).

In the 2010s, feminist theories on embodiment started to move beyond the consumer research field onto the broader marketing field, particularly connecting with the critical marketing tradition. Feminist embodiment theories were used in a study related to social marketing (Gurrieri et al. 2013), critically scrutinizing the way idealized bodies are used in campaigns related to e.g. breastfeeding and weight-control, and paying attention to the ethico-political aspects of embodiment in marketing. Another study analyzed the bodies of service employees, engaging in gendered practices of aesthetic and emotional labor (Stevens 2012). The focus of these studies was on how bodies are politicized and governed through different discourses and technologies in society, including, for instance, date-labeling practices (Yngfalk 2016) and managerial athleticism (Johansson et al. 2017).

Many studies in the 2010s drew from practice theory and performativity (Butler 1990, 1993; Gherardi 2009; Goffman 1956). These studies focused on how the gendered body is practised or performed in everyday life (see e.g. Valtonen 2013; Valtonen and Närvänen, 2015, 2016; Veijola and Valtonen 2007). Studies also explored consumers' transgressions of idealized bodies, such as Goulding and Saren's (2009) study on goth women celebrating their voluptuous bodies and gender play in the subculture through clothing practices. Patterson and Schroeder (2010) study on heavily tattooed women (how they challenge myths of the feminine body as a conveyer of femininity) and Harju and Huovinen's (2015) work on fatshionistas – drawing from Butler and postfeminism (see also Scaraboto and Fischer 2013). Hence, the focus of these studies moved from representations and images of the body to doings – what people do socially, materially, and sensorially – and how especially gendered practices shape their agency and relations and interactions with the material and social world (Valtonen 2013). These studies thus sought inspiration from the materialist turn as well, denoting the agency of material entities such as consumption objects like the bed (Valtonen and Närvänen 2015) to sustain, shape, and constrain gendered practices. Furthermore, this stream of research highlighted bodies as affective and affecting – emotions are performed and experienced in a bodily manner, yet they are also discursively constructed in social situations (Kuuru and Närvänen 2019; Valtonen 2013).

In the very recent years, studies on embodiment in consumer research and marketing have begun to consider the materiality of the body more closely (see e.g. Brace-Govan and Ferguson 2019; Valtonen and Närvänen 2015, 2016). In this, they follow feminists who challenge the discursive and performative focus of poststructural feminism – arguing instead that bodies are corporeal and material (e.g. Alaimo and Hekman 2008; Grosz 1994). For instance, Matich et al. (2019) explore the #freethenipple campaign, which addresses the sexualization and censorship of female bodies through online activism. In their treatise, they also explore the digital aspects of embodiment and technofeminism. Next, we introduce feminist materialist approaches to the body in more detail.

Feminist new materialist approach to the body

Recently, feminist new materialism has gained increasing ground across social sciences. Donna Haraway, Karen Barad, or Elisabeth Grosz – to mention a few key representatives of this scholarship – have influenced the work of many scholars in a range of disciplines. Feminist new materialism emerged as a response to an over-emphasis of language, culture, and discourse in the analysis of social realities, including bodies. As Stacy Alaimo and Susan Hekman point out in the introduction of their seminal book *Material Feminisms* – the purpose is to "bring the material, specifically the materiality of the human body, and the natural world, into the forefront of feminist theory and practice" (Alaimo and Hekman 2008, 1). While they acknowledge that the linguistic turn has been most valuable for the development of feminist accounts on the body, they share a conviction that a focus on language, discourse, and representations *only* is insufficient for providing an adequate understanding of the constitution of bodies, and associated ethical and political questions. Therefore, feminist new material scholars seek to develop "a new way of understanding the relationship between discourse and matter that does not privilege the former to the exclusion of the latter" (ibid., 6). Accordingly, attention is directed to the 'stuff' of the body – fleshy, biological, material body, and evolving corporeal practices – and the way it relates to the discourse about the body, and the socio-material surroundings. Below, we outline some of the key ideas of how the body is conceived of in this way of theorizing.

Central to this scholarship is the extension of agency to the material and biological body, instead of considering it as a passive target of cultural inscription. In other words, it challenges the tendency to regard the socio-cultural body as active and endlessly malleable (via cultural inscription and marketplace practices such as tattooing or surgery), and the biological one as pre-social, fixed, and passive. Instead, this scholarship highlights the active role of both the biological body – the genes, bones, blood, muscles, nerves, and hormones – and the cultural body, signified by practices, norms, values, myths, and materiality.

Another central idea is the recognition of the inextricable entanglement of the material and socio-cultural aspects of the body, including its surroundings. Such a reconceptualization of the body departs from producing binaries, such as outer-inner body, or nature-culture, and is instead interested in how material, discursive, human, more-than-human, corporeal, biological, or technological phenomena – or any other relevant aspect to the study in question – entangle. As Elisabeth Grosz puts it, there is a need for "reconceptualising the relations between the natural and the social, between the biological and the cultural, outside the dichotomous structure in which these terms are currently enmeshed" (Grosz 2008, 43). These various aspects *intra-act*, to use Baradian oft-quoted expression, and in doing so co-constitute bodies (Barad 2007).

This way of thinking leads to consider the body as always open and permeable, instead of viewing it as a clearly bounded and easily definable entity. It is, after all, not always clear where the body begins and where it ends. The literature has conceptualized this phenomenon using notions such as 'porosity', 'fluidity', or 'transcorporeality', for instance. In the words of Stacy Alaimo (2008, 238):

> Imagining human corporeality as trans-corporeality, in which the human is always intermeshed with the more-than-human world, underlines the extent to which the corporeal substance of the human is ultimately inseparable from "the environment." It makes it difficult to pose nature as a mere background for the exploits of the human, since "nature" is always as close as one's own skin.

The notion of transcorporeality is illustrated in a study that explores the encounter of the body of a tourist and that of a mosquito. When the mosquito lands on the human skin and sucks the blood, these two bodies become entangled via the blood (Valtonen et al. 2020). Indeed, the inclusion and problematization of human and non-human bodies – and their interconnections – is a typical endeavor for feminist new materialist scholars. They have for long argued that a human body is always also a non-human body (Alaimo 2008; Barad 2012; Haraway 2016). In other words, human bodies are nature already. For instance, Grosz thinks of the body in terms of 'open materiality', which exists "in continuity with organic and inorganic matter" (Grosz 1994, 22). To exemplify, 60–70% of human bodies consist of water, and human bones are the result of the process of mineralization that occurred during evolution (Valtonen and Pullen 2021).

Much of the work inspired by the seminal work of Donna Haraway (2008) have explored the messy interrelation, or contact zones, between human and non-human bodies, often referring to the bodies of animals, such as dogs (Syrjälä 2016) or fish (Markuksela and Valtonen 2019). This echoes the overall aim to decenter the human in social scientific inquiry and to highlight the equally important role of non-human when bodies (and the world) are investigated.

Many of the ideas discussed above are shared within ongoing 'material turn' (Borgerson 2013; Scott et al. 2014). However, feminist new material scholars seek to challenge the masculinist, human-centric, and dichotomist onto-epistemology that privileges humans over other creatures and maintains fantasies of mastery, control, and rationality (Zylinska 2014). Instead, it recognizes the uncertain, entangled, messy, and relational character of the common worlding of earthly creatures. Another key characteristic of feminist new material scholarship is a concerted concern for ethical and political issues – that are being reformulated in line with relational onto-epistemologies. One of the key issues relevant for our chapter is a shift from ethical principles to ethical practices, which are embodied and situated actions unfolding in time and space (Puig de la Bellacasa 2017; Zylinska 2014). Ethics of care, a core notion in feminist theorizing, is rethought, as Puig de la Bellacasa aptly notes: "care is a human trouble, but this does not make of care a human-only matter" (2017, 2). Therefore, the significance and the liveliness of the more-than-human world is taken seriously; after all, ethical practices emerge from material realities and they have multiple material consequences.

Then again, the recent turn to affect closely relates to the debates on materiality and non-representationalism. While the turn to affect involves a range of different modes of thought (Blackman and Venn 2010), studies commonly share a focus on the body – acknowledging its social and material dimensions – and on the exploration of sensations, emotions, energies, and intensities that circulate between bodies (Katila et al. 2019). Affects influence our bodily capacities, making, for instance, consumers to feel energetic and capable, or phlegmatic. The body, in this way of thinking, is conceived as a capacity to affect and be affected by other bodies (Massumi 2002), including non-human bodies (Bennett 2010). The affect lens directs attention to bodily pre-linguistic sensations, visceral perceptions, and autonomic responses that precede cognition. While these are felt in the individual body, affects circulate and transfer between bodies – it is rather a social than an individual phenomenon. Think of, for instance, affects resonating between bodies in a movie festival (Haanpää 2017). Affects may be mobilized and transferred by cultural practices, such as media texts, and they may 'stick' to objects. Kuruoğlu and Ger's (2014) analysis of the use of Kurdish music cassettes in Turkey exemplifies how an object becomes laden with affects through various circulation practices. Our case that is discussed next exemplifies how certain artifacts such as the bed may arouse (dis)pleasure and shape our relation to it – the affects invested in the bed may make us avoid it or long for it.

Case: sleeping bodies

This case is based upon our co-authored study that explores gendered aspects of sleeping bodies in the bed (Valtonen and Närvänen 2015). The study is part of a wider project on sleep cultures led by the first author, and it employs bricolage as its method, using various empirical materials ranging from (auto)ethnographic observations to song lyrics, advertisements, and interviews. The fieldwork was conducted in Finland in 2007–2013. These varied empirical materials allowed us to analyze how socio-historically constructed discourses of sleep entangle with the materiality of bodies and sleep-related artifacts, such as the bed. Material feminism and theories of affect equipped us with appropriate ways of conceiving the complex ways in which the materiality of the bed and the body are woven together, and how gender is implicated in it. As a result, the study offers an extended view of the gendered body that interacts with the material world: one that is biological and cultural, sleeping and waking, and can affect and be affected. Here, we exemplify how feminist materialism and affect lens enabled us to explore the interrelation of the bed and the body.

The bed can be found in most Western homes. Consumers spend approximately one-third of their lives in a bed that involves a network of other objects, such as mattresses or a bedside table. The materiality of the bed (e.g. smoothness of mattresses) and that of the surrounding sleep environment from lights to the temperature and sounds exemplify how a range of material aspects are involved when bodies go to bed and seek to sleep.

The bed is, actually, more than a mere piece of furniture. It is culturally regulated as a place to be used for the dual purposes of sex and sleeping – as illustrated by many bed advertisements. It also is an important site for consumers' affective life. It is in the bed that much of the emotions and sensations are corporeally sensed and lived – flow moments provided by sexual experiences, creative insights passing through the mind at the moment of falling asleep, frightening, shaming or pleasurable memories, moments of passion as well as those of loneliness, sorrow, and pain are experienced while lying in the bed or while being in the world of dreams. No wonder, therefore, that many of the sleep-related objects and practices that the bed assumes are, in one way or another, directed to managing or mobilizing affects. Think, for instance, of the practices of evening prayer, deep breathing, or singing lullabies, or the material practices of closing doors or leaving lights on to ensure safety. Then again, the use of various biochemical and technical devices has become popular, such as sleeping pills or sleep trackers. This points to the way 'technology' and 'body, and the 'inner' and 'outer' body entangle with cultural discourses that accentuate the significance of 'good sleep'.

The bed itself can be attached with 'sticky' affects. It may become an object of desire in itself that makes one long for the warmth and comfort it affords. Or, the bed may become a problem space – one that frightens the sleeper. This is particularly the case when the bed is not able to provide the body, for a range of reasons, with sweet slumber. Our data include several stories of women who relate that they prefer to sleep on sofas; in armchairs, aircraft, or cars; or anywhere other than in their own bed, simply because they are not able to sleep in their bed and have developed a hate relation to their bed. These stories often take the form of 'confessional tales', as they run against the prevailing cultural norm, according to which 'good sleep' equals eight hours of uninterrupted nocturnal sleep in one's own bed.

In the bed, the entire body – head, neck, back, hips, arms, legs, toes – is in close contact with it: the body senses the bed either directly through the skin or as mediated by nightwear. And the body is, as Grosz (1994) reminds us, a culturally and sexually specific body: the physical shape of the male body differs from that of the female body both in terms of body parts and bodily fluids. While sweating and losing hair, for instance, may concern both sexes, the biological signs from menstruation to sperm are sex-specific. The signs of the corporeal life of the sexed body are perhaps more visible (and sensible) in the bed than in any other domestic artifact. Think of sweats of the body going through the menopause years, traces of hair loss due to stress, or signs of sexual encounters. This intimate relationship between the body and the bed is indeed thoroughly material: the bed leaves signs on the body in the form of traces in the face or pain in the back and – vice versa – the body leaves signs on the bed.

With this case, we suggest that material feminism and affect lens help us to achieve a more nuanced understanding of the way consumers, as embodied and affective beings, interact with material objects (see also Salmela et al. 2017). The material object, such as the bed, cannot fully be understood apart from the body; we can open up a novel path for thinking about agency. While the current literature has cogently argued that material artifacts also hold agency, our study provides a reminder of the need to consider agency in terms of interaction and to acknowledge that in this interaction the material body (and its constituents) also holds agency.

Case: bodies caring for food waste

This case is based on a research project undertaken by the second author and her colleagues, which focused on studying the reduction of food waste, especially in consumer households. The perspective discussed here is more specifically based on findings that have been published in Finnish (Koskinen et al. 2018, see also Mattila et al. 2019). The data for the study entail netnographic data from food blogs, accompanied by food blogger interviews as well as ethnographic observations from food waste workshops organized as part of the larger project. The study was conducted in Finland in 2015–2017. The data focus on how food bloggers engage in food waste reduction as part of their daily lives, as well as part of a collective quest to impact their own and their followers' food waste behaviors. For this particular study, we focused on a more-than-human approach to care – how care manifests in different food waste reduction practices, with embodied practices playing a key role. We utilized the work by Maria Puig de la Bellacasa (2010, 2011, 2012, 2017) and Ann Marie Mol (2008) among others to theorize food waste as a matter of care. Here, we discuss how feminist materialism informed our understanding of how consumers care for food waste in embodied ways.

Food waste is a sustainability challenge from environmental, ethical/social, and economic viewpoints. It entails a loss of resources that go to waste. When this resource is food that could be eaten by those suffering from hunger, it is also morally questionable. According to food waste statistics, most of the problems in developed countries relate to consumer households. However, consumers are not careless or intentionally wasteful – instead, they often feel guilty and anxious about throwing food away. Hence, food waste is an affect-laden issue. On the other hand, how we experience food/waste is also thoroughly embodied – we smell, taste, feel, and see food through our senses. The materiality of the food itself – that it perishes more or less quickly as it is biological in nature – causes further complication to the project of food waste reduction.

In our study, we consider reducing food waste in everyday life as a commitment to preventing food from becoming waste – from moving beyond the edibility boundary. Hence, we analyze food/waste not as static categories, but as vibrant matter (Bennett 2010) that has the ability to affect people (see Kinnunen 2017). Reducing food waste requires care not only in relationships with other humans but concerning more-than-human worlds such as animals, materials, environment, and forces of nature (Puig de la Bellacasa 2010, 2011, 2017). Furthermore, the nature of care is voluntary, and it is always seen to be open for situation-specific solutions – how to care in a way that leads to the best possible outcome when it is often impossible to reach perfection.

Caring for food waste is mundane and often remains invisible for anyone not involved in it themselves – consider, for instance, the meal plans made before going to the store, storing food correctly to avoid spoilage, inserting leftovers to new meals, using the freezer to lengthen food's timeframe as well as evaluating the edibility of previously opened food packages. In our data, we found that this work is still very much gendered in nature – women are mainly responsible for cooking and provisioning family meals, and hence, they mainly carry out these tasks as well. Men and children either did not participate in the everyday practices of food waste reduction or they could even sabotage them, for instance, by refusing to eat leftovers. Furthermore, consumers' bodies are crucial in these practices. In our study, consumers engaged in embodied practices of, for instance, tasting, feeling, and touching food, as well as skillful use of kitchen appliances and devices to constantly tinker (Mol 2008) with food so that it would remain edible. The embodied practices are also affective. Consider tasting food that is possibly already beyond the edibility boundary. It is truly scary, as you may catch food poisoning. Hence, it is a sacrifice that the consumer makes to avoid food waste. Caring for one's own body and the bodies of loved ones is thus sometimes in contradiction with care for food/waste.

In our study, we also highlight the way people do not engage in changing their everyday habits alone, but as a part of and in relation to a collective entity (Puig de la Bellacasa 2010, 157). Hence, it is always already a political activity. Acting ethically and sustainably is not only about making ethical choices or having such attitudes, but it is about everyday embodied doings. Observing food waste reduction from the point of view of care brought the feminization of care to the forefront. However, relying on feminist theoreticians, we can argue that care as an ethical and political act can move from private homes to involve the maintenance of relations between humans and non-human worlds. Our study also highlighted food waste reduction as entering into relations with food/waste that do not need to involve guilt or leaving the problem onto the responsibility of the waste management system.

Closing words

What is the benefit of the above-suggested theorizing for marketing and consumer scholars? We suggest, first, that it helps to advance the current debate on the body. While feminist theories have been employed in explorations of the body since the 1990s, the new materialist and affect lens enable marketing scholars to take the next theoretical step and achieve a better and more fruitful balance between discursive and material dimensions. This would widen the ethico-political concerns from bodily representations to a wide range of bodily issues such as the inclusion and exclusion of different bodies, bodies as part of everyday ethical consumption, and human bodies' interrelationships with non-humans.

More generally, we posit that the focus on embodiment and the employment of feminist theories enable to enrich several key debates in the field of marketing and consumer research. Debates around sustainability, ethical consumption, food, tourism, mobility, biohacking, and technology, or human-animal relations would benefit from the inclusion of the theories and approaches we have discussed above. New methods such as sensory, mobile, and affective ethnography may offer marketing and consumer researchers' ways to access these phenomena empirically (Moisander et al. 2020). Moreover, more concerted and critical attention to the role of the body and materialities in the practice of doing and representing research would advance methodological and epistemological discussions of marketing (see Salmela et al. 2019).

Finally, the proposed feminist new materialist lens provides a much-needed perspective for the proliferating 'non-human' or 'material' turns. Much of the existing investigations have drawn from Actor-Network Theory or assemblage theory, which can be criticized for mobilizing a rather technical and mechanical, 'entity-based' world view, without thoroughly acknowledging the entangled and intra-active nature of the world. The current Covid-19 provides an apt case for feminist new material analysis of the inevitably entangled and intra-active nature of humans and non-humans, and the way it is co-constituted via a range of discursive and material practices. Consider, for instance, the representation of the virus through a microscope in the media, and the affects circulating around it. The pandemic also highlights the powerful agency of one tiny non-human body, once entangled to the human body: the socio-political and economic effects are tremendous, and not distributed equally in terms of gender, class, race, residence, etc. Feminist materialist analyses are urgently needed. Commonly, feminist theories are poorly represented in the (mainstream) business academy, and yet "feminism provides opportunities for distinctive practices of knowledge production that challenge the patriarchal social formations which characterize academic work" (Bell et al. 2019, 4). This challenge is to be taken now.

References

Alaimo S. 2008. "Trans-corporeal feminisms and the ethical space of nature". In *Material feminism*, edited by Stacey Alaimo and Susan Hekman, 237–263. Bloomington: Indiana University Press.
Alaimo, S. and Hekman, S. 2008. *Material feminism*. Bloomington: Indiana University Press.
Askegaard, S., M. Gertsen, and R. Langer. 2002. "The body consumed: Reflexivity and cosmetic surgery." *Psychology & Marketing* 19 (10): 793–812.
Barad, K. 2007. *Meeting the universe halfway: Quantum physics and the entanglement of matter and meaning*. Durham, NC: Duke University Press.
Bell, E., S. Meriläinen, S. Taylor, and J. Tienari. 2019. "'Time's up! Feminist theory and activism meets organization studies." *Human Relations* 72 (1): 4–22. doi: 10.1177/0018726718790067.
Bennett, J. 2010. *Vibrant matter. A political ecology of things*. Durham and London: Duke University Press.
Blackmann, L. and C. Venn. 2010. Affect. *Body & Society* 16(1): 7–28. doi: 10.1177/1357034 X09354769.
Bordo, S. 1993. "Reading the slender body". In *Unbearable weight: Feminism, western culture, and the body*, edited by Susan Bordo, 185–212. Berkeley: University of California Press.
Borgerson, J. L. 2013. "The flickering consumer: New materialities and consumer research." *Research in Consumer Behavior* 15: 125–144.
Brace-Govan, J. 2010. "Representations of women's active embodiment and men's ritualized visibility in sport." *Marketing Theory* 10(4): 369–396.
Brace-Govan, J. and S. Ferguson, S. 2019. "Gender and sexed bodies: Embodiment, corporeality, physical mastery and the gaze." In *Handbook of research on gender and marketing*, edited by, 63–100. Northampton, MA: Edward Elgar Publishing.
Buchanan-Oliver, M., A. Cruz, and J.E. Schroeder. 2010. "Shaping the body and technology: Discursive implications for the strategic communication of technological brands." *European Journal of Marketing* 44(5): 635–652.

Butler, J. 1990. *Gender trouble. Feminism and the subversion of identity*. London: Routledge.
Butler, J. 1993. *Bodies that matter: On the discursive limits of sex*. London: Routledge.
Gherardi, S. 2009. "Introduction to the special issue – The critical power of the 'practice lens'." *Management Learning* 40(2): 115–128.
Goffman, E. 1956. *The presentation of self in everyday life*. Edinburgh: University of Edinburgh Social Sciences Centre.
Goulding, C. and M. Saren. 2009. "Performing identity: An analysis of gender expressions at the Whitby goth festival." *Consumption, Markets and Culture* 12(1): 27–46.
Grosz, E. 1994. *Volatile bodies: Toward a corporeal feminism*. Bloomington: Indiana University Press.
Gurrieri, L., J. Previte, and J. Brace-Govan, J. 2013. "Women's bodies as sites of control: Inadvertent stigma and exclusion in social marketing." *Journal of Macromarketing* 33(2): 128–143. doi: 10.1177/0276146712469971.
Haanpää, M. 2017. *Event co-creation as choreography: Autoethnographic study on event volunteer knowing*, 358. Rovaniemi: Acta Universitatis Lapponiensis, Lapin yliopistopaino. ISBN 978-952-337-023-4; ISSN 0788-7604..
Haraway, D. 2008. *When species meet*. Minneapolis: University of Minnesota Press.
Haraway, D. 2016. *Staying with the trouble: Making kin in the Chthulucene*. Durham, NC: Duke University Press.
Harju, A.A. and A. Huovinen. 2015. "Fashionably voluptuous: Normative femininity and resistant performative tactics in fatshion blogs." *Journal of Marketing Management* 31(15–16): 1602–1625. doi: 10.1080/0267257X.2015.1066837.
Hewer, P. and K. Hamilton. 2010. "On emotions and salsa: Some thoughts on dancing to rethink consumers." *Journal of Consumer Behaviour* 9(2): 113–125.
Johansson, J., J. Tienari, and A. Valtonen. 2017. "The body, identity and gender in managerial athleticism." *Human Relations* 70(9): 1141–1167. doi: 10.1177/0018726716685161.
Joy, A. and A. Venkatesh. 1994. "Postmodernism, feminism, and the body: The visible and the invisible in consumer research." *International Journal of Research in Marketing* 11(4): 333–357.
Joy, A. and J.F. Sherry Jr. 2003. "Speaking of art as embodied imagination: A multisensory approach to understanding aesthetic experience." *Journal of Consumer Research* 30(2): 259–282.
Katila, S, A, Kuismin, and A. Valtonen. 2019. "Becoming upbeat: Learning the affecto-rhytmic order of organizational practices." *Human Relations* 73(9): 1308–1330. doi: 10.1177/00/18726719867753.
Kinnunen, V. 2017. "Bokashi composting as a matrixal borderspace." In *Living ethics in a more-than-human world*, edited by Veera Kinnunen and Anu Valtonen, 66–73. Rovaniemi: University of Lapland.
Koskinen, O., M. Mattila, E. Närvänen, and N. Mesiranta, N. 2018. "Hoiva ruokahävikin vähentämisen arkisissa käytännöissä." *Alue ja ympäristö* 47(2): 17–31. doi: 10.30663/ay.72986
Kuruoğlu, A. and G. Ger. 2014. "An emotional economy of mundane objects." *Consumption Markets & Culture* 18, 209–238. doi: 10.1080/10253866.2014.976074.
Kuuru, T.K. and E. Närvänen. 2019. "Embodied interaction in customer experience: A phenomenological study of group fitness." *Journal of Marketing Management* 35(13–14): 1241–1266.
Markuksela, V. and A. Valtonen. 2019. "Dance with a fish? Sensory human-nonhuman encounters in the waterscape of match fishing." *Leisure Studies* 38 (3): 381–393. doi: 10.1080/02614367.2019.1588353.
Matich, M., R. Ashman, and E. Parsons. 2019. "# freethenipple–digital activism and embodiment in the contemporary feminist movement." *Consumption Markets & Culture* 22(4): 337–362. doi: 10.1080/10253866.2018.1512240.
Mattila, M., N. Mesiranta, E. Närvänen, O. Koskinen, and U.M. Sutinen. 2019. "Dances with potential food waste: Organising temporality in food waste reduction practices." *Time & Society* 28(4): 1619–1644. doi: 10.1177/0961463X18784123.

Moisander, J., E. Närvänen, and A. Valtonen. 2020. "Interpretive marketing research: Using ethnography in strategic market development." In *Marketing management: A cultural perspective*, edited by Lisa Penaloza, Luca Visconti, and Nil Ozcaglar–Toulouse, 237–253, 2nd Edition. London: Routledge.

Mol, A. 2008. *The logic of care. Health and the problem of patient choice*. London, New York: Routledge.

Östberg, J. 2010. "Thou shalt sport a banana in thy pocket: Gendered body size ideals in advertising and popular culture." *Marketing Theory* 10(1): 45–73.

Patterson, M. and R. Elliott. 2002. "Negotiating masculinities: Advertising and the inversion of the male gaze." *Consumption, Markets and Culture* 5(3): 231–246.

Patterson, M. and J. Schroeder. 2010. "Borderlines: Skin, tattoos and consumer culture theory." *Marketing Theory* 10(3): 253–267.

Pekkanen, A., E. Närvänen, and P. Tuominen. 2017. "Elements of rituality in consumer tribes: The case of crossfit." *Journal of Customer Behaviour* 16(4): 353–370. doi:10.1362/1475392 17X15144729108144.

Peñaloza, L. 1998. "Just doing it: A visual ethnographic study of spectacular consumption behavior at Nike Town." *Consumption, Markets and Culture* 2(4): 337–400.

Puig de la Bellacasa, M. 2010. "Ethical doings in naturecultures." *Ethics, Place and Environment* 13(2): 151–169. doi: 10.1080/13668791003778834.

Puig de la Bellacasa, M. 2011. "Matters of care in technoscience: Assembling neglected things." *Social Studies of Science* 41(1): 85–106. doi: 10.1177/0306312710380301.

Puig de la Bellacasa, M. 2012. "'Nothing comes without its world': Thinking with care." *The Sociological Review* 60(2): 197–216. doi:1 0.1111/j.1467-954X.2012.02070.x.

Puig de la Bellacasa, M. 2017. *Matters of care: Speculative ethics in more than human worlds*. Minneapolis: University of Minnesota Press.

Salmela, T., A. Valtonen, and D. Lupton. 2019. "The affective circle of harassment and enchantment: Reflections on the ŌURA ring as an intimate research device." *Qualitative Inquiry* 25(3): 260–270. doi: 10.1177/1077800418801376.

Salmela, T., A. Valtonen, and S. Miettinen. 2017. "An uncanny night in a nature bubble: Designing embodied sleeping experiences." In *Design science in tourism*, edited by Daniel R. Fesenmaier, 69–93. Cham: Springer.

Sassatelli, R. 2010. *Fitness culture. Gyms and the commercialisation of discipline and fun*. Basingstoke: Palgrave.

Sayre, S. 1999. "Using introspective self-narrative to analyze consumption: Experiencing plastic surgery." *Consumption, Markets and Culture* 3(2): 99–128.

Scaraboto, D. and E. Fischer. 2013. "Frustrated fatshionistas: An institutional theory perspective on consumer quests for greater choice in mainstream markets." *Journal of Consumer Research* 39(6): 1234–1257. doi: 10.1086/668298.

Schouten, J.W. 1991. "Selves in transition: Symbolic consumption in personal rites of passage and identity reconstruction." *Journal of Consumer Research* 17(4): 412–425.

Schroeder, J.E. and J.L. Borgerson. 1998. "Marketing images of gender: A visual analysis." *Consumption, Markets and Culture* 2(2): 161–201.

Schroeder, J.E. and D. Zwick. 2004. "Mirrors of masculinity: Representation and identity in advertising images." *Consumption, Markets and Culture* 7(1): 21–52.

Scott, K., D.M. Martin, and J.W. Schouten. 2014. "Marketing and the new materialism." *Journal of Macromarketing* 34: 282–290. doi: 10.1177/0276146714532471.

Stevens, L. 2012. "'Feeling bodies' in marketing: Aesthetics, emotions and gender." *The Marketing Review* 12(2): 141–159.

Syrjälä, H. 2016. "Turning point of transformation: Consumer communities, identity projects and becoming a serious dog hobbyist." *Journal of Business Research* 69 (1): 177–190. doi: 10.1016/j.jbusres.2015.07.

Thompson, C.J. and E. C. Hirschman. 1998. "An existential analysis of the embodied self in postmodern consumer culture." *Consumption, Markets and Culture* 2(4): 401–447.

Thompson, C.J. and E.C. Hirschman. 1995. "Understanding the socialized body: A poststructuralist analysis of consumers' self-conceptions, body images, and self-care practices." *Journal of Consumer Research* 22(2): 139–153.

Valtonen, A. 2013. "Height matters: Practicing consumer agency, gender, and body politics." *Consumption Markets & Culture* 16(2): 196–221.

Valtonen, A. and A. Pullen. 2021. "Writing with rocks". *Gender, Work and Organization.* doi: 10.1111/gwao.12579.

Valtonen, A. and E. Närvänen. 2015. "Gendered reading of the body in the bed." *Journal of Marketing Management* 31(15–16): 1583–1601. doi: 10.1080/0267257X.2015.1061038.

Valtonen, A. and E. Närvänen. 2016. "The everyday intimacy of sleeping: An embodied analysis of intimate practices." *Consumption Markets & Culture* 19(4): 370–386.

Valtonen, A., T. Salmela, and O. Rantala. 2020. "Living with mosquitoes." *Annals of Tourism Research* 83: 102945. doi: 10.1016/j.annals.2020.102945.

Veijola, S. and A. Valtonen. 2007. "Body in tourism industry." In *Tourism and gender. Embodiment, sensuality and experience*, edited by Annette Pritchard, Nigel Morgan, Irina Atelejevic and C. Harris, 13–31. Oxfordshire: CABI.

Venkatesh, A., A. Joy, J.F. Sherry Jr., and J. Deschenes. 2010. "The aesthetics of luxury fashion, body and identity formation." *Journal of Consumer Psychology* 20(4): 459–470.

Yngfalk, C. 2016. "Bio-politicizing consumption: Neo-liberal consumerism and disembodiment in the food marketplace." *Consumption Markets & Culture* 19(3): 275–295.

Zylinska, J. 2014. *Minimal ethics for the Anthropocene*. Ann Arbor: Open University Press, University of Michigan Library.

12 Transformations

Is there a role for feminist activism in women's sport?

Jan Brace-Govan

Introduction

There is a welcome upsurge in activity and visibility around women's rights. Examples of this include corporatized interventions in development (Koffman and Gill 2014), a political speech going viral [i.e. Julia Gillard] or female political leaders being venerated [i.e. Jacinta Ardern]. As well, there is the focus of significant international organisations such as the United Nations, celebrity uptake of key issues of discrimination through #MeToo and the academic activism and digital engagement of #EverydaySexism. Harnessing digital media, and sometimes referred to as a fourth wave of feminism (Maclaran and Kravets 2019), these recent upsurges of activism focus on the disrespectful treatment of women and issues of the body.

The body is a critically important topic for feminist theory, and feminist work on the body and embodiment from a range of disciplines has had a profound impact. While philosopher Judith Butler's (1990) notions around performativity have held sway bolstered by third-wave feminism, more important, complex debates in sociology, anthropology, cultural and media studies draw on a broad spectrum of views on the role of the body in social interaction, social cohesion, rituals and the exercise of power (Cregan 2006; Douglas (1996) 2002; Martin (1987) 2018; Shilling 2003; Turner 2012). The significance of the body to feminist theory began with their challenge to the assumed naturalness of the Enlightenment's Cartesian dualism which associated the feminine subject with the body and emotionality, and the masculine subject with the mind and rational thought. Young's (1989) classic 'Throwing Like a Girl' and MacKinnon (1987) argue that women are trained to be physically weak not only captured an embodied state that lacked strength, but also asserted that women should access positions of power. Connell's (1987, 1995) hugely important work on gender and hegemonic masculinity identifies the vital role of sport in generating the dominant social position of some men that is symbolically reinforced by the visibility of men's professional sport which also works to maintain men's validated access to violence (Brace-Govan 2010). While there are multiple masculinities and localised social conditions, the prevalence of a dominating masculinity embodied in the spectacle of football codes is international, and a highly lucrative business. The athletic body is even argued to be essential to contemporary managerial identities (Johansson, Tienari, and Valtonen 2017). Indeed, gender differences in engagement with competitive sport are presented as a reason for a lack of women in top-level positions in business, science and politics (Comeig et al. 2016). Generally, marketing's focus has been on supporting the highly lucrative business of sport, with its masculine bias, particularly in media broadcast professional games that

DOI: 10.4324/9781003042587-15

carry significant social symbolism, thus leaving women's sport somewhat neglected. However, increasingly the women's game has been in the media, especially in the football codes. Several leagues have been launched to wide acclaim, and women's international matches have attracted large crowds.

Given the significance of men's sport and the recent shift in the visibility of women's sport, this chapter ponders the role of feminist activism. If transformations for women in sport are to gain a foothold and become an enduring social phenomena, what is required. This chapter begins by briefly considering the apparent upsurge in women's football and assessments of its emancipatory potential. Today's young Australian women express a passion for 'footy' with their numbers jumping from 380,000 nationally in 2016 to 600,000 in 2021 (Graham 2021, 8). However, that the physicality of sport affects women and their perception of themselves is not in doubt (Brace-Govan 2002, 2004, 2010). So, the focus here moves away from the individualised experience of women to a macro level question that asks what is the next step for feminist activism in women's sport? The lack of women in the management and leadership of sport is widely noted (Adriaanse 2016; Evans and Pfister 2020). It is asserted that women should be included in the management of sport, just as it is important that they join government and the executive suites and boardrooms of other businesses. Given the lack of progress in sport management, successful transformations driven by leading local feminist activists across the domains of government and business are drawn on from which some potential research implications are identified. Following this, the contemporary state of women's leadership in sport, recent feminist activism and academic activism are then considered separately. This chapter closes by pointing to some challenges and potential research topics.

Women's sport: A feminist breakthrough?

The recent upsurge in the visibility of women playing professional sport is heartening, but is it novel? Women singles tennis players receive significant media coverage, and the women's soccer teams are followed closely. The successful Australia and New Zealand bid for the Women's Soccer World Cup in 2023 was met with much celebration, as was the Australian women's cricket team's record in one day matches. Forays into professional football codes are widespread and, in Australia, rugby [NRLW] and Australian Football League [AFLW], or 'footy', were announced as ground-breaking and drew surprising audience numbers and support (Brace-Govan and Ferguson 2019). In the UK, 2017 was called the 'summer of women's sport' (McLachlan 2019, 10–12; Petty and Pope 2019, 499). The interest and enthusiasm for professional women's sport has concomitant government support for women's everyday physical activity and community sport: for example, the 2015 launch of 'This Girl Can' in England and its 2018 launch in Victoria, Australia.[1]

This flurry of attention begs the question: is this as ground-breaking as touted? Petty and Pope (2019) are cautiously positive, which is appropriate given the well-documented and long-standing lack of media coverage of any women's sport as well as the trivialisation or denigration of sportswomen, especially in the sporting activities perceived to be masculine such as the football codes. However, McLachlan's historical study demonstrates that such enthusiasm is not novel, in fact the narratives of progress and success have echoes going back through the 1900s to the 1880s, and she notes an 1887 women's cricket match expected to attract a large crowd (2019, 16). Moreover, in

Australia in 1929 the *Sunday Times* included a page devoted to women's sport and in 1935 *The Sun* followed suit (McLachlan 2019, 17). Therefore, despite lower visibility, women have long engaged with a competitive active embodiment.

Post-World War II (WWII) women were perceived to be active in leisure-based pursuits. Wearing's (1990) poststructuralist proposition that access to leisure was important for women to give them personal time away from childcare and housework touched on the burgeoning aerobics movement, and an active embodiment that valued health and shaping one's body. At this time Western governments' policies embraced a liberal feminist approach of personal choice which was often co-opted and commercialised through brands such as *Nike* into a commodity feminism (Cole and Hribar 1995), but these offered limited change to the structural inequalities women faced (Brace-Govan 2010). The increasing impact of neoliberalism and responsibilisation of the self (Gurrieri, Previte, and Brace-Govan 2013) created a subjectification amongst women (Gill 2011) whereby their focus on self-management and empowerment led to contradictions that McRobbie (2009) calls the 'double entanglement' and generates questionable embodied endeavours for young women (Ferguson, Brace-Govan, and Welsh 2020).

Physical activity has offered women different freedoms and been embraced for reasons that vary over time (Brace-Govan 2010; Brace-Govan and Ferguson 2019). Women's contemporary visibility as professional athletes has the potential to provide many and varied opportunities for role modelling (Brace-Govan 2013). But there is a shift that draws on the discourse of empowerment provided by third-wave feminism, to be powerful *and* pretty, a *both/and* framing that opens up a fissure for women to embrace the feminisation that was accused of being trivial while at the same time demonstrating physical prowess (Heywood 2018). The usual heroine here is the tennis player Serena Williams, or the focus is on what are termed 'lifestyle' sports (Wheaton 2014) or 'action sports' (Thorpe and Olive 2016) including surfing, roller derby, skate boarding and rock climbing. Negotiating a space for themselves, it is asserted that these sportswomen engage in activism, agency and politics, and authors often draw on their own experiences of challenging systems and structures of discrimination in the sport-media-industrial complex (Ferguson, Brace-Govan, and Martin 2020; Mansfield et al. 2018; Silk, Andrews, and Thorpe 2017; Thorpe and Olive 2016; Toffoletti, Thorpe, and Francombe-Webb 2018). But Snyder (2008) is less enamoured with third-wave feminist claims and questions their lack of detail and their lapses into over-statement. Others point out that the *both/and* discourse of empowerment is culpable in the renewal of impossible body shapes as goals for women promoted by Instagram Influencers (Ferguson et al. 2020). Furthermore, as Caudwell (2011) and McRobbie (2009) carefully document, many third-wave discourses erase prior feminist work on corporeal feminism, diversity and the fluidity of gender. In essence, recognition of the complexity and longevity of feminist theorising is required (Maclaran and Kravets 2019; Maclaran and Stevens 2019) but often lost in the metaphor of waves (Rome, O'Donohoe, and Dunnett 2019). It is suggested that activism is in a fourth wave which is more about connection and finding community through the internet (Maclaran 2015), and this contemporary response will be revisited in more detail later.

The transformative capacity of contemporary women's sport leagues is also less certain. Burke raises serious questions around the viability of women's professional football to make a difference and instead deems them to be simply market extensions of the men's league primarily to ensure the financial stability of men's sport (2019, 507). Key here is lack of women's control over decision-making and access to those organisational positions which allows the maleness of sporting authority to continue unchecked. While individual women's experience is transformative, the gender hierarchy of sport remains intact as the "most publicly mediatized demonstrations of difference between the sexes" (Burke 2019, 499). And the argument has wide support. For example, national and international sport associations where, despite numerous initiatives for women's equality in sport, the pace of change has been glacial (de Soysa and Zipp 2019). An important agenda for feminist activism and feminist theorising is to move away from individualised notions of empowerment to engage collective action in order to generate enduring structural transformation. Reminiscent of second-wave feminism, Burke advocates for consciousness-raising that maintains an honest history, building women-centred collective organisations and challenging the patriarchal discourse through a redistributive affirmative action (2019, 508).

In sum, there is a congratulatory discourse around women's football leagues which on closer inspection does not adequately cover the issues. While sportswomen may well experience personal empowerment, act as role models and draw substantial crowds, there is no evidence of improvement in sports management, nor sport's symbolic role that presents the gender binary as unchallenged. If feminist activism is to make a transformative difference to sport, how might that be organised? With the lack of progress for women in the management of sport, either in government or in business, casting a wider net to women who have led and managed successful feminist transformations in their field could offer some clues to such an agenda and potential research topics. It is to these that we now turn.

Activist interviews and method

Interviews were taken with highly regarded women leaders who had successfully progressed a feminist agenda in government or business. Their work continued despite times of 'backlash' or low visibility and, in some instances, over several decades. The transformations they achieved endure and are the seeds of further positive change for women thus offering potential pathways for feminist activism in sports organisation. The interviews were taken in early 2017, before #MeToo was given an injection of celebrity fame (Mendes, Ringrose, and Keller 2018), and were originally intended for a team project investigating successes in addressing gender injustice. Participants were invited to have a conversational, taped interview about their experiences as activists and practitioners. They were told the conversation would revolve around three questions: (1) how do you, as a practitioner, navigate institutions and institutional injustice; (2) what do you focus on transforming and why; (3) what are the goals of your organisation for gender justice. Institutional ethical permission was obtained and addressed the identifiability of high-profile interviewees by giving them a verbatim transcript of the interview with options to delete or alter any of the content, or to withdraw themselves and their commentary entirely. The interviewees were informed that their conversation would be shared in team meetings and that their commentary could be published with extensive quotations. All agreed to the material subsequently analysed and presented here. However, the team took the decision to move the project in a quite different direction, and these interviews have not been published before and were not extended into a larger project.

Table 12.1 Summary of Participants

Position	Organisation	Problem	Action	Level
Politician	State Electorate	Leadership of local community groups	Identifying and training potential leaders	Community
Lawyer	Law Firm	HR and unconscious bias training	Awareness raising within work contexts	Business and legal profession
Co-ordinator	Emily's List	Redress the lack of women in Federal politics	Funding and mentoring for aspiring politicians	Federal Politics
CEO	NFP	Improve women's access to well-paid work	Coaching, mentoring, provision of resources	Individual women
Trade Unionist	ACTU	Establish and defend workers' rights	Strategic campaigning	National policy and law

The interviewees were chosen because they had played a significant role in challenging gender injustice with widely recognised success. They were informally approached to ascertain their level of interest at an event organised by the Victorian Women's Trust, 'Breakthrough', which was held on the 25th and 26th of November 2016.[2] The women invited to participate were selected to represent diverse fields and contrasting experience bases rather than consistency. The participants, who will be described in more detail shortly, included a lawyer, a State politician, a public servant who also volunteered for a key initiative for the advancement of women, a CEO for a women-focused NGO and high-ranking trade union official. All were interviewed at a place of their choosing where it was possible to tape the conversation, which as noted was transcribed verbatim. Interviews lasted for between 60 and 90 minutes. Despite being identifiable, all five participants were content to use their real names at the time of the interviews, but these are avoided partly due to the time lapse and in part because at least three interviewees have moved on from these positions. All interviewees were women, and these initial conversations were intended to explore starting points for further research and not to represent any kind of holistic or integrated perspective. Nevertheless, across their experiences, a narrative analysis (Cresswell 2013) uncovered ideas and points of connection that were important to achieve long-term change. As is usual, the narrative analysis is presented with(in) context to enhance comprehension by situating knowledge and is reported here in the order in which the interviews were taken. The leadership of these women and the transformations they generated offer implications for further research summarised here and re-visited towards the end of this chapter.

Interview 1: State politician and local community organising

The first interview was with a State level politician for an area of Melbourne renowned for disadvantage and cultural diversity. The area was highly industrialised, on a major trucking route, with a significant communities from recent migration. These factors culminated in local women from diverse backgrounds becoming what she called 'accidental activists' to address local issues that affected their families such as pollution or lack of kindergartens or keeping green spaces. She was in her 50s and had been an activist most of her adult life with a focus on local politics, women and the environment. In our conversation we reflected on what had changed for women over the last 30 years and how slow change was. Her focus had always been at the local, extended community level and relied on alliances of diverse community groups, finding connections and networks. Importantly, the organising was informal and highly flexible in order that women could contribute: finding a suitable location for meetings might be the park so that children could play or facilities where childcare could be arranged; food and timing would accommodate women's responsibilities for children and paid work; and women's limited time led to tasks being broken down so that they could be completed in small batches or across a number of women. Communicating across multiple languages by being simple and direct without rhetoric was also important. She noted the "women were a dynamic leading force" but often "overshadowed by men who have louder voices but don't do the work", and to remedy this she arranged cost-free training for leadership, including public speaking. She would encourage women to take part, often those who did not recognise their own potential to find what she called the 'hidden women' and was pleased that this counterbalanced the men who thought "the sound of their own voice was just miraculous". For this activist what usually failed was formality, or imposing structures.

Interview 2: Lawyer and unconscious bias training

The next interview was with a lawyer who specialised in workplace relations and regularly presented training to the firm's business clients on unconscious bias and how to challenge these attitudes. Offered to employees as personal development her tactic was to focus on what she called 'Hot Spots', or areas of organisational process that exposed discrimination. She was usually engaged to address gender and most often leadership was the 'hot spot'. She approached this by having employees consider questions such as who is a leader, what is the pathway, what 'stretch' opportunities are available and for whom. The next step was to workshop for solutions. Despite its applicability to intersectionality, this was rarely pursued with the profile of gender issues in the media driving interest in this direction. Having undertaken this work for several years and with high ranking organisations and clients, she was of the opinion that 'quotas' were the best approach to managing numbers of women in various layers of business.

Interview 3: Co-coordinator of Emily's List giving support and mentoring to women federal politicians

Emily's List is an American initiative that was adopted in Australia in 1996 by the Australian Labor Party (ALP). While not nearly as wealthy as the American version, Emily's List has been successful in supporting many women into parliament with a focus on the Australian Federal Parliament. EMILY stands for 'Early Money Is Like Yeast'. The third interviewee was a volunteer and co-coordinator of the list, in addition to her paid employment in the public service. She spoke at length about the development and impact of Emily's List as it shifted from telephone trees to social media and the value of the mentoring program. Committed to equality, diversity, equal pay, access to childcare and pro-choice, Emily's List supports women into politics through funding, mentoring and what she called 'gender-based campaigning' where women were polled in electorates when women were standing to find out what were the key issues for them. She commented on the late 1990s and early 2000s as a time of generational differences when the women's movement seemed perceived to be almost unnecessary. As a Gen Xer she fondly remembered gathering with other women on university campus. She lamented the loss of the women's rooms where women's solidarity had been able to flourish but is now absorbed into the LBGTI identity movements of Gen Y. However, Julia Gillard's experience as Prime Minister had 'rejuvenated anger' and raised the profile of the disadvantages that continue to exist for women. Although Australian politics is, as she said, still run by the 'pale male whales', there have been significant activist achievements. The ALP committed in 2014, in its constitution, to 50% women's representation by 2025. This initiative is underpinned by the consequence that if quotas are not met then *all* candidates are spilled. She asserts that this level of accountability is essential for significant cultural change. Furthermore, it was achieved only incrementally over an extended period of time and with a great deal of informal reinforcement. She called herself an 'incrementalist' and that if significant change is to occur one 'can't be impatient' therefore, mentoring and a succession plan are essential.

Interview 4: CEO of a NFP that supported disadvantaged women into work

Following the women only focus of Emily's List the next interview was with the CEO of an NFP that helped disadvantaged women into the workforce and supported them to keep that work for a year. The organisation provided women with entire outfits including accessories for interviews and matched them to a mentor as well as giving them training in interview techniques and CV presentation. Mentoring was especially important because she noted that a lack of self-confidence and self-esteem along with destructive internal dialogue was common amongst their clients. The organisation had secured a contract with a company to place women into traditionally male work with great success which was important on two counts. First, it demonstrated that, given appropriate support initially, women were also good candidates for this work, and second, given the gender pay gap these women were able to earn a significantly better income than they would otherwise.

Interview 5: Trade Unionist of peak trade union body

The final interview shifted to the highest strategic level for worker organisations, a high-ranking officer of the Australian Council of Trade Unions (ACTU). Noting that "women pretty much carry the inequality load" and that a new social compact was needed, this interviewee had a very clear, articulated strategic agenda for change, albeit not solely for women, and one that took diversity into account. Aiming for tax justice to adjust 'corporate greed' and campaigning for workers' rights that included portable entitlements, free childcare, paid parental leave and domestic violence leave, the organisation's remit was to represent and advocate for workers' rights which included addressing discrimination and disadvantage. She remarked that unconscious bias often underpinned taken-for-granted views that needed to be challenged. Affirmative action, targets and quotas were useful ways to provide benchmarks and rationales for audits. She saw audits as circuit breakers that exposed the unintended consequences of company policies. For example, gender pay gaps that arose due to company policies around flexible working hours or part-time work only being available to the lower paid positions. Getting attention for these and other issues of disadvantage was key, as was the language used to express them. She commented that there had been a strong shift in community views around domestic violence, so this was achieving some traction, but parental leave and equal pay continue to be 'tough to explain' and therefore difficult to make progress on. But by 'starting the conversation' her organisation "made it safe for them [politicians] to be brave". She was also an 'incrementalist' expecting that change takes a long time and relies on alliances.

Distilling ideas and points of connection for transformations

Clearly, as intended, these activist leaders/managers are embedded in quite disparate organisations that varied in size, focus and the level of social structure that they addressed, as summarised in Table 12.1. Importantly though, their activism was not a *cul de sac* of women but engaged widely with various segments of society, drawing organisations and others into the frame of understanding. Emily's List, for example, is an independent entity but to achieve quotas for women in the ALP and have that enshrined in the Party's constitution required significant broad-based advocacy. The NFP that supports women into work engages with a range of businesses to seek work opportunities for their female clients. The other three activists tackling local politics, HR policy and national strategies for change in worker conditions bring their activism to more obviously mixed audiences. In short, these activist leaders were working 'at the coalface' and had found ways to 'move the needle'.

Overall, acknowledging the limitations of these brief vignettes and the women's diversity, there emerge some broad dimensions which are instructive. First, they all commented that simply being a woman was, for them, the primary and substantive disadvantage. Whether or not a woman had actually become a mother, the effect of women bearing the main burden for childcare and household unpaid labour continues to underpin a range of significant inequalities. In their different fields the interviewees responded to this through the goals of their organisations and recognised that other facets often compounded and exacerbated these disadvantages, such as migration, religion, ethnicity, and age, academically referred to as intersectionality. Second, although strategies for achieving change varied, their focus for transformation, advocacy and activism responded to the social locus of women. Some drew on informality and local connections to expand the potential of 'hidden women'. Others provided objective information and solutions based on research to bring change management to a business. Identifying the shortfalls in women's experience and resources was an important starting point, whether that is to gain high office or steady well-paid work or steers a highly formal clearly articulated national level strategy.

Third, to navigate institutionalised injustice there was a commonly held recognition that women needed training in leadership accompanied by continued support through mentoring. All interviewees touched on this remedy, albeit in different arenas. Furthermore, and fourth, there was consistency amongst these activists in the value of targets, auditing for accountability and the usefulness of quotas. This sequence was perceived to offer moments of intervention when discrimination and disadvantage can be 'discovered' (exposed), then compared to a standard or benchmark to assess what is absent or what could be included which can then be reviewed to ensure that change moves, however slowly, in the desired direction, or better still towards a set point at a set time (quota and date). Finally, there was the sheer tenacity of women who persisted, despite popular narratives that past feminisms were unwanted or unnecessary and that '*grrl*' power had arrived. Their tenacity recognised that change was slow and incremental, took time, demanded patience and long-term strategic thinking, as well as cross-generational input. They had contributed and persevered for several decades: advocacy and leadership shortfalls in local community politics; challenged biases in the workplace; overcoming obstacles that prevented women being elected, or their difficulties finding work opportunities and lacking self-confidence; adjusting policy and laws that discriminate against women leaving them with the heaviest burdens. As the Trade Unionist said, "We made the laws. We can change the laws. ... We need a new social compact".

List of key points from narrative analysis of activists' interviews

1   Simply being a women is a source of disadvantage
2   The social locus of women defined the way forward tactically and strategically
3   Training in leadership and long-term supportive mentoring is essential
4   The value of targets and quotas for setting benchmarks and pace of change
5   The slow, incremental pace of change demands patience and resilience

Women's sport leadership and academic activism

This chapter began by noting the significance of feminist theories and gender inequality to academic discussions of the body, embodiment, physical activity and sport. Besides being a lucrative business, it was noted that sport is a significant social institution that carries highly important symbolism. Bearing in mind the activists' insights, let us now examine the parlous state of women in sport's leadership at the national and international levels. Then, before drawing the threads together to consider areas for potential research, we will reflect on academic activism, particularly for feminists and young women academics.

The status of women's leadership in sport business

It comes as no surprise that there is a preponderance of men in the leadership of sport. Gender equality is Sustainable Development Goal 5 for the United Nations (UN) which recognises the benefits of gender equality in leadership but also the serious shortfall of women at senior levels in business (Women Rising 2030, 2018, 35). Surveys at a global level identify the largest gender disparity is the 'Political Empowerment gap' (World Economic Forum 2020, 5). Despite the commitment of the UN and organisations like the International Working Group (IWG) on Women and Sport (created in 1994), there has been only limited progress for women in leading sports organisations at the national and international level (de Soysa and Zipp 2019). A recent systematic review confirmed a consensus in the literature that women are under-represented at these higher levels but also identified patriarchal selection practices and organisational cultures as significant barriers for women's leadership in sports organisations and a heavy reliance in research on 'Western' experiences (Evans and Pfister 2020). Other work documented the international situation through data collected from 1,600 national sports organisations across

45 countries to reveal that 41 countries "failed to achieve a critical mass of women's presence on its boards" (Adriaanse 2016, 157), where 'critical mass' was set at only 30%. Arguing the ethical case of adequate stakeholder representation and the business case of organisational performance, Adriaanse (2016) finds only the Cook Islands have 'balanced' representation and a further three achieve critical mass, Norway, Sweden, Fiji. Many other works confirm this finding in single country contexts and international committees (see Evans and Pfister 2020, 9 for a list). There are proactive approaches to gender equality, often undertaken with the backing of government. However, these are criticised for 'fixing' women or 'add women and stir' approaches that rarely aim to adjust the setting and culture from which the issue emerges (Evans and Pfister 2020, 10; Fox 2017). Recently, Piggott and Pike (2020) investigated the informal 'naturalised' ways and means by which the hegemony of men continues to govern sport. Gendered organisational practices included dress codes with a focus on branded blazers, sexist language, informal gender segregation which undermined women's efforts to collaborate or be included, and long, inflexible, unsociable hours that clashed with care giving (Piggott and Pike 2020). Moreover, there is a dogged adherence to the sexed binary male/female which arises directly out of the structure and organisation of sports' competition and needs closer attention. In short, women and leadership in sport is a long-standing challenge that is yet to be rectified indicating that there is scope for a feminist research lens onto the business of sport. First though, let us reflect on activism in academic research as well as recent developments in feminist activism, and the implications this might contain.

Where to from here? Activism and/in academic research

Just as there is a case for women managing businesses, women also deserve access to the leadership positions and management of sport organisations. Moreover, the stubborn nature of the problem seems to require a fresh standpoint because, as shown, the older liberal style of feminism has made little headway. However, business academics in the neoliberal university are claimed to be lacking in challenge to the status quo (Brewis 2017; Dunne, Harney, and Parker 2008; Rhodes, Wright, and Pullen 2017). Spicer, Alvesson, and Karreman (2016, 241) assertively argue the case for 'waste disposal' because:

> [B]usiness schools are veritable junkyards filled with the ideological wreckage of long discredited ideas. Usually, companies are even worse.

Furthermore, the lack of political engagement across 20 top management and marketing journals is remarkable, including those journals of a reputedly critical stance (Dunne, Harney, and Parker 2008), although some have since attempted to address these criticisms (Tadajewski 2016). It is suggested that the call for academic activism (Burawoy 2014) can be responded to through a critical stance (Shankar 2009). But the effects of peer review (Brewis 2017) and the evaluation of academic output for impact are asserted to act as policing functions reducing any potential political impact instead enhancing the status quo (Rhodes, Wright, and Pullen 2017). Recognising the limitations of the neoliberal academic environment, Dallyn, Marinetto and Cederstrom (2015) define the senior academic with a public profile differently to the more critical non-conformist. Describing the "cul-de-sac of peer-induced conformity" (2015, 1034) and "professional insularity" (2015, 1038), Dallyn, Marinetto and Cederstrom argue for the critical intellectual as a temperament that sidesteps the confines of metrics and auditing, less celebrity and public, instead more alternative, "subterranean" even (2015, 1042).

In marketing, Handelman and Fischer's (2018) thorough review of the main perspectives of activism adopts a quite functional approach through a framework of three questions over four journals for articles post-2000: what actors matter, what is mobilised and what is achieved. Beyond the opportunities they identify as blind spots, there is limited attention paid to the role of emotions and emotional work in activism (Jasper 2011) and the significance of private experiences to public and political standpoints. The part played by feminist theory in these academic spaces is profound. Recent developments in feminist activism, sometimes referred to as a fourth wave, have revitalised the public debate of personal experiences reminiscent of the second wave through movements facilitated by the internet and digital media, such as #MeToo, #EverydaySexism and #DestroyingTheJoint (DtJ). The wave metaphor can be clumsy and mask the diversity that resides in feminist activism (Rome, O'Donohoe, and Dunnett 2019). Here it serves to bring attention to the revival of some agendas that are unfinished, the comfort that women have experienced in collectivities, the consciousness raising that occurs across generations, as well as the social power that gathering together enables. Most recently, the connectivity of social media has assuaged the wounds of 'going public', as the following examples record.

#MeToo initiated in the USA in 2006 by Tarana Burke and picked up by celebrity Alyssa Milano late in 2017 became a media phenomenon. The high profile of this digital feminist activism certainly created visibility and support, generating a community (Mendes, Ringrose, and Keller 2018) but the shift in its focus from the original intention towards powerful, rich celebrities was questionable (Zarkov and Davis 2018). Moreover, the labour involved in maintaining this kind of digital space can be onerous and emotionally demanding as women are subjected to aggressive trolling (Mendes et al. 2018). In spite of these difficulties the feminist solidarity experienced online was positive and contrasted to the challenge of being feminist in offline locations (Mendes et al. 2018). Another activist initiative that garnered much attention is the #EverydaySexism project started by academic Laura Bates in the UK in 2012 which exposed and documented through personal postings the systemic sexism experienced by all kinds of women in so many settings (Bates 2014). Vachhani and Pullen (2018) describe the affective solidarity that emerges from this revitalised feminism as women share their embodied experiences of discrimination. A different example of solidarity and contemporary feminism arose in DtJ. DtJ was a 2012 Australian feminist response to a 'shock jock' rant (conservative male radio host with extreme views) describing the then Prime Minister Julia Gillard's initiative to fund a Pacific women's leadership program as an example of women leaders 'destroying the joint'. The misogynistic comment was picked up by businesswoman and social commentator, Jane Caro, in an ironic tweet that launched a movement and received international press attention (Caro 2013, x). The DtJ administrators describe the collective and its work to "create a safe place to talk about important issues" (DtJ Administrators 2013, 104). These feminist digital spaces brought together disparate women to offer a safe place to express their feelings in an affective solidarity that undermined the atomising effects of neoliberalism (Vachhani and Pullen 2018, 40). The digital space offered the experience of collectivity and, in spite of the emotional labour required, challenged the language that denigrated women's leadership. So, what does that imply for feminist academic activism?

Along with much renewed enthusiasm and visibility for feminism (Bell et al. 2018; Contu 2018; Vachhani and Pullen 2018) there are lively debates around critical performativity about how this should proceed (Tadajewski 2016). Although feminist academics are visible and active (Phipps 2016, 307) and the prominence of a feminist resurgence is welcomed (Bell et al. 2018, 3), others offer warnings not only of failures but of the complicity of the Academy in those failures (Bell and de Gama 2019; Brewis 2017; Callahan and Elliott 2020). Lund and Tienari (2019) utilise Smith's (2005) institutional ethnography method to investigate the standpoint of junior academic women in a leading university and find a vulnerability that the exhortations to activism overlook. They bring real experiences to the hegemonic practices of academic writing in the masculine space that is the competitive neoliberal university. An embeddedness both politically and institutionally has consequences for individuals (Fleming and Banerjee 2015, 263). Constructing feminist knowledge is a precarious activity (Hemmings 2012; Phipps 2016) that challenges hierarchies and has long decried the use of obscure, jargonised theory (Bell et al. 2018, 11). As well there are enduring concerns about male feminists and the risk they pose as users of feminism for simply another theoretical position to advance themselves (Bell et al. 2018, 7).

The activist leader interviews have practical suggestions which are most relevant to women academics who would engage in feminist research, such as the need for mentoring and leadership training, and importantly, supportive funding with a long-term view. They also strongly encouraged a contextualised awareness and sensitivity to the processes that include and incorporate women, not simply an echo of the masculinised neoliberal academy. Notably, the echoes of second-wave feminism in the digital fourth wave point to need to engage in cross-generational and intersectional dialogues to find coherence, affective solidarity and to combat divisive critiques. Negative voices allow others to frame feminist theorising as a "perspective" (Cresswell 2013) or dismiss feminist concerns as too political for business research, rather than the serious re-interpretation of human society that it provides. Quotas and targets can help sustain shifts towards transformation by recording and comparing activities and outcomes. However, there is a strong cautionary note that the neoliberal business academy is not necessarily transparent and supportive of feminist research. In spite of this, some research pathways are considered next.

Future research – and final summation

Sport is big business and a social institution that creates, maintains and makes visible the dominance of hegemonic masculinity. Marketing has engaged deeply with the lucrative business of sport but paid less attention to a critical review of its social consequences. Although professional sportswomen are on the football field, women are less visible in sports' boardrooms. For a transformation of sport to endure, it is argued that this imbalance needs to change and therefore there is a role for feminist activism in women's sport. Bearing the noted pitfalls in mind, there is much scope here for academics to engage in "intellectual activism" (Contu 2018). Finding clarity on what needs to be transformed and why, and what might be the goals for gender justice in sport are important places to start. Shifting the focus from individualised empowerment to the enduring value of collective action that generates structural transformation is essential (Table 12.2).

Table 12.2 Summary of Activists' Key Points and Implications for Research

Activists' Key Points	Implications for Research
Being a women is a source of inequality	Women together despite differences
Respond to the social locus of women	Institutional Ethnography finds and recognises how women's places are specific different and design research for coherence not division
Women needed training in leadership followed by continued support through mentoring	Generate organisations like Emily's List Generate cohorts of role models and mentors and give them support to engage and be welcomed
Value of targets, auditing for accountability and the usefulness of quotas	What are the acceptable starting points for targets, accountability and quotas and explain the resistance to these?
Pay attention to language	Challenge the male as neutral/human framing of 'natural' difference
	Deconstruct the 'equal to men' discourse for the 'phallacy' it is – and rebuild the equity discourse to give appropriate support for identified disadvantages that includes the maleness of power and understands the tentacles of discrimination
Tenacity recognised that change was slow and incremental, took time, demanded patience and long-term strategic thinking, as well as cross-generational input	Develop and nurture cross-generational listening and learning by first recognising that 'divide and conquer' is a well-worn strategy of control and power – find the ways and means to undermine, challenge and overcome its insidious and ubiquitous disempowering effects to combat the disadvantages of incremental, slow change

The activist leaders asserted that simply being a woman is a disadvantage bearing the weight of inequality. A powerful, illuminating lens developed to acknowledge the standpoint of women is institutional ethnography (Smith 2005). Revealing the perils that young women academics confront (Lund and Tienari 2019) also shows how the documentation of women's experiences can identify pathways for change. The locus of women and their needs was the starting point for the activist leaders who addressed the shortfalls women must contend with whether training for leadership, finding well-paid work or revealing the inadvertent discrimination of company policies. Further research in the management of sport across these topics could offer starting points for consolidated action.

Another pathway might challenge the critical mass women need to achieve to make a difference in management and leadership which has been set at only 30% (Adriaanse 2016). This seems low especially when Emily's List aims for 50% in political positions. Moreover, given that quotas have been shown to be successful (Gillard and Okonjo-Iweala 2020; Wallace 2018), setting the benchmark is significant. As Emily's List enabled change in political arenas, for women to challenge the homosociality of both the academy (Broadbridge and Simpson 2011) and sport leadership (Adriaanse 2016) they will require funding to be heard and to fashion the adept communication that presents a persuasive case for critical mass. As well, investigating what kind of support, training and funding would encourage and enable women to move into sports management in greater numbers offers important policy starting points.

There are also strong threads of collectivity and connection running through recent feminist activism and the activist leader commentaries. Although role models have value in leadership (Gillard and Okonjo-Iweala 2020) simple visibility is insufficient (Brace-Govan 2013). Research needs to identify the processes that provide broad, ongoing support through mentoring (Brace-Govan and Powell 2005) and the communication that can facilitate across differences and over time. Intersectionality offers a solid foundation from which to work on these agendas in order to critique the commodified, depoliticised binary of sport. The profound effect of the gender binary so valorised in sport demands a complex challenge. Theoretically, intersectionality offers such pathways (McCall 2005), as does decolonisation (Mohanty 2013), particularly in recognition of the variability of the effects of neoliberalism internationally (Connell and Dados 2014).

Implementing change required not only patience and determination, it also relied on garnering support externally and establishing new rules and regulations. Research designed to facilitate change management in a range of organisations would be beneficial, fostering not only a better understanding of digital collectivities and commonalities, but also better communication beyond the group's boundaries. It is insufficient for individual women to declare empowerment rather feminist activism demands systemic transformation providing long-lasting change. Challenging discourses of natural difference embedded in the language of sport and deconstructing the symbolism of sport are useful research pathways. As noted by the activists, language is crucial to framing perceptions and the language of sport is pervasive. But, if enduring change is to be achieved, then the diversity within feminism needs to be embraced as a resource (Gill 2011) and innovative approaches to research informed by feminist ethics engaged (Pullen and Vachhani 2020). Research that addressed these important topics would be valuable, in particular redressing the lack of acknowledgement of the emotional demands and labour embedded in activism. Effective activism is rarely a short-term, and the leader activists all commented on the longevity of their involvement. A feminist examination of the emotional work of activism could integrate insights into theories of transformational change generated by social movements.

Overall, then, the contribution of feminist academic work to women's sport has been substantial but it is clear there is still much to be done. This chapter has shown that although women continue to demonstrate remarkable persistence and resilience in both sport and activism, despite the challenges, there is a role for feminist activism in women's sport.

Notes

1 Detail about the development and current status of these women's sporting initiatives can be found at the following:
Australian Football League Women's competition https://womens.afl/; see also https://en.wikipedia.org/wiki/AFL_Women.
National Rugby League Women's competition https://www.nrl.com/womens/nrlw-premiership/; see also https://en.wikipedia.org/wiki/NRL_Women%27s_Premiership.
The English government campaign to encourage women to take up physical activity https://www.sportengland.org/campaigns-and-our-work/this-girl-can and the only license granted so far is to the Australian state, Victoria https://thisgirlcan.com.au/.
2 Victorian Women's Trust, "Breakthrough" Conference, Melbourne, Victoria, Australia, 2016: Held over two days with 100 speakers, the focus of the event was to ask: how can we move beyond old world views so that everyone has the freedom, security and space to reach their full potential? (Breakthrough 2016. vwt.org.au). It was one of the most inspiring and broad ranging feminist events I have attended.

References

Adriaanse, J. 2016. "Gender Diversity in the Governance of Sport Associations: The Sydney Scoreboard Global Index of Participation." *Journal of Business Ethics* 137: 149–160. DOI:10.1007/s10551-015-2550-3.

Bates, L. 2014. *Everyday Sexism*. London: Simon & Schuster.

Bell, E., S. Merilainen, S. Taylor and J. Tienari. 2018 "Times Up! Feminist Theory and Activism Meets Organization Studies." *Human Relations* 72 1: 4–22. DOI:10.1177/0018726718790067.

Bell, E. and N. de Gama. 2019. "Taking a Stand: The Embodied, Enacted and Emplaced Work of Relational Critique." *Organization* 24 1: 36–58. DOI:10.1177/1350508418815424.

Brace-Govan, J. 2002. "Looking at Bodywork: Women and Three Physical Activities." *Journal of Sport and Social Issues* 26 4: 403–420. DOI:10.1177/0193732502238256.

Brace-Govan, J. 2004. "Weighty Matters: Control of Women"s Access to Physical Strength." *Sociological Review* 52 4: 503–531. DOI:10.1111/j.1467-954X.2004.00493.x

Brace-Govan, J. 2010. "Representations of Women's Active Embodiment and Men"s Ritualized Visibility in Sport." *Marketing Theory* 10 4: 369–396. DOI:10.1177/1470593110382825.

Brace-Govan, J. 2013. "More Diversity Than Celebrity: A Typology of Role Model Interaction." *Journal of Social Marketing* 3 2: 111–126. DOI: 10.1108/JSOCM-05-2012-0079.

Brace-Govan, J. and S. Ferguson. 2019. "Gender and Sexed Bodies: Embodiment, Corporeality, Physical Mastery and the Gaze." In *Handbook of Research on Gender and Marketing*, edited by S. Dobscha, 63–100. Cheltenham: Edward Elgar.

Brace-Govan, J. and I. Powell. 2005. "Real World Transfer of Professional Knowledge: A Modification to Internship Learning." In *Educating Managers Through Real World Projects*, edited by C. Wankel and R. deFillippi, 115–148. Greenwich, CT: Information Age.

Brewis, J. 2017. "On Interference, Collegiality and Co-authorship: Peer Review of Journal Articles in Management and Organization Studies." *Organization* 15 1: 21–41. DOI:10.1177/1350508417703472.

Broadbridge, A. and R. Simpson. 2011. "25 Years On: Reflecting on the Past and Looking to the Future in Gender and Management Research." *British Journal of Management* 22: 470–483. DOI:10/111/j.1467-8551.2011.00758.x.

Burawoy, M. 2014. "Sociology as a Vocation: Moral Commitment and Scientific Imagination." *Current Sociology Monograph* 62 2: 279–284. DOI:10.1177/0011392113515796.

Burke, M. 2019. "Is Football Now Feminist? A Critique of the Use of McCaughey's Physical Feminism to Explain Women's Participation in Separate Leagues in Masculine Sports." *Sport in Society* 22 3: 499–513. DOI:10.1080/17430437.2018.1504772.

Butler, J. 1990. *GenderTtrouble: Feminism and the Subversion of Identity*. New York: Routledge.

Callahan, J. L. and C. Elliott. 2020. "Fantasy Spaces and Emotional Derailment: Reflections on Failure in Academic Activism." *Organization* 27 3: 506–514. DOI:10.1177/1350508419831925.

Caro, J. 2013. "Introduction: Sometimes you just have to laugh." In *Destroying the Joint. Why Women Have to Change the World*, edited by J. Caro, ix–xiv. St Lucia: University of Queensland Press.

Caudwell, J. 2011. "Sport Feminisms: Narratives of Linearity?", *Journal of Sport and Social Issues* 352: 111–125. DOI:10.1177/0193723511406132.

Cole, C. and Hribar, A. 1995. "Celebrity Feminism: Nike Style Post-Fordism, Transcendence, and Consumer Power." *Sociology of Sport Journal* 12: 347–369.

Comeig, I., A. Grau-Grau, A. Jaramillo-Gutiérrez and F. Ramírez. 2016. "Gender, Self-confidence, Sports, and Preferences for Competition", *Journal of Business Research*, 694: 1418–1422. DOI:10.1016/j.busres.2015.10.118.

Connell, R. W. 1987. *Gender and Power*. St. Leonards: Allen and Unwin.

Connell, R. W. 1995. *Masculinities*. St. Leonards: Allen and Unwin.

Connell, R. W. and N. Dados. 2014. "Where in the World does Neoliberalism Come From? The Market Agenda in Southern Perspective." *Theory & Society* 43: 117–138. DOI:10/1007/s11186-014-9212-9.

Contu, A. 2018. "… the Point Is to Change It – Yes, But in What Direction and How? Intellectual Activism as a Way of "Walking the Talk" of Critical Work in Business Schools." *Organisation* 252: 282–293. DOI:10.1177/1350508417740589.

Cregan, K. 2006. *The Sociology of the Body*. London: Sage.

Cresswell, J. W. 2013. *Qualitative Inquiry and Research Design. Choosing From Five Approaches*. 3rd ed. Thousand Oaks: Sage.

Dallyn, S., M. Marinetto and C. Cederstrom. 2015. "The Academic as Public Intellectual: Examining Public Engagement in the Professionalised Academy." *Sociology*. 496: 1031–1046. DOI:10.1177/0038038515586681.

de Soysa, L. and S. Zipp. 2019. "Gender Equality, Sport and the United Nation's System. A Historical Overview of the Slow Pace of Progress." *Sport in Society* 2211: 1783–1800. DOI:10/1080/17430437.2019.1651018.

Destroying the Joint Administrators. 2013. "Birth of a Movement." In *Destroying the Joint. Why Women Have to Change the World*, edited by J. Caro, 99–106. St Lucia: University of Queensland Press.

Douglas, M. (1966) 2002. *Purity and Danger: An Analysis of Concepts of Pollution and Taboo*. London: Routledge.

Dunne, S., S. Harney, and M. Parker. 2008. "The Responsibilities of Management Intellectuals: A Survey." *Organization* 152: 271–282. DOI:10.1177/1350508407087871.

Evans, A. B. and G. Pfister. 2020. "Women in Sport Leadership: A Systematic Narrative Review." *International Review for the Sociology of Sport* online first. DOI:10.1177/1012690220911842.

Ferguson, S., J. Brace-Govan, and D. M. Martin. 2020. "Gender Status Bias and the Marketplace." *Journal of Business Research* 107: 211–221. DOI:10.1016/j.jbusres.2018.11.047.

Ferguson, S., J. Brace-Govan, and B. Welsh. 2020. "Complex Contradictions in a Contemporary Idealised Feminine Body Project." *Journal of Marketing Management*. DOI:10.1080/0267257X.2020.1721553.

Fleming, P. and S. B. Banerjee. 2015. "When Performativity Fails: Implications for Critical Management Studies." *Human Relations* 692: 257–276. DOI:10.1177/0018726715599241.

Fox, C. 2017. *Stop Fixing Women*. Sydney NSW: NewSouth.

Gill, R. 2011. "Sexism Reloaded, or, It's Time to Get Angry Again!" *Feminist Media Studies* 111: 61–71. DOI:10.1080/14680777.2011.537029.

Gillard, J. and N. Okonjo-Iweala. 2020. *Women and Leadership. Real Lives, Real Lessons*. London: Vintage.

Graham, J. 2021. "Girls Hungry for Footy: 'It Makes Me Who I Am'." *The Age*, Saturday 17th April, 8.

Gurrieri, L., J. Previte, and J. Brace-Govan. 2013. "Women's Bodies as Sites of Control: Inadvertent Stigma and Exclusion in Social Marketing." *Journal of Macromarketing* 332: 128–43. DOI:10.1177/0276146712469971.

Handelman, J. and E. Fischer. 2018. "Contesting Understandings of Contestations: Rethinking Perspectives on Activism." In *The SAGE Handbook of Consumer Culture*, edited by O. Kravets, , P. Maclaran, S. Miles, and A. Venkatesh. London: Sage. DOI:10.4135/9781473998803.n15.

Hemmings, C. 2012. "Affective Solidarity: Feminist Reflexivity and Political Transformation." *Feminist Theory* 132: 147–161. DOI:10.1177/1464700112442643.

Heywood, L. 2018. "Third-Wave Feminism and Representation." In *The Palgrave Handbook of Feminism and Sport, Leisure and Physical Education*, edited by L. Mansfield, J. Caudwell, B. Wheaton and B. Watson, 463–477. London: Palgrave Macmillan. DOI:10.1057/978-1-137-53318-0_29.

Jasper, J. M. 2011. "Emotions and Social Movements: Twenty Years of Theory and Research." *Annual Review of Sociology* 37: 285–303. DOI:10.1146/annurev-soc-081309-150015.

Johansson, J., J. Tienari, and A. Valtonen. 2017. "The Body, Identity and Gender in Managerial Athleticism." *Human Relations* 709: 1141–1167. DOI:10.1177/0018726716685161.

Koffman, O. and R. Gill. 2014. ""I Matter and So Does She": Girl Power, Postfeminism and the Girl Effect." In *Youth Cultures in the Age of Global Media*, edited by D. Buckingham, 242–257. Basingstoke: Palgrave Macmillan.

Lund, R. and J. Tienari. 2019. "Passion, Care, and Eros in the Gendered Neoliberal University." *Organization* 261: 98–121. DOI:10.1177/1350508418805283.

MacKinnon, C. A. 1987. *Feminism Unmodified. Discourses on Life and Law.* Boston, MA: Harvard University Press.

Maclaran, P. 2015. "Feminism's Fourth Wave: A Research Agenda for Marketing and Consumer Research." *Journal of Marketing Management* 31 15/16: 1732–1738. DOI:10.1080/0267257x.2015.1076497.

Maclaran, P. and O. Kravets. 2019. "Feminist Perspectives in Marketing." In *The Routledge Companion to Critical Marketing*, edited by M. Tadajewski, M. Higgins, J. Denegri-Knott, and R. Varman, 64–82. Abingdon: Routledge.

Maclaran, P. and L. Stevens. 2019. "Thinking Through Feminist Theorising: Poststructuralist Feminist, Ecofeminism and Intersectionality." In *Handbook of Research on Gender and Marketing*, edited by S. Dobscha, 229–251. Cheltenham: Edward Elgar.

Mansfield, L., J. Caudwell, B. Wheaton, and B. Watson. 2018. *The Palgrave Handbook of feminism and Sport, Leisure and Physical Education.* London: Palgrave Macmillan. DOI:10.1057/978-1-137-53318-0.

Martin, E. (1987) 2018. *The Woman in the Body: A Cultural Analysis of Reproduction.* Revised ed. Boston, MA: Beacon.

McCall, L. 2005. "The Complexity of Intersectionality." *Signs* 303: 1771–1800.

McLachlan, F. 2019. "It's Boom Time! Again: Progress Narratives and Women's Sport in Australia." *Journal of Australian Studies* 431: 7–21. DOI:10.1080/14443058.2019.1575262.

McRobbie, A. 2009. *The Aftermath of Feminism: Gender, Culture and Social Change.* London: Sage Publications.

Mendes, K., J. Ringrose, and J. Keller. 2018. "#MeToo and the Promise and Pitfalls of Challenging Rape Culture Through Digital Feminist Activism." *European Journal of Women's Studies* 252: 236–246. DOI:10.1177/1350506818765318.

Mohanty, C. T. 2013. "Transnational Feminism Crossings: On Neoliberalism and Radical Critique." *Signs* 384: 967–991.

Petty, K. and S. Pope. 2019. "A New Age for Media Coverage of Women's Sport? An Analysis of English Media Coverage of the 2015 FIFA Women's World Cup." *Sociology* 153: 486–502. DOI:10.1177/0038038518797505.

Piggott, L. V. and E. C. J. Pike. 2020. "'CEO Equals Man': Gender and Informal Organisational Practices in English Sport Governance." *International Review for the Sociology of Sport* 557: 1009–1025. DOI:10.1177/1012690219865980.

Phipps, A. 2016. "Whose Personal Is More Political? Experience in Contemporary Feminist Politics." *Feminist Theory* 173: 303–321. DOI:10.1177/1464700116663831.

Pullen, A. and S. Vachhani. 2020. "Feminist Ethics and Women Leaders: From Difference to Intercorporeality." *Journal of Business Ethics* online first. DOI:10.1007/s10551-020-04526-0.

Rhodes, C., C. Wright, and A. Pullen. 2017. "Changing the World? The Politics of Activism and Impact in the Neoliberal University." *Organization* 151: 139–147. DOI:10.1177/1350508417726546.

Rome, A. S., S. ODonohoe, and S. Dunnett. 2019. "Rethinking Feminist Waves." In *Handbook of Research on Gender and Marketing*, edited by S. Dobscha, 252–272. Cheltenham: Edward Elgar.

Shankar, A. 2009. "Reframing Critical Marketing." *Journal of Marketing Management* 257–8: 681–696. DOI:10.1362/026725709x471569.

Shilling, C. 2003. *The Body and Social Theory.* 2nd ed. London: Sage.

Silk, M. L., D. L. Andrews, and H. Thorpe. 2017. *Routledge Handbook of Physical Culture Studies.* Abingdon: Routledge.

Smith D. E. 2005. *Institutional Ethnography. A Sociology for People.* Lanham, MD: Rowman Altamira.

Snyder, R. C. 2008. "What is Third-Wave Feminism? A New Direction Essay." *Signs* 341: 175–196. DOI:0097-9740/2008/3401-0021.

Spicer, A., M. Alvesson, and D. Karreman. 2016. "Extending Critical Performativity." *Human Relations* 692: 225–249. DOI:10.1177/0018726715614073.
Tadajewski, M. 2016. "Relevance, Responsibility, Critical Performativity, Testimony and Positive Marketing: Contributing to Marketing Theory, Thought and Practice." *Journal of Marketing Management* 3217–3218: 1513–1536. DOI:10.1080/026727x.2016.1244974.
Thorpe, H. and R. Olive. 2016. *Women in Action Sport Cultures. Identity, Politics and Experience*. London: Palgrave Macmillan.
Toffoletti, K., H. Thorpe, and J. Francombe-Webb. 2018. *New Sporting Femininities Embodied Politics in Postfeminist Times*. Cham: Springer International Publishing.
Turner, B. 2012. *Routledge Handbook of Body Studies*. Abingdon: Routledge.
Vachhani, S. and A. Pullen. 2018. "Ethics, Politics and Feminist Organizing: Writing Feminist Infrapolitics and Affective Solidarity into Everyday Sexism." *Human Relations* 721: 23–47. DOI:10.1177/0018726718780988.
Wallace, C. 2018. "Quotas Are Not Pretty But They Work – Liberal Women Should Insist on Them." *The Conversation*, 21st September. https://theconversation.com/quotas-are-not-pretty-but-they-work-liberal-women-should-insist-on-them-103517.
Wearing, B. 1990. "Beyond the Ideology of Motherhood: Leisure as Resistance." *Journal of Sociology* 26 1: 36–58.
Wheaton, B. 2014. *The Cultural Politics of Lifestyle Sports*. New York: Routledge.
Women Rising 2030. 2018. *Better Leadership Better World*. London: Business & Sustainability Development Commission, United Nations Foundation.
World Economic Forum. 2020. *Global Gender Gap Report 2020*. Geneva: World Economic Forum. http://reports.weforum.org/glbal-gender-gap-report-2020/dataexplorer.
Young, I. 1989. "Throwing Like a Girl." In *The Thinking Muse. Feminism and Modern French Philosophy*, edited by J. Allen and I. Young, 51–70. Bloomington: Indiana University Press.
Zarkov, D. and K. Davis. 2018. "Ambiguities and Dilemmas Around #MeToo: #ForHowLong and #WhereTo?" *European Journal of Women's Studies* 251: 3–9. DOI:10.1177/1350506817749436.

13 Women's sexual practices

The B-spot of marketing and consumer research

Luciana Walther

Introduction

I have been researching what I like to call women's erotic consumption since 2007, when I was just starting my doctoral studies in marketing. Since then, different scholars have called it feminized sexual consumption (Rome and Lambert 2020), women's sex shopping (Wood 2019), sexuality-related consumption (Piha et al. 2018), among other terms. There were not many scientific marketing studies on this topic at that time, and the ones that struck me the most were Stephen Gould's early 1990s papers in the proceedings of the Association for Consumer Research Conference, calling for more scholarly work on what he named "the sexuality-consumption connection" (1991b, 381), or "the consumer sexual behaviour sequence" (1992, 304). I will get back to Gould's call later. In the late 2000s, as a Brazilian woman and then young scholar, I had to face much resistance to this research topic, in particular because of its novelty as a consumption context, and in general because women's sexual practices were surrounded by taboo, outside and within the academy. This chapter will show that, when it comes to the marketing academy specifically, they still might be.

In theory, the objectives of this chapter are: (1) to provide a thorough but non-exhaustive overview of current scholarship at the intersection of marketing, women's erotic consumption and feminism, serving as a single up-to-date repository of relevant literature; (2) to describe some uses of feminist theories in the referred research context; and (3) to reflect on where the research agenda is likely to advance in the future.

In practice, to fulfill those objectives, I broke them down into three sections. In the first section, I present a compendium of scholarly literature on women as sexualized consumers, produced by different fields of knowledge. I proceed to justify the present chapter's title, arguing that, despite some marketing researchers claiming the existence of a large body of research on sexuality within the field, women's sexual practices remain a blind spot of marketing scholarship, in comparison to other scientific domains. I also argue that, although some studies assert that taboo around erotic products has been destructed (Bardzell and Bardzell 2011; Wilner and Huff 2017; Piha et al. 2018), this is not true for all cultures, Brazil being an alarming counterexample. In the second section, I acknowledge that most of my work published in the English language has, indeed, celebrated the emancipatory aspects of women's participation in erotic consumption, instead of criticizing its underlying neoliberal postfeminist project, like pointed out by Rome and Lambert (2020) – although I have called out a problematic system of gender hierarchies (Walther 2019b) and its double moral standard (Walther 2019a). To redress that and to respond to Rome and Lambert's call (2020), I briefly address the subset of my findings that relate to the paradoxes and contradictions of women's erotic

DOI: 10.4324/9781003042587-16

consumption, interrogating them with the lens of poststructuralist feminism (Butler 1990, 1993; Fischer and Bristor 1994; Maclaran and Stevens 2019). Finally, in the concluding section, I reflect on what a sexuality-related consumption arena and its entailing marketing research might look like in the future.

An epistemological blind spot

The definition and the scope of women's erotic consumption that I usually adopt in my research come from the emic discourse offered by consumers and industry professionals I have interviewed (for more details, please see Walther and Schouten 2016; Walther 2017, 2019a, 2019b). This way, women's erotic consumption may refer to all goods, services, experiences, people, information and ideas consumed by women in order to perform sexual practices and to construct and communicate sexual identities – before, during or after intercourse, alone or with someone else. Many of these products and services are sold by sex shops, like vibrators, lingerie, erotic cosmetics, condoms, costumes, BDSM accessories and workshops on sexual practices, positiveness or health. Pornographic media products (books, films, magazines, websites, etc.) are also included in the scope of women's erotic consumption. So is prostitution, as a service to be consumed. In Brazil, motels are used almost exclusively for sexual encounters and were frequently mentioned during my fieldwork. Besides products intentionally meant for erotic use by industry, my research has also tapped into what Toffler (1981, 271) called "prosumption" and Arnould and Thompson (2005, 871) called "productive aspects of consumption". So, a back massager, not intended by industry for erotic purposes, but adapted by consumers for clitoral masturbation, is also part of women's erotic consumption. The same goes for a belly-dancer costume, for instance, put together at home by the consumer to be used during sensual play with her partner. This demonstrates that boundaries between erotic and romantic practices are blurred for the scope of my research, thus including candlelight dinners, alcoholic beverages, flowers and whatever products, services or activities the interviewed consumers might infuse with eroticism.

Epistemologically, ontologically and methodologically, my research and the marketing studies I discuss in this chapter adhere to the school of thought known as Consumer Culture Theory (CCT) (Arnould and Thompson 2005), which preconizes a cultural and social understanding of consumption phenomena, under the micro, meso and macrosocial scales of observation, in opposition to biological or psychological approaches. Following this criterium, besides searching for the still scant marketing scholarship on women's erotic consumption, I visited the abundant scientific literature on the same topic by sociology, anthropology, communications and other adjacent fields. I will also refer to some health studies that might be useful for the reader who wishes to dig into the intersection of marketing, feminism and women's sexual practices. But I am excluding from this discussion all cognitive, behavioural and evolutionary marketing research that attempts to link biological sexuality to consumption (for excluded examples, see Sanbonmatsu and Kardes 1988; Sundie et al. 2008; Vohs, Finkenauer, and Burger 2008; Durante and Arsena 2015; Buss and Foley 2020).

I organized the following literature review chronologically and by field of study, rather than thematically. I believe that a temporal account of how marketing debates around women's sexuality evolved across different disciplines might shed light not only on the reasons for which certain themes came to the forefront, but also on why other themes were silenced, becoming epistemological blind spots.

In 1991, Stephen Gould presented a provocative piece at the Association for Consumer Research Conference, challenging marketing scholars and denouncing their silence around sex, which he claimed to be one of consumer behaviour's most important and least comprehended phenomena. He predicted that, in a 100 years, we should witness a "sex revolution" in marketing research (Gould 1991b, 383). Among his contributions to this revolution was the theoretical model he named "consumer lovemaps" (Gould 1991b, 1992, 1995), which offered a methodological pathway to unveil, map and grasp sexually related aspects of consumption as experiential phenomena at fundamental levels of being. He also published a controversial (Arnould and Thompson 2005) paper in the *Journal of Consumer Research*, articulating product usage with different levels of his own sexual energy, under an introspective-praxis perspective (Gould 1991a). Thirty years have gone by, and the aforementioned revolution is yet to happen. As this chapter will show, some marketing scholars have woken up to the importance of the study of sexuality as a means to examine consumers, markets and societies. Some of them also perceived feminism as a critical lens to scrutinize those institutions. But is the revolution coming any time soon?

Until the late 2000s, consumers' sexual practices remained largely ignored by marketing scholars. Marketing literature, with or without a feminist approach, had been profusely dissecting sexualized and stereotyped depictions of women in advertising (Gilly 1988; Stern 1991; Reichert and Lambiase 2003; Stevens and Maclaran 2007). That was the closest to sex that mainstream marketing academia would get. Some marketing studies peripherally addressed sex, when examining hedonism, pleasure, desire, subcultures or gender (Hirschman and Holbrook 1982; Belk, Ger, and Askegaard 2003; Kates 2002; Maclaran and Stevens 2004; Goulding and Saren 2009; Goulding et al. 2009). But marketing research that focused specifically on sexual practices and the ensuing consumption was scarce and unconventional (see Table 13.1).

During that time, research at the intersection of sex and consumption in general, and on sex shops and vibrators in particular, was abundantly produced by other scientific fields, like sociology, anthropology, psychology, media and communications, philosophy and a little less so by history, education, health and technology (see Table 13.1).

It turns out that most of those marketing studies that addressed sexuality focused on advertising, with the objective of criticizing women's portrayal in ads as sexual objects. In hindsight, it becomes evident that what was being criticized by marketing scholars was also practised by them, because their research framed women chiefly as objects, ignoring women's subject position as sexualized consumers. This does not mean that, nowadays, scholarly critique to women's objectivation became outdated or unwelcome (Maclaran 2015); nor does it mean that the subjectification of women as erotic consumers is unproblematic (Gill, 2003; Rome and Lambert 2020). It simply means that the marketing field could benefit from deeper and more frequent dives into cultural aspects of women's sexuality, revealing its many nuances.

Framing sexuality as relevant almost exclusively to LGBTQ+ consumers was also a problem of previous marketing research tending to the intersection of sex and consumption (Bettany et al. 2016). Again, this acknowledgement does not denote that these consumers' sexuality became irrelevant. Rather, it pinpoints that sexual practices are central to identity building in current Western societies (Bozon 2004), being therefore relevant to the comprehension of consumers of all sexual orientations.

In 2011 and 2012, the *Fifty Shades* novel series (James 2011, 2012a, 2012b) was published, followed by the movie trilogy in 2015, 2017 and 2018. Several academic and non-academic spheres took interest in the globally best-selling phenomenon, documenting and analysing it exhaustively (see Table 13.1). With BDSM sexual practices and porn literature brought to the limelight by media and scholarly discourses, women as sexualized consumers gained more visibility in the marketing academia as well, which increased the number of publications, by this field, on consumer and industry practices

192 *Luciana Walther*

related to the *Fifty Shades* ethos in particular (see Table 13.1), and on the intersection of sex and consumption in general (see Table 13.1). Still a modest increase, if compared to the scholarly production on similar topics by other disciplines (see Table 13.1). Next, I will succinctly describe some examples of recent marketing scholarship at the intersection of consumer subjectivity and women's sexual lives.

Wilner and Huff (2017) conducted a media analysis in the United States to uncover what role product design played in the transformation of a market historically shrouded by taboo: the sex toy market. They concluded that product designers, together with mass media and changing social mores, have contributed to the mainstreaming of what used to be a counternormative market. By changing sex toys' form, function and material, designers have aligned these products with culturally acceptable meanings, like hedonism, sexual well-being and tasteful naughtiness, instead of fear, shame and wickedness. The authors acknowledge that the legitimation of a product is different from the legitimation of a practice. While marketing and consumption activities involving vibrators may have evolved, in the United States, towards normative legitimacy, both the practice and discourse about masturbation are still considered sensitive topics.

Piha et al. (2018) also delved into sex toys' departure from taboo to healthy products, this time in the Finish context. Like Wilner and Huff's (2017), this study points to a cultural liberalization of the sex toy market at a societal level, adding, however, reasons for taboo construction and maintenance at the individual level. With a mixed-methods approach that included a consumer survey and interviews with experts, this research found that self and status protection was the core force behind taboo maintenance. Moreover, consumers may voluntarily construct taboos regarding sex toys because the controlled violation of a taboo may be associated with sexual excitement.

Rome and Lambert (2020) investigated women's sexual practices considering neoliberalism and postfeminism as relevant consumer culture categories that give rise to a field of possible subjectivities. They claim, and I agree, that feminist problematizations of the sovereign consumer could help dismantle patriarchal interests and widen the scope of critique in marketing, since the few existent studies on women's sexual practices have, so far, celebrated the mainstreaming of erotic consumption, instead of criticizing it. Utilizing a critical feminist self-reflexive approach (Bettany and Woodruffe-Burton 2009) throughout data collection and interpretation, the authors interviewed young women in the southern United States about their intimate and sexual relationships, "one of marketing's most fundamental exchanges" (Murgolo-Poore et al. 2003, 236). Research participants manifested a postfeminist subjectivity in two key ways: first, by attempting to establish an authoritative positioning in their relationships, as the empowered women they are expected to be; and second, by a seemingly contradictory submissive sexual positioning, in order to grant variety to sexual encounters, as the sexually liberated women they are expected to be. Besides being interpellated by postfeminist discourses that stress a variety imperative, these consumers must also adhere to a sex imperative, which underpins their accounts of unwanted sex, and an orgasm imperative, underlying their accounts of faked orgasms. Justifiably alarmed, Rome and Lambert (2020, 18) vent out: "what is most disconcertingly stark is the inherent contradiction between participants' perception of themselves as free, able, and equal, and the constraining, subjugating experiences shaping their relationships and (sexual) lives". Therefore, their work sheds light onto neoliberal notions of choice and agency that actually mask patriarchal influences and gendered inequalities.

Table 13.1 Scholarly Literature at the Intersection of Sex and Consumption (Sex in Advertising Excluded)

	Marketing and Consumption	Other Areas
Before Fifty Shades	Gould (1991, 1992, 1995) Hirschman (1991) Malina and Schmidt (1997) Belk, Østergaard and Groves (1998) Brown (1998) O'Donnell (1999) Murgolo-Poore, Pitt and Berthon (2003) Kent (2005) Amy-Chinn (2006) Amy-Chinn, Jantzen and Østergaard (2006) Jantzen, Østergaard and Vieira (2006) Kates (2002) Kent and Brown (2006) Basil (2007) Østberg (2010) Fernandez and Lastovicka (2011)	Bataille (1986) Laqueur (1992) Foucault (1994, 1997a, 1997b) Davis et al. (1996) Juffer (1998) Butler (1999) Maines (1999) Giddens (2000) McCaughey and French (2001) Taylor and Ussher (2011) Storr (2003) Curtis (2004) Reece, Herbenick and Sherwood-Puzzello (2004) Attwood (2005, 2006, 2011) Radner (2005) Heineman (2006, 2011) Herbenick and Reese (2007) Smith (2007) Zelizer (2009) Coulmont and Hubbard (2010) Evans, Riley and Shankar (2010a, 2010b) Fisher et al. (2010) Johnson (2010) Bardzell and Bardzell (2011) Better (2011) Daneback, Mansson and Ross (2011) Eaglin and Bardzell (2011) Fahs (2011) Harvey and Gill (2011)
About Fifty Shades	Prasad (2014) Northey et al. (2019) Knudsen (2019) Buchanan-Oliver, Schau and Schau (2020) Gopaldas and Molander (2020)	Comella (2013) Deller and Smith (2013) Dymock (2013) Harman and Jones (2013) Martin (2013) Whitehead (2013) Colbjørnsen (2014) Jones (2014) Parry and Light (2014) Click (2015) Heljakka (2016) Tripodi (2017) Drdová and Saxonberg (2020)
After Fifty Shades	Zayer et al. (2012) Ourahmoune (2013) Blanchette (2014) Valtonen and Närvänen (2015) Patterson and Larsen (2016)	Blinne (2012) Voss (2012) Fahs and Swank (2013) McNair (2013) Schick et al. (2013)

(*Continued*)

	Marketing and Consumption	Other Areas
After Fifty Shades	O'Sullivan (2016) Walther and Schouten (2016) Scott (2017) Walther (2017, 2019a, 2019b) Wilner and Huff (2017) Cervellon and Brown (2018) Farley (2018) Neal (2018) Piha et al. (2018, 2020) Thompson, Henry and Bardhi (2018) Varman, Goswami and Vijay (2018) Veer and Golf-Papez (2018) Yalkin and Veer (2018) Lanier and Rader (2019) Drenten, Gurrieri and Tyler (2020) Macleod (2020) Mayr (2020, 2021a) McVey, Gurrieri and Tyler (2020) Rome and Lambert (2020) Sobande, Mimoun and Torres (2020) Takhar (2020) Zanette and Daskalopoulou (2020)	Evans and Riley (2015) Hakim (2015) Wood (2015, 2017) Martin (2016) Rossolatos (2016, 2017) Scholes-Balog, Francke and Hemphill (2016) Watson et al. (2016) Comella (2017) Crewe and Martin (2017) Hubbard, Collins and Gorman-Murray (2017) Lieberman (2017a, 2017b, 2018) Nixon (2017) Smith, Attwood and McNair (2017) Barker, Gill and Harvey (2018) Döring and Pöschl (2018) Huff (2018) Paasonen (2018) Rullo et al. (2018) Chesser, Parry and Light (2019) Fiaveh (2019) Agoos (2020) Daskalopoulou and Zanette (2020) Fennell (2020) Kingston, Hammond and Redman (2020) Møller (2020) Ronen (2020) Sundén (2020) Waskul and Anklan (2020) Mayr (2021b)

By focusing my previous paragraphs on marketing's scientific production, I am not discarding the studies from other areas, mainly sociology and anthropology, which have been so necessary and enlightening to those marketing scholars who have ventured, so far, in sex research. Cross-pollination from such fields remains beneficial. Surveys about sexual practices in certain cultures may also be useful as secondary data, providing building blocks for CCT studies on sex. It is possible to find surveys about sexual behaviour conducted in various countries: Canada (Wood et al. 2017), the United States (Herbenick et al. 2009, 2010, 2011), Australia (Richters et al. 2014), Germany (Döring and Poeschl 2020) and Brazil (Abdo 2004), to name just a few.

Analysing erotic consumption through feminism

Together, the recent marketing studies I described in the previous paragraphs imply that there are both long-lasting and new constraints on women's sexual lives. In my published research, I argue that taboo might not have been lifted as much as some overgeneralizing scientific accounts claim. It still needs to be fought, especially in cultures where patriarchal injunctions endure. These are the long-lasting restrictions. A critical feminist perspective applied to my findings may bring to light the new constraints that come with postfeminism and with neoliberal notions of emancipation via consumption.

Listening earnestly to Rome and Lambert's (2020, 20) foreboding,

> (…) we argue that failing to critically attend to wider power structures in this context may promote a sexually agentic female consumer subjectivity that risks propagating erroneous, disrespectful, and potentially dangerous notions of consumer sovereignty and responsibilization,

in this section, I use a poststructuralist feminist approach (Butler 1990, 1993; Fischer and Bristor 1994; Maclaran and Stevens 2019) to discuss a few of the contradictions and paradoxes I have found during my research on women's erotic consumption. The following is, thus, intended as a short account, zooming in a subset of findings from my larger study, in order to demonstrate an attempt to think of data through feminism.

My fieldwork comprised 35 in-depth interviews with female consumers of erotic products and industry professionals. Observation sessions were held in sex shop and trade events (for more details, please see Walther and Schouten 2016; Walther 2017, 2019a, 2019b). Participants expressed a great diversity of preferences and views on erotic consumption. Contradictions emerged, like in every cultural experience (Miller 2010).

Fieldwork signalled that erotic consumption can be the expression of women's autonomy and independence, allowing them to be authors and protagonists of their own pleasure, or, on the contrary, it can reinforce conservative views that condemn the practice of casual sex by women, facilitating solitary orgasms when they are not in a steady relationship. Conjugal use of erotic products can restore a relationship's sexual health, or it can cause addiction, which is viewed by some participants as pathological and scary. Interactions between mothers and daughters may include sharing information about erotic products, or may repudiate such an intimate confidence. The industry that empowers women, offering products designed specifically to grant autonomy of pleasure, can, at the same time, objectivate women, by portraying them as consumable bodies to men. Women who visit erotic boutiques may be financially independent, but may also want their male partners to pay the bill. Women's search for erotic products can be disapproved and understood as conjugal betrayal and as an attempt to supplant men, but women who fail to reach orgasms can also be frowned upon and viewed as defective or incomplete.

Feminist thought may reveal the dangers of accepting these contradictions merely as reminiscent traces of a long-lasting double moral standard (that encourages men to exercise their sexuality when and how it suits them, while imposing restrictions and social sanctions on women). Feminist thought may expose the risks of blindly trusting that a process of taboo destruction already under way (Wilner and Huff 2017; Piha et al. 2018) will eventually legitimize women's sexual liberty and erotic consumption. Who is to say that, in some specific contexts, this process has not stagnated or has not been reversed, considering the rise of right-wing nationalist populism and the revival of oppressive forms of tradition (Lambert 2019) taking place in several parts of the world? By inspecting how discourse constructs binary oppositions, like masculinity/femininity, culture/nature, production/consumption, street/home, work/leisure, which depend on each other to maintain power hierarchies (Maclaran and Stevens 2019), poststructuralist feminism may help deepen insights into the aforementioned contradictions and advance the pursuit of gender equality in the context of women's erotic consumption.

Let us look specifically at how the binary opposition virgin/whore may explain some paradoxes in women's erotic consumption. In the interaction between Brazilian men and women, it is possible to identify several aspects that contribute to the maintenance of a complex system of hierarchies and symbolic dominations. One of them is the opposition between the virgin and the whore, the former being an essential representation not only of female sexuality, but of the control that men exert over that sexuality (Parker 1991). Thus, the virgin represents both the woman who has never engaged in sexual intercourse and, more often, the woman who will only have sex under specific conditions, like being in a steady relationship. At the other extreme is the whore, who may be both the prostitute and the woman who practises sex outside of marriage or with multiple partners with no strings attached. The virgin's behaviour is associated with femininity, while the whore's behaviour is associated with masculinity, therefore perceived as unsuitable for women.

In my research, participants' discourses have testified to a binary opposition virgin/whore still at play in Brazil, but in new ways resulting from neoliberalism and postfeminism. The contradiction between the vibrator as a tool for women's empowerment and as a tool for preventing casual sex was revealed when comparing consumer discourses, like: "When you want to feel pleasure, you just feel it. It's available right there. You don't need (…) anyone" (Pamela, 51 years old), "[Before erotic consumption] It was up to the guy to make me come or not. And the vast majority were bad at it. (…) From then on, I became the person who dominates intercourse. I make myself come." (Francine, 35 y.o.),"Being a mother and a grandmother, I cannot go around fucking everyone, meeting everyone, so it's complicated. But [after the divorce] I needed to feel (…) pleasure too, right?" (Maria, 59 y.o.), and "Instead of screwing around, I have my toys to use at home" (Bianca, 36 y.o.). Above, the first couple of quotes express the empowering character of erotic consumption, while the last two indicate that erotic consumption assists these consumers in complying with conservative cultural principles.

Bianca praises vibrators as tools for self-knowledge: "I did discover how to come because of the device. (…) And when you discover the power of an orgasm, how wonderful it is… Many women haven't discovered that". But she does not buy condoms, expecting men to provide the item: "I think it's ugly, actually, the woman who has a condom in her drawer. (…) It looks slutty. Like she's just waiting the next guy to fuck her". So, the association of femininity with the virgin still stands, when the vibrator is used to prevent women from "screwing around". The association of masculinity with the whore becomes evident when the woman who performs tasks traditionally framed as masculine, like buying condoms, is called a "slut". In participants' discourse, we also see postfeminism's orgasm imperative (Rome and Lambert 2020), both when the vibrator is seen as a means to self-discovery and when it is seen as a means to sexual abstinence in the lack of a steady partner.

Poststructuralist feminism indicates that the conflation of binary oppositions does not serve patriarchy, because, in gender hierarchies, the privileged term (masculinity) is dependent on the other term's (femininity) inferior position. Therefore, the conflation of the virgin with the whore, fostered by postfeminist sex and orgasm imperatives and supported by neoliberal notions of self-realization through consumption, has been problematic in Brazil. Postfeminism exhorts women to be virgins and whores, without diluting these conceptual opposites. That is, occupying the two categories at the same time creates an illusion that they have been erased and substituted by a new category of truly independent, sexualized women. But this third type of subjectivity does not seem possible yet in Brazil, where women are now pressured to be virgins and pressured to be whores.

So, the paradoxes found in emic discourse are not just a matter of old values still lingering, and there is no guarantee that they will naturally subside. There are new influences at stake, like postfeminism and neoliberalism, thwarting a full transformation towards gender equality. A fourth wave of feminism, in lieu of postfeminism, is therefore necessary to expose and to fight the current reasons for adopting or maintaining old patriarchal values.

Conclusion

What does the future hold? I believe future marketing research on women's erotic consumption should, first, become more prolific. Second, it should work as an instrument to understand, disclose and redress gender and power struggles, embracing intersectionality, especially in more conservative cultures. And third, it should include technology among researched phenomena.

Dating apps have already become mediators of many romantic and sexual encounters. Currently, they serve to initiate contact; after that, the physical relationship goes offline. In the coming decades, steps following the first contact may increasingly happen online, in a futuristic version of intercourse. My research has shown that the touch of someone's skin is still extremely valued by consumers, which indicates that face-to-face interactions may not be expendable in the near future. But there may be a rise in erotic products that mediate sexual interplay, such as teledildonics (remote sex with the use of haptic devices), multiplayer sex games (virtual worlds where consumers customize their avatars and interact with each other) and robotics. These products and apps, however, will also demand a process of taboo destruction before they become normatively legitimate. Besides the issues regarding cultural resistance to technological sex products, marketing research will also have to deal with ethical issues that relate to human (and non-human) safety, dignity and morality, like alerted by Belk and colleagues in their research on artificial life and transhumanism (Belk 2019, 2020; Belk, Humayun, and Gopaldas 2020).

My intent here was not to create a quantitative census of all scholarly work on women's erotic consumption published by each scientific area. Rather, I intended to show, with a qualitative perspective, how more or less pervasive the topic might be within the scholarly production of certain fields. Therefore, counting publications is not what matters. What matters is the fact that, in an effortful and thorough search, one might find all scientific literature on women's erotic consumption issued by the marketing field with a cultural approach (sex in advertising excluded). But to find all papers, articles, chapters or books on this topic produced by fields like sociology, anthropology and communications seems like an impossible task. The epistemological silence around women's sexual practices I encountered when I first started studying this topic has been timidly broken in the past decade. But unfortunately women's sexuality remains a blind spot of cultural consumption studies. Until Gould's revolution (1991b) is fulfilled, I will keep challenging the idea that taboo regarding sex has been lifted and I will go on claiming that, in our marketing field, women's sexual practices are underresearched in general, and underexplored with a critical feminist approach in particular.

The epistemological silence around sexual practices in the Brazilian marketing academia specifically goes hand in hand with the social sanctions still bestowed on women who consume erotic products. This explanation for the blind spot may differ in other cultures not rooted in Catholicism's conservatism and patriarchal sexism, yet informed by institutional inequality due to other cultural and political tenets (Dowsett 2014; Irvine 2014). Should an early career researcher jeopardize her future by shedding light onto the power struggles both women consumers and women scholars must endure in a predominantly white, masculine-dominated, heteronormative, wealthy, senior marketing research community? My answer to that has been yes, because I want to be part of the change.

References

Abdo, Carmita. 2004. *Descobrimento Sexual do Brasil*. São Paulo: Summus.
Agoos, Ella. 2020. "Women's Erotic Consumption: Articulating the Sexual Self Under Late Capitalism." *Inquiries Journal* 12 (7). http://www.inquiriesjournal.com/a?id=1785.
Amy-Chinn, Dee. 2006. "This is just for Me(n): Lingerie Advertising for the Post-Feminist Woman." *Journal of Consumer Culture* 6 (2): 155–175.
Amy-Chinn, Dee, Christian Jantzen, and Per Østergaard. 2006. "Doing and Meaning: Towards an Integrated Approach to the Study of Women's Relationship to Underwear." *Journal of Consumer Culture* 6 (3): 379–401.
Arnould, Eric J., and Craig J. Thompson. 2005. "Consumer Culture Theory (CCT): Twenty Years of Research." *Journal of Consumer Research* 31 (4): 868–882.
Attwood, Feona. 2005. "Fashion and Passion: Marketing Sex to Women". *Sexualities* 8 (4): 392–406.
Attwood, Feona. 2006. "Sexed Up: Theorizing the Sexualization of Culture." *Sexualities* 9 (1): 77–94.
Attwood, Feona. 2011. "Sex and the Citizens: Erotic Play and the New Leisure Culture." In Bramham, Peter, and Stephen Wagg, eds. *The New Politics of Leisure and Pleasure*, 82–96. London: Palgrave Macmillan.
Bardzell, Jeffrey, and Shaowen Bardzell. 2011. "Pleasure Is Your Birthright: Digitally Enabled Designer Sex Toys as a Case of Third-Wave HCI." In *Proceedings of the SIGCHI Conference on Human Factors in Computing Systems*, 257–266, Vancouver, Canada.
Barker, Meg-John, Rosalind Gill, and Laura Harvey. 2018. "Mediated Intimacy: Sex Advice in Media Culture." *Sexualities* 21 (8): 1337–1345.
Basil, Michael. 2007. *Japanese Love Hotels: Protecting Privacy for Private Encounters*. ACR European Advances. Provo: Association for Consumer Research.
Bataille, Georges. 1986. *Erotism: Death and Sensuality*. San Francisco, CA: City Lights Books.
Belk, Russell W. 2019. "Machines and Artificial Intelligence." *Journal of Marketing Behavior* 4 (1): 11–30.
Belk, Russell W. 2020. "Ethical Issues in Service Robotics and Artificial Intelligence." *The Service Industries Journal*: 1–17. doi: 10.1080/02642069.2020.1727892.
Belk, Russell W., Güliz Ger, and Søren Askegaard. 2003. "The Fire of Desire: A Multisited Inquiry into Consumer Passion." *Journal of Consumer Research* 30 (3): 326–351.
Belk, Russell W., Mariam Humayun, and Ahir Gopaldas. 2020. "Artificial Life." *Journal of Macromarketing* 40 (2): 221–236.
Belk, Russell W., Per Østergaard, and Ronald Groves. 1998. "Sexual Consumption in the Time of AIDS: A Study of Prostitute Patronage in Thailand." *Journal of Public Policy & Marketing* 17 (2): 197–214.
Bettany, Shona, Lisa Penaloza, Diego Rinallo, Gillian Oakenfull, Ekant Veer, David Rowe, Nacima Ourahmoune, Luciana Walther, Christian Eichert, Katherine Sredl, Alexandra Rome, Ana-Isabel Nolke, and Jack Coffin. 2016. "Vive la Sexual Revolution! Liberté, Égalité (and Beyond) Fraternité in CCT Sexuality Research." *Roundtable held at the Consumer Culture Theory Conference*, Lille, France.
Bettany, Shona, and Helen Woodruffe-Burton. 2009. "Working the Limits of Method: The Possibilities of Critical Reflexive Practice in Marketing and Consumer Research." *Journal of Marketing Management* 25 (7–8): 661–679.
Better, Alison. 2011. "Pleasure for Sale. Feminist Sex Stores." In Seidman, Steven, Nancy Fischer, and Chet Meeks, eds. *Introducing the New Sexuality Studies*, 348–353. New York: Routledge.
Blanchette, Annie. 2014. "Revisiting the 'Passée': History Rewriting in the Neo-Burlesque Community." *Consumption Markets & Culture* 17 (2): 158–184.

Blinne, Kristen C. 2012. "Auto (Erotic) Ethnography." *Sexualities* 15 (8): 953–977.
Bozon, Michel. 2004. *Sociologia da Sexualidade*. Rio de Janeiro: FGV.
Brown, Stephen. 1998. "Romancing the Market: Sex, Shopping and Subjective Personal Introspection." *Journal of Marketing Management* 14 (7): 783–798.
Buchanan-Oliver, Margo, Hope Jensen Schau, and Alexander Schau. 2020. "The Dark Side of Brand-Fan Relationships: Lessons from Twilight and Fifty Shades." In Wang, Cheng Lu, ed. *Handbook of Research on the Impact of Fandom in Society and Consumerism*, 441–459. Hershey: IGI Global.
Buss, David M., and Pete Foley. 2020. "Mating and Marketing." *Journal of Business Research* 120: 492–497.
Butler, Judith. 1993. *Bodies that Matter: On the Discursive Limits of Sex*. New York: Routledge.
Butler, Judith. 1990. *Gender Trouble: Feminism and the Subversion of Identity*. New York: Routledge.
Butler, Judith. 1999. "Revisiting Bodies and Pleasures." *Theory, Culture & Society* 16 (2): 11–20.
Cervellon, Marie-Cécile, and Stephen Brown. 2018. "Reconsumption Reconsidered: Redressing Nostalgia with Neo-Burlesque." *Marketing Theory* 18 (3): 391–410.
Chesser, Stephanie, Diana Parry, and Tracy Penny Light. 2019. "Nurturing the Erotic Self: Benefits of Women Consuming Sexually Explicit Materials." *Sexualities* 22 (7–8): 1234–1252.
Click, Melissa. 2015. "Fifty Shades of Postfeminism: Contextualizing Readers' Reflections on the Erotic Romance Series." In Levine, Elana, ed. *Cupcakes, Pinterest, and Ladyporn. Feminized Popular Culture in the Early Twenty-First Centry*, 15–31. Urbana: University of Illinois Press.
Colbjørnsen, Terje. 2014. "The Construction of a Bestseller: Theoretical and Empirical Approaches to the Case of the Fifty Shades Trilogy as an eBook Bestseller." *Media, Culture & Society* 36 (8): 1100–1117.
Comella, Lynn. 2013. "Fifty Shades of Erotic Stimulus." *Feminist Media Studies* 13 (3): 563–566.
Comella, Lynn. 2017. *Vibrator Nation: How Feminist Sex-Toy Stores Changed the Business of Pleasure*. Durham, NC: Duke University Press.
Coulmont, Baptiste, and Phil Hubbard. 2010. "Consuming Sex: Socio-Legal Shifts in the Space and Place of Sex Shops." *Journal of Law and Society* 37 (1): 189–209.
Crewe, Louise, and Amber Martin. 2017. "Sex and the City: Branding, Gender and the Commodification of Sex Consumption in Contemporary Retailing." *Urban Studies* 54 (3): 582–599.
Curtis, Debra. 2004. "Commodities and Sexual Subjectivities: A Look at Capitalism and its Desires." *Cultural Anthropology* 19 (1): 95–121.
Daneback, Kristian, Sven-Axel Mansson, and Michael W. Ross. 2011. "Online Sex Shops: Purchasing Sexual Merchandise on the Internet." *International Journal of Sexual Health* 23 (2): 102–110.
Daskalopoulou, Athanasia, and Maria Carolina Zanette. 2020. "Women's Consumption of Pornography: Pleasure, Contestation, and Empowerment." *Sociology* 54 (5): 969–986.
Davis, Clive M., Joani Blank, Hung-Yu Lin, and Consuelo Bonillas. 1996. "Characteristics of Vibrator Use among Women." *Journal of Sex Research* 33 (4): 313–320.
Deller, Ruth A., and Clarissa Smith. 2013. "Reading the BDSM Romance: Reader Responses to Fifty Shades." *Sexualities* 16 (8): 932–950.
Döring, Nicola, and Sandra Pöschl. 2018. "Sex Toys, Sex Dolls, Sex Robots: Our Under-Researched Bed-Fellows." *Sexologies* 27 (3): e51–e55.
Döring, Nicola, and Sandra Poeschl. 2020. "Experiences with Diverse Sex Toys among German Heterosexual Adults: Findings from a National Online Survey." *The Journal of Sex Research* 57 (7): 885–896.
Dowsett, Gary W. 2014. "'Dirty Work' Down Under: A Comment on Janice Irvine's 'Is Sexuality Research 'Dirty Work'?'." *Sexualities* 17 (5–6): 657–661.
Drdová, Lucie, and Steven Saxonberg. 2020. "Dilemmas of a Subculture: An Analysis of BDSM Blogs about Fifty Shades of Grey." *Sexualities* 23 (5–6): 987–1008.
Drenten, Jenna, Lauren Gurrieri, and Meagan Tyler. 2020 "Sexualized Labour in Digital Culture: Instagram Influencers, Porn Chic and the Monetization of Attention." *Gender, Work & Organization* 27 (1): 41–66.

Durante, Kristina M., and Ashley Rae Arsena. 2015. "Playing the Field: The Effect of Fertility on Women's Desire for Variety." *Journal of Consumer Research* 41 (6): 1372–1391.

Dymock, Alex. 2013. "Flogging Sexual Transgression: Interrogating the Costs of the 'Fifty Shades Effect'." *Sexualities* 16 (8): 880–895.

Eaglin, Anna, and Shaowen Bardzell. 2011. "Sex Toys and Designing for Sexual Wellness." In *CHI'11 Extended Abstracts on Human Factors in Computing Systems* , 1837–1842, Vancouver, Canada.

Evans, Adrienne, and Sarah Riley. 2015. *Technologies of Sexiness: Sex, Identity, and Consumer Culture*. New York: Oxford University Press.

Evans, Adrienne, Sarah Riley, and Avi Shankar. 2010a. "Postfeminist Heterotopias: Negotiating 'Safe'and 'Seedy'in the British Sex Shop Space." *European Journal of Women's Studies* 17 (3): 211–229.

Evans, Adrienne, Sarah Riley, and Avi Shankar. 2010b. "Technologies of Sexiness: Theorizing Women's Engagement in the Sexualization of Culture." *Feminism & Psychology* 20 (1): 114–131.

Fahs, Breanne, and Eric Swank. 2013. "Adventures with the 'Plastic Man': Sex Toys, Compulsory Heterosexuality, and the Politics of Women's Sexual Pleasure." *Sexuality & Culture* 17 (4): 666–685.

Fahs, Breanne. 2011. "Sexuality on the Market: An Irigarayan Analysis of Female Desire as Commodity." In Rawlinson, Mary C., Sabrina L. Hom, and Serene J. Khader, eds. *Thinking with Irigaray*, 179–200. New York: State University of New York Press.

Farley, Melissa. 2018. "Risks of Prostitution: When the Person is the Product." *Journal of the Association for Consumer Research* 3 (1): 97–108.

Fennell, Julie. 2020 "It's Complicated: Sex and the BDSM Subculture." *Sexualities*. doi: 10.1177/1363460720961303.

Fernandez, Karen V., and John L. Lastovicka. 2011. "Making Magic: Fetishes in Contemporary Consumption." *Journal of Consumer Research* 38 (2): 278–299.

Fiaveh, Daniel Yaw. 2019. "Phallocentricism, Female Penile Choices, and the Use of Sex Toys in Ghana." *Sexualities* 22 (7–8): 1127–1144.

Fischer, Eileen, and Julia Bristor. 1994. "A Feminist Poststructuralist Analysis of the Rhetoric of Marketing Relationships." *International Journal of Research in Marketing* 11 (4): 317–331.

Fisher, Christopher, Debby Herbenick, Michael Reece, Brian Dodge, Sonya Satinsky, and Dayna Fischtein. 2010. "Exploring Sexuality Education Opportunities at In-Home Sex-Toy Parties in the United States." *Sex Education* 10 (2): 131–144.

Foucault, Michel. 1994. *Histoire de la sexualité, tome I: La volonté de savoir*. Paris: Gallimard.

Foucault, Michel. 1997a. *Histoire de la sexualité, tome II: L'usage des plaisirs*. Paris: Gallimard

Foucault, Michel. 1997b. *Histoire de la sexualité, tome III: Le souci de soi*. Paris: Gallimard.

Giddens, Anthony. 2000. *The Transformation of Intimacy: Sexuality, Love and Eroticism in Modern Societies*. Stanford, CA: Stanford University Press.

Gill, Rosalind. 2003. "From Sexual Objectification to Sexual Subjectification: The Resexualisation of Women's Bodies in the Media." *Feminist Media Studies* 3 (1): 100–106.

Gilly, Mary C. 1988. "Sex Roles in Advertising: A Comparison of Television Advertisements in Australia, Mexico and the United States", *Journal of Marketing* 52 (Apr): 513–525.

Gopaldas, Ahir, and Susanna Molander. 2020. "The Bad Boy Archetype as a Morally Ambiguous Complex of Juvenile Masculinities: the Conceptual Anatomy of a Marketplace Icon." *Consumption Markets & Culture* 23 (1): 81–93.

Gould, Stephen J. 1991a. "The Self-Manipulation of My Pervasive, Perceived Vital Energy through Product Use: An Introspective-Praxis Perspective." *Journal of Consumer Research* 18 (2): 194–207.

Gould, Stephen J. 1991b. *Toward a Theory of Sexuality and Consumption: Consumer Lovemaps*. ACR North American Advances. Provo: Association for Consumer Research.

Gould, Stephen J. 1992. "A Model of the Scripting of Consumer Lovemaps: The Consumer Sexual Behavior Sequence." *ACR North American Advances*. Provo: Association for Consumer Research.

Gould, Stephen J. 1995. "Sexualized Aspects of Consumer Behavior: An Empirical Investigation of Consumer Lovemaps." *Psychology & Marketing* 12 (5): 395–413.

Goulding, Christina, and Michael Saren. 2009. "Performing Identity: An Analysis of Gender Expressions at the Whitby Goth Festival." *Consumption, Markets and Culture* 12 (1): 27–46.

Goulding, Christina, Avi Shankar, Richard Elliott, and Robin Canniford. 2009. "The Marketplace Management of Illicit Pleasure." *Journal of Consumer Research* 35 (5): 759–771.

Hakim, Catherine. 2015. "Economies of Desire: Sexuality and the Sex Industry in the 21st Century." *Economic Affairs* 35 (3): 329–348.

Harman, Sarah, and Bethan Jones. 2013. "Fifty Shades of Ghey: Snark Fandom and the Figure of the Anti-Fan." *Sexualities* 16 (8): 951–968.

Harvey, Laura, and Rosalind Gill. 2011. "Spicing it up: Sexual Entrepreneurs and the Sex Inspectors." In Gill, Rosalind, and Christina Scharff, eds. *New Femininities: Postfeminism, Neoliberalism and Subjectivity*, 52–67. London: Palgrave Macmillan.

Heineman, Elizabeth D. 2006. "The Economic Miracle in the Bedroom: Big Business and Sexual Consumption in Reconstruction West Germany." *The Journal of Modern History* 78 (4): 846–877.

Heineman, Elizabeth D. 2011. *Before Porn was Legal: The Erotica Empire of Beate Uhse*. Chicago, IL: University of Chicago Press.

Heljakka, Katriina. 2016. "Fifty Shades of Toys: Notions of Play and Things for Play in the Fifty Shades of Grey Canon." *Intensities: The Journal of Cult Media* 8: 59–73.

Herbenick, Debby, and Michael Reece. 2007. "Sex Education in Adult Retail Stores: Positioning Consumers' Questions as Teachable Moments." *American Journal of Sexuality Education* 2 (1): 57–75.

Herbenick, Debra, Michael Reece, Stephanie Sanders, Brian Dodge, Annahita Ghassemi, and J. Dennis Fortenberry. 2009. "Prevalence and Characteristics of Vibrator Use by Women in the United States: Results from a Nationally Representative Study." *The Journal of Sexual Medicine* 6 (7): 1857–1866.

Herbenick, Debra, Michael Reece, Stephanie A. Sanders, Brian Dodge, Annahita Ghassemi, and J. Dennis Fortenberry. 2010. "Women's Vibrator Use in Sexual Partnerships: Results from a Nationally Representative Survey in the United States." *Journal of Sex & Marital Therapy* 36 (1): 49–65.

Herbenick, Debra, Michael Reece, Vanessa Schick, Kristen N. Jozkowski, Susan E. Middelstadt, Stephanie A. Sanders, Brian S. Dodge, Annahita Ghassemi, and J. Dennis Fortenberry. 2011. "Beliefs about Women's Vibrator Use: Results from a Nationally Representative Probability Survey in the United States." *Journal of Sex & Marital Therapy* 37 (5): 329–345.

Hirschman, Elizabeth C. 1991. "Exploring the Dark Side of Consumer Behavior: Metaphor and Ideology in Prostitution and Pornography." *ACR Gender and Consumer Behavior Conference*. Provo: Association for Consumer Research.

Hirschman, Elizabeth C., and Morris B. Holbrook. 1982. "Hedonic Consumption: Emerging Concepts, Methods and Propositions." *Journal of Marketing* 46 (3): 92–101.

Hubbard, Phil, Alan Collins, and Andrew Gorman-Murray. 2017. "Introduction: Sex, Consumption and Commerce in the Contemporary City." *Urban Studies* 54 (3): 567–581.

Huff, April. 2018. "Liberation and Pleasure: Feminist Sex Shops and the Politics of Consumption." *Women's Studies* 47 (4): 427–446.

Irvine, Janice M. 2014. "Is Sexuality Research 'Dirty Work'? Institutionalized Stigma in the Production of Sexual Knowledge." *Sexualities* 17 (5–6): 632–656.

James, E. L. 2011. *Fifty Shades of Grey*. New York: Random House.

James, E. L. 2012a. *Fifty Shades Darker*. New York: Random House.

James, E. L. 2012b. *Fifty Shades Freed*. New York: Random House.

Jantzen, Christian, Per Østergaard, and Carla M. Sucena Vieira. 2006. "Becoming a 'Woman to the Backbone': Lingerie Consumption and the Experience of Feminine Identity." *Journal of Consumer Culture* 6 (2): 177–202.

Johnson, Naomi R. 2010. "Consuming Desires: Consumption, Romance, and Sexuality in Best-Selling Teen Romance Novels." *Women's Studies in Communication* 33 (1): 54–73.

Jones, Bethan. 2014. "Fifty Shades of Exploitation: Fan Labor and Fifty Shades of Grey." *Transformative Works and Cultures* 15: 115–123.

Juffer, Jane. 1998. *At Home with Pornography: Women, Sex, and Everyday Life*. New York: NYU Press.

Kates, Steven M. 2002 "The Protean Quality of Subcultural Consumption: An Ethnographic Account of Gay Consumers." *Journal of Consumer Research* 29 (3), 383–399.

Kent, Tony. 2005. "Ethical Perspectives on the Erotic in Retailing". *Qualitative Market Research* 8 (4), 430–439.

Kent, Tony, and Reva Berman Brown. 2006. "Erotic Retailing in the UK (1963-2003): The View from the Marketing Mix." *Journal of Management History (*12) 2: 199–211

Kingston, Sarah, Natalie Hammond, and Scarlett Redman. 2020. "Transformational Sexualities: Motivations of Women who Pay for Sexual Services." *Sexualities*. doi: 10.1177/1363460720904646.

Knudsen, Gry Hongsmark. 2019. "Critical Consumers: Discourses of Women, Sexuality, and Objectification." In Dobscha, Susan, ed. *Handbook of Research on Gender and Marketing*. Cheltenham: Edward Elgar Publishing.

Lambert, Aliette. 2019. "Psychotic, Acritical and Precarious? A Lacanian Exploration of the Neoliberal Consumer Subject." *Marketing Theory* 19 (3): 329–346.

Lanier Jr, Clinton D., and C. Scott Rader. 2019. "The Irrepressible and Uncontrollable Urge: Sex, Experience, and Consumption." *Consumption Markets & Culture* 22 (1): 17–43.

Laqueur, Thomas. 1992. *Making Sex: Body and Gender from the Greeks to Freud*. Cambridge, MA: Harvard University Press.

Lieberman, Hallie. 2017a. *Buzz: The Stimulating History of the Sex Toy*. New York: Pegasus Books.

Lieberman, Hallie. 2017b. "Intimate Transactions: Sex Toys and the Sexual Discourse of Second-Wave Feminism." *Sexuality & Culture* 21 (1): 96–120.

Lieberman, Hallie, and Eric Schatzberg. 2018. "A Failure of Academic Quality Control: The Technology of Orgasm." *Journal of Positive Sexuality* 4 (2): 24–47.

Maclaran, Pauline. 2015. "Feminism's Fourth Wave: A Research Agenda for Marketing and Consumer Research." *Journal of Marketing Management* 31 (15–16): 1732–1738.

Maclaran, Pauline, and Lorna Stevens. 2004. "Special Session: Gender and the Erotics of Consumption." *ACR Gender and Consumer Behavior Conference*. Provo: Association for Consumer Research.

Maclaran, Pauline, and Lorna Stevens. 2019. "Thinking through Feminist Theorising: Poststructuralist Feminism, Ecofeminism and Intersectionality." In Dobscha, Susan, ed. *Handbook of Research on Gender and Marketing*: 229-251. Cheltenham: Edward Elgar Publishing.

Macleod, Patrick J. 2020. "Influences on Ethical Decision-Making among Porn Consumers: The Role of Stigma." *Journal of Consumer Culture*. doi: 10.1177/1469540520970247.

Maines, Rachel P. 1999. *The Technology of Orgasm: "Hysteria," the Vibrator, and Women's Sexual Satisfaction*. Baltimore, MD: Johns Hopkins University Press.

Malina, Danusia, and Ruth A. Schmidt. 1997. "It's Business Doing Pleasure with You: Sh! A Women's Sex Shop Case." *Marketing Intelligence & Planning* 15 (7): 352–360.

Martin, Amber. 2013. "Fifty Shades of Sex Shop: Sexual Fantasy for Sale." *Sexualities* 16 (8): 980–984.

Martin, Amber. 2016. "Plastic Fantastic? Problematising Post-Feminism in Erotic Retailing in England." *Gender, Place & Culture* 23 (10): 1420–1431.

Mayr, Cornelia. 2020. "Symbolic Vibration: A Meaning-Based Framework for the Study of Vibrator Consumption." *Journal of Consumer Culture*. doi: 10.1177/1469540520926233.

Mayr, Cornelia. 2021a. "Beyond Plug and Play: The Acquisition and Meaning of Vibrators in Heterosexual Relationships." *International Journal of Consumer Studies* 45 (1): 28–37.

Mayr, Cornelia. 2021b. "Toy Stories: The Role of Vibrators in Domestic Intimacies." *Sexualities*. doi: 10.1177/13634607211000194.

McCaughey, Martha, and Christina French. 2001. "Women's Sex-Toy Parties: Technology, Orgasm, and Commodification." *Sexuality and Culture* 5 (3): 77–96.
McNair, Brian. 2013. *Porno? Chic!: How Pornography Changed the World and Made it a Better Place*. Oxfordshire: Routledge.
McVey, Laura, Lauren Gurrieri, and Meagan Tyler. 2020. "The Structural Oppression of Women by Markets: The Continuum of Sexual Violence and the Online Pornography Market." *Journal of Marketing Management* 37 (1–2): 1–28.
Miller, Daniel. 2010. *Stuff*. Cambridge: Polity.
Møller, Kristian. 2020. "Hanging, Blowing, Slamming and Playing: Erotic Control and Overflow in a Digital Chemsex Scene." *Sexualities*. doi: 10.1177/1363460720964100.
Murgolo-Poore, Marie E., Leyland F. Pitt, and Pierre R. Berthon. 2003. "Three Theoretical Perspectives on One of Marketing's Most Fundamental Exchanges: Propositions on Personal Relationships." *Marketing Theory* 3 (2): 235–265.
Neal, Mark. 2018. "Dirty Customers: Stigma and Identity among Sex Tourists." *Journal of Consumer Culture* 18 (1): 131–148.
Nixon, Paul G. 2017. "Sex Toys." In Nixon, Paul G., and Isabel K. Düsterhöft, eds. *Sex in the Digital Age*: 16-32. Oxfordshire: Routledge.
Northey, Gavin, Rebecca Dolan, Patrick van Esch, Felix Septianto, Vicki Andonopoulos, and Michael Barbera. 2019. "Fifty Shades of Gay: the Effects of Gender and LGBT Imagery on Politically Conservative Viewers." *ACR North American Advances*. Provo: Association for Consumer Research.
O'Donnell, Kathleen A. 1999. "Good Girls Gone Bad: The Consumption of Fetish Fashion and the Sexual Empowerment of Women." *ACR North American Advances*. Provo: Association for Consumer Research.
O'Sullivan, Stephen R. 2016. "The Branded Carnival: The Dark Magic of Consumer Excitement." *Journal of Marketing Management* 32 (9–10): 1033–1058.
Østberg, Jacob. 2010. "Thou Shalt Sport a Banana in thy Pocket: Gendered Body Size Ideals in Advertising and Popular Culture." *Marketing Theory* 10 (1): 45–73.
Ourahmoune, Nacima. 2013. "Gender, Women and Sexual Experiences of Tourism." *ACR North American Advances*. Provo: Association for Consumer Research.
Paasonen, Susanna. 2018. *Many Splendored Things: Thinking Sex and Play*. Cambridge: MIT Press.
Parker, Richard G. 1991. *Bodies, Pleasures and Passions: Sexual Culture in Contemporary Brazil*. Boston, MA: Beacon Press.
Parry, Diana C., and Tracy Penny Light. 2014. "Fifty Shades of Complexity: Exploring Technologically Mediated Leisure and Women's Sexuality." *Journal of Leisure Research* 46 (1): 38–57.
Patterson, Maurice, and Gretchen Larsen. 2016. "Pornographication and the Advertising of Sexual Services." *ACR North American Advances*. Provo: Association for Consumer Research.
Piha, Samuel, Leila Hurmerinta, Elina Järvinen, Juulia Räikkönen, and Birgitta Sandberg. 2020. "Escaping into Sexual Play: A Consumer Experience Perspective." *Leisure Sciences* 42 (3–4): 289–305.
Piha, Samuel, Leila Hurmerinta, Birgitta Sandberg, and Elina Järvinen. 2018. "From Filthy to Healthy and beyond: Finding the Boundaries of Taboo Destruction in Sex Toy Buying." *Journal of Marketing Management* 34 (13–14): 1078–1104.
Prasad, Ajnesh. 2014. "Psychoanalytically Reading Hedonic Consumption in the 50 Shades Trilogy." *ACR North American Advances*. Provo: Association for Consumer Research.
Radner, Hilary. 2005. *Shopping Around: Feminine Culture and the Pursuit of Pleasure*. Oxfordshire: Routledge.
Reece, Michael, Debby Herbenick, and Catherine Sherwood-Puzzello. 2004. "Sexual Health Promotion and Adult Retail Stores." *Journal of Sex Research* 41 (2): 173–180.
Reichert, Tom, and Jacqueline Lambiase, eds. 2003. *Sex in Advertising: Perspectives on the Erotic Appeal*. Mahwah, NJ: Lawrence Erlbaum.
Richters, Juliet, Richard O. de Visser, Paul B. Badcock, Anthony MA Smith, Chris Rissel, Judy M. Simpson, and Andrew E. Grulich. 2014. "Masturbation, Paying for Sex, and Other Sexual

Activities: The Second Australian Study of Health and Relationships." *Sexual Health* 11 (5): 461–471.
Rome, Alexandra S., and Aliette Lambert. 2020. "(Wo)men on Top? Postfeminist Contradictions in Young Women's Sexual Narratives." *Marketing Theory* 20 (4): 501–525.
Ronen, Shelly. 2020. "Gendered Morality in the Sex Toy Market: Entitlements, Reversals, and the Irony of Heterosexuality." *Sexualities*. doi: 10.1177/1363460720914601.
Rossolatos, George. 2016. "Good Vibrations: Charting the Dominant and Emergent Discursive Regimes of Sex Toys." *The Qualitative Report* 21 (8): 1475–1494.
Rossolatos, George. 2017. "Toy Stories: On the Disciplinary Regime of Vibration." *Semiotica* 218: 145–164.
Rullo, Jordan E., Tierney Lorenz, Matthew J. Ziegelmann, Laura Meihofer, Debra Herbenick, and Stephanie S. Faubion. 2018. "Genital Vibration for Sexual Function and Enhancement: Best Practice Recommendations for Choosing and Safely Using a Vibrator." *Sexual and Relationship Therapy* 33 (3): 275–285.
Sanbonmatsu, David M., and Frank R. Kardes. 1988. "The Effects of Physiological Arousal on Information Processing and Persuasion." *Journal of Consumer Research* 15 (3): 379–385.
Schick, Vanessa, Debby Herbenick, Kristen N. Jozkowski, Sofia Jawed-Wessel, and Michael Reece. 2013. "The Sexual Consumer: Characteristics, Expectations, and Experiences of Women Attending In-Home Sex Toy Parties." *Journal of Sex & Marital Therapy* 39 (2): 160–175.
Scholes-Balog, Kirsty, Nicole Francke, and Sheryl Hemphill. 2016. "Relationships between Sexting, Self-Esteem, and Sensation Seeking among Australian Young Adults." *Sexualization, Media, & Society* (2): 1–8.
Scott, Sue. 2017. "Sexual Embodiment and Consumption." In Keller, Margit, Bente Halkier, Terhi-Anna Wilska, and Monica Truninger, eds. *Routledge Handbook on Consumption*, 372–383. Yorkshire: Routledge.
Smith, Clarissa. 2007, "Designed for Pleasure: Style, Indulgence and Accessorized Sex." *European Journal of Cultural Studies* 10 (2): 167–184.
Smith, Clarissa, Feona Attwood, and Brian McNair, eds. 2017. *The Routledge Companion to Media, Sex and Sexuality*. Yorkshire: Routledge.
Sobande, Francesca, Laetitia Mimoun, and Lez Trujillo Torres. 2020. "Soldiers and Superheroes Needed! Masculine Archetypes and Constrained Bodily Commodification in the Sperm Donation Market." *Marketing Theory* 20 (1): 65–84.
Stern, Barbara B. 1991. "Two Pornographies: A Feminist View of Sex in Advertising." *ACR North American Advances*. Provo: Association for Consumer Research.
Stevens, Lorna, and Pauline Maclaran. 2007. "The Carnal feminine: Womanhood, Advertising and Consumption." *ACR European Advances*. Provo: Association for Consumer Research.
Storr, Merl. 2003. *Latex & Lingerie. Shopping for Pleasure at Ann Summers Parties*. New York: Berg.
Sundén, Jenny. 2020. "Play, Secrecy and Consent: Theorizing Privacy Breaches and Sensitive Data in the World of Networked Sex Toys." *Sexualities*. doi: 10.1177/1363460720957578.
Sundie, Jill, Vladas Griskevicius, Douglas Kenrick, and Joshua Tybur. 2008. "Peacocks, Porsches and Thorstein Veblen: Romantic Motivations For Conspicuous Consumption." *ACR North American Advances*. Provo: Association for Consumer Research.
Takhar, Jennifer. 2020. "The Voice Inside." *Marketing Theory* 20 (2): 167–174.
Taylor, Gary W., and Jane M. Ussher. 2001. "Making Sense of S&M: A Discourse Analytic Account." *Sexualities* 4 (3): 293–314.
Thompson, Craig J., Paul C. Henry, and Fleura Bardhi. 2018. "Theorizing Reactive Reflexivity: Lifestyle Displacement and Discordant Performances of Taste." *Journal of Consumer Research* 45 (3): 571–594.
Toffler, Alvin. 1981. *The Third Wave*. New York: Bantam Books.
Tripodi, Francesca. 2017. "Fifty Shades of Consent?." *Feminist Media Studies* 17 (1): 93–107.
Valtonen, Anu, and Elina Närvänen. 2015. "Gendered Reading of the Body in the Bed." *Journal of Marketing Management* 31 (15–16): 1583–1601.

Varman, Rohit, Paromita Goswami, and Devi Vijay. 2018. "The Precarity of Respectable Consumption: Normalising Sexual Violence against Women." *Journal of Marketing Management* 34 (11–12): 932–964.

Veer, Ekant, and Maja Golf-Papez. 2018. "Physically Freeing: Breaking Taboos Through Online Displays of the Sexual Self." *Journal of Marketing Management* 34 (13–14): 1105–1125.

Vohs, Kathleen, Catrin Finkenauer, and Nina Burger. 2008. "Sexual Behavior as Predicted by a Social Exchange Model: Three Tests of Sexual Economics." *ACR North American Advances*. Provo: Association for Consumer Research.

Voss, Georgina. 2012. "'Treating It as a Normal Business': Researching the Pornography Industry." *Sexualities* 15 (3–4): 391–410.

Walther, Luciana. 2017. *Mulheres que não ficam sem pilha: Como o consumo erótico feminino está transformando vidas, relacionamentos e a sociedade*. Rio de Janeiro: Mauad.

Walther, Luciana. 2019a. "Patriarchal Myths Debunked: Applying a Dialectic of Extremes to Women's Erotic Consumption." In Dobscha, Susan, ed. *Handbook of Research on Gender and Marketing*: 117-167. Cheltenham: Edward Elgar Publishing.

Walther, Luciana. 2019b. "The Life and Death of Anthony Barbie: A Consumer Culture Tale of Lovers, Butlers, and Crashers." In Bajde, Domen, Dannie Kjelgaard, and Russell W. Belk, eds. *Research in Consumer Behavior: Consumer Culture Theory*: 23-38. Bingley: Emerald Publishing.

Walther, Luciana, and John W. Schouten. 2016. "Next Stop, Pleasure Town: Identity Transformation and Women's Erotic Consumption." *Journal of Business Research* 69 (1): 273–283.

Waskul, Dennis, and Michelle Anklan. 2020. "Best Invention, Second to the Dishwasher: Vibrators and Sexual Pleasure." *Sexualities* 23 (5–6): 849–875.

Watson, Erin D., Léa J. Séguin, Robin R. Milhausen, and Sarah H. Murray. 2016. "The Impact of a Couple's Vibrator on Men's Perceptions of Their Own and Their Partner's Sexual Pleasure and Satisfaction." *Men and Masculinities* 19 (4): 370–383.

Whitehead, Deborah. 2013. "When Religious 'Mommy Bloggers' Met 'Mommy Porn': Evangelical Christian and Mormon Women's Responses to Fifty Shades." *Sexualities* 16 (8): 915–931.

Wilner, Sarah J.S., and Aimee Dinnin Huff. 2017. "Objects of Desire: The Role of Product Design in Revising Contested Cultural Meanings." *Journal of Marketing Management* 33 (3–4): 244–271.

Wood, Jessica, Sara Crann, Shannon Cunningham, Deborah Money, and Kieran O'Doherty. 2017. "A Cross-Sectional Survey of Sex Toy Use, Characteristics of Sex Toy Use Hygiene Behaviours, and Vulvovaginal Health Outcomes in Canada." *The Canadian Journal of Human Sexuality* 26 (3): 196–204.

Wood, Rachel. 2015. "Sexual Consumption within Sexual Labour: Producing and Consuming Erotic Texts and Sexual Commodities." *Porn Studies* 2 (2–3): 250–262.

Wood, Rachel. 2017. *Consumer Sexualities: Women and Sex Shopping*. Oxfordshire: Routledge.

Yalkin, Cagri, and Ekant Veer. 2018. "Taboo on TV: Gender, Religion, and Sexual Taboos in Transnationally Marketed Turkish Soap Operas." *Journal of Marketing Management* 34 (13–14): 1149–1171.

Zanette, Maria Carolina, and Athanasia Daskalopoulou. 2020. "Women Who Watch Porn: Market-Mediated Gendered Discourses and Consumption of Pornography." *ACR European Advances*. Provo: Association for Consumer Research.

Zayer, Linda Tuncay, Katherine Sredl, Marie-Agnes Parmentier, and Catherine Coleman. 2012. "Consumption and Gender Identity in Popular Media: Discourses of Domesticity, Authenticity, and Sexuality." *Consumption Markets & Culture* 15 (4): 333–357.

Zelizer, Viviana A. 2009. *The Purchase of Intimacy*. Princeton, NJ: Princeton University.

14 Taking off the blindfold

The perils of pornification and sexual abjectification

Alexandra S. Rome

Introduction

Porn has gone mainstream. Its tropes and narratives have infiltrated the most intimate aspects of our lives, from our screens and social media platforms to the relationships we foster with others as well as with ourselves (Dines 2010). Notwithstanding the porn industry's increasing presence within the global economy (McVey, Gurrieri, and Tyler 2020), the process by which pornography has seeped into our everyday lives has been unfolding over nearly a century. The porn industry took off in the 1950s following the debut of *Playboy* magazine (Dines 2010), but it wasn't until the 1970s, following the box office success of the pornographic film *Deep Throat*, that porn shifted towards the mainstream (Paasonen, Nikunen, and Saarenmaa 2007). Since then, the use of pornographic references and imagery has been well-documented in areas as diverse as primetime and reality television, music, self-help literature, video games, sports, education, fashion and beauty practices, and digital forums (Tyler and Quek 2016). Though it is not possible – nor desirable – to untangle pornography from this process of pornification (Tyler 2011), the focus of this chapter is to examine how discourses related to porn shape and are shaped by consumer culture and women's lived experiences.

The data for this chapter are drawn from a six-year longitudinal study exploring how young American women discursively construct (discuss, negotiate, and justify) their intimate lives (Shankar, Elliott, and Fitchett 2009), i.e., their sexual experiences, sexuality, relationships, etc. Initial in-depth interviews took place in the US in 2014, as described in Rome and Lambert (2020). Multiple follow-up interviews were conducted with eight of the women who participated in the original study over the summer and fall of 2020. These took place over the phone or on Zoom, and lasted on average 2.5 hours. Rapport between myself and respondents was already well established and the conversations flowed naturally, focusing on their experiences relating to, e.g., sex, relationships, dating, marriage, motherhood, menstruation, porn, feminism, and sexual violence. All interviews were transcribed verbatim, and NVivo 12 was used to generate and compare themes within and across participants over the six-year time span. The research findings indicate a shift in sexual subjectivities afforded to women, which, at first glance, appear to be shaped by the repudiation of neoliberal values – those which foster competitiveness, individuality, autonomy, and meritocracy. Critical reflection, however, suggests a disconnect between how women understand, enact, and experience their intimate experiences and sexualities.

The remainder of this chapter is organized as follows. First, the debates around pornification are outlined. In subsequent sections, I articulate two distinct shifts within the pornification of culture and discuss the impact on women's sexual subjectivities. In the

DOI: 10.4324/9781003042587-17

first section, I discuss the emergence of the ideal neoliberal subject and briefly reflect on the original study (Rome and Lambert 2020). In the second section, I document the rise of an abject subjectivity, which begets new forms of self-policing and commodification. Abjectification, in this context, refers to that which "disturbs identity, system, order" and "what does not respect borders, positions, rules" (Kristeva 1982, 4). Its usage is premised on – yet is more encompassing and less pejorative than – an emerging 'grossout' feminism that works by normalizing women's bodies, their bodily functions (flatulence, menstruation, lactation), body hair, smells, fat, and so forth (Strimpel 2016), as well as 'corporal' feminism, marked by a reclaiming of the material and biological body (Grosz and Probyn 1995). Drawing on examples from contemporary media culture and making use of selected data excerpts, three of these practices are explored in-depth. I conclude with a critical analysis illustrating the intersections of abjectification, subjectification, and objectification, and offer avenues for future research.

Pornification

The pornification of Western post-industrial cultures is marked by both the "increasing accessibility and acceptability of pornography, as well as the ways pornography and pornographic imagery are fragmenting and blurring into traditionally nonpornographic forms of popular culture" (Tyler and Quek 2016, 1). Although there is no single way pornification manifests in popular culture, its ubiquity naturalizes, normalizes, and commodifies particular types of and narratives around sexuality (Paasonen, Nikunen, and Saarenmaa 2007).

Pornification is not a spontaneous or naturalistic process, but is instead inherently linked and continuously informed by the porn industry (Boyle 2018). Presently, there is much debate surrounding the implications of porn and pornification. These debates are reminiscent of the Sex Wars in the 1970s and 1980s when feminists argued the merits of pornography and whether it contributed to women's domination or liberation (Mikkola 2019). Critics of pornification under the 'negative effects paradigm' argue that porn leads to the internalization of harmful body ideals and sex practices that perpetuate cruelty and violence towards women, cause desensitized sexual response, disrupt daily life, damage relationships, and lead to the sexual exploitation of children (e.g., Dines 2010; McCormack and Wignall 2017; McVey, Gurrieri, and Tyler 2020; Tyler and Quek 2016). Women under this paradigm are reduced to faceless bodies (or objects), modified and adapted to maximize male pleasure (Dworkin 1981). Others maintain that the outright condemnation of pornification is problematic, particularly without accounting for the specificities around its "production, consumption, and textual forms" (Smith 2010, 107). From this point of view, porn and pornification are believed to install new meanings, representations, and performances of sexuality, leading to a "democratization of desire" (McNair 2013) that offers, e.g., sexual minorities and women new ways of articulating, learning about, and making sense of their sexual experiences and proclivities (Attwood 2010; Paasonen, Nikunen, and Saarenmaa 2007; Smith 2010).

The ambiguity around pornification has led some to distinguish between sexualization, which refers, more broadly, to the visibility of sexual representation in mainstream culture (Attwood 2010), and pornification, which espouses *particular types* of commodified sex that eroticize violence and gender inequality (Boyle 2018; McVey, Gurrieri, and Tyler 2020; Tyler and Quek 2016). This distinction, however, proves problematic in the current climate for two main reasons. First is the issue of *who* decides what constitutes pornified sex and from *what standard* such an evaluation should rightfully occur. Indeed, to censure forms of sexuality which fall outside 'normative' conceptions (e.g., sex as heterosexual, monogamous, private, and rooted in passionate love) is to reinforce views that non-normative sex is perverted, undignified, shameful, and/or harmful (Rubin 1993; Smith 2010). Second, this distinction omits issues around the production and consumption of pornography and pornification. Specifically, it fails to account for a rising female audience (Attwood, Smith, and Barker 2021): an oversight, Och (2019, 215) warns, that threatens to reify "long-standing imaginations of women as uncritical and naïve with pleasures that should be hidden, mocked, and shamed." With respect to production, it overlooks the evolution and expansion of porn and popular media, which increasingly employ female producers and promote feminist, queer, and other egalitarian genres, many of which work to subvert conventionally harmful, hegemonic, and/or exploitive representations and industry practices (Jacobs 2014). Thus, meaning is more complex and less stable than what a simplified distinction between pornification and sexualization can account for (Mikkola 2019). In addition, the rise of (free or low-cost) online and content-sharing platforms and do-it-yourself (DIY) porn has drastically shifted the way individuals create, access, and pay for porn content, further blurring the boundaries between porn, pornification, and sexualization (Drenten, Gurrieri, and Tyler 2019; Ruberg 2016).

In an effort to account for these rising changes and ambiguities, some have argued for a more expansive approach to conceptualize porn and pornification discourses. Gregory and Lorange (2018), for example, introduce a post-pornographic approach, which "understands sex (as a practice), gender (as a complicated identity) and sexuality (as a set of orientations or modes of being in relation) as co-constitutive and, above all, inherently social" (140). Their approach differs from other conceptualizations of post-porn as a genre which undermines the conventions of mainstream pornography (Jacobs 2014) and instead, acts as a lens from which to interrogate "contemporary ideas about the body, desire, sex and technology that cannot be reduced to seeking natural or truthful insights into sexuality and sex itself" (146). Thus, given the ambiguity surrounding contemporary mediations of sexuality, sexual desire, and sexual pleasure, such an approach may prove useful in exploring both the oppressive *and* subversive elements which are not easily subsumed into the (pro) sexualization/(anti) pornification dichotomy. In the following sections, I explore how these trends and debates drive new subjectivities in women.

Sexual subjectification

The 1990s ushered in a new, liberated sexuality for women, premised on a postfeminist sensibility that allowed women to be feminine, attractive, and feminist all at the same time (Gill 2007). While pornified discourses were prevalent in mainstream media prior to the 1990s, what distinguished this era from those preceding it was its conflation with feminist discourses. Specifically, feminism was at once taken into account and fiercely repudiated, buttressed by claims that gender equality had been achieved (McRobbie 2009). The intersection of these two trends signified a shift from *objectification*, women being portrayed as passive, desirable, and demure sexual objects, to *subjectification*, women being addressed as active, confident, and desiring sexual subjects (Gill 2003). Representations of this new sexually savvy woman were abound in consumer culture and popular media (Gill 2007), captured most poignantly perhaps, by the HBO series

Sex and the City (*SATC*; 1998–2004). This series normalized casual sex and popularized sex toys such as vibrators for an entire generation of women, marking one of the first instances of sex being re-imagined on-screen as liberating – something women do to please themselves rather than their male counterparts. Subsequent marketization, from burlesque and pole-dancing to vibrators and bondage kits, reimagined women's sexuality in ways that ostensibly celebrated their autonomy, femininity, and sexual power (Evans, Riley, and Shankar 2010).

This shift, consequently, introduced a new repertoire of self-policing practices that were outlined in the original study (Rome and Lambert 2020). The findings of this research illustrate how a postfeminist positioning manifests in women's sexual and intimate experiences in two main ways. First, young women strive to maintain a sense of agency, despite appearing disempowered in broader financial and economic domains and disconnected from their embodied (sexual) experiences. Second, by embracing a submissive sexual positioning, young women prioritize male pleasure and reenact taboo and often painful sex practices in ways that (re)eroticize traditional power relations. These findings not only underscore how entrenched patriarchal and pornified ideals are masked by postfeminist discourses, they also illustrate how women have come to embody the ideal neoliberal subject.

Sexual abjectification

The 2010s witnessed yet another shift in the representation and address of women in Western post-industrial cultures. The election of Donald Trump in 2016 signaled not only a stark rejection of feminist ideals, but also a radical departure from the neoliberal status quo (Fraser 2016). This prompted a resurgence of feminist activism that reached new heights at the onset of the #MeToo movement. This movement gave rise to a revived collective feminist activism, foregrounding a 'call-out' or 'cancel' culture that sanctions the public shaming of sexist, misogynist, racist, or otherwise offensive remarks and wrongdoings (Banet-Weiser 2018). At the same time, it has exacerbated expressions of popular misogyny (Banet-Weiser 2018), from men's rights activism, the growing acceptance of so-called 'locker room talk,' to the ascendance of radical online communities and networks that promote antifeminist, sexist, and violent behavior against women and other minorities (Dignam and Rohlinger 2019).

Amidst this socio-political backdrop, the 2010s saw a boom in media content created by and for women that started to push back against prescriptive neoliberal standards of women's appropriate behavior and appearance (Darling 2020). At the forefront of this trend was another HBO series – *Girls* (2012–2017), created, written, and starring Lena Dunham. Much like its predecessor (*SATC*), *Girls* sparked new sexual subjectivities for young women struggling to cope with the expectations and demands placed on them in this contemporary neoliberal society (Weitz 2016). Yet, in contrast to *SATC* and other postfeminist media, the mode of female sexual subjecthood created and performed in *Girls* is one premised on an emerging 'gross-out' feminism that attempts to politicize, embrace, and normalize all aspects of women's bodies, bodily functions, and strange carnalities, particularly those that have long been labeled as 'private' or 'shameful' (Grosz and Probyn 1995; Strimpel 2016; Whelan 2016). Dunham's body, in particular – often presented as nude, untamed, and unwieldly in the show – has drawn both criticism and praise in its capacity to perform shocking and subversive body politics whilst simultaneously functioning as a site onto which others (characters and the audience) can project their fears and anxieties (Ford 2016; Woods 2015). Related media, e.g., *Bridesmaids* (2011), *Insecure* (2016–2021), *Fleabag* (2016–2019), have honed in on women's experiences of economic, social, and sexual precarity (Wanzo 2016), advancing this characterization of a 'failed' neoliberal subjectivity, in which the female grotesque, defined by excess, obscenity, and looseness, is both celebrated and ridiculed (Darling 2020; Petersen 2017; Rowe 1995).

A second catalyst, though not entirely separate from the first, is the rise of female stand-up comedians like Amy Schumer, Nikki Glaser, Ali Wong, and Jenny Slate, who "exaggerate tropes of self-authorization through the abject aesthetics of grotesque bodily exposure and humiliating self-depreciation" (Hennefeld 2020, 88). Employing comedic devices such as mockery, irony, and satire, these comedians simultaneously highlight the unrealistic standards placed on women, whilst pushing the boundaries of femininity and female sexuality in ways that challenge neoliberalism's privileging of the perfect (Darling 2020; Lauzen 2014). Utilizing the positioning of the abject (Grosz and Probyn 1995; Middleton 2017), these representations contribute to the formation of new subjectivities, whereby women invert their abjection in obscene, grotesque, or perverse ways, in an attempt to reclaim the material and biological body and subvert dominant narratives or modes of power, like sexism, heteronormativity, and racism.

In culmination, these trends have given rise to a new type of sexually agentic femininity premised on *abjectification*, which calls upon women to embrace their imperfections, acknowledge their shortcomings, and live 'authentically.' Notably, the abjectification of women is not altogether new; Roseanne Barr exemplified this subjectivity, par excellence, as far back as the 1980s. What distinguishes this cultural moment from those proceeding it is "how thoroughly unruly women have come to dominate the zeitgeist" (Petersen 2017, 6; Rowe 1995). While this indicates a marked detour from women being portrayed as sexual objects and as successful, self-contained, sexual subjects (Gill 2003), it does not entirely dispel notions of a pornified ideal. In contrast, it emphasizes how women and their bodies, minds, and sexualities are incessantly open to the scrutiny and judgment of voyeurs (Ford 2016), reinforcing the many ways in which women are still in need of patriarchal management (Darling 2020). This contributes to the creation of ever-new forms of self-policing and commodification. I explore some of these in the following sections focusing on the unruly body, psychic excess, and sexual (dis) empowerment.

Managing the unruly body

In the original study, participants often expressed disdain and on some level disgust and shame with their bodies; the vagina, in particular, emerging as a site of intense self-surveillance (Rome and Lambert 2020). The current findings suggest that, on the whole, women feel more comfortable with their bodies ("*My body's not perfect, but I love it*" – Khloe; "*I don't care about like looking super hot anymore. Like, of course, I wanna be attractive for myself. But, I'm not freaking out because I have a little bulge where my skin has stretched out*" – Angela). These sentiments align with the body politics advanced in media advocating sexual abjectification (Ford 2016). As such, there appears to be less of an impetus to hide or conceal the body, and more emphasis on managing or enhancing it. For example, Khloe, who in 2014 fervently avoided receiving cunnilingus because "I just don't think you can ever be fully 100% clean down there" (Rome and Lambert

2020, 511), recently turned to social media to learn how to clean her vagina, which was previously inconceivable:

> There's a gynecologist on TikTok talking about how to clean your vagina. … She's talking about how you clean the vulva in the shower and like went in detail, like 'get in the folds.' And I've never heard that before. I'm like why do I always smell bad? How do I like wash myself? Like, we've never been taught that, you know. And so that was really cool and **now I don't have that fishy smell anymore. You know, every girl has that but you don't know how to get rid of it**. And when you use the wrong stuff, you don't realize it's actually making it worse.
>
> (Khloe)

In pinpointing the decidedly unappealing aspect of her vagina ("*that fishy smell*"), Khloe is able to control and modify her vagina in a way that allows her to participate in oral sex, even if she "*[doesn't] really like down there a lot*." Although she now recognizes hers is not a personal failure or unusual problem ("***we've*** *never been taught that*" and "***every girl*** *has that [smell]*"), she nonetheless employs an individual-solution to manage a social stigma. Thus, while the vagina is still problematized, increasing types of and access to marketplace solutions (Gurrieri 2020) enables her to control rather than conceal her physical body.

Other examples of this acceptance-control paradox are apparent in women's discussions around their metaphorically 'leaky' bodies:

> My periods sometimes are semi-heavy, but usually **they're like manageable.** … When I was younger [my period] was way more taboo and it was like hush-hush to talk about. So, I think a part of that was just **unlearning that it's not a gross thing**. It's **a very natural thing**.
>
> (Ivy)

> Coz that shit [breastfeeding] sucks too. …We'd be at dinner with our friends or something and I'd be like, '**guys I gotta go, my boobs are leaking**.' Like I have to go. There's no option. There's no like pushing it or hiding. It's gonna come out whether it's got some place to go or not. And they get hard and sore. Oh my god. But they look great, so it's worth it, right [*Laughing*]?
>
> (Angela)

Neither Ivy nor Angela express an outright discomfort with regard to their period (Ivy) or lactation (Angela). For Ivy, this was a so-called "*unlearning*" curve, and although she – along with the other women in this study – recognizes that menstruation is "*a very natural thing*," it is nonetheless something which needs to be managed (Ivy), "*tracked*" (Krista), and "*kept up with*" (Mia). Marketing discourse has capitalized on this trend, promoting menstruation as a natural occurrence, albeit one that requires management so as to rescue women from the shame and embarrassment of blood (Malefyt and McCabe 2016). Likewise, though Angela candidly discusses her leaky breasts, this is mediated by her humorous invocation of the male gaze ("*But they look great, so it's worth it, right?*"), reinforcing how even the 'abject' female body is subject to men's approval and desire. Notably, the emphasis here is less on changing or erasing the 'troublesome' body, but rather on *reinscribing* it with new meaning. Such is similarly evidenced in Aaliyah's decision to pierce her nipples:

> I have always been self-conscious about my nipples while growing up. ... I never realized that **my nipples were not normal** until [high-school boyfriend] said something. But at that point in time, we had both been exposed to pornography and had engaged with it. ... and **a lot of women that are portrayed in pornography don't have big areolas or they don't have like nipples like mine, and they're not brown like mine**, coz a lot of them are very white. ... And since then, I've been comparing my [breasts] to other women's breasts. And **piercing my nipples made me feel confident about my breasts again.**
>
> (Aaliyah)

Aaliyah is reflexive in referring to an ideal porn standard, albeit one which is decidedly white. Lamenting on the lack of sexualized representations of women of color, Aaliyah's story speaks to how pornography, as a medium of representation, has the potential to "train people's erotic tastes" (Zheng 2017, 188), including her own. By modifying this *"not normal"* part of her body, Aaliyah is able to reclaim a sexuality that prior to elicited feelings of shame. This is all the more significant given that women of color are not only underrepresented in the media, but are also hypersexualized (Harrison, Thomas, and Cross 2017). For Aaliyah, piercing her nipples inverts what Zheng (2017, 186) terms a "respectability politics" that maintains "because women of color are hypersexualized as 'naturally' promiscuous and as having excessive or deviant sexualities, they must expend extra effort in order to appear 'respectable'—to conform to traditional normative expectations of women's sexuality." Similar inversions are evidenced in sexually provocative pop-songs and music videos that borrow from the tradition of hip-hop-porn (Hunter and Cuenca 2017), such as Nicki Minaj's (2014) *Anaconda* (https://www.youtube.com/watch?v=LDZX4ooRsWs) and Cardi B and Megan Thee Stallion's (2020) *WAP* or *Wet Ass Pussy* (https://www.youtube.com/watch?v=siTGRbeq5K8). In this context, abjectification is less conspicuous – save for the lyrics of *WAP* – illustrating the double burden facing women of color to legitimize existing *and* reimagine new sexualities.

Emotional outsourcing

Postfeminist media throughout the 1990s and 2000s embraced powerful, successful, and often hyperfeminine women, resulting in the expectation that women should be perfect, resilient, confident, and happy (McRobbie 2015). In turn, the original study found that women tended to deny or repudiate feelings of vulnerability – even in profoundly disempowering situations involving, e.g., sexual assault, in lieu of establishing an authoritative and empowered sense of self (Rome and Lambert 2020). In recent years, however, therapeutic narratives have begun to redefine ideals of well-being and authentic selfhood (Illouz 2008). This gives way to a burgeoning self-help marketplace (Riley et al. 2019), and is increasingly evidenced in (feminist) porn and pornification discourse emphasizing authenticity, i.e., the representation of 'real' bodies, unscripted sex, and genuine pleasures (Attwood, Smith, and Barker 2021; Macleod 2020). Thus, for the women in this follow-up study, projecting a sense of 'realness' or authenticity has become a priority. In pursuit of this aim, all but one of the participants has seen and/or continues to see a counsellor or therapist since the original study in 2014. For Natasha, therapy has become a cornerstone of living an authentic life and maintaining a healthy relationship:

> I think people who aren't [in therapy] are generally people **who aren't being fully honest**. … I've done personal therapy for years, like five years. We started our couples' therapy actually during Covid [*laughing*]. We've been talking about it for a while and then we began. … I would say, half the people I talk to and I mention it to, they're like, 'oh, are you ok?' We're like, 'yeah, [*laughing*] we are. That's why we're going to therapy.'
>
> (Natasha)

Natasha's embrace of imperfection as a testament to her "*honest*" and authentic relationship hints toward a departure from "the perfect" as a realistic, attainable, or even desirable aspiration (McRobbie 2015). At first glance, this shift appears to be productive in terms of combating unrealistic standards placed on women. Specifically, the imperative for women to always be in control – that was so apparent in our original study (Rome and Lambert 2020) – seems to have loosened its stranglehold. Upon critical reflection, however, it becomes clear how imperfection, as a measure of authenticity, has become commodified and transformed into a technology of self in its own right (Riley et al. 2019). This gives way to a re-alignment of abjection that arises not from a disgust *attached* to women's hidden or unruly 'excess,' but rather from a failure to *recognize* and *enunciate* it (Gilleard and Higgs 2011; Grosz and Probyn 1995; Kristeva 1982). Indeed, in the current epoch, to deny or discount one's abjection (e.g., personal and relational problems) is to be rendered unintelligible – without agency, autonomy, or self-control – which is where the core of abjection lies (Gilleard and Higgs 2011).

However, for many women, the enunciation and requisite working through of psychic excess tends to increase the burden of emotional work, which has long fallen disproportionately on women (Hochschild [1983] 2012). In response, a wide range of marketized solutions – therapists, pharmaceuticals, and a slew of self-help materials – are employed as a way to outsource or offload some of this weight, as demonstrated by Ivy and Khloe:

> Losing [my ex-boyfriend] was also a moment of time where I was like, hm, I should probably get in therapy coz **I can't deal with this by myself**.
>
> (Ivy)

> I was really hesitant about medication for the longest time, coz I'm very like holistic. Like, I'm gonna try to fix it with like nutrition and lifestyle. And **I just had to accept that I cannot fix this** [*laughing*]. And that's hard for me because I know with the pharmaceutical industry, I'm not like a huge fan. It was a hard decision for me to finally [feel] like, ok fine, I will take the damn pill.
>
> (Khloe)

Feeling flooded by a situation such as a breakup (Ivy) and/or one's emotions ("*I felt out of control*" – Aaliyah; "*I wasn't able to handle my emotions*" – Kris) were common triggers that led participants to seek out external support. Still, as indicated by Khloe, this process was not entirely without remorse ("*it was a hard decision for me*").

In some cases, emotional outsourcing was employed as a preemptive measure to ensure or guarantee a future healthy relationship:

> Before marriage, we're both going to seek counselling apart and together, not just due to Covid, but just because we both know that we have some unresolved issues with our pasts and baggage and stuff. And **we wanna go to counselling together to open up and be able to discuss all of our past relationships**. But also to discuss what is our plan of action for marriage.
>
> (Kris)

Herein, Kris sheds light on the importance afforded to emotional and relational transparency, key indicators of what it means to secure a 'healthy' intimate relationship. Such a viewpoint is similarly affirmed by Angela:

> I'm pretty open with my emotions and feelings and stuff. … Like, **we have full access** to each other's phones … To think that you should be embarrassed in front of the person that you're choosing – hopefully the one time – to spend your life with would make me sad. That you shouldn't feel like you should be able to be anything but your full self – good and bad – that'd be a disservice to you and to them. Kinda like, **take it or leave it, me and my poops,** you know?
>
> (Angela)

As Angela makes clear, this emerging authenticity imperative is tightly intertwined with 'gross-out' discourses, suggesting that intimacy is premised on transparency and an acceptance of the abject ("*me and my poops*").

Reconciling sexual (dis)empowerment

October 2020 marked the third anniversary of the #MeToo movement, which has worked to both undermine and capitalize on female sexuality in a myriad of ways. Among some of the participants in this follow-up study, the effects of #MeToo are readily apparent. For Natasha and Ivy, the language and discourse around specific publicized cases were central to unearthing memories that had been previously neglected:

> It wasn't until some of the **conversations around Weinstein and some of the language that was used** that I realized that when I was younger, I was actually sexually assaulted when I was at a church camp. And it wasn't until I started to hear some of the [details] – specifically **talking about like the massages** that it started to unpack memories that I think I had rewritten and that had also been rewritten for me.
>
> (Natasha)

> I certainly remember **relating heavily to Dr. Ford's experiences**. The first time I remember being assaulted I was in middle school. And like Dr. Ford's experiences, remembering the laughter of the boys at the time, I still have those pressing memories.
>
> (Ivy)

For many women, therefore, #MeToo proved instrumental in raising awareness around the pervasiveness of sexual assault; shedding light on issues around consent ("*it made me realize that I haven't always given consent*" – Krista); justifying expressions of female rage

Pornification and sexual abjectification 215

("*#MeToo was very therapeutic for me [because] the army of women that are like, 'well fucking me too, so let's bind together and burn some fucking tables down'*" – Ivy); and buttressing the importance of setting boundaries ("*I will make sure that my boundaries are respected or like [my partners] know what I don't want and what I do wan*t" – Aaliyah). Indeed, these findings diverge quite significantly from those of the original study, whereby women's desire for sexual agency and control often obfuscated instances of subjugation, vulnerability, and disempowerment (Rome and Lambert 2020).

Yet, while the emergence of a call-out culture has enabled some women to *retrospectively* identify instances of disempowerment, *theoretically* express psychic 'excess' in the form of anger or rage, and *anticipate* future interpersonal conflict, its manifestation in practice is far less conspicuous. This is particularly true in the context of women's extant relationships, as Khloe and Natasha illustrate below in reflecting on their experiences around anal sex:

> [My husband] had been very interested in like anal sex and stuff and that was something I wasn't comfortable with for a while. …**He never forced me** or anything. But … **I feel like it's kind of like the compromise**, like, 'hey, if I can't get you pregnant, can I at least [have anal sex]?'
>
> (Khloe)

> To be honest, we've always been very – like pretty drunk whenever we had anal sex, so my detailed memory of it's a little hazy. But I think **it feels like something that I generally express not really being interested in.** And [my husband] is. And then, when we aren't drunk… there's like weird remorse and then awkward like – I'm like uncomfortable, just in pain and uncomfortable. **And then he feels bad**.
>
> (Natasha)

Though their rationalizations have become more nuanced, these findings reinforce those of the original study that find women tend to prioritize masculine meanings of sexual pleasure and struggle with discerning the boundaries between sex and violence when partners or friends are involved (Rome and Lambert 2020). Khloe, for example, may not comply with her husband's pleas for anal sex in order to afford him a position of superiority, per se, but rather as a way to placate his desires to, e.g., have children, forgo condoms. Similarly, though Natasha is privy to the fact that having anal sex causes her both physical and mental anguish, she stops short of characterizing it in terms of assault.

Two key factors seem to contribute to the ambiguity surrounding this type of sexual interaction. First, intimate acts – even unwanted ones – which involve one's romantic partner are framed as something that must be endured rather than enjoyed, regardless of the consequences (e.g., unwanted pregnancy, STDs, pain, etc.). Such antiquated notions have long been exemplified in pornified discourse that insinuates or shows disinterested wives having dutiful sex with their husbands (e.g., *Desperate Housewives* [2004–2012], *Good Girls* [2018–2021], *Working Moms* [2017–]). Far from innocuous, this discourse risks legitimizing intimate partner sexual violence, reinforces dominate rape myths that maintain sexual assault is only perpetrated by a stranger, and has increasingly come to define modern day 'hook-up' culture. For example, in the pilot episode of *Fleabag*, Phoebe Waller Bridge turns to the audience (mid-intercourse with "Arsehole guy") and, with a nonchalant coolness, says: "After some pretty standard bouncing, you realize he's edging towards your arsehole. But you're drunk, and **he made the effort to come all the way here** so, you let him. He's thrilled." The humorous notion that women *should* sexually appease or reward men perpetuates patriarchal notions that women are responsible for men's behavior – good or bad – which complicates sexual victimization and sustains pervasive victim-blaming discourse (Gilson 2016).

Second, and perhaps most troubling, is the women's acknowledgment of their partners' intentions and/or sentiments, whereby through an inverted logic, men become characterized as victims. This speaks to how an emerging 'himpathetic' culture (Manne 2018) – whereby victimhood and sympathy are disproportionately afforded to men – has come to influence popular understandings of sex, intimacy, and rape (Lanius 2019). And indeed, the widespread skepticism and backlash that succeeded #MeToo (Lanius 2019) appears to inform how many of the women think, talk, and pass judgment about sexual assault, coercion, and victimhood ("*I just have such a hard time digesting those stories because I just don't know who to believe*" – Angela; "*I think that there are people out there that also use [#MeToo] as a way to abuse certain powers*" – Kris). Further, because the notion of male oppression and expression of male vulnerability is both foreign and unusual, men's emotions have come to inhabit a more 'authentic' space, compared to women's, which have long been pathologized as hysteria or dismissed as paranoia (Kay and Banet-Weiser 2019). This not only implores women to self-police or exercise restraint over themselves and their emotions (Orgad and Gill 2019), but positions them as the arbitrators of men's as well. Mia reflects on this when describing the obligation she felt to assuage her boyfriend after *she* was sexually harassed:

> A guy walked past me and just slapped my butt and didn't even know him. …I was with my boyfriend at the time and he was like pissed …and then **it quickly turned from that situation to me trying to calm my boyfriend down** and you know, take care of the situation in that way.
>
> (Mia)

Mia's recounting of this experience notably centers not on her perpetrator, but on her partner, who – by assuming he needs to come to Mia's rescue (what Veer, Zahrai, and Stevens [2020] refer to as 'White Knighting') – essentially robs her of her ability to express and process her feelings towards the situation in that moment.

Thus, although shifts in public discourse may have succeeded in raising awareness around the pervasiveness of sexual assault in general, the ways in which women reflect on, experience, and negotiate sex appear to be framed by competing narratives. Efforts to reconcile these inconsistencies tend to manifest in an outward ambivalence, illustrating the underlying power relations that render women disempowered. Exacerbating these inconsistencies is the encroachment of popular misogynistic – not to mention racist and violent – discourses circulating in porn, popular culture, social media, and increasingly politics (Banet-Weiser 2018; Dignam and Rohlinger 2019), which thwart a closing of the awareness-action gap, but also – most worrisome – obscure the victim–victimizer divide.

Discussion

The data in this chapter illustrates how changing pornification discourses engender new types of sexual subjectivities and modes of discipline among women. In particular, the abundance, variety, and ubiquity of pornography, coupled with social and cultural changes, has led to notable shifts in the representation, construction, and consumption of female sexuality, ultimately driving new subjectivities in women. Different from objectification and subjectification, abjectification calls upon women to embrace their physical, psychic, and sexual 'shortcomings.' In some ways, these findings are encouraging. The participants in this follow-up study express greater confidence and are more reflexive in their discussions around their bodies, sexuality, mental health, and relationships than they were six years ago. While this may, in part, reflect their transition from emerging adulthood to middle age, in other cases, it appears more directly attributable to emerging discourses which challenge dominant narratives of, e.g., sexism, heteronormativity, and racism.

However, though it may be tempting to think of abjectification as a radical or transgressive subjectivity which challenges hegemonic and patriarchal conventions of gender and sex, this chapter shows how it also serves to fortify certain dominant norms, resulting in a disconnect between how women understand, enact, and experience their intimate lives and sexualities. In particular, the findings of this study suggest that pushing against prescriptive standards of women's appropriate behavior and appearance paradoxically leads to an internalization of the 'women as abject' trope. Thus, the interpretive repertoires women use to produce, understand, and interpret their lived experiences are increasingly informed by a borderline uncertainty they hold of and about themselves, i.e., the idea that they (or parts of themselves) are flawed, disgusting, ambiguous, perverse, and frightening (Grosz and Probyn 1995; Kristeva 1982). This is evidenced most clearly in the variety of 'equitable' marketplace solutions and discursive materials they rely on to help them manage and/or enhance their unruly bodies, psychic excess, and complicated sexual experiences. Indeed, as women come to terms with the previously hidden or messy parts of themselves, there is still a narcissistic drive to want to tame or control the narrative around these. This compulsion begets forms of covert self-policing practices that range from the innocuous (cleaning) to the more injurious (a desire to reconcile irreconcilable sexual experiences).

At the core of each of these practices is a desire to live, love, and fuck more *authentically*. This pervasive yearning for authenticity – women's desire to know and give (of themselves) and receive (from others) "*full access*" (Angela) – appears to stem from a fetishization of intimacy that has been at the forefront of shifting porn and pornification discourses. The rise of amateur (Ruberg 2016) and feminist porn (Stewart 2019) coupled with platforms granting users personal access to performers (Bernstein 2019; Ruberg 2016) gives way to truth/transparency obsessed culture that transcends on-screen performances. Further, the rise of 'real' porn correlates with the fact that more women are watching it. Authenticity, in particular, has been identified as a key factor driving women's consumption of pornography (Attwood, Smith, and Barker 2021; Macleod 2020). Drawing on a Kristevian lens of abjection, the problem with conceptualizing authenticity in relation to porn is that it tends to reify 'realness' (Macleod 2020) and conflate it with notions of intimacy, transparency, relatability, and intensity (Attwood, Smith, and Barker 2021). This, in turn, risks undermining non-normative depictions of sex (Macleod 2020), contributes to the devaluation of sexual labor (Drenten, Gurrieri, and Tyler 2019), but also – as this study demonstrates – calls on women to perform authenticity via new forms of self-governance through which they attempt to manage, mediate, and/or temper (rather than subvert) their perceived abjection.

Consequently, rather than displace prior conceptions of an ideal (agentic, autonomous, and desiring) postfeminist subject (Evans, Riley, and Shankar 2010), the so-called abject subject (unruly, flawed, vulnerable) appears to emerge in parallel. Whereas sexual subjectification imagines autonomous and empowered women willingly participating in sexually objectifying practices (Gill 2003), sexual abjectification inverts these, yet, does so in ways that do not transgress, but rather foreground the harms of neoliberalism. Both the ideal neoliberal subject and the undisciplined grotesque abject derive from hegemonic patriarchal discourses; neither are viable or desirable without the fantasy of the other (Hennefeld 2020, 90). Thus, abjectification does not repudiate neoliberal values, nor does it exempt women from patriarchal management (Darling 2020); rather, it operates at the obscene limit of postfeminism, engendering new insidious technologies of neoliberal governmentality that mirror patriarchal and antiquated notions of female sexuality as flawed, dangerous, and perverse (Grosz and Probyn 1995). Foregrounding the ascension of this governmentality that places the onus of responsibility on women to manage their self and life course (Gill and Scharff 2011) allows for the conceptualization of multiple and shifting permutations of representational practice – that is, subjectification *and* abjectification – as fundamentally objectifying.

Moving forward: the perils (and promises?) of pornification

To the extent that sexual abjectification is tightly bound with patriarchal and neoliberal ethics, identifying opportunities for resistance and emancipation remain limited (Rome and Lambert 2020). In spite of the persistence and adaptability of neoliberalism, there is some indication that a post- or reformed-neoliberal era is on the cusp (Fraser 2016). Sexual abjectification, in particular, presents significant opportunities for postfeminist research. More work is needed – particularly from an intersectional feminist approach – to explore the contours and transgressive potential of this subjectivity in marketing and the media, and its impact on women, men, and so forth.

In the context of pornification, more research is needed to interrogate how existing power relations operate through and/or are challenged by the creation, distribution, and consumption of new counter-hegemonic representations in porn and pornified discourse. Recent changes in the production and distribution of pornography have given rise to feminist and alternative genres that claim to honor the experiences of under- or mis-represented groups (Jacobs 2014) and may function as mediums to eroticize consent, mutual respect, and gender equality (Zheng 2017). Still, others have warned that the rise of online amateur pornography perpetuates existing power relations, harmful stigmas about paid-sex work, and the exploitation and alienation of sexualized labor (Drenten, Gurrieri, and Tyler 2019; Ruberg 2016).

Finally, building on existing feminist and consumption scholarship, researchers are encouraged to explore consumer engagements with porn and pornified media, which is generally lacking (McVey, Gurrieri, and Tyler 2020). Special attention might be paid to issues of reflexivity and media literacy (Borgerson and Schroeder 2002) that are central to fostering critical disengagement from pornographic texts (Albury 2014). From a policy perspective, various efforts have already been implemented around the world including a new campaign ad (https://www.youtube.com/watch?v=f29mh5ntlw4) released by the New Zealand government that used real-life porn stars to highlight the differences between 'mediated' and 'real' sex. Exploring the pedagogical implications of and for pornified discourse, particularly from a post-pornographic (Gregory and Lorange 2018) or feminist intersectional approach, may shed light on the promises, in addition to the perils, of pornification.

References

Attwood, Feona. 2010. *Mainstreaming Sex: The Sexualization of Western Culture*. New York: I.B. Tauris.
Attwood, Feona, Clarissa Smith, and Martin Barker. 2021. "Engaging with pornography: An examination of women aged 18–26 as porn consumers." *Feminist Media Studies* 21 (2): 173–188. doi: 10.1080/14680777.2019.1681490.
Albury, Kath. 2014. "Porn and sex education, porn as sex education." *Porn Studies* 1 (1–2): 172–181. doi: 10.1080/23268743.2013.863654.
Banet-Weiser, Sarah. 2018. *Empowered: Popular Feminism and Popular Misogyny*. Durham, NC: Duke University Press.
Bernstein, Jacob. 2019. "How OnlyFans Changed Sex Work Forever." *The New York Times*, February 9. https://www.nytimes.com/2019/02/09/style/onlyfans-porn-stars.html.
Borgerson, Janet L., and Jonathan E. Schroeder. 2002. "Ethical issues of global marketing: Avoiding bad faith in visual representation." *European Journal of Marketing* 36 (5–6): 570–594. doi: 10.1108/03090560210422399.
Boyle, Karen. 2018. "The implications of pornification: Pornography, the mainstream and false equivalences." In *The Routledge Handbook of Gender and Violence*, edited by Nancy Lombard, 85–96. Oxon and New York: Routledge.
Darling, Orlaith. 2020. "'The moment you realise someone wants your body:' Neoliberalism, mindfulness and female embodiment in Fleabag." *Feminist Media Studies*. Advance online publication. doi: 10.1080/14680777.2020.1797848.
Dignam, Pierce Alexander and Deana A. Rohlinger. 2019. "Misogynistic men online: How the red pill helped elect Trump." *Signs: Journal of Women in Culture and Society* 44 (3): 589–612. doi: 10.1086/701155.
Dines, Gail. 2010. *Pornland: How Porn Has Hijacked Our Sexuality*. Boston, MA: Beacon Press.
Drenten, Jenna, Lauren Gurrieri, and Meagan Tyler. 2019. "Sexualized labour in digital culture: Instagram influencers, porn chic and the monetization of attention." *Gender, Work & Organization* 27 (1): 41–66. doi: 10.1111/gwao.12354.
Dworkin, Andrea. 1981. *Pornography: Men Possessing Women*. London: The Women's Press.
Evans, Adrienne, Sarah Riley, and Avi Shankar. 2010. "Technologies of sexiness: Theorizing women's engagement in the sexualization of culture." *Feminism & Psychology* 20 (1): 114–131. doi: 10.1177/0959353509351854.
Ford, Jessica. 2016. "The 'smart' body politics of Lena Dunham's Girls." *Feminist Media Studies* 16 (6): 1029–1042. doi: 10.1080/14680777.2016.1162826.
Fraser, Nancy. 2016. "Progressive neoliberalism versus reactionary populism: A choice that feminists should refuse." *NORA-Nordic Journal of Feminist and Gender Research* 24 (4): 281–284. doi: 10.1080/08038740.2016.1278263.
Gill, Rosalind. 2003. "From sexual objectification to sexual subjectification: The resexualization of women's bodies in the media." *Feminist Media Studies* 3 (1): 100–106. doi: 10.1080/1468077032000080158.
Gill, Rosalind. 2007. "Postfeminist media culture: Elements of a sensibility." *European Journal of Cultural Studies* 10 (2): 147–66. doi: 10.1177/1367549407075898.
Gill, Rosalind and Christina Scharff. 2011. *New Femininities: Postfeminism, Neoliberalism and Subjectivity*. Basingstoke: Palgrave Macmillan.
Gilleard, Chris and Paul Higgs. 2011. "Ageing abjection and embodiment in the fourth age." *Journal of Aging Studies* 25 (2): 135–142. doi: 10.1016/j.jaging.2010.08.018.
Gilson, Erinn Cunniff. 2016. "Vulnerability and victimization: Rethinking key concepts in feminist discourses on sexual violence." *Signs: Journal of Women in Culture and Society* 42 (1): 71–98. doi: 10.1086/686753.
Gregory, Tim and Astrid Lorange. 2018. "Teaching post-pornography." *Cultural Studies Review* 24 (1): 137–49. doi:10.5130/csr.v24i1.5303.

Grosz, Elizabeth and Elspeth Probyn. 1995. *Sexy Bodies: The Strange Carnalities of Feminism.* London and New York: Routledge.

Gurrieri, Lauren. 2020. "Patriarchal marketing and the symbolic annihilation of women." *Journal of Marketing Management.* Advance online publication. doi: 10.1080/0267257X.2020.1826179.

Harrison, Robert L., Kevin D. Thomas, and Samantha N. N. Cross. 2017. "Restricted visions of multiracial identity in advertising." *Journal of Advertising* 46 (4): 503–520. doi: 10.1080/00913367.2017.1360227.

Hennefeld, Maggie 2020. "Abject feminism, grotesque comedy, and apocalyptic laughter on Inside Amy Schumer." In *Abjection Incorporated: Mediating the Politics of Pleasure and Violence,* edited by Maggie Hennefeld and Nicholas Sammond, 86–111. Durham, NC and London: Duke University Press.

Hochschild, Arlie Russell. (1983) 2012. *The Managed Heart: Commercialization of Human Feeling.* Berkeley and Los Angeles: University of California Press.

Hunter, Margaret and Alhelí Cuenca. 2017. "Nicki Minaj and the changing politics of hip-hop: Real blackness, real bodies, real feminism?." *Feminist Formations* 29 (2): 26–46.

Illouz, Eva. 2008. *Saving the Modern Soul: Therapy, Emotions, and the Culture of Self-Help.* Berkeley and Los Angeles: University of California Press.

Jacobs, Katrien. 2014. "Internationalizing porn studies." *Porn Studies* 1 (1–2): 114–119. doi: 10.1080/23268743.2014.882178.

Kay, Jilly Boyce and Sarah Banet-Weiser. 2019. "Feminist anger and feminist respair." *Feminist Media Studies* 19 (4): 603–609. doi: 10.1080/14680777.2019.1609231.

Kristeva, Julia. 1982. *Powers of Horror: An Essay on Abjection.* Translated by Leon S. Roudiez. New York: Columbia University Press.

Lanius, Candice. 2019. "Torment porn or feminist witch hunt: Apprehensions about the #MeToo movement on/r/AskReddit." *Journal of Communication Inquiry* 43 (4): 415–436. doi: 10.1177/0196859919865250.

Lauzen, Martha. 2014. "The funny business of being Tina Fey: Constructing a (feminist) comedy icon." *Feminist Media Studies* 14 (1): 106–117. doi: doi.org/10.1080/14680777.2012.740060.

Och, Dana. 2019. "The mainstream cult of Fifty Shades of Grey: Hailing multiple women audiences." *Communication Culture & Critique* 12 (2): 213–229. doi: 10.1093/ccc/tcz017.

Orgad, Shani, and Rosalind Gill. 2019. "Safety valves for mediated female rage in the #MeToo era." *Feminist Media Studies* 19 (4): 596–603. doi: 10.1080/14680777.2019.1609198.

Macleod, P. J. 2020. "How feminists pick porn: Troubling the link between 'authenticity' and production ethics." *Sexualities.* Advance online publication. doi: 10.1177/1363460720936475.

Malefyt, Timothy de Waal, and Maryann McCabe. 2016. "Women's bodies, menstruation and marketing 'protection:' Interpreting a paradox of gendered discourses in consumer practices and advertising campaigns." *Consumption Markets & Culture* 19 (6): 555–575. doi: 10.1080/10253866.2015.1095741.

Manne, Kate. 2018. Brett Kavanaugh and America's 'Himpathy' Reckoning, *The New York Times,* September 26. https://www.nytimes.com/2018/09/26/opinion/brett-kavanaugh-hearing-himpathy.html.

McCormack, Mark, and Liam Wignall. 2017. "Enjoyment, exploration and education: Understanding the consumption of pornography among young men with non-exclusive sexual orientations." *Sociology* 51 (5): 975–991. doi: 10.1177/0038038516629909.

McVey, Laura, Lauren Gurrieri, and Meagan Tyler. 2020. "The structural oppression of women by markets: The continuum of sexual violence and the online pornography market." *Journal of Marketing Management.* Advance online publication. doi: 10.1080/0267257X.2020.1798714.

McNair, Brian. 2013. *Porno? Chic! How Pornography Changed the World and Made It a Better Place.* Abingdon: Routledge.

McRobbie, Angela. 2009. *The Aftermath of Feminism: Gender, Culture and Social Change.* London: Sage.

McRobbie, Angela. 2015. "Notes on the perfect: Competitive femininity in neoliberal times." *Australian Feminist Studies* 30 (83): 3–20. doi: 10.1080/08164649.2015.1011485.

Middleton, Jason 2017. "A rather crude feminism: Amy Schumer, postfeminism, and abjection. *Feminist Media Histories* 3 (2): 121–140. doi: 10.1525/fmh.2017.3.2.121.

Mikkola, Mari. 2019. *Pornography: A Philosophical Introduction*. New York: Oxford University Press.

Paasonen, Susanna, Kaarina Nikunen, and Laura Saarenmaa. 2007. *Pornification: Sex and Sexuality in Media Culture*. New York: Berg.

Petersen, Anne Helen. 2017. *Too Fat, Too Slutty, Too Loud: The Rise and Reign of the Unruly Woman*. New York: Plume.

Riley, Sarah, Adrienne Evans, Emma Anderson, and Martine Robson. 2019. "The gendered nature of self-help." *Feminism & Psychology* 29 (1): 3–18. doi: 10.1177/0959353519826162.

Rome, Alexandra S., and Aliette Lambert. 2020. "(Wo) men on top? Postfeminist contradictions in young women's sexual narratives." *Marketing Theory* 20 (4): 501–525. doi: 10.1177/1470593120926240.

Rowe, Kathleen. 1995. *The Unruly Woman: Gender and the Genres of Laughter*. Austin: University of Texas Press.

Ruberg, Bonnie. 2016. "Doing it for free: Digital labour and the fantasy of amateur online pornography." *Porn Studies* 3 (2): 147–159. doi: 10.1080/23268743.2016.1184477.

Rubin, Gayle. 1993. "Misguided, dangerous and wrong: An analysis of anti-pornography politics." In *Bad Girls and Dirty Pictures: The Challenge to Reclaim Feminism*, edited by Alison Assiter and Avedon Carol, 18–40. Pluto Press: London.

Shankar, Avi, Richard Elliott, and James A. Fitchett. 2009. "Identity, consumption and narratives of socialization." *Marketing Theory* 9 (1): 75–94. doi: 10.1177/1470593108100062.

Smith, Clarissa. 2010. "Pornographication: A discourse for all seasons." *International Journal of Media & Cultural Politics*, 6 (1): 103–108. doi: 10.1386/macp.6.1.103/3.

Stewart, Robert Scott. 2019. "Is feminist porn possible?." *Sexuality & Culture* 23 (1): 254–270. doi: 10.1007/s12119-018-9553-z.

Strimpel, Zoe. 2016. "Welcome to The New Feminism – Where The Aim Is to Gross You Out." *The Conversation*, September 28. https://theconversation.com/welcome-to-the-new-feminism-where-the-aim-is-to-gross-you-out-65579.

Tyler, Megan. 2011. *Selling Sex Short: The Pornographic and Sexological Construction of Women's Sexuality in the West*. Newcastle: Cambridge Scholars.

Tyler, Megan, and Kaye Quek. 2016. "Conceptualizing pornographication: A lack of clarity and problems for feminist analysis." *Sexualization, Media, & Society* 2 (2): 1–14. doi: 10.1177/2374623816643281.

Veer, Ekant, Kseniia Zahrai, and Susannah Stevens. 2020. "I stood by: The role of allies in developing an inclusive and supportive academic environment post #MeToo," *Journal of Marketing Management* 37 (1–2): 162–179. doi: 10.1080/0267257X.2020.1772344.

Wanzo, Rebecca 2016. "Precarious-girl comedy: Issa Rae, Lena Dunham, and abjection aesthetics." *Camera Obscura: Feminism, Culture, and Media Studies* 31 (2 [92]): 27–59. doi: 10.1215/02705346-3592565.

Weitz, Rose. 2016. "Feminism, post-feminism, and young women's reactions to Lena Dunham's Girls." *Gender Issues* 33 (3): 218–234. doi: 10.1007/s12147-015-9149-y.

Whelan, Ella. 2016. "Gross-Out Feminism Is Just Plain Gross." *Spiked*, October 6. https://www.spiked-online.com/2016/10/06/gross-out-feminism-is-just-plain-gross/.

Woods, Faye. 2015. "Girls talk: Authorship and authenticity in the reception of Lena Dunham's Girls." *Critical Studies in Television* 10 (2): 37–54. doi: 10.7227/CST.10.2.4.

Zheng, Robin. 2017. "Race and pornography." In *Beyond Speech: Pornography and Analytic Feminist Philosophy*, edited by Mari Mikkola, 177–189. New York: Oxford University Press.

15 The quest for masculine to-be-looked-at-ness?

Exploring consumption-based self-objectification among heterosexual men

Jacob Ostberg

The connection between heterosexual (sexual) relationships and the patriarchal order of society is an issue that has been debated at length by feminist scholars (see, e.g., the edited volume *New Sexual Agendas* [Segal 1997a]). While the issue is far more complex than men being dominant/active and women being submissive/passive—research even suggests that this is anything but the norm in actual relationships (Vanwesenbeeck 1997)—the *idea* of the dominant/active male is a pervasive cultural ideal continuously perpetuated by the arts, popular culture, the media, and not least market communication (Goffman 1979; Schroeder & Zwick 2004). Such marketplace myths, regardless of whether they are rooted in social facts or not, tend to shape consumers' expectations of available subject positions. Consequently, in "doing gender" (West & Zimmerman 1987) such distinctions are routinely played out by consumers in order to conform to internalized social expectations of how to behave.

Masculinity is irrevocably connected with, opposed to, and in relation to femininity (see e.g., Schroeder & Zwick 2004). One important semiotic dichotomy that structures our understanding of masculinity and femininity, especially in relation to heterosexual sexuality, is that between subjects and objects, where men tend to be regarded as subjects and women as objects. As suggested by Vanwesenbeeck "*[dominant] discourses of heterosexuality and connected (institutional and social) practices provide an unequal distribution of subject and object positions for women and for men*" (1997, 171). While interrelationships between subjects and objects on the one hand are at the center of marketing and consumer culture research, they are on the other hand notoriously undertheorized (Bettany 2018). Bettany (2018) critiques the conventional view of the hierarchy between objects and subjects where "*the subject is largely seen as hierarchically superior, with agency, and human, and the object is seen as secondary to, non-agentic, often non-sentient, and non-human*" (378). While such simple division is thus not viable—even with regard to inanimate objects, and much less so with human beings—it is nevertheless an understanding that has impact on consumers' lived lives, as it solidifies hierarchical positions within the current patriarchal system.

This chapter looks at the intricate ways in which heterosexual men on the one hand attempt to construct a sufficiently attractive and sexualized public persona, but on the other hand attempt not to turn themselves into sexual objects. This might perhaps sound like a narrow topic of marginal interest to a broader audience, especially an audience interested in feminist perspectives on marketing and consumer research. The proposal of this chapter, however, is that this refusal to self-objectify (Fredrickson & Roberts 1997) or self-sexualize (Smolak, Murnen & Myers 2014) on behalf of heterosexual, middleclass, white, cisgender men, and the ensuing condemnation of those who

DOI: 10.4324/9781003042587-18

do is a way of "*policing appropriate masculine behaviors and identities, regulating normative sexuality*" (Gill, Henwood & McLean 2005, 37–38). In their extensive survey of gender and feminist knowledge construction in marketing and consumer research Hearn and Hein (2015) point to a general lack of attention to feminist politics and gender power relations, especially in the domain of men and masculinity studies that tend to lack "*attention to men's structural position(s) within the gender system called patriarchy*" (1636). Following Hearn and Hein (2015) I view feminism as a set of theories, politics, and practices that contest the dominant gender order. In this chapter I therefore aim to shed light on certain aspects of one pervasive element of the dominant gender order, namely, that which tends to construct heterosexual males as dominant and active subjects and others—most clearly women—as subordinate passive objects. I argue that this cultural construction of women as objects and men as subjects is at the heart of the patriarchal order as it is currently constructed in Western cultures. The justification for looking at the issue at this particular time is that we are currently witnessing a "'crack' in the phallocentric order" (Vanwesenbeeck 1997, 172) where men are increasingly constructed as objects of desire in popular culture and marketing communication. As suggested by Gill, Henwood, and McLean (2005) the coding of the male body as "to be looked at" (Mulvey 1989) disrupts conventional patterns of looking in which "men look at women and women watch themselves being looked at" (Berger 1972, 47). Men have thus increasingly become an object of the gaze rather than simply the bearer of the look. This inevitably leads to re-negotiations of how masculinity is constructed, as men—especially heterosexual, middleclass, white, cisgender men at the intersection of various positions of privilege (Gopaldas & Fischer 2012; Hearn & Hein 2015)—are anxious not to lose their hierarchical positions within the current patriarchal system.

In this chapter I will explore self-objectification among heterosexual, middleclass, white, cisgender men, partly by comparing and contrasting with the research that has been conducted on self-objectification of women. More particularly, I will look at the role that consumption plays—or does not play, as it appears—in men's construction of a sexualized public persona. While there is a virtual lexicon of consumption objects that are coded as sexy for girls and women (Goodin et al. 2011), there is a relative dearth of similarly coded objects for men. This, however, is not a natural state of things but rather a convention that might be changing as men are increasingly portrayed as objects in the public sphere (Bordo 1999; Gill, Henwood & McLean 2005; Jobling 2003; Mort 1996; Patterson & Elliott 2002; Schroeder & Zwick 2004), and as young women are increasingly adopting "predatory sexual behaviors" (Chatterton & Hollands 2003) where men are treated as objects to be conquered. In order to explore this in more detail I will first make a theoretical exploration of relevant research that touches upon these issues. Thereafter I will present preliminary findings from a study where I have interviewed men involved in fashion, broadly speaking, about their perspectives on male sexuality and consumption.

To self-objectify or not to self-objectify, that's the question?

No, that is not the question, actually, as self-objectification is less something that an individual chooses voluntarily and more something an individual is coerced into engaging in depending on the position the person inhabits in a given societal structure. Social research has clearly indicated that girls and women tend to internalize an observer's perspective as a primary view of their physical self. They thus engage in self-objectification

(Fredrickson & Roberts 1997)—and many times self-sexualization, defined as "intentionally engaging in activities expressly to appear more sexually appealing" (Smolak, Murnen & Myers 2014, 379)—in order to live up to the narrowly defined standards of attractiveness. From early age girls are socialized into measuring their social worth in terms of how sexy they are (Daniels, Zurbriggen & Ward 2020; Goodin et al. 2011). According to objectification theory (Fredrickson & Roberts 1997) women from Western cultures are widely portrayed and treated as objects of the male gaze. Martins, Tiggeman, and Kirkbridge (2007) suggest that "membership in sexually objectifying Western societies gradually socializes women to adopt an observer's perspective on their physical self. This leads to negative consequences, including body shame and restricted eating behavior." Girls and women thus engage in self-objectification, in which the societal messages of what is sexualized attractiveness become internalized and used as a measuring tool that they constantly compare themselves with. Considerable amounts of time, energy, and money are therefore typically used in order to construct a sufficiently sexualized public persona, leaving less time, energy, and money to pursue all the other interests that make up a person.

As suggested by Mulvey (1989), in a world ordered by sexual imbalance, pleasure in looking has traditionally been split between active/male and passive/female. According to this order, the determining male gaze projects its fantasy onto the female figure, which is styled accordingly. This is essentially the same argument put forth in the self-objectification and self-sexualization literature, even though they typically do not pay tribute to Mulvey's pioneering work. Mulvey (1989), who builds her argument on an analysis of films, shows that in their traditional exhibitionist role women are simultaneously looked at and displayed. This is achieved by having their appearance coded for strong visual and erotic impact so that they can be said to connote "to-be-looked-at-ness" (Mulvey 1989, 19). Heterosexual men, however, have hitherto been relatively relieved of the pressure to live up to such standards of attractiveness and sexiness, and there is not the same code in play for how heterosexual men should achieve to-be-looked-at-ness.

It appears that currently heterosexual men have not viewed themselves—and perhaps cannot view themselves, due to the ways in which masculinity is currently framed—as sexual objects to the same degree as women. Fredrickson et al. (1998) provide an interesting case in point when they report findings from an experimental study where men and women tried on swimwear in a dressing room. This situation of assessing oneself in a swimsuit triggered feelings of insufficiency among the female participants who reported feeling shame and disgust for not meeting "physical attractiveness ideals" (Fredrickson et al. 1998, 280). The men, on the other hand, experienced the situation as "rather light-hearted" (280). Rather than feeling "disgust, distaste, and revulsion," the men reported feeling "silly, awkward, and foolish [and some] were even heard to laugh through the closed dressing room door" (280).

From this we can infer that thinking of oneself as a sexual object makes heterosexual men laugh, it is apparently funny, and it can be brushed off as a joke. And consequently, failing at it is not a big deal. Being sexy is not an important part of heterosexual men's self-understanding. The way patriarchal society is rigged men at the intersection of multiple levels of privilege (Gopaldas & Fischer 2002)—i.e., heterosexual, able-bodied, white, middle-class cis-men—has so many other things working in their favor that being sexy is not currently important. These men will, it appears, be OK regardless of their potential sexiness or not. They can live a socially successful life despite low levels of "erotic capital" (Hakim 2010). This is not without consequence for how social life is organized. In continuing the study Fredrickson et al. (1998) studied how the women who had tried on the swimsuit and thus experienced body shame performed on a math test. They found that these women scored lower on the test than the ones that did not experience body shame. In comparing to the men, the results came out differently. Their lack of conforming to standards of beauty and attraction did not reflect on their mental capabilities. This is an illustration of how men that do not continually have to assess whether they live up to a supposed standard of sexual attractiveness can focus on other domains in life that thus reinforces the positive rewards they are already reaping from living in a patriarchal society. Gender researchers who have explored the effects of the ways in which women's bodies are treated as objects and commodities have viewed men as enjoying considerable psychological benefits by virtue of their gender (Bordo 1992).

Becoming the sexy man

The arguments put forth in the above section are not, of course, intended to suggest that sex is unimportant to men. On the contrary, research suggests that sex is indeed quite an important element in men's self-understanding (Montemurro 2021). The view of how we create a sense of who we are, of our self, has moved from a view of us forming a static identity early on in life to a view of the construction of self being a constantly ongoing perpetual project (Giddens 1991). This construction also includes a "sexual self" (Jackson 2007) that requires that one understands oneself as sexual and learns various sexual scripts for sexual interaction (Simon & Gagnon 1984). For heterosexual men this sexual self, however, is less about being seen as a sexual object that should be pleasing to others and more about viewing oneself as an agentic sexual subject. Furthermore, research suggests that heterosexual male sexuality is largely defined in terms of exhibiting a constant desire for sex and taking all opportunities at "getting some," to quote the respondents in Murray's (2018) study.

The construction of the sexual self is largely homosocial insofar as research indicates that men use sexuality as a means to demonstrate what kind of man they are in relation to other men and their compliance with and articulation of hegemonic masculinity (Montemurro 2021). Hegemonic masculinity (Connell 1995) in Western cultures is grounded in the ability to demonstrate sexual mastery and to garner the sexual attention and favors of women (Wade 2017). So, while research suggest that self-sexualization does not have the same prevalence amongst men as it does among women (Smolak, Murnen & Myers 2014), men still seem to attempt to construct a public persona that is seen as desirable. Part of men's ability to garner sexual attention and favors of women (Wade 2017) has to do with physical attractiveness which is socially valued and can be considered a status characteristic (Sarpila 2013). This is echoed in work on men's compliance with standards of attractiveness that tend to focus on the body, especially on losing weight and building muscles (Elliott & Elliott 2005; Rosenmann et al. 2018). In doing this, however, heterosexual men tend to find functional justifications for building muscles, stating that they want to be strong and agile rather than pleasurable to look at (Elliott & Elliott 2005; Rosenmann et al. 2018). Research attempting to connect self-objectification to the project of building a more muscular body found a relationship between these two variables for gay men but no similar relationship for heterosexual men (Martins, Tiggeman & Kirkbridge 2007). This is consistent with research indicating that gay men overall tend to self-objectify to a higher degree than heterosexual men (Kozak, Frankenhauser & Roberts 2009). Body projects connected to both losing weight and building a more muscular body can thus be connected to the increased objectification of men in public. Still, as theorized by Henwood et al. (2002) the focus on muscular masculinity as a cultural ideal may be a form of resistance to alternative masculinities—i.e., those focusing on the use of marketplace resources that are extrinsic to the body, such as grooming products or clothes—that potentially contest power hierarchies among men. When it comes to other ways in which marketplace resources can be used in order to comply to the new standards of "to-be-looked-at-ness" the work has been of a slightly different kind focusing on what has typically been constructed as "The New Masculinity," which has gradually been overtaking some older, primitive, or perhaps even natural masculinity (Edwards 2009). This discussion has been especially true in the realms of clothing and fashion. In the 1980s men's lifestyle magazines wrote about, and companies tried to sell products and services to, the "New Man" (Mort 1996). This creature was subsequently shuffled off the stage by the "New Lad" in the 1990s (MacKinnon 2003), only to be quickly and forcefully replaced by the so-called Metrosexual (Rinallo 2007).

The idea of a new masculinity largely came out of a shift from more traditionally masculine consumer roles that focus on rationality and usability, and the more feminized consumer roles that focus on appearance. Contemporary male consumers, especially in the younger age groups, must negotiate these seemingly contradictory roles in their everyday consumption to construct a (appropriately suave) male consumer identity. Tuncay (2005) theorizes that contemporary heterosexual male consumers need to find a balance between conforming to gender roles while still expressing individuality and between caring too much about appearance and thus running the risk of appearing homosexual, and expressing sufficient levels of heterosexuality. Rinallo (2007) puts forth a similar argument and shows that in between the polar opposites of effeminacy and sloppiness, there is a "safe zone" where heterosexual men can safely experiment with consumption activities and objects. On either side of this "safe zone" lies a "danger zone." If a man shows no care of self, he will suffer negative social consequences, and if a man is too careful with his appearance he will be viewed as effeminate. One should be careful, however, to take the outcries about new masculinities at face value and think that they implied a substantial change to masculinity that was qualitatively different than previous changes.

Classic masculinity meets gray sweatpants

The degree to which men have sought to construct a sexualized public persona via clothing and how this has been visually represented has shifted over time (Harvey 2015). A trend that has lasted ever since the late 18th century when the so-called "Great Masculine Renunciation" occurred (Flugel 1930) is that men's clothing has been simplified, producing uniformity and decorative reduction, and contrasting with the "erotic exposure" of women's dress (Harvey 2015, 798). This tendency to not construct men as sexual objects has been mirrored in art historical conventions where portrayals of men in partial or full nudity often required some sort of alibi so that their position as active agents was intact, such as portraying a shipwreck with men swimming in ripped clothing (Lucie-Smith 2003).

Visual conventions are not static, however, and for decades we have seen a shift whereby men in the media, the arts, and advertising are increasingly assuming the position of objects (Bordo 1999; Gill, Henwood & McLean 2005; Jobling 2003; Mort 1996; Ostberg 2010, 2012). The styles of portrayals have also changed insofar as the unclothed male body used to occur only in "appropriate situations (e.g., at the beach)" (Martins, Tiggeman & Kirkbridge 2007, 634), whereas today the male bodies are used extensively in, e.g., advertising to sell a vast variety of products. The increased interest in and prevalence of such portrayals parallels the growth of the men's movement, the gay liberation movement, and the rising commercial value of men (Bordo 1999; Gill, Henwood & McLean 2003; Patterson & Elliott 2002). Both the overall number and the number of objectifying portrayals of men have risen dramatically over the last couple of decades (Rohlinger 2002). Beginning in the 1980s and gaining in frequency during the 1990s, men were increasing portrayed as "to-be-looked-at" (Gill, Henwood & McLean 2003; Mulvey 1989), without the aforementioned alibis or the protective shelter of humor, degradation, or ridicule that has also been used in order to not overtly objectify men. In 1982, Calvin Klein posted a "tantalizing voyeuristic advertisement [on a] traffic-stopping billboard in New York's Times Square" (Jobling 2003, 147); and about ten years later Calvin Klein took a new turn and introduced even more overtly sexual representation of males in a series of underwear ads running in mainstream media outlets. In 1985 Nick Kamen's classic ad for Levi's 501 jeans, where he undresses in a 1950s launderette, aired for the first time which marked a shift in representations of men in TV ads. Mort (1996) suggests that much of the new imagery of men is implicitly directed towards a homosocial audience, i.e. towards a community of heterosexual men, much like the inverted gaze suggested by Patterson and Elliott (2002). The increased objectification of men also impacts on the intersection of traditional media and social media. The last couple of years there has been a yearly media buzz around gray sweatpants season (Elle 2018; GQ 2020; Vox 2019). Countless memes have been created around the phenomena, and several online outlets have devoted space to it (Bored Panda 2020; Elite Daily 2015). The idea is quite simply that there are plenty of people out there who derive pleasure from looking at guys wearing gray sweatpants. Perhaps because of the "the faint outline of the wearer's dick they allow" to quote GQ as they try to explain the phenomenon to their primarily male readers (GQ 2020). Gray sweatpants thus become a real-life example of the visual convention of "phallic packaging" (Schroeder and Borgerson 1998, 170), whereby shadows are put to creative use in order to simultaneously show and hide. The recent fixation with gray sweatpants is perhaps not interesting in and of itself but it is significant of a larger trend whereby heterosexual men are more explicitly objectified by women. The gray sweatpants phenomenon represents a kind of collective scopophilia, Freud's term for the pleasure in looking, whereby the looker takes other people as objects, subjecting them to a controlling and curious gaze (Mulvey 1989).

While there are thus frequent reports of the increased objectification of men in media and advertising, research suggests that this has not hitherto been matched by an increased self-objectification among heterosexual men (Fredrickson et al. 1998). There have previously been indications that this might be changing (Rohlinger 2002), but this has only partially been corroborated by more recent studies, then typically focusing on the body as such and not on other means of adhering to standards of attractiveness (Daniel, Bridges & Martens 2014; Kozak, Frankenhauser & Roberts 2009; Martins, Tiggeman & Kirkbridge 2007; Visser et al. 2014).

From sexual subject to sexual object

In a series of texts feminist thinker Rosalind Gill (2003, 2008, 2011) has proposed that there has been a shift in the portrayal of women in popular culture and advertising entailing a "knowing and deliberate re-sexualization and re-commodification of women's bodies" (2003, 101). As accounted for above, this increased sexualization is prevalent for men too (Bordo 1999; Gill, Henwood & McLean 2003, 2005; Jobling 2003; Mort 1996; Patterson & Elliott 2002; Schroeder & Zwick 2004). On the surface this re-sexualization and re-commodification of women's bodies might look like a backlash against the systematic work of feminist scholars and activists to raise public awareness of the problems related to objectifying women's bodies in public. The interesting perspective that Gill brings to the table is that it is not merely a backlash, but that it has been accompanied by a shift in outlook so that it is constructed as something that would ultimately benefit women. The

> pervasive re-inscription of women as sexual objects is happening at a moment when we are being told that women can 'have it all' and are doing better than ever before—in school, university, and the workplace. Publications by think tanks, articles by journalists, and research by marketing agencies cohere around the notion that there has been a 'genderquake' in contemporary society, that tomorrow's values are 'feminine' and that 'women are winning'.
>
> (Gill 2003, 102)

The proposal is thus that we are witnessing the construction of a new type of femininity organized around sexual confidence and autonomy. A large part of this is that women are increasingly portrayed, not as passive objects that was previously the norm, but as knowing, active, and desiring sexual subjects.

Gill's argument is not, it should be noted, that this shift in representations of women in popular culture and advertising is necessarily followed by a subsequent shift in women's lived lives and in the power relations between men and women in society overall. On the contrary, Gill's analysis is rather that women who subscribe to the postfeminist ideas behind this supposed shift—"the battle has been won, now let's take what we want"—are inadvertently doing a disservice to the feminist project of achieving a more equal society. For the purpose of the present chapter, however, it is sufficient to stay at the level of popular media and advertising portrayals and the subsequent shift in public imaginations that this might result in. In what Gill (2011) calls "midriff advertising" women are much less likely to be shown as passive sexual objects than as empowered, heterosexually desiring sexual subjects, operating playfully in a sexual marketplace. This marketplace, in turn, is presented as more egalitarian than it used to be or even as *more* favorable to women. There has thus been a shift from women being portrayed, and consequently viewing themselves, as objects of sexual desire towards sexual subjects with agency.

For men, however, there has been a reverse tendency where they have increasingly been objectified in mainstream popular media and not least advertising. If marketing imagery indeed does, as suggested by Schroeder and Zwick (2004, 23), give partial answers to the question "what does it mean to be a man?" then this has impacts for men's self-understanding. When the imagination of the "sexual marketplace," to use Gill's (2011) term, shifts into one wherein active women go out to take what they want, is this likely to imply a subsequent shift wherein men start contemplating whether they should turn themselves increasingly into attractive objects to be chosen? If so, this might pose problems for men as there is a dearth of clothes, styles, and accessories that are explicitly coded as sexy for men in the same way that they are for women. While there is a virtual lexicon of sexually coded clothes, styles, and accessories available for women (Goodin et al. 2011), for men there is a much vaguer notion of what are legitimate ways in which to use consumption to enhance one's erotic capital. While a muscular and toned body is coded as sexy, there has traditionally not been an established set of clothes, styles, and accessories for heterosexual men that are coded for strong visual and erotic impact so that they can be said to connote "to-be-looked-at-ness" (Mulvey 1989).

In marketing and consumer culture studies it has been stressed how consumption, not least of clothes (Marion & Nairn 2011) and brands (Elliott and Wattanasuwan 1998), plays an important role in the ever-ongoing quest to form a self. This appears to be true also in the domain of forming a sexual self. Sarpila (2013, 311) addresses this issue and contends that "consumerism in people's lives can play a key role in understanding how people see the meaning of performing and developing erotic capital." Through consumption individuals attempt to enhance their beauty, sexual attractiveness, and social representation (Sarpila 2013). These are all elements that contribute to what is conceptualized as "erotic capital," Hakim's (2010) suggested addition to the conventionally accepted elements cultural, economic, and social capital in the makeup of symbolic capital. Hakim asserts that "In sexualized individualized modern societies, erotic capital becomes more important and more valorized, for both men and women" (2010, 499). While being seen as desirable, having sufficient levels of erotic capital, and complying with articulations of hegemonic masculinity by demonstrating sexual mastery and garnering sexual attention and favors of women are thus important for heterosexual, middleclass, white, cisgender men, self-objectification and self-sexualization are still not widespread in this group (Daniel, Bridges & Martens 2014; Visser et al. 2014). It appears that the subject position of a heterosexual man as an object of desire is not a tried and tested one in our contemporary consumer culture. There are no ready-made templates of how this should be achieved. We will now turn to reporting some preliminary findings from a study that seeks to explore the consumer culture resources that men have at their disposal in constructing themselves as objects of desire connoting a sense of to-be-looked-at-ness.

Method

The preceding sections of this chapter has attempted to anchor the idea that it is likely that we are witnessing a change whereby men are increasingly encouraged to view themselves as potential objects of desire. Regardless of whether previous research has correctly identified that heterosexual men are engaging in self-objectification and self-sexualization to a lower degree than women—as implied by, e.g., Fredrickson et al. (1998), Goodin et al. (2011), Kozak, Frankenhauser, and Roberts (2009), and Smolak, Murnen and Myers (2014)—it appears that we know relatively little about the role that marketplace resources—such as clothes, styles, and accessories—play in self-objectification and self-sexualization of heterosexual men.

In order to explore this empirically this chapter reports findings from interviews with men connected to the fashion scene in Sweden, such as journalists, PR-experts, influencers, and designers. The geographical connection to Sweden is not without consequence, as Sweden is a country influenced by decades' worth of a state ideology of gender equality (Molander, Kleppe & Ostberg 2019). As a consequence, men with a somewhat more nuanced way of talking about differences between men and women and at least rudimentary insights about male privilege are likely to be more frequently occurring in Sweden. The Swedish fashion scene is also rather attuned to issues of gender. Many brands are, for example, actively problematizing the traditional division of male and female fashion by introducing gender neutral collections (Andersen, Lindberg & Ostberg 2021). While the interviewees are thus likely to produce a rather nuanced discourse compared to settings in which questions of gender are less part of the public agenda, they are nevertheless part of a larger Western fashion system adhering to certain structures dictating the borders of available legitimate subject positions for heterosexual men.

Apart from being connected to the fashion scene, these men are also consumers who navigate these issues on a day-to-day basis, not least in their ongoing endeavors to construct an attractive public persona. They can be regarded as expert consumers who have spent considerable amounts of time and energy on how to carefully construct masculinity in order not to digress into the "danger zones" (Rinallo 2007) surrounding the fairly narrow path available for heterosexual, middleclass, white, cisgender men, and thus risk being dismissed. While these respondents might be seen as outliers, as extreme cases obsessed with appearance whose insights have little relevance for the common man on the streets, I would rather view them as guardians of traditional values. From their privileged position they function as cultural intermediaries who leverage their expertise in setting the standards for others. Perhaps they can even be seen as "defenders of the phallocentric order" (Segal 1997b). The data produced as these men reflect on what makes a man sexy, and the roles that clothes, styles, and accessories, or the market if you will, play in this, provides interpretive inroads to understand larger issues connected to the respective role of men and women as subjects and objects in contemporary consumer culture.

The data set consists of 20 interviews that lasted for about an hour each. The interviews were recorded and subsequently transcribed in order to allow for analysis. The interviews were held in a conversational style circling the topic of what clothes, styles, and accessories a man can use in order to exude an aura of sexiness. While no strict interview template was used I made sure that each conversation covered topics of specific times, places, and occasions when it was more likely that sexiness would be an element to consider in choosing how to dress, and how this supposed sexiness was supposedly achieved, of fashion *faux-pas* connected to attempting to increase one's sexiness, and of how behaviors connected to attempting to be sexy would change throughout a person's life.

In order to get the conversation started I initiated each interview with presenting a rather stereotypical scenario that went something like this:

> Imagine that it is time for the annual Christmas party at a company that is sufficiently large for the employees not to be acquainted with each other. One of the younger women feels that she would like to use the Christmas party as an occasion to initiate a flirt with one of her male colleagues as this would add an extra layer of excitement to her somewhat dull workdays. In getting ready for the party, she thus wants to present herself to the world as sexy and available. What stylistic elements can we imagine that she can work with?

As I was introducing this scenario I would leave plenty of space for the interviewees to contribute to the scenario and they would typically nod with approval and make affirmative comments that signaled that this was a scenario that they could relate to. Towards the end of the scenario they would also typically volunteer a list of stylistic elements that the woman in the story could use to achieve the desired effect, such as using a short skirt, high heels, cleavage, showing plenty of skin, wearing red lipstick, a lace bra showing a little bit, and so forth. While the scenario was stereotypical in the sense of introducing a woman who constructed herself as an object of desire, I made sure not to impose the specific stylistic elements in use to achieve this objectification. Still, all the interviewees clearly showed that they were in possession of a cultural competence regarding clothes, styles, and accessories coded as sexy for women.

Having thus prompted the interviewees to consider clothes, styles, and accessories coded as sexy for women, I asked them to think of a young, heterosexual man in the same situation. If a man wants to present himself to the world as sexy and available, what stylistic elements are at his disposal? The opening scenario was intended to sensitize the interviewees to the topic of self-objectification and self-sexualization, to imagining what it is like to construct a sexualized public persona. Rather than talking about this in the abstract, I opted for a scenario method in which we could begin talking about this in concrete terms. Once the general practice of self-objectification and self-sexualization was introduced we could move on to the domain of men, after which the conversations unfolded.

Preliminary results

The general sentiment among the interviewees after having listened to the opening scenario was some sort of bewilderment over how hard it was to give a list of clothes, styles, and accessories that would enable a man to exude an aura of sexiness. The interviewees were typically amused when they realized that they did not have a simple answer to this relatively straightforward question. They had, they almost unanimously conceded, never quite framed the question in such a way. Instead they referred to adjacent terms such as being handsome, manly, or neat and clean. These concepts, while potentially overlapping with sexiness, were still seen as different as one could be handsome, manly, and neat and clean without exuding an aura of sexiness at all. In analyzing the conversations that unfolded there were a number of recurrent themes that captures how these men from the world of fashion viewed the issue.

Don't try too hard

One of the most recurring themes during the interviews was that while men could no doubt be viewed as sexy by both other men and women, this aura of sexiness would instantly vanish if it looked like the man was trying to be sexy. In their view, this was a sharp contrast to the dynamics for females where the visible attempts at "sexing things up" could be coded as sexy in themselves.

Rather than "putting on sexiness" by using marketplace resources, the view was that sexiness had to come from the inside, more particularly from the confidence of the individual men. Many of the interviewees were engaged in the world of fashion and had thus styled models as well as celebrities for photo shoots and the catwalk. In doing this they said that they never attempted to force a surface of sexiness, but that they rather tried to unearth the true character of the men. This echoes an idea of men as active subjects rather than passive objects.

In addressing the issue of what happens when men do indeed appear to be trying hard to exude an aura of sexiness they came up with examples of illegitimate compensatory consumption. In terms of marketplace resources some brands were singled out as representative of a "trying too hard" aesthetic. Dolce & Gabbana, for example, was mentioned as an overtly sexy brand that could be seen as catering to a homosexual audience where there is more room for actively portraying sexiness. Many straight men, however, did not pick up on these cues but considered themselves as a suitable target audience, something that is typically described as "gay vagueness in advertising" (Campbell 2015). They thus adopted the Dolce & Gabbana aesthetic nevertheless, which resulted in them looking like clichés trying too hard (John, fashion editor at *Dude*). Another frequent reference was the "reality TV aesthetic" where young men with muscular bodies strut around wearing very "skimpy clothes" (Magnus, fashion editor at *Nordic Sense*). This was written off as a poor attempt to compensate for the fact that they had very poor mental capabilities. It was suggested that this type of aesthetic probably had "an audience" but that it was not to be legitimately labeled sexy but perhaps rather as "horny" or some other term that enabled them to write it off as not really manly. In their view a man who obviously tried to get attention for his looks, especially his body, thereby diminished his value in other areas that they considered to be important in the construction of masculinity, especially areas connected to mental faculties, which is a classic marker of masculinity.

These judgments are certainly not unique for men, as research has shown that women who dress in a way invoking sexiness are judged as less competent (Howlett et al. 2015). There is something else at play here as well, however, connected to the issue of not trying too hard. Gill, Henwood, and McLean (2005, 51) suggest that the desire to achieve a particular look, whether focused on sexiness or not, "*must simply be presented in a way that does not transgress the taboo about appearing vain.*" For the participants in this study, displaying vanity was certainly not eschewed. They wanted to look good, they wanted to look manly, and they were not anxious about their ambitions being detected. In a sense, they were too vested in the fashion world to deny it. When it came to attempting to look "sexy," however, they had a rather different outlook. This would be taking things one step too far, and this would imply making a spectacle out of oneself, of appearing desperate. I suggest that this is because it would challenge the patriarchal order in which men are constructed as subjects.

Neat and clean

Another aspect of that many of the respondents spontaneously brought up was to keep a basic standard of hygiene, such as showering and using a deodorant. After some more contemplation they typically circled back to these statements and revised them by saying that sticking to some sort of basic hygiene factors such as being neat and clean really could not be said to constitute sexiness or attractiveness. Rather it was something that should be checked off in order not to be rejected, of not ending up on the negative end of the spectrum.

These types of discussions unearthed a more complex meaning universe behind the dichotomy of sexy/attractive and turn-off/repulsive, such that the assertion of being sexy/attractive needs to be complemented by a characteristic of being non-repulsive.

At the same time, many of the responded reasoned around the notion that according to their understanding, some men—bikers and rock stars were typically brought up as examples—were typically viewed as potentially sexy despite not necessarily living up to this standard of hygiene. This is yet another example where the male subject is brought to the fore and where a particular agentic character trumps the notion of being "merely" an object of desire. These types of ambiguities are discussed in Gopaldas and Molander's (2019) account of the bad boy archetype where juvenile masculinities—more specifically being aggressive, rebellious, and sexual, which corresponds rather well to the idea of bikers and rock stars—can easily turn into toxic masculinities if taken too far. Still, the ambiguity and constant maneuvering between these two ends of the spectrum is what makes the bad boy interesting and keeps the audience engaged.

Suit up

If there was one particular object that was typically brought up as potentially sexy it was the suit, which is not strange given that the suit has been one of the most enduring markers of masculinity for over two centuries. In a move that is typically labeled the "the great masculine renunciation" after psychoanalyst Flügel's observations, extravagance in male dress was eschewed around the turn of the 19th century (McNeil & Karaminas 2009). Before this, men's clothing had rivaled women's clothing in using ornamentation, bright colors, embroidery, etcetera. After "the great masculine renunciation" masculinity in dress became much more subdued and organized around conservatively tailored suits, typically in the colors black, grey, and navy blue. While there has indeed been a fair deal of ornamentation and fanciness still going on in male fashion since the turn of the 19th century, the general idea is that it is manly to dress conservatively and potentially emasculating to ornament oneself in an extravagant fashion. Given this connection between traditional masculinity and the suit (Hollander 1994) it is not strange that the respondents saw this as a potential object coded as sexy.

Discussions, however, revolved around how a common garment worn by, e.g., bank clerks, and undertakers, could be charged with sexiness. It was clear that it was not the object per se that was coded as sexy—in the same way that, e.g., a lace bra or a pair of high heels could be coded as sexy for women—but a specific combination of subject and object. A man had to "own his suit" (Mats, owner of an underwear brand) in order to exude an aura of sexiness in it. The active subject wearing the suit needed to shine through, which is not always an easy task given the iconicity of the suit as a marker of masculinity. It is easy for "a man to be owned by his suit" (Mats). In order to achieve this sense of "owning one's suit" a certain type of carelessness was required. One metaphor that was used to illustrate this was that one should "sleep in one's suit for a couple of nights so one wears it with as little respect as one would one's pyjamas" (Mats).

Tomas, editor-in-chief of an international fashion magazine and co-owner of a high-end tailoring house, is known globally in sartorial circles for his exquisite taste. He wears a lot of suits on a daily basis, and most of them are tailormade for him and clearly show that he is a man that goes to great lengths to curate a particular style. In talking about the potential sexiness of suits he exclaimed that "Wearing this type of suit is basically a chastity belt…" The reason, he argued, was that he was clearly paying too much attention to nerdy details that were appreciated by a homosocial audience. For a female audience, however, this particular interest in sartorial detail was seen as emasculating and thereby made him less attractive.

Concluding discussion

This chapter addresses a fairly simple state of affairs in contemporary Western consumer cultures: there is a virtual lexicon of clothes, styles, and accessories coded as sexy for women, whereas there is a relative dearth of such consumption resources for men. Throughout this chapter I have attempted to show that this is not a natural consequence of men and women being different, but that it is connected to the fact that we are living in a patriarchy. One way in which such a system is upheld is by constructing women as sexual objects whose worth in society is (partly) connected to whether they are seen as sexy or not. To privilege subjects over objects and to view them as hierarchically superior, with agency, is a taken-for-granted and undertheorized position in Western consumer cultures (Bettany 2018). And while this understanding of available subject and object positions certainly does not reflect the experiences of men or women in their daily lives, such taken-for-granted notions still shape our expectation of how life should be lived. In this sense they are ideological.

In a patriarchal system, men are typically not construed as sexual objects in the same sense and erotic capital (Hakim 2010) thus seems to be relatively less important in the overall makeup of their symbolic capital. Rather, the traditional view has been that heterosexual men are sexual subjects whose position of relative power in society—e.g., as breadwinners and "family heads" in a heterosexual marriage—would legitimate them (and give them access to sex) regardless of whether they are seen as sexy or not. The #MeToo movement exposed to the broader public this system whereby men in positions of power had viewed access to women, and to sex in particular, as an indispensable feature of their social position. While the cases that were exposed during this movement in many instances represented criminal acts, they nevertheless reflect and illustrate a broader social system where men are constructed as sexual subjects and women are constructed as sexual objects. This is not news, of course, for anyone versed in feminist theory, but the issue was brought to public attention in a new way post #MeToo. Since men have not traditionally had to construct themselves as sexual objects, there is a lack of codified, marketized means that are used to consecrate a man as sexy. This is not to say that men cannot be sexy or are not objectified, but merely that the means by which this happens is more ambiguous than in the case of women. Male and female bodies are sexualized differently, and this is a way of upholding the patriarchy. Perhaps this dynamic is about to change, however, as postfeminist ideas of female sexual agency are becoming more widespread. The argument is not that this necessarily reflects a real-life shift in power relations between men and women, but that the popular images of men as sexual subjects are reflected in an increased self-objectification and self-sexualization on behalf of men.

In reflecting on the findings of the empirical work of this project it is important to point out how careful the respondents were to actively avoid coding marketplace resources as overtly sexy. Instead, most of the objects and practices that were singled out as potentially sexy were simultaneously also considered absolutely normal and used by virtually everyone: take a shower, wear deodorant, look reasonably neat and clean, wear a suit, and perhaps show that you have put a little effort into your outfit, but not too much as you might then fall into the "danger zone" and be called out as effeminate (cf. Rinallo 2007). Connected to this idea is the notion that a man, in the view of the respondents, risked losing face and thus any potential to exude sexiness, if it was apparent that he was trying too much. There was a distinct horror in even imagining the situation of "serving oneself up on a silver platter, holding oneself up to public inspection, staring at people with needy eyes, begging 'here I am, please have a piece of me, consume me for your pleasure!'" (Carl-Philip, influencer, and fashion entrepreneur). This reflects what Goldman (1992, 122) describes as "the diverse forms of terror experienced by [wo]men who objectify themselves." Goldman discusses this in the case of women, but the men in this study similarly described the "the mundane psychic terror associated with not receiving 'looks' of admiration—i.e. of not having others validate one's appearance" (ibid.), especially if one had made a concerted effort to appear sexy. This is corroborated by Bordo (1999, 297) in her discussion of how "needy" men can be where she suggest that men "*really do come from the same planet as women [...] and that 'we're all earthlings, desperate for love, demolished by rejection'.*" Instead of taking this risk, sexiness should appear as an unintended side-effect of just being oneself, seemingly coming from the inside (cf. Stevens & Ostberg's 2020, discussion of Frigo underwear). Opening up for a potential reading that one would be explicitly trying to be sexy would invite the speculation that one would be compensating for something. Such signs of insecurity, in turn, would be antithetical to the type of dominant agency connected to male sexuality (Montemurro 2021) and would, to borrow Ostberg's (2010, 66) term, make men feel "anxious about their anxiousness and embarrassed about their embarrassment."

In concluding it is important to acknowledge that this exploration of the topic of marketplace resources coded as sexy for men is built upon a rather homogeneous heterosexual, able-bodied, middleclass, white, cisgender man perspective. These men speak from a position of multiple intersecting privileges. While on the one hand it would be reasonable to argue that they thereby have many more degrees of freedom in expressing themselves through marketplace resources, they are on the other hand also bound by conventions. Perhaps even more so since they have more to lose by transgressing the boundaries of legitimate consumption. It is important therefore in closing this chapter to stress that the goal is not to study these men merely as "negotiators of norms" (Hearn & Hein 2015). They do not, despite their privileged positions, have unlimited choice to maneuver these norms. Gender is not a question of lifestyle, of which "option from the menu to choose," within given consumer cultures (Maclaran 2012). Furthermore, the perspective represented by these men has prevalence in, e.g., the mainstream fashion press and in the marketing communication of mainstream fashion brands, and thus influences men that are not part of this particular group. Still, it is likely that a study exploring similar dynamics among a different set of men would produce alternative viewpoints of how men can achieve a status of sexiness. This would be an appropriate topic for further research in this area.

References

Andersen, L. P., F. Lindberg and J. Ostberg. 2021. "Unpacking Nordic Branding: The Value Regimes of Nordicness." *Journal of Place Management and Development*, ahead-of-print. doi: 10.1108/JPMD-12-2019-0113

Berger, J. 1972. *Ways of Seeing*. London: Penguin Classics.

Bettany, S. 2018. "Subject/Object Relations and Consumer Culture." In O. Kravets, P. Maclaran, S. Miles and A Venkatesh (eds.) *The Sage Handbook of Consumer Culture*. London: Sage, 365-383.

Bordo, S. 1992. *Unbearable Weight: Feminism, Western Culture, and the Body*. Berkeley: University of California Press.

Bordo, S. 1999. *The Male Body: A New Look at Men in Public and in Private*. New York: Farrar, Straus and Giroux.

Bored Panda. 2020. "Guys in Gray Sweatpants 2020 Calendar Is Here and the Thirst Is Real." Available at: https://www.boredpanda.com/guys-in-gray-sweatpants-2020-calendar-is-here-and-the-thirst-is-real/?utm_source=google&utm_medium=organic&utm_campaign=organic (accessed October 5th 2020).

Campbell, J. E. 2015. "Gay and Lesbian/Queer Markets/Marketing." In D.T. Cook and J.M. Ryan (eds.) *The Wiley Blackwell Encyclopedia of Consumption and Consumer Studies*, Oxford: John Wiley & Sons, 313–315.

Chatterton, P. and R. Hollands. 2003. *Urban Nightscapes: Youth Cultures, Pleasure Spaces and Corporate Power*. London: Routledge.

Daniel, S., S. K. Bridges, and M. P. Martens. 2014. "The Development and Validation of the Male Assessment of Self-Objectification (MASO)." *Psychology of Men & Masculinity*, 15(1), 78–89.

Daniels, E. A, E. L. Zurbriggen and L. M. Ward. 2020. "Becoming an Object: A Review of Self-Objectification in Girls." *Body Image*, 33, 278–299.

Edwards, T. 2009. "Consuming Masculinities: Style, Content and Men's Magazines." In P. McNeil, and V. Karaminas (eds.) *The Men's Fashion Reader*. Oxford: Berg Publishers, 462–471.

Elite Daily. 2015. "Women Are Going Crazy Over Guys in Grey Sweatpants This Season (Photos)." Available at: https://www.elitedaily.com/envision/grey-sweatpants-season-photos/1299222 (accessed October 5th 2020).

Elle. 2018. "Just a Bunch of Hot Guys in Sweatpants to Warm You Up." Available at: https://www.elle.com/culture/celebrities/g25243925/hot-guys-in-sweatpants-celebrities/ (accessed October 5th 2020).

Elliott, R. and C. Elliott. 2005. 'Idealized Images of the Male Body in Advertising: A Reader-Response Exploration.' *Journal of Marketing Communications*, 11(1), 3–19.

Elliott, R. and K. Wattanasuwan. 1998. "Brands as Symbolic Resources for the Construction of Identity." *International journal of Advertising*, 17(2), 131–144.

Flugel, J. C. 1930. *The Psychology of Clothes*. London: Hogarth Press.

Fredrickson, B. L. and T.-A. Roberts. 1997. Objectification Theory: Toward Understanding Women's Lived Experiences and Mental Health Risks. *Psychology of Women Quarterly*, 21(2), 173–206.

Fredrickson, B. L., T. A. Roberts, S. M. Noll, D. M. Quinn, and J. M. Twenge. 1998. "That Swimsuit Becomes You: Sex Differences in Self-Objectification, Restrained Eating, and Math Performance." *Journal of Personality and Social Psychology*, 75(1), 269–284.

Giddens, A. 1991. *Modernity and Self-Identity: Self and Society in the Late Modern Age*. Stanford, CA: Stanford University Press.

Gill, R. 2003. "From Sexual Objectification to Sexual Subjectification: The Re-Sexualisation of Women's Bodies in the Media." *Feminist Media Studies*, 3(1), 100–106.

Gill, R. 2008. "Empowerment/Sexism: Figuring Female Sexual Agency in Contemporary Advertising." *Feminism & Psychology*, 18(1), 35–60.

Gill, R. 2011. "Supersexualize Me! Advertising and the Midriffs." In F. Attwood and R Cere (eds.) *Gender, Race, and Class in Media: A Critical Reader*. London: Sage, 278–284.

Gill, R., K. Henwood and C. McLean. 2003. 'A Genealogical Approach to Idealized Male Body Imagery.' *Paragraph* 26(1/2), 187–197.

Gill, R., K. Henwood and C. McLean. 2005. "Body Projects and the Regulation of Normative Masculinity." *Body & Society*, 11(1), 37–62.

Goffman, E. 1979. *Gender Advertisments*. New York: Harper & Row.

Goldman, R. 1992. *Reading Ads Socially*. London: Routledge.

Goodin, S. M., A. Van Denburg, S. K. Murnen, and L. Smolak. 2011. "'Putting on' Sexiness: A Content Analysis of the Presence of Sexualizing Characteristics in Girls' Clothing." *Sex Roles*, 65(1–2), 1–12.

Gopaldas, A. and E. Fischer. 2012. "Beyond Gender: Intersectionality, Culture, and Consumer Behavior." In C. Otnes and L. T. Zayer (eds.) *Gender, Culture, and Consumer Behavior*. New York: Routledge, 394–408.

Gopaldas, A and S. Molander. 2019. "The Bad Boy Archetype as a Morally Ambiguous Complex of Juvenile Masculinities: The Conceptual Anatomy of a Marketplace Icon." *Consumption Markets & Culture*, 23(1), 89–93.

GQ. 2020. "How Gray Sweatpants Became the Unofficial Symbol of Fall Horniness." Available at: https://www.gq.com/story/grey-sweatpants-meme-explained (accessed October 5th 2020).

Hakim, C. 2010. "Erotic Capital." *European Sociological Review*, 26(5), 499–518.

Harvey, K. 2015. "Men of Parts: Masculine Embodiment and the Male Leg in Eighteenth-Century England." *Journal of British Studies*, 54(October), 797–821.

Henwood, K., R. Gill and C. McLean. 2002. "The Changing Man." *The Pshychologist*, 15(4), 182–86.

Hollander, A. 1994. *Sex and Suits: The Evolution of Modern Dress*. London: Bloomsbury.

Howlett, N., J. J. Pine, N. Cahill, İ. Orakçıoğlu and B. C. Fletcher. 2015. "Unbuttoned: The Interaction between Provocativeness of Female Work Attire and Occupational Status." *Sex Roles*, 72(3–4), 105–116.

Jackson, S. 2007. "The Sexual Self in Late Modernity." In M. Kimmel (ed.) *The Sexual Self: Construction of Sexual Scripts*. Nashville, TN: Vanderbilt University Press, 3–15.

Jobling, P. 2003. "Underexposed: Spectatorship and Pleasure in Men's Underwear Advertising in the Twentieth Century." *Paragraph* 26(1/2), 147–162.

Kozak, M., H. Frankenhauser and T. A. Roberts. 2009. "Objects of Desire: Objectification as a Function of Male Sexual Orientation." *Psychology of Men & Masculinity*, 10(3), 225–230.

Lucie-Smith, E. 2003 "Kitsch and Classicism: The Male Nude in the Twentieth Century." *Paragraph* 26(1/2), 42–51.

MacKinnon, K. 2003. *Representing Men: Maleness and Masculinity in the Media*. London: Arnold.

Maclaran, P. 2012. "Marketing and Feminism in Historic Perspective." *Journal of Historical Research in Marketing*, 4(3), 462–469.

Marion, G. and A. Nairn. 2011. "'We Make the Shoes, You Make the Story' Teenage Girls' Experiences of Fashion: Bricolage, Tactics and Narrative Identity." *Consumption, Markets and Culture*, 14(1), 29–56.

Martins, Y., M. Tiggemann and A. Kirkbride. 2007. "Those Speedos Become Them." *Personality and Social Psychology Bulletin*, 33(5), 634–647.

McNeil, P. and V. Karaminas. 2009. "Introduction: The Field of Men's Fashion." In P. McNeil and V. Karaminas (eds.) *The Men's Fashion Reader*. London: Berg, 2–4.

Molander, S., I. A. Kleppe and J. Ostberg. 2019. "Hero Shots: Involved Fathers Conquering New Discursive Territory in Consumer Culture." *Consumption, Markets and Culture*, 22(4), 430–453.

Montemurro, B. 2021. "'If You Could Just See Me': The Construction of Heterosexual Men's Sexual Selves and the Hierarchy of Desirability." *Sexualities*, 24(3), 303–321.

Mort, F. 1996. *Cultures of Consumption: Masculinities and Social Space in Late Twentieth Century Britain*. London and New York: Routledge.

Mulvey, L. 1989. *Visual and Other Pleasures*. Basingstoke: Macmillan.

Murray, S. H. 2018. "Heterosexual Men's Sexual Desire: Supported by, or Deviating from, Traditional Masculinity Norms and Sexual Scripts?" *Sex Roles*, 78(1–2), 130–141.

Ostberg, J. 2010. "Thou Shalt Sport a Banana in Thy Pocket: Gendered Body Size Ideals in Advertising and Popular Culture." *Marketing Theory*, 10(1), 45–73.

Ostberg, J. 2012. "Masculine Self-Presentation." In R. W. Belk and A. A Ruvio (eds.) *The Routledge Companion to Identity and Consumption*. New York: Routledge, 129–136.

Patterson, M. and R. Elliott. 2002. "Negotiating Masculinities: Advertising and the Inversion of the Male Gaze", *Consumption, Markets and Culture*, 5(3), 231–246.

Rinallo, D. 2007. "Metro/Fashion/Tribes of Men: Negotiating the Boundaries of Men's Legitimate Consumption." In B. Cova, R. Kozinets and A. Shankar (eds.) *Consumer Tribes*. London: Elsevier/Butterworth-Heinemann, 76–92.

Rohlinger, D. A. 2002. "Eroticizing Men: Cultural Influences on Advertising and Male Objectification." *Sex Roles*, 46(3–4), 61–74.

Rosenmann, A., D. Kaplan, R. Gaunt, M. Pinho and M. Guy. 2018. "Consumer Masculinity Ideology: Conceptualization and Initial Findings on Men's Emerging Body Concerns." *Psychology of Men & Masculinity*, 19(2), 257–72.

Sarpila, O. 2013. "Attitudes Towards Performing and Developing Erotic Capital in Consumer Culture." *European Sociological Review*, 30(3), 302–314.

Schroeder, J. E. and D. Zwick. 2004. "Mirrors of Masculinity: Representation and Identity in Advertising Images", *Consumption Markets & Culture*, 7(1), 21–52.

Schroeder, J.E. and J. L. Borgerson. 1998. "Marketing Images of Gender: A Visual Analysis." *Consumption, Markets and Culture* 2(2), 161–201.

Segal, L. (ed.) 1997a. *New Sexual Agendas*. London: Palgrave Macmillan.

Segal, L. 1997b. "Feminist Sexual Politics and the Heterosexual Predicament." In L. Segal (ed.) *New Sexual Agendas*. London: Palgrave Macmillan, 77–89.

Segal, L. 2007. *Slow Motion, Changing Masculinities, Changing Men* (revised edition). London: Palgrave Macmillan.

Simon, W. and J. H. Gagnon. 1984. "Sexual scripts." *Society*, 22(1), 53–60.

Smolak, L., S. K. Murnen and T. A. Myers. 2014. "Sexualizing the Self: What College Women and Men Think About and Do to Be 'Sexy'." *Psychology of Women Quarterly*, 38(3), 379–397.

Stevens, L. and J. Ostberg. 2020. "Gendered Bodies: Representations of Femininity and Masculinity in Advertising Practices." In N. Toulouse, L. Visconti and L. Peñaloza (eds.) *Marketing Management: A Cultural Perspective* (2nd edition). London: Routledge, 392–407.

Tuncay, L. 2005. "How Male Consumers Construct and Negotiate Their Identities in the Marketplace: Three Essays." PhD Diss., University of Illinois.

Vanwesenbeeck, I. 1997. "The Context of Women's Power(lessness) in Heterosexual Relations." In L. Segal (ed.) *New Sexual Agendas*. London: Macmillan, 171–179.

Visser, B. A., F. Sultani, B. L. Choma and J. A. Pozzebon. 2014. "Enjoyment of Sexualization: Is It Different for Men?" *Journal of Applied Social Psychology*, 44(7), 495–504.

Vox. 2019. "The Enduring, Endearing Cult of Gray Sweatpants Thirst." Available at: https://www.vox.com/the-goods/2019/3/12/18246515/gray-sweatpants-season-challenge-meme (accessed October 5th 2020).

Wade L. 2017. *American Hookup: The New Culture of Sex on Campus*. New York: W.W. Norton.

West, C., and D. H. Zimmerman. 1987. "Doing Gender." *Gender & Society*, 1(2), 125–151.

Section 4
Difference, diversity, and intersectionality

16 Are all bodies knitworthy?

Interrogating race and intersecting axes of marginalization in knitting spaces

Alev Pınar Kuruoğlu

In 2021, despite all moves and aspirations toward a more liquid and postmodern world, in which humans are less attached to or grounded in singular places and identities (see, e.g., Bardhi and Eckhardt 2017; Firat and Venkatesh 1995), dichotomies still continue to color the way many people not only see, but also experience the world, and also build their resistance toward it: female – male; crafts – arts; domestic – public. These dichotomies, and the unequal distribution of worth across their poles, have long occupied feminist thought. French feminist philosopher Simone de Beauvoir (1948) took a Hegelian approach to delineating between two forms of activities – the immanent and transcendent. The transcendent, she argued, was the domain of the male, and comprised the forms of activity and labor that are exploratory and creative, productive, and expressive – these allow an individual to extend one's self and senses out into the world. Immanent activities, on the other hand, are reproductive and serve to maintain the status quo – and of course, these comprise activities that are typically associated with women: giving birth, raising children, cooking, cleaning, and all manners of "domestic" labor. Iris Marion Young (1980), drawing on Merleau Ponty's phenomenology, complemented de Beauvoir's conceptualization with the "bodily experience" of femininity, particularly in terms of the body's relation to its social and physical surroundings, its orientations and movements within space. From a young age, Young argued, "girls" are taught to embody a feminine comportment and motility. They learn that their body is fragile and incapable of extending itself out into the world with the forcefulness of a boy's. While de Beauvoir located the feminine "immanence" as a social construction, Young relocated it as an inscription onto the body that throughout a woman's life, imposes itself upon the body's "comportment, motility, and spatiality" (Young 1980, 141), delimiting the body's possibilities and range of action.

This framework is apt for understanding the relegation of knitting as a domestic, feminine practice (Bratich and Brush 2011; Maciel and Wallendorf 2021), a form of "immanent" labor mirrored by the bodily posture and motion range of the knitter: arms held close to the body, hands making small movements, balls of yarn held close to avoid unraveling or to prevent them from getting caught by the claws of domestic companions such as cats and young children. Knitting appears to be performed with the body closing in on oneself rather than "reaching out" into the world. Research on knitting and other forms of craft-activism has shown, however, that knitters *have* been extending themselves, in order to take up public space and make their voices heard: from supporting war efforts (Bratich and Brush 2011) to engaging in knitting in unexpected public places and occasions (Maciel and Wallendorf 2021) – such as academic conferences (guilty as charged) – to other spatial tactics (de Certeau 1984; Tonkiss 2004).

DOI: 10.4324/9781003042587-20

Quite recently, the "Pussy Hat Project" was an instance of knitting serving to "materialize" resistance (Kuruoğlu and Ger 2015): thousands of women wearing pink hats with ears participated in Women's March demonstrations in early 2017 following the election of Donald Trump in the USA (Black 2017). These hats, a clever reference to Donald Trump's infamous interview, created a striking visual representation of what I can only imagine must have been an exuberant atmosphere of resistance. In 2019, the knitting and crochet portal Ravelry further took part in a cultural-political branding move, banning open support of Donald Trump and his administration on the website, "in the form of forum posts, projects, patterns, profiles, and all other content."[1] "Craftivism" is the term that some have used to describe such endeavors that employ feminine bodies as well as their crafts to "challenge patriarchal hegemony, advocate for political and social rights, and promote the recognition of women's traditional art forms" (Literat and Markus 2020, 141).

These are significant and visible instances of solidarities. However they also bring forth the trouble with assuming a uniform "feminist" crafting body that resists spatial and ideological constrictions. How so? Several commentators have addressed the ambivalences and tensions within the Pussyhat Project and the Women's March. Gokariksel and Smith (2017), for example, note that the Women's March initially did not include non-white organizers. The organizers responded by including non-white voices, and trying to signal that they were committed to practicing intersectional feminism – yet some participants read the Women's March as a "white space" (e.g., Rose-Redwood and Rose-Redwood 2017) to which Black Women were called upon to lend support (Lemieux 2017), rather than one in which they were, from the start, involved as organizers in an equal capacity. The pussyhat itself was criticized by some as "reducing women's identity to female genitalia" (May 2020) and thereby also excluding trans women.

Attending to these tensions and ruptures within social movements and solidarities (Chatzidakis, Maclaran and Varman 2021) is important, as they draw attention to how feminist or other politicized spaces have their own ways of folding upon and delimiting the participation of some bodies, more than others (see also Bilge 2013). This is a premise upon which intersectionality as well as other critical feminist epistemologies – such as postcolonial feminism or decoloniality is built. Black, postcolonial, and anti-racist feminisms have long since argued for the inadequacy of a "universal" understanding of women's experiences of domination. They have stressed the importance of culturally and historically situating the intersections of class, gender, race, sexuality, (dis)ability, religion, citizenship, and other categories that operate, and differentially create specific and varied patterns of inequality and discrimination (Collins and Bilge 2016; Mirza 2009). These approaches call for the centering of the experiences of those who constitute the "gaps," and draw attention to the vitality of bringing forth the "subjugated knowledge" (Collins 2002) of differentially relegated groups and subjectivities. Therefore, I turn to think with some critical – and in particular, non-white – feminist theorists to argue that we need to look into the differences and hierarchies *within* the embodied feminine experience of knitting – and, by extension, to also critically interrogate hierarchies of knowledge and praxis among various groups of resistive and activist feminist subjectivities.

Sara Ahmed's body of work, for example, situated at the intersections of phenomenology, queer theory, as well as Black feminist and postcolonial thought, guides our attention to production of the gendered and racialized body in predominantly heteronormative and white institutional spaces, ranging from the family (Ahmed 2004) to academia (Ahmed 2012) and also to the Nation (Ahmed 2000). In line with the phenomenological tradition, Ahmed centers the body in her work "Queer Phenomenology" (2004), noting "the significance of nearness or what is ready-to hand, and the role of repeated and habitual actions in shaping bodies and worlds" (2). Spaces within which bodies are emplaced, in turn, "impress" themselves upon the body. With this in mind, how, then, do public spaces impress themselves upon the knitting body? How does the knitting body push back? And is every knitting *body* oriented and aligned with other bodies who knit, such that they can push back collectively?

Nirmal Puwar's (2004) work helps reorient my gaze toward the "double encroachment" that takes place when it's not just women, but Black women – or other individuals of color and individuals who are non-conforming to mainstream imaginings of knitters – who move into the public spaces. Non-white, non-heterosexual, non-middle class knitters – all of whom are not only marked but also *produced* as "non-" in their relation to the white space of knitting – can be disruptive, not only because they are performing an activity that was supposed to be confined to the domestic sphere; but *also* because the figure of the knitter is so engrained in the public (and even researchers') imagination as a white woman. What happens when non-white or otherwise non-conforming bodies insert themselves into these spaces? Nirmal Puwar talks about "space invaders" who are often not only gendered but also racialized subjects, and who are doubly marked when they are – invoking Doreen Massey (1996) – "of and in a space, while at the same time not quite belonging to it" (Puwar 2004, 8) and thereby causing disruption. These moments of disruption are revealing, as they are perceived of threats to the "unity" of the previously homogeneous (imagined) space.

It is precisely in moments of disruption that I find it possible to see knitting as not only a space of solidarity but also a space of exclusion. What I have seen is that non-white or otherwise non-conforming knitters are not merely "taking" space (as white women do, when they knit in public) but are "invading" it in a way that creates unease in the previous occupants, as the surfaces of the space they occupied is now being challenged, to also accommodate different types of bodies. Following Sara Ahmed, a "queering" of the phenomenological project requires an understanding of how spaces and institutions *produce* racialized bodies. I therefore would like to propose that a critical phenomenology, which looks at the relationships between gendered and racialized bodies and the spaces they occupy, would give us valuable insights into how and why both the online and physical spaces of knitting can also become battlegrounds for its occupants.

Such an account would require the centering of the voices and lived experiences of a "willful" (Ahmed 2014) knitter who does not fit into the white spaces of knitting – a kind of centering that is also at the core of intersectional (Collins 2002, 2019; Crenshaw 1989) approaches and epistemologies. I thus turn to think with Black feminist thinkers, who are familiar but also disruptive figures to academic as well as public imaginaries. The term "intersectionality" was first used by Crenshaw, though the phenomenon itself was identified and critiqued by several Black feminist thinkers that preceded Crenshaw, perhaps starting with Soujourner Truth's question, "Ain't I a Woman" and its re-citation by bell hooks (1981). Audre Lorde (1984) significantly drew attention to the inadequacy of mainstream feminism, noting "As white women ignore their built-in privilege of whiteness and define *woman* in their terms of their experience alone, then women of Color become 'other,' the outsider whose experience and tradition is too 'alien' to comprehend" (110). Lorde's words call upon the reader to recognize that the sexism, marginalization, and devaluation of labor experienced by a white woman, is not the same as the sexism and marginalization and devaluation of labor as experienced by a Woman of Color. Intersectionality offers a critical and analytical lens – a flexible "heuristic" toolbox (Collins 2019) to center this "alien" experience – this marking of certain bodies (such as bodies that are queer, fat, poor, chronically ill, disabled) in multiple and intersecting ways. How do such intersecting marginalizations and relegations then shape the experiences of knitting? Do all of these bodies "fit" into knitting spaces? And might such varied forms of "markedness" become a conduit as well as barrier to coalitions (Carastathis 2013)?

Online/digital intersectionality

Increasingly, critical intersectional and Black feminist approaches to studying the Internet have also drawn attention to the not only gendered but also racialized (and otherwise differentiated) experiences of online participation which affords creative and liberatory possibilities as well as the reproduction of social injustices that fold upon racialized bodies.

Extant literature recognizes the affordances of online spaces in supporting intersectional political activism, and as providing resources for discriminated actors to engage in resistive activities. For example, in the context of marketplace discrimination (Crockett, Grier and Williams 2003) in the USA, Ekpo and colleagues (2018) find that Black consumers draw on their engagement with online technologies, to become equipped to combat "offline" racialized encounters, as well as to withdraw permanently or temporarily into online shopping to avoid such encounters (Ekpo et al. 2018). Sobande and colleagues (2020; see also Sobande 2017) note the rich digital lives of Black British women, highlighting their engagements with and disengagements with from digital media in "personal, political and purposeful ways" (415). They situate Black British women's resistive activities in relation to mainstream media, in ways that are shaped by but also sometimes run counter to the more prevalent US-centric Black feminist/intersectional discourses (Sobande, Fearfull and Brownlie 2020). Other situated examinations of Black women's usage of expressive rhetorical devices, such as "sass" and "shade," also bring forth the potential of digital mediation and language in serving as a means to "expose individual and institutional folly and attempts to upend systems of power" (Monk-Payton 2017, 16).

While these accounts demonstrate the pedagogical potentiality of online discourse in generating transformative knowledge, through engaging with anger and discomfort with the lived experience of marginalized others, and of creating spaces and resources for women (of various marginalized subject positions) to thrive, these works also draw attention to the limitations of encounters and engagements in online spaces (see also Nakamura 2015), in their failure to adequately address the systemic effects of racial capitalism, or to generate non-oppressive coalitions that would lead to structural change.

Where does knitting fit in?

Maciel and Wallendorf (2021) note that in contradiction to what one would expect based on Bourdieusian analyses of symbolic power, the field of knitting does not engender status competitions that aim to "outdo others," arguing that, "when an entire arena of consumption is culturally devalued, we believe it is more likely that individuals will focus on raising the status of the identity associated with it rather than on their own within-field status." This implies that within a devalued identity or consumption category, there is a primary (if not singular) force of domination that unites all involved in resistive praxis. Yet, feminisms, in the plural, increasingly draw attention to the multiple and intersecting structures of domination that operate within social fields and spaces and invite us to reckon with these intersections, beyond the devaluation of feminine labor.

Discussions and debates within feminisms have allowances for the forming of solidarities and coalitions (Carastathis 2013) similar to the ones described by Maciel and Wallendorf (2021), yet they also point toward some deeply rooted fault lines that are difficult to surmount, and which become intensified throughout these debates. Platformization and social media have afforded the possibility of increased visual representation of knitted goods and bodies inhabiting spaces and products of knitting, and as such they have also made some of the visibilities and exclusions more salient. They thus also become spaces where one finds interrogations of some of the following: the universality of a white, older, respectable female "knitting" subject; the assumptions underlying normative bodies as well as the availability of size ranges in patterns; the status and benefits afforded to knitters and designers (who often become "influencers") who are able to work with expensive fibers, the accessibility of knitting platforms and spaces to individuals with disabilities.

While it is important to recognize that knitters socio-materially and symbolically resist the relegation of their labor and its products, an equally vital task is to recognize the further marginalization, even within this "community of resistance," of some bodies and subjectivities. Moreover, this further marginalization leads to a disproportionate burden of engaging in pedagogical activities that seek to redress societal inequalities, which I also see reflected and reproduced in the knitting community. But first, I would like to present my personal story – to afford a sense of what I "carry on my body" (Puwar 2020) as a researcher and a knitter, I will try to present a "work-in-progress" account of conflict in online knitting spaces.

My knitting story

I started taking yarn seriously in 2016; starting out with crochet, educating myself with YouTube videos, and in the meantime, moving to Denmark, the homeland of the infamous "The Killing Sweater." I threw myself further into tutorials, learned to knit properly, and finished my first sweater in November that year: an extremely whimsical red wool jumper with a yoke that featured rabbits.

A couple of years down the road, I had knit several items and was a regular on "Ravelry," an online repository of knitting patterns (where independent designers as well as companies are able to sell their designs) as well as yarns, knitting diaries, forums, and the like. By late 2018 I was "following" many of my favorite designers, yarn companies, and knitters on the social media platform Instagram, and I was a member of several Facebook groups dedicated to knitting.

In January 2019, I saw a flurry of posts, criticizing someone for engaging in cultural appropriation and racism. After some online excavation work, I managed to find the post that had started the conversation: a blogger had posted, with great excitement, about her upcoming trip to India, as part of her overall aim to live the upcoming year "in color." In this post, she compared her trip to India to travel to Mars. A commenter called "Alex" opened the floodgates, commenting, "I'd ask you to re-read what you wrote and think about how your words feed into a colonial/imperialist mindset toward India and other non-Western countries."[2] Several commenters followed suit. The blogger, at first defensive, later on issued an apology as well as a new blog post in which she detailed the ways in which she had learned from the experience that her original post served to essentialize India and Indian people as the "other."

The initial conversation centered around colonialism and essentialization: several of the commenters demonstrated their familiarity, at the very least, with a vernacularized form of orientalist and postcolonial critique. They were bothered by the thought of "India" serving only as a resource and inspiration for a white woman's "color pallette." However, as the discussion reverberated through other social media platforms, including Instagram, it expanded to a broader discussion on racism in knitting communities. This was met with surprise by some (mostly white) knitters, as knitting and other feminine crafts worlds are often characterized as conducive to "kind" and "polite" interactions. A great deal of online discussion followed, delineating the various ways in which kindness and conviviality did not extend to all knitting individuals.

As these discussions took place, I observed them on social media and felt moved by some of the posts that highlighted the forms of discrimination that "BIPOC" (Black, Indigenous, and People of Color) individuals faced in knitting-related spaces of leisure or commerce. This is also the point where I became aware of the term BIPOC – which, reportedly, has been in use since 2013 (Garcia 2020) and gained mainstream visibility around 2019–2020. I noticed that this term had a performative (in Judith Butler's usage of the term) capacity – inscribing those who feel the call of the term into an affectively charged and politicized solidarity. I came to recognize many posts on Instagram as *testimonies* from self-identified BIPOC knitters, as forms of knowledge that aim to highlight how racialization is central to the experience of some knitters' everyday encounters (Donnor and Ladson-Billings 2017) and that bring to fore the sites and bodies that have been previously subjected to "epistemic erasure" (Thomas 2020). Such use of words and testimonial autoethnographic writing has been essential in conveying, centering, and theorizing the experiences of marginalized and especially racialized subjects (see, e.g., Boylorn 2008; Eguchi 2015; Goitom 2019; Griffin 2012; Lorde 1984; Ono 1997) – an act that takes place through many forms of dissemination, including social media today.

I thus now turn to an exploratory analysis of what I witnessed happening in online communities, by drawing on publically available[3] testimonies of discrimination and exclusion. These range from outright hostility to less visible (but still discernible, to the recipient) racial microaggressions (Pérez Huber and Solorzano 2015; see also Pierce 1969) in knitting communities. These discussions show that embodied differences – ethnic/racial to begin with but also gender identity and sexual orientation, body-size, (dis)ability, and class are central to the experiences as well as resistive solidarities of knitters – many of whom are situated within multiple and intersecting axes of domination. I continue by "thinking with" feminism(s) to understand these testimonies as well as a series of events that have unfolded in the world of knitting.

Do Black People knit?

Dana Williams-Johnson (2020), a Black knitter and academic noted, "When I started blogging on Yards of Happiness five years ago, I did it because I didn't see a lot of faces like mine talking about knitting." Black women were not only absent from knitting discourse – Black North American women's testimonies indicate that physical spaces, including yarn shops, knitting groups, yarn and knitting conventions, and other events are sites where Black and otherwise racialized individuals do not always feel welcome. Felicia Eve, a Black woman, and owner of a yarn shop, described her experiences of racial microaggressions in knitting spaces,[4] such as a visit to a yarn shop with two other Black friends, where they received a lukewarm greeting, "tart responses" to their questions, and were even encouraged to shop elsewhere. Eve also cites the commonplace assumption that black women do not knit, and also notes how many of her customers at her own store assume that her white employees are the shop owners. This sentiment is echoed in a piece titled "Black People Do Knit" by Jeanette Sloan (2019), published by *Knitting* magazine. Sloane notes that, despite having less visibility in knitting magazines, public spaces, and conventions, there are many talented knitters, designers, and other "fiber artists" of color. Sloan took action to this oversight and established a website called "BIPOC in Fiber," which provides a directory as well as opportunities for marketing and networking.

These experiences of exclusion or invisibility extend to digital spaces: many knitters/designers/dyers have noted that they felt a difference in their online engagements when they made it known that they were not white. In a published interview (Saxena 2019), yarn dyer Ocean Rose says she noticed that

> she'd post a photo of herself, or part of herself, after long stretches of only showing yarn or other images. "I just noticed the space was easier to navigate when I didn't show who I was, because then you wouldn't assume that I was a black person," she said. "When I didn't show myself, people would assume that the picture was from a white person."

Rose's testimony in particular affirms that the Internet is not and cannot be a "raceless space" (see, e.g., Cottom 2020; Daniels 2013; Noble 2018), in terms of how its algorithmic affordances have been designed in a way to (re)produce racialized knowledge and inequalities (e.g., Benjamin 2019; Noble 2018) and also in terms of how online spaces of communication and discussion – the "networked society" (Daniels 2013) – reflect and exacerbate the wider societal and political-economic dynamics of racial capitalism in which they are embedded (Cottom 2020).

The *Vox* article covers several instances in which the Instagram posts and other online media of several knitters (or other fiber artists) of color drew attention to the issues of racism and "whitewashing" in the knitting community – for example, the disproportionate featuring of white (and thin, young, able-bodied) women as models for knitting patterns, on Instagram as well as magazines. This piece also notes the "backlash" – the polarizing responses – especially from individuals and organizations in the knitting scene who have high number of followers, and whose political orientations are conservative; as well as those who perceive themselves as already being anti-racist and who express discomfort with their positionalities questioned. I turn to examine the toll as well as the rewards of sharing testimonies with the knitting community on social media (and beyond).

Anger and talking back: the burdens, rewards, and appropriation of pedagogy

bell hooks (1986), in *Talking Back*, refers to the practice of speaking "as an equal" to authority figures, as something that one had to dare to do, in the face of one's elders (as a child) or as a "right of speech" to ears that are unwilling to hear you – something for which black women writers, including herself, are punished, as is evidenced by the harsh criticism she received for her seminal work, *Ain't I a Woman*, but it also performs as a most powerful act. In her words,

"[m]oving from silence into speech is for the oppressed, the colonized, the exploited, and those who stand and struggle side by side, a gesture of defiance that heals, that makes new life, and new growth possible. It is that act of speech, of 'talking back' that is no mere gesture of empty words, that is the expression of moving from object to subject, that is, the liberated voice" (hooks 1986, 128). Gloria Anzaldua, in *Borderlands*, also says: "wild tongues can't be tamed, they can only be cut out" (1987, 54) reflecting upon the violence inflicted upon her as a child and a young person, to force her to adhere to a "tradition of silence," to speak English at school, and to get rid of her accent; and then the sit also for speaking English, her colonizer's language; for feeling inferior while speaking Chicano Spanish with other Latinas.

A great deal of "talking back" involves Black women asking white people to examine their own relation to race and racism in America. bell hooks has argued that

> [s]exist discrimination has prevented white women from assuming the dominant role in the perpetuation of white racial imperialism, but it has not prevented white women from absorbing, supporting, and advocating racist ideology or acting individually as racist oppressors in various spheres of American life.
>
> (hooks 1981/2015, 124)

This is echoed in critical posts on Instagram and beyond: that the white women who are trying to be their allies are still not critically assessing the ways that they have been complicit in structures of domination (which are built upon white supremacy). Even while the so-called fourth wave of feminism – which is increasingly mobilized and experienced in/through social media platforms – emphasizes intersectionality, many self-identified BIPOC knitters find that they continue to experience disparities in their online as well as offline knitting-related adventures. Their testaments to this effect, however, are found antagonistic by some.

Oftentimes, these testimonies are perceived as merely "angry," even when their anger is directed toward the systemic injustices of their social worlds. This reminds me of Audre Lorde's piece on the "Uses of Anger," in which she notes, "Women responding to racism means women responding to anger; the anger of exclusion, of unquestioned privilege, of racial distortions, of silence, ill-use, stereotyping, defensiveness, misnaming, betrayal, and cooptation." She continues,

> My anger is a response to racist attitudes and to the actions and presumptions that arise out of those attitudes. If your dealings with other women reflect those attitudes, then my anger and your attendant fears are spotlights that can be used for growth in the same way I have used learning to express anger for my growth. But for corrective surgery, not guilt. Guilt and defensiveness are bricks in a wall against which we all flounder; they serve none of our futures.
>
> (Lorde 1984, 117)

Yet, the pedagogical promise of "speaking out of anger" is not always realized in a way that Lorde has cautioned. The exchange between women, in such cases, reminds me of one of the scenarios Audre Lorde presents, involving her exchanges with white women:

I speak out of direct and particular anger at an academic conference, and a white woman says, 'Tell me how you feel but don't say it too harshly or I cannot hear you.' But is it my manner that keeps her from hearing, or the threat of a message that her life may change?

(Lorde 1984, 118)

Many knitters of color express that their manner of engagement is met with "tone policing" from white women – a popular vernacular term used in discussing racism (Nuru and Arendt 2019), "when someone (usually the privileged person) in a conversation or situation about oppression shifts the focus of the conversation from the oppression being discussed to the way it is being discussed" (Oluo 2019). This is also echoed in larger discussions around race and other issues of social (and in particular, gendered) inequality: great deal of "back talk" has been branded as "cancel culture" or "call-out culture" (Nagle 2017) by its critics.

The work of anti-racist activism, as well as the labor of moderating online discussions, is disproportionately undertaken by women of color (Lawson 2020; Nakamura 2015). Relatedly, this labor also involves encountering and countering accusations of perpetuating a "cancel culture," or the dismissal of such efforts as "identity politics," especially by individuals, groups, and publications leaning conservatively. This also leads to BIPOC individuals receiving personal attacks in comments or private messages. Nakamura (2015) talks about an emotional toll of moderating online discussions, that reminds me of Audre Lorde's conversation with Adrienne Rich (1981), in which Lorde recalls a period during which she taught (mostly white) students a class on racism in education. "…I began to feel by the end of two terms that there ought to be someone white doing this. It was terribly costly emotionally" (Lorde and Rich 1981, 725) she says.

These labors and injuries of engaging in anti-racist activism, especially by BIPOC women, are nonetheless also accompanied by followership and admiration, and in some instances, visible change. Several anti-racist knitter influencers' accounts have thousands or tens of thousands of followers, with many people posting their acknowledgement and gratitude, and sometimes making payments to "Patreon" or "buying ko-fi" toward these individuals. I observe many other knitters engaging in activism – online as well as offline, including financial support to anti-racist organizations, participating in marches, writing to politicians, in response to calls from BIPOC knitter-influencers. Various knitting-related organizations (such as publications, festivals, online/offline courses) have responded to calls for inclusion.[5] This has, however, also brought about a debate of what has been referred to as "performative allyship[6]" within the knitting community. An incisive argument here is that one does not become "anti-racist" by reading anti-racist books or by hiring a diversity consultant to the workplace or by "tokenizing" racialized individuals in their daily experiences and encounters (see, e.g., the platform https://www.unfinishedobject.com/).

These processes highlight or generate new market spaces as well as entrepreneurial opportunities for various actors. Some BIPOC designers, knitters, or other actors in the field of knitting have gained visibility and also economic capital. There are online political activists (or influencers) who offer paid content or consultancies through social media (e.g., membership on Patreon). On the one hand, this can be seen as an adoption of a marketplace logic by political activists – on the other, it is also possible to read this as a way to adopt the marketplace to further a political agenda. Manuals, workbooks, or other publications that are geared at the "lay audience" draw upon the intellectual heritage of Black feminist thought – and sometimes also cite them in their posts or books – and these publications and their reverberations on social media seem to generate new experts on Racism and Diversity. The popularity of some of these books – as well as the fact that some that have been written by white women – is accompanied by well-paid career paths as "speaker" or "educator." This also deserves attention in terms of marketplace appropriation of radical concepts in a way that is relevant to organizational and market-based "woke-washing" (Sobande 2019). Whether this form of activism may be compatible with anti-racist ideals that seek to expose the racial foundations of capitalism also deserves thought in relation to the longstanding discussions on marketplace co-optation of radical or oppositional ideologies (see, e.g., Heath and Potter 2004).

"Other" marginalities and axes of domination

Other issues of marginality that have been discussed in the knitting communities included body-size and weight stigma, economic access in relation to prices of patterns as well as independently produced/dyed yarns, and disability-related access.

Discussions on body-size issues especially deserve attention, as it is one that cuts across different crafts and "maker" communities, and has also reverberations with discussions related to inclusion in the mainstream fashion world (Scaraboto and Fischer 2013). In the knitting world, the discussion has ranged from the lack of patterns that extend to some of the larger sizes; the lack of representation of fat bodies as models for knitwear, on pattern pages, in knitting magazines and other visual media, as well as accessibility to physical spaces (Cieslak 2020). An intersectional lens to these discussions allows us to notice how racialization or other axes of marginalization may change the experience of weight stigma (Cieslak 2020). Commenters have drawn attention to fatphobia having a racial origin, citing sociologist Sabrina Strings' work "Fearing the Black Body: The Racial Origins of Fat Phobia" (2019) which historically traces colonialist beauty ideals including being "svelte" and having an "ascetic aesthetic" and argue for the recognition of this history in explaining fatphobia and size-based marketplace exclusion as it is experienced today.

A criticism I saw voiced during discussions on size inclusivity was that many white knitters – some who have not been active in discussing racism, have, on the other hand, been comfortable discussing inclusivity in relation to body-size, as well as some of the other issues brought up in the knitting community, including yarn and pattern pricing,[7] as well as the (in)accessibility of knitting spaces to disabled individuals.[8] These debates draw attention to not only the variety of disagreements and debates that take place within the social spaces of knitting, but also to the disparities in terms of the "battles" that the mainstream knitting culture is willing to fight.

These have been discussions that took place and caught my eye in waves (sometimes in cycles, waning and waxing again). While my intention has not been to conduct an extensive "archaeology" of knitting-related discussions, one thing that I have noticed is the less visibility of various positionalities, even within the discussions based on intersectional perspective or critical frameworks. One point that has been voiced by a few is that there is less visibility of (visibly) Muslim or other minority knitters of religious minority groups (situated in North America/Europe and beyond) and their perspectives on inclusion–exclusion: an interesting dynamic, as especially in Europe, racialization often takes place at the confluence of ethno-religious identities. Echoing

Weinberger's (2015) findings on social boundaries and relational difficulties experienced by non-participation in Christmas in the USA; some Jewish knitters have expressed feeling frustrated at the emphasis on Christmas-related knitting traditions (especially "advent calendar" activities), but also in some cases, being subject to anti-Semitic racism within their knitting groups. Another point of interest is the dominance of a North American Black feminist perspective within critical knitting circles – which also echoes Sobande's (2019) findings in her research with Black British women, who may have followed different historical trajectories into the UK and thereby possess different situated knowledges that are aligned with/conducive to different critical epistemologies. Some thoughts that this work and my (somewhat limited) observations of "non-participation" in knitting cultures leads to, for example, the question of to what extent might intellectual lineages of Intersectionality be also compatible or conciliatory with other critical/decolonial/Islamic/secular (and the list goes on) feminist movements (see, e.g., Lugones 2010; Thomas 2020)? How can these different intellectual traditions, and different forms of situatedness be resources for coalitions rather than barriers toward it?

My continued bodily entanglements

I continue to carry the joy of knitting, which seems to be shared across the political divisions, the forms of engagement with activism, across social media platforms and physical spaces. If there is one thing that unites this practice, it is this *joy*, this exuberance in the "making" of objects and wearing and exchanging them. I knit on trains and sometimes exchange smiles and knowing glances with other passengers who are knitting – during one memorable train journey, we were three women (strangers to each other) with seats around the same table in the silent section, knitting in quiet companionship. One Danish women commented on how "hyggelig" (loosely translated, cozy) this trip was, as we were leaving the train. Knitting made me feel less *strange* in that encounter. However, knowing what I know from my online explorations, I can't help but feel fragmented about my knitting.

I am an immigrant and am coded as non-white in Denmark, yet I have privileges that are not always shared by other people of my background. I was not raised in Denmark, and am not fluent in the Danish language, but rather, communicate in English at yarn shops. I am usually not immediately categorized as an immigrant, an *invanderer*, but as a "foreigner." Upon hearing of my Turkish background, I have heard expressions of surprise from people in various walks of society, including one woman who saw me knitting on the train, asked me about my project, and as we continued to talk she admitted that I was the first "educated" person of Turkish background she had ever conversed with. My experiences in yarn shops and knitting groups have been cordial and pleasant, with shop assistants sometimes complimenting my knitwear. Not having had conversations or done fieldwork with other BIPOC knitters in Denmark, I cannot claim to have a comprehensive understanding of racialized encounters in the Danish knitting scene. However, based on scholarship problematizing the integration of migrants in Danish society (Rytter 2019; Wren 2001), as well as my own research in commercial spaces in Denmark (Kuruoğlu and Woodward 2021), there is evidence of ways – sometimes more visible, oftentimes more subtle – through which public and commercial spaces accommodate or hinder individuals of different ethnic/racial backgrounds, to different extents and in different ways.

In lieu of a conclusion

Knitting offers joy and relaxation to many who engage in it, but not all aspects and spaces of knitting are joyful, and not everyone who wants to be involved in this craft as a social practice is able to do so in equal ways. While knitters have been challenging the dichotomies of the domestic-immanent vs. public-transcendent divide (a la de Beauvoir) and have been extending their bodies (Young 1980) into all kinds of spaces, the dominant masculine culture is not the only wall that they hit. Some bodies are not cozily enveloped by knitting communities, and some clothes do not "fit" the knitters' bodies. Spaces fold onto bodies, bodies tear into clothes. Some bodies are seen as invasive (Puwar 2004), and as disrupting the "straight lines" (Ahmed 2006) of the knitting community, veering it into political discussions that some of its participants do not want to have. Within this community, not every body is deemed "knitworthy" (to borrow a phrase and hashtag used by knitter-activists, including Jacqueline Cieslak)) in the community – and this is a challenge that in itself simultaneously generates solidarity as well as fault lines.

Gender-sensitive approaches in consumer research have focused on the potentiality for, as well as limitations of, solidarity and social action in online (Matich, Ashman and Parsons 2019; Scaraboto and Fischer 2013) as well as physical spaces (Maciel and Wallendorf 2021), but these accounts have attended less to the inequalities, disagreements, and challenges within these action-communities. The lack of an intersectional agenda within some of these movements has been noted (Matich, Ashman and Parsons 2019) and deserves a closer gaze. Without gaining deeper insights into these challenges, it is hard to argue for a "transformative" (Steinfield et al. 2019) potential or capacity of feminism, intersectionality, or other critical theories in the market or within institutions (Ahmed 2012). Moreover, even approaches such as intersectionality or decoloniality, which are cognizant of the hierarchies of power and knowledge, may become buzzwords that signal that 'something' is being done – but that 'something' becomes non-performative (Ahmed 2004) as it does not perform the output that its utterances would signify (Butler 1997).

In the conversation between Audre Lorde and Adrienne Rich, there is a snippet that I have been carrying with me. Lorde invokes the imaginary conversations she has with Rich, mentioning that she writes them down in her journal and that these come across in her published writings as well – because "stereotypically or symbolically these conversations occur in a space of black woman/white woman, where it's beyond Adrienne and Audre, almost as if we're two voices" (Lorde and Rich 1981, 731). Lorde goes on to say how there are different pitfalls, and remembers a phone conversation in which Rich impatiently said to her "It's not enough to say to me that you intuit it." Lorde explains how this, despite Rich's intentions, came across as a "total wipeout of my modus, my way of perceiving and formulating." Rich defends herself, saying it was not a wipeout of Lorde's modus, but a request for "documentation," as she "simply cannot assume that I know what you know, unless you show me what you mean." Lorde then counters that this request for documentation has been, for her, "a questioning of my perceptions, an attempt to devalue what I'm in the process of discovering." This conversation has been valuable to me in unpacking some of the discussions and interactions around race and exclusion in the social field of knitting as well as beyond: the burden of providing documentation falling upon the Black woman – but the white woman also, with good intentions, not wanting to collapse the Black woman's experience with her own and the difficulty of finding the common ground: A difficulty that persists, even between two women whose friendship emanates off the pages.

Notes

1 https://www.ravelry.com/content/no-trump.
2 https://fringeassociation.com/2019/01/07/2019-my-year-aof-color/.
3 My entry into the field of testimonies I draw from was initiated by my observations on Instagram. However, in this chapter I choose not to directly reference Instagram posts or stories, as these require membership to the platform. I only do so to the extent that these texts have been shared (with their owners' consent) on other forms of media, such as magazine articles. Moreover, some of the accounts I followed have become private or have changed usernames – thus making me aware that privacy and anonymity might be an issue.
4 https://www.youtube.com/watch?v=cm6MFKZOccE.
5 For example, the periodical *Vogue Knitting* now has a diversity advisory council.
6 The term performative has increasingly become used in lieu of "fake" or "false" allyship for personal gain (see, e.g., Saad 2020). "Performative" here seems to refer to what Sara Ahmed terms "non-performative", in that the words fail to perform the resignification of racial hierarchies that is promised by the allyship, and is actually not an instance of true solidarity. In this sense, this term of "performative allyship" also aligns with "ornamental intersectionality" (Bilge 2011; Nash 2017).
7 For example, https://www.reddit.com/r/craftsnark/comments/hrnmk0/can_we_have_a_conversation_about_yarn_cost_with/.
8 For example, https://www.reddit.com/r/knitting/comments/i2qmuk/thoughts_on_ravelry_accessibility_controversy/.

References

Ahmed, S. 2000. Strange encounters: Embodied others in post-coloniality. London: Routledge
Ahmed, S. 2004. The Cultural Politics of Emotion. Edinburgh: Edinburgh University Press.
Ahmed, S. 2006. Queer phenomenology: Orientations, objects, others. Durham, NC: Duke University Press.
Ahmed, S. 2012. On being included: Racism and diversity in institutional life. Durham, NC: Duke University Press.
Ahmed, S. 2014. Willful subjects. Durham, NC: Duke University Press.
Anzaldua, G. 1987. Borderlands/La frontera: The new mestiza. San Francisco, CA: Aunt Lute Books.
Bardhi, F., and G.M. Eckhardt. 2017. "Liquid consumption". Journal of Consumer Research 44(3), 582–597.
Benjamin, R. 2019. Race after technology: Abolitionist tools for the new Jim code. New York: John Wiley & Sons.
Bilge, S. 2013. "Intersectionality undone? Saving intersectionality from feminist intersectionality studies". Du Bois Review 10(2): 405–424.
Black, S. 2017. "KNIT+ RESIST: Placing the Pussyhat project in the context of craft activism". Gender, Place & Culture 24(5): 696–710.
Boylorn, R.M. 2008. "As seen on TV: An autoethnographic reflection on race and reality television" Critical Studies in Media Communication 25(4): 413–433.
Bratich, J.Z., and H.M. Brush. 2011. "Fabricating activism: Craft-work, popular culture, gender. Utopian Studies 22(2), 233–260.
Butler, J.P. 1997. Excitable speech: A politics of the performative. New York: Routledge.
Carastathis, A. 2013. "Identity categories as potential coalitions". Signs: Journal of Women in Culture and Society 38(4): 941–965.
Chatzidakis, A., P. Maclaran, and R. Varman. 2021. "The regeneration of consumer movement solidarity". Journal of Consumer Research. doi: 10.1093/jcr/ucab007
Cieslak, J. 2020. "Liminal bodies". Pompom Magazine, 32. https://pompommag.com/blogs/blog/liminal-bodies
Collins, P.H. 2002. Black feminist thought: Knowledge, consciousness, and the politics of empowerment. New York: Routledge.

Collins, P.H. 2019. Intersectionality as critical social theory. Durham, NC: Duke University Press.
Collins, P. H., and Bilge, S. 2016. Intersectionality. Chicester: John Wiley & Sons.
Daniels, J. 2013. "Race and racism in Internet studies: A review and critique". New Media & Society 15(5): 695–719.
Cottom, T.M. 2020. "Where platform capitalism and racial capitalism meet: The sociology of race and racism in the digital society" Sociology of Race and Ethnicity 6(4): 441–449.
Crenshaw, K. W. 1989. "Demarginalizing the Intersection of Race and Sex: A Black Feminist Critique of Antidiscrimination Doctrine". University of Chicago Legal Forum, 1989: 139–168.
Crockett, D., S.A. Grier, and J.A. Williams. 2003. "Coping with marketplace discrimination: An exploration of the experiences of black men". Academy of Marketing Science Review 4(7): 1–21.
de Beauvoir, S. 1948. The ethics of ambiguity. Trans. Bernard Frechtman. Secaucus, NJ: Citadel Press.
de Certeau, M. 1984. The practice of everyday life. Berkeley: University of California Press.
Donnor, J.K., and G. Ladson-Billings. 2017. "Critical race theory and postracial imaginary". In The Sage handbook of qualitative research, edited by N.K. Denzin & Y.S. Lincoln, 5th ed., pp. 195–213. Thousand Oaks, CA: Sage.
Eguchi, S. 2015. "Queer intercultural relationality: An autoethnography of Asian–Black (dis)connections in white gay America" Journal of International and Intercultural Communication 8(1): 27–43.
Ekpo, A.E., B. DeBerry-Spence, G.R. Henderson, and J. Cherian. 2018. "Narratives of technology consumption in the face of marketplace discrimination". Marketing Letters 29(4): 451–463.
Firat, A.F., and A. Venkatesh. 1995. "Liberatory postmodernism and the reenchantment of consumption". Journal of Consumer Research 22(3) 239–267.
Garcia, S E. 2020. Where did BIPOC come from. The New York Times, 17 June 2020.
Goitom, M. 2019. "'Legitimate knowledge': An auto-ethnographical account of an African writing past the white gaze in academia". Social Epistemology 33(3): 193–204.
Gökarıksel, B., and S. Smith. 2017. "Intersectional feminism beyond US flag hijab and pussy hats in Trump's America" Gender, Place & Culture 24(5): 628–644.
Griffin, R.A. 2012. "I am an angry black woman: Black feminist autoethnography, voice, and resistance". Women's Studies in Communication 35(2): 138–157.
Heath, J., and A. Potter. 2004. The rebel sell: Why the culture can't be jammed. New York: HarperCollins.
hooks, b. 1981/2015. Ain't I a woman?: Black women and feminism. New York: Routledge.
hooks, b. 1986. "Talking back". Discourse Fall-Winter 86/87: 123–128.
Kuruoğlu, A.P., and G. Ger, 2015. "An emotional economy of mundane objects". Consumption Markets & Culture 18(3): 209–238.
Kuruoğlu, A.P., and I. Woodward. 2021. "Textures of diversity: Socio-material arrangements, atmosphere, and social inclusion in a multi-ethnic neighbourhood". Journal of Sociology 57(1): 111–127.
Lawson, C.E. 2020. "Skin deep: Callout strategies, influencers, and racism in the online beauty community". New Media & Society. doi: 10.1177/1461444820904697
Lemieux, J. 2017. "Why I'm skipping the women's march on Washington". Color Lines, January 17. https://www.colorlines.com/articles/why-im-skipping-womens-march-washington-opinion
Literat, I., and S. Markus. 2020. "'Crafting a way forward': Online participation, craftivism and civic engagement in Ravelry's Pussyhat project group". Information, Communication & Society 23(10): 1411–1426.
Lorde, A. 1984. Sister outsider. New York: Random House.
Lorde, A., and A. Rich. 1981. "An Interview with Audre Lorde". Signs: Journal of Women in Culture and Society 6(4): 713–736.

Lugones, M. 2010. "Toward a decolonial feminism". Hypatia 25(4): 742–759.
Maciel, A.F., and M. Wallendorf. 2021. "Space as a resource in the politics of consumer identity". Journal of Consumer Research. doi: 10.1093/jcr/ucab002/6117380
Matich, M., R. Ashman, and E. Parsons. 2019. "# freethenipple–Digital activism and embodiment in the contemporary feminist movement". Consumption Markets & Culture 22(4): 337–362.
Massey, D. 1996. Space, place and gender. Oxford: Polity Press.
May, K. 2020. "The Pussyhat project: Texturing the struggle for feminist solidarity". Journal of International Women's Studies 21(3): 77–89.
Mirza, H. S. 2009. "Plotting a History: Black and Postcolonial Feminisms in 'new times'". Race Ethnicity and Education, 12(1): 1–10.
Monk-Payton, B. 2017. "# LaughingWhileBlack: Gender and the comedy of social media blackness". Feminist Media Histories 3(2): 15–35.
Nagle, A. 2017. Kill all normies: Online culture wars from 4chan and Tumblr to Trump and the alt-right. New Alresford: John Hunt Publishing.
Nakamura, L. 2015. "The unwanted labour of social media: Women of colour call out culture as venture community management". New Formations 86: 106–112.
Noble, S.U. 2018. Algorithms of oppression: How search engines reinforce racism. New York: NYU Press.
Nuru, A.K., and C.E. Arendt. 2019. "Not so safe a space: Women activists of color's responses to racial microaggressions by white women allies". Southern Communication Journal 84(2): 85–98.
Oluo, I. 2019. So you want to talk about race. Paris: Hachette.
Ono, K. 1997. "A letter/essay I've been longing to write in my personal/academic voice". Western Journal of Communication 61: 114–125.
Pérez Huber, L., and D.G. Solorzano. 2015. "Racial microaggressions as a tool for critical race research". Race Ethnicity and Education 18(3): 297–320.
Pierce, C. 1969. "Is Bigotry the basis of the medical problem of the Ghetto?" In Medicine in the Ghetto, edited by J. Norman, 301–314. New York: Meredith Corporation.
Puwar, N. 2004. Space invaders: Race, gender and bodies out of place. Oxford: Berg.
Puwar, N. 2020. "Carrying as method: Listening to bodies as archives". Body & Society. doi: 10.1177/1357034X20946810
Rose-Redwood, C., and R. Rose-Redwood. 2017. "'It definitely felt very white': Race, gender, and the performative politics of assembly at the women's march in Victoria, British Columbia". Gender, Place & Culture 24(5): 645–654.
Rytter, M. 2019. "Writing against integration: Danish imaginaries of culture, race and belonging". Ethnos 84(4): 678–697.
Saad, L. 2020. Me and white supremacy: How to recognise your privilege, combat racism and change the world. Paris: Hachette.
Saxena, J. 2019. "The knitting community is reckoning with racism" https://www.vox.com/the-goods/2019/2/25/18234950/knitting-racism-instagram-stories
Scaraboto, D., and E. Fischer. 2013. "Frustrated fatshionistas: An institutional theory perspective on consumer quests for greater choice in mainstream markets". Journal of Consumer Research 39(6): 1234–1257.
Sloan, J. 2019. "Black people do knit". Knitting Magazine, 187. https://www.jeanettesloandesign.com/blackpeopledoknit.html
Sobande, F. 2017. "Watching me watching you: Black women in Britain on YouTube". European Journal of Cultural Studies 20(6): 655–671.
Sobande, F. 2019. "Woke-washing: 'Intersectional' femvertising and branding 'woke' bravery". European Journal of Marketing 54(11): 2723–2745.
Sobande, F., A. Fearfull, and D. Brownlie. 2020. "Resisting media marginalisation: Black women's digital content and collectivity". Consumption Markets & Culture 23(5): 413–428.

Steinfield, L., M. Sanghvi, L.T. Zayer, C.A. Coleman, N. Ourahmoune, R.L., Harrison, W. Hein, and J. Brace-Govan, 2019. "Transformative intersectionality: Moving business towards a critical praxis". Journal of Business Research 100: 366–375.

Strings, S. 2019. Fearing the black body: The racial origins of fat phobia. New York: NYU Press.

Thomas, K.B. 2020. "Intersectionality and epistemic erasure: A caution to decolonial feminism". Hypatia 35(3): 509–523.

Tonkiss, F. 2004. "Urban cultures: Spatial tactics". In Urban culture: Critical concepts in literary and cultural studies, edited by C. Jenks, 236–248. London: Routledge.

Weinberger, M.F. 2015. "Dominant consumption rituals and intragroup boundary work: How non-celebrants manage conflicting relational and identity goals". Journal of Consumer Research 42(3): 378–400.

Williams-Johnson, D. 2020. "See me, not just what I knit". https://www.moderndailyknitting.com/2020/06/05/danas-edit-see-me-not-just-what-i-knit/

Wren, K. 2001. "Cultural racism: Something rotten in the state of Denmark?". Social & Cultural Geography 2(2): 141–162.

Young, I.M. 1980. "Throwing like a girl: A phenomenology of feminine body comportment motility and spatiality". Human Studies 3(1): 137–156.

17 Marketing and the missing feminisms

Decolonial feminism, and the Arab Spring

Nacima Ourahmoune and Hounaida El Jurdi

In this chapter, we participate in addressing the issue of "missing feminisms" (Hearn and Hein 2015; Maclaran 2015; Scott 2017) in marketing and the consideration of gender issues in non-Western contexts per the recent calls from marketing journals special issues (Dobscha and Ostberg 2021). More specifically, we focus on the MENA region as a missing and misrepresented gendered space within the marketing and gender literature. In this meta-region, gender activism and feminisms are mobilized by various actors while they remain perceived as either exotic and estranged to Western challenges, or modernizing only when conformed to Western thoughts. The "Arab Spring," as referred to by Western media, shows women and men invariably asking for rights, including rights in relation to gender justice even though the revolutions were not centered on gender issues (El-Jurdi and Ourahmoune 2021). Examining the Arab Spring phenomenon in various countries, we witness a variety of references to feminisms by different actors not necessarily intra-regionally and in an ideologically fragmented space as well. While commonalities can be noted, we invite scholars to consider socio-historic realities within the meta-region to depart from distortions and simplifications that echo and reproduce colonial discourses about the homogenous Other, the Orient. We will first show how women in the Global South and local feminisms are a missing conversation in marketing scholarship, we will follow up with how social movements lack a gender lens in marketing after focusing our chapter on decolonial feminism and Arab feminisms as two interrelated constructs that are under-mobilized in marketing and feminist scholarship. Marketplace phenomena are entangled with gender justice issues and require an enlargement of our current repertoire of references at a moment where decolonizing research has become a trans-disciplinary concern.

Introduction

When examining the history of marketing (see Maclaran, 2015) we see how first-, second-, and third-wave feminisms traverse the discipline with rich debates, leading fruitful insights for theory and practice. We also note that these insights share common concepts and sites of investigations that focus predominantly on Anglo-Saxon and European contexts, yet how these concepts transfer to realities outside these cultural spaces has been little discussed. This is not only true of gender and feminism research in marketing, but also of marketing and consumer research constructs. In the pursuit of knowledge and inclusivity, these must be examined in other cultural contexts. Jafari et al. (2012) labeled Non-Western contexts as the 'invisible half' in marketing and encouraged scholars to dig into other realities to solidify and innovate in terms of marketing knowledge production. As Karababa (2012) notes, "A very common but futile practice in scientific research investigating non-western consumer cultures and markets is the imposition of concepts that are derived from a single historical trajectory of western modernization."

This is particularly problematic as we witness macro-level transformations in emerging economies when it comes to gender relations, with strong implications for marketing. This disconnect between the changing socio-political spaces and the marketplace, and the paucity of marketing research at the intersection of gender and emerging economies contexts creates an opportunity to question taken-for-granted phenomena and assumptions. This disconnect also evokes an urge to build new knowledge, knowledge that is non-Anglo/European centric, which will enrich the discipline and benefit societies. For instance, according to a Boston Consulting Group (Zakrewski et al. 2020) report,

> The expected rise in women's wealth in the Middle East is especially noteworthy. Greater political and economic stability across the region and improving healthcare and educational access for women are fanning the expected 9% CAGR. Girls' rates of primary and secondary school participation are now similar to boys', and women outnumber men at the university level in 15 of 22 Arab countries. Women are making the most of these educational opportunities. In Bahrain, for example, girls consistently make up the majority of top-ten high school graduates, based on academic performance.

We note a range of marketing studies tackle gender issues with a sociocultural standpoint in emerging economies. For instance, the gendered structure and agency interplay that inform gendered power issues behind fashion (Ourahmoune and Özçağlar-Toulouse 2012), Joy, Belk and Bhardwaj's (2015) discussion of sexual assault in India, the normalizing of sexual violence against women in India (Varman et al. 2018), the transformative gender justice framework and the case of sex tourism in the Dominican Republic (Hein et al. 2016), and the power issues involved in the contraception market in Uganda (Steinfield et al. 2019). While these studies signal a need to further unpack the relationship between feminism, gender, and marketing in Non-Western contexts, we note a wealth of social marketing research on issues relating to women in the Global South. Still, a critical approach and a consideration for cultural contexts and socio-historical processes are lacking. The application of Western constructs without considering local knowledge can lead to unintended consequences. For example, social marketing research and practice has contributed to the solidification of the idea of the "poor woman" from the global south who lacks agency, is dependent, and needs saving by international/Western intervention and knowledge. This invariably reproduces colonial discourses and scholars outside marketing call for decolonizing knowledge and practices. Marketing areas such as social marketing tend to either ignore or freeze women from the Global South in the colonized, passive position, and feminisms discussed in marketing do not evoke or build from third world feminisms, postcolonial, or decolonial feminisms. Issues of gender politics, stigma, and gender equality (Gurrieri et al. 2013), power (Brace-Govan 2015), unintended consequences (Peattie et al. 2016), and non-Western voices (Badejo et al. 2019) are now emerging.

The aim of the chapter is to introduce decolonial feminism and the relationship with Arab feminisms. This will help show how women who live in the Arab world, while faced with patriarchal issues, are not yet passive victims but rather active with traditional modes of resistance and at the forefront of digitally led revolutions.

Decolonial feminism

Feminism is not a monolith movement. Just as feminism has evolved from the first wave to subsequent waves, we do not speak of feminism but of feminisms; white, postcolonial, inter-sectional, Marxist, and most recently decolonial feminism, among others. These evolved approaches have not made their way into marketing scholarship despite the increasing interest in feminist and gender-related research in marketing. Why are such perspectives important? Decolonial feminist approaches argue that it is important to recognize the feminisms involved in any given context. After all, women are not a monolithic category, hence attempts to "empower" them as a monolithic category fail to recognize the social, cultural, and historical traditions and experiences of women from non-dominant categories, thereby essentializing marginalized women and women from the global south (Lugones 2010; Tlostanova 2010).

Despite the presence of multiple feminisms and multiple perspectives, there are two main constants across various feminist positions: the first is the idea of subordination or oppression of women as a gender. This is explained by the existence of a gendered and structural system of power that puts men in control of social, political, and cultural institutions. This invariably produces a gendered construction of knowledge about the social order and results in a gendered system of power. The second view is the need for a social movement to bring women together to challenge and overturn the order of power they are subjected to. However, to achieve this, a critical stance must be taken since not all women are subject to similar forms of subjugation and this goes beyond intersectionality (Asher 2013). For example, postcolonial feminists call for the study of gender-related power structures in postcolonial nations under the structures left by colonialism (Spivack 1988). In such contexts, women suffer from subjugation in a twofold way – imperialism and male dominance.

Decolonial feminism builds on intersectional forms of feminism such as black feminism, postcolonial feminism, and post-structural feminism to question the unity and equality of all women (Lugones 2010, 2014). Decolonial feminism questions the project of modernity and opposes the salvationist claim of classical feminism given its complicity with coloniality. Indigenous feminists (see, e.g. the works of Aileen Moreton-Robinson, and Linda Tahuwai-Smith to name a few) provide a deep analysis of historical conditions that give rise to social organizations that sustain and enforce hierarchical structures of subjugation. They argue that such structures are not only explained by gender, emphasizing power structures of privilege in addition to the lack of diversity and inclusion within the classical feminist movements. In other words, classical feminist approaches reproduce modernist colonial discourses; hence, the oppression and subordination of women in the global south cannot be explained only in terms of patriarchy.

Decolonial feminists highlight the complicity of Eurocentric feminism in feeding on colonialist structures and overshadow local movements that draw attention to the possibility of other meanings of communal life. Lugones (2010, 2014) argues that understanding the power matrix of overlapping oppressions and profiting from counter-hegemonic knowledge is necessary for the success of the emancipatory project. Rather than thinking of intersections of racism and gender oppression, Lugones conceives of oppression in terms of a matrix – the racist modern/colonial gender matrix. Lugones (2010, 2014) points out that decolonial feminism lies at the intersection of intersectionality, the coloniality of power, the coloniality of knowledge, and the coloniality of being. Hence, engaging with indigenous knowledge and the voices of the subaltern and the marginalized is central to understanding gender systems in the global south and how they are shaped by coloniality. For example, Rodriguez Moreno (2018) argues that the colonial project maintains its continuity through public policies for gender equality through the apparatus of development aid. Rodriguez shows that discourses on gender equality and public gender policy at the national level – reflect colonial gender discourses and technologies.

Arab feminisms

"Arab" is a non-homogenous category, and this invariably applies to gender issues and feminisms in the Arab world. To assume that all Arab women face similar experiences and levels of oppression would be a fallacy; for their conditions and experiences are shaped by different socio-cultural histories (Abukhalil 1993). Arab countries also exhibit diversity of cultures and religions and lack uniformity in social and economic conditions. The subjugation of women in the Arab world has its roots in tribalism, colonialism, local culture, as well as religion (Bryan 2012). In any discussion of gender issues in the Arab world there is a need for a comparative approach to underline the similarities and the differences in the lives and conditions of Arab women.

Cultural, historical, economic, and social debates influence and shape the principles underlying the work produced by feminists in the Arab and Islamic worlds, and feminist Arabs have made great contributions to theory and practice (Valassopoulos 2010); see, for example, the works of Saadawi, Mernissi, Moghissi, Abulughod, and Mughaddam to name a few. In other words, we do not speak of Arab feminism but rather of Arab feminisms; for there are the works of Islamic Arab feminists, secular Arab feminists, queer Arab feminists, etc. For example, Islamic feminism is grounded in the Quran as a guiding text, whereas secular feminism draws on secular universal discourses for gender equality (Badran 2005). Queer Arab feminism calls for the inclusion of the experiences of non-binary genders that are specific to the Arab world (Hamdan 2015a,b).

Furthermore, the debate about the locus of feminist change – women's organizations or national governments – demarcates regional variations in Arab women's organizing strategies. For example, feminists from Lebanon and from the Gulf disagree about the role national governments could play in improving the status of women and in advancing feminist agendas (Robinson 2016). Lebanese activist Jean Said Makdisi describes how the language of women's rights has been appropriated by governments and political forces for political gains. On the other hand, gulf activists Hatoon Ajwad el-Fassi and Suad Zayed al-Oraimi argue that national governments have a lot of potential in helping secure women's rights.

Arab women face many challenges. For example, the link between Arab women's liberation, national liberation, and the modernization project has always been a double-edged sword (Abukhalil 1993). Women in the Arab world have always been burdened with the impossible task of simultaneously being both the icons of tradition and the trail-blazers of modernity; or in other words, to be "modern but modest" (6). It also meant that any discussion of women's status in society inevitably became a discussion of something else: national identity; the relation with the West; the necessity or lack of safeguarding cultural specificity; how to emulate the Western model of modernity while fighting Western colonialism, etc. Invariably, this symbolic dimension of the "woman question" contributed to the complication of women's liberation struggle. Also, that women were responsible for their own advancement while maintaining their traditional social role in Arab society has been another obstacle. Gender issues in the Arab world are further stifled by the "cultural authenticity" argument – used to constrain women's rights by arguing that they are incompatible with cultural values.

In addressing cultural, political, and social factors particular to the Arab world and to Arab women, with an eye to feminism as it is practiced globally, Arab feminists have shown that a productive Arab feminism needs to engage both nationally and transnationally (Moghissi 2005). A strong women's rights movement in the Arab world requires the production of local knowledge on women and gender in Arab cultural history. The socio-historical origins of prejudices against women and the nature of power relations that shape and are shaped by the cultural norms and structures need to be unearthed. Dominant cultural discourses on Arab women, regionally and internationally, whether shaped by neo-colonial, nationalist, or Islamist discourses, are often manipulated for political agendas (El-Sadda 2020). They feed on reductionist stereotypes of the Arab woman who lacks agency and overlook cultural diversity in the region. Western assumptions of Arab women's complicity have also been critiqued by Arab feminist scholars (Kandiyoti 1988; Lengel 1997, 2004), and re-interpreted from local and post-colonial perspectives as using Western standards to interpret something that had to be understood from the Othered point of view (Abouzeid 2008; Abu Lughod 2001; Mohanty 1986; Said 1978).

Women in the Arab world are often held to "moral standards" in the name of religion and tradition. Deniz Kandiyoti (1991) insists that women in the Middle East must not be studied in terms of an

> undifferentiated "Islam" or Islamic culture but rather through the differing political projects of nation-states, with their distinct histories, relationships to colonialism and the West, class politics, ideological uses of an Islamic idiom, and struggles over the role of Islamic law in state legal apparatuses.
>
> (p. 5)

Moghissi (2005) argues that changes to social and political policies toward women need to be read and understood as arising from specific interpretations of Islam that come into contact with varying economic, historical, and contextual specificities and realities. Thus, feminist critics working from outside of this context need to be attentive to these issues rather than be uncritically drawn to signifiers that appear to reveal uncomplicated 'realities' (such as the veil, polygamy, etc.).

Arab feminists have always faced challenges related to the burden of colonialism, accusations of Westernization, isolation from their cultural heritage, and elitism, but the biggest challenge of all has been the fact that their activism and their entire lives have all been in the context of authoritarian postcolonial states (Elsadda 2020). Arab feminisms cannot be understood unless contextualized within the postcolonial legacy that shapes politics in the region and regulates political discourses. Arab feminists are continually reminded that their discourse emanates from the mindset of Western colonial powers (Elsadda 2020). The existence of long-term Western hegemony through colonial powers in the Middle East marks all political and social movements in the region, which not only look inward toward achieving change, but also look outwards, to the West, for the West provides resources and knowledge.

Arab feminisms, marketing, and the Arab Spring

The participation of women in national liberation movements in Arab countries has well been acknowledged and documented (Arenfeldt and Golley 2012). Yet, the history of Arab feminisms is a history of appropriation and negotiation with power in authoritarian postcolonial states (Elsadda 2020). Arab women's rights activists often agree to give precedence to national demands over their demand for rights. The classic example is Algeria. In 1958, as a reaction to a call by French colonialists to Algerian women asking them to burn their veils in a public square and chant Algeria is French, Algerian women wore veils as a symbolic confirmation of their national identity and immersed themselves in the struggle for independence postponing their struggle for gender rights. Despite women's huge sacrifices in the war of liberation in Algeria, they were asked by their comrades to return to their homes.

Arab women's participation in national independence movements rarely resulted in a transformation of gender relations or even into an acknowledgement of their demands after independence in postcolonial nation states. Cole and Cole (2011) explain:

> But with such bold gestures go fears. As women look to the future, they worry that on the road to new, democratic parliamentary regimes, their rights will be discarded in favor of male constituencies, whether patriarchal liberals or Muslim fundamentalists. The collective memory of how women were in the forefront of the Algerian revolution for independence from France from 1954 to 1962, only to be relegated to the margins of politics, thereafter, still weighs heavily.

Yet, that does not mean that no gains have been made in terms of transforming gender relations. The Arab Spring was a series of pro-democracy uprisings, began in early 2011, was marked by heavy participation of women. The uprisings/protests resulted in regime changes in some Arab countries and increased cultural freedoms. The protests were marked by a strong presence for activists on social media. A main slogan of the protests across the Arab world was "الشعب يريد اسقاط النظام" "the people want to bring down the regime."

Both online and in the streets, Marzouki (2011) commended the "impressive visibility of women" in demonstrations and how the revolutions were situated in contrast to "stereotypes about the 'Arab street' that propagate the image of a male-dominated public space" (p. 37). In Egypt, feminists seized the opportunity which opened-up political spaces for mobilization and activism – online and offline. They formed feminist coalitions; joined new political parties and various initiatives; organized campaigns; organized and participated in street demonstrations; participated in negotiations with official bodies and state actors to push for legal reforms and constitutional reforms; and led media campaigns to raise consciousness regarding gender justice. Despite the vilification campaigns against Egyptian right groups and the heavy closing down of political spaces, there was a positive change. One such change was breaking the taboo about sexual violence, where a law has been passed criminalizing harassment and where the topic is no longer a taboo but a social problem to be dealt with.

The impact of the Arab Spring revolutions on enhancing gender equality in the Middle East and North Africa has been challenged by multiple feminist scholars and activists, including Arab feminists (Bohn and Lynch 2011; Brown 2011; Fathi 2011; Younis 2011). To have a more nuanced understanding of the impact of the Arab Spring on Arab women, transnational and Western feminist scholars must examine and question and reflect on their role in contributing to essentializing of the Arab woman and must be aware of genuine and relevant local knowledge (Newsom et al. 2011).

The Arab Spring is said to be one of the first digitally led revolutions, yet the gendered dimensions have been largely overlooked by marketing scholars despite the heavy participation of women across contexts. During the revolutions across the Arab world, women and activists used social media to aid social change, they mobilized, produced knowledge, and shared resources online and offline (see, for instance, Al Jaber 2009; Fandy 1999; Faris 2008; Jansen 2010; Tatarchevskiy 2011; Wheeler 2009). Yet, simultaneously, both traditional and social media cite the absence of gendered revolution or gender-based social change (UPF Office of Peace and Security Affairs, 2012, February 12).

In our research on the recent revolutions in Algeria and Lebanon where we employed hermeneutic analysis of online, media, and activists' messages and images to note competing inter and intra discourses of objectification and subjectification. In media representations of the protests, whether by private media outlets or social media activists, images of women were used as icons of the uprising, as sources of empowerment, resilience, and unity. This was often juxtaposed with representations of women as synonymous with oppression, objectification, and otherness. We note an exploitation of women as catalysts for change and to sensualize the revolutions. Women and their bodies were used to legitimate and delegitimize the revolutions in competing discourses by competing actors and parties through representations, political communications, anti-revolution protestors, the media, and online and offline activists. Performances in the street were gendered, and oppression overlapped with patriarchal oppression. Women became icons of empowerment and liberation while representing oppression and exploitation.

We locate feminist activism in the Arab spring in a space of contained empowerment, specifically in the context of women's role and agency in the protests. The protests are revealed as sites where normative rules are suspended in favor of generating alternative norms that disappear after the revolutions die down. In these spaces (online and offline), gender boundaries are transgressed, and gender divides are recreated. Spaces of protests and activism are spaces for challenging corruption, power structures, and political divides, where participation in these spaces is empowering yet the spaces remain restrained by patriarchal hegemonic forces (Newsom 2004). The power in these spaces is neither patriarchal nor completely removed from patriarchy, hence it is betwixt and between these potential states. Such contained empowerment can provide the potential to generate new types of power which can be transferred to hegemonic space. Yet, this power is limited temporally – the duration of the protests and activities. The woman becomes the face of resistance but not of salvation and transformation.

For critical marketing scholars, examining closely the variety of marketplace manifestations occurring in this space in relation to feminisms is very instructive. After all, the Arab Springs were among the first digitally lead-revolutions in terms of female e-activism, starting in 2005 thereby preceding #MeToo movements. The case of Nemeena a female blogger who launched a campaign to address sexual harassment, through the silent protest of women wearing black, holding signs calling for an end to the sexual harassment in Cairo's Streets, had a major impact (Norderson 2017). She inspired thousands of Egyptian female bloggers to voice their concerns and gender issues on-line, a space where statistically they are more equally represented than in the workplace and where anonymity grants enhanced capabilities. Another interesting case is that of Aliaa Al-Mahdy, author of "A Rebel's diary" blog. Her blog mixed art, politics, and the body (naked male and female bodies) to protest oppression and express her call to freedom – political, social, and cultural. She was met with widespread condemnation from all political and revolutionary groupings for transgressing social and political boundaries. Sociologist Marwan Kraidy, in his book *The Naked Blogger of Cairo* writes "The revolutionary public sphere was hostile to a woman's sexually and politically provocative body" (Kraidy 2016, p. 160) but not the naked male body. "The uproar itself was not surprising, but its one-sidedness was startling." Furthermore, Al-Mahdy was lambasted as inauthentic politically and culturally and therefore not a "true revolutionary" because her mode of activism mimicked Western notions of sexuality that were rejected by local society.

This avant-gardist usage of digital spaces, the body, and the semiotics of signs by female consumers toward a transformative approach to gender equality aligns with the acculturation of citizens to marketing techniques for protests mobilized in recent female social movements in Chile, Mexico, the USA, France (Ourahmoune 2020). Market targeting of female consumers in Egypt and in Arab countries at large requires a nuanced understanding of both emancipatory and ultra-modern consumer patterns that emulate the West while drawing on specific local dynamics that inform gender impediments instead of the tale of passive victim. Marketing efforts need to address these transformative aspects beyond colonial hegemonic discourses or standardized campaigns that fail to connect with local representations.

Conclusions

In historically patriarchal regions, cultural, religious, and social values often do not match the values promoted by feminism as a global movement, therefore the need for recognition of local values is particularly strong (Newsom and Lengel 2003; Newsom et al. 2011). Nonetheless, the call for indigenous solutions for indigenous problems should not distract attention from the fact that women in non-Western contexts face issues that are culture bound in addition to universal issues relating to women's rights. In other words, indigenized versions of feminism should not preclude core ideas of feminism, like the right to choose or not to choose, self-autonomy, gender justice, and sexual democracy.

There is a need to engage in more research on the role of women and in the Arab Spring from a critical marketing perspective, and how marketing can support activist efforts toward social change in advancing feminist agendas across the Arab world where the effects of the revolutions are still unfolding. What needs to be kept in mind is the distinctive nature of the governance structures that will emerge after the revolutions and how patriarchal structures can be prevented from reproducing themselves, and how marketing (e.g. gendered messages and representation) can contribute to positive social transformation when it comes to gender relations and gender justice. Critical marketing scholarship should focus on how different forms of media, particularly social media, as well as various marketing practices and representations can continue to facilitate the building of feminist civil society for social transformation.

References

Abouzeid, O. 2008. *Projects of Arab women empowerment: Current status and future prospects*. Cairo: Arab Women Organization.

AbuKhalil, A. 1993. "Toward the study of women and politics in the Arab world: The debate and the reality." *Feminist Issues* 13(1): 3–22. https://doi.org/10.1007/BF02685645

Abu Lughod, L. 2001. "Orientalism and Middle East feminism." *Feminist Studies* 27 (1): 101–113.

Asher, K. 2013. "Latin American decolonial thought, or making the subaltern speak. *Geography Compass* 7(12): 832–842.

Al Jaber, H. 2009. Opening remarks. Advancing Arab women in technology leadership workshop, April 15. Retrieved from http://www.scribd.com/doc/34512014/Advancing-ArabWomen-in-Technology

Arenfeldt, P., and N. A. H. Golley, eds. 2012. *Mapping Arab women's movements: A century of transformations from within*. Oxford: Oxford University Press

Askegaard, S., and J. T. Linnet. 2011. "Towards an epistemology of consumer culture theory: Phenomenology and the context of context." *Marketing Theory* 11 (4): 381–404.

Badejo, F. A., S. Rundle-Thiele, and K. Kubacki. 2019. "Taking a wider view: A formative multi-stream approach to understanding human trafficking as a social issue in Nigeria." *Journal of Social Marketing* 9 (4): 467–484. https://doi.org/10.1108/JSOCM-10-2017-0062

Badran, M. 2005. "Between secular and Islamic feminism/s: Reflections on the Middle East and beyond." *Journal of Middle East Women's Studies* 1 (1): 6–28.

Bohn, L. E., and S. Lynch. 2011. "Women and the revolution: What does the new democratic future hold for Egyptian women?" *Foreign Policy, the Middle East Channel*, March 2. http://www.foreignpolicy.com/articles/2011/03/02/women_and_the_revolution?page=0,1

Brace-Govan, J. 2015. "Faces of power, ethical decision making and moral intensity. Reflections on the need for critical social marketing." In: Wymer, W. (eds) *Innovations in social marketing and public health communication. Applying quality of life research (best practices)*, 107–132. Springer, Cham. https://doi.org/10.1007/978-3-319-19869-9_6

Brown, W. 2011. "Is the Egyptian revolution sidelining women?" *Notebook, The Independent blogs*, March 8. http://blogs.independent.co.uk/2011/03/08/egyptian-revolution-siveliningwomen

Bryan, D. (2012). Women in the Arab world: A case of religion or culture. *E-International Relations Studies*, 2: 12.

Cole, J., and S. Cole. 2011. "An Arab Spring for women." *CBS News*, April 26. http://www.cbsnews.com/stories/2011/04/26/opinion/main20057432.shtml

Dobscha, S., and J. Ostberg. 2021. "Gender impacts: Consumption, markets, marketing and marketing organisations." *Journal of Marketing Management* 37 (3–4): 181–187. https://doi.org/10.1080/0267257X.2021.1880163

El Jurdi, H. and N. Ourahmoune (2021). "Revolution is a Woman: The Feminization of the Arab Spring." *Journal of Marketing Management* 37 (3–4): 360–363. https://doi.org/10.1080/0267257X.2021.1880162

Elsadda, Hoda. 2020. "Against all odds: A Legacy of Appropriation, Contestation, and Negotiation of Arab Feminisms in Postcolonial States." *Journal of Feminist Scholarship* 16 (Fall): 53–64. https://doi.org/10.23860/jfs.2019.16.04

Fandy, M. (1999). "CyberResistance: Saudi opposition between globalization and localization." *Comparative Study of Society and History*, 41(1), 124–147.

Faris, D. 2008. "Revolutions without revolutionaries? Network theory, Facebook, and the Egyptian blogosphere." *Arab Media and Society* 6: 1–11.

Fathi, Y. 2011. "After the revolution: Egyptian women yet to win equality." *Ahram Online*, June 12. http://english.ahram.org.eg/NewsContent/1/2/14071/Egypt/Society/After-therevolution-Egyptian-women-yet-to-win-equ.aspx

Ger, G., M. C. Suarez, and T. C. D. Nascimento. 2019. "Context and theorizing in the global south: Challenges and opportunities for an international dialogue." *BAR-Brazilian Administration Review* 16 (3), e180069. https://doi.org/10.1590/1807-7692bar2019180069.

Gurrieri, L., J. Previte, and J. Brace-Govan. 2013. "Women's bodies as sites of control: Inadvertent stigma and exclusion in social marketing." *Journal of Macromarketing* 33 (2): 128–143.

Hamdan, S. 2015a. "Becoming-Queer-Arab-activist: The case of Meem." *Kohl: A Journal for Body and Gender Research* 1(2): 66–82.

Hamdan, S. 2015b. "Re-orienting desire from with/in queer Arab shame: Conceptualizing queer Arab subjectivities through sexual difference theory in a reading of Bareed Mista3jil." *Kohl: A Journal for Gender and Body Research* 1(1): 55–69.

Hearn, J., and W. Hein. 2015. "Reframing gender and feminist knowledge construction in marketing and consumer research: missing feminisms and the case of men and masculinities." *Journal of Marketing Management* 31(15–16): 1626–1651.

Hein, W., L. Steinfield, N. Ourahmoune, C. A. Coleman, L. T. Zayer, and J. Littlefield. 2016. "Gender justice and the market: A transformative consumer research perspective." *Journal of Public Policy & Marketing* 35(2), 223–236.

Jafari, A., F. Fırat, A. Süerdem, S. Askegaard, and D. Dalli. 2012. "Non-western contexts: The invisible half." *Marketing Theory* 12 (1): 3–12.

Jansen, F. 2010. "Digital activism in the Middle East: Mapping issue networks in Egypt, Iran, Syria and Tunisia." *Knowledge Management for Development Journal* 6 (1): 37–52. https://doi.org/10.1080/19474199.2010.493854

Joy, A., R. Belk, and R. Bhardwaj. 2015. "Judith Butler on performativity and precarity: Exploratory thoughts on gender and violence in India." *Journal of Marketing Management* 31 (15–16): 1739–1745.

Kandiyoti, D., ed. 1991. *Women, Islam and the state*. Philadelphia, PA: Temple University Press.

Kandiyoti, D. 1988. "Bargaining with patriarchy." *Gender & Society*, 2(3): 274–290.

Karababa, E. 2012. "Approaching non-western consumer cultures from a historical perspective: The case of early modern Ottoman consumer culture." *Marketing Theory* 12 (1): 13–25.

Kraidy, M. 2016. *The naked blogger of Cairo*. Cambridge, MA: Harvard University Press.

Lengel, L. 2004, April. *The UN World Summit on the information society: Implications for phase II of the summit in Tunisia*. Paper presented at the Union for Democratic Communications, St. Louis, Missouri.

Lengel, L. 1997. *Identity, representation and disempowerment: Arab women and the media*. Paper presented at the National Communication Association Convention, Chicago.

Lugones, M. 2010. "Toward a decolonial feminism." *Hypatia* 25 (4): 742–759.

Lugones, M. 2014. "Indigenous movements and decolonial feminism." Undergraduate and graduate seminar, Department of Women's, Gender and Sexuality Studies, The Ohio State University, March 21, Vol. 50. https://wgss.osu.edu/sites/wgss.osu.edu/files/LugonesSeminarReadings

Maclaran, P. 2015. "Feminism's fourth wave: A research agenda for marketing and consumer research." *Journal of Marketing Management* 31 (15–16): 1732–1738.

Marzouki, N. 2011. "Tunisia's wall has fallen". *Third World Resurgence* 245/246 (January/February 2011): 37–40.

Moghissi, H., ed. 2005. *Women and Islam: Social conditions, obstacles and prospects*. Vol. 2. London: Taylor & Francis.

Mohanty, C. T. 1986. "Under western eyes: Feminist scholarship and colonial discourses." *Chandra Talpade Mohanty Boundary* 12 (3): 333–358 and *Journal of International Women's Studies* 13 (5).

Moreno, C. R. 2018. "Las políticas públicas de mujer y género: radiografía de una tecnología de género moderno colonial." *Los saberes múltiples y las ciencias sociales y políticas* 2: 321–338.

Newsom, V. 2004. "Theorizing contained empowerment: A critique of activism and power in third wave feminist spaces." *Dissertation Abstracts International* (UMI No. 0496051229).

Newsom, V., and L. Lengel. 2003. "The power of the weblogged word: Contained empowerment in the Middle East North Africa region." *Feminist Media Studies* 3 (3): 360–363.

Newsom, V., L. Lengel, and C. Cassara. 2011. "The Arab Spring|local knowledge and the revolutions: A framework for social media information flow." *International Journal of Communication* 5: 10.

Norderson, J. 2017. *Online activism in the Middle East: Political power and Authoritarian Governments from Egypt to Kuwait.* London: I.B. Tauris.

Ourahmoune, N. 2020. "Aucun champ de la vie sociale n'échappe aujourd'hui au marketing." *Revue Politique et Parlementaire.* https://www.revuepolitique.fr/author/nacima-ourahmoune/

Ourahmoune, N., and N. Özçağlar-Toulouse. 2012. "Exogamous weddings and fashion in a rising consumer culture: Kabyle minority dynamics of structure and agency." *Marketing Theory* 12(1): 81–99.

Peattie, K., S. Peattie, and R. Newcombe. 2016. "Unintended consequences in demarketing antisocial behaviour: Project Bernie." *Journal of Marketing Management* 32 (17–18): 1588–1618.

Robinson, N. 2016. "Arab feminisms: Gender and equality in the Middle East." In Makdisi, J. S., N. Bayoumi, and R. R. Sidawi, eds. *Women's history review* 25 (3): 470–472. https://doi.org/10.1080/09612025.2015.1078171

Said, E. 1978. *Orientalism: Western conceptions of the Orient.* New York: Pantheon.

Scott, L. 2017. "Consumption on the feminist agenda." In John, E. M. F. and F. Sherry, eds. *Contemporary consumer culture theory.* London: Routledge: 107–129.

Spivack, G. C. (1988). "Can the Subaltern speak?" In Nelson, C. and L. Grossberg, eds. *Marxism and the interpretation of Culture.* Chicago: University of Illinois Press: 271–313.

Steinfield, L., M. Sanghvi, L. T. Zayer, C. Coleman, N. Ourahmoune, R. Harrison, W. Hein, and J. Brace-Govan. 2019. "Transformative intersectionality: Moving business towards a critical Praxis." *Journal of Business Research* 100 (July): 366–375.

Steinfield, L. A., C. A. Coleman, L. Tuncay Zayer, N. Ourahmoune, & W. Hein. (2019). "Power logics of consumers' gendered (in)justices: Reading reproductive health interventions through the transformative gender justice framework." *Consumption Markets & Culture* 22 (4): 406–429.

Tatarchevskiy, T. 2011. "The 'popular' culture of Internet activism." *New Media & Society* 13 (2): 297–313. https://doi.org/10.1177/1461444810372785

Tlostanova, M. 2010. "Decolonial feminism and the decolonial turn". In *Gender epistemologies and Eurasian borderlands.* New York: Palgrave Macmillan: 19–60.

Valassopoulos, A. 2010. "Arab feminisms." *Feminist Theory* 11 (2): 205–213.

Varman, R., P. Goswami, and D. Vija. 2018. "The precarity of respectable consumption: Normalising sexual violence against women." *Journal of Marketing Management,* 34 (11–12): 932–964.

Wheeler, D. 2009. "Working around the state: Internet use and political identity in the Arab world." In Chadwick A. and P. Howard, eds. *Handbook of Internet politics.* Abington: Routledge: 305–320.

Younis, J. 2011. "Egypt's revolution means nothing if its women are not free." *The Guardian,* March 9. http://www.guardian.co.uk/commentisfree/2011/mar/09/egypt-revolutionwomen

Zakrzewski, Anna , Kedra Newsom Reeves, Michael Kahlich, Maximilian Klein, Andrea Real Mattar, and Stephan Knobel (2020). Managing the Next Decade of Women's Wealth, Boston Consulting Group. Retrieved from https://www.bcg.com/publications/2020/managing-next-decade-women-wealth

Zayer, L. T, W. Hein, J. Brace-Govan, R. Harrison, C. Coleman, N. Ourahmoune, M. Sanghvi, and L. Steinfield (2020). "Renaissance of gender equality research." In Tay, T. K., P. Flynn, and M. Gudic, eds. *Struggles and successes in the pursuit of sustainable development for the Principles of Management Education (PRME) Series.* Abington: Routledge: 139–150.

18 Unfolding climate change inequities through intersectionality, Barad's new materialism, and post/de-colonial Indigenous perspectives

Laurel Steinfield

Intersectionality theory and its theoretical perspective of a critical praxis hold the promise of moving scholars from researching the occurrences and effects of overlapping oppressions and/or privileges to using this knowledge to help challenge the resulting social injustices. Indeed, marketing and consumer behavior scholars have recently argued for a refocus and "re-radicalization" of intersectionality studies so that they address the elements that actions (praxis) can change—that is, the economic, political, and sociocultural forces that give rise to experiences of overlapping oppression or privileges for consumers (Steinfield et al. 2019, 367, see also Steinfield et al. 2020). However, despite these forays, scholars (and practitioners) continue to largely overlook a key element: the contributing power and actions of the non-human world. In this chapter, I accordingly expand the analytical lens of intersectionality, blending it with Karen Barad's concept of agential realism while giving recognition to its foundational roots of Indigenous knowledge (Rosiek, Snyder, and Pratt 2020)[1] and Gloria Anzaldúa's (1987) postcolonial queer feminist concept of mestiza consciousness. Such a lens produces what I call a 'holistic agential praxis'. A holistic agential praxis recognizes the dynamic intra-activity of human and non-human forces so that we might be able to identify the multiple elements that give rise to the realities of oppressions/privileges we study and seek to address. Moreover, the combination of these theories pushes us to consider our own role in bringing about these realities and how we might enact change through pursuing a politics of possibilities. To illustrate for readers the implications and analytical power of these combined lenses, I explore the phenomenon of an intervention related to climate change.

Before proceeding to demonstrate the analytical power of this combined lens and the holistic agential praxis it offers, I lay the foundations by describing what various components of these lenses entail and their usage in marketing and consumer behavior theory. I provide a more in-depth description of these perspectives, with the goal of aiding scholars less familiar with the theoretical lenses to understand the key elements and their usage in the field so that scholars might employ them and continue to develop their theoretical and practical insights.

Intersectionality theory

Intersectionality theory offers an analytical perspective that illuminates the ways "systems and practices can magnify oppressions versus privileges when identity categories overlap" (Steinfield et al. 2019, 366). We all have overlapping identity categories, such as one's biological sex, race, age, expressed gender, ethnicity, class, designated nationality,

DOI: 10.4324/9781003042587-22

etc. Those with identity categories that differ from the naturalized norm (e.g., White, educated, middle/upper class, Western male), however, face multiple modes of oppression, given that social practices, institutional arrangements, and cultural ideologies were (and continue to be) created by dominant groups to maintain their privileged position and ways of living (MacKinnon 2013). Oppressions can include "discrimination (unjust treatment), additional hardships, disadvantages, marginalization, invisibilities, and/or (mis)recognitions" and can augment vulnerabilities (Steinfield and Holt 2020, 565), while privileges signal the existence of social structures, practices, and discourses that (re)produce multiple benefits, advantages, visibilities, and recognitions. Raising awareness of the ways people's social locations, due to their overlapping identity categories, result in experiences of intersectional oppressions versus privileges is one important step in rectifying social injustices. However, the roots of intersectionality theory call for a centering of research on the *systemic elements* that need to change. This focus reflects the historical legacy of intersectionality studies.

The history of intersectionality theory is one that stems from a merger of activism and intellectual pursuits in critical race and feminist studies. It was the work of Black feminists who coined and advanced the term to draw attention to the oppressions that African American women experienced so that they might change the laws that disadvantaged them. As Crenshaw (1989) related, African American women's reality could not be assessed in a unidimensional way—that is, a way that focused on gender *or* race. Rather, what was needed was an understanding of how laws and institutional practices caused gender- *and* race-based discriminations to interact, leading Black women to face multiple oppressions simultaneously. Although in intersectionality's canonical legacy, Gloria Anzaldúa's (1987) concept of mestiza consciousness is often given limited recognition (e.g., Dill and Kohlman 2012; Sanghvi 2019; Steinfield et al. 2019), it does express similar perspectives. It captures the conflicting space Chicanas experience in which their White culture attacks their Mexican culture and both attack their Indigenous culture. Chicanas thus simultaneously experience privileges and oppressions, and must navigate an ongoing "duel of oppressor and oppressed" (Anzaldúa 1987, 79).

What is key to note from this brief recount is that the origins of intersectionality theory stem from academic knowledge projects that sought to highlight the multiplicity and interactions of social inequities and the intersecting systems of power that foster them. Imperatively, the purpose was to support social justice projects (Collins 2015, 2020). This is known as adopting a 'critical praxis.' As Collins (2015, 16,17) describes:

> Intersectionality is not simply a field of study to be mastered or an analytical strategy for understanding; rather, intersectionality as critical praxis sheds light on the doing of social justice work… [Its knowledge projects should] critique social injustices that characterize complex social inequalities, imagine alternatives, and/or propose viable action strategies for change.

Since the term was coined in 1989, intersectionality has become an enriched yet contested concept as scholars stretch it across disciplines, apply different approaches, and veer toward various foci and priorities of analysis (see overviews in: Bilge 2013; Carbado et al. 2013; Collins 2015; 2020; Davis 2008; the collection of works in Lutz, Vivar, and Supik 2011; Nash 2008; Rodriguez et al. 2016; Walby, Armstrong, and Strid 2012). These traverses have been no different in marketing and consumer behavior studies. Initially, scholars positioned intersectionality theory primarily as a means to study the "multiplicity and interactivity of social identity structures such as race, class, and gender" and how "every person in society is positioned at the intersection of multiple social identity structures and is thus subject to multiple social advantages and disadvantages" (Gopaldas 2013, 91). This, however, resulted in an over-emphasis on what (consumer) identities to include versus a study of the systemic elements and power dynamics that result in the social advantages and disadvantages. For example, Corus et al. (2016), in advocating for an intersectionality perspective for poverty studies, reiterate McCall's (2005) typology of various approaches to studying social groups: intra-categorical (comparing disadvantages within a social group); inter-categorical (contrasting disadvantages between social groups); and anti-categorical (questioning and deconstructing the categories themselves). Pushing scholars to correct for the limited deliberation on the "power structures and practices of domination," Steinfield et al. (2019) urge marketing, consumer behavior and management scholars to "re-radicalize" intersectionality with its social justice mission (pp. 368, 367). They repeat Chun, Lipsitz and Shin's (2013, 923) call to study "the way things work rather than who people are." This is because it is not the race, gender or class identities of consumers that are themselves problematic and that need change but the "oppressions and 'isms'—racism, sexism, classism—that result from historically rooted power asymmetries, which make overlapping categories of identities problematic" (Steinfield et al. 2019, 368). As MacKinnon (2013, 1023) aptly states:

> [C]ategories and stereotypes and classifications are authentic instruments of inequality. And they are static and hard to move. But they are the ossified outcomes of the dynamic intersection of multiple [power] hierarchies, not the dynamics that create them. They are there, but they are not the reason they are there.

Thus, if intersectionality was (and is) to regain its critical praxis and be used by scholars and practitioners to push for change, a shift was (and is) needed from a concentration on identities to a focus on "the processes (such as economic exploitation) or combination of systems (such as the family, workplace, market, and nation) that (re)produce interlocking oppressions" (Steinfield et al. 2019, 368).

This shift, however, has limitations. As the prior quote from Steinfield et al. (2019) exemplifies, in marketing as well as wider intersectionality studies (e.g., Collins 2020; Gopaldas and Siebert 2018; Hopkins 2019; Lassalle and Shaw 2021; Noble 2018; Steinfield et al. 2020), the critical praxis perspective is primarily centered on the 'human' or 'social world' and on related processes, systems, structures, practices, beliefs, or ideologies, or what Anthias (2013, 3) calls the "societal arenas of investigations." What remains under-explored are the modes of oppression and/or privileges that stem from power exercised by non-human-related elements, particularly in the natural world. This becomes obvious in studying the effects of climate change. Indeed, I have made initial forays into identifying how human and non-human power dynamics interact and contribute to intersectional oppressions versus privileges by proposing an 'ecological-intersectionality perspective' (Steinfield and Holt 2020). However, a clear articulation of the theoretical underpinnings and, in turn, methodological implications, has yet to be fully considered. The remainder of this chapter provides this clarity by merging intersectionality theory with Karen Barad's feminist perspective of agential realism. In relating Barad's work, I also seek to recognize Indigenous knowledges and postcolonial queer feminist concepts that have come before but that largely remain overlooked

(Rosiek, Snyder, and Pratt 2020; Sundberg 2014). Such a move is necessary and one that others should consider embracing to avoid whitesplaining, creating the illusion of the lone White scholar-genius, and reproducing the colonial, heteronormative Whiteness that has plagued academia and caused violence through citational and knowledge erasures (Arvin, Tuck, and Morrill 2013; Harris and Ashcraft 2019; Todd 2016).

Agential realism: making matter matter

Situating agential realism: dismantling the binaries of Euro-Western academic thought

At its essence, "agential realism"—a term coined by Barad (1998)—explores how "matter comes to matter" (Barad 1998, 87). As a form of feminist new materialism, Barad's notion of agential realism pushes against the limited understandings of reality produced by the historical, artificial binaries in Euro-Western thought. These binaries include the divisions created between: humans/non-humans, subjects/objects, culture/nature, representation/materiality, language/matter, and the scientific-knower/object-under-investigation. Barad's work parallels arguments of Indigenous scholars, such as Leroy Little Bear (2011), Juanita Sundberg (2014), Vanessa Watts (2013), and Gregory Cajete (2000), who note that these binaries have for centuries reproduced a colonial mindset that has separated humans from the world and awarded humans a special capacity for reasoning, representing the world, and taking meaningful action. These hierarchical divisions have helped to justify humans' conquership—both of the natural world and of each other (Rosiek, Snyder, and Pratt 2020)—and they have centered Euro-Western research on human-social interpretations of reality. Before delving into the specificities of agential realism, it is helpful to understand the history of the binaries and their legacy in marketing, consumer behavior, gender and intersectionality studies, given that agential realism seeks to dismantle and transcend them.

To start, consider the human/non-human binary. Under empiricists' preoccupation with studying nature and a desire to describe and determine generalizable laws that represented reality, non-human matter took on the form of inert, self-contained objects that humans (through their unique capacity to think and act) had the ability to study (Barad 2007). The agency of non-human matter—a key element long recognized in Indigenous knowledge (Battiste 2011; Cajete 2000; Rosiek, Snyder, and Pratt 2020; Todd 2016; Watts 2013)—became overlooked. What was left in its place was a positivist approach in which objects were described with "inherent properties that follow deterministic trajectories," proven through experimentation (Barad 2007, 472). For example, laws of gravity explained why the inert, passive apple fell from the tree.

Secondly, as feminist new materialists (Barad 2007; Haraway 1991) and Indigenous scholars (e.g., Cajete 2000; Watts 2013) relate, in their desire to achieve generalizable laws, empiricists unnaturally separated nature from the cultural context. Humans, like non-humans, became reduced to essentializing descriptions that often conveyed a sense of biological determinism (i.e., one is born this way), and culture became overlooked (Van der Tuin and Dolphijn 2010).

Counteracting these reductive explanations of reality came a wave in Euro-Western thought of social constructivism, (post)structuralist, and performative accounts that sought to reaffirm the importance of culture, language, and social interactions, and to recognize differences in perspectives and representations that give shape not to one generalizable, determinable reality but to a plurality in how the world is experienced and viewed (e.g., Barthes 1974; Berger and Luckmann 1991; Bourdieu 1984). For example, scholars explored how reality was produced through socially constructed discourses (meanings, language, representations), how humans imbued things with a variety of symbolic and cultural meanings (e.g., Barthes 1974; Butler 1990; Foucault 2001; Goffman 1976), and how a person's life was shaped by different societal systems or structures (e.g., Bourdieu 1984; Durkheim 2014; Lévi-Strauss 1969; Marx 1977). Similar forays occurred in the marketing and consumer behavior disciplines. Consumer culture theory, for instance, was originally premised on similar ideas: studies examined how (agentic) human subjects ascribed meaning to (passive) objects, used objects in their experiences, and derived their identities from objects (Bettany 2007). These views, however, rather than eliminating divisive binaries, emphasized the binaries between humans/non-humans, culture/nature, language/matter, representation/materiality, subjects/objects.

The resultant shortcomings of these binary divisions are made evident by Barad (1998, 2007) in their questioning of Judith Butler's work on the performative power of discourse. To briefly summarize Butler's argument, Butler (1990, viii) contends that gender, sex, and sexuality, despite their appearance, are not innate, naturally existing elements of identities; they are products of "discursively constrained performance acts," which, in turn, "produce the body." Discursive scripts are passed down, generation to generation, that relate what one can be (e.g., male or female) and how one should behave (masculine, feminine, heteronormatively). These scripts establish socially acceptable meanings that we internalize and perform; to contest them a person risks punishment and marginalization (Butler 1988). By performing them, we entrench their repetition, or an "iterative citationality" (Barad 2007, 184), and continue to allow them power over our bodies and what we do with our bodies so that we are not marginalized. While Buter's work is insightful, the focus of Butler (and others, such as Foucault) on discursive dynamics or how language and representations determine our material existence, only tells part of the story. As Barad (2007) surmises, what remains missing are: (i) considerations of non-human bodies; (ii) the material dimensions of regulating practices that enable discourse to produce effects on bodies (e.g., books, magazines); and (iii) recognition of the material aspects of the body—the anatomy and physiology—and their effects. The role of matter needed (and needs) to be acknowledged.

Notably, the concerns Barad levels at these scholars are points that also ring true in how many scholars have approached intersectionality studies and the study of gender. In order to push against an essentializing, positivistic, biological determinism, scholars have given prioritization to the social, structural, cultural, and discursive elements of human life. Yet in so doing, they have often overlooked the (biological) material conditions of human and non-human matter, and thus the ways the dynamism of these elements matters to the materialization of reality. For example, in marketing and consumer behavior scholarship, Gopaldas and Sibert (2018) explore how the discursive power of marketing images creates "mirrors of intersectionality," which shape how people think, feel, and behave, and cultivate biased assumptions, stereotypes, and "favorable or unfavorable misconceptions of particular intersections" (18). Saatcioglu and Corus (2014) assess how multiple structural disadvantages for low-income community members stem from overlaps in the healthcare, financial, and welfare systems. Noble (2018) documents the way human-created algorithms on Google perpetuate "technological redlining," thereby reproducing oppressive social relations and racial profiling. Steinfield et al. (2020) trace how various social structures and ideologies (neo-liberal, neo-imperialistic capitalism, and patriarchy) influence the responses of female versus male subsistence prosumers to environmental disruptions (such as those caused by climate change). And Steinfield et al. (2019) contemplate why diversity initiatives fail by breaking down the intersectional and interacting sources of (dis)advantages, including "pervading beliefs, norms and regulatory structures…, practices, discourses or representations…, and [human] agentic actions" (370).

Similarly in gender-focused studies, to counteract essentializing tendencies that equate sex with gender (e.g., females have innate caregiver instincts), scholars propose studying various elements that shape how people behave. As Hein et al. (2016, 224) summarize, per McCall's (1992) definition, these various elements include:

(1) gender symbolism and representations, or "durable cultural expressions of gender differences" (McCall 1992, 837) rooted within binary categories of male/female, masculine/feminine; (2) gender identities, or the multiple experiences that relate to individual circumstances and personal embodiment of gender, found, for example, in experiencing motherhood or masculinity; and (3) gender organization and institutions that affect socioeconomic structuring, such as the gendered division of labor.

While the insights regarding societal and discursive dynamics gained from queer (e.g., Butler, Foucault) and gender studies are of significant value, a more encompassing perspective is needed if we are to grapple with the multiple components that contribute to intersectional oppressions. In line with Barad and postcolonial queer and decolonial[2] Indigenous theorists, such as Gloria Anzaldúa (1987), Juanita Sundberg (2014), and Sebastian De Line (2016), I thus argue that studies of gender and intersectional dynamics could benefit from transcending the binaries—the anthropocentric prioritization of humans over non-humans, culture/nature, representation/materiality. Studies need to adopt a more holistic view of how discourse and socio-cultural dynamics merge with human bodies and actions and non-human material elements to create the world we perceive and experience. Playing with words to visually represent this shift in perspective (as Barad so often does), I note that this calls for the removal of the dividing "/" of binaries so that we focus on the *relational* intra-activities that occur—that is, the connecting "-" or blurred boundaries of things. Thus, rather than the 'material/discursive' we need to acknowledge the 'material-discursive' (also called material-semiotics) or, as subsequently described, to recognize the even more blurred entanglements of *material-discursive*, which other scholars have called "spacetimematter" (Barad 2007, 181), "Place-Thought" (Watts 2013, 21), and All My-Our Relations[3] (De Line 2016).

In marketing and consumer behavior studies there are scholars that have heeded this call to recognize relational ontologies by considering the connectedness of things. However, when doing so, the majority of scholars employ theories of new materialists that allow boundaries to still remain. Works that draw on Barad (e.g., Steinfield 2019) or that highlight Indigenous knowledge (e.g., Kennedy, McGouran, and Kemper 2020) are scarce. Many scholars take inspiration from actor-network theorists Latour (2008), Callon (1984), and Law (2009), who demonstrate how non-human matter is alive, dynamic, and agentic, and has a performative quality that impacts other things: Non-human matter acts on and with humans to create social activity. (For applications in marketing and consumer behavior studies see: Bajde 2013; Bettany and Kerrane 2011; Bettany, Kerrane, and Hogg 2014; Buchanan-Oliver, Cruz, and Schroeder 2010; Canniford and Bajde 2015; Cluley 2018; Giesler 2012; Lucarelli and Hallin 2015; Mason, Kjellberg, and Hagberg 2015; Scott, Martin, and Schouten 2014.) Yet in taking this view of new materialism forward, scholars have, at times, fallen prey to the same trap as Butler. Instead of discourse, they give objects more power in shaping humans, negating to adopt an ontology that recognizes how all elements mutually co-create and co-constitute each other (Gamble, Hanan, and Nail 2019). Thus, the subject/object binary becomes flipped to be the object/subject binary, with things still viewed as separate entities. Moreover, by tracing how networks or assemblages of humans and non-human things unfold, they give objects a taken-for-granted nature, largely overlooking how discursive practices are also involved in the shaping of reality. For instance, variables such as gender, race, nationality, class, and sexuality become viewed as "properties of individual persons" instead of discursive renderings (Barad 2007, 57).

To overcome these object/subject or non-human/human dichotomies, some scholars draw on the work of Donna Haraway (see Bettany 2007; Bettany and Daly 2008; Campbell, O'Driscoll, and Saren 2010 for examples in marketing and consumer behavior literature). Donna Haraway (1991, 2008) supplements new materialism with a stronger post-humanist[4] slant: Her concept of a cyborg and exploration of companion species (e.g., dogs) blurs the boundaries between objects and subjects, humans and non-human matter, nature and culture, and the natural and artificial. As related in the next section, Barad, in dismantling the binaries, takes forward Haraway's post-humanist blurring of boundaries between things. Barad draws together all things—human and non-human matter and discourse—in accounting for the unfolding of reality. Although the origins of these thoughts are often attributed to Haraway and Barad, it should be noted that Haraway's work, and thus Barad's by extension, draws inspiration from Anzaldúa's (1987) concept of mestiza consciousness "where the possibility of uniting all that is separate occurs" (80) and Indigenous perspectives of the world (e.g., Harris and Ashcraft 2019; Watts 2013). The key difference between Barad and Indigenous perspectives is that the former assumes the splits have been universal, when in fact they are merely a product of how Euro-Western scholarship has emerged (Sundberg 2014). Because Barad's agential realism is vested in bridging the Euro-Western false divides, they propose an approach that draws together the strengths of the different theories: Barad creates an "enriched understanding" of reality by cross-pollinating empiricists' recognition of the nature of nature and use of apparatus to study reality, social scientists' and feminists' acknowledgement of sociocultural dynamics, Butler's queer performative account of discourse, actor-network theory's recognition of the dynamism of objects, Haraway's strong post-humanist slant, and new materialists' focus on the human and non-human co-production of knowledge.

Before delving into agential realism, there is one other key Euro-Western binary that Barad aims to dismantle: that of the scientific-knower/object-under-investigation. Under Cartesian and Newtonian modes of scientific knowledge, scholars assumed that the subject conducting the agencies of observations could be separate from the object being observed. This had the effect of making the human observer and the facilitating apparatus disappear, leaving only the object as the focal point of studies. For example, for scientists it might be their lab analysis of different micro-organisms or monkeys, and for economists it may be the maps of supply and demand curves of various goods. However, as Barad (2007) and other new materialists (e.g., Haraway 1991; Latour 2008) recognized, rather than the human observer and apparatus disappearing, the human scholar and apparatuses actively shaped how matter is perceived. Scholars are not distant from that which they are studying: they are actors who act on and with things to create facts, knowledge. and meanings. While other new materialists have noted this dynamic of academic knowledge creation (Haraway 1991; Latour and Woolgar 1979), they have largely documented *other* academics' production of knowledge. Distinct from these views, Barad, in parallel with Indigenous views of science (Cajete 2000) and ethics of reciprocity (Rosiek, Snyder, and Pratt 2020), recognizes how the 'I' (or 'you') as a researcher is caught up in the blurring of boundaries or entanglements between materialdiscursive dynamics. As Barad (2007) surmises: "We don't obtain knowledge by standing outside the world; we know because we are *of* the world. We are part of the world and its differential becomings" (p. 185, emphasis original). Or, as the Chinese-Métis scholar, Sebastian De Line (2016) relates, All My-Our Relations reveals the relationality of everything while "operating from within process and [making] this process personal, intimate and shared" (n.p.).

Key elements of agential realism and post/de-colonial, Indigenous perspectives that extend intersectionality theory

In Euro-Western centric terms, agential realism can largely be described as a "posthumanist performative account" of *how* the world becomes or emerges (Barad 2007, 32). While Barad's theory is full of complexities and continues to evolve, and Indigenous and post/de-colonial theories diverse (Battiste 2011; Kohn and Reddy 2017), there are a few elements and perspectives I wish to highlight given their centrality to the 'holistic agential praxis' I propose. As an aid to readers, I summarize some of these elements in Table 18.1, noting areas of alignments versus extensions of the two feminist theories, and implications for methods. In the subsequent section, I illustrate the analytical process and power of this combined lens through the case of a climate change intervention.

Agentic REALISM

First, the *realism* stance of Barad's work is one that attempts to provide "an accurate description" of reality, or phenomena (which are "basic units of reality"), by purposefully adopting post-humanist perspectives to challenge binaries (Barad 2001, 87). For example, the human/non-human binary collapses as Barad's agential realism recognizes how "nonhumans play an important role in naturalcultural practices, including everyday social practices, scientific practices, and practices that do not include humans" (Barad 2007, 32). Although Barad does not mention Indigenous perspectives, as subsequently related, their theory draws similarities to Indigenous philosophies that have as their foundations a reality composed of an intimate relationship between humans and non-humans (Cajete 2000; Little Bear 2011). Indeed, as the Blackfoot philosopher Leroy Little Bear (2011, 78) notes, the very language of Indigenous people allows for the "transcendence of boundaries" because it aims to describe happenings, processes, or actions, rather than objects. Everything has the capacity to think, act, talk, thus everything is involved in the ongoing flow of motions and energy (Spirit) that bring about the world.

Table 18.1 A Comparison and Merger of Feminisms—Intersectionality Theory + Barad's New Materialism

Concept Per Intersectionality Theory	Concept Per Barad's Feminist New Materialism	Alignment vs. Extension	Methodological Implications
Critical praxis—examines, critiques, and seeks to change realities of oppression/privilege to create more socially just human experiences; employs critical social theory—focus on human-created socio-cultural, political, and economic dynamics and discourse (e.g., "societal arenas of investigation" (Anthias 2012, 4))	Agential REALISM and the study of phenomena	Expands beyond a focus of humans, their power dynamics, and resulting, overlapping human-created structures of oppression/privilege to recognize how realities (phenomena) and forces of oppression/privilege also include non-human matter. The unit of analysis moves beyond individual/overlapping "societal arenas of investigation" to be the phenomena as a whole; phenomena are the unit of analysis in which the entanglements of materialdiscursive elements create oppressions/privileges.	Broaden scope of elements included in the study of phenomena to include human and non-human matter, and discourse.
Agency exercised by or denied to humans Agentic power of words (e.g., discursive power per Foucault or performativity per Butler)	AGENTIAL Realism Agency Discourse	Agency is not something someone is denied or expresses, or something that is vested in discourse and its performative power; agency represents the (im)possibilities of future becomings of the reality or phenomenon we live and study. Discourse is redefined. It is not a signifier for language or symbols but denotes the practices that simultaneously exclude and include, create visibilities and invisibilities, draw attention to and away from, and constrain and enable what can be said.	We might "recognize agency in different forms," stemming out of "relations, movements, repetitions, silences, distances, architecture, structures, feelings, things, us/them/it, words" (Sauzet 2018, n.p.). We investigate "how discourse sets the boundaries of what can and cannot be said, and what it makes visible versus invisible" (Steinfield 2019, 325–326). We identify the dynamisms and (im)possibilities that unfold from material-discursive intra-activities.

Applies critical social theory in a way that treats causal socio-cultural, political, and economic structures, practices, and systems as separate yet overlapping entities that cause certain experiences of oppression/privilege. Key approaches: studying the interactions of intersecting sources of oppressions & power asymmetries, i.e., material-discursive interactions	Intra-actions (instead of interactions) Relational ontology that explores materialdiscursive entanglements of a phenomena Diffractive reading of data	Rather than questioning cause and effects, the question is how realities/phenomena are produced through entanglements of intra-activity. Recognize that (non)human elements are not distinct things but come into being with and through each other (i.e., boundaries are blurred). Instead of applying an interpretivist/phenomenological or positivist lens, one engages in a diffractive reading of the data to identify differences that are made to matter and marks on bodies.	Diffractive reading involves: paying close attention to details, "reading" data through each other to find "patterns of thinking… that might take you somewhere interesting that you never would have predicted" (Barad in interview, Juleskjaer and Schwennesen 2012, 13). "Goal is to think the social and the natural together, to take account of how both factors matters… without defining one against the other or holding either nature or culture as the fixed referent for understanding the other" (Barad 2007, 30).
Oppressions and privileges are context (space and time) specific	Spacetimemattering	Extends beyond a specific time/context. Recognizes how space, time, and matter enfold within each other—how the past and future, local, regional, national, and global are intra-actively produced through one another. Instead of comparing and contrasting differences in social injustices pending different spaces and times, one conducts a genealogical analyses, examining data to ascertain how the spaces and moments of oppressions/privileges are "made through one another" (Barad 2007, 246).	Genealogical analyses: Data gathering goes beyond the specific time/context to understand the history and events in other spaces that have contributed to the current experiences of oppression/privileges, as well as the potential future implications.

(*Continued*)

Concept Per Intersectionality Theory	Concept Per Barad's Feminist New Materialism	Alignment vs. Extension	Methodological Implications
Self-reflexivity	Ethico-onto-epistem-ology	Goes beyond a reflection of one's actions or involvement to being a-count-able for the agential cuts and marks on bodies we make, and response-able for intra-acting from within (responsible for the effects our knowledge-making processes have on the world).	A-count-able approaches acknowledge agential cuts and marks on bodies that unfold from our intra-action within the phenomenon, and consider the (im)possibilities these may create. "Response-able methodologies involve careful attentiveness, responsibility/accountability, rendering each other capable and the ability to respond" (Murris and Bozalek 2019, 10).
Adoption of different perspectives: an inter-categorical (comparing experiences/sources of oppression between different social groups), intra-categorical (comparing experiences/sources of oppression within a social group), or anti-categorical (questioning the essence of the categorizations of the social groups—e.g., the demarcation of racial or gender identities).	Recognition of agential cuts made by apparatus in the study of phenomena and the boundaries these make. Adoption of diffractive methods to identify (de)stabilizing boundaries.	Expands beyond inter-categorical and intra-categorical to capture what agential cuts are made. Thus, similar to anti-categorical, the phenomenon under study and the agential cuts made in placing boundaries around phenomena need to be questioned. Focus changes from "questions of correspondence between descriptions and reality (e.g., do they mirror nature or culture?) to matters of practices of doings or actions" (Barad 2007, 28).	Research why the materialdiscursive elements of a phenomena even come to matter, or as Barad states, investigate "the material-discursive boundary-making practices that produce 'objects' and 'subjects', and other differences out of, and in terms of, a changing relationality" (Barad 2007, 92–93). Research is "attuned to the entanglements of apparatuses of production, one that enables genealogical analyses of how boundaries are produced" (Barad 2007, 30), and to the stabilization and destabilization of boundaries.
Critical praxis' focus on a politics of identity, which directs and stimulates political and social actions.	Politics of possibility	Move beyond a politics of identity bounded by temporal dimensions and/or politics of location, which fail to recognize the intra-connectedness of things, to a "politics of possibilities" that responsibly imagines and intervenes "in the (re)configurations of power" and inequities (Barad 2007, 246).	Adopt a stance that is open to explore the possibilities of (re)configurations, being responsive to "the possibilities that might help us" and the world "flourish" (Barad 2007, 396).

These ideas of a more holistic rendering of reality address the aforementioned critical gap in intersectionality theory: they can recognize the way non-human things also act recursively with humans and socio-cultural elements to produce phenomena of oppressions and/or privileges. The implications for scholars and practitioners are not only to rethink how they view non-human things, but to also cast a wider net when collecting data. As detailed in the proceeding section, data should seek to capture human *and* non-human elements and experiences.

AGENTIAL Realism

Second, Barad's *agential* (action or performance-orientated) perspective captures the ways (non)human matter and discourse are co-constitutively produced and materialize through iterative entanglements with each other. Notably, similar to Indigenous perspectives, Barad's theory: (i) changes the study of casual interactions to relational intra-actions and a focus on processes; (ii) alters the meaning of agency and discourse; (iii) expands the conceptualization of time and space; and, in turn, (iv) calls for methods of diffraction instead of reflection.

Intra-activities: Barad contends that to understand phenomena require Euro-Western thought to shift ontologically (in our theory of being) and epistemologically (in our theory of knowing) in how the world is perceived and studied. Typically, Euro-Western scholars examine the world in terms of interactions, which means they conceive of things as pre-existing, independent entities that act on or cause each other. This perspective, however, is what has led to the aforementioned academic debates and binaries regarding what should receive primacy and what determines reality: Is it nature or nurture (culture) that governs outcomes? Does human agency (action) create structures? Or is it language, representations, and/or societal structures that shape material existences and our bodies?

In contrast to this interaction perspective, a focus on intra-activity blurs boundaries between (non)human things and discourse, centering attention on the *relational entanglements*. Consequently, the binaries are prevented from flipping. Instead of neglecting or giving supremacy to one over the other (e.g., non-human over humans; culture over nature; language over matter; and vice versa), or arguing about what leads to what, the notion of intra-activity captures how human and non-human, culture and nature, language and matter mutually inform each other and their evolution or becoming. As Barad (2007, ix) describes:

> To be entangled is not simply to be intertwined with another, as in the joining of separate entities, but to lack an independent, self-contained existence. Existence is not an individual affair. Individuals do not pre-exist their interactions; rather, individuals emerge through and as part of their entangled intra-relating.

While the words of "intra-activity" may be unique to Barad, the relationality it captures has origins in Indigenous and post/de-colonial thought. Consider, as examples, the Anishnaabe and Haudenosaunee concept of Place-Thought shared by Watts (2013). Place-Thought recognizes that "we are the very extension of the land we walk upon" (p. 23): the "land is alive and thinking" and "humans and non-humans derive agency through the extensions of these thoughts" (p. 21). Moreover, because "non-human beings are active members of society," and "choose how they reside, interact, and develop relationships with other non-humans," they "directly influence how humans organize themselves into society" (Watts 2013, 23). Similarly, Little Bear (2011) describes the Blackfoot philosophy that sees all things as animate and views Spirit, which is akin to energy waves, as existing in all things. Because "everything, those rocks, those trees, those animals all have spirit just like we do as humans," they are referred to as "all my relations," or as De Line (2016) reframes, as "Niw_hk_m_kanak,"[5] meaning "All My/Our Relations" (n.p.). Barad's relational account of reality also holds similarities to Anzaldúa's (1987) postcolonial queer rendering of the world in which the mestiza consciousness transcends dualities by "breaking down the unitary aspect" of paradigms to create a "new mythos" that recognizes our interconnectedness (p. 80).

In regards to intersectionality theory, while perspectives of relationality complement its critical praxis by acknowledging the ways elements of oppression and privileges blur together, they also amend it. Rather than viewing elements as pre-existing independently or having inherent boundaries, the focus for Barad and many Indigenous post/de-colonial perspectives is to question how things of the phenomena under study co-emerge through intra-actions, or, per De Line (2016) and Little Bear (2011), how the energy waves (Spirit) move—composing, decomposing, and recomposing everything.

Agency & Discourse: Building on the relational perspective, Barad reconceptualizes agency and discourse. Similar to how Indigenous scholars acknowledge the animation created by Spirit (energy waves) (Little Bear 2011) or the thoughts of land (per Place-Thought) (Watts 2013), Barad conceives agency as representing the *dynamism* of entanglements/intra-activities and the "ongoing reconfigurations of the world" of phenomena (Barad, 2003, 818). Agency is thus no longer an attribute of discourse (per Butler) or humans (as commonly viewed in intersectionality theory) or non-human things: it represents a continual flow of dynamism through which the local material-discursive "causal structures, properties and boundaries" of phenomena "are stabilized and destabilized" (Barad, 2003, 817). Agency is thus productive: It is akin to possibility, producing the possible and impossible ways intra-activities of phenomena can unfold. It allows intra-activities and phenomena to always be open to change.

In addressing Euro-Western divisions, Barad also reframes discourse. Instead of being a synonym for words, language, and signified meanings (per theories of representation), it denotes the practices that simultaneously exclude and include, create visibilities and invisibilities, draw attention to and away from, and constrain and enable what can be said (Barad 2003). Studying discourse is, accordingly, "not an examination of what has been said," as is commonly the case in intersectionality studies (e.g., Gopaldas and Siebert 2018), "but rather an investigation of how discourse sets the boundaries of what can and cannot be said, and what it makes visible versus invisible" (Steinfield 2020, 325–326).

Time and Space: Barad's concept of intra-activity and agency means that time and space also have their boundaries blurred: they become enfolded into the intra-activity. This has implications for how time and space are conceived. Typically in intersectionality studies, the context-specific nature of oppressions and privileges is emphasized. As Hulko (2009) states, "systems of oppression [are] historically and culturally situated" (53). However, if we focus on the relational dynamics of intra-activities, we see that phenomena do not happen in specific spaces or in specific times. Rather, akin to a wave, intra-acting elements can exist in multiple places at once, or as Indigenous perspective acknowledge: "All things are related and interconnected, everywhere and at all times"

(Cajete 2000, 36). The past, present, and future are not distinct time points. The past (what one experienced at that time), the present (what they are experiencing now), and the future (what they will experience) blend together. Akin to Butler's *iterative citationality*, Barad notes that it is through *iterative intra-actions* and the shifting boundaries around these intra-actions that "temporality and spatiality are produced and... reconfigured" (Barad 2007, 180). Space, time, and matter are not static but dynamically intra-act and become blended, informing (through the resulting agency) time and place possibilities. The materialization of phenomena emerges from a constantly shifting "spacetimematter" manifold (Barad 2007, 181).

Diffractive Methods: Typically, in studying interactions, scholars use positivist approaches, such as experiments or statistical analysis, to test a cause and effect. Or they use interpretivist/phenomenological approaches to capture and describe the experiences of people and to theorize what causes these experiences to occur (as an intersectionality lens often does). These methods encourage reflection (mirroring reality and looking for sameness). Barad, drawing from their physics background and from the work of Donna Haraway, argues that instead of reflection we should employ methods of diffraction. If one were to visualize diffractive methods it would be akin to studying the diffractive patterns or changes in direction that occur when waves encounter a barrier. Diffractive methods seek to attend to "patterns of difference" and "how different differences [and boundaries] get made, what gets excluded, and how those exclusions matter" (Barad 2007, 30). They are thus a means through which we can critically examine the practices by which the varied and changing boundaries of phenomena and within phenomena (i.e., (non)human and discursive intra-activities) are drawn. By studying or looking for diffractive patterns, entanglements become visible.[6]

One way to accomplish this is to view things from different viewpoints, or as Barad details, to think "the social and natural together" (Barad 2007, 30). Barad describes one such approach as:

> [Rethinking] the nature of nature based on our best scientific theories, while rethinking the nature of scientific practices in terms of our best understanding of the nature of nature and our best social theories, while rethinking our best social theories in terms of our best understanding of the nature of nature and the nature of scientific theories. The goal is...to take account of *how* both factors matter (not simply to recognize that they both do matter).
>
> (Barad 2007, 30, emphasis original)

The reason for making entanglements visible, however, is not merely to describe intra-activities; it is concerned with capturing how phenomena's agentic intra-activities ("ongoing reconfiguring of spacetimemattering") are productive, creating (im)possibilities (Juelskjær and Schwennesen 2012, 12). As Barad (2001) stresses, "who and what are excluded through...entangled practices matter: different intra-actions produce different phenomena" (56). For example, imagine if researchers and their publications recognized the long-lasting fluorinated gases as the key contributor to the greenhouse gas (GHG) problem instead of carbon dioxide. The intra-activity we see around the phenomena of achieving "carbon neutrality" or "net zero by 2050" (UN News 2020) and the agentic (im)possibilities that unfolds would drastically change. Instead of a promotion of clean energy or hybrid car solutions, we and other things (e.g., publications, innovations) may critique and curb them, drawing awareness to the fluorinated gases produced by their electronic components (including semi-conductors), as well as the existence of fluorinated gases in aerosols and heating and cooling systems. This would bring in different actors to the intra-activities to bring down GHGs—such as focusing on curtailing semiconductor makers versus coal mines—unfolding into different possible solutions. Electric cars, due to the fluorinated gases emitted in the production of their batteries, may become an impossible or excluded solution, giving space for other possible innovations to emerge. A different manifold of intra-activity would emerge. Acknowledging (im)possibilities such as these ties into one last critical piece of Barad's theory: its ethical dimension or fusion of ethics with ontology and epistemology.

Ethico-onto-epistem-ology

Barad's ethical dimension adds substance to new materialism theories by grounding it in an ethically charged ontological and epistemological disposition—an inseparable "ethico-onto-epistem-ology" (Barad 2007, 90). In so doing, Barad challenges the scientific-knower/object-under-investigation binary by calling scientific-knowers to recognize how they are a part of the agential intra-activities of the world's becoming. As Barad emphasizes (2010), we obtain our knowing of reality by being within the intra-activity of the phenomenon we are trying to study, and our presence in this intra-activity means that we can no longer pretend to be innocent, disconnected, and objective bystanders—we must bear "a-count-ability" and "response-ability" (p. 251). This ethical prerogative expands the realism of Barad's theory: It is not only "about the representations of an independent reality" (per philosophical realism), but about "the real consequences, interventions, creative possibilities, and responsibilities of intra-acting within and as part of the world" (Barad 2007, 37).

These ideas mirror the longstanding Indigenous belief in an 'ethics of reciprocity' (Rosiek, Snyder, and Pratt 2020), and are at the essence of 'all my-our relations' (De Line 2016). They likewise have similarities with intersectionality theory and its: (i) demand for "scholars and practitioners to be self-reflexive of their own actions, involvement, and impact, and how privileges or oppressions affect their own worldviews" (Steinfield and Holt 2020, 566); as well as (ii) social justice and critical praxis goals. However, Barad reframes and extends these components as related by the concept of agentic cuts of apparatuses, ideals of a-count-ability and response-ability, and a shift to a politics of possibilities.

Agential Cuts of Apparatuses: Barad (drawing on their physics background) contends that scholars need to understand how *apparatuses* make *agential cuts*, which cause things (spacetimematter) to be (momentarily) included or excluded from the phenomena under study. Similar to how apparatuses employed in science influence experiments by shaping results and causing some things to be seen or included and others to be not seen or excluded, apparatuses are "*specific interventions/practices involving humans and nonhumans*" that reconfigure the material-discursive (im)possibilities (Barad 2001, 87, emphasis original). The agential cuts they produce "radically rework" the relations of entangled things (Barad 2010, 265).

The self-reflexivity processes encouraged by intersectionality theory (Steinfield and Holt 2020) align closely with this idea: a researchers' apparatus (interventions/practices) and their ability to draw from their social location and the oppressions/privileges it entangles into their lives, influences what they uncover. Moreover, similar to intersectionality approaches that seek to question the social categories themselves (i.e., anti-categorical approaches), the social locations we identify in our studies and as mattering to our interpretation of data, such as racial, gender, and/or class identities, are products of "enacted cuts" (Barad 2014, 174).

Barad, however, goes further. They recognize that apparatuses are not a scientific instrument nor are they static. Apparatuses enable the agency or dynamism of intra-activities: They produce momentary boundaries, which a self-reflexive lens or an anti-categorical intersectionality approach may identify. Yet they are also always open to be reconfigured, hence the agential descriptor of *cuts*. The implications of these ideas for scholars is that when they are enacting intersectionality theory's self-reflexivity and anti- (as well as intra/inter) categorical approaches, they need to: i) attend to the ways we perform agential cuts—reflecting on what things and social locations they are bringing in versus keeping out; and ii) recognize how we become entangled in diffractive patterns and the (im)possibilities these create.

Additionally, as Barad notes (2007), agential cuts are not a human-only endeavor—all things are capable of enacting agential cuts or, as framed in Indigenous knowledge, directing events and processes (Rosiek, Snyder, and Pratt 2020; Little Bear 2011). Consider, for example, how plants, during the photosynthesis process decide to include (absorb) versus exclude certain CO_2 particles. Yet even the amassed CO_2 particles, joining with other GHGs, enact cuts: while they exclude some energy, such as the energy produced when sunlight reflects from the earth, by letting it go into space, they trap others, re-emitting the energy waves (and the heat they give off) in all directions (American Chemical Society 2021). Everything thus has the potential to enact cuts, which, in turn, adds to the complexities and agential possibilities of intra-activities.

According to Barad (2007), tracing apparatuses and their agential cuts is done by focusing on the diffractive patterns (or marks demarcating differences) they leave in their wake. This makes it possible to "perform a genealogical account" or to identify the materialdiscursive practices that make things matter (Barad 2007, 169). (The prior GHGs example is a case in point.) This extends to time and space as well, meaning one is not only assessing specific material demarcations *in* certain spaces and times but also identifying the material demarcations *of* space and time made through cuts of apparatuses (spacetimematterings). That is, we, as well as other (non)humans and discourse, enact cuts that include/make visible versus exclude/make invisible certain time frames (such as past occurrences or future possibilities) and places. These spacetimematterings have implications for the enfolding (what gets included) and unfolding (agential possibilities) of phenomena's intra-activities.

A-count-ability and Response-ability: Barad emphasizes that because we (and our apparatuses and agential cuts) are a part of the entanglements and the different reconfiguration of what is and what may yet be possible, questions of a-count-ability and response-ability constantly present themselves.

A-count-ability amplifies accountability: It acknowledges that we need to: (i) consider *what* is made to count or to matter, and what is excluded from counting or mattering and (ii) to account for "marks on bodies" or *how* "different cuts produce differences that matter," and how apparatuses "enact determinate casual structures, boundaries, properties, and meanings" (Barad 2007, 348, 340). Scholars can achieve a-count-ability by adopting diffractive methods that pay "care-full" attention to detail, to "what is and is not being expressed," and to "our complex histories of entanglements" (Murris and Bozalek 2019, 8, 10). By tracing entanglements, we can make "our obligations and debts"—those things we need to care about—visible, which is a required step toward "reconfigur[ing] relations of spacetimemattering" so that they are more equitable (Juelskjær and Schwennesen 2012, 20). This approach of care-full attentiveness corrects for the common 'care-less' critical approaches scholars take with intersectionality studies, which are often negative and destructive, closing down (instead of opening up) possibilities, and in which scholars negate to recognize or to take care with their agential cuts and contributions to the entanglements (Dolphijn and Tuin 2012; Murris and Bozalek 2019).

To achieve this level of care-full attentiveness, Barad and others who adopt diffractive methods (e.g., Murris and Bozalek 2019; Taguchi 2012) propose approaches that draw similarities to Indigenous experiential practices that sense connections and flows of energy to *and* with things (Cajete 2000; De Line 2016): scholars are to use all their faculties to sense and inhabit the entanglements. As Barad (2007, x) describes, to be attentive means to engage in an "ongoing practice of being open and alive to each meeting, each intra-action, so that we might use our ability to respond, our responsibility to help awaken, to breathe life into ever new possibilities for living justly."

Building on a-count-ability, Barad thus adds an obligation of response-ability. Entanglements, as Barad (2010) emphasizes, "are relations of obligations—being bound to the other" (265). We must be responsible for the impact we, our research, and agential cuts have on phenomena's ongoing reconfigurations. Indigenous philosophies have long recognized this, noting how all my-our relations means there is a "responsibility of animate bodies for each other" (De Line 2016, n.p.) and an ethics of reciprocity. An ethics of reciprocity attends to "the way our existence is interdependent with…other humans and non-humans," and considers "the consequences of our actions—including our research—for all the communities with which we are in relation and on which our being depends" (Rosiek, Snyder, and Pratt 2020, 340).

Additionally, Barad's response-ability is also about being responsive to those things that are in the entanglements or intra-activities with us. For example, if one is reading a report or article, to "*do justice* to a text" one should take "what you find inventive… and work carefully with the details of patterns of thinking that might take you somewhere interesting that you never would have predicted" (Juelskjær and Schwennesen 2012, 13, emphasis original). One needs to respond to the text. Similar to the way Indigenous people converse with (non)humans, response-ability involves listening, "inviting and enabling response" (Juelskjær and Schwennesen 2012, 22). It also involves having an "obligation to be responsive to the other" (Dolphijn and Tuin 2012, 69). Response-ability after attentive a-count-ability thus allows us to answer the question: "what should be done…what commitments to ourselves and [those in the intra-activity with us] are we willing to take on" (Murris and Bozalek 2019, 10)?

Politics of Possibilities: For Barad, because spacetimematter intra-activities and spacetimematterings are constantly being reworked, and because agency means that boundaries of intra-activities and phenomena can/are being shifted and exclusions can/are being included, what is possible is always open. Consequentially agential realism adapts intersectionality's critical praxis. Rather than forming political agendas around social identities or social locations to change oppressions (i.e., a politics of identity), what is needed is a politics of possibility. A politics of possibility entails "ways of responsibly imagining and intervening in the configurations of power, that is, intra-actively reconfiguring spacetimematter" (Barad 2007, 246). It is thus by identifying how matter comes to matter that we can then be responsive to the (in)visibilities and (im)possibilities that unfold.

Applying a holistic agential praxis: the case of a climate change intervention

In the remaining space, I want to briefly draw on a case of a climate change intervention to demonstrate the implications of combining an intersectionality lens with Barad's agential realism and the Indigenous and post/de-colonial perspectives from which it draws. I will begin with a brief overview of the intervention, and then work to detail how a 'holistic agential praxis' is achieved by expanding the research questions we ask, data we collect, analysis we perform, and the findings and (im)possibilities we bring into existence.

The intervention

The intervention was initially premised on testing the effectiveness of a tool—the planter—that could help a group of subsistence farmers in a semi-rural area of Kenya limit soil disruption during planting. My research colleague and the elderly farmer who invented the planter posited that by limiting soil disruption the soil's microbiology would have the capability to regenerate and heal itself, thereby improving its ability to absorb the erratic rainfall when and if it came. Our goal was to correct a debilitating cycle of intra-actions that reduced farmers' yields. In brief, as the International Panel on Climate Change (IPCC 2007, 2014) reports relate, the erratic rainfall and prolonged dry seasons and droughts the area experienced were connected to the CO_2 released through the burning of fossil fuels (petroleum, coal, gas) and industrial processes (e.g., cement production) in other geographical areas (e.g., China, the USA). CO_2 is viewed as the main driver of the human-induced growth in GHGs, contributing to an additive layer that prevents the natural dispersion of energy waves. As GHGs cause more and more waves to remain trapped in the atmosphere, the heat emitted from them increases temperatures. Yet just as waves stretch across spaces, so too do the effects of these temperature changes: they are geographically dispersed, and, as the IPCC notes (Allen et al. 2018), they disproportionately affect those least responsible, such as the subsistence farmers our intervention sought to support. The warmer temperatures caused by GHGs accelerate the drying of land surfaces and unfold into longer dry seasons and droughts, yet they also increase the water stored in the atmosphere, causing erratic rainfalls or floods (IPCC 2007). These water stresses cut into the lifespan of microorganisms key to soil fertility, leading to lower yields. These conditions give rise to a recursive cycle: to secure sufficient crops, farmers intensify farming through either planting more often (often over-tilling their land) or engaging in deforestation to expand their cropping lands (UNDP 2019). These actions can further the release and growth of CO_2 (which is otherwise sequestered in the soil and absorbed by trees and plants (Ontl 2012). The detrimental conditions of climate change continue.

While the planter, the soil, and the subsistence farmers, who were mostly women, were our initial focal points of study, just as agential realism predicts the ways boundaries shift, unfolding and enfolding new intra-activities, our study, which involved multiple field visits over three years, expanded as other interventions, involving other (non)humans, became visible to us. For example, because the planter alone was insufficient to heal the land, we also had to: provide the farmers with fertilizers, pesticides, and genetically modified seeds (things that reflect further intra-activities of global markets); demonstrate how to use the planter; and encourage the farmers to find something akin to mulch to cover the ground (residual corn stalks, leaves, or branches from trees, grass). It was an odd combination of conservation agriculture with modern farming necessities. There were also other things marking the land, such as the presence of empty and abandoned water ponds versus water-filled and effectively used water ponds that stemmed from the government and a prior NGO's intervention in the community. Water ponds opened up possibilities for farmers to grow their own kitchen gardens, helping them to increase familial sources of food.

The research questions—acknowledging the 'agential'

Initially, I approached the research questions from an intersectionality lens, focused on discerning why certain farmers did and did not adopt these climate-resilience strategies, such as the farming practices we encouraged and the water ponds. I asked: *what* were the overlapping sources of (dis)advantage that affected uptake? To answer the 'what', I supplemented intersectionality theory's assessment of social (human) structures with an 'ecological-intersectionality perspective' (Steinfield and Holt 2020), which captures both social/human and nature/non-human elements (as Indigenous scholarship and agential realism encourages). Understanding the 'what' or essence of overlaps or entanglements and intra-activities, however, does not sufficiently capture the agential nature of reality. To acknowledge the agential component of a 'holistic, agential praxis' requires shifting from an analysis of *what* to questions of *how* (Barad 2007), drawing attention to the *process* of entanglements or relationalities (Little Bear 2011). Thus, although an intersectionality analysis provides a good starting point in that it captures the elements surrounding our phenomenon of inquiry—the production of social inequities—it needs to be further supplemented with a recognition of: *how* the dynamism (agency) produced through intra-activities (per Barad) or flows of energy (per Indigenous thought) emerges, *how* the agential cuts we and other (non)humans make have implications and leave 'marks on bodies,' and *how* we create and are going to respond to the (im)possibilities of agential intra-activities.

Data collection—enabling a holistic rendering

Answering both sets of research questions—the *what* and the *how*—demands that scholars extend their data collected. For example, we collected data that could shed light on the social, political, and economic structures (per intersectionality theory), as well as the ecological elements (in line with agential realism and Indigenous recognition of the non-human). Collectively, this data allowed us to understand how and why people experienced climate change and our interventions in different ways. The data included: our interviews with and observations of farmers that documented their experiences with non-human matter (e.g., the planter, water ponds, crop infestations, weather, seeds) as well as their life stories and intra-actions with other humans; visits to government agencies and interviews with government officials to identify localized structures and practices; news items, articles, and reports that captured additional overlapping macro-meso-micro social and ecological dynamics (e.g., government reports and IPCC documents); photos of (non)human bodies (e.g., corn stalks); experiences of touching things, such as the soil, crops, and mulch substitutes, and samples of soil and water so that I could sense and make visible the composing microorganisms of non-human matter. Additionally, to capture a more expansive rendering of space and time (or spacetimematter), we identified the (non)human things across different places (e.g., the human actions, government policies, and international protocols that support or limit the generation of CO_2 in other countries) and times (e.g., historical versus current documents related to Kenya's (limited) investments in education systems or agricultural research and development). Finally, I turned the data collection inward, tracing (through reflexive fieldnotes and memos) the effects of the agential cuts made by us and our intervention (apparatus). Notably, by being able to continually go back to the field I was able to capture the evolution of these effects, and thus how we were/are a part of the intra-activities and contribute to the (im)possibilities. Varied data points, such as these, are necessary to achieve a 'holistic' rendering of reality that can capture the wide-reaching agential intra-actions and possible, unfolding, praxis.

Analysis & findings—moving from critical praxis to a holistic agential praxis

With any analysis of inequities, an ecological-intersectionality theory provides a good starting point to accomplish a more holistic perspective. Although it focuses on critically assessing interactions (versus intra-actions), it does enable one to map out or make visible the various (non)human elements that create (dis)advantages, in this case, those that contributed to farmers being supported versus constrained in their capacity to adopt the climate change interventions. For example, we identified how neocolonial practices enacted predominately by Global North policy makers overlap with localized ethnocentric practices of government officials to limit state investments in research and development as well as educational opportunities. Insufficient investments in research and development reduced the effectiveness of the local maize seed to withstand the erratic weather. Limited educational opportunities, which intersected with heteronormative, patriarchal practices and norms that viewed young women's bodies as appropriate for marriage, childbirth, and care work versus education, marked many female farmers' bodies with low literacy. Low literacy affects the uptake and reproduction of social innovations like our conservation agricultural practices and the water ponds (Steinfield and Holt 2019). A neoliberal, patriarchal capitalism further marks women's bodies: interventions (including are own) were (and are) premised on an ideology or mentality (accepted by the farmers) of 'empower-yourself-through-the-market', or for women, 'empower-your-family-through-the-market'. However, this ideology assumes equal access to the market. It can make invisible the challenges less-abled (i.e., elderly, low literate) females, who bear the majority of care and household duties due to patriarchal norms, may face. Additionally, economic exclusions versus inclusions and the (under) valuation of work gave rise to differing socioeconomic positions, which influenced a farmers' willingness and ability to adopt social innovations. Farmers in lower socioeconomic positions, who were also often low literate, faced greater trade-offs in adopting the social innovations. The necessity for producing crops reduced their ability to risk trying new things. And they had limited ability to contribute required monetary or time/energy investments (poorer farmers go and work on richer farmers' fields). The (dis)advantages created by these social dynamics further interact with ecological dynamics (e.g., GHGs, localized erratic weather patterns, sunshine, rain, plant infestations, soil quality, type, and microorganisms), to create significant disadvantages for very poor, less-abled females (i.e., elderly, low literate) in comparison to their male counterparts or richer, and literate females. Resultantly, interventions like ours or the water ponds, which do not challenge the neoliberal patriarchal capitalism, can exacerbate time poverty, particularly for women in disadvantaged positions: their survivalist tasks are not reallocated, they are merely expected to do more (i.e., empower themselves/their families). A recursive cycle can ensue: their time poverty can prevent them from adopting social innovations, but by foregoing the social innovations, their time poverty remains or is even exacerbated. In turn, the gap between the haves and the have nots—the advantaged and disadvantaged farmers—can widen. Indeed, in casting a self-reflexive lens back on our actions, we recognize that we may have inadvertently contributed to widening this gap.

In this brief summary of our ecological-intersectionality findings (Steinfield and Holt 2020) we see many contributing elements that interact with each other. To achieve a 'holistic agential praxis,' however, requires that we identify how the boundaries of these time- and space-spanning (non)human elements and discourse blur into agential intra-activities, or how Spirit connects and animates everything, giving way to (im)possibilities. To explore this process of the phenomena's becoming, I apply a diffractive method of reading the natural through the social and vice versa. In adopting this method, my goal is to find other ways to view the data so that I can increase my attentiveness and discern *how* marks on bodies are made.

For example, if I read the ecological data with a social lens that seeks to discern flows of power and the dynamism it produces, I perceive how the growing power of GHGs creates a recursive flow of intra-activities, and causes different things to matter. As space-spanning GHGs entangle energy waves and their heat in the atmosphere and then disperse the heat through unequal increases in temperature, localized erratic weather patterns intra-act with the historically ladened farming tools and methods employed by farmers. For (female) farmers, the intra-actions of the aforementioned social dynamics (which reach back in time) and their present-day experiences of these dynamics (e.g., low literacy, economic exclusion, time poverty) blur into their intra-action with the weather patterns, farming tools and social innovations (the planter, water ponds), creating marks on the body of the land. Some land is well-nourished, with its microorganisms helping to prevent the growth of GHGs' power by absorbing CO_2. Other land is over-tilled. Over-tilled land marks/destroys the soil's microorganisms and releases CO_2 into the atmosphere. The power of GHGs thus grows, and the process risks being repeated. Over-tilled land gives way to limited food production, and to farmers further over-tilling the land in attempts to secure sufficient food. These recursive intra-actions blur into the scientific studies and publications that mark the bodies of female farmers, making them visible in a way that paints farmers in developing countries as vulnerable (e.g., Nellemann, Verma, and Hislop 2011). These ecological-social entanglements provide opportunities (agency) for relationships to form with NGOs, Green Climate Fund projects, and even our own research project, which unfold into other intra-actions and (im)possibilities.

Although this is just a brief recount of some of the agential intra-actions, it demonstrates how viewing things from a different perspective (e.g., by tracing power in ecological things) can allow us to make different bodies visible: We find that the bodies marked by (dis)advantages are not only human bodies (female farmers) but also include the land and its microorganisms. Moreover, the continual, agential intra-actions of these marked bodies open up possibilities for the constituted nature of their oppression to be addressed.

In contrast, when reading the social through the natural, I consider the different wavelengths of waves, and how humans and non-humans have differing capacities for seeing and hearing a light or sound wave depending on its length. This gives me pause to question: are there energy flows or intra-activities others see and hear that I cannot (or do not want to)? What intra-activities might the soil, crops, or farmers identify? I expand upon the visible elements mapped out in the initial ecological-intersectionality and intra-activity analysis to probe for the invisible and to turn the lens inward to acknowledge my involvement in the intra-activity and the agential cuts I make. I engage in response-ive activities—listening to, learning from, and responding to (non)human things. In walking through the fields, I feel the soil and observe the presence or absence of fungi on crops and microorganisms in the soil. The importance of water comes to the fore. Too much water and fungi appear; too little and micro-organisms disappear. I learn to appreciate and respect the many factors that go into maintaining a balanced ecosystem. I look for marks on the body of soil, becoming aware of whether it has been or has not been plowed, and how these actions enact cuts in microorganisms. I learn from some farmers how to be more response-able in maintaining a balanced ecosystem by using local practices (e.g., substituting ash for pesticide) and I pass on these words of wisdom, encouraging other farmers to be more response-able in maintaining a balanced ecosystem. These shared insights form new intra-actions and possibilities of restoring the land and alleviating farmers' disadvantages.

I also question whether there are wavelengths that the farmers and I see differently. Indeed, while I view the female farmers' duties of care as an impediment to their well-being and capacity to adopt the social innovations, they view it as a source of pride and a key part of their identities. We each bring different personal wavelengths (histories and societal-informed stories) that cause us to see marks on bodies differently. Response-able responding would thus entail a recognition and celebration of marks that I once renounced. I sit with the truth that I struggle to change my wavelengths to positively acknowledge these marks. But by not recognizing their wavelengths, I am contributing to marking their bodies and allowing a certain critical discourse to prevail. What emerges is the need for a mestiza consciousness (Anzaldúa 1987) that can push against the tendency to mark bodies as this or that, that can acknowledge the emergence of multiple identities and recognize the multi-faceted nature of reality. It implores me to be careful in how I am a-count-ing for bodies and to be response-able to the intra-actions and (im)possibilities that may unfold. A different, diffractive reading of reality makes visible what we may (sub)consciously make invisible, thereby opening up possibilities for discourse to be destabilized and different (im)possibilities to emerge.

Thus, the final consideration in my analysis is to recognize these (im)possibilities and to advance a praxis—a politics of possibilities—that encourages others to continue to recognize how different bodies—human and non-human—matter. One body that matters is that of the farmer, yet as we found, not all farmers have the same marks on their bodies, and thus interventions need to adjust or target their approach so that a more equitable level of possibilities occurs. Our follow-up interviews, for example, made visible how the interventions (conservation agriculture techniques, water ponds) unfolded helpful possibilities for some farmers: by achieving better yields, they secured more sources of food and income and could reallocate funds to education or to time saving devices (e.g., gas cookers). Yet for other farmers, nothing seemed to change, in part because of the intra-actions surrounding their social locations. Desires to continue the intervention were disrupted by other new intra-activities (medical emergencies) or the historical legacies of neocolonialism/ethnocentrism (low literacy), economic exclusion (limited funds and willingness to take risk/enact change) and patriarchy (limited time). As we withdrew from the field, new impossibilities likely sprung up as those reliant on us for support may have resorted to the familiar, traditional ways of intra-acting with the land, foregoing what could be possible. The marks of oppressions on their human bodies and on the land may be deeply ingrained. A very care-full engagement process is accordingly needed—one that allow us (scholars, practitioners, readers) to consider how the intra-activities of which we are apart and the bodies we make matter versus not matter can create (in)visibilities, breed feelings of hope or despair, and perpetuate intersectional advantages or disadvantages and the gap between the haves and the have nots.

Lastly, I want to stress that the words we write in articles, publications, and grants can also result in (im)possibilities. They join the intra-activities, enacting agential cuts. For instance, our research enabled us to achieve academic publications (Steinfield and Holt 2020, 2019; Steinfield et al. 2020). These may become entangled in other conversations about climate change or open up opportunities for further research. But in achieving these publications we also had to silence certain stories as we became entangled with the academic standards and editorial processes demanded to achieve publication. The silences we produced have agency, creating implications for how phenomena unravel. We never did tell the full story of ecological-matter's dynamism. It is there, however, waiting to be told. In the same way we make visible the marks on human bodies, the marks on non-human bodies need to be made visible. My praxis or adoption of a politics of possibilities is my response-ability to this silence, which in part, is this very publication.

Notes

1 While this chapter touches on some Indigenous-based theories and scholarship, I also recognize that Indigenous knowledge is diverse. This chapter is thus merely a starting point. I encourage scholars to continue to explore the wide and rich terrain of Indigenous knowledge, and to work to decolonialize prevailing Anglo-Eurocentric perspectives through cultivating what the Sami scholar, Rauna Kuokkanen (2011) describes as "multiepistemic literacy" (57).
2 The difference between postcolonialism and decolonialism is a matter of conceptualization and lines of thought that are predicated on historical emergence. In brief, 'post' implies a recognition of the effects of colonialism and reworking of representations to correct for said effects. Postcolonialism analysis, like Anzaldúa's (1987) work, seeks to introduce another way of viewing the world. On the other hand, 'de'-colonialism acknowledges that things existed before colonialism, such as Indigenous knowledges. The 'de' escapes the Western demarcations of time in which 'post'-colonialism is trapped. It is "neither new or post" (Mignolo 2017, n.p.). The knowledge project of the 'de' has "the goal of re:—epistemic reconstitutions, re-emergence, resurgence, re-existence" (ibid.). In some accounts, decolonialism is also viewed as more radical—concerned with revolution, inequities, violence, and political identity—while postcolonialism studies concentrate on knowledge/power hierarchies, representations, narratives, and issues of hybridity and diaspora (Kohn and Reddy 2017).
3 De Line (2016) originally describes the blurred relationship between human and non-human things as "All My/Our Relations". I have intentionally replaced the "/" with a "-" to ensure it is not confused with the arguments I am making with respect to the other academic-created binaries and hierarchies (e.g., human/nonhuman).
4 Post-humanism, of which new materialism is a subset, reconceptualizes the human/non-human or subject/object relationship established by the Renaissance era's humanist approach. Under this latter view, humans were viewed as supreme to all other non-humans, as autonomous given their mind's capacity to think and control their body, and as "uniquely capable of and motivated by speech and reason" (Keeling and Lehman 2018, n.p.). The post-humanism movement challenges the idealization of the human by demonstrating how humans and their

mind, speech, and reason are shaped by the social, cultural, and discursive environmental factors. That is, they are not autonomous but bound up with the "larger evolving ecosystem" (ibid.). What I refer to as Haraway's stronger post-humanist slant is one that not only disrupts the humanist's ideals of human supremacy through a flat ontology but also seeks to critique and call into question what we mean by 'human,' including disrupting the typical bodily boundaries we view as defining humans from non-human. Although post-humanist works tend to claim authority over a flat ontology, readers should note that Indigenous perspectives of the world did not hold these binary views: they have always seen humans and non-humans as co-existing and as co-evolving (Sundberg 2014).

5 Niw_hk_m_kanak are the words used by the Cree and Metis nations (which include Blackfoot and Haudenosaunee Confederacies) in opening and closing ceremonies. "The words acknowledge and bless all that is in the continuum, continually in flux, in all our relations; all matter, all energy waves that are in contingent relationality through a familial network" (De Line 2016).

6 Barad's employment of diffractive methods to identify the relations of things is perhaps well-suited for Euro-Western scholars who are familiar with gaining knowledge based on what they examine. In contrast, Indigenous approaches to understanding relationality are often achieved by sensing or communing with things. That is, Indigenous practices center on experiences of relationality versus merely identifying them (Cajete 2000; De Line 2016).

References

Allen, Myles R., Opha Pauline Dube, William Solecki, Fernando Aragón-Durand, Wolfgang Cramer, Stephen Humphreys, Mikiko Kainuma, et al. 2018. "Framing and Context." In *Global Warming of 1.5°C*, edited by V. Masson-Delmotte, P. Zhai, H. Pörtner, D. Roberts, J. Skea, P.R. Shukla, A. Pirani, et al., 49–91. Geneva: Intergovernmental Panel on Climate Change.

American Chemical Society. 2021. "What Is the Greenhouse Effect?" American Chemical Society. https://www.acs.org/content/acs/en/climatescience/climatesciencenarratives/what-is-the-greenhouse-effect.html.

Anthias, Floya. 2013. "Intersectional What? Social Divisions, Intersectionality and Levels of Analysis." *Ethnicities* 13 (1): 3–19.

Anzaldúa, Gloria. 1987. *Borderlands: The New Mestiza = La Frontera*. San Francisco, CA: Aunt Lute Books.

Arvin, Maile, Eve Tuck, and Angie Morrill. 2013. "Decolonizing Feminism: Challenging Connections between Settler Colonialism and Heteropatriarchy." *Feminist Formations* 25: 8–34.

Bajde, Domen. 2013. "Consumer Culture Theory (Re)Visits Actor–Network Theory: Flattening Consumption Studies." *Marketing Theory* 13 (2): 227–242. https://doi.org/10.1177/1470593113477887.

Barad, Karen. 1998. "Getting Real: Technoscientific Practices and the Materialization of Reality." *Differences: A Journal of Feminist Cultural Studies* 10 (2): 87–91.

———. 2001. "Re (Con) Figuring Space, Time, and Matter." In *Feminist Locations: Global and Local, Theory and Practice*, edited by Marianne DeKoven, 75–109. New Brunswick, NJ: Rutgers University Press.

———. 2003. "Posthumanist Performativity: Toward an Understanding of How Matter Comes to Matter." *Signs: Journal of Women in Culture and Society* 28 (3): 801–831. https://doi.org/10.1086/345321.

———. 2007. *Meeting the Universe Halfway: Quantum Physics and the Entanglement of Matter and Meaning*. Durham, NC: Duke University Press.

———. 2010. "Quantum Entanglements and Hauntological Relations of Inheritance: Dis/Continuities, Spacetime Enfoldings, and Justice-to-Come." *Derrida Today* 3 (2): 240–268.

———. 2014. "Diffracting Diffraction: Cutting Together-Apart." *Parallax* 20 (3): 168–187. https://doi.org/10.1080/13534645.2014.927623.

Barthes, Roland. 1974. *S/Z*. New York: Hill and Wang.
Battiste, Marie, ed. 2011. *Reclaiming Indigenous Voice and Vision*. Vancouver: UBC Press.
Berger, Peter L., and Thomas Luckmann. 1991. *The Social Construction of Reality: A Treatise in the Sociology of Knowledge*, 10. London: Penguin.
Bettany, Shona M. 2007. "The Material Semiotics of Consumption or Where (and What) Are the Objects in Consumer Culture Theory?" In *Consumer Culture Theory*, 41–56. Bingley: Emerald Group Publishing Limited. https://doi.org/10.1016/S0885-2111(06)11003-0.
Bettany, Shona M., and Rory Daly. 2008. "Figuring Companion-Species Consumption: A Multi-Site Ethnography of the Post-Canine Afghan Hound." *Journal of Business Research* 61 (5): 408–418. https://doi.org/10.1016/j.jbusres.2006.08.010.
Bettany, Shona M., and Ben Kerrane. 2011. "The (Post-Human) Consumer, the (Post-Avian) Chicken and the (Post-Object) Eglu: Towards a Material-Semiotics of Anti-Consumption." *European Journal of Marketing* 45 (11/12): 1746–1756. https://doi.org/10.1108/03090561111167388.
Bettany, Shona M., Ben Kerrane, and Margaret K. Hogg. 2014. "The Material-Semiotics of Fatherhood: The Co-Emergence of Technology and Contemporary Fatherhood." *Journal of Business Research* 67 (7): 1544–1551. https://doi.org/10.1016/j.jbusres.2014.01.012.
Bilge, Sirma. 2013. "Intersectionality Undone: Saving Intersectionality from Feminist Intersectionality Studies." *Du Bois Review* 10 (2): 405–24. https://doi.org/10.1017/S1742058X13000283.
Bourdieu, Pierre. 1984. *Distinction: A Social Critique of the Judgement of Taste*. Translated by Richard Nice. Cambridge, MA: Harvard University Press.
Buchanan-Oliver, Margo, Angela Cruz, and Jonathan E. Schroeder. 2010. "Shaping the Body and Technology: Discursive Implications for the Strategic Communication of Technological Brands." *European Journal of Marketing* 44 (5): 635–652.
Butler, Judith. 1988. "Performative Acts and Gender Constitution: An Essay in Phenomenology and Feminist Theory." *Theatre Journal* 40 (4): 519–531.
———. 1990. *Gender Trouble: Feminism and the Subversion of Identity*. New York: Routledge.
Cajete, Gregory. 2000. *Native Science: Natural Laws of Interdependence*. Santa Fe: Clear Light Publishers.
Callon, Michel. 1984. "Some Elements of a Sociology of Translation: Domestication of the Scallops and the Fishermen of St Brieuc Bay." *The Sociological Review* 32 (1_suppl): 196–233. https://doi.org/10.1111/j.1467-954X.1984.tb00113.x.
Campbell, Norah, Aidan O'Driscoll, and Michael Saren. 2010. "The Posthuman: The End and the Beginning of the Human." *Journal of Consumer Behaviour* 9 (2): 86–101. https://doi.org/10.1002/cb.306.
Canniford, Robin, and Domen Bajde, eds. 2015. *Assembling Consumption: Researching Actors, Networks and Markets*. New York: Routledge.
Carbado, Devon W., Kimberlé Williams Crenshaw, Vickie M. Mays, and Barbara Tomlinson. 2013. "Intersectionality: Mapping the Movements of a Theory." *Du Bois Review* 10 (2): 303–312. https://doi.org/10.1017/S1742058X13000349.
Chun, Jennifer Jihye, George Lipsitz, and Young Shin. 2013. "Intersectionality as a Social Movement Strategy: Asian Immigrant Women Advocates." *Signs* 38 (4): 917–940. https://doi.org/10.1086/669575.
Cluley, Robert. 2018. "The Construction of Marketing Measures: The Case of Viewability." *Marketing Theory* 18 (3): 287–305. https://doi.org/10.1177/1470593117753981.
Collins, Patricia Hill. 2015. "Intersectionality's Definitional Dilemmas." *Annual Review of Sociology* 41: 1–20.
———. 2020. "Intersectionality as Critical Inquiry." In *Companion to Feminist Studies*, 105–128. John Wiley & Sons, Ltd. https://doi.org/10.1002/9781119314967.ch7.
Corus, Canan, Bige Saatcioglu, Carol Kaufman-Scarborough, Christopher P. Blocker, Shikha Upadhyaya, and Samuelson Appau. 2016. "Transforming Poverty-Related Policy with Intersectionality." *Journal of Public Policy & Marketing* 35 (2): 211–222. https://doi.org/10.1509/jppm.15.141.

Crenshaw, Kimberle. 1989. "Demarginalizing the Intersection of Race and Sex: A Black Feminist Critique of Antidiscrimination Doctrine, Feminist Theory and Antiracist Politics." *University of Chicago Legal Forum* 1 (8): 139–167.

Davis, Kathy. 2008. "Intersectionality as Buzzword: A Sociology of Science Perspective on What Makes a Feminist Theory Successful." *Feminist Theory* 9 (1): 67–85.

De Line, Sebastian. 2016. "All My/Our Relations." *Open! Platform for Art, Culture and the Public Domain.* https://onlineopen.org/all-my-our-relations.

Dill, Bonnie Thornton, and Marla H. Kohlman. 2012. "Intersectionality: A Transformative Paradigm in Feminist Theory and Social Justice." In *Handbook of Feminist Research: Theory and Praxis*, edited by Sharlene Nagy Hesse-Biber, 2:154–74. Thousand Oaks, CA: Sage.

Dolphijn, Rick, and Iris van der Tuin, eds. 2012. *New Materialism: Interviews & Cartographies*. Ann Arbor, MI: Open Humanities Press.

Durkheim, Emile. 2014. *The Division of Labor in Society*. New York: Simon and Schuster.

Foucault, Michel. 2001. *Madness and Civilization: A History of Insanity in the Age of Reason*. Abingdon: Routledge.

Gamble, Christopher N., Joshua S. Hanan, and Thomas Nail. 2019. "What Is New Materialism?" *Angelaki* 24 (6): 111–134. https://doi.org/10.1080/0969725X.2019.1684704.

Giesler, Markus. 2012. "How Doppelgänger Brand Images Influence the Market Creation Process: Longitudinal Insights from the Rise of Botox Cosmetic." *Journal of Marketing* 76 (6): 55–68. https://doi.org/10.1509/jm.10.0406.

Goffman, Erving. 1976. *Gender Advertisements*. Cambridge, MA: Harvard University Press. http://eric.ed.gov/?id=ED187633.

Gopaldas, Ahir. 2013. "Intersectionality 101." *Journal of Public Policy & Marketing* 32 (special issue): 90–94. https://doi.org/10.1509/jppm.12.044.

Gopaldas, Ahir, and Anton Siebert. 2018. "Women over 40, Foreigners of Color, and Other Missing Persons in Globalizing Mediascapes: Understanding Marketing Images as Mirrors of Intersectionality." *Consumption Markets & Culture*, May. http://www.tandfonline.com/doi/abs/10.1080/10253866.2018.1462170.

Haraway, Donna. 1991. *Simians, Cyborgs, and Women: The Reinvention of Nature*. New York: Routledge.

———. 2008. *When Species Meet*. Minneapolis: University of Minnesota Press.

Harris, Kate Lockwood, and Karen Lee Ashcraft. 2019. "Doing Power, Deferring Difference: Gendered-Raced Processes and the Case of Karen Barad." https://www.egosnet.org/jart/prj3/egos/releases/de/upload/Uploads/TIA-2019_st-10_Harris_Ashcraft.pdf.

Hein, Wendy, Laurel Steinfield, Nacima Ourahmoune, Catherine Coleman, Linda Tuncay Zayer, and Jon Littlefield. 2016. "Gender Justice and the Market: A Transformative Consumer Research Perspective." *Journal of Public Policy & Marketing* 35 (2): 223–236. https://doi.org/10.1509/jppm.15.146.

Hopkins, Peter. 2019. "Social Geography I: Intersectionality." *Progress in Human Geography* 43 (5): 937–947. https://doi.org/10.1177/0309132517743677.

Hulko, Wendy. 2009. "The Time-and Context-Contingent Nature of Intersectionality and Interlocking Oppressions." *Affilia* 24 (1): 44–55.

IPCC. 2007. *Climate Change 2007: The Physical Science Basis. Contribution of Working Group I to the Fourth Assessment Report of the Intergovernmental Panel on Climate Change*. Cambridge: Cambridge University Press.

———. 2014. *Climate Change 2014: Mitigation of Climate Change. Contribution of Working Group III to the Fifth Assessment Report of the Intergovernmental Panel on Climate Change*. Cambridge: Cambridge University Press. https://www.ipcc.ch/report/ar5/wg3/.

Juelskjær, Malou, and Nete Schwennesen. 2012. "Intra-Active Entanglements—An Interview with Karen Barad." *Kvinder, Køn & Forskning* 1–2: 10–23.

Keeling, Diane Marie, and Marguerite Nguyen Lehman. 2018. "Posthumanism." *Oxford Research Encyclopedia of Communication*, April 26. https://doi.org/10.1093/acrefore/9780190228613.013.627.

Kennedy, Ann-Marie, Cathy McGouran, and Joya A. Kemper. 2020. "Alternative Paradigms for Sustainability: The Māori Worldview." *European Journal of Marketing* 54: 825–855.

Kohn, Margaret, and Kavita Reddy. 2017. "Colonialism." In *The Stanford Encyclopedia of Philosophy*, edited by Edward N. Zalta. Metaphysics Research Lab, Stanford University. https://plato.stanford.edu/archives/fall2017/entries/colonialism/.

Kuokkanen, Rauna. 2011. *Reshaping the University: Responsibility, Indigenous Epistemes, and the Logic of the Gift*. Vancouver: UBC Press.

Lassalle, Paul, and Eleanor Shaw. 2021. "Trailing Wives and Constrained Agency among Women Migrant Entrepreneurs: An Intersectional Perspective." *Entrepreneurship Theory and Practice*. https://doi.org/10.1177/1042258721990331.

Latour, Bruno. 2008. *Reassembling the Social: An Introduction to Actor-Network-Theory*. Oxford: Oxford University Press.

Latour, Bruno, and Steve Woolgar. 1979. *Laboratory Life: The Construction of Scientific Facts*. Los Angeles, CA: Sage.

Law, John. 2009. "Actor Network Theory and Material Semiotics." In *The New Blackwell Companion to Social Theory*, edited by Bryan S. Turner, 141–158. Chichester: Blackwell Publishing Ltd.

Lévi-Strauss, Claude. 1969. *The Elementary Structures of Kinship*. Rev. ed. Boston, MA: Beacon Press.

Little Bear, Leroy. 2011. "Jagged Worldviews Colliding." In *Reclaiming Indigenous Voice and Vision*, edited by Marie Battiste, 77–85. Vancouver: UBC Press.

Lucarelli, Andrea, and Anette Hallin. 2015. "Brand Transformation: A Performative Approach to Brand Regeneration." *Journal of Marketing Management* 31 (1–2): 84–106. https://doi.org/10.1080/0267257X.2014.982688.

Lutz, Helma, Maria Teresa Herrera Vivar, and Linda Supik, eds. 2011. *Framing Intersectionality: Debates on a Multi-Faceted Concept in Gender Studies*. Surrey: Ashgate Publishing, Ltd.

MacKinnon, Catharine A. 2013. "Intersectionality as Method: A Note." *Signs* 38 (4): 1019–1030. https://doi.org/10.1086/669570.

Marx, Karl. 1977. *Capital: A Critique of Political Economy*. Translated by Ben Fowkes. New York: Vintage Books.

Mason, Katy, Hans Kjellberg, and Johan Hagberg. 2015. "Exploring the Performativity of Marketing: Theories, Practices and Devices." *Journal of Marketing Management* 31 (1–2): 1–15. https://doi.org/10.1080/0267257X.2014.982932.

McCall, Leslie. 1992. "Does Genderfit? Bourdieu, Feminism, and Conceptions of Social Order." *Theory and Society* 21 (6): 837–67. https://doi.org/10.1007/BF00992814.

———. 2005. "The Complexity of Intersectionality." *Signs* 30 (3): 1771–1800. https://doi.org/10.1086/426800.

Mignolo, Walter D. 2017. "Interview—Walter Mignolo/Part 2: Key Concepts." *E-International Relations* (blog), January 21. https://www.e-ir.info/2017/01/21/interview-walter-mignolopart-2-key-concepts/.

Murris, Karin, and Vivienne Bozalek. 2019. "Diffraction and Response-Able Reading of Texts: The Relational Ontologies of Barad and Deleuze." *International Journal of Qualitative Studies in Education* 32 (7): 872–886.

Nash, Jennifer C. 2008. "Re-Thinking Intersectionality." *Feminist Review* 89: 1–15.

Nellemann, Christian, Ritu Verma, and Lawrence Hislop. 2011. *Women at the Frontline of Climate Change: Gender Risks and Hopes, a Rapid Response Assessment*. Norway: United Nations Environment Programme.

Noble, Safiya Umoja. 2018. *Algorithms of Oppression: How Search Engines Reinforce Racism*. New York: NYU Press.

Ontl, Todd A. 2012. "Soil Carbon Storage." *Nature Education Knowledge* 3 (10): 35.

Rodriguez, Jenny K., Evangelina Holvino, Joyce K. Fletcher, and Stella M. Nkomo. 2016. "The Theory and Praxis of Intersectionality in Work and Organisations: Where Do We Go from Here?" *Gender, Work & Organization* 23 (3): 201–222. https://doi.org/10.1111/gwao.12131.

Rosiek, Jerry Lee, Jimmy Snyder, and Scott L. Pratt. 2020. "The New Materialisms and Indigenous Theories of Non-Human Agency: Making the Case for Respectful Anti-Colonial Engagement." *Qualitative Inquiry* 26 (3–4): 331–346.

Saatcioglu, Bige, and Canan Corus. 2014. "Poverty and Intersectionality A Multidimensional Look into the Lives of the Impoverished." *Journal of Macromarketing* 34 (2): 122–132. https://doi.org/10.1177/0276146713520600.

Sanghvi, Minita. 2019. *Gender and Political Marketing in the United States and the 2016 Presidential Election: An Analysis of Why She Lost*. Gender and Politics. Palgrave Macmillan. https://doi.org/10.1007/978-1-137-60171-1.

Scott, Kristin, Diane M. Martin, and John W. Schouten. 2014. "Marketing and the New Materialism." *Journal of Macromarketing* 34 (3): 282–90. https://doi.org/10.1177/0276146714532471.

Steinfield, Laurel. 2020. "1, 2, 3, 4. I Declare…empowerment? A Material-Discursive Analysis of the Marketisation, Measurement and Marketing of Women's Economic Empowerment." *Journal of Marketing Management* 37 (3/4): 320–356. https://doi.org/10.1080/0267257X.2019.1699850.

Steinfield, Laurel, and Diane Holt. 2019. "Toward A Theory on the Reproduction of Social Innovations in Subsistence Marketplaces." *Journal of Product Innovation Management* 36 (6): 764–799. https://doi.org/10.1111/jpim.12510.

———. 2020. "Structures, Systems and Differences That Matter: Casting an Ecological-Intersectionality Perspective on Female Subsistence Farmers' Experiences of the Climate Crisis." *Journal of Macromarketing* 40 (4): 563–582. https://doi.org/10.1177/0276146720951238.

Steinfield, Laurel, Minita Sanghvi, Linda Tuncay Zayer, Catherine A. Coleman, Nacima Ourahmoune, Robert L. Harrison, Wendy Hein, and Jan Brace-Govan. 2019. "Transformative Intersectionality: Moving Business Towards a Critical Praxis." *Journal of Business Research* 100 (July): 366–75. https://doi.org/10.1016/j.jbusres.2018.12.031.

Steinfield, Laurel, Srinivas Venugopal, Samuelson Appau, Andres Barrios, Charlene Dadzie, Roland Gau, Diane Holt, Mai Nguyen Thi Tuyet, and Clifford Shultz. 2020. "Across Time, Across Space and Intersecting in Complex Ways: A Framework for Assessing Impacts of Environmental Disruptions on Nature-Dependent Prosumers." *Journal of Public Policy & Marketing* 40 (2): 262–284. https://doi.org/10.1177/0743915620976563.

Sundberg, Juanita. 2014. "Decolonizing Posthumanist Geographies." *Cultural Geographies* 21 (1): 33–47.

Taguchi, Hillevi Lenz. 2012. "A Diffractive and Deleuzian Approach to Analysing Interview Data." *Feminist Theory* 13 (3): 265–281. https://doi.org/10.1177/1464700112456001.

Todd, Zoe. 2016. "An Indigenous Feminist's Take on the Ontological Turn:'Ontology'Is Just Another Word for Colonialism." *Journal of Historical Sociology* 29 (1): 4–22.

UN News. 2020. "The Race to Zero Emissions, and Why the World Depends on It." *UN News*, November 30. https://news.un.org/en/story/2020/12/1078612.

UNDP. 2019. *Combatting Land Degradation—Securing a Sustainable Future*. New York: UNDP. https://www.undp.org/publications/combatting-land-degradation-securing-sustainable-future.

Van der Tuin, Iris, and Rick Dolphijn. 2010. "The Transversality of New Materialism." *Women: A Cultural Review* 21 (2): 153–171.

Walby, Sylvia, Jo Armstrong, and Sofia Strid. 2012. "Intersectionality: Multiple Inequalities in Social Theory." *Sociology* 46 (2): 224–240. https://doi.org/10.1177/0038038511416164.

Watts, Vanessa. 2013. "Indigenous Place-Thought and Agency amongst Humans and Non Humans (First Woman and Sky Woman Go on a European World Tour!)." *Decolonization: Indigeneity, Education & Society* 2 (1): 20–34.

19 Consumption beyond the binary

Feminism in transgender lives

Sophie Duncan Shepherd and Kathy Hamilton

Introduction

Gender is so deeply embedded in our sociocultural worldview that its influence is often hidden. Marketing has an unavoidable influence on gendered perceptions in society; through representation in advertising, segmentations, and brand meanings, marketers decide what (and in what ways) to promote (Visconti, Maclaran and Bettany 2018). Consumer socialisation of men and women to perform certain roles and to maintain particular identities is implicit, which not only creates conflict in those endeavouring to conform, but a foundational conflict in those who identify as distinct from a male/female gender binary. Sexuality is so closely linked to a person's conception of gender, that non-normative identities cause disruption across both categories. An individual cannot be intelligible without being gendered (Butler 1990), and cisheteronormativity enforces repetition of culturally recognisable practices deemed to represent either being male and masculine, or female and feminine. The emergence of increasingly visible non-normative gender identities challenges cisheteronormativity through disruption and subversion of consumer identity practices and norms, creating space for the expression of transgender and gender diverse identities. As Marques (2019, 203) puts it, "a focus on transgender people's lives, experiences, discourses, and expectations helps to critically reflect upon gender by recognising and exploring existing gender diversity". Thus, understanding the relationship between consumption and gender, encompassing non-normative experiences of consuming gender, is vital for marketing as academic discipline, business practice, and site of social change.

In defining the term transgender, it must be acknowledged that the language used by the LGBT+ community is often contested and varied; for some, a word such as 'queer' is fundamentally harmful, for others it is a reclaimed slur, which can be used for self-description despite its historical connotations. For our purposes here, the term 'transgender' is defined as "an umbrella term that refers to individuals whose gender presentation is so different from ideals for the sex assigned to them at birth that it defies traditional notions of what it means to be male or female" (Levitt and Ippolito 2014, 1728). Where transgender identity is referred to, it is vital to be aware that this encompasses an unstable landscape of gender non-conformity. Within the transgender umbrella, there are a variety of nonbinary and binary trans identities. As Vincent (2018) points out, there has historically been a delineation in research between those who seek access to medical transition via hormone therapy and surgery, and those who do not. Some trans people choose not to pursue medical transition, and instead socially transition (changing gender presentation, pronouns, etc.). Binary transitions from male to female or female to male

DOI: 10.4324/9781003042587-23

do not represent the only ways to transition either; many (though not all) nonbinary people also identify as trans (Vincent 2016), where the term 'trans' simply represents a discontinuity between gender identity and assigned gender at birth. The complex relationships within the transgender umbrella oblige an awareness of the nuance at play in gender diverse identities. We suggest that it is this very instability of identity that enables new perspectives on gender to be expressed.

This chapter will begin with positioning transgender and gender non-conforming consumers within a broader overview of gender in consumer and marketing research. Following a discussion of transgender representation in current research, the chapter then turns to the analysis, insights, and perspectives accessible to marketing scholars through transgender, queer, and feminist theorising. In doing so, we seek to deepen our understanding of heterogeneous non-normative gender, sexuality, and consumer identity. We will also draw inspiration from these studies to suggest areas for future research along with suggestions of appropriate methodologies for accessing the voices of these often invisible and marginalised consumers.

Consuming (trans)gender

Gender studies in marketing have roots in social and cognitive psychology, where "consumers' gender is generally understood as biological, fixed or constructed as 'choice', reflecting the discipline's evolution from behaviourist perspectives" (Hearn and Hein 2015, 1640). Following the interpretive turn in consumer research in the 1990s, researchers began to explore gender in more depth as socioculturally constructed. Creating and recreating meanings through social practices is a theme which appears in several consumer research studies on gender. Looking at the ways in which an individual becomes gendered through social interactions, conventions and norms, and ideals of behaviour has helped consumer researchers to apply a gender lens to various phenomena, including gift giving (Fischer and Arnold 2002), motherhood and caring responsibilities (Thompson 1996), and the construction of masculinity (Holt and Thompson 2004).

The degree of congruity between gender identity and consumer behaviour has also been investigated but with an assumed static nature:

> the consumer's gender has tended to be viewed as fixed based on biological sex, that is, male consumers will be masculine and prefer a masculine brand or product, while female consumer will seek congruity between their feminine self-concept and their preferred brands and products.
>
> (Oakenfull 2012)

Doing gender, as proposed by West and Zimmerman (1987), is a framework on which many consumer studies of gender have drawn. In this influential chapter, the authors conduct a sociological examination of how the 'doing' of gender emerges in social situations as "a routine, methodological, and recurring accomplishment" (126). The doing of gender as described here also links to the early gender performativity work of Judith Butler, which is explored in more detail later in this chapter.

Contrary to much other research of transgender identities, trans doings of gender have received considerable attention, for example, through the work of symbolic interactionists in the field of sociology examining the navigation of the sex/gender system (Darwin 2017). Connell (2010) also notes in their work exploring the workplace experiences of trans people that 'doing' gender can involve an ongoing negotiation that challenges the assumed static link between gender identity and behaviour noted above. For Connell (2010, 51), these "moments of interactive resistance to gender stability" are not specific to trans people alone, as cisgender people also navigate, (de)construct, and challenge gender norms. Transgender and cisgender people "use certain pronouns; adjust their voice tones; let their hair grow or have it cut short or shaved; and choose certain items of clothes, shoes and accessories" in order to be perceived as masculine or feminine (Marques 2019, 210).

However, masculinities and femininities, gender identity, and the body, are generally described in marketing using binary terms despite acceptance of fluidity in the concept of gender (Bettany, Dobsch, O'Malley and Prothero 2010). Often, gender consumer research is skewed towards white, middle-class women (Maclaran 2015), and this unacknowledged bias is perpetuated through the stereotypes and gendered subjectivities produced and created by marketers (a criticism which has also been levelled at feminism itself). The dominance of heteronormative perspectives in gender studies of consumer culture is being challenged by researchers exploring the practices and performances of gender by LGBT+ consumers (Kates 2002, 2004; Oakenfull 2012, 2013), but this also reproduces a presumably unintended bias, this time towards white, middle-class gay men. This bias is again reflected in advertising to LGBT+ markets, recognising the assumed financial power of gay male consumers, prioritised over presumably poorer lesbian, bisexual, or other LGBT+ consumers (Oakenfull 2007).

Here, a difficulty for transgender research arises – "all too often transgender phenomena are misapprehended through a lens that privileges sexual orientation and sexual identity as the primary means of differing from heteronormativity" (Stryker 2004). As noted earlier, sexuality and gender are intimately linked such that without gender, sexuality becomes unintelligible. These identities overlap so that LGBT+ is itself a somewhat problematic umbrella; bringing together multiple identities of sexuality and gender, LGBT+ is often viewed as a subculture, which further complicates and homogenises consumers labelled as such (Visconti, Maclaran and Bettany 2018). In reducing identity to be solely based on sexuality, we risk overlooking other important markers of identity for trans and gender diverse consumers. This has resonance with Baker's (2006, 42) conceptualisation of consumer normalcy that reveals how consumers seek to achieve distinction in the marketplace from their personal tastes and expressions of individuality, and "not because of a category".

To date, very few studies in consumer research have centred the experiences of trans and gender diverse consumers. Mckeage, Crosby and Rittenburg (2017) have explored how these consumers experience vulnerability; the authors seek to revisit Baker, Gentry and Rittenburg's (2005) established model of consumer vulnerability through the lens of transgender people's lives. The authors reconceptualise consumer vulnerability as an iterative, cyclical system in which antecedent forces, vulnerability trigger events, and consumer responses are presented as impacting groups of consumers both singularly and as part of the system. Due to marketplace structures (product design, retail store layout, advertising, etc., can all be heavily gendered towards binary male/female, man/woman distinctions), transgender consumers must "navigate a marketplace that is unfriendly and places them at a distinct disadvantage" (McKeage, Crosby and Rittenburg 2017, 77). Drawing on interviews with trans and gender diverse participants, the authors further examine social gender norms in marketplace contexts and how these and other macro factors affect the experiences of trans individuals. The significant power of marketing in shaping normative gender is emphasised again as marketing actions "can have both positive and negative ramifications for these individuals far beyond the marketplace" (ibid., 86). It is important to note that, at time of writing, this chapter is the only consumer research specifically addressing trans and gender diverse identities. While it is reasonable to assume that transgender consumers may be vulnerable and marginalised in the marketplace, this assumption ignores the variability of expression and experience among trans consumers. The transgender experience presented in consumer research thus far is one of vulnerability, but we suggest that there is a much more comprehensive narrative of trans consumers' lives waiting to be told.

Normative gender culture is challenged by trans and nonbinary individuals; heteronormativity is so deeply embedded in institutional and cultural practices that it goes unseen and unquestioned in daily life, but is disrupted by 'deviant' practices which subvert gender (Wight 2011; Maclaran 2018). The ways in which consumers express gender identity has been explored in marketing research through the work of Judith Butler, whose theorising of gender performativity has become somewhat synonymous with the concept of gender fluidity.

Gender performativity is a useful lens which challenges the notion of a "fixed and stable gendered subject", proposing that "gender identity is constructed by performing (and repeating) specific acts within a culture" (Maclaran 2018, 228). The repetition of conventional gendered activities can be so commonplace as to be "treated as social facts" (Thompson and Ustuner 2014, 238), whereas resignifying practices, which contest and destabilise conventional gender norms can create backlash directed to those who challenge dominant cisheteronormativity. For example, Thompson and Ustuner (2014) analyse the ways in which naturalised femininity is challenged by women's roller derby participants, to highlight the juxtapositions and subversions of gendered boundaries in marketplace performances. In employing performativity, researchers can investigate the (re)significations and practices of gender, brought into being through speech and embodied acts of consumption. As Visconti (2015) discusses in their commentary article looking at consumer vulnerability, performativity can contextualise consumers' actions and strategies within broader settings of norms, power structures, space, and time, and also enables researchers to reveal the mutual influence of identity and performativity itself.

Butler's work does have its critics; Brickell (2003, 166) argues that "Butler appears reluctant to grant actors any capacity for enacting gender", and argues that the confusion produced by this apparent contradiction of gender as something one does without acknowledging 'one' as an agentic subject, means that researchers must adapt performativity to include subject performance despite their original discussion rebuffing this. However, as Schep (2012, 871) points out, it is impossible to account for "all gender dynamics within a single theory". Butler's work on gender performativity offers a way to explore the potential for disruption, the now paradigmatic linkage of gender and trouble (Stryker 2004); "It is precisely the idea that gender is done through human agency and social interaction that led authors to defend the possibilities of not only challenging the gender binaries and inequalities, but also of moving to a non-gendered social order, where gender can be dismantled and undone" (Marques 2019, 206). Such a non-gendered utopia, where social categories and norms are critically and constantly reworked, may at first seem unachievable, but consistent challenging and questioning is one of the key tenets of queer and transgender theorising.

Trans theory: insights for consumer research

In the 1990s, transgender theorising in the humanities and social sciences sought to question the medical construction of trans identity, challenging its socio-biological focus (Hines and Sanger 2010). Many transgender studies scholars are themselves trans; challenging exclusion from society, transgender scholars create an academic platform for political activism through which sociocultural assumptions of gendered identity are critically addressed. The implications of troubling social categories, resisting supposedly stable binaries, and questioning norms can create space for recognition of those who do not adhere or conform (Sanger 2010). These attributes can also be found in queer and feminist theory, where power structures are problematised and stability is redundant.

What queer, trans, and feminist theory have in common then, argues Enke (2012, 61) is that they "all pull hard on the seams of conventional sex/gender nomenclatures". The destabilisation of taken-for-granted social categories, and the examination of power structures at play in the creation, recreation, and reinforcement of these categories, is central to how phenomena can be viewed through queer, feminist, and trans lenses. Transgender scholarship has embraced the core of queer theory, ways of thinking that Hausman (2001, 467) describes as informed by queer theory's "attack on heteronormativity; its emphasis on performativity over essence, its insistent denaturalization of sexuality". Queer theory redeveloped to further challenge societal norms and inclusion/exclusion in society (Maclaran 2015). Recognising the instability of identity, queer theory represents not a single methodology or conceptualisation, but an assortment of thinking about the relationships between gender, sex, and sexuality (Spargo 1999).

There has been limited acknowledgement of consumption and its role in creating queer identities, with transgender and gender non-conforming identities remaining particularly invisible. In a study of female-to-male trans consumers, Hyatt (2002) notes that transitioning by physical and/or social means is not given consideration by consumer researchers, an important oversight given that the participants in their exploratory research encountered significant changes in shopping experience. The significance of consumption in popular culture (speaking from a Westernised, usually Anglo-American perspective) as context for the development of transgender theorising is also worth noting: "the vehement expansion of consumer culture in the 1980s… is an indispensable historical backdrop to this new theoretical field and continually emerging cultural phenomenon" (Hausman 2001, 486). This would seem to suggest that there could be much fruitful work to be done in consumer research using concepts and ideas from transgender theorising. In particular, investigating the ways in which consumer culture reinforces and/or subverts wider sociocultural structures, and how this reinforcement/subversion impacts on consumers, recognising the instability of consumer identities. Utilising insights provided through transgender theorising could help to highlight the specific intersecting forms of social marginalisation which impact transgender consumers themselves.

Consumer research has a long-established history of borrowing and applying theorising and concepts from varied disciplines like sociology, social and behavioural psychology, and cultural studies. Transgender theory acknowledges the instability of identity categories. In similar ways to queer theory, it can provide a useful lens to explore how consumers (de)construct fluid identities. In terms of feminist research approaches, trans theorising allows for the inclusion of trans masculine and men's perspectives, which have not received as much attention from scholars looking at consumer gender identities. There is scope for consumer research to borrow insights from transgender theorising, but there should also be recognition that, broadly, transgender people have not received the most respectful treatment in research.

The pathologisation of trans identity, challenged by emergent transgender theorising in the 1990s to today, stems from work in the late 19th and early 20th centuries which conceptualised being trans as an inversion, a condition of psychosexual development where trans people were the object of medical knowledge and legal discussion. The medicalised view of transness meant that much research prior to the 1990s was conducted by medical practitioners and clinicians who held keys to the gates of gender affirming treatment for trans people, thus creating a severe power differential in the research relationship (Stryker and Whittle 2006). Outside of clinical and legal contexts, an othering of trans people is unfortunately also commonplace, even when the researchers' intentions are to explore queer and trans experiences and theory. Referring to "transgenders" rather than transgender people has the effect of situating a marginalised group as objects of research; the difference between research on a population and research with a population is starkly shown. A specific example of what this means is an overview of transgender theorising for social work by Nagoshi and Brzuzy (2010) which, despite its interesting arguments and comprehensive consideration of queer and trans theory, intermittently uses othering wording. The fluidity of language in the realm of gender identity and expression cannot be emphasised enough; terms become outdated and meanings change so frequently among such a heterogeneous community so that even the most well-meaning researcher may trip up on occasion. This does not mean however that researchers should neglect trying to appreciate the nuances of meanings in the trans community, just as would be expected of researchers studying disability, race, class, or any other intersection of marginalised identity.

Awareness of the long history of transphobia in many disciplines, and as a result the feelings of alienation and suspicion of researchers on the part of trans people, can help ensure work in consumer research is sensitive to the specific concerns of trans people as a marginalised group. As Vincent (2018, 103) notes: "if a researcher is unaware of how (and by who) trans people have received ethically dubious, or even outright traumatic treatment in research contexts, there is a risk of problematic practices being repeated". Feminist methodologies, intersectional analysis, and reflexive approaches to work with (not on) transgender populations can alleviate some of the research fatigue that increased visibility has brought.

In the first author's PhD study, for example, interviews have been approached with a collaborative attitude, working with participants to investigate various marketplace topics and experiences relating to gender diversity and consumption. Sharing their own vulnerabilities as they developed and discovered an understanding of themselves as a nonbinary/genderqueer person made possible access to participants who would otherwise have been closed off to the research. Reflexive field notes have offered the opportunity to explore how personal feelings about the researcher's own gender identity shifted and transformed over the course of the research process. This adds a further autobiographical element to data collection, enabling reflection on the discourses and power dynamics at work from both a personal and an academic feminist perspective.

Why feminism matters for trans consumers

Feminism and gender are intrinsically linked; one of the key aims of feminism is to address gender-based imbalances and inequalities. The category of 'woman' oppressed by a patriarchal society which deems them inferior to men has formed the basis of much second wave feminist thought, making sexuality and gender political as well as personal. Where women and trans people seem to have common goals in struggling with societal oppression and would appear to be natural allies in destabilising gender, there exists a deep, acrimonious schism within feminism with regard to the inclusion of trans identities (Carrera-Fernández and DePalma 2020). In 2017, the UK government announced plans to reform the Gender Recognition Act (2004) in the UK, which enables trans people to change the sex marker on their birth certificate through a lengthy and often traumatically bureaucratic process. This has been met with a backlash to the very existence of trans people, which is itself a "contextual expression of a wider trans-exclusionary political climate with international dimensions" (Pearce, Erikainen and Vincent 2020, 680).

Historically, transgender people in mass media provided tabloid-style titillation; Christine Jorgensen's outing via the New York Daily News headline "Ex-GI Becomes Blonde Bombshell" in the US in 1952 mirrored the outing of British model April Ashley by the Sunday People in 1961. Narratives based in the shock value of transitioning from male to female set the format for portraying trans lives in the press for the next 50 or so years. The sensational nature of these narratives means that public awareness of the real issues impacting transgender people is still relatively low, which can create misunderstandings and incorrect assumptions. This highlights the need for more transformative representations. As Moscovici (1984, 24) explains, "the purpose of all representations is to make the unfamiliar, or unfamiliarity itself, familiar". As a key agent of social representations, the media has a crucial role. Media representations inform gender practice and vice versa. Schroeder and Borgerson (1998, 164) note the role that visual media plays in the construction of gender identity, as images do not simply "reflect or portray". Advertising gives meaning to visual images, creating cultural form through what Kang (1997) calls "signifying practices". The authors then expand on this, suggesting that consumers utilise raw materials produced by marketing images to construct identities and are thereby actively choosing how to appropriate symbolic meaning (Schroeder and Borgerson 2015). Advertising meanings become absorbed into society through what we read, view, our beliefs about how we live, and these meanings are constantly being recreated in our cultural context; "Advertising is a social practice, and it does not operate in a vacuum" (980). The sociocultural and political environment in which advertising is created affects gender portrayals as norms shift and change; advertising and social representations iteratively work within a cultural context, making marginalised identities visible or not depending on contemporary norms.

The invisibility of trans people in media and advertising can contribute to feelings of isolation as much as hyper-visibility can create an atmosphere of hostility. Much of the focus of hostility is on trans women; the question of who 'is' a woman has been central to divisions within UK feminism since the second wave of the 1970s and 1980s. The position that biological sex is immutable and cannot be chromosomally changed, thus gender is an expression of biological sex, can be seen in Janice Raymond's polarising 1979 work *The Transsexual Empire* (Hines 2019). What is now often described in broader social conversation, online, and in news media, as trans-exclusionary radical feminism (with proponents known as TERFs or in their own words, 'gender-critical' feminists), stems from some of Raymond's work and speaks to a "contemporary manifestation of older sex/gender essentialist discourses", where trans women are categorised as a threat to cis women's safety (Pearce, Erikainen and Vincent 2020, 680). Debates in both the UK and the US media have concentrated on granting (or prohibiting) access to 'women's-only' spaces, with toilets providing an unexpected arena of conflict. The arguments made by 'gender-critical' feminists around access to 'single-sex' spaces are grounded in a historical conception of woman as cisgender, white, wealthy, non-disabled, and heterosexual (Jones and Slater 2020). The existence, lives, experiences, and perspectives of trans men are often overlooked in feminist discourse and their identities at the intersection of being male and being transgender are not easily accepted as feminist (Deroest 2018).

The tide appeared to be turning in recent years and in 2015, American *Vogue* magazine declared it was the 'year of trans visibility' (Burns 2018). Representations of trans experiences have begun appearing in media, with widely acclaimed shows like *Orange Is the New Black*, *Pose*, and Netflix documentary *Disclosure* featuring trans characters played by trans actors, and trans people speaking about being trans in media. Despite this apparently positive visibility, there has been intense discussion particularly in UK newspapers of 'trans ideology'. In the 'post-truth era' where differently positioned knowledge claims coexist in extensive but fragmented digital spaces, 'gender critical' narratives conflict with the ways in which trans people themselves describe and discuss their experiences (Pearce, Erikainen and Vincent 2020).

These issues are important to consider given the reciprocal roles of media and the marketplace in shaping cultural attitudes, especially attitudes towards and (de)stigmatisation of marginalised communities and identities. In offering the stigma turbine as a conceptual framework for investigating marketplace stigma, Mirabito et al. (2016) point to how sociocultural institutions reinforce norms and social codes, and note "the need for research and public policy agendas dedicated to improving consumer welfare and social justice" (171). Feminist critiques of marketing have discussed the need to focus on welfare and social justice as feminist researchers seek to question power dynamics, arguing that inadequacies in mainstream philosophical dichotomies privilege one of a pair (e.g. male perspectives privileged over female) (Catterall, Maclaran and Stevens 2000). Critiquing the role of consumption in culture, Siebler (2012, 96) states that "consumption is a way of life, a way to validate one's existence, a way to display one's status and worth… the Digital Age has obliterated the transqueers who embrace the borderlands of gender fluidity and replaced it with 'gender as consumption'". This quote speaks to the generational differences within the umbrella of transness. Those who transitioned without the support of online communities, accessible regardless of geographical barriers, often view gender fluidity through sociocultural lenses temporally situated during times of Section 28, the AIDS pandemic, and much other hostility to non-conforming identities. This critique also highlights the power and role of marketing in individual lives, where consumption has transgressed so deeply into identity that gender is itself a consumer product.

Conclusion and suggestions for future research

This chapter has positioned transgender and gender non-conforming consumers within a broader overview of gender in consumer and marketing research. Following a discussion of transgender representation in current research, the chapter then looked to the analysis, insights, and perspectives accessible to marketing scholars through transgender, queer, and feminist theorising. Feminist perspectives allow previously unheard voices to be raised to the fore by examining and challenging power structures, dynamics and discourses. Below, we outline some suggestions for future research that may enable a more comprehensive understanding of the lives of transgender consumers.

The male/female gender binary is most starkly represented in Western conceptions of gender, which creates tension between the powerful Anglo-American perspectives replete in gender research, and understandings of gender which originate in the Global South. As Stryker (2004, 204) notes, "it is appallingly easy to reproduce the power structures of colonialism by subsuming non-Western configurations of personhood into Western constructs of sexuality and gender". We suggest that future research could usefully engage with the rich stream of non-English language transgender research, which is often overlooked. This would mark an important step in addressing the centrality of Anglo-American feminist thinking within consumer research. For example, in Brazil there is a growing body of work published in Portuguese which is written by and with *travesti*, in areas like healthcare, politics, gender and sexuality studies, law, and migration (Coacci 2011; Teixeira 2013; Amaral, Silva, Cruz and Toneli 2014; Carvalho 2018). These are just a few examples and as noted in the introduction to a special issue of *Contexto Internacional*, there are multiple narratives of gender, race, ethnicity, and class across a complex geographical space encompassing the Global South (Souza 2018).

We would also welcome future research that recognises greater diversity in the lived experience of transgender consumers. Although McKeage, Crosby and Rittenburg (2017) conduct a thorough study which considers multiple aspects of trans consumer experience, the majority of participants (17 of 24) are binary trans identified, i.e. trans man or trans woman. Given that 'transgender' as an umbrella term encompasses a wide variety of identities as noted previously, there is scope for research to investigate the nuances of unstable gender identities, where gender is constantly in flux, exploring the impacts of such instability of identity on consumer lives. Studies could also explore intersecting forms of social marginalisation to understand how gender identity is interdependent with other categories of social identity such as race, class, and poverty. An equally important area for consideration is the structuring forces that perpetuate such experiences of social marginalisation in the first instance.

Given the paucity of existing consumer research that explores the experiences of gender diverse consumers, there are many possible directions for studies to explore particular aspects of consumption. We suggest that future research could explore how trans consumers experience various consumption spaces, for example, the utilisation of online sharing platforms, similar to Rotaro, Rent the Runway, and Endless Wardrobe, for clothing rental. In the circumstances of the 2020/2021 global pandemic, trans consumers may seek experimentation from the relative safety of their own homes as they explore their gender identity and expression.

Feminist scholars have an obligation to address "what is happening at and what is being pushed into the margins of the socially prescribed, heteronormative gender order" (Elliot 2016, 8). Given the importance of consumption in gender expression and the power of the marketplace to shape perceptions of gender norms, taking trans lived experiences into account is vital for holistic understanding of the complex relationship between gender, identity, and consumer culture.

References

Amaral, M. S., T. C. Silva, K. O. Cruz, and M. J. F. Toneli (2014) '"From travestism to travestilities": A critical review of Brazilian academic production (2001–2010)', *Psicologia e Sociedade*, 26 (2) 301–311. Available at: https://www.researchgate.net/publication/289373720_From_travestism_to_travestilities_A_critical_review_of_Brazilian_academic_production_2001-2010 (Accessed: 7 September 2020).

Baker, S. M., J. W. Gentry, and T. L. Rittenburg (2005) 'Building understanding of the domain of consumer vulnerability', *Journal of Macromarketing*, 25 (2) 128–139. doi: 10.1177/0276146705280622.

Baker, S.M., 2006. 'Consumer normalcy: Understanding the value of shopping through narratives of consumers with visual impairments', *Journal of Retailing*, 82(1) 37–50.

Bettany, S., S. Dobscha, L. O'Malley, and A. Prothero (2010) 'Moving beyond binary opposition: Exploring the tapestry of gender in consumer research and marketing', *Marketing Theory*. 10 (1) 3–28. doi: 10.1177/1470593109355244.

Brickell, C. (2003) 'Performativity or performance? Clarifications in the sociology of gender', *New Zealand Sociology*, 18 (2) 158–178.

Burns, C., ed. (2018) *Trans Britain: Our Journey from the Shadows*. London: Penguin Books Ltd.

Butler, J. (1990) *Gender Trouble*. Abingdon: Routledge.

Carrera-Fernández, M. V. and R. DePalma (2020) 'Feminism will be trans-inclusive or it will not be: Why do two cis-hetero woman educators support transfeminism?', *Sociological Review*, 68 (4) 745–762. doi: 10.1177/0038026120934686.

Carvalho, M. (2018) '"Travesti", "transsexual woman", "trans man" and "non binary": Generation and class intersectionalities in the production of political identities', *Cadernos Pagu*, 2018 (52). Universidade Estadual de Campinas UNICAMP. doi: 10.1590/1809444920100520011.

Catterall, M., P. Maclaran, and L. Stevens (2000) *Marketing and Feminism: Current Issues and Research*. Abingdon: Routledge.

Coacci, T. (2011) 'A transexualidade no/pelo judiciário mineiro:: um estudo dos julgados do TJMG correlatos à transexualidade no período de 2008 a 2010', *Revista Três Pontos* 8 (2): 81–92. Available at: https://www.researchgate.net/publication/283498778_A_Transexualidade_nopelo_Judiciario_Mineiro_um_estudo_dos_julgados_do_TJMG_correlatos_a_transexualidade_no_periodo_2008_a_2010 (Accessed: 7 September 2020).

Connell, C. (2010) 'Doing, undoing, or redoing gender?: Learning from the workplace experiences of transpeople', *Gender and Society*, 24 (1) 31–55. doi: 10.1177/0891243209356429.

Darwin, H. (2017) 'Doing gender beyond the binary: A virtual ethnography', *Symbolic Interaction*, 40 (3) 317–334. doi: 10.1002/symb.316.

Deroest, A. (2018) *Critiquing Feminism: A Trans Man Perspective*. Academic Excellence Showcase Proceedings 105. Available at: https://digitalcommons.wou.edu/aes/105 (Accessed: 2 April 2019).

Elliot, P. (2016) *Debates in Transgender, Queer, and Feminist Theory: Contested Sites*. Abingdon: Routledge. doi: 10.4324/9781315576008.

Enke, A. (2012) 'The education of little Cis: Cisgender and the discipline of opposing bodies'. In *Transfeminist Perspectives in and Beyond Transgender and Gender Studies*, edited by Enke, A., 60–77. Temple University Press. Available at: https://www.jstor.org/stable/j.ctt14bt8sf (Accessed: 16 July 2020).

Fischer, E. and S. J. Arnold (2002) 'More than a labor of love: Gender roles and Christmas gift shopping', *Journal of Consumer Research*, 17 (3) 333–345. doi: 10.1086/208561.

Hausman, B. L. (2001) 'Recent transgender theory', *Feminist Studies*, 27 (2) 465–490. Available at: https://www.jstor.org/stable/3178770 (Accessed: 13 April 2019).

Hearn, J. and W. Hein (2015) 'Reframing gender and feminist knowledge construction in marketing and consumer research: Missing feminisms and the case of men and masculinities', *Journal of Marketing Management* 31 (15–16) 626–1651. doi: 10.1080/0267257X.2015.1068835.

Hines, S. (2019) 'The feminist frontier: On trans and feminism', *Journal of Gender Studies*, 28 (2) 145–157. doi: 10.1080/09589236.2017.1411791.

Hines, S. and T. Sanger (2010) *Transgender Identities: Towards a Social Analysis of Gender Diversity*. New York: Routledge.

Holt, D. B. and C. J. Thompson (2004) 'Man-of-action heroes: The pursuit of heroic masculinity in everyday consumption', *Journal of Consumer Research*, 31 (2) 425–440. doi: 10.1086/422120.

Hyatt, E. M. (2002) 'An explanatory investigation of the shopping behaviour of female-to-male consumers: Before, during, and after transition', *Gender and Consumer Behaviour*, 6, ed.

Maclaran, P., Association for Consumer Research, 323–336. Available at: http://www.acrwebsite.org/volumes/15733/gender/v06/GCB-06.

Jones, C. and J. Slater (2020) 'The toilet debate: Stalling trans possibilities and defending "women's protected spaces"', *The Sociological Review*, 68 (4) 834–851. doi: 10.1177/0038026120934697.

Kang, M.E., 1997. 'The portrayal of women's images in magazine advertisements: Goffman's gender analysis revisited', *Sex roles*, 37 (11) 979–996.

Kates, S. (2002) 'The protean quality of subcultural consumption: An ethnographic account of gay consumers', *Journal of Consumer Research*, 29 (3) 383–399. doi: 10.1086/344427.

Kates, S. (2004) 'The dynamics of brand legitimacy: An interpretive study in the gay men's community', *Journal of Consumer Research*, 31 (2) 455–464. doi: 10.1086/422122.

Levitt, H. M., and M. R. Ippolito (2014) 'Being transgender: The experience of transgender identity development', *Journal of Homosexuality*, 61 (12) 1727–1758. doi:10.1080/00918369.2014.951.262.

Maclaran, P. (2015) 'Feminism's fourth wave: A research agenda for marketing and consumer research', *Journal of Marketing Management*, 31 (15–16) 732–1738. doi: 10.1080/0267257X.2015.1076497.

Maclaran, P. (2018) 'Judith Butler: Gender performativity and heterosexual hegemony'. In *Canonical Authors in Consumption Theory*, edited by Askegaard, S. and Heilbrunn, B., 227–233. Abingdon: Routledge.

Marques, A. C. (2019) 'Displaying gender: Transgender people's strategies in everyday life', *Symbolic Interaction*, 42 (2) 202–228. doi: 10.1002/symb.412.

McKeage, K., E. Crosby, and T. Rittenburg (2017) 'Living in a gender-binary world: Implications for a revised model of consumer vulnerability', *Journal of Macromarketing*, 38 (1) 73–90. doi: 10.1177/0276146717723963.

Mirabito, A. M., C. C. Otnes, E. Crosby, D. B. Wooten, J.E. Machin, C. Pullig, N. Ross, S. Dunnett, K. Hamilton, K. D. Thomas, M. A. Yeh, C. Davis, J. F. Gollnhofer, A. Grover, J. Matias, N. A. Mitchell, E. G. Ndichu, N. Sayarh, and S. Velagaleti . (2016) 'The stigma turbine : a theoretical framework for conceptualizing and contextualizing marketplace stigma', *Journal of Public Policy & Marketing*, 35 (2) 170–184. doi: 10.1509/jppm.15.145.

Moscovici, S. (1984). 'The myth of the lonely paradigm: A rejoinder', *Social research*, 51 (4) 939–967.

Nagoshi, J. L. and S. Brzuzy (2010) 'Transgender theory: Embodying research and practice', *Affilia – Journal of Women and Social Work*, 25 (4) 431–443. doi: 10.1177/0886109910384068.

Oakenfull, G. (2007) 'Effects of gay identity, gender and explicitness of advertising imagery on gay responses to advertising', *Journal of Homosexuality*, 53 (4) 49–69. doi: 10.1080/00918360802101278.

Oakenfull, G. (2012) 'Gay consumers and brand usage: The gender-flexing role of gay identity', *Psychology and Marketing*, 29 (12) 968–979. doi: 10.1002/mar.20578.

Oakenfull, G. (2013) 'Unraveling the movement from the marketplace: Lesbian responses to gay-oriented advertising', *Journal of Marketing Development & Competitiveness*, 7 (2) 57–72.

Pearce, R., S. Erikainen, and B. Vincent (2020) 'TERF wars: An introduction', *Sociological Review*, 68 (4) 677–698. doi: 10.1177/0038026120934713.

Sanger, T. (2010) 'Beyond gender and sexuality binaries in sociological theory: The case for transgender inclusion'. In *Transgender Identities: Towards a Social Analysis of Gender Diversity*, edited by Hines, S. and T. Sanger., 259–276. New York: Routledge.

Schep, D. (2012) 'The limits of performativity: A critique of hegemony in gender theory', *Hypatia*, 27 (4) 864–880. doi: 10.1111/j.1527–2001.2011.01230.x.

Schroeder, J.E. and Borgerson, J.L., 1998. 'Marketing images of gender: A visual analysis'. *Consumption, Markets and Culture*, 2 (2) 161–201.

Schroeder, J. E. and J. L. Borgerson (2015) 'Critical visual analysis of gender: Reactions and reflections', *Journal of Marketing Management*, 31 (15–16) 1723–1731. Routledge. doi: 10.1080/0267257X.2015.1077883.

Siebler, K. (2012) 'Transgender transitions: Sex/gender binaries in the digital age', *Journal of Gay and Lesbian Mental Health* 16 (1) 74–99. doi: 10.1080/19359705.2012.632751.

Souza, N. M. F. de. (2018) 'Introduction: Gender in the Global South: Disturbing International Boundaries', *Contexto Internacional*, 40 (3) 429–434. FapUNIFESP (SciELO). doi: 10.1590/s0102–8529.2018400300001.

Spargo, T. (1999) *Foucault and Queer Theory: Postmodern Encounters*. Duxford, Cambridge: Icon Books; Totem Books.

Stryker, S. (2004) 'Transgender studies: Queer theory's evil twin', *GLQ: A Journal of Lesbian and Gay Studies*, 10 (2) 212–215. Available at: https://muse.jhu.edu/article/54599 (Accessed: 13 April 2019).

Stryker, S. and Whittle, S. eds. (2006) *The Transgender Studies Reader*. 1st edn. Routledge. doi: 10.1017/CBO9781107415324.004.

Teixeira, F. (2013) *Dispositivos de dor : saberes, poderes que (con)formam as transexualidades*. 1a ediciao. Sao Paulo SP Brasil: Fapesp; Annablume.

Thompson, C. J. (1996) 'Caring consumers: Gendered consumption meanings and the juggling lifestyle', *Journal of Consumer Research*, 22 (4) 388–407. doi: 10.1086/209457.

Thompson, C. J. and Ustuner, T. (2014) 'Women skating on the Edge: Marketplace Performances as Ideological Edgework', *Journal of Consumer Research*, 42 (2) 235–265. doi: 10.1093/jcr/ucv013.

Vincent, B. W. (2016) 'Non-binary gender identity negotiations: Interactions with Queer communities and medical practice'. PhD diss., University of Leeds. Available at: http://etheses.whiterose.ac.uk/15956/ (Accessed: 1 October 2020).

Vincent, B. W. (2018) 'Studying trans: Recommendations for ethical recruitment and collaboration with transgender participants in academic research', *Psychology and Sexuality*, 9 (2) 102–116. doi: 10.1080/19419899.2018.1434558.

Visconti, L. M. (2015) 'A conversational approach to consumer vulnerability: Performativity, representations, and storytelling', *Journal of Marketing Management*, 32 (3–4) 1–15. doi: 10.1080/0267257x.2015.1122660.

Visconti, L. M., Maclaran, P., and Bettany, S. (2018) 'Gender, consumption, and markets'. In *Consumer Culture Theory*, edited by Arnould, E. J. and Thompson, C. J., 180–206 London: Sage.

West, C. and Zimmerman, D. H. (1987) 'Doing gender', *Gender and Society*, 1 (2) 125–151. Available at: https://www.jstor.org/stable/189945 (Accessed: 25 May 2019).

Wight, J. (2011) 'Facing gender performativity: How transgender performances and performativity trouble facework research', *Kaleidoscope: A Graduate Journal of Qualitative Communication Research*, 10 (1) 73–90. Available at: https://opensiuc.lib.siu.edu/kaleidoscope/vol10/iss1/6.

20 Ageism, sexism, and women in power

Minta Sanghvi and Phillip Frank

The American population is rapidly aging. In 2019 about 16.5% of the American population was over 65 years old. By 2050 that number will be 22%. The median age in the United States has been going up steadily from 30 years in 1980 to hovering close to 40 years today. The US Congress, which is supposed to reflect the populace, has also seen a significant increase of older members. In the 116th US Congress, about a third of the Representatives in the House were over 65 years of age, while the US Senate has almost half of its members over 65. Joe Biden replaces Donald Trump as the oldest person elected president in US history. The Speaker of the House of Representatives, Nancy Pelosi is 80. The outgoing Senate majority leader, Mitch McConnell is 78, while the incoming senator majority leader, Chuck Schumer is 70. While Mr. Schumer may seem young, in comparison to the leadership in Congress, he is well above the retirement age in the United States. One of the reasons why we have older politicians in Congress is because we not only have an older electorate but also one that votes in larger numbers. For example, in the 2016 presidential election over 23% of the US electorate was over 65, and over 71% of them voted in the elections, in comparison to the US electorate under 29 which stood at 15% of which only 46% voted (Noah 2019).

Apart from Vice President Kamala Harris, Speaker of the House Nancy Pelosi is the most powerful woman in the United States. And yet she has received sustained attacks on her age which focus on her appearance and her mental faculties. She is not the only one targeted because of age. In the 2016 US Presidential election, Hillary Clinton received (Balcerzak and Nielek 2016; Bock, Byrd-Craven, and Burkley 2017; Lau, Bligh and Kohles 2020; Lytle et al. 2018; Muñoz and Towner 2017; Sanghvi 2019). Her ageist coverage was especially remarkable because Hillary Clinton was six years younger than Bernie Sanders, her main opponent in the Democratic Primaries, and one year younger than Donald J. Trump, her main opponent in the 2016 US Presidential elections. Women holding political power, such as, Margaret Thatcher (UK), Indira Gandhi (India), Julia Gillard (Australia), and Hillary Clinton and Nancy Pelosi in the United States are often demonized and deemed as 'witches,' 'bitches,' 'crones,' and 'hags' by the patriarchy that is threatened by the disruption of gender hierarchies (Balcerzak and Nielek 2016; Rosen 2017; Sanghvi 2014). Many of these terms are specifically employed on older, post-menopausal women.

Ageism impacts women in a myriad of ways. Between a country that values feminine youth, and the visual culture of politics, female politicians face a harder time than their male counterparts. To combat the adverse impact of ageism and manage impressions of competence women, especially those in the public arena, attempt to obfuscate their visible signs of aging and show they are aging successfully (Clarke and Griffin 2008;

DOI: 10.4324/9781003042587-24

Jefferys 2014). Aging successfully is a marketplace intervention that includes neoliberal solutions, such as cosmetic products and procedures, and exercise and fitness regimens to combat the appearance of aging. However, for several female politicians such as Nancy Pelosi, this leads to commentaries about their Botox or face-lifts (Sanghvi 2019). Furthermore, claims about Nancy Pelosi's mental acuity have also surfaced.

Using a feminist critical discourse analysis we attempt to uncover the complex social phenomena of aging as it impacts women of power (Lazar 2007; Phelan 2018). By going beyond language, and images to gendered social practices, we hope to examine the ageist narratives of Nancy Pelosi using a feminist critical discourse analysis and highlight how ageism and sexism are used to strip women of their power by creating a dynamic that is unsuitable for their campaigns, candidacies, and rise in politics.

Literature review

In marketplaces, whether historical or contemporary, women were often depicted in three life stages. Either the life stages were depicted as virginity, motherhood, and middle-ages (Ozane, Moscato and Kunkel 2012) or the women were depicted as the maiden, mother, and crone (Stevens, Maclaran and Kravets 2020). Women are subject to the male gaze as maidens and mothers, and are often rewarded by the fruits of the patriarchy as long as they follow the expectations of traditionally feminine women, as dutiful daughters, wives, and mothers (Rosen 2017). However, as women pass the child-bearing ages, enter menopausal years, and get old, the male gaze disappears and older women are made to feel devalued and invisible (Rosen 2017; Stevens, MacLaran and Kravets 2020).

Marketing has largely looked at aging from a consumption perspective – whether it is understanding the changing consumption patterns of elderly consumers (Barnhart and Peñaloza 2013; Gregoire 2003; Moschis 2003) or as a segmentation issue (Sudbury and Simcock 2009; Tepper 1994), or advertising to older consumers (Chevalier and Moal-Ulvoas 2018; Smith, Moschis, and Moore 1985). However, not much attention has been paid to gender and intersectionality issues around aging. The aging process is different for men and women. And while there has been some literature on women's body image and fashion choices as they age (Holmlund, Hagman and Polsa 2011; Joung and Miller 2006; Sobh 2011), it does not do justice to intersectional aspects of aging. There are few studies in marketing regarding race, gender, disability, sexuality, and gender expression as it relates to aging (Gopaldas and Siebert 2018; Veresiu and Parmentier 2021) presenting a vast and rich opportunity for critical research in the area. We believe there is a greater need to study aging from an intersectional perspective and hope to add to this growing body of research.

Ageism

Ageism was coined in 1968 by Dr. Robert Butler as the prejudice, stereotyping and casual and systemic discrimination against older people (Raynor 2015). Human aging is not just a biological maturing but a gradual deterioration of the mind and body. It is embedded in social contexts and impacted by social factors (Calasanti 2005; Nelson 2016). Studies show older adults have hard time gaining employment, getting access to financial resources (Raynor 2015), and often have a lower quality of healthcare and that their health concerns often get dismissed by healthcare professionals (Chrisler 2016). Within social gerontology, double or multiple jeopardy hypothesis suggests that along with advancing age there is a worsening of any inequalities existing between men and women (Sherman and Schiffman 1984). The weathering hypothesis forwarded by Geronimus (1992) suggests that socioeconomically disadvantaged persons such as women "may be subjected to many sets of health risks, the consequences of which may accumulate with age" (210) as evidenced in the next section.

Aging women

Women earn less than men in the workplace, and hold a larger percent of student loans, which diminishes their capacity to save money for retirement (AAUW 2018; Blau and Kahn 2017). Furthermore, women live about five years longer than men according to the CDC mortality data. Hence their retirement savings need to last longer than men's. Then it is no surprise that out of the 7.1 million older adults living in poverty in the United States, two third of them are women. Women over 80 had the highest poverty level among elderly men and women of all age groups. Moreover, the reports state that women of color are two times as likely to live in poverty than older white women. Similarly lesbian, bisexual, and transgender elderly women face not only greater economic disparity because of years of discrimination and lack of opportunities but also significantly increased health disparities with regard to mental and physical health and well-being and access to healthcare (Averett, Yoon and Jenkins 2011; Emlet 2016; Fredriksen-Goldsen et al. 2015).

Women face greater age discrimination in the workplace often based on their appearance or sexuality (Sobh 2011). Older women are judged more negatively and at an earlier age than men (Lytle et al. 2018), which influences their career and peak earnings (Sobh 2011). Lookism or discrimination based on one's appearance seems to impact older women in much greater numbers and to a much greater degree than men (Jyrkinen and McKie 2012). This is not surprising since the social worth of women is often tied to their appearance and child rearing ability. Beauty and body are largely linked to youth as the lack of aging female bodies, pervades American media, marketing, and culture (Loos and Ivan 2018; Woodward 2006). Women face an onslaught of young, slender, unblemished bodies through various forms of media from magazines to television (Lewis, Medvedev and Seponski 2011).

Ageism is a complex, multi-layered problem. Apart from societal perspectives, women (and men) may believe that their aging bodies negatively impact their body image, social status, and self-worth (Clarke and Griffin 2008). Norms about beauty, and aging are often internalized by men and women creating anxiety and discomfort about one's appearance and identity (Hatch 2005). Youth is often paired with the notion of beauty and old age is symbolically tied to ugliness (Muecke 2005). For some men and women, it impacts their satisfaction in their partner, marriage and fidelity (Calasanti 2005). In the visual culture of the film and television industry, female actors are aged out quicker, and face a paucity of roles as they get older (Hatch 2005; Woodward 2006).

Several researchers have remarked on a double standard in aging, wherein, signs of aging such as gray hair or facial lines, may make a man look distinguished and wise and yet the same signs of aging will make a woman look 'old' (Chrisler, Barney and Palantino 2016; Hatch 2005; Sanghvi 2014, 2019). Sanghvi (2014) discusses how words describing old women have largely negative connotations, such as, crone, hag, and witch. Similarly, words such as wrinkly, saggy which are associated with aging, and lack of control are often applied to women and not men (Calasanti 2005; Muecke 2005). As a result, it is unsurprising that women often deny or obscure their age, use cosmetic interventions to evade signs of aging, or in a more recent trend, demonstrate how they are aging gracefully or successfully (Loos and Ivan 2018; Tortajada, Dhaenens and Willem 2018).

Aging successfully

From a young age there is a greater objectification of girls, and the male gaze continues well into their reproductive years. As women reach an older age, they are reviled, ignored, or devalued often termed as hags, witches, or crones (Calasanti 2005; Greer 2018; Woodward 2006). Post-menopausal women are often portrayed as "physically repulsive, argumentative and difficult" and viewed with "horror, fear and revulsion" (Stevens, Maclaran, and Kravets 2020). Judgment is passed about women's mental acuity, productivity, health, and (in)dependence based on the appearance of their aging bodies (Calasanti 2005).

Considering the material and social impacts of aging illustrated above, women often strive to change their appearance to look younger or, as a new dominant discourse has taken hold, to age successfully. Successful aging is defined as "encompassing the avoidance of disease and disability, the maintenance of high physical and cognitive function, and sustained engagement in social productive activities" (Rowe and Kahn 1997, 433). To showcase successful aging the focus is often put on the body and avoiding graying hair, wrinkles, sagging body parts, or weight gain with an emphasis on being fit (Lewis, Medvedev and Seponski 2011). Exercise and fitness regimens, plastic surgery, and cosmetics are key marketplace interventions to age successfully. There is an entire industry of cosmetic interventions from anti-aging creams to surgical procedures estimated to be over $100 billion globally with the United States being one of the major markets. Interestingly, the pandemic saw a surge in cosmetic procedures such as body contouring, Botox, fillers, face-lifts and neck lifts, despite many workspaces and social gatherings being moved online. Some of these are motivated by how people appear on Zoom calls (Edgar 2020; Ellwood 2020).

Women in the public eye often feel a greater pressure to adhere to societal expectations of appearance and body image. Hollywood actresses have talked about how they are aged out of lead roles much younger than their male co-stars. Several studies show older adults are often under-represented in film and television programming or shown as posing a financial burden on society (Loos and Ivan 2018; Roy and Sanyal 1997). Similarly, older female politicians are judged more harshly than their male counterparts. When she ran in 2008, conservative radio commentator Rush Limbaugh forecast then Senator Clinton's loss in the primaries because he believed Americans did not want to "watch a woman get older before their eyes" (Dowd 2008). Similarly news stories proposed a choice between grandmotherhood and running for president in 2014 for Hillary Clinton suggesting that once a woman achieved grandmotherhood, she was not fit to be president (Sanghvi 2019). However, there were no stories about Donald Trump's ability to lead after being a grandfather during his run in the 2016 US presidential race.

The opposite of successful aging is the decline of cognitive and bodily faculties and a loss of independence . A new trend in media, health, and aging discourses shows older adults being broken into two categories, one in which they are often shown as healthy and vibrant or aging successfully and one in which they are shown as inactive and needing help with their daily routines (Loos and Ivan 2018). This new discourse is similar to some of the findings from Barnhart and Peñaloza (2013) and this notion of older adults moving from independence to dependence, from active to inactive. We believe both these discourses are important to understanding how aging female politicians are treated in the public domain.

Methodology

We utilize a case study approach to provide a deeper, nuanced understanding of the phenomenon of how ageism impacts female politicians (Kravets, Preece and Maclaran 2020). This allows us to explore the socio-political context of a specific episode while also understanding the deeper history and meaning surrounding it while we overlay it with the contemporary discourse. We use the feminist critical discourse analysis to analyze our data to highlight the nuanced and complex gendered assumptions and examine all the modes in which "hegemonic power relations are discursively produced, sustained, negotiated, and challenged" (Lazar 2007: 142).

We analyzed a corpus of 45 articles, radio, and TV interviews that specifically focused on the age of House Representative Nancy Pelosi of the US Congress. Following the established principles of qualitative research we believe corpus achieved theoretical saturation. She has received significant coverage about her age especially as she assumed positions of power in Congress. Nancy Pelosi became the Speaker of the House amidst hue and cry about her advanced age.

Analysis

Congresswoman Nancy Pelosi represents the 12th District of California and has served in Congress since 1987. She is a member of the Democratic Party and the leader of the House Democratic Caucus. Nancy Pelosi was the most powerful woman in the United States till the election and inauguration of Vice President Kamala Harris. As Speaker of the House, she is first in line to succession after the president and vice president and the commentary about her age, gender, and appearance (often as it relates to her age) has been relentless in the media. As Jennifer Pozner, Executive Director of Women in Media and News, articulates in the documentary *MissRepresentation*, "The fact that the media are so derogatory to the most powerful women in the country, then what does it say about media's ability to any woman in America seriously?" Ageism and sexism are serious issues that impact women not just in politics but all over the country. Our data analysis broke down the coverage about Nancy Pelosi's age into three main categories. They are (1) Demean, (2) Displace, and (3) Desecrate. We will explain them in greater detail below.

Demean

The coverage in media, and social media, about Nancy Pelosi's age was largely demeaning in nature. Demeaning nicknames were not just based on her age, and her appearance, but also her mental faculties with the implication her climbing age necessarily indicated a cognitive decline. Especially from her opponents, such as Donald Trump calling her, "tired, old Nancy Pelosi" or the House minority leader, Kevin McCarthy calling her the face of "the old, old past" on Fox News (Doyle 2018). This, in turn, gave permission for more people to call her demeaning nicknames such as popular CNBC host Jim Cramer calling Nancy Pelosi during an interview, "crazy Nancy" (Sunstein 2020). Similarly during discussions on Syria at the White House when Pelosi, as the only woman in a room full of men rose to speak, Trump called her "unhinged" (Dvorak 2019).

Apart from calling her demeaning names, there was a robust discussion about her aging appearance. During his first impeachment, Trump also made a jab about her teeth implying she had dentures which "were falling out of her mouth" (Demirjian 2019). Several commentators on Fox News, as well as some politicians such as Senator Lindsey Graham have commented on Nancy Pelosi's "surgeries" implying she had cosmetic plastic surgery or procedures done to alter her physical appearance and mask the signs of aging (McCabe 2015). Plastic surgeons speculated about possible procedures Nancy Pelosi may have undertaken such as "an eyelid lift and…a facelift" (Dingfelder 2011) with Republicans giving her the nickname "Botox Nancy" (Dowd 2019). Megyn Kelly made a jibe about Pelosi's face being expressionless because of the numerous procedures on her face and former Governor Sarah Palin also suggested Pelosi had surgery when she accused Pelosi of telling a "tight-faced lie" (Mcabe 2015). In fact, Dingfelder (2011) concludes that for aging female politicians, "looking your age isn't just a cosmetic disadvantage; it's often interpreted as a sign of advancing senescence – like buttoning your coat wrong or wearing two different shoes." Consequently, discussions of Nancy Pelosi's mental faculties and cognitive declines have also dominated stories of her aging.

There were several videos of Nancy Pelosi that were circulated on social media that were doctored to look like she was slurring her words and appearing intoxicated and shared thousands of times (Denham 2020). This led to discussions of dementia and cognitive declines over several groups on social media platforms. Donald Trump also circulated a doctored video of her where she tore his State of the Union speech interweaved with clips of him honoring groups of people such as the Tuskegee airmen and young women receiving scholarships (Levenson 2020). When Pelosi reached out to social media companies such as Facebook or Twitter, they often ignored or denied her requests (Levenson 2020).

Displace

While Nancy Pelosi has faced sexism and ageism from members of the Republican Party, she has also faced opposition based on her age within the Democratic Party. This came to sharp relief during her bid to return as the Speaker of the House in 2018 as several members of her own party have also made several attempts to displace her. Some Democrats argued that Nancy Pelosi's "septuagenarian reign" was not keeping in line with young Democratic voters' ideals and desires (Doyle 2018). However, the same members had no qualms about supporting two older septuagenarians, Bernie Sanders and Joe Biden as front runners for the Democratic ticket for President. Doyle (2018) argues that the campaign to destabilize Pelosi's bid for Speakership was based solely on her age, that there was "no coherent progressive politics" behind that campaign and that Democrats were "casting her as a desperate crone, clinging to relevance at any cost."

Similarly, young activists, such as gun control advocate and Parkland shooting survivor David Hogg, told *New York* magazine, "Older Democrats just won't move the fuck off the plate and let us take control. Nancy Pelosi is old" (Miller 2018). The media starting as early as 2012 and continuing since has consistently asked Nancy Pelosi if she is too old to lead and she has replied every single time to the reporters, 'Have you asked Mitch McConnell that?' (CBS 2014; CNN 2012).

In 2006, when Nancy Pelosi became the Speaker of the House for the first time, breaking a glass ceiling for women in the United States, she did not dawn a single mainstream magazine cover such as *Time* or *Newsweek* during her tenure as the first female Speaker of the House. While her successor John Boehner dawned the covers of several magazines such as *Time*, *Newsweek*, *The New Yorker*, *The Economist*, and *The National Journal* within the short period from his election (Shields 2011). In 2010, Republicans spent over $65 million attacking Pelosi in political ads while the Republican National Committee hung a banner at their headquarters that read "Fire Pelosi" (Draper 2018). Whether it is the Republican Party trying to fire her or the Democratic Party trying to upend her campaign for Speakership, Nancy Pelosi seems to face a consistent barrage of men and women who are attempting to displace her from positions of power.

Desecrate

In political ads Republicans have portrayed her as a "satanic figure in the flames of deficit spending, or a 50-foot monster" (Collins 2010). In 2018 Republicans and Trump ran more than 61,000 ads, one of which compared her to a prostitute (Zernike 2018). Considering how reviled Nancy Pelosi is among Republicans, considering how they have demeaned her with corrosive nick names and how much time, money, and effort Republicans and Democrats have spent trying to displace her, it comes as no surprise that when domestic terrorists led an insurrection at the United States Capitol Building on January 6, 2021, they broke into and desecrated her office space. These terrorists that imbibed notions of "white male power" and were goaded by a President who boasts about assaulting women, chose to specifically target the most powerful woman in the United States (Krook 2021). Members of the mob vandalized her office space breaking a mirror, stealing her mail, her gavel, her nameplate, her signage, her laptop, and her lectern. As the terrorists stormed the Capitol building with some carrying zip-tie handcuffs as they entered her office space, amidst shouted chants such as "Get her out" specifically targeting Nancy Pelosi.

Krook discusses two specific cases of gendered violence against Nancy Pelosi during the insurrection. One was a photo of Richard "Bigo" Barnett with his feet up on a desk in Nancy Pelosi's office who later told a reporter, "I wrote her a nasty note, put my feet up on her desk, and scratched my balls" (Rosenberg 2021). Krook (2021) explains that his actions were about "putting a woman in her place by violating and defiling her space." Another terrorist, Cleveland Meredith, who is being charged by the FBI was found with texts stating, "Thinking about heading over to Pelosi cunt's speech and putting a bullet in her noggin on live TV" and "Dead bitch walking."

Discussion

The heteronormative focus on female politician's body and appearance creates a paradox with regard to aging. Aging women are made to feel invisible by society and media and often experience a loss of self-esteem, feel trepidation about intimacy, and often face loss of opportunities and resources in the workplace (Clarke and Griffin 2008). Older women are judged on their competency based on their physical appearance and perceived health (Lewis, Medvedev and Seponski 2011). The more visible their aging, the more invisible women feel (Clarke and Griffin 2008). The dominant cultural forces drive women to look young for as long as possible (Tortajada, Dhaenens and Willem 2018). Thus to gain visibility and social currency, women choose to obfuscate their age by aging successfully. This forces her to choose market interventions in an effort to age successfully in the public eye. As Veresiu and Parmentier (2021) discuss, the discourses on successful aging are both "inward and outward oriented" creating a neoliberal ideology on aging that aims at changing cultural conceptions through individual actions. Through condemnation, patriarchal marketing problematizes and shames women's bodies, offering up a variety of marketplace 'solutions' that are unnecessary at best and risky or dangerous at worst (Guirrieri 2020).

For women in politics, ageism adds a layer of complexity to an already fraught path to success. Aging male politicians gain power and prominence while aging female politicians are demeaned, devalued, and displaced. This is not a new phenomenon. Women attempting to gain power have faced severe backlash, whether it was in historical or contemporary society (Okimoto and Brescoll 2010; Rosen 2017). For older women, such as Nancy Pelosi, Hillary Clinton, and other women politicians in Congress, who are gaining power and prominence that is due to them based on seniority, the backlash utilizes their age to discredit them.

Similarly, while there is some evidence that male politicians also use some beauty procedures to obfuscate their age, the target of commentary on the subject is largely directed to and endured by older female politicians trying to fit American societal standards and the emphasis on their appearance. The convention of American society is a tendency to degrade and reduce older women to sexless and irrelevant beings especially in media (Woodward 2006). As Doyle (2018) explains, "Pelosi's age is cast as ugly and scary and freakish in a way her male colleague's ages aren't; she is defined by being an old woman, whereas they are politicians."

Powerful women in the United States are criticized largely on "their looks and sexuality" (Dowd 2019). Calling women ugly nicknames is a form of "character assassination" (Sunstein 2020). Years of demeaning commentary, sexist, and ageist remarks, attempts to displace women in power created an atmosphere that led to the desecration and violence against the most powerful woman in the United States. Research shows us that degradation and dehumanizing of women, whether it is through media or advertising, are linked to violence against them (Jhally and Kilbourne 2010). Marketing is also to blame for this, as Gurrieri (2021) points out, as patriarchal marketing reinforces sexism and ageism by promoting societal stereotypes regarding women's bodies, bodily functions, women's work and trivializing their work and accomplishments.

Nancy Pelosi, as one of the most prominent women in power, bears the brunt of aging in the public eye and her attempts to age successfully have been derided and shamed by the media, her colleagues. Even those who come to defense end up hurting her and women in power in the long run. Articles defending Nancy Pelosi called her "purposeful" (Draper 2018), a "remarkable authority" (Dvorak 2019), a "master legislator" and "political fairy godmother" (Zernike 2018), and observed her remarkable productivity (Collins 2010). The same articles also trivialized her achievements by calling her the "Lady Gaga of American Politics" (Zernike 2018), focused on her appearance by claiming she has powerful "stiletto stamina" (Dowd 2019), called her "ultra-programmed and ultra-intense" (Collins 2010) and "Machiavellian" (Draper 2018). While they may not mean to devalue or demean her ascendancy, we know the discourse around women and power often has shades of deception to explain her achievement (Sanghvi 2019), or focuses on appearance in a way that is stereotypical or transgressive and is often detrimental not only to her success as well as that of the feminist cause the authors may be espousing (Lazar 2007). Several of these articles referred her wardrobe, her Catholic faith, her husband, five children, grandchildren, the food she likes and how she eats it. Research shows that women get more coverage about their appearance and family than they do about substantial issues such as policy, campaign and politics (Carlin and Winfrey 2009; Falk 2010; Sanghvi 2014). Research also explains how such coverage is detrimental to women even when it is from a positive perspective (Lee 2014).

The feature story about Nancy Pelosi in Harper's Bazaar which was an attempt to show Pelosi in a better light discussed in detail her beauty regimen and talks about how she used to exercise and splash water on her face every morning but now relies on "her good Italian skin" while also suggesting that Botox and face creams in her mind were about the same thing (Dowd 2019). Dowd (2019) defends Pelosi's beauty procedures by suggesting that there are many male politicians getting Botox.

In an article titled, 'Nancy Pelosi is showing women how to age fearlessly and ferociously' in *The Washington Post*, Dvorak (2019) wrote that when Pelosi is demeaned she "purses her lips and mercy claps at them, refusing to engage in the profane, ugly language that swirls around her." Dvorak (2019) then goes further by comparing her to Lorena Bobbitt (the woman who after years of being abused by her husband cut off his penis) and her knife or Carrie Nation (an American temperance movement activist) with a hatchet to showcase how threatening she was to men in Washington, DC. Such comparisons create a "restrictive structure" in gender roles by pitting men against (powerful) women (Lazar 2007, 153). This does not end up benefiting women in the end.

Beyond Pelosi

While we have chosen to focus on Pelosi for this book chapter, there is no dearth of additional material. In the 2016 US Presidential elections, focus on Hillary Clinton's advanced age, tired appearance and her fainting episode triggered widespread claims of her frailty, questioning her 'fitness' to lead and delegitimizing her candidacy (Neville-Shepard and Nolan 2019). Claims about her physical health and use of adult diapers led to assumptions about her diminished intellectual capacity (Sanghvi 2019; Smith 2016).

Another example of powerful aging women in US politics is that of Senator Dianne Feinstein of California. She is a ranking member of the US Committee on the judiciary, an important and critical position as the committee providing oversight of the Department of Justice and agencies such as the Federal Bureau of Investigation, and Department of Homeland Security and plays a critical role in nominations of judges, especially to the US Supreme Court. Of those eight octogenarians serving in the Senate in 2020, she was the only woman. And while many of the senators have received age related questions, only Dianne Feinstein had an investigative report written about her age and cognitive declines, and was pushed by her party leadership to step down as a ranking member of the judicial committee.

A more intersectional example comes from 82-year-old Congresswoman Maxine Waters from California, a ranking member of the House Committee on financial services in the US Congress. She is fondly known as "Auntie Maxine" which during slavery was a term used to refer to someone who was servile and Mammy-like but in the current context is being used by the Black community as a form of endearment toward a woman who is "smart, strong, sassy, tell-it-like-it-is woman" (Patton and Small 2020). However, Republicans have demeaned by calling her a "useful idiot" who has grown "progressively bizarre" and "dangerous" with "Tourette-syndrome like ranting" (Chumley 2018). She was "slapped" with a censure and a call to resign by a colleague from the Republican Party as a way to displace her from a position of power (Chumley 2018).

From executive to legislative branches of government, from Hillary Clinton to Nancy Pelosi, Maxine Waters, and Dianne Feinstein as women assume or attempt to attain positions of power, the twin edge of ageism and sexism stymies their success. From demeaning characterizations about their appearance, their age and their mental faculties, attempts to displace them from positions of power, to desecrating their work, all efforts are made to devalue and diminish women's authority and power. For example, in 2018, Texas State Board of Education decided that the schools would no longer study Hillary Clinton as the first woman to win a major party nomination for President in an effort to "streamline" the state's social studies standards. Deleting women's achievements is another yet another mode of the patriarchy trying to dominate women.

Conclusion

Nancy Pelosi is a small part of a larger, broader issue of how ageism impacts women leaders in a youth-oriented, visual culture. Using this case study and focusing on the discourse regarding her age, we showcase how Pelosi's attempt to age successfully in the public eye is fraught with complications and how it impacts her ability to succeed in politics.

Apart from these specific scenarios that examine ageism as it impacts women in power, future research can focus on how ageism impacts women of all ages in politics and beyond. Ageism is not an issue that impacts only older women. Representative Alexandria Ocasio Cortez (AOC) has publicly addressed issues of ageism and specifically how young women in power are treated by media and society (Scott 2018). Similarly, Senator Barbara Boxer and Senator Kirsten Gillibrand have spoken about how they have faced accusations of being bad mothers or are questioned about care-giving duties to their young children (Sanghvi 2019). Moreover, ageism toward younger woman is a phenomenon that goes beyond politics and is also found in the workplace and affects careers of young women and mothers (Jyrkinen and McKie 2012).

Ageism impacts women in a myriad of ways that are detrimental to their success in politics and beyond. Patriarchal marketing and neoliberal ideologies that focus on marketplace interventions on beauty, body image, and ideal self-create a panopticon which ensnares women in its scrutiny creating a no-win condition. As one Twitter writer observed, "Between AOC[1] being 'too young' and Pelosi being 'too old' I'm getting the sense that for some people the only right age for a woman in politics is 'male'" (Teaberry 2019).

Reclaiming witches

There is a small but affirming movement, heralded by older women that is working on reclaiming words, symbols, and ideas such as witches, and crones. In popular culture and academia, there is a growing effort to remove the negative stereotypes and stigmas around these words, add more positivity and re-establish the sacredness of these terms (Stevens, Maclaran and Kravets 2020). According to Stevens, Maclaran and Kravets (2020), the crone was a third aspect of the "Triple Goddess" and one that was sacred and wise. Feminist groups, pop culture (such as the popularization of witches in Harry Potter), religious groups, and counter cultural movements, such as Neopaganism and Wicca are reimagining the notion of witches and crones across Western cultures. There is also a growing body of work that is reimagining conversations about aging, including removing the stigma from words such as wrinkles (Muecke 2005) and reframing conversations about ageism and sexism especially for women in power (Stevens, Maclaran and Kravets 2020).

Note

1 Alexandria Ocasio Cortez, the youngest US Representative in Congress, is often referred to as AOC.

References

AAUW (2018). The simple truth about the gender pay gap. Retrieved from: https://ww3.aauw.org/research/the-simple-truth-about-the-gender-pay-gap/

Averett, Paige, Yoon, Intae, and Jenkins, Carol. 2011. "Older lesbians: Experiences of aging, discrimination and resilience." *Journal of Women and Aging, 23* (3): 216–232.

Barnhart, Michelle, and Peñaloza, Lisa. 2013. "Who are you calling old? Negotiating old age identity in the elderly consumption ensemble." *Journal of Consumer Research, 39* (6): 1133–1153.

Balcerzak, Bartlomiej, and Nielek, Radoslaw. 2016. "Of Hags and bitches. Ageist attitudes in 2016 presidential debate on twitter." arXiv preprint arXiv:1611.03616.

Blau, Francine D., and Kahn, Lawrence M. 2017. "The gender wage gap: Extent, trends, and explanations." *Journal of Economic Literature, 55* (3): 789–865.

Bock, Jarrod, Byrd-Craven, Jennifer, and Burkley, Melissa. 2017. "The role of sexism in voting in the 2016 presidential election." *Personality and Individual Differences, 119* (1): 189–193.

Calasanti, Toni. 2005. "Ageism, gravity, and gender: Experiences of aging bodies." *Generations, 29* (3): 8–12.

Carlin, Diana B., and Winfrey, Kelly L. 2009. "Have you come a long way, baby? Hillary Clinton, Sarah Palin, and sexism in the 2008 campaign coverage." *Communication Studies, 60* (4): 326–343.

CBS News (2014). Nancy Pelosi: Nobody asks Mitch McConnell if he's too old to lead. Retrieved from: https://www.cbsnews.com/video/nancy-pelosi-nobody-asks-mitch-mcconnell-if-hes-too-old-to-lead/#x

Chevalier, Corinne, and Moal-Ulvoas, Gaelle M. 2018. "The use of mature models in advertisements and its contribution to the spirituality of older consumers." In E. W. Wang & M. Zhang (Eds.), *Asia-Pacific Advances in Consumer Research* (Volume 12, pp. 59–60). Duluth, MN: Association for Consumer Research.

Chrisler, Joan C., Barney, Angela, and Palatino, Brigida. 2016. "Ageism can be hazardous to women's health: Ageism, sexism, and stereotypes of older women in the healthcare system." *Journal of Social Issues, 72* (1): 86–104.

Chumley, Cheryl. 2018. "Maxine waters finally slapped with House call to censure, resign." *The Washington Times.* Retrieved from: https://www.washingtontimes.com/news/2018/jun/26/maxine-waters-finally-slapped-house-call-censure-r/

Clarke, Laura H., and Griffin, Meredith. 2008. "Visible and invisible ageing: Beauty work as a response to ageism." *Ageing and Society, 28* (5): 653.

CNN. 2012. "Pelosi: You wouldn't ask a man about his age." *CNN.* Retrieved from: https://www.youtube.com/watch?v=NbVrYF8-oOc

Collins, Gail. 2010. "The age of Nancy." *The New York Times.* Retrieved from: https://www.nytimes.com/2010/06/26/opinion/26collins.html

Demirjian, Karoun. 2019. "Trump goes after Pelosi's teeth as the House gears up for impeachment vote." *The Washington Post*. Retrieved from: https://www.washingtonpost.com/politics/trumps-goes-after-pelosis-teeth-as-the-house-gears-up-for-impeachment-vote/2019/12/15/51aacf46-1f8d-11ea-a153-dce4b94e4249_story.html

Denham, Hannah. 2020. "Another fake video of Pelosi goes viral on Facebook." *The Washington Post*. Retrieved from: https://www.washingtonpost.com/technology/2020/08/03/nancy-pelosi-fake-video-facebook/

Dinglefelder, Sadie. 2011. "Pelosi, plastic surgery and the expression of emotion in politics." *The Washington Times*. Retrieved from: https://www.washingtontimes.com/news/2011/nov/7/facing-the-voters/

Dowd, Maureen. 2008, October 26. "A makeover with an ugly gloss." *The New York Times*. Retrieved from http://www.nytimes.com/2008/10/26/opinion/26dowd.html

Dowd, Maureen. 2019. "Nancy Pelosi on Trump and the future." *Harper's Bazaar*. Retrieved from: https://www.harpersbazaar.com/culture/features/a28900588/nancy-pelosi-on-donald-trump/

Doyle, Jude, Ellison. S. 2018. "Nancy Pelosi is old. Good." *GEN Medium*. Retrieved from: https://gen.medium.com/nancy-pelosi-is-old-good-e7b7d8a4a2fc

Draper, Robert. 2018, November 19. "Nancy Pelosi's Last Battle." *The New York Times Magazine*. Retrieved from: https://www.nytimes.com/2018/11/19/magazine/nancy-pelosi-house-democrats.html

Dvorak, Petula. 2019. "Nancy Pelosi is showing women how to age fearlessly and ferociously." *The Washington Post*. Retrieved from: https://www.washingtonpost.com/local/nancy-pelosi-is-showing-women-how-to-age-fearlessly-and-ferociously/2019/12/19/70c1d52a-2283-11ea-bed5-880264cc91a9_story.html

Edgar, Jolene. 2020, October 27. "The demand for plastic surgery is booming despite an ongoing pandemic. Why? *Allure*. Retrieved from: https://www.allure.com/story/plastic-surgery-fillers-demand-covid-19-pandemic

Ellwood, Mark. 2020, August 7. "The pandemic has caused a boom in plastic surgery." *Bloomberg*. Retrieved from: https://www.bloomberg.com/news/articles/2020-08-07/pandemic-plastic-surgery-is-booming-what-are-people-getting-done

Emlet, Charles. A. 2016. "Social, economic, and health disparities among LGBT older adults." *Generations*, 40 (2): 16–22.

Falk, Erica. 2010. *Women for President: Media Bias in Nine Campaigns*. Urbana: University of Illinois Press.

Fredriksen-Goldsen, Karen I., Hoy-Ellis, Charles P., Muraco, Anna, Goldsen, Jayn, and Kim, Hyun Jun. 2015. The health and well-being of LGBT older adults: Disparities, risks, and resilience across the life course. In N. A. Orel & C. A. Fruhauf (Eds.), *The Lives of LGBT Older Adults: Understanding Challenges and Resilience* (pp. 25–53). Washington, DC: American Psychological Association.

Geronimus, Arline T. 1992. "The weathering hypothesis and the health of African-American women and infants: Evidence and speculations." *Ethnicity and Disease*, 2, 207–221.

Gopaldas, Ahir, and Siebert, Anton. 2018. "Women over 40, foreigners of color, and other missing persons in globalizing mediascapes: Understanding marketing images as mirrors of intersectionality." *Consumption Markets & Culture*, 21 (4): 323–346.

Greer, Germaine. 2018. *The Change: Women, Aging, and Menopause*. New York: Bloomsbury Publishing.

Gregoire, Yany. 2003. "The impact of aging on consumer responses: What do we know?" In P. A. Keller & D. W. Rook (Eds.), *NA – Advances in Consumer Research* (Volume 30, pp. 19–26). Valdosta, GA: Association for Consumer Research.

Gurrieri, Lauren 2021 "Patriarchal marketing and the symbolic annihilation of women." *Journal of Marketing Management*, 37 (3–4): 364–370.

Hatch, Laurie R. 2005. "Gender and ageism." *Generations*, 29 (3): 19–24.

Holmlund, Maria, Hagman, Anne, and Polsa, Pia. 2011. "An exploration of how mature women buy clothing: Empirical insights and a model." *Journal of Fashion Marketing and Management*, 15 (1): 108–122.
Jefferys, Sheila. 2014. *Beauty and Misogyny: Harmful Cultural Practices in the West*. London: Routledge.
Jhally, Sut, and Kilbourne, Jean. 2010. *Killing Us Softly 4 Advertising's Image of Women*. Northampton, MA: Media Education Foundation.
Joung, Hyun-Mee, and Miller, Nancy J. 2006. "Factors of dress affecting self-esteem in older female." *Journal of Fashion Marketing and Management*, 10(4), 466–478.
Jyrkinen, Marjut, and McKie, Linda. 2012. "Gender, age and ageism: Experiences of women managers in Finland and Scotland." *Work, Employment and Society*, 26 (1): 61–77.
Kravets, Olga, Preece, Chloe, and Maclaran, Pauline. 2020. "The uniform entrepreneur: Making gender visible in social enterprise." *Journal of Macromarketing*, 40 (4): 445–458.
Krook, Mona Lena. 2021. "Misogyny in the Capitol: Among the insurrectionists, a lot of angry men who don't like women." *The Conversation*. Retrieved from: https://theconversation.com/misogyny-in-the-capitol-among-the-insurrectionists-a-lot-of-angry-men-who-dont-like-women-153068
Lau, Vienne W., Bligh, Michelle C., and Kohles, Jeffrey C. 2020. "Leadership as a reflection of who we are: Social identity, media portrayal, and evaluations of Hillary Clinton in the 2016 US presidential election." *Sex Roles*, 82 (7): 422–437.
Lazar, Michelle. 2007. "Feminist critical discourse analysis: Articulating a feminist discourse praxis." *Critical Discourse Studies*, 4 (2): 141–164.
Lee, Yu K. 2014. "Gender stereotypes as a double-edged sword in political advertising: Persuasion effects of campaign theme and advertising style." *International Journal of Advertising*, 33 (2): 203–234.
Levenson, Michael. 2020. "Pelosi clashes with Facebook and Twitter over video posted by Trump." *The New York Times*. Retrieved from: https://www.nytimes.com/2020/02/08/us/trump-pelosi-video-state-of-the-union.html
Lewis, Denise C., Medvedev, Katalin, and Seponski, Desiree M. 2011. "Awakening to the desires of older women: Deconstructing ageism within fashion magazines." *Journal of Aging Studies*, 25 (2): 101–109.
Loos, Eugene, and Ivan, Loredana. 2018. "Visual ageism in the media." In L. Ayalon and C. Tesch-Römer (Eds.), *Contemporary Perspectives on Ageism* (pp. 163–176). Cham: Springer.
Lytle, Ashley, Macdonald, Jamie, Dyar, Christina, and Levy, Sherri R. 2018. "Ageism and sexism in the 2016 United States presidential election." *Analyses of Social Issues and Public Policy*, 18 (1): 81–104.
McCabe, D. 2015. "Lindsay Graham mocks Pelosi's 'surgeries', apologizes." *The Hill*. Retrieved from: https://thehill.com/blogs/blog-briefing-room/234515-lindsey-graham-mocks-pelosis-surgeries-apologizes
Miller, L. 2018. "David Hogg, after Parkland." *New York Magazine*. Retrieved from: https://nymag.com/intelligencer/2018/08/david-hogg-is-taking-his-gap-year-at-the-barricades.html
Moschis, George P. 2003. "Marketing to older adults: An updated overview of present knowledge and practice." *Journal of Consumer Marketing*, 20 (6): 516–525.
Muecke, Patricia. 2005. "Wrinkles: A depth psychological view through the lens of story." PhD diss., Pacifica Graduate Institute.
Munoz, Caroline L., and Towner, Terri L. 2017. "The image is the message: Instagram marketing and the 2016 presidential primary season." *Journal of Political Marketing*, 16 (3–4): 290-318.
Nelson, Todd D. 2016. "The age of ageism." *Journal of Social Issues*, 72 (1): 191–198.
Neville-Shepard, Ryan, and Nolan, Jaclyn. 2019. "She doesn't have the stamina": Hillary Clinton and the hysteria diagnosis in the 2016 presidential election. *Women's Studies in Communication*, 42 (1): 60–79.
Noah, T. 2019. "America, the gerontocracy." *Politico*. Retrieved from: https://www.politico.com/magazine/story/2019/09/03/america-gerontocracy-problem-politics-old-politicians-trump-biden-sanders-227986

Okimoto, Tyler G. and Brescoll, Victoria L. 2010. "The price of power: Power seeking and backlash against female politicians." *Personality and Social Psychology Bulletin*, 36 (7): 923–936.

Ozanne, Julie L., Moscato, Emily M., and Kunkel, Danylle R. 2013. "Transformative photography: evaluation and best practices for eliciting social and policy changes." *Journal of Public Policy & Marketing* 32 (1): 45–65.

Patton, Tracey O., and Small, Nancy. 2020. "Maxine waters's black feminist and womanist rebuke of supremacist hegemony." In M. N. Goins, J. F. McAlister, & B. K. Alexander (Eds.), *The Routledge Handbook of Gender and Communication* (pp. 243–258). London, UK.

Phelan, Amanda. 2018. "Researching ageism through discourse." In L. Ayalon & C. Tesch-Römer (Eds.), *Contemporary Perspectives on Ageism* (pp. 549–564). Cham: Springer.

Raynor, Barbara. 2015. "Ageism in action? Ageism inaction!" *Generations*, 39 (3): 58–63.

Rosen, Maggie. 2017. "A feminist perspective on the history of women as witches." *Dissenting Voices*, 6 (1): 5.

Rosenberg, Matthew. 2021. "He looted Speaker Pelosi's office, and then bragged about it." *The New York Times*. Retrieved from: https://www.nytimes.com/2021/01/06/us/politics/richard-barnett-pelosi.html

Rowe, John W., and Kahn, Robert L. 1997. "Successful aging." *The Gerontologist*, 37 (4): 433–440.

Roy, Subhadip, and Sanyal, Shamindra N. 2017. "Perceived consumption vulnerability of elderly citizens: A qualitative exploration of the construct and its consequences." *Qualitative Market Research*, 20 (4): 469–485.

Sanghvi, Minita. 2014. *Marketing the Female Politician: An Exploration of Gender, Appearance, and Power*. Greensboro: The University of North Carolina.

Sanghvi, Minita. 2019. *Gender and Political Marketing in the United States and the 2016 Presidential Election: An Analysis of Why She Lost*. New York: Palgrave-MacMillan.

Scott, E. 2018, December 11. "Is there a double standard for Alexandria Ocasio-Cortez?" *The Washington Post*. Retrieved from: https://www.washingtonpost.com/politics/2018/12/11/is-there-double-standard-alexandria-ocasio-cortez/

Sherman, Elaine, and Schiffman, Leon G. 1984. "Applying age-gender theory from social gerontology to understand the consumer well-being of the elderly." In L. Scott & E. Arnould (Eds.), *Advances in Consumer Research* (Volume 11, pp. 569–573). Provo, UT: Association for Consumer Research.

Shields, A. 2011. "Boehner Bias?" *Ms. Magazine*. Retrieved from: http://msmagazine.com/blog/2011/01/07/boehner-bias/

Smith, Michelle. (2016). Performing femininity. The conversation. Retrieved from: http://dro.deakin.edu.au/eserv/DU:30090185/smith-notfittobepresident-2016.pdf

Smith, Ruth B., Moschis, George P., and Moore, Roy L. 1985. "Some advertising influences on the elderly consumer: Implications for theoretical consideration." *Current Issues and Research in Advertising*, 8 (1): 187–201.

Sobh, Rana. 2011. "Approaching what we hope for and avoiding what we fear: A study of women's concern with visible signs of skin aging." *Australasian Marketing Journal*, 19 (2): 122–130.

Stevens, Lorna, Maclaran, Pauline, and Kravets, Olga 2020. "Reclaiming the crone: Reimagining old age and feminine power." Presented at *Association for Consumer Research 2020 Virtual Conference*, Paris, France.

Sudbury, Lynn, and Simcock, Peter. 2009. "A multivariate segmentation model of senior consumers." *Journal of Consumer Marketing*, 26 (4): 251–262.

Sunstein, Cass. 2020. "Trump's nasty nicknames spread like a virus." *Yahoo Finance*. Retrieved from: https://www.yahoo.com/now/trumps-nasty-nicknames-spread-virus-133004668.html

Teaberry Blue. Jan 16, 2019. https://twitter.com/teaberryblue/status/1085642277299470336

Tepper, Kelly. 1994. "The role of labelling process in elderly consumers' responses to age segmentation cues." *Journal of Consumer Research*, 20 (4): 503–518.

Tortajada, Iolanda, Dhaenens, Frederick, and Willem, Celia. 2018. "Gendered ageing bodies in popular media culture." *Feminist Media Studies*, *18* (1): 1–6.
Veresiu, Ela, and Parmentier, Marie. 2021. "Advanced style influencers: Confronting gendered ageism in fashion and beauty markets." *Journal of the Association for Consumer Research*, *6* (2). https://doi.org/10.1086/712609
Woodward, Kathleen. 2006. "Performing age, performing gender." *NWSA Journal*, *18* (1): 162–189.
Zernike, K. (2018). "Nancy Pelosi: Demonized or celebrated, she refuses to agonize." *The New York Times*. Retrieved from: https://www.nytimes.com/2018/11/04/us/politics/nancy-pelosi-house-leader-women.html

21 Our aging bodies, ourselves

Lisa Peñaloza

Introduction

A powerful aging woman, Bonnie Raitt's rock'n, riff'n rendition of John Prine's lyrics came to my mind writing this (https://www.youtube.com/watch?v=MaHNUY-AKDn4). Prine's words attest to the legacy passed from mother to daughter and the love, desire, and need to believe that continues, even gains force with aging. The documentary film, *A Secret Love*, also inspired this chapter. The film spans Terry Donohue and Pat Henschel's couple through six decades, from professional baseball players to career women, retirees, and wives. The song and film tap many of the issues discussed in this chapter: dreams and desires, some achieved, some not; family traditions and scars; the way experience challenges beliefs and changes love over time; and care—for loved ones as well as those not so loved, those with deep roots and bank accounts and those without, and those moved into elderly residences with and without their will. In grasping the process of aging for women from a feminist perspective, attending to the lows and highs along the way is vital in its comprehension.

Qualifier: I'm as ambivalent in claiming my age as I am in claiming my status as a US resident in France. They say life happens when you're doing something else. Well, aging entails a *lot* of something else: relationships, work, play, health, and home. As time passes, one day here, another month or year there, we come to recognize our aging... or not.

In the feminist tradition, I write introspectively, as a 30-year veteran in consumption and market studies, adding *the personal is academic* to the well-known feminist slogan, the personal is political. Explicitly dealing with subjectivity has been a strength of feminist writings in our field and remains a key foundation for our contributions (Catterall et al., 2000). Aging for women is no small task, certainly not for 'sissies,' as Bette Davis caustically advises those embarking on this rite of passage. It creeps up on us gradually, in a range of shocking stares and smiles to the image in our mirrors, others' knowing nods and idiotic statements, and reassuring and devastating trips to a doctor. As colleagues, friends, lovers, and informants, aging women command a paradoxical place in our field, as in society, where crones and grandmas, post and mid-menopausal mothers and others are everywhere and invisible. We are powerful and meek at once, at the backbone of our families, our cultures, and our professional associations.

Social tendencies show a progressive leap regarding gender diversity, in contrast to a regression of sorts from the 1990s in the consumption and marketing discipline, when gender scholarship was cutting edge and social relations lagged. With the social diffusion of concepts and realities of gender and age fluidity, and the vast, numerable, and

DOI: 10.4324/9781003042587-25

significant contributions of elderly women, 'No' increasingly has come to mean 'No!' and biology is less and less destiny—at home and at work. And yet, as with former backlashes, such social integration and empowerment is accompanied by increasing politicization, institutional setbacks and back steps, and continued market specialization and fragmentation, with a new twist, intensifying cyborgian human-technological interfaces that benefit some, even while—or perhaps *because*—others face privations of shelter, food, and health care.

The reversal in our field is a somewhat different paradox. While women have made substantial gains as journal editors and associate editors, presidents of academic associations, deans, and department heads, research on gender published in mainstream journals remains scarce (Prothero and McDonagh, 2021). GENMAC seeks to remedy this, in building upon a strong feminist tradition in consumption and market scholarship that interrogates and extends beyond binary treatments of gender, as encouraged by Bettany et al. (2010). Our last conference, 14th in the series, featured panels, presentations, and posters by women and men of multiple academic cohorts. The topic of aging women represents another promising arena for GENMAC, as there is much work to be done to challenge and build upon research juxtaposing optimistically positive perspectives and findings with those demonstrating physiological and mental decay.

The scope of this chapter is selective, in providing an overview of theoretical approaches and topics regarding aging women that include history, demographics, abilities, subjectivities, and institutions, with consideration of intersectionalities of race/ethnicity and class. The game plan is consciousness-raising in sprinkling academic work with insights drawn from creative writing, media, film, and market practice. Discussion of trends and future opportunities for research and practice concerning aging women concludes the chapter.

What we know to date

While working with Michelle Barnhart on "Who are you calling old" (Barnhart and Peñaloza, 2013), and with Carol Kelleher on "Aging and consumption" (Kelleher and Peñaloza, 2017), we laughed from time to time with irony and horror that we were writing our future. We would, with some luck and good fortune, support from loved ones, and competent health care, grow old, and we dared to wonder what that will look like. Deciphering the multi-agentic forces and dynamics of identity for aging women consumers, was, and remains, as Davis coined, 'no place for sissies!'

History

Our past is one of chattel. Remnants of women's status as property remain in wedding rings and some marriage rites. Rosalind Miles (1988) reminds us that it wasn't always this way: aging women once were leaders, monied land owners, purveyors of agriculture, custodians of animal 'husbandry,' religious practitioners, and guardians of cultural knowledge. Her work, *Who Cooked the Last Supper*, reminds us just how much ground has been lost and remains to be reclaimed still—in the potential contributions of aging women for our quality of life, families, businesses, and societies. As to consumption and the market, both have proven again and again to be tool (Kang and Ridgway, 1996) and foe, remarkably adaptive and adaptable, and so weaving through these diverse manifestations (Saren et al., 2007) is crucial in navigating the road ahead.

Miles (1988) begins with an archeological foundation, citing evidence of goddess worship in many parts of the world (also well documented by Stone, 1976). She continues in tracing the shift in power from women to men, as a function of physical and then institutional acumen, and culminates on a positive note in recognizing the many, taken-for-granted accomplishments of the women's movement through the 1970s and 1980s. It's an exhilarating read, from the wonder and resonating sense of the early place of women in human civilization, tending crops and children; harvesting, storing, and preparing foods; making crafts and art; and controlling money, property, and their body; to the violent horror of beatings, forced marriage, and childbearing, and usurpation of money and property ushered in by the reinvention of creation from the womb to the mind, that of a male god and his legacy in secular science. Transubstantiation, indeed!

Lerner (1994) picks up key threads that fall within Miles' (1988) historical reckoning. Her account of the development of feminist consciousness necessarily challenges religious doctrine and subsequent scientific objectivity, respectively, for their far from holy, blatantly interested justification and support for male dominance.

I had the pleasure to visit Lascaux two years ago. Its 22,000 years old imagery is an amazing ark of exiting horses, elk and cattle of various sizes and shapes, richly colored ochre, blood red, and black. In between, stenciled hands pattern waves of presence within the dark recesses of the cave, an emblematic womb of consciousness. Well-buried in tourist brochures is growing recognition that this art/work is by women, in giving credit to its creators.

It's important that we retain and transmit this history, lest we continue to repeat it, Miles and Lerner warn. Their invocation of Santayana's dictum adds sobering inspiration to feminist consumer and marketing research that challenges the use of evolutionary biological perspectives that relegate women to gathering shoppers and men to hunters in the shops and in ads, with relatedly limited treatments of sexuality (Dennis et al., 2018). Noteworthy is the masculine bias that continues to romanticize and favor hunting over gathering. You can almost feel the adrenaline of the kill; seldom mentioned is the compelling evidence of a predominantly plant-based diet and the rarity of meat as a food source that remains on teeth in ancestors' graves, residues of food in archeological digs, and predominantly flattened, contemporary chewing surfaces.

Demographics

Of the 617 million persons in the world over the age of 65, 342 million (55%) are women, and projections are that this number will increase to 862 million by the year 2050 (Roberts et al., 2018). While women's life expectancy continues to rise across the globe, it varies markedly, from a high of 88 years in 2015 in Japan, as compared to approximately 85 in Europe 55 years in many African nations (He et al., 2016). A number of factors contribute to these trends: advances in nutrition and health care, lower birth-rates, supportive household living arrangements, and state- and employment-supported retirement and housing programs, as well as the ability to choose to marry and to divorce, and to co-habit or live alone.

In the US, where much of the consumer research in our field is carried out, 50 million persons (55%) over the age of 65 are women, with a life expectancy of just under 80 years that has declined in recent years (Kamal 2019). If US Census projections hold, by the year 2050 there will be over 46 million women over the age of 65 in the nation (Ortman et al., 2014, pp. 1, 10). Regarding education, one of every five women in the

US holds a bachelor's degree, compared to 1 of every 3 men, while aging women's median income amounted to $41,720, as compared to $56,850 for men (Roberts et al., 2018, pp 12, 18). Continuing with the profile of women over the age of 65 in the US, 14.2% continue to work, compared to 21.9% of men (Roberts et al., 2018, p. 16). This difference in employment partly is due to the absence of funds, volition, and the erosion of pensions and retirement benefits. Related to wealth and work is home ownership; roughly 78% of women over the age of 65 in the US own their residence, as compared to 63% of those under 65 years, and 80% are connected to internet technology at home, either through their phone or computer (Roberts et al., 2018, pp. 14, 13). Taking a deeper look into the living arrangements for women over the age of 65 in the US, 2.6 million women live alone and 14 million are married and live with spouses (Roberts et al., 2018, p. 6). Of the former, those living alone are six times more likely to live in poverty than their married cohorts (Roberts et al., 2018, p. 20). Contributing to this statistic is lower education, employment, and occupation levels, outliving a spouse, and not having children.

However, the above figures are *not* representative of the situation of aging women in the US. When we consider the intersectionalities of race/ethnicity and class, disparities of life expectancy, lower rates of education, lower paid jobs/careers, and lower income come to the fore. According to US Census figures, elderly Black women comprise 8.4% of Black persons and 62.5% of elderly Black persons, and one in three lives in poverty (U.S. Bureau of the Census, 1993a, pp. 5, 10). The figures for elderly Hispanic women are somewhat similar, in comprising 5% of Hispanic persons in the US and 56% of elderly Hispanics, with one in four living in poverty (U.S. Bureau of the Census, 1993c, pp. 6, 9). It is vital that we keep in mind these dramatic differences in demographics and experience for aging women in our research, teaching, and work with firms and activists, as these differences ripple through consumption and in the market.

Generational and cohort analysis

Social views and stereotypes have changed remarkably over time, framing expectations and experience in ways that coalesce generational differences and conflict (Mannheim, 1952). Regarding the study of aging for women, it is valuable to consider cross-generational differences in activity, life expectancy, and views of the body, as well as formative gender roles, expectations, norms, and aspirations for the way each frames and impacts consumption experience (Castaño et al., 2012). As valuable in comprehending and profiling the consumption of cohorts of aging women is directing attention to formative and contemporary market conditions, to include work conditions and benefits, as well as service provision and accessibility. As illustrative examples, challenges in using technologies impact consumption and quality of life for aging women (Castaño et al., 2012; Gilly et al., 2012) that play out in extended families (Quintanilla et al., 2019).

TV and film are good sites to track such generational and cohort differences, as is advertising (Yoon and Powell, 2012; Carrigan and Szmigin, 2002). Consider the role changes from the dedicated mother and housewife, June Cleaver in *Leave it to Beaver*, to the single apartment life of compassionate, independent career gal, *Mary Tyler Moore*, to the divorced single mother in *Reba*, and the spirited grandmas in the blended and gay families in *Modern Family*. It is less rare to see men cleaning and cooking, although older men doing so remain scarce.

The family life cycle

Considering generational differences and cohort experiences in women's roles, we can appreciate early work on the consumption implications of the increasing prevalence of working women (Venkatesh, 1980), and adaptations of the family life cycle (FLC) model to incorporate then novel family forms (Gilly and Enis, 1982). At the time this work was published, families supported by a single earner with pension benefits were more common, at least among professionals and some in the working class, and it made sense then to focus on the nuclear family and cast elderly women as part of an elderly couple or as a solitary survivor.

Later work recenters aging women and consumption in broader social and market circumstance. For example, Schau et al. (2009) noted a 'renaissance' for post-retirement elderly in recuperating identities they had crafted prior to their work. In again updating the Family Life Cycle (FLC) as it pertains to the consumption of elderly women, the earlier stage of work culminating in retirement will be usefully recrafted to encompass work after work, and in some cases multiple work after multiple work. As important is considering the current situation for elderly women: living the trauma of COVID in the wake of the early 21st-century financial crisis that dwindled the interest rates banks paid, eroding savings and retirement accounts for those who had them, and shifting savings and retirement strategies to stock markets.

Notably, engagement gives life meaning. Elizabeth Warren, US Senator from Massachusetts in her 70s, and Vanessa Redgrave, acting in her 90s, are exemplary upper-class aging women. Warren pitched a strong presidential campaign for the democratic party on a platform of restoring financial regulations separating investments from other bank operations and continues to work for graduated income tax levels that have been eroded by tax cuts. At 90, Vanessa Redgrave's most recent work was as the mother of renowned artist L.S. Lowrey in *Mrs. Lowrey and son*. In an interview between rehearsals for Richard III at the Almedia theater in London, Redgrave spoke about her heart attack the previous year (Hattenstone, 2016). Admitting that she wanted to die, "because trying to live was just too tiring" (p. 8), she credited her friend Joely for helping her by giving her permission to do just that, which "released" her. She also linked her childhood during WWII to her activism for human rights and spoke about the importance of embracing contradictions, warning, "if you don't, you're not going to get very far in understanding anything," adding in reference to religion and Marxism, humans need "to explain things they can't explain and acknowledge the existence of things they want to explain but can't" (p. 8). We feminist consumption and market scholars will benefit from her wisdom. About working into her 90s, she quipped, "if you have too much time to think you can drown in grief" (pp. 8–9). Viewed in this light, those continuing to work for wages and to volunteer well into retirement merit consideration in our research, teaching and service.

Mind and body

Another form of 'generational differences' in aging manifests in changing views and approaches from neighboring academic fields, and with increases in the age of those writing! Feminist perspectives on the body are useful in approaching the topic of consumption among aging women. For Butler (1993, pp. 29–30), bodies matter as the means of enabling political aims. For her, the body is more than an irreducible materiality useful to feminism in speaking about women. Instead, she argues for the motivated and conscious treatment of doings and sayings regarding the body as an anchor for political subjectivity and agency, pointing to the interests at work in such metaphysical placements, and challenging the related presumptions that physicality could somehow exist outside the realm of social construction. The focus on gender categories and their legitimizing and exclusionary effects in *Bodies that Matter* and *Gender Trouble* serves as theoretical lens addressing the major concerns of identity, social visibility, and inclusion pertinent to aging women.

Third age

Mixing science and new age philosophy, scholars examining the phenomena of aging ushered in the third age (Laslett 1989). Representing positive aging in consumer research is Pettigrew's (2007) work on the importance of companionship and Wilkes' (1992) early distinction between 'younger' older people in terms of their confidence, activity and better life outcomes than 'older' older people. This approach is the guiding principle of the Taos Institute, Kenneth Gergen and Mary McConnel Gergen's (2000) center featuring seminars, workshops, and a cadre of faculty. The late Madame Gergen is an icon of both feminism (1988) and positive living. Her life and ideas have served, and continue to serve as a beacon to others on this path https://www.socialsciencespace.com/2020/10/mary-gergen-1938-2020-pioneer-in-social-constructionism-and-feminist-psychology/.

Yet which comes first for aging women, positive aging or favorable life circumstance? While it would seem much easier for those in a good life situation to have a positive mindset about aging, work on materialism shows lower happiness ratings for those with more stuff (Rudmin and Richins, 1992). For post-war and boomer cohorts, life wasn't supposed to be like this; it was supposed to get better. Always. Not so for previous cohorts, who lived the ravages of one or even two world wars, a pandemic, and the depression. Expectations then were less. As my mom recalled her mother telling her, a good husband was a 'good supporter who didn't beat you.' So, while there are similarities between then and now, including the growing gulf between the 1% and the other 99%, material and emotional expectations steadily had risen, and now COVID and climate change are again tempering and dividing them.

Fourth age

The fourth age scholarship on aging returns attention to physical, mental, and social deterioration, loss, and marginalization (Higgs and Gilleard, 2015; Twigg, 2004). Consumer research categorizable as such highlights physical and mental decay in aging, to include the loss of information processing (Drolet, Schwartz and Yoon, 2010) and decision making abilities (Cole et al., 2008), memory (Roedder-John and Cole, 1986), and adaptability (Lambert-Pandraud and Laurent, 2010), which, in turn, pose market vulnerabilities with technology (Griffiths and Harmon, 2011) and in service encounters (Grougiou and Pettigrew, 2011). Some will experience these aspects of aging more than others. Important for us to not ignore, as researchers and as aging women and those who later will age, is this range of ability and consumption/market experience.

Crucial in enriching our knowledge and understanding of aging is people's conscious experience of 3rd and 4th age as shaped in consumption in interactions with others. As such, we can learn more about the involvement of family and service providers in consumption for elderly persons, in addition to how their collaborative recognition of differences in the consumption of elderly persons interacts with the reluctance of the elderly to identify as such due to their determination to live positively and combat negative stereotypes ((Barnhart and Peñaloza 2013). As an example, Kelleher et al. (2019) detail the importance of carers in orchestrating the elderly's reception of services.

Subjectivities

Subjective accounts of aging are conveyed poignantly in writing, film, and photography. The Feminist Collective's *Our Bodies, Ourselves* (1973) and Des Femmes' (2020) updated *Notre Corps, Nous-Mêmes* attest to the subjective understanding of aging so vital to humanistic and scientific advancement in consumption and marketing scholarship. Freed from the homages citing previous work, wonky theoretical framing and contributions, and methodological justification, their contents are informative and instructive on a range of topics from bodily awareness and beauty norms, to gender identity and sexuality, work, pregnancy and menopause, illness, and harassment and self-defense. The section on aging in *Notre Corps* is small, yet features resonant testimonies. In addition, collaborative subjectivity has been the life work of Betty Dodson. This heroine of self-pleasure gave scores of instructive, hands-on workshops and talks during her life (Green, 2020), including explaining different kinds of orgasms in "The pleasure is ours," episode 3 of Gwyneth Paltrow's Netflix series.

In academic writing many steadily have worked to include consumers' and marketers' 'voices' and the contexts which they construct and from which they emerge. Recent examples presented at the online ACR conference go into depth and social context pertaining to women's aging. Godefroit-Winkle et al. (2020) detail the wisdom accorded Moroccan grandmothers after menopause, as those who've born sons gain status and social recognition in their families and society. Aging women are a force like this in many families, in keeping the financial books and stocking cupboards in families, even as they put forward their men in public (Lindridge et al., 2016). Gaviria et al. (2020) provide a spirited account of the playful child post-menopausal women rejuvenate, now that they're less objectified and reclaiming their sensuality and sexuality apart from childbearing. Stevens et al. (2020) invoke the crone, that archetype of wisdom and irreverence attained by aging women who have reflected on their past and made peace with it. Aging on our terms means not giving in to what society deems appropriate.

Institutions

For Gallop (1988), thinking through the body proves a useful means of recuperating an embodied perspective from the mind–body split and its progeny: disinvested, institutionalized 'objective' intellectual discourse. Her early studies of de Sade, Barthes and Freud highlight the systemic masking of social violence in the church, the state, and the academy, respectively. Her interrogations remind us of the power in such objectivity, as well as its usefulness in strategically generating thought-provoking questions and answers.

Overall, gains and setbacks characterize treatment of aging women at institutional levels, from leaders and crones, dependents and loners, to agentic grey panthers. The present scenario features encouraging initiatives in response to aging populations, to include the particular concerns and circumstances of women. Concomitantly, there are

330 Lisa Peñaloza

alarming reversals of hard-fought gains in gender rights, against which people—aging and younger women and men—are mobilizing (see Figure 21.1). In the photo women sporting robes resembling the cast in *The Handmaiden's Tale* protest the nomination of 'conservative' Supreme Court justices by the 45th US president and their confirmation by the US Senate, advanced with blatant intention to repeal Roe vs. Wade, the landmark decision establishing women's right to *choose* whether to carry a fetus to term. These appointments are a stab in the hearts of those mourning the passing of Justice Ruth Bader Ginsburg, champion of gender justice. Another formidable aging woman, Justice Ginsburg worked for 27 of her 87 years on the US Supreme Court, having been appointed in 1993 by President Bill Clinton. Her life and career demonstrate a series of tests: at Harvard and then graduating with honors at Columbia Law School, and when no law firm would hire her, teaching on the faculty at Rutgers Law School, where she won landmark cases with the American Civil Liberties Union in establishing women's rights and gender parity.

Also working at the level of institutional engagement is GENMAC. Join us, in highlighting the importance of gender-related activity and research in our field, in showcasing its diverse expressions, which include aging, in striving for gender parity and justice in consumption and market activity, and in drawing attention to the loss and injury

Figure 21.1 Women's march for the right to choose. Austin, Texas, January 2018.
Photo: Lisa Peñaloza.

resulting in their absence. To highlight the blend of academics and practitioners at the conference in Dallas in 2018: a changemakers' panel featuring Lucinda Guinn from Emily's List, a group fostering women in political office, and Shannon Moorman from the TimesUp Movement, and a transformative agenda for gender research, practice, and teaching organized by Wendy Hein and Linda Tuncay Zayer.

In the marketplace there is a somewhat different version of the paradoxical ubiquity and invisibility regarding aging women found in research. With marketers' increasing savvy regarding those with 'grey' dollars, less common are packaging and ad copy promising anti-aging with the application of skin crème modeled on flawless young faces, as they are replaced by the somewhat visible lines of Hellen Mirren and Jane Fonda. Important is disentangling personal agency within a web of social and market interests medicalizing aging, illness, and dying. While marketers promise to 'solve the aging problem' (https://www.alwaysbestcare.com/), and others suggest auditors to monitor care homes (Csanady, 2015), activists such as Diane Rehm work for the right to die with dignity (Washington Post, 2015).

In film, aging women are increasingly found in agentic roles, from the touching portrait of a loving couple dealing with Alzheimer's in *Away from Her*, to the comic romps of Meryl Streep in *It's Complicated* and Diane Keaton in *Something's Gotta Give*, and the type A, business savvy, Jane Fonda and her hippie roommate, Lily Tomlin in *Grace and Frankie*. Sarah Polley's *Away from Her* provides a sobering window into an affliction that pushes thousands of persons into the fourth age each year, with projections by the Alzheimer's Association (2020) that the total number will reach 14 million in the US alone by 2050. In the film, we see the progression from compromised work, through diagnosis and assisted living. Treatments are somewhat encouraging, however. In Denmark's House of Memories, Dorthe Bentsen (2020), director of the Center on Autobiographical Memory Research at Aarhus University, furnishes apartments with objects from the 1950s that reinvoke some former mental and physical capabilities. Music appears to work in similar ways. In Hawaii, Jen McGeehan, founder of iPods For the Elderly, provides the devices to patients on the Big Island. In one of their videos neurologist-narrator Oliver Sacks refers to Henry, animatedly answering questions about his youth while listening to his favorite music, in stark contrast from his earlier unreachable state. These effects involving the possessions of elderly women merit further work, in building on Price et al. (2000).

The other films offer a comic glimpse into aging women's lives. In *Something's Gotta Give*, Keaton plays a successful playwright, who reluctantly allows her daughter's weekend date, played by Jack Nicholson, to recuperate from a heart attack at her beach house, and then transforms parts of their later heartbreaking affair into another Broadway hit. The play begins with the protagonist's biting indictments of her lover's ageism, machismo, and inability to commit in serially dating women half his age, and then cuts to scenes of her in the arms of his younger doctor, played by Keanu Reeves. Ultimately, she chooses the older man's attention and vulnerability over the young doctor's adoration. Hope springs eternal that old dogs learn, her and him!

Streep is smart, funny, and sexy, in *It's Complicated*. She's an empty nesting mom, and her adult children are not the main axis of her life any more than she is at the center of theirs. Brought together at the graduation of their youngest child, the exes embark on an affair. For her, it's sexual reaffirmation, revenge, and 'been there, done that' at the inability of the since remarried ex, played by Alec Baldwin, to relate emotionally, juxtaposed with a building and competing romance with her architect, played by Steve Martin.

Jane Fonda and Lily Tomlin are forces not to be reckoned with in *Grace and Frankie,* an aging women's odd couple set in a roomy Malibu beach house. Both recover from the long-closeted affair of their husbands by steering a thriving dildo business in between amorous adventures and the trials and tribulations of their respective broods. The gal's friendship triumphs through the thick and thin of divorce, health crises, financial pit- and windfalls, assisted suicide, colorful foodie spreads, and lots of pot (hey, it's California!).

In photography, Cindy Sherman's latest exhibit at the Metro Pictures Gallery in New York represents her efforts at age 62 to come to terms with 'health issues and getting older' (Gopnik, 2016). Of the self-portraits, her black and white image is intent and serene, looking ahead, yet not directly, her blonde bangs fall just to the top of her eyelids, wrinkles visible at her neck and along pressed lips. In the set of images Sherman casts herself as veteran leading ladies of Hollywood's Golden Age, Gloria Swanson and Greta Garbo, among others. In them art critic Gopnik observes 'a tenderness that hasn't been seen in her work for several decades,' adding that in her interview Sherman credited Mary Beard's campaign for a woman's right to age today. Particularly inspiring was Beard's message to men, "You are looking at a 59-year-old-woman. That is what 59-year-old women who have not had work done look like. Get it?" (Gopnik, 2016, p. 16). We all should be so lucky to age like this.

Many are, notes Douglas (2020a) in a manifesto charting the legacies of 'radical elders of the tribe.' Among the many feminists *in their prime* Douglas (2020b) mentions is Maggie Kuhn. Kuhn is relevant to this chapter for having midwifed a movement, the Grey Panthers. Predating the fatshionistas featured by Scaraboto and Fischer (2012), this institutional entrepreneur gave thousands of speeches and appeared on numerous talk shows through the 1970s mobilizing likeminded activists and shattering the glass ceilings of discrimination and marketing myopia (Leavitt, 1960) shackling aging persons. Among their accomplishments: accommodating public transportation, cost of living increases in social security allotments, and a powerful nonprofit organization, the American Association of Retired Persons (AARP).

Regarding fashion, Scott's (2005) historical tour de force documents a long trajectory of puritanical class struggles to hold on to power by policing beauty standards. The affordable fashion that manufacturers and retailers made available to the working class posed a threat to US agrarian aristocrats, Scott explains. Pointing to feminists' interests at various times in denouncing corsets, large skirts and pointed small shoes in the 1800s, lipstick on young flappers and immigrants, the busty Gibson girls of the 1950s, and the flannels, jeans, and unshaved legs in the 70s and 80s, Scott urges contemporary feminists to end such division and instead focus on equality, empowerment, and advancement.

Fashion is an important means of self-expression and rebellion, Scott reminds us, highlighting notable brand stewards who worked well into their later years: Estée Lauder, Mary Kay, and Harriet Hubbard Ayer. Scott's work implores feminists to move beyond reducing the forms of self-presentation we are uncomfortable with to sexual allure, and striving to control other women, and instead foster women's desire to be beautiful as a source of our power. For aging women, dealing with our greying hair (Hurd and Korotchenko, 2010) and the pull of gravity on our faces (Twigg and Majim, 2014) and breasts (Risius et al., 2014) are forms of consumption where we may find that power in navigating the market.

Future trends and directions

1. **We are aging as a people worldwide**. While this is happening faster and to a greater degree in 'developed' nations than in those 'less developed,' this is happening everywhere. Encouraging is the compelling support for the elderly among the next generation, united in the quest for equal opportunity and social justice. Working against this alliance is resentment at a skewed distribution of wealth largely driven by home ownership, pensions, and benefits of at least some elderly persons that is less accessible for younger persons, and a minimum wage that does not keep up with the rising costs of living and is dwarfed further by the overgrown ratio between CEO pay and bonuses. Dramatic tax cuts over the last decades have exacerbated this gulf in wealth distribution. Creative market and social solutions based on and fostering mutual understanding, care, and tolerance are needed, as is further research attuned to the circumstance of, and the relations between, these different generations and cohorts.

2. **Changing Household configurations**. For decades, demographers have noted increasing trends for persons living alone, both aging and youth (U.S. Census, 1993b). In *Critical Theory of the Family*, Poster (1978) attributed the nuclear family household trend to industrial society. Will the service/information economy reverse this trend? Recent economic and social circumstances portend an increasing incidence of extended families. A counter-trend, with profound implications for aging women consumers and the marketers accommodating us, is brought about by 'mature' adults in their 40s and 50s, jobs, less financially able to accommodate parents, and spatially encumbered and constrained by jobs as well, and perhaps less willing, in instead prioritizing themselves and their children. At the higher end of the 'grey market,' a host of senior living resorts and facilities compete to keep depression, post-war, and boomer cohorts with pensions/savings/IRA's living alone as long as possible. These are the extremes, a tale not of two cities, but of two colliding worlds of experience for aging women, and reconciling them within our nations, our cultures, and our families marks important areas for further work.

3. **The COVID 19 pandemic**. This is hitting elderly persons particularly hard, accounting for an estimated 80% of its mortality. Elderly women are affected somewhat less than men, yet afflicted nonetheless. Had our great grandmothers lived, they could've talked about their experiences with the misnamed Spanish Flu, since traced to Kansas (*The Spanish Flu & How the World Recovered*, 1918–1929, https://www.youtube.com/watch?v=d0AoRkmj9YM). Also notable in the documentary is the back to the future scenario of our present predicament. Visible in the film are photos showing obligatory masks and sumptuary fines for not wearing them in St. Louis, Missouri, and those refusing to wear them in Philadelphia, Pennsylvania, with correspondingly different numbers of cases and deaths.

    Riled now with the daily risk of COVID contagion and uncertainty are those in retirement homes, frontline workers, and those living in densely populated cities. Lives are less affected for those living with comfortable financial means, access to food/drink, spacey homes—maybe more than one, spacey gardens, and living with loved ones and/or maybe a pet. While history shows previous pandemics to run for two to three years, this one seems eternal. One thing is sure: COVID puts particularly at risk older people, overweight persons, and especially those with respiratory ailments and compromised immune systems.

Each day, as if the rising number of deaths and cases weren't bad enough, politicians across the globe are politicizing this virus, some refusing knowledge and practices that have been proven effective in shielding *us and others* from its wrath, and worse, attacking those working to arrest the transmission and save lives. Consumers and business persons again are part of the problem; consumers refusing to be vaccinated and wear masks and doggedly assaulting or otherwise preventing those who do, and businesswomen and men capitalizing on these circumstances in shedding jobs and mortgages they'd been wanting to drop before.

Regarding solutions, Eileen Fischer (2020) diagnosed well so many problems with COVID in her recent Association for Consumer Research (ACR) presidential address: consumers lacking enough food and not having access to affordable health care, debt, lost jobs and businesses, front line health and service workers' risk of transmission, illness, uncertainty, and death; children at home, isolated, angry; and systemic racism that contributes to the disproportionate affliction among those of color. Fischer encouraged us as consumer researchers to do what we do best, research, teach, and inspire others in crafting solutions, mentoring others, and incorporating intersectionality in our work. In doing so, let's interrogate how such vulnerabilities at the nexus of age, gender, race, and class are exacerbated by the increasing egoism and skewed distributions of wealth fostered by consumer culture and neoliberal economy, and work for collaborative remedies.

4 **Technological u/dystopias**. Doris, 77, an informant once said to me with a gleam in her eye, "If my Ipad were a woman, I'd marry her" (Peñaloza et al., 2020). Following up with her a few years later, I could see that the honeymoon was over, ended by the saturated memory of the device and her fear and reticence to change a lost password, due to a cascade of connected apps. Recently, she was diagnosed with cancer, a slow growing form, and is just over the nauseating effects of initial treatment. Her numbers are looking good, and bolstered by the pleasure of being able to eat a full meal, the last one being Tex-Mex, she is determined to enjoy life while she can, spend time at a distance with loved ones, and make amends in trying to understand and come to grips with the beauty and fear of the end of her life.

Technology is a huge issue, offering promises for connectivity to loved ones and advances in health care and quality of life. Here, too, are important intersectionalities, in the unevenness of access, affordability, and abilities with regard to technology, as displaced, middle-class 'gig' workers (Cook, 2020) join the historical circumstance of working-class people who always have worked more than one job, and as the routines of many women giggers include family care and housework when they do get home (Hochschild 1990). The mix of promise, access, and abilities for aging women are particularly acute, as evident in the example featuring Doris above, and represent important topics for future work.

Several writers have penned their visions of the future, and I close with a few. I mentioned already Margaret Atwood's novel, *The Handmaiden's Tale*, which features a futuristic account of a caste of women channeled into the life work of childbearing for those who can't or won't. Richard Fleischer's cult classic film, *Soylent Green*, depicts aging professor Sol Roth (played by Edward G. Robinson), going to a facility to die, where he is dressed in white robes and surrounded by images and sounds of how the world once looked, plush and green with colorful flowers, abundant wildlife, and clean air and water. Later he will be processed into food for a population that long exceeded the world's carrying capacity.

In Tom Wolfe's (1984) futuristic UK, three-fourths of the nation work in tourism, walking about in clothes resembling the mid-1800s. In homage to Orwell's *1984*, Wolfe situates Winston and Julie in an amphitheater in 2020, where a hologram (somewhat akin to our COVID-adapted teaching) jeers his 'best of Britain.' By then Marxists are relegated to 'the zone,' a marginal netherland, and have become a fading memory. Asked by someone in the audience why there has been no fascism in the US, the hologram calmly compares the 'Yanks' to sharks that do not announce they will kill and do not think of themselves as killers, even as they suppress "the largest concentration of black people outside Africa"... and supply "instruments and training for mayhem and slaughter" (p. 22). The voice taunts the audience, "Just as you... don't *think* of them as fascists!" The performance closes with the question, "Do you think a shark is a shark?" to hoots and laughter from the audience (p. 22). Oh, the "priceless lunacy" (p. 22) of that century. Winston and Julie chant, louder and louder, the "time-tried chorus of Xenophobia, Resentment and Wounded Chauvinism." And as the audience responds, first with an isolated shout and then an echoing jeer through the auditorium, they kiss.

Our kiss? Another future. Not Ortega y Gasset's tryanny by the majority, but by the minority instead? Let's hope not. That future is now. Let's make it a good one, where intellectuals, including Marxists, inspire more inclusive and just policy. Toward that end, I offer this link https://www.youtube.com/watch?v=J4n_jDe0JsQ to aging women, to those who have cared for us all, and to those we care for. In the video Demi Lovato sings Bill Withers' song, *Lovely Day*, accompanied by the diverse voices and grooves of enthusiastic health-care workers, to President Biden and the nation for his inauguration. Just as they find moments of hope and joy mid-pandemic, so can we in our difficult times. In moments of unbearable thoughts and seemingly impossible days or weeks, turn to others: "Then I look at you, and the world's all right with me. Just one look at you..." At the end, Lovato and the workers chorus another Withers' song, *Call me*, flanked with images of Rosie the Riveter flexing her muscle and the adage, "We're all in this together." Wise words and gests for third age, fourth age, and now—by, with and for aging women.

References

Barnhart, M. and Peñaloza, L. (2013), "Who are you calling old? Negotiating old age identity in the elderly consumption ensemble," *Journal of Consumer Research*, 39:6 (April), 1133–1153.

Bettany, S., Dobscha, S., O'Malley, L., and Prothero, A. (2010), "Moving beyond binary opposition: Exploring the tapestry of gender in consumer research and marketing," *Marketing Theory*, 10:1, 3–28.

Butler, J. (1990), *Gender Trouble*, New York: Routledge.

——— (1993), *Bodies that Matter*, New York: Routledge.

Carrigan, M. and Szmigin, I. (2002), "Advertising in an aging society," *Aging and Society*, 20, 217–233.

Castaño, R., Quintanilla, C. and Perez, M.E. (2012). "Aging and the changing meaning of consumption experiences." Documentary Film, 20 min., Association of Consumer Research Film Festival, Vancouver, Canada.

Catterall, M., Maclaran, P., and Stevens, L. (2000), *Marketing and Feminism: Current Issues and Research*, London: Routledge.

Cole, C., Laurent, G., Drolet, A., Ebert, J., Gutchess, A., Lambert-Pandraud, R., Mullet, E., Norton, M.I., and Peters, E. (2008), "Decision making and brand choice by older consumers," *Marketing Letters*, 19:3/4 (July), 355–365.

Cook, K. (2020), "Economic inequality and employment," in her book *The Psychology of Silicon Valley: Ethical Threats and Emotional Unintelligence in the Tech Industry*, Chapter 7, New York: Palgrave Macmillan, pp. 167–195.

Dennis, C., Brakus, J.J., Ferrer, G.G., McIntyre, C., Alamanos, E., and King, T. (2018),"A cross-national study of evolutionary origins of gender shopping styles: She gatherer, he hunter?" *Journal of International Marketing*, 26:4, 38–53.
Des Femmes (2020), *Notre Corps, Nous-Mêmes*, Marseille: Hors d'attente.
Douglas, S. (2020a), *In Our Prime: How Older Women Are Reinventing the Road Ahead*, New York: W.W. Norton and Company.
——— (2020b), "The forgotten history of the radical 'elders of the tribe'," *New York Times*, Sept. 8, online edition, https://www.nytimes.com/2020/09/08/opinion/gray-panthers-maggie-kuhn.html.
Drolet, A., Schwartz, N., and Yoon, C. (2010), *The Aging Consumer: Perspectives from Psychology and Economics*, New York: Routledge.
Feminist Collective (1973), *Our Bodies, Ourselves*, New York: Simon and Schuster.
Fischer, Eileen (2020), "2020 ACR Presidential Address: Where to From Here?", in North American Advances in Consumer Research, Vol. 48, Jennifer Argo, Tina M. Lowrey, and Hope Jensen Schau eds., Duluth, MN: Association for Consumer Research, pp. 1–3. https://vimeo.com/465479728
Gallop, J. (1988), *Thinking through the Body*, New York: Columbia University Press.
Gaviria, P., Del Bucchia, C. and Quental, C. (2020), "'The Foreigner Within Us': Catharsis Amid Horror and Confusion in Menopause", in North American Advances in Consumer Research, Volume 48, Jennifer Argo, Tina M. Lowrey, and Hope Jensen Schau eds., Duluth, MN: Association for Consumer Research, pp. 1107–1108, https://www.acrwebsite.org/volumes/2661468/volumes/v48/NA-48.
Gergen, K. and Gergen, M.M. (2000), "The new aging: Self-construction and social values," in The evolution of the aging self: the societal impact on the aging process, H.W. Schaie and J. Hendrick, eds., New York: Springer, pp. 281–306.
Gergen, M.M., ed. (1988), *Feminist Thought and the Structure of Knowledge*, New York: New York University Press.
Gilly, M.C. and Enis, B. (1982), "Recycling the family life cycle: A proposal for redefinition," in *Advances in Consumer Research*, A. Mitchell, ed., Ann Arbor, MI: Association for Consumer Research, Vol. 9, pp. 271–276.
Gilly, M., Celsi, M.W., and Schau, H.J. (2012), "It don't come easy: Overcoming obstacles to technology use within a resistant consumer group," *Journal of Consumer Affairs*, 46(Spring), 62–89.
Godefroit-Winkel, D., Schill, M., and Hogg, M. (2020), "Wisdom examined via a qualitative investigation of the bathing rituals of aging Moroccan women and their granddaughters," *in* North American Advances in Consumer Research, Volume 48, Jennifer Argo, Tina M. Lowrey, and Hope Jensen Schau eds., Duluth, MN: Association for Consumer Research, pp. 1109–1111, https://www.acrwebsite.org/volumes/2661468/volumes/v48/NA-48.
Gopnik, B. (2016), "Ready for her close-up," *New York Times, International Edition*, April 23–24, pp. 16–19.
Green, P. (2020), "Betty Dodson, women's guru of self-pleasure, dies at 91," *New York Times*, Nov. 3, online edition, https://www.nytimes.com/2020/11/03/style/betty-dodson-dead.html.
Griffiths, M.A. and Harmon, T.R. (2011), "Aging consumer vulnerabilities influencing factors of acquiescence to informed consent," *Journal of Consumer Affairs*, 45:3, 445–466.
Grougiou, V. and Pettigrew, S. (2011), "Senior customers' service encounter preferences," *Journal of Service Research*, 14:4 (Nov.), 475–488.
Hattenstone, S. (2016), "The g2 interview," *The Guardian*, June 13, pp. 6–9.
He, W., Goodkind, D., and Kowal, P. (2016), *An Aging World: 2015, International Population Reports*, Washington, DC: U.S. Census Bureau, U.S. Government Publishing Office.
Higgs, P. and Gilleard, C. (2015), *Rethinking Old Age: Theorising the Fourth Age*, London: Palgrave Macmillan.
Hochschild, A.R. 1990, *The Second Shift*, New York: Avon Books.

Hurd Clarke, L. and Korotchenko, A. (2010). "Shades of grey: To dye or not to dye one's hair in later life," *Ageing and Society*, 30:6, 1011–1026.

Kamal, R. (2019), "How does U.S. life expectancy compare to other countries?" Petersen Center on Health Care and Kaiser Family Foundation, https://www.healthsystemtracker.org/chart-collection/u-s-life-expectancy-compare-countries/#item-start.

Kang, Y.S. and Ridgway, N.M. (1996). "The importance of consumer market interactions as a form of social support for elderly consumers," *Journal of Public Policy and Marketing*, 15:1 (Spring), 108–117.

Kelleher, C., O'Loughlin, D., Gummerus, J., and Peñaloza, L. (2019), "Shifting arays of a kaleidoscope: Orchestration of value co-creation," *Journal of Service Research*, 23:2 (Nov.), 211–228.

Kelleher, C. and Peñaloza, L. (2017), "Aging and consumption," in Part V of *The Routledge Handbook on Consumption*, M.t Keller, B. Halkier, T.-A. Wilska, and M. Truninger, eds., London: Routledge, pp. 326–338.

Lambert-Pandraud, R. and Laurent, G. (2010), "Why do older consumers buy older brands? the role of attachment and declining innovativeness," *Journal of Marketing*, 74:5 (Sept.), 104–121.

Laslett, P. (1989), *A Fresh Map of Life: The Emergence of a Third Age*, London: Weidenfeld and Nicolson.

Leavitt, T. (1960), "Marketing myopia," *Harvard Business Review*, 38:4 (July–Aug.), 45–56.

Lerner, G. (1994). *The Creation of Feminist Consciousness: From the Middle Ages to Eighteen-Seventy* (Vol. 2), Oxford: Oxford University Press.

Lindridge, A., Peñaloza, L., and Worlu, O. (2016), "Agency and empowerment in consumption in relation to a patriarchal bargain: The case of Nigerian immigrant women in the UK," *European Journal of Marketing*, 50:9/10, 1652–1671.

Mannheim, K. 1952. "The problem of generations," In *Essays on the Sociology of Knowledge*, P. Kecskemeti, ed., New York: Routledge, pp. 276–320.

Miles, R. (1988), *Who Cooked the Last Supper*, New York: Random House.

Ortman, Jennifer, Velkoff, V., and Hogan, H. (2014), "An Aging Nation: The Older Population in the U.S.," *Current Population Reports*, Washington, DC: U.S. Department of Commerce, (May), p. 6, https://www.census.gov/prod/2014pubs/p25-1140.pdf.

Peñaloza, Lisa, Barnhart, M., and Kelleher, C. (2020), "Opportunities and challenges for aging women in cocreating value in the elderly consumption ensemble," *in* North American Advances in Consumer Research, *Volume 48, Jennifer Argo, Tina M. Lowrey, and Hope Jensen Schau eds., Duluth, MN : Association for Consumer Research, p. 1107.*

Pettigrew, S. (2007), "Reducing the experience of loneliness among older consumers," *Journal of Research for Consumers*, 12, 1–14.

Poster, M. (1978), *Critical Theory of the Family*, New York: Seabury Press, Continuum.

Price, L., Arnould, E., and Curasi, C. (2000), "Older consumers' disposition of special possessions," *Journal of Consumer Research*, 27:2, 179–201.

Prothero, A. and McDonagh, P. (2021), "'It's hard to be what you can't see' – Gender representation in marketing's academic journals," *Journal of Marketing Management*, 37:3, 1–12.

Quintanilla, C., Pérez, M.E., Castaño, R., and Peñaloza, L. (2019), "Inverse socialization with technology: Understanding intergenerational family dynamics," *Journal of Consumer Marketing*, 36:6 (Sept.), 818–826.

Risius, D., Thelwell, R., Wagstaff, C.R., and Scurr, J. (2014). "The influence of ageing on bra preferences and self-perception of breasts among mature women," *European Journal of Ageing*, 11:3, 233–240.

Roberts, A., Ogunwole, S., Blakeslee, L., and Rable, M. (2018), *The Population 65 Years and Older in the United States: 2016: American Community Survey Reports*, Washington, DC: United States Census Bureau, U.S. Department of Commerce, Economics and Statistics Administration.

Roedder-John, D. and Cole, C. (1986), "Age differences in information processing: Understanding deficits in young and elderly consumers," *Journal of Consumer Research*, 13:3 (Dec.), 297–315.

Rudmin, F.W. and Richins, M.L. eds. (1992), *Meaning. Measure and Morality of Materialism*, Provo, UT: Association for Consumer Research.
Saren, M., Maclaran, P., Goulding, C., Elliott, R., Shankar, A., and Catterall, M. eds. (2007), *Critical Marketing: Defining the Field*, Oxford: Elsevier.
Scaraboto, D. and Fischer, E. (2012), "Frustrated fatshionistas: An institutional theory perspective on consumer quests for greater choice in mainstream markets," *Journal of Consumer Research*, 39:6, 1234–1257.
Schau, H.J., Gilly, M.C., and Wolfinbarger, M. (2009), "Consumer identity renaissance: The resurgence of identity-inspired consumption in retirement," *Journal of Consumer Research*, 36:2, 255–276.
Scott, L.M. (2005), *Fresh Lipstick: Redressing Fashion and Feminism*, New York: Palgrave Macmillan.
Stevens, L., Maclaran, P., and Kravets, O. (2020), "Reclaiming the crone: Reimagining old age and feminine power," *in* North American Advances in Consumer Research, *Volume 48, eds. Jennifer Argo, Tina M. Lowrey, and Hope Jensen Schau, Duluth, MN : Association for Consumer Research, pp. 1106–1107*, https://www.acrwebsite.org/volumes/2661468/volumes/v48/NA-48.
Stone, M. (1976), *When God was a Woman*, New York: Harcourt Brace Jovanovich.
Twigg, J. (2004). "The body, gender and age: Feminist insights in social gerontology," *Journal of Aging Studies*, 18, 59–73.
——— and Majim, S. (2014), "Consumption and the constitution of age: Expenditure patterns on clothing, hair and cosmetics among post-war 'baby boomers'," *Journal of Aging Studies*, 30, 23–32.
U.S. Census Bureau (1993a), *We are the Americans: Blacks*, U.S. Department of Commerce, Washington, DC: U.S. Printing Office.
——— (1993b), *We are the Americans: Elderly*, U.S. Department of Commerce, Washington, DC: U.S. Printing Office.
——— (1993c), *We are the Americans: Hispanics*, U.S. Department of Commerce, Washington, DC: U.S. Printing Office.
Venkatesh, Alladi (1980), "Changing Roles of Women – A Life-Style Analysis," September, 7:2, pp. 189–197. DOI: 10.1086/208806.
Washington Post (2015), "NPR hose a key force in the right to die movement," *San Antonio Express-News*, February 22, p. K20.
Wilkes, R.E. (1992), "A structural modeling approach to the measurement and meaning of cognitive age," *Journal of Consumer Research*, 19 (September), 292–301.
Wolfe, T. (1984), "Viddies in the Scepter'd Isle," *The Telegraph Sunday Magazine*, 399: June 17, pp. 16–22.
Yoon, H. and Powell, H. (2012), "Older consumers and celebrity advertising," *Aging & Society*, 32:1319–1336.

Select Websites

Alzheimer's Association, https://alz-journals.onlinelibrary.wiley.com/doi/full/10.1002/alz.12068
AARP American Association for Retired Persons, https://www.aarp.org/
Denmark's House of Memories, https://www.npr.org/sections/parallels/2016/09/13/493744351/denmarks-house-of-memories-recreates-1950s-for-alzheimers-patients?t=1602503561241
iPods for the Elderly, https://www.westhawaiitoday.com/2019/12/02/hawaii-news/ipods-for-the-elderly-program-helping-pull-memories-in-alzheimers-patients/ https://www.youtube.com/watch?v=fyZQf0p73QM
Taos Institite, https://www.taosinstitute.net/
The pleasure is ours, https://www.youtube.com/watch?v=Pj3L39LLRMg
The right to die movement, https://www.pbs.org/wgbh/frontline/article/the-evolution-of-americas-right-to-die-movement/

Section 5

Gendering digital technologies in marketing

22 Black women's digital media and marketplace experiences

Between buying, branding, and Black Lives Matter

Francesca Sobande

Introduction

The digital media experiences of Black women are relatively rarely the focus of critical scholarship at the nexus of feminism and consumer culture, despite the advertising industry's expanding recognition of Black women's impactful marketplace activities. Nielsen's (2017) report on "African-American Women: Our Science, Her Magic" is a key example of how Black women's online encounters have been monitored and analysed as part of data and consumer behaviour insights. The report includes discussion of hashtags and Twitter discourse generated by Black women and claims that Black women have a "unique place of power at the intersection of culture, commerce and consciousness" (Nielsen, 2017, p. 2). This report by Nielsen (2017, p. 2) is referred to as being their "seventh look at African-American consumers and the second time we've focused our attention on Black women. Now more than ever, African-American women's consumer preferences and brand affinities are resonating across the U.S. mainstream, driving total Black spending power toward a record $1.5 trillion by 2021". Similar industry discourse about Black women's media and marketplace experiences in Britain is somewhat scarce in comparison to the amount of attention that has been directed at such matters in the US. However, in recent years, the digital experiences of Black women in Britain have been a source of much interest among media and marketing professionals who are in search of creative content, viral threads, and the influence of individual "digital-trendsetters" (Sobande, 2020a).

There is a need for more scholarly considerations and critiques of how brands and the advertising industry are engaging with the digital experiences and work of Black women in Britain, and how Black women in Britain are experiencing different digital technologies and spaces. Furthermore, more research related to the digital experiences of Black women in Britain and "how the Internet has amplified and reworked existing social relations" (Cottom, 2020, p. 442) can enhance understandings of the entanglements of feminism and blackness in media and the marketplace—including the pervasiveness of racial capitalism which contours contemporary consumer culture and how Black women navigate digital domains. Such research can also contribute to social marketing scholarship and continue fruitful conversations that have been led by scholars such as Grier and Poole (2020, p. 378) who posed the question, "Will Social Marketing Fight for Black Lives? An Open Letter to the Field".

Thus, drawing on Black feminist work and critical studies of the interdependent racist and sexist dynamics of media and the marketplace, this chapter focusses on Black women's digital experiences and forms of corporate commodification and co-optation

DOI: 10.4324/9781003042587-27

that can be involved in them. Such writing builds upon my prior work on the digital lives of Black women in Britain and digital (re)presentations of Black people (Sobande, 2017, 2020a, 2021a, 2021b, Sobande et al., 2019). In conversation with extant Black feminist work and research regarding Black women's marketplace and digital experiences (Bobo, 1995, 2002; Bruce, 2019; Ndichu and Upadhyaya, 2019), and the specifics of the lives of Black women in Britain (Bryan et al., 2018, Dadzie and Lewis, 2020), this chapter highlights that scholarship on marketing and feminism must account for intersecting oppressions and the particularities of Black women's lives which cannot be meaningfully understood through a lens that treats race and gender as separable social constructs.

This chapter is aligned with the principles of Black feminist citational practice which involves recognition of the many different forms that knowledge production takes, including beyond the content of traditional academic journal articles and texts. Therefore, the discussion in this piece connects to a wide range of conventional academic sources but also includes citations that stem from insightful blogs, journalistic and industry pieces, podcasts, and online videos discussions. In agreement with Gilmore's (2019, p. xvii) view that "[i]n this world of social media, we are often tempted by a clever meme, even a deep one but even the best are inadequate to the many struggles we must engage", I recognise the limitations of theorising and analysis that solely springs from the study of such digital content and without due engagement with other texts. Then again, part of what is discussed in my chapter is how the knowledge production of Black women in digital spaces (Bailey, 2021) is often dismissed, including due to its perceived brevity and ephemerality. So, I tread carefully when considering the drawbacks of social media texts such as memes which can be a vivid vessel of significant socio-political analysis and generative theorising and critique (Mina, 2019; Sobande, 2019).

While this chapter is influenced by over five years of empirical research on the digital and media experiences of Black women in Britain, in this work I am especially concerned with theorising that can help to further articulate the mechanics of the digital media and marketplace spheres that affect Black women's lives. For this reason, empirical examples are discussed but this writing predominantly delves into the conceptualising that surrounds them. The next section outlines the Black feminist and critical media and marketplace theoretical framework at the core of this chapter. Then there is discussion of key developments in terms of how Black women's digital media and marketplace experiences in Britain have attracted industry and brand interest, as well as reflection on crucial challenges faced by Black women online. Such analysis accounts for how the COVID-19 (coronavirus) pandemic and galvanising visibility of Black Lives Matter (BLM) organising in Britain in 2020 have impacted the varying degrees of online visibility that Black women navigate (Sobande, 2021a). Finally, this chapter concludes with comments concerning the importance of Black feminist work with respect to critical research on media and the marketplace and crystallises some of the ways that Black feminist approaches contribute to nuanced understandings of media and marketplace activities.

Black feminist and critical studies of media and the marketplace

There is a rich history of feminist approaches to the study of media and the marketplace (Catterall et al., 2000) but there is still much work to be done to address knowledge gaps in this area due to the tendency for Black women's experiences to be overlooked amid aspects of scholarship on feminism and marketing. Moreover, the normativity of whiteness within the practice and discipline of marketing (Burton, 2009; Davis, 2018; Mitchell, 2020) means that work that emphatically centres the perspectives and research of Black women is seldom homed in academic journals and spaces that are regarded as the locus of canonical material. Still, since the turn of the 21st century there has been an increase in scholarly work on feminism and marketing which tarries with how gender *and* race are interrelated social constructs that mould how different demographics move through and are moved by marketplace terrains. In an attempt to yield insights related to how racial capitalism impacts the digital experiences of Black women in Britain, this chapter is bolstered by work that contributes to "the long battle to end colonialism, imperialism, racism, and inequality" (Gilmore, 2019, p. xi) and which explicitly examines how gendered issues are raced and how raced issues are gendered.

Understanding the matrix of oppression and intersectionality

As Catterall et al. (2000, p. 5) maintain in the foundational edited collection, *Marketing and Feminism: Current Issues and Research*, "Gender is not a sole defining category or experience, since no woman is only a woman. Race, class and sexuality can intersect with gender in ways that problematise talk of oppression on the basis of gender alone". Baked into the base of Black feminist thought is an understanding of "the matrix of domination characterized by intersecting oppression" (Hill Collins, 2000, p. 26) and which undeniably impacts the lives of Black women in ways that are particular to them. To be precise, the intersections of antiblackness, sexism, and misogyny—known as misogynoir (Bailey, 2010, 2021; Bailey and Trudy, 2018)—affect Black women's media and marketplace encounters in ways that cannot be comprehended by a feminist perspective that centres a concern with gender at the expense of an equal focus on race, blackness, and what hooks (2000, p. xiv) terms "imperialist, white supremacist, capitalist patriarchy". Allied with the Black feminist roots of much writing and work on the matrix of oppression and intersectionality (Crenshaw, 1989, 1991; Hill Collins, 2000), my chapter foregrounds the experiences of Black women.

As such, this chapter emerges from a Black feminist position that is typically side-lined, if not, erased, within much marketing scholarship, even critical marketing approaches. Although this chapter focusses on the digital media and marketplace experiences of Black women, in doing so it reiterates calls for more work on how racialised subjectivities are experienced online (Lindridge et al., 2015), and echoes requests for more work that evocatively deals with "the neoliberal co-optation of social marketing" (Tadajewski et al., 2014, p. 1735), as well as how both racial capitalism and antiblackness are implicated in the practice and discipline of marketing. Academics, researchers, activists, and other individuals interested in work at the intersection of marketing and feminism must contend with "an economy of visibility" (Banet-Weiser, 2018, p. 2), which fuels the commodification of identities, including the spectacularisation and marketisation of Black women and other individuals from structurally marginalised groups. Different dimensions of digital visibility are an inherent part of how Black women may forge a sense of connection, collectivity, and community with other Black women online, but may also find themselves on the receiving end of vitriolic abuse and under the disciplining institutionally white gaze of commercial organisations seeking out people and content to profit from.

Reckoning with racial capitalism and the commodification of feminism

Deeply embedded racial capitalism is one of the central components of consumer culture that must be understood as part of feminist efforts that take seriously the intersecting nature of oppression and its maintenance in marketplace contexts. When speaking in an Antipode Foundation film about geographies of racial capitalism, Gilmore (2020) states that "the relationship between slavery and race, race and unfreedom, and freedom and labour is one that we constantly try to untangle and at our peril we ignore it but also at our peril we make it too simplistic…". When offering examples of how racial capitalism manifests today, Gilmore refers to forms of it such as austerity and neoliberalism which are reflective of how "capitalism requires inequality and racism enshrines it". This chapter is approached from a sociological point of view that is sensitive to how centuries of racial capitalism have culminated in the anti-Black and racist underpinnings of contemporary consumer culture.

Cottom (2020, p. 442) observes that "sociological practice does not systematically engage with the social relations of Internet technologies as analytical equals to the object of study". Inspired by the words of Cottom (2020), as well as those of Kravets et al. (2018, p. 2) who acknowledge that "most theories [of consumer culture] emanating from sociological or anthropological sources fail to take account of the market and marketing system itself", my analysis in this chapter includes a consideration of the market logic that buttresses elements of Black women's digital experiences and is directly related to racial capitalism and the workings of the Internet. Motivated by vital critical race and digital studies scholarship (Cottom, 2020; Hamilton, 2020), this chapter dances between the disciplinary boundaries of marketing, digital sociology, media, race and ethnicity, and gender and feminism studies. Hence, this chapter may be perceived as being part of a broader body of interdisciplinary and transdisciplinary work that deals with issues to do with inequalities, ideologies, and the marketplace.

In the poignant words of Bruce (2019, n.p.n.), "[i]n thinking about Digital Blackness I contemplate the ways and conditions that hard technologies (computers, video games, smart phones) meet with soft technologies (race, gender)". Bruce's (2019) framing of race and gender as technologies is fundamental to understanding the structural and processual ways that both function and how their application in society influences perceptions of knowledge, such as what is knowledge, who possesses knowledge, and how that knowledge has been yielded. In addition to Bruce's (2019) reflections on digital blackness, Cottom's (2020, p. 1) extensive work on Black digital experiences and "where platform capitalism and racial capitalism meet" is essential to efforts to effectively grapple with how race and racism is embroiled in digital media and marketplace encounters. As Cottom (2020, p. 441) puts it, "Internet technologies are now a totalizing sociopolitical regime and should be central to the study of race and racism". Cottom's (2020, p. 441) innovative work on racial capitalism and digital society articulates the following:

> …that there are two turns in the political economy of race, ethnicity, and racism: networked capital that shapes a global racial hierarchy that varies across spatial geographies and the privatization of public and economic life. Internet technologies produced the first turn, and they accelerate the second turn.

My work is shaped by Cottom's (2020) analysis of how racial capitalism is a framework that can aid studies of race, racism, and digital experiences. Hence, the sections that follow involve scrutiny of how racial capitalism and the rise of neoliberal feminist notions of self-empowerment through consumption are entangled with how Black women in Britain experience digital spaces. In other words, my chapter is based on the premise that critical studies of feminism and marketing can be advanced by unpacking how racial capitalism and the commodification of feminism is enmeshed with how consumer culture is constructed and experienced, including in digitally mediated settings. It is by considering how racial capitalism and commodified notions of feminism contribute to marketplace activity that burgeoning brand interest in Black women's digital experiences can be grasped.

Buying, branding, and BLM: industry interest in Black digital experiences

The digital experiences of Black women in Britain can involve forms of social bonding and collective and community-building (Sobande, 2020a), which is akin to the Black digital diasporic dynamics that scholars such as Everett (2009) researched and wrote about over ten years ago. Also, the digital experiences of Black women in Britain can be closely linked with matters pertaining to buying, branding, and how media and marketing institutions in Britain have attempted to respond to the Black Lives Matter (BLM) social justice movement in the context of 2020.

Black Pound Day and Black Influencers

Black Pound Day launched in June 2020, shortly after a notable increase in national media coverage of BLM and Black activist organising in Britain in response to anti-Black police brutality in the US and the UK. Referred to on the Black Pound Day (2020) website as "a solution-based approach set up to support the growth of the UK Black economy", Black Pound Day (#BlackPoundDay) involves a day each month being dedicated to encouraging people to spend money on the products and services of Black-owned businesses in Britain. It may therefore be unsurprising that both the spending power and digital influence of Black people has attracted the attention of brands, advertising agencies, and consumer behaviour analysts in Britain in the first quarter of the 21st century.

In the weeks that followed mounting media, public, and political discourse on BLM in Britain in Spring and Summer of 2020, various "brands pledged to 'hire more Black people' and claimed they would 'amplify Black voices', and 'diversify' their industries. Many commercial organisations' carefully crafted PR statements still circulate and may signal the ongoing attempt to frame brands and the ad industry as 'woke'" (Sobande, 2020b). Nevertheless, prior to the increase in British media and marketing industry discussions to do with Black lives in the first half of 2020 there was also ample indication of how marketing practitioners and commercial organisations were taking note of what Black people do, create, and say online. In 2019 Twitter organised a Black Twitter UK event at their London HQ which is one of myriad examples of how, in recent years, businesses have attempted to formally recognise the digital work and words of Black people in Britain, and arguably, position themselves in proximity to Black people's cultural capital.

Since first embarking on my research related to Black women's digital experiences in 2015, I have witnessed a sometimes start and stop swell in media and marketing industry interest in Black women's lives and digital encounters. In the first half of 2020, in a similar way to many other Black people, I experienced a surge in the number of industry requests for my comments and thoughts on the digital experiences of Black people and how brands were attempting to align themselves with Black social justice movements in often superficial ways. I remain cynical of the extent to which such industry interest is ever motivated by anything but the potential to pursue profit and manage reputational risk, yet, I am intrigued, but not convinced, by the possibility of Black women's digital work and labour in Britain being treated with more care, respect, and recognition of its value by different institutions.

The year 2020 has involved UK advertising trade bodies and leaders from ad agencies pledge their alleged "solidarity with the Black community" when signing an open letter which stated an intention to "maintain inclusive cultures that are sensitive to the enduring injustice and pain of racism" (Stewart, 2020). In turn, media and marketing institutions in Britain continually seek out ways to suggest that they are not anti-Black, and, furthermore, they are not anti-Black *or* sexist. One of the ways that such brands may endeavour to signal their regard for Black lives, and, specifically, Black women, is by platforming the digital content and creativity of Black women, but often without critically considering the limitations of such visibility with respect to tackling racial capitalism and the societal antiblackness that movements such as BLM exist in response to.

Visibility ≠ combating antiblackness and intersecting oppressions

There is yet to be a British equivalent to Nielsen's (2017) "African-American Women: Our Science, Her Magic" report. However, more and more brands in Britain are attempting to incorporate or call on the images, ideas, and digital innovations of Black women—perhaps partly due to how social media has spurred on the visibility of their digital experiences, and in response to research such as Nielsen's (2017) which originates in the US where marketing practitioners have more explicitly and aggressively attempted to track and target Black consumer markets for decades. As is emphasised in the leading work of both Benjamin (2019) and Warner (2017), media visibility and economic recognition should not be mistaken for the redistribution of resources, power, and the dismantlement of structural oppression such as intersecting antiblackness, sexism, and classism. Such points are clear when reflecting on pay disparities between Black and non-Black influencers in Britain (Katsha, 2020; Tait, 2020), which are symptomatic of the fact that the visibility and (self)branding opportunities that Black influencers experience does little, if anything, to address the structural inequalities that result in them being underpaid and more precariously positioned in the influencer economy and labour market in comparison with their non-Black peers. The intersections of the race and gender pay gap mean that Black women often face the sharpest end of pay disparities within the influencer and digital content creator economy.

The Drum's (2020) article "After a decisive year, how are brands celebrating Black History Month UK?" lists many examples that illustrate how Black people's social media and digital experiences are a source of interest to brands. Instagram's "#ShareBlackStories" work for Black History Month UK involved them partnering with iconic and influential Black people in Britain to catalyse conversations on the platform. Bumble's "#MyLoveIsBlackLove" approach platformed leading Black artists, actors, athletes, entrepreneurs, and activists in Britain who drove online discourse on Black love. Additionally, TikTok's "#MyRoots" in-app and out-of-home brand campaign focussed on telling the stories of TikTok creators and artists who were celebrating "their Afro-Caribbean heritage". These are just three of countless cases which exemplify branding and advertising industry interest in Black content creation and the digital experiences of Black women in Britain. But what does all of this mean for Black women in Britain, beyond the reality that they may experience heightened levels of visibility when brands are mobilised to highlight Black content creators during Black History Month and in response to the increasing momentum of BLM?

More than just the male gaze

Feminist studies of marketing have demonstrated how women are frequently objectified in the content of advertising campaigns that portray them in sexist and misogynistic ways (Catterall et al., 2000; Matich et al., 2019; Schroeder and Borgerson, 1998). Further still, work such as that of Davis (2017) on *Pioneering African-American Women in the Advertising Business: Biographies of MAD Black WOMEN* elucidates the specific ways that Black women have encountered structural barriers during their work and labour experiences in the areas of marketing and advertising. Relatedly, the present-day digital experiences of Black women in Britain are affected by the particular ways that their images may be spectacularised and weaponised by brands as part of these organisations' opportunistic efforts to tap into on-trend discourse on race, gender, blackness, and feminism (Sobande, 2020a, 2020b). A wealth of feminist studies of marketing address how representations of women often take shape in relation to the cis-male heteronormative gaze. In spite of this, there has been less detailed discussion of how images of women in marketing are often formed via the distinctly institutionally white gaze of brands, regardless of the gendered nature of such a gaze, and which can result in depictions of Black women being (mis)used as part of ultimately oppressive narratives that maintain the very normativity of whiteness that Burton (2009) critiqued over a decade ago.

When interviewing 26 Black women in Britain (aged 19–47 years-old) about their media and digital experiences, one of the key themes that arose was how the digital, creative, and cultural industry experiences of Black women may be typified by extractive and unequal dynamics between them and institutions that attempt to co-opt and commodify their work to propel surface-level equality, diversity, and inclusion (EDI) goals, such as increasing the number of Black people who feature on a brand's social media accounts (Sobande, 2020a). Table 22.1 outlines some of the concerns expressed by Black women who I interviewed whose digital images, content, and experiences have received attention from commercial organisations, particularly organisations located in the creative and cultural industries. The second column details how such concerns link to issues of racial capitalism and feminism.

Some brands may mistakenly view increasing the digital visibility of Black women who they employ (if they employ any) or who engage with their products and services as a meaningful anti-racist, or, even, Black feminist action. However, changes to the content of brands' social media posts and marketing material means nothing without substantial internal changes that drastically improve the work and labour opportunities and experiences of Black women, as well as the lives of Black women in general.

Table 22.1 Black Women's Concerns about Corporate Co-Optation and Their Digital Content

Concern Expressed	Connection to Racial Capitalism and Feminism
Black women's digital content will be decontextualised and reframed by institutionally white organisations attempting to improve their EDI image	Due to racial capitalism and the intense commodification and mainstreaming of facets of feminism in the 21st century, brands can profit from performing a proximity to Black women, and by extension, Black feminism which such women may be assumed to embody
Black women's creative digital content, commentaries, critiques, and knowledge-production will be stolen by organisations that do not credit or compensate such women	Due to racial capitalism being predicated on the exploitation of Black people's labour and lives, which is also shaped by the intersections of antiblackness, sexism, and misogyny, the exploitation of Black women's labour and lives is societally normalised in ways that enable organisations to mistreat Black women without facing significant consequences for their actions

Conclusion

The digital media and marketplace experiences of Black women in Britain are influenced by matters concerning buying, branding, and the recent focus on Black Lives Matter (BLM)—all of which is always affected by issues to do with both race and gender, and the relationship between these social constructs and how they are operationalised in marketplace environments. The potential trappings of the male gaze may be a source of anguish for feminist scholars who scrutinise how marketing reinforces objectifying and heteronormative gendered power relations and oppression, but such a concern should not eclipse a much-needed attentiveness to how depictions of Black women in digital media and marketing can be subject to an innately raced and gendered gaze that props up and is part of "imperialist, white supremacist, capitalist patriarchy" (hooks, 2000, p. xiv). Since the emergence of the COVID-19 (coronavirus) pandemic in 2020, digital media has been playing an even bigger part in the daily lives of many people, and as is suggested by research by Glitch (2020) which is a not-for-profit organisation working towards ending online abuse, such digital experiences during this time of crisis may involve an intensification of misogynoir and relentless online harassment and harm.

Since increased media interest in BLM organising and Black activism in Britain in Spring and Summer of 2020, many media and marketing industry institutions have continued to seek out, share, and engage with the digital content of Black women. It is through a Black feminist perspective of such marketing activity that we can critically reckon with the fact that brands' interest in Black women's digital content and online experiences is motivated by predominantly self-serving intentions such as rebranding attempts and shallow EDI goals which are a by-product of racial capitalism rather than a way in which racial capitalism can be challenged. The future of feminist studies of marketing should involve more work that analyses how the digital media and marketplace experiences of women are impacted by intersecting oppressions which are tethered to deeply entrenched racial capitalism, sexism, misogyny, and an economy of visibility which enables brands to capitalise on the creative content and work of marginalised individuals.

References

Bailey, M. (2010) "They aren't talking about me...", *Crunk Feminist Collective*, 14 March. Available at: http://www.crunkfeministcollective.com/2010/03/14/they-arent-talking-about-me/

Bailey, M. and Trudy (2018) "On misogynoir: citation, erasure, and plagiarism", *Feminist Media Studies* 18(4): 762–768.

Bailey, M. (2021) *Misogynoir Transformed: Black Women's Digital Resistance*. New York: New York University Press.

Banet-Weiser, S. (2018) *Empowered: Popular Feminism and Popular Misogyny*. Durham, NC: Duke University.

Benjamin, R. (2019) *Race after Technology: Abolitionist Tools for the New Jim Code*. Cambridge, MA: Polity Press.

Bobo, J. (1995) *Black Women as Cultural Readers*. New York: Columbia University Press.

Bobo, J. (ed.) (2002) *Black Feminist Cultural Criticism*. Malden, MA: Blackwell Publishers.

Bruce, K. (2019) "Reflections: #DigitalWhileBlack", *In Search of Blackness: Digital Blackness, Ephemerality & Social Media*, 24 February. Available at: https://digitalblacknessphd.wixsite.com/dbphd

Burton, D. (2009) "'Reading' whiteness in consumer research", *Consumption, Markets & Culture* 12(2): 171–201.

Bryan, B., Dadzie, S and Scafe, S. (2018) *The Heart of the Race: Black Women's Lives in Britain*. London: Verso.

Catterall, M., Maclaran, P. and Stevens, L. (eds.) (2000) *Marketing and Feminism: Current issues and research*. New York: Routledge.

Cottom, T. M. (2020) "Where platform capitalism and racial capitalism meet: The sociology of race and racism in the digital society", *Sociology of Race and Ethnicity*, October 2020. doi: 10.1177/2332649220949473

Crenshaw, K. (1989) "Demarginalizing the intersection of race and sex: A Black feminist critique of antidiscrimination doctrine, feminist theory and antiracist politics", " University of Chicago Legal Forum 1 (8): 139–167.

Crenshaw, K. (1991) "Mapping the margins: Intersectionality, identity politics, and violence against women of color", Stanford Law Review 43 (6): 1241–1299.

Dadzie, S. and Lewis, C. (2020) "E108 the surviving society alternative to woman's hour: Stella Dadzie" [podcast recording] *Surviving Society*. Available at: https://soundcloud.com/user-622675754/e108-the-surviving-society-alternative-to-womans-hour-stella-dadzie

Davis, J. F. (2017) *Pioneering African-American Women in the Advertising Business: Biographies of MAD Black WOMEN*. London: Routledge.

Davis, J. F. (2018) "Selling whiteness? – A critical review of the literature on marketing and racism", *Journal of Marketing Management* 34 (1–2): 134–177.

Everett, A. (2009) *Digital Diaspora: A Race for Cyberspace*. Albany: SUNY Press.

Gilmore, R. W. interviewed by Antipode Foundation (2020). *Geographies of Racial Capitalism with Ruth Wilson Gilmore – An Antipode Foundation Film*.

Gilmore, R. W. (2019) cited in Quan, H. L. T. (ed.) (2019) *Cedric J. Robinson: On Racial Capitalism, Black Internationalism, and Cultures of Resistance*. London: Pluto Press.

Glitch (2020) "The ripple effect: Covid-19 and the epidemic of online abuse", *Glitch*. Available at: https://fixtheglitch.org/covid19/

Grier, S. A. and Poole, S. M. (2020) "Will social marketing fight for black lives? An open letter to the field", *Social Marketing Quarterly* 26(4): 378–387.

Hamilton, A. (2020) "A genealogy of critical race and digital studies: past, present, and future", *Sociology of Race and Ethnicity* 6(3): 292–301.

Hill Collins, P. (2000) *Black Feminist Thought: Knowledge, Consciousness, and the Politics of Empowerment*. New York and Routledge: London.

hooks, b. (2000) *Feminist Theory: From Margin to Center*. London: Pluto Press.

Katsha, H. (2020) "Black influencers shortchanged by big brands are starting to talk", *Huffington Post*, 26 June. Available at: https://www.huffingtonpost.co.uk/entry/black-influencer-pay-gap_uk_5ef32959c5b6aa825ac96254

Kravets, O., Maclaran, P., Miles, S., and Venkatesh, A. (eds.) (2018) *The Sage Handbook of Consumer Culture*. London: Sage.

Lindridge, A., Henderson, G. R. and Ekpo, A. E. (2015) "(Virtual) ethnicity, the Internet, and well-being", *Marketing Theory* 15(2): 279–285.

Matich, M., Ashman, R. and Parsons, E. (2019) "#freethenipple – digital activism and embodiment in the contemporary feminist movement", *Consumption, Markets & Culture* 22(4): 337–362.

Mina, A. X. (2019) *Memes to Movements: How the World's Most Viral Media Is Changing Social Protest and Power*. Boston, MA: Beacon Press.

Mitchell, T. (2020) "Critical race theory (CRT) and colourism: a manifestation of whitewashing in marketing communications?", *Journal of Marketing Management* 36(13–14): 1366–1389.

Ndichu, E. G. and Upadhyaya, S. (2019) ""Going natural": black women's identity project shifts in hair care practices", *Consumption, Markets & Culture* 22(1): 44–67.

Nielsen (2017) "African-American Women: Our Science, Her Magic", *Nielsen*, 21 September. Available at: https://www.nielsen.com/us/en/insights/report/2017/african-american-women-our-science-her-magic/

Schroeder, J. and Borgerson, J. (1998) "Marketing images of gender: a visual analysis", *Consumption, Markets & Culture* 2(2): 161–201.

Sobande, F. (2017) "Watching me watching you: black women in Britain on YouTube", *European Journal of Cultural Studies* 20(6): 655–671.

Sobande, F. (2019) "Memes, digital remix culture and (re)mediating British politics and public life", *IPPR Progressive* 26(2): 151–160.

Sobande, F, Fearfull, A. and Brownlie, D. (2019) "Resisting media marginalisation: black women's digital content and collectivity", *Consumption Markets & Culture*. https://doi.org/10.1080/10253866.2019.1571491.

Sobande, F. (2020a) *The Digital Lives of Black Women in Britain*. Cham: Palgrave Macmillan.

Sobande, F. (2020b) "The revolution will not be branded", *Disegno*. Available at: https://disegnojournal.com/newsfeed/the-revolution-will-not-be-branded.

Sobande, F. (2021a) "The politics of digital peace, play, and privacy during the COVID-19 pandemic: Between digital engagement, enclaves, and entitlement", *Sociological Review*. Available at: https://www.thesociologicalreview.com/the-politics-of-digital-peace-play-and-privacy-during-the-covid-19-pandemic-between-digital-engagement-enclaves-and-entitlement/

Sobande, F. (2021b) "Spectacularized and branded digital (re)presentations of black people and Blackness", *Television & New Media* 22(2): 131–146.

Stewart, R. (2020) "UK ad bosses pledge to support black talent in open letter amid George Floyd outrage", *The Drum*, 3 June. Available at: https://www.thedrum.com/news/2020/06/03/uk-ad-bosses-pledge-support-black-talent-open-letter-amid-george-floyd-outrage

Tadajewski, M., Chelekis, J., DeBerry-Spence, B., Figueiredo, B., Kravets, O., Nuttavuthisit, K., Peñaloza, L. and Moisander, J. (2014) "The discourses of marketing and development: towards 'critical transformative marketing research'", *Journal of Marketing Management* 30: 17–18.

Tait, A. (2020) "'Influencers are being taken advantage of: the social media stars turning to unions", *The Guardian*, 10 October. Available at: https://www.theguardian.com/media/2020/oct/10/influencers-are-being-taken-advantage-of-the-social-media-stars-turning-to-unions

The Drum (2020) "After a decisive year, how are brands celebrating Black History Month UK?", *The Drum*, 5 October. Available at: https://www.thedrum.com/news/2020/10/05/after-decisive-year-how-are-brands-celebrating-black-history-month-uk

Warner, K. (2017) "Plastic representation", *Film Quarterly Winter* 71(2). Available at: https://filmquarterly.org/2017/12/04/in-the-time-of-plastic-representation/

23 The symbolic violence of digital (anti-)feminist activism

Aliette Lambert and Ana-Isabel Nölke

The overarching question at the heart of this chapter is what drives people to act seemingly against their own interests. This question is all the more relevant in a political climate where elected political candidates unashamedly promote policies violating their electorate's economic and social interests. The UK's 'Brexit' vote, for instance, was supported by those potentially most affected by ensuing economic destabilisation, while some American minority groups and women campaigned for Donald Trump, a president who endorsed racist policies (e.g., the 'Muslim ban') and openly expressed misogynistic attitudes. A more relevant question for the development of critical, feminist marketing theory, and indeed the focus of this chapter, is why many women[1] do not identify with feminism.[2] The context for examining this question is the proliferation of social media activism that has facilitated a fourth wave of feminism (Munro 2013; Maclaran 2015) along with reactionary anti-feminist sentiment.

In a virtual space, feminist activism has flourished with 'viral' hashtags campaigns like #MeToo and #TimesUp on social network sites (SNSs) generating increased visibility of women's issues (Rottenberg 2019) and exposing the pervasiveness of sexual harassment and abuse, with material consequences for some perpetrators. However, there remains concern about whether these consequences have 'trickled down' to initiate significant change on the ground (ibid). Likewise, neo-conservative values have flourished. This is encapsulated by vitriolic 'trolling' of feminist posts (Lumsden and Morgan 2018) and by platforms such as Reddit, a hotbed for anti-feminist discourse, in extremes demarcated by 'incel' (involuntarily celibate) men who berate women for depriving them of romantic and sexual relationships (Scaptura and Boyle 2020). In other cases, women turn to social media to voice their rejection of feminism, using hashtags such as '#tradwife' that indicate a choice to embrace traditional roles à la 1950s housewife consumer subject position.

The backlash against feminism by women themselves is obdurate and enduring (Faludi 1992), and is categorised theoretically as 'postfeminism', or the assertion that feminism is anachronistic as the battle for women's rights has already been won (Catterall et al. 2005; Gill et al. 2016; Rome and Lambert 2020). Postfeminist discourse is steeped in a neoliberal ideology that emphasises individual responsibility and personal competence in resolving structural inequalities (Gill 2008). It obfuscates or ignores obvious universal markers that indicate structural gendered oppression, such as women's representation in politics, on corporate boards, or in professorial positions, as well as an enduring gender wage gap (Blau and Khan 2017). Within the context of a fourth wave of feminist activism (Munro 2013; Maclaran 2015; Mendes et al. 2018), a more specific and relevant

DOI: 10.4324/9781003042587-28

question here is whether and how digital feminist activism reproduces or contributes to a backlash that encapsulates a postfeminist ideology.

Addressing this question, in this chapter we take a historical perspective to examine a feminist campaign at the genesis of digital feminist political action: *Who Needs Feminism?* (WNF?). WNF? was launched as a Tumblr page in the spring of 2012 (active until 2015) by Duke University students to spark conversation around the 'disturbingly apathetic sentiment toward feminism' (Petronzino 2012). In July 2013 a reactionary page materialised that we also analyse here: *Women Against Feminism* (WAF). The Tumblr site asked women to share their 'voices against modern feminism and its toxic culture' – 'judging feminism by its actions, not by dictionary definitions' (Tumblr 2015). We perform a critical discourse analysis of posts on both sites, informed by a feminist reading of Pierre Bourdieu's theory of symbolic power, to show how brief personal accounts encompassing the preponderance of posts on both sites are predicated on postfeminist ideals of individual choice and agency. This focus, we argue, not only weakens feminist critique but gives rise to a reactionary sentiment from women wanting to assert their agency and embrace a traditional feminine subjectivity.

In what follows, we first discuss the intersection of fourth-wave feminism and postfeminist sentiment. Next, we describe our methodological approach and how Bourdieu's theory of symbolic power informed our analysis. Third, we illustrate our findings by addressing three topics central to discourse on both sites: agency, embodiment, and tradition. We conclude by reflecting on what our findings mean for feminist theorising and critique in marketing, as well as discussing avenues for future research.

Feminism's 'fourth wave': digital activism in a postfeminist climate

In an increasingly neoliberal, postfeminist climate (Gill et al. 2016), a fourth wave of feminism has emerged (Munro 2013; Maclaran 2015), broadly characterised by online activism from an array of intersectional voices re-asserting the need for feminism (Dean 2010). Nearly a decade on, feminist movements such as Everyday Sexism and #TimesUp intending to illustrate the extent of women's oppression have exploded in the digital sphere and permeate everyday parlance. There can be no doubt that these digital campaigns have increased visibility of persistent gendered issues and have added to the feminist toolkit (Rottenberg 2019).

As Baer (2016) highlights, digital feminist activism departs from conventional modes of 'doing' feminist politics for three key reasons. First, digital tools such as memes and hashtags bring attention to feminist issues, thereby mobilising 'new modes of feminist critique and collectivity' (Thrift 2014, 2). Second, SNSs particularly provide reflexive spaces for discussion of intersectional issues related to access, privilege, and difference (Thelandersson 2014), thus 'doing meaningful and worthwhile work in building networks of solidarity' which 'often transform into a feminist consciousness' (Mendes et al. 2018, 238). This is exemplified by sites and hashtags that expose persistent sexist practices, such as *#MeToo* (ibid.). In light of disillusionment with pursuing gender equality through conventional legislative channels, these digital spaces third facilitate 'a provocative and risky space for an emergent feminist politics situated in the interplay between female bodies and feminist (online) protest' (Baer 2016, 18; Salime 2014). Digital modes of feminist organising are thus considered more participative, inclusive, and global.

Despite its promise, there are significant concerns around the efficacy of fourth-wave digital activism, the complicity of digital feminist organising with a neoliberal logic, and the composition of online voices. Though digital feminist organisation sometimes produces meaningful, global action, such as the 2016 *Women's March*, critics note that online activism – dubbed 'slacktivism' – typically lacks connection to 'real-world', structural change (Christensen 2011). Instead, it often takes the form of disparate 'micro-rebellions' marked by 'entrepreneurial forms of self-promotion, self-reliance and self-governance' (Salime 2014,16). It is thus not 'a mode of political action' (Dean 2010, 127) but rather subverts the traditionally anti-capitalist movement by converting it into a marketised version of feminism (Catterall et al. 2005). Of further concern is the preponderance of white, Western voices representing this wave (Butler 2013). #MeToo, for instance, began as black feminist activist Tarana Burke's 2006 MySpace campaign to increase the visibility of sexual violence against women of colour, but the viral campaign's main material outcome has been to condemn mostly white powerful men (Rottenberg 2019). This obscures insidious, everyday gendered and raced violence (symbolic and otherwise) by creating a dichotomy between 'good guys' and powerful, sexist 'bad guys' whose reputations are publicly sullied on social media (Zarkov and Davis 2018).

A final, and significant, concern is fourth-wave feminism's complicity with neoliberal postfeminism. Not only is digital activism predicated on individual, affective narratives of experience that may further perpetuate a neoliberal focus on the individual (Phipps 2016); it has fostered a resurgence of anti-feminist activism (Baer 2016; García-Favaro and Gill 2016), including 'trolling' and harassment (Rentschler and Thrift 2015; Mendes et al. 2018) of feminist content. What is broadly termed 'postfeminism' denotes contention around feminism's necessity and purpose, characterised by: 'the prominence accorded to 'choice' and 'agency', the emphasis upon individualism, the retreat from structural accounts of inequality, and the repudiation of sexism and (thus) of the need for feminism' (Gill et al. 2016, 2). In a postfeminist milieu, women in particular are exhorted to engage in self-management and self-discipline, 'and to present all their actions as freely chosen' (Catterall et al. 2005, Gill 2008, 443; Rome and Lambert 2020).

In short, although digital feminist activism may be potentially emancipatory, there are also worrying implications for feminist theorising/critique. As feminist marketing scholars have not significantly explored digital feminist activism (Maclaran 2015), questions around whether feminist solidarity can emerge in an online environment marked not only by a postfeminist ethic but also by anti-feminist voices therefore remain unaddressed.

Context and methodological framework

With the above in mind, we analysed 400 posts on WAF and WNF? Tumblr sites from 2012 to 2015 that represent two digital activism campaigns at the inception of online (anti)feminist action. Tumblr is a public micro-blogging network associated with the expression of political views, and in particular feminist and queer activism as 'users experience freedom specifically related to gender and sexuality' (Oakley 2016, 7). Tumblr users are not connected to 'real life' identities: content is constructed via 'anonymous' pages comprised of microblog posts. Tumblr does not facilitate direct conversation: if users want to comment on a post, they must re-blog it on their own page. Hence, Tumblr is described as an 'intimate' discursive public (Berlant 2008) that 'flourishes as a porous, affective scene of identification amongst strangers that promises a certain experience of belonging' (Berlant 2008, viii).

To analyse posts on both sites, we employed critical discourse analysis (Fairclough 1992) informed by a feminist reading (Moi 1991) of Pierre Bourdieu's theory of symbolic power and symbolic violence. This theory captures how the oppressed are complicit with, if not propagating, their own domination and builds on a series of concepts detailed in Table 23.1.

While coercive and physical violence is obvious, the theory of symbolic power captures imperceptible power, power that is interwoven into the fabric of our society and being: 'For symbolic power is that invisible power which can be exercised only with the complicity of those who do not want to know that they are subject to it or even that they themselves exercise it' (Bourdieu 1991, 64). This form of power is difficult, if not impossible, to detect or defend against because it is exercised not only by those in material positions of power (with social, economic, cultural, and symbolic capital) but also by those who are themselves the target of domination or oppression. This elucidates why women would be complicit in gendered power dynamics that keep men in positions of power, or why some women reject feminism (e.g., on WAF), as well as how those who do support emancipatory politics such as feminism (e.g., on WNF?) may too be complicit in propagating gendered and asymmetrical power relations. As Bourdieu describes of symbolic power: 'resistance is more difficult, since it is something you absorb like air, something you don't feel pressured by; it is everywhere and nowhere and to escape from that is very difficult' (Eagleton and Bourdieu 1991, 115).

Symbolic violence is the exercising of symbolic power. It is enmeshed within all forms of violence (Thapar-Björkert et al. 2016); it is multidirectional, perpetrated not only by the 'strong' and 'powerful' but also the 'weak' and 'vulnerable', even by its very target. Importantly, Bourdieu (2001) described masculine domination to be a particularly insidious and durable form of symbolic power and violence, gender relations being the fundamental mechanism of the symbolic order (Krais 1993). Feminism is therefore vital to a symbolic power struggle: the movements' actions are not only working to expose symbolic power and ensuing symbolic violence, but also may somehow be implicated in the consolidation of masculine domination and gendered violence against women that continues today. To understand this, we turn to our analysis of discourse on the WAF and WNF? Tumblr pages.

Aligned with Bourdieu's interest in examining 'the social conditions of the production of utterances' (Eagleton and Bourdieu 1991, 111), we focussed our analysis on processes of naturalisation within intimate discourses on Tumblr. Bourdieu (1977) foregrounds language as integral to analyses of symbolic power; we must speak in certain ways given the universe of discourse that structures the habitus and distribution of capital in a given field (Bourdieu 1991). Bourdieu's view of language has been critiqued for its focus on social practices as constitutive of language, rather than language shaping social practices (Chouliaraki and Fairclough 1999). However, our interest here is with the role of language in the perpetuation of symbolic power. As Thapar-Björkert et al. (2016, 148) remark, 'Language itself is a form of domination. Language can constitute violence and be co-constituted by it. Language includes and excludes, it frames discourses through which social reality is constructed, and consequently has implications for power'. Symbolic power is 'euphemized' through language and thereby contributes to its misrecognition (Bourdieu 1991); this theory thus offers a compelling account of the social forces that influence language and underpin performativity (Myles 2010).

Table 23.1 Theoretical Concepts Underpinning the Theory of Symbolic Power

Concept	Definition
Doxa	Doxa is the hegemonic order of the world; the social mores and norms that are somehow taken for-granted, or 'broadly respected' (Bourdieu 2001, 1). It is everything that appears normal or commonplace
Habitus	The internalisation of doxa forms an individual's tacit dispositions, or habitus: 'a way of being, a habitual state (especially the body) and, in particular, a predisposition, tendency, propensity or inclination' acquired over time (Bourdieu, 1977, 214)
Economic capital	Capital that is materially financial, convertible into money or in the form of property rights and so forth (Bourdieu 1986)
Cultural capital	Capital that can be convertible to economic capital but not as a rule, and takes three forms: embodied, i.e., 'long-lasting dispositions of the mind and body'; objectified, or cultural goods (e.g., art, machines, technologies, instruments, books, etc.); and institutionalised such as educational qualifications (ibid.)
Social capital	Capital that is comprised of social obligations and connections, such as friendship and peer groups, club or society memberships, or more institutionalised forms such as a title of nobility (ibid).
Symbolic capital	Symbolic capital can be any of the forms of capital or all three whereby the person who has the symbolic capital is assumed (or misrecognised) to be the one with power. Bourdieu (1985, 731) describes symbolic capital 'as nothing other than capital, in whatever form, when perceived by an agent endowed with categories of perception arising from the internalization (embodiment) of the structure of its distribution, i.e., when it is known and recognized as self-evident'
Symbolic power	Power that is unseen yet perpetuated, even by those subject to its consequences. Bourdieu (1991, 170) describes symbolic power as 'a power of constituting the given through utterances, of making people see and believe, of confirming or transforming the vision of the world' that can be exercised 'only if it is recognized, i.e., misrecognized as arbitrary'
Symbolic violence	Symbolic violence is the exercising of symbolic power. It is a sophisticated and dispersed form of 'everyday' violence; the violence that no one seems to be responsible for (especially those who appear to benefit from it), a violence that is 'imperceptible, insidious and invisible' (Thapar-Björkert et al. 2016, 148)

We were guided by Bourdieu and Wacquant (1992), and Bourdieu (1991) in conducting our discursive analysis as an iterative process, generating inductive codes which were synthesised into second-order themes (Duffy and Hund 2015). Codes such as 'housewife vs career'; 'violent submission'; 'housework as empowering', e.g., were grouped into the second-order theme of tradition, linked to the discursive struggle 'feminism as oppressor' (orthodoxy) vs. 'patriarchy as oppressor' (heterodoxy). We continued adding images until themes began significantly repeating, at around 80 images for WAF and 100 images for WNF. We then increased the data set to 200 images for each site to enrich the themes identified.

In addition to thematic analysis, we followed Bourdieu (1991, 150) in seeking to 'fully explicate processes of communication, why something is said or not said, by whom, what is meant and understood, and, most importantly, with what social effects'. We conducted a transitivity analysis of the use of pronouns as well as passive and active voice, paying particular attention to 'modal auxiliary verbs' such as 'can('t)', 'should(n't)', and 'will(won't)'. This helped determine posts' point-of-view, underpinning (societal) ideals, as well as the poster's relation to such ideals and 'others' implicated in them. WNF posters, e.g., tended to use 'should' or 'can't', deontic modalities (Bybee and Fleischman 1995), combined with passive voice, as in the sentence 'I should not be afraid to go out alone', juxtaposing their expectation of how the world, and their subjectivity, ought to be.

Given that figures of speech often act to denote (obscured) power relations (Bourdieu, 1991), we noted metaphors, euphemisms and sarcasm (e.g., a WAF poster writing: 'I need FEMINISM because I am a self-centred hipster brat'). We also expanded each argument to consider its discursive consequences; e.g., I don't need feminism, because 'I am a female gamer and never was harassed online' implies 'If I had been harassed playing games online, I would need feminism'. We took note of words that were emphasised (bold, underlined, cursive, coloured) and coded images (Duffy and Hund 2015), relating text to visual context, noting overall composition, social distance conveyed in the statement (text-only, face hidden or visible), the posters' gaze, body language, as well as attitude (power, detachment versus involvement) in relation to the text (Kress and van Leeuwen 2006).

Findings: agency, the body, and tradition

The key findings we present in the following sections illustrate the discursive struggles between WNF? and WAF. Discourse on each site, marked by affect and personal experience, is 'aimed at imposing the definition of the social world that is best suited to [posters'] interests' (Bourdieu 1991, 167). We illustrate, first, the prominence of the neoliberal assumption of and desire for free choice and agency. This, we show, acts to cement an agent (postfeminist subject) versus victim (feminist subject) binary that weakens fourth-wave feminist activism given that, in a neoliberal doxa, agents are celebrated, and victims denigrated (Fraser 2013). From this, we demonstrate how this discourse is organised around notions of the (female) body, with feminist posters defending their position to be any type of gendered subject they desire, and anti-feminist posters defending the essence of their femininity. We conclude by reflecting on the discursive construction of roles for women through the notion of 'tradition', with feminist posters desiring to break free from gendered roles, and anti-feminist posters rejecting an imagined 'feminist' subjectivity and embracing gendered roles.

The role of agency

The key finding from our analysis is the doxic (neoliberal) desire for freedom of choice and agency apparent on both sites as posts are predominately written in the first-person singular rather than plural 'we'. The individualised discursive construction of this contestation fosters binary 'agent' (WAF) and 'victim' (WNF?) subject positions. Over half of WAF posts draw on variations of the utterances 'I take responsibility for my actions/decisions/problems', 'I am able to choose for myself', 'I have power/control/am empowered/free' in constructing their rejection of 'modern' feminisms and feminists. Written in active voice through variations of the modal auxiliary verb 'can', posts assert agency; e.g., 'I can defend myself'. 'Will not' is similarly used to distinguish themselves from the berated feminist positioned as a wily victim; e.g., 'I will never play the victim to get ahead'. Conversely, WNF? posts are often constructed through deontic modalities 'should not' or 'can't', using passive voice – e.g., 'I should not be afraid to go out alone' – indicating desire for (and lack of) agency. The agent/victim distinction is further reflected by WNF? and WAF images. Only 26 WNF? posts show a full face or body, the rest an even mix of text-only images or images in which the face is obscured by a placard. Inversely, over half of all WAF posts were selfies showing face/body, one-third partially covering their faces, a mere 22 text-only images. This suggests assertiveness (agency) of WAF's disavowal of feminism, contrasted by tentativeness (victim) of WNF?

The rejection of feminism on the basis of personal agency is central to the struggle for symbolic capital. From our perspective, WAF's agentic positioning serves to (mis)identify feminists as denigrated victims in an attempt to gain symbolic capital for embracing traditional roles. While dependency became stigmatised as a psychological/moral deficiency during industrial times given emergent discourses of independence associated with wage labour, its association with the (white) housewife consumer subject position was socially acceptable (De Grazia and Furlough 1996; Fraser 2013). In post-industrial neoliberal capitalism, more women are able to claim such formerly male independence, 'while a more stigmatized but still feminized sense of "dependency" attaches to "deviant" groups who are considered "superfluous"' (Fraser 2013, 8). As such, with 'worker' becoming the 'universal social subject' (Kelan 2008; Fraser 2013), WAF posts seek to maintain symbolic capital by avoiding the identification of 'housewife' with 'deviant' dependency, instead consigning feminists to this 'dependent' association. This leads to (mis)recognition of the patriarchy as a feminist construction used to excuse personal failings: 'I got to where I am today by working hard and not adopting a victim complex by blaming "the patriarchy" for my first world problems'; 'I do NOT use my gender as an excuse for failures'.

Structural influences are thereby rejected by WAF, as women are constructed as agents unaffected by an 'invented' patriarchy ('the "patriarchy" does NOT control or influence my choices'). By this logic, those women who 'need' or support feminism are rendered 'victims', unable or unwilling to take control of their lives, 'living under the lazy assumption that I have no power or control over ME :)'. As such, many posts construe feminists as 'whining, lazy female[s] who pretends everything with no effort'. The implication of this discourse is that women who identify as feminists may be construed as 'using' feminism to excuse poor performance, instead of 'leaning in' (Rottenberg 2014). Rather than 'depending on' the feminist movement, WAF posts assert individualism, positioning posters as intelligent and self-sufficient ('I am capable of critical thinking and I do not need other women representing me'). Sentiment on WAF is captured by the following post, rejecting a feminist movement that oppresses these assumptions: 'I am an independent + intelligent girl + I have free will to make my own decisions'.

WNF? posts reinforce this victim position by conveying a need for feminism through personal accounts of victimisation that (mis)recognise a desire for agency. Posts are situated in affective experiences in which a need for feminism could be likened to a longing for agency. Sentiment on WNF? is broadly captured by the posts: 'I need feminism because I am sick of girls being shamed for making their own choices with what to do with their bodies'; and, 'I need feminism because I want a family and home life to be a choice that I [underlined three times] choose, not an expectation'. This highlights WAF posters' conviction in their ability to choose in a society unaffected by structural inequality, and WNF? posters' desire for such choice in a society perceived as structurally misogynistic. This is further reflected in posts that identify gendered expectations of women's competence as hindering (personal) choices: 'several CAPABLE women in my battalion would be placed in office jobs, instead of being allowed to train and participate in the jobs they signed up for'; or 'My adviser's only "advice" on my major was; "Are you sure you want to go into engineering? It's not exactly oriented for females"'. The sexist 'other' presupposes women's cultural capital through gendered competencies and capabilities that construe women as intellectually and physically less able (Gatrell 2013). This restricts women to certain roles, thereby making it more difficult to live out their desired subject position.

From the above, we surmise that symbolic violence operates in the neoliberal assumption of free choice and agency on both sites, obfuscating structural inequalities and perpetuating patriarchal interests. But it may also operate in a feminist interpretation of WAF's reactionary discourse as wrong, given that this is precisely what WAF is organised around: rejection of a collective voice of modern feminisms. Many WAF posts note that they do not want 'these women to be MY VOICE' because 'I'VE GOT MY OWN OPINION'. As one WAF poster writes from the imagined feminist position: 'I need FEMINISM because I am a self-centred hipster brat and I think I know everything because I took a liberal studies class in college'. The feminist subject position is constructed sarcastically as liberal, upper-middle-class, intellectual elitism that WAF posters reject. In the next section, we illustrate how WAF posts use WNF? concerns to further this argument, rejecting the notion of restrictive norms and instead embracing their (natural) femininity as a source of agency and symbolic capital.

Embodied habitus: being a woman and the role of femininity

The embodiment of (gendered) habitus (Moi 1991) plays a distinctive role in the discursive struggles between both sites. This is reflected in WAF discourse that locates feminism as a mechanism of support for lazy, dependent 'victims'. However, as we discuss here, WNF? posts express frustration with an embodied (female) habitus still structured by an oppressive women-as-object subject form whereby women are pressured to manage their bodies to stem 'uncontrollable' male desire (Gill 2008; Dobson 2016). This contrasts with WAF posters who celebrate their heteronormative femininity and control over their bodies with the aim of re-asserting femininity. Hence, whereas WAF posters position gender as a positive form of symbolic capital, on WNF? it is described as negative. WNF? posters describe embodied experiences that illustrate the restrictions placed on their bodies: 'I'm required to dress modestly, practice bending over and sitting down, and be mindful of my underwear choices. This is not to keep up professional appearances, but because "it's distracting to the students especially the boys"'. Posts demonstrate how the female body renders women as irrational and weak, undermining the ability to be the ideal (male) neoliberal subject:

> I need feminism because during class discussion, a guy said that unlike men, women are too emotional to properly run a country.
> ...my fiancé is free to do his jogging in public without fearing being assaulted. When I want to go running he comes with me so that no one attacks or violates me. [...] I wish I wasn't afraid of every man that I cross in public.

Fear of gender-based violence is prevalent across WNF?, often situated in relation to the dangerous 'stranger'. Of the 200 WNF? posts, 94 reference violence against women and use variations of 'I am' or 'I shouldn't be (so) scared/afraid/terrified' – e.g.: 'I'm so scared that someone will follow me and harass me or even jump out and grab me'. Fear is compounded by the (structural) lack of recognition for victims of violence: 'I need feminism because I'm tired of being shamed into believing that I wasn't raped.' A deep sense of injustice stems from this cultural tendency to blame victims. Reflected on WNF?, as the 'stigmatised' dependent, women are told to take responsibility for their actions through, for instance, managing the body through dress ('my dad told me I asked for it because my pants were too tight'), by controlling substance intake, and not inviting male attention. This fosters misrecognition of gendered violence. Responsibility is not placed on violators but victims who are personally deficient (Fraser 2013), seen to be 'asking for it' or seeking attention: 'a female police officer [...] said the system is "fucked" and victims "do it for attention"'.

Posts also indicate indignation over being the object of male sexual desire, a desire posters cannot express without fear of being branded, in the words of one, a 'THOT' [that ho over there]. These posts do not reject femininity or a gender binary per se, but the stereotypes that enforce certain subjectivities ('If a girl doesn't like to cook or clean does that make her any less of a woman? If a man likes to cook and clean does that make him less of a man?'). These statements convey a desire for freedom in expressing dispositions that do not strictly adhere to pre-ordained gendered expectations. Notably, only five posts speak directly to issues with non-binary gender and sexuality: e.g., 'a guy at my school had to leave for crossdressing'. WNF? posts are thus embedded in, and misrecognise a gender binary, expressive of oppressive social fields in which female bodies are viewed as objects of desire to be managed by women, with those who do not fit gendered expectations excluded.

The excerpt from the post below – text placed next to a selfie collage held by a woman, face and torso visible – captures sentiment on WAF, one of the few to address rape:

> ...I was raped – thankfully, I live in a society where he was arrested, put on trial and received a lengthy custodial sentence. He was not representative of men. It was actual men, those that worked tirelessly to find justice, that put him behind bars. (...) I am not a victim and I don't need anyone to speak for me. (...) Every time a woman uses the word rape out of context it trivialises this crime; Someone looking at you is not rape. Besides any man that cat-calls me in the street. He won't do it twice. I can speak for myself. (...) I can vote, work, attend University, pick my own spouse and society will protect me – there are people that need feminism – I am not one of them. I don't need third wave feminism because I am already a WOMAN.

WAF posts embrace (natural) female bodies, experiencing femininity as positive symbolic capital (Skeggs 1997): 'Women are wired to be more emotional, motherly and sensitive than men! – I like when men compliment my looks & body (even if they are strangers!)'. Gender differences are celebrated, inequality refuted – 'Men and women are different from each other – not superior and/or inferior' – or embraced (discussed below). This facilitates misrecognition of structural inequalities, argued to be a consequence of women's natural proclivities: 'The "wage gap" is feminists' cherry picking at the fact that women tend to pick careers that pay less than those that men pick'. Furthermore, as evidenced above, men are constructed as 'allies', more supportive than (feminist) women:

> FEMINISTS TELL ME: I am weak, vulnerable and a victim I can only be successful if I act like a man. Being feminine is shameful and stupid. MEN TELL ME: I am beautiful and strong. I am good enough as I am. Being a 'real' woman is admirable and deserves respect.

Contrary to WNF?, WAF posts seek to embrace a feminine embodied habitus they perceive as under attack by a version of feminism they interpret as imploring women to reject femininity, which – however inadvertently – affirms a woman-as-object position. They further place the onus of responsibility on women to control their appearance and sexuality: 'Promiscuity is NOT okay!!'; 'I don't believe exposing my body is "confidence"'. Thus, women's bodies are objects to be self-regulated based on a masculine rationality that sees female bodies as the objects of male desire (Dobson 2016). Paradoxically this presents on WAF as simultaneous acceptance and rejection of the 'pressure [on women] to create and maintain erotic capital' (Maclaran 2015, 1735) fostered by contemporary marketing messaging.

In this struggle for symbolic capital, WAF posters fend off feminist 'attacks' on men and their status as 'real' women, situating their defence through embodied cultural capital. Feminists (often referred to as 'feminazis') are imagined as oppressors of women and men. WAF posters accuse feminists of supressing certain points of view, such as the naturalisation of gender norms: 'As a Christian, I follow the Bible's commands that I SUBMIT to my husband in all things. This brings me joy and makes my marriage stronger! Feminists would never open their minds to this, they will only judge and attack me for my beliefs! Feminists oppress me more than my husband ever could'. This is further reflected in posts detailed in the previous section that reject a liberal feminist collective that rejects traditional roles in favour of roles embracing working life.

Somewhat perversely, similar to reconfiguring the position 'housewife' to align with agent, WAF posts appropriate the very femininity that they defend to undermine feminists, arguing that feminists posit 'shrill, illogical' arguments: 'I deem it offensive to be determined by (the use of) my uterus: I WILL ALWAYS CHOOSE MY BRAIN and never be represented by a bunch of hystericals'. This works to justify 'natural' gender norms while concurrently aligning women with 'rational', androcentric notions of independence, and not the deviant dependent and feminised feminist. Thus, in the struggle for symbolic capital, WAF defends an embodied form of capital, i.e., being an agentic woman who recognises and celebrates the natural differences between men and women: 'I DON'T NEED FEMINISM BECAUSE IT DESTROYS THE VERY ESSENCE OF BEING A WOMAN'.

Desire for/desire to escape 'tradition'

Central to issues of (feminine) embodiment outlined above is contestation around what it means to be a woman. WNF? discourse is constructed around frustration with gendered expectations that encourage traditional subjectivities. As one poster writes: 'A woman's choices shouldn't be reduced to having babies. My family shouldn't call me selfish for putting all my efforts on my professional growth instead of finding the right man to have kids with'. Posts suggest an orthodoxy in which women's ambitions should be centred on pregnancy and/or marriage, rather than professional goals. This implies that women are 'selfish' for aspiring to challenge traditional roles: 'When I answered to my colleagues that I'm not dreaming about a marriage, they looked down on me and acted like I'm not "normal"'. WNF? discourse thus demonstrates that women feel pressured to embrace domestic responsibilities, indicating the persistence of a traditional labour division (Kelan 2008). Many WNF posts suggest the dominance of men over women:

> **…when telling my male co-workers that I would never give up my career to be a stay-at-home mom, they tried to convince me why I should by saying:**
> You'll probably change your mind once you have kids.
> Well, I was my mother's number one priority. She would've dropped her job on the spot if I had wanted her to.
> You can still be ambitious. Did you know our CEO's wife is a stay-at-home mom?

The patriarchal control of women is often depicted on WNF? by violently enforced submission. One post – handwritten in red – describes:

> As a 14-year-old girl (Or any age at all), I should not be told by my parents that they hope my husband (when or if I get one) beats me for not wanting to clean every day and for not wanting to become a 24/7 housewife […].

This post relates women to the oppressive subject position of housewife symbolised by domestic servitude, implying that a feminist subject position is free of violence and oppression. The family is constructed as oppressive, invoking the male breadwinner subject who engages in physical violence to enforce traditional roles. This enacts symbolic (and physical) violence of masculine domination (Bourdieu 2001) that casts women as weak homemakers. Online activism that challenges the persistence of traditional roles and lack of choice is executed by posting personal experiences of resistance, thus forming a community of individuals with similar experiences in everyday life – a series of 'I's' comprising an amorphous 'we'.

WAF posts are the other side of the discursive coin, as posts on both sites advocate choice. That which is constructed as obstructing choice on WAF is not patriarchal, however, but feminist. WAF posts relate shame to embracing traditional roles, propagated by 'feminists' who prioritise career instead: 'Feminists keep trying to shame me for my CHOICE to be a monogamous, young, happily married, stay-at-home mother'. Those who normatively value becoming workers instead of domestic subjects are construed as judging those 'choosing' their children over work: 'There is NOTHING wrong with wanting kids, having to stay at home with them, or choosing them over work'. This triggers declarations on WAF that reject feminism on the basis that their choices are disrespected by feminists' neoliberal ideals of working life. Motherhood and career are constructed as binary (Kanji and Cahusac 2015). Posters do not advocate a 'have it all' mentality, instead suggesting that the choice for one subjectivity negates the possibility of the other. The binary construction of choice constitutes a 'symbolic struggle for the production of common sense' (Bourdieu 1991, 239) in an effort to preserve capital:

362   *Aliette Lambert and Ana-Isabel Nölke*

WNF? discourse denotes desire to be respected for the choice to engage professionally, whereas WAF discourse denotes a desire to fend off heterodoxic feminist discourse that undermines their gendered capital.

In this struggle for symbolic capital, WAF posters contend that feminist goals of liberation and empowerment can be attained by embracing traditional roles. Over a third of WAF posts indicate a desire to 'stay home to cook, clean, and care for my future family [rather] than go to work full-time'. Being a caretaker is seen as liberating over 'slaving away' for a corporation:

> I WILL NEVER UNDERSTAND HOW STAYING AT HOME DOING HOUSEWORK ON YOUR OWN SCHEDULE IS SOME KIND OF "OPPRESSION" BUT GETTING UP EVERY MORNING, PUNCHING A TIME CLOCK AND HAVING TO SUCCUMB TO THE DEMANDS OF AN EMPLOYER 40 HOURS A WEEK IS "LIBERATION"

This post rejects working life in favour of what are considered more fulfilling pursuits of caring for family. This is reflected by studies indicating that many women choose to opt-out of a masculine, competitive workplace (Gatrell 2013). The (patriarchal) corporation is (mis)recognised as oppressive in contrast to a (patriarchal) breadwinner who is defended: 'My husband is not a monster for wanting me to stay home and I am not brainwashed for agreeing with him!'. As such, feminist goals of empowerment and equality can, according to the posts' logic, emerge from adherence to traditional roles that should be coveted rather than eschewed. This is further reflected by these selfie posts, text written on a placard held over the face just below the eyes:

> MY HUSBAND IS MY EQUAL. I MAY COOK BUT HE CLEANS. WE'RE BOTH BREADWINNERS, BUT FIGHT ABOUT WHO WILL BE THE LUCKY ONE TO STAY HOME + RAISE OUR KIDS.
>
> I WILLING [sic] quit my job & put my dream of becoming a mechanic on hold to be a housewife/stay at home mom. ★Gasp★ My husband respects me and I Serve him.

Here (mis)recognition of gender equality is located in both marriage and career, as women are evidenced to have access to traditionally masculine spaces ('I [worked] twenty years in a traditionally male dominated career field'). This juxtaposes emancipation and the ability for women to engage in men's work with a traditionally feminine role, ostensibly against feminist expectations ('★gasp★'). Associating 'feminism' with 'employer' is not accidental: on WAF, feminism seems to have become synonymous with a neoliberal subject position that is encouraged to 'lean in' to a feminist subjectivity that is associated with work (Rottenberg 2014) to the detriment of some women's more 'traditional' pursuits.

Discussion

Disheartening as they may be for feminist marketing scholars, these findings speak for themselves: women continue to experience subjugation related to gendered roles and their embodied habitus, and some women find those identifying as 'feminists' to be threatening of traditional, gendered choices and embodied femininity. This inherently pits women against one another in a battle for symbolic capital over what it is to be a woman. The focus of our discussion is not to rehearse this argument. Instead, we draw conclusions as to the role of social media platforms in the construction of discourse that operates as a form of symbolic violence, resulting in the propagation of gender inequality by *both* feminist and anti-feminist digital activists. Our findings demonstrate in particular two forms of symbolic violence in which both 'sides' are complicit: the focus on agency and the perception of feminism.

First, both sites are centred on agency. On WAF, a postfeminist sentiment pervades in which 'modern' feminism is rejected given its purported success; posts exude agency through active voice and assertions of 'I can/will', taking personal responsibility; traditional roles and femininity are embraced on the basis of personal choice and naturalised gender norms. In these posts, a traditional, orthodox form of femininity is a distinctly positive form of symbolic capital (Skeggs 1997). A market logic is incorporated into the self-project, which is evaluated based on the ability to incorporate this 'freely chosen' form of femininity. Conversely, on WNF? posters identify with heterodoxic feminist discourse that constructs a need for feminism as a desire for individual agency. This is depicted by personal accounts of victimisation often associated with traditional gender roles that complicate access to feminist subjectivities, subjectivities largely defined by the oppression generated by such traditional – and consumer-oriented – roles predicating a need to participate in working life. A passive discursive positioning contrasts the active positioning of WAF, reinforcing WAF posters' convictions of feminists as victims unwilling to take personal responsibility, thereby weakening the symbolic legitimacy of feminism in a neoliberal postfeminist doxa in which victims are denigrated (Fraser 2013).

Feminist activism's complicity in this doxa is reinforced by the use of social media platforms that facilitate activism predicated on disjointed, ephemeral declarations. Individual posts are scattered, hindering cohesive, sustained arguments that might lead to substantive, structural action. These fragmented arguments are situated in personal experiences, fostering intimate publics based on the authority of the individual (Phipps, 2016). Personal experiences are thereby essentialised, intensifying a neoliberal focus on the individual over a community predicated on social bonds (Dean 2010). The self-subjectified subject (Gill 2008) is firmly anchored in a self-branding culture, always there, always introspectively regulating itself. As a result of this hyper-individualisation, posters seem incapable of moving beyond their micro experiences. WAF posters, for instance, draw on myths such as 'men are rapists' that are dismissed for their inaccuracy given individual experience, without empathic consideration of others' experiences. WNF? posts centred on individual accounts of victimisation do little to further activism, instead fuelling this reactionary discourse centred on feminists' lack of agency. Feminism's embeddedness in a politics of recognition is thereby exacerbated by its harnessing of social media to revive activism. This calls into question the ability of fourth-wave feminism to effect structural change, when its very medium seems to foster symbolic violence.

The second form of symbolic violence relates to perceptions of feminism. As feminist marketing scholars, we must acknowledge how these perceptions, depicted on WAF and arguably exacerbated by digital activism, shape a rejection of feminism. WAF posts (mis)recognise a feminist subjectivity as one that rejects traditional roles historically associated with the construct of 'consumer' (De Grazia and Furlough 1996) in favour of 'independent' (i.e., masculine) engagement with the labour market (Fraser 2013). Defending symbolic capital of hegemonic femininity and domesticity, WAF posters blur WNF?'s victim discourse with posters' desire to eschew 'tradition' in favour of work and independence. Thereby, WAF posters construe feminists as victims who use feminism to bolster an inherently 'weak' disposition shaped by an inability to take initiative to resolve personal incompetence. This, paradoxically, aligns WAF with the cultural capital of agentic, neoliberal subjects who can choose to reject working life and act/think independently, misrecognising feminists as victims of neoliberal subjectivities. Symbolic violence is enacted by WAF posters rejecting feminist activism that seeks to provide them with choices – whatever those may be – and by WNF? feminist activism as complicit with a neoliberal, postfeminist doxa that magnifies individual identity politics to the detriment of communal, structural change.

As feminist marketing scholars (and activists), where do we go from here? We suggest that rather than recoiling at discourse on the WAF Tumblr (as, based on our initial reaction, we suspect some readers may have done), we take the concerns presented seriously in shaping our response and a future research agenda. Bourdieusian theory compels us, as academics, to question our collusion with symbolic power – here a form of liberal, elitist feminism captured by a WAF poster sketching feminists as well-educated, 'self-centred hipster brats'. We must ask ourselves how our own liberal, feminist, academic beliefs influence the way we critically analyse discourse, and the effects this has on feminist theory and on the very subjects of our analysis.

Beneath the surface, WAF posts echo concerns that feminist theorising has become disengaged from practice (Munro 2003) as post-structural understandings arguably propagate a politics of recognition (Fraser 2013) to the detriment of programmes for structural change. Moreover, WAF posters seek to embrace a sense of gendered and embodied femininity that they perceive as denigrated by progressive and feminist discourses. By focussing on micro-experiences of oppression and by rejecting some women's embodied sense of gender, feminist activism is therefore complicit in a neoliberal doxa that forms the universe of possible discourse and propagates hegemonic (patriarchal) power. Instead, feminist scholarship and activism *could* highlight macro-practices that propagate structural inequalities, seeking solutions for collective action and using digital technologies to that end. Likewise, scholars could heed the concerns that posters on both 'sides' are expressing related to agency and embodiment, by exploring the potential emancipation of embodied experiences and empowering forms of femininity. Notably, extant work on both of these topics is often framed as distinctly anti-capitalist.

We conclude this chapter by arguing for a new wave of feminism (Rome et al. 2019) that rejects any focus on the individual and instead uses forms of (social) media to accrue and consolidate evidence of structural gendered and raced oppressions. This would also allow a diversity of audiences to come together to challenge such oppressions and provide new alternatives for change without undermining experiences of the individual. Future research could therefore focus on discursive analyses of feminist speeches and media content, to understand how they may be hindering progress through the use of the same passive discursive positioning and neoliberal focus on micro-experiences found on WNF?, while also suggesting avenues for sparking structural change. As we show here, marketing messaging that increasingly incorporates feminist discourse by suggesting feminist subjectivities can be achieved through consumption (Maclaran and Catterall 2000; Catterall et al. 2005) fosters feminist subjectivities that alienate the very women feminism needs to create meaningful change. To critically evaluate our complicity with this alienation is the first step towards a more unifying wave of feminism.

Notes

1 We use the term 'women' to refer to cis women – those born female and identifying as women – given that this is the term and identification on which discourse on the social media sites analysed is centred.
2 Acknowledging that there are many variations of feminisms, we refer to feminism throughout this chapter in the singular to capture the essence of that to which the posters on the sites refer: a broad sweeping movement intending to bring about equality of all genders, with a focus on dismantling patriarchal forces that oppress women.

References

Baer, H. 2016. "Redoing Feminism: Digital Activism, Body Politics, and Neoliberalism." *Feminist Media Studies* 16(1): 17–34.
Berlant, L. 2008. *The Female Complaint: The Unfinished Business of Sentimentality in American Culture*. Durham, NC: Duke University Press.
Blau, F.D. and L.M. Kahn. 2017. "The Gender Wage Gap: Extent, Trends, and Explanations." *Journal of Economic Literature* 55(3): 789–865.
Bourdieu, P. 1977. "Outline of a Theory of Practice". In *Cambridge Studies in Social Anthropology*, edited by J. Goody, 248. Cambridge: Cambridge University Press.
Bourdieu, P. 1985. "The Social Space and The Genesis of Groups." *Theory and Society* 14(6): 723–744.
Bourdieu, P. 1986. "The Forms of Capital." In *Handbook of Theory of Research for the Sociology of Education*, edited by J. G. Richardson, 241–258. New York: Greenwood Press.
Bourdieu, P. 1991. *Language and Symbolic Power*. Cambridge, MA: Harvard University Press.
Bourdieu, P. 2001. *Masculine Domination*. Stanford, CA: Stanford University Press.
Bourdieu, P. and L.J. Wacquant. 1992. *An Invitation to Reflexive Sociology*. Stanford, CA: University of Chicago Press.
Butler, J. 2013. "For White Girls Only? Postfeminism and the Politics of Inclusion." *Feminist Formations* 25(1): 35–58.
Bybee, J. and S. Fleischman. 1995. *Modality in Grammar and Discourse*. Amsterdam: John Benjamins Publishing.
Catterall, M., P. Maclaran, and L. Stevens. 2005. "Postmodern Paralysis: The Critical Impasse in Feminist Perspectives on Consumers." *Journal of Marketing Management* 21(5–6): 489–504.
Chouliaraki, L. and N. Fairclough. 1999. *Discourse in Late Modernity: Rethinking Critical Discourse Analysis*. Edinburgh: Edinburgh University Press.
Christensen, H. 2011. "Political Activities on the Internet: Slacktivism or Political Participation by Other Means?" *First Monday* 16(1): 2–7.
Dean, J. 2010. *Rethinking Contemporary Feminist Politics*. Basingstoke: Palgrave Macmillan.
DeGrazia, V. and E. Furlough. (eds.). 1996. *The Sex of Things: Gender and Consumption in Historical Perspective*. Berkeley: University of California Press.
Dobson, A.S. 2016. *Postfeminist Digital Cultures: Femininity, Social Media, and Self-Representation*. New York: Palgrave Macmillan.
Duffy, B.E. and E. Hund. 2015. "'Having It All' on Social Media: Entrepreneurial Femininity and Self-Branding Among Fashion Bloggers." *Social Media + Society* 1(2): 2–12.
Eagleton, T. and P. Bourdieu. 1991. "Doxa and Common Life." *New Left Review* 1(191): 111–121.
Fairclough, N. 1992. "Discourse and Text: Linguistic and Intertextual Analysis within Discourse Analysis." *Discourse & Society* 3(2): 193–217.
Faludi, S. 1992. *Backlash: The Undeclared War Against American Women*. New York: Broadway Books.
Fraser, N. 2013. *Fortunes of Feminism: From State-Managed Capitalism to Neoliberal Crisis*. London: Verso.
Gatrell, C. J. 2013. "Maternal body work: How Women Managers and Professionals Negotiate Pregnancy and New Motherhood at Work." *Human Relations* 66(5): 621–644.

García-Favaro, L. and R. Gill. 2016. "Emasculation Nation has Arrived: Sexism Rearticulated in Online Responses to Lose the Lads' Mags Campaign." *Feminist Media Studies* 16(3): 379–397.

Gill, R. 2008. "Culture and Subjectivity in Neoliberal and Postfeminist Times." *Subjectivity* 25(1): 432–445.

Gill, R., E.K. Kelan, and C. Scharff. 2016. "A Postfeminist Sensibility at Work." *Gender, Work & Organization* 24(3): 226–244.

Kanji, S. and E. Cahusac 2015. "Who am I? Mothers' Shifting Identities, Loss and Sensemaking After Workplace Exit." *Human Relations* 68(9): 1415–1436.

Kelan, E. 2008. "Gender, Risk and Employment Insecurity: The Masculine Breadwinner Subtext." *Human Relations* 61(9): 1171–1202.

Krais, B. 1993. "Gender and Symbolic Violence: Female Oppression in the Light of Pierre Bourdieu's Theory of Social Practice." In *Bourdieu: Critical Perspectives*, edited by C. Calhoun, E. LiPuma, and M. Postone, 156–177. Chicago: University of Chicago Press.

Kress, G.R. and T. van Leeuwen. 2006. *Reading Images*. London: Routledge.

Lumsden, K. and H.M. Morgan. 2018. "Cyber-Trolling as Symbolic Violence." In *The Routledge Handbook of Gender and Violence*, edited by N. Lombard, 121–132. Abingdon: Taylor and Francis.

Maclaran, P. 2015. "Feminism's Fourth Wave: A Research Agenda for Marketing and Consumer Research." *Journal of Marketing Management* 31(15–16): 1732–1738.

Maclaran, P. and M. Catterall. 2000. "Bridging the Knowledge Divide: Issues on the Feminisation of Marketing Practice." *Journal of Marketing Management* 16(6): 635–646.

Mendes, K., J. Ringrose, J., and J. Keller. 2018. "#MeToo and the Promise and Pitfalls of Challenging Rape Culture Through Digital Feminist Activism." *European Journal of Women's Studies* 25(2): 236–246.

Moi, T. 1991. "Appropriating Bourdieu: Feminist Theory and Pierre Bourdieu's Sociology of Culture." *New Literary History* 22(4): 1017–1049.

Munro, V.E. 2003. "On Power and Domination: Feminism and The Final Foucault." *European Journal of Political Theory* 2(1): 79–99.

Munro, V.E. 2013. "Feminism: A Fourth Wave?" *Political Insight* 4(2): 22–25.

Myles, J.F. 2010. *Bourdieu, Language and the Media*. London: Palgrave Macmillan.

Oakley, A. 2016. "Disturbing Hegemonic Discourse: Nonbinary Gender and Sexual Orientation Labelling on Tumblr." *Social Media + Society* 2(3): 1–12.

Petronzino, M. 2012. *'Who Needs Feminism?' New Tumblr Promotes Gender Equality*. Mashable. Available from: http://mashable.com/2012/04/13/tumblr-who-needs-feminism/ (accessed 7 December 2017).

Phipps, A. 2016. "Whose Personal Is More Political? Experience in Contemporary Feminist Politics." *Feminist Theory* 17(3): 1–19.

Rentschler, C.A. and S.C. Thrift. 2015. "Doing Feminism in The Network: Networked Laughter and the 'Binders Full of Women' Meme." *Feminist Theory* 16(3): 329–359.

Rome, A.S., S. O'Donohoe, and S. Dunnett. 2019. "Rethinking Feminist Waves." Chap. 11 in *Handbook of Research on Gender and Marketing*, edited by S. Dobscha, 252–272. Northampton, MA: Edward Elgar Publishing.

Rome, A.S. and A. Lambert. 2020. "(Wo)men On Top? Postfeminist Contradictions in Young Women's Sexual Narratives." *Marketing Theory* 20(4): 501–525.

Rottenberg, C. 2014. "The Rise of Neoliberal Feminism." *Cultural Studies* 28(3): 418–437.

Rottenberg, C. 2019. "# MeToo and the Prospects of Political Change." *Soundings* 71(71): 40–49.

Salime, Z. 2014. "New Feminism as Personal Revolutions: Microrebellious Bodies." *Signs* 40(1): 14–20.

Scaptura, M.N. and K.M. Boyle. 2020. "Masculinity Threat, 'Incel' Traits, and Violent Fantasies Among Heterosexual Men in The United States." *Feminist Criminology* 15(3): 278–298.

Skeggs, B. 1997. *Formations of Class & Gender: Becoming Respectable*. Thousand Oaks, CA: Sage.

Thapar-Björkert, S., L. Samelius, L., and G.S. Sanghera. 2016. "Exploring Symbolic Violence in the Everyday: Misrecognition, Condescension, Consent and Complicity." *Feminist Review* 112(1): 144–162.

Thelandersson, F. 2014. "A Less Toxic Feminism: Can the Internet Solve the Age-Old Question of How to Put Intersectional Theory into Practice?" *Feminist Media Studies* 14(3): 527–530.

Thrift, S. 2014. "#YesAllWomen as Feminist Meme Event." *Feminist Media Studies* 16(6): 1090–1092.

Tumblr. 2015. "Women Against Feminism (WAF)." *Tumblr.* Available from: http://womenagainstfeminism.tumblr.com/ (accessed 7 December 2017).

Zarkov, D. and D. Kathy. 2018. "Ambiguities and dilemmas around# MeToo:# ForHow long and# WhereTo?" *European Journal of Women's Studies* 25(1): 3–9.

24 Big Brother is monitoring

Feminist surveillance studies and digital consumer culture

Lauren Gurrieri and Jenna Drenten

In recent times we have witnessed the intersecting rise of surveillance, digital technologies, marketing and consumption. Whether in the form of Facebook data informing targeted advertising practices, beauty filters that minimise 'imperfections' in selfies or the rise of 'femtech' apps that monitor menstruation, fertility and pregnancy, digital technology increasingly plays a role in tracking and monitoring our everyday lives. How data, business models and digital culture have come to inform one another in these ways is encapsulated by the term 'surveillance capitalism' (Zuboff 2019). This describes how private human experiences are monitored and captured through technologies and translated into behavioural data that is packaged and monetised to enable businesses to better understand, predict and target future consumers. Yet, the surveillant opportunities afforded through the consumption of technologies that monitor, track and produce 'data doubles' (Haggerty and Ericson 2000) are highly gendered (Nakamura 2015)—as evidenced even in the colloquial term 'Big Brother.' This gives rise to effects ranging from the perpetuation of normative stereotypes and assumptions about women and men (Lupton 2015) to a heightened regulatory gaze upon women (Elias and Gill 2018).

Consequently, how digital technologies are consumed in everyday life, their capacities for surveillance and the implications for the construction of subjectivities needs to be understood as a feminist priority. Here, the emerging field of feminist surveillance studies offers important insights. This chapter explores how this approach can help interrogate and understand the elisions in consumer culture between digital technologies, surveillance and gender. We provide an overview of extant literature that explores these intersections at the levels of individuals, their social relations and the broader constitution of consumer categories. This ranges from wearable technologies that record individual moods, activities and biometrics giving rise to the 'quantified self'; to apps that structure and facilitate our social relationships and how we appear to others; through to the organisation and valuing of consumers through data generated profiles. Across these topics, we discuss how a feminist surveillance studies approach (Dubrofsky and Magnet 2015) offers insights into the gendered dynamics at play and map directions for future research to understand the gendered implications of digital technology consumption intensifying tracking and monitoring in our lives.

Feminist surveillance studies

Early feminist examinations of gender and digital culture—known as cyberfeminism—signalled the subversive potential of Internet technologies for resisting oppressive gendered regimes. This included the possibilities of identity tourism (Nakamura 2002;

DOI: 10.4324/9781003042587-29

Turkle 1997), disembodiment (Hansen 2012; Nouraie-Simone 2005) and the boundary transgression of the part human and part machine cyborg (Haraway 1985). However, this utopian vision has been subsequently problematised, whereby it is acknowledged that digital technologies can both resist and reinforce hierarchies of gender (Daniels 2009). Indeed, feminist scholars across a range of disciplines now point to the gendered configurations of unequal power relations within various technocultural contexts. Here, one area of emerging focus is the role of surveillance, namely, "any collection and processing of personal data, whether identifiable or not, for the purposes of influencing or managing those whose data have been garnered" (Lyon 2001, p. 2). Surveillance has been highlighted as a feminist issue that warrants greater attention (Gill 2019), while digital technologies are noted for inviting new and unique surveillance possibilities (Fuchs 2011a).

The contemporary state of ever-evolving digital technologies collecting exponentially increasing amounts of information about our identities and lives has recast power formations from a mode of discipline to control. Under societies of control (Deleuze 1992), surveillance shifts from a panopticon model that is top-down, instrumental and focussed on crafting docile bodies to becoming more networked, abstract and focussed on moulding 'dividuals' whose fragmented data-bodies come to matter (Deleuze 1992; Galič, Timan, and Koops 2017; Haggerty and Ericson 2003). Under this post-panoptic dynamic, surveillance has become liquid—taking on an ever-changing character that spreads and seeps into many areas of modern life—and is less focussed on fixing and containing victims as opposed to seeking out volunteers to be surveilled (Bauman and Lyon 2013). As a consequence, more horizontal forms of surveillance that operate across society have come to emerge, including social, lateral and participatory surveillance (Albrechtslund 2008; Andrejevic 2004; boyd and Marwick 2011; Marwick 2012). These surveillance forms speak to the use of digital technologies for peer-related data gathering and monitoring where power hierarchies are more or less flattened. As part of these 'surveillance societies' (Wood and Webster 2009), how we come to be watched and monitor both ourselves and others now operates in ubiquitous and inescapable ways.

To date, there has been a strong focus on the implications for privacy across studies of surveillance and our digitally mediated lives. Yet, examinations of surveillance also reveal deep structures of inequality in how dynamics of watching and being watched are borne out. An emerging body of research that brings a critical feminist approach to surveillance through the adoption of an explicitly feminist praxis is feminist surveillance studies (Dubrofsky and Magnet 2015). This perspective broadly adopts an intersectional critical feminist perspective to examine 'white supremacist capitalist heteropatriarchal surveillance,' namely, "the use of surveillance practices and technologies to normalise and maintain white-ness, able-bodiedness, capitalism, and heterosexuality, practices integral to the foundation of the modern state" (Dubrofsky and Magnet 2015, p. 7). Through such a prism, feminist surveillance studies opens up examinations of how subjectivities come to be remade in ways that highlight othered forms of racialised, gendered, classed, sexualised and abled and disabled identities. In doing so, it focusses on illuminating what surveillance constitutes, who comes to be scrutinised, why, and at what cost (Dubrofsky and Magnet 2015).

A feminist surveillance studies approach problematises a conception of technologies as 'neutral' and instead focusses on how issues of oppression, discrimination and disenfranchisement come to be both practiced and resisted. In a rapidly evolving surveillance society, there are both longstanding and newly emerging surveillance technologies that reproduce inequalities. Increasingly, these involve subjects taking on the roles of both producers and consumers of cultural content in the guise of prosumers (Fuchs 2011b), adding further complexities to the power relations produced and reproduced accordingly. Moreover, such actions take place within spaces that blur the conventional lines between public and private. For example, social media facilitates the presentation of women as willingly placing themselves under surveillance through the 'voluntary' posting of lifestyle oriented photographs, with gendered and racialised implications for the display of bodies, agency and the invitation to gaze (Dubrofsky and Wood 2015). This speaks to how technologies have enabled a surveillant gaze that disproportionately targets marginalised and stigmatised groups, in turn, making them more comprehensively observed and trackable than ever before (Nakamura 2015). Accordingly, a feminist surveillance studies lens enables an examination of how technology comes to scrutinise certain identities and reward others in consumer culture.

Feminist surveillance studies and digital consumer culture

Relevant to understanding the theoretical value of feminist surveillance perspectives in consumer research and marketing, we identify three key conversations across studies of gender, surveillance and digital consumer culture and identify opportunities to build upon this existing research. The following section examines these conversations, namely: surveillance and the tracking of selves through technology, surveillance and technologically mediated relationships and surveillance and the categorisation of consumers. After reviewing relevant existing research at the intersection of surveillance, digital technologies, marketing and consumption, we contextualise future opportunities across these conversations through proposing a feminist surveillance research agenda accordingly.

Surveillance and tracking selves through technology

Self-tracking describes how people monitor and record specific features of their lives, such as activities, bodily functions and behaviours, in real time. This phenomenon is also referred to as lifelogging, personal analytics and personal informatics and is regarded as part of a broader history of self-monitoring that includes practices such as journaling and diary keeping (Lupton 2016b). As self-tracking technologies have advanced and developed as a large consumer market, self-tracking has become a widespread cultural phenomenon (Didžiokaitė, Saukko, and Greiffenhagen 2018; Pantzar and Ruckenstein 2015). Such technologies range from devices that can be inserted into the body, worn on the body, carried or placed in the home and workplace; and operate jointly with apps or platforms that enable users to view, monitor, analyse, visualise and share collected data (Lupton 2019). While some technologies require users to manually input data, most devices are now designed to automatically record data for users through accelerometers, gyroscopes, magnetometers, global positioning systems, compasses, microphones, cameras and wireless devices embedded with sensors (Bode and Kristensen 2016). Consequently, the self-monitoring of steps taken, moods, sleep patterns or menstrual cycles through digital technologies has become normalised as part of modern life, in turn, heightening the possibilities for surveillance. Yet, who comes to be scrutinised, and in what ways, through self-tracking operates in highly gendered ways. For example, that women are more likely to engage in calorie tracking speaks to broader gendered inequalities related to the regulation of women's bodies, norms of feminine embodiment and unattainable standards that fuel regimes of self-perfection (Sanders 2017).

Digital self-tracking is strongly associated with the Quantified Self (QS) movement, a loosely structured community that upholds the idea of 'self-knowledge through numbers.' QS embraces datafication towards greater self-understanding and self-improvement (Wolf 2010), with this 'numerical self' defined by transparency, optimisation, feedback loops and biohacking (Ruckenstein and Pantzar 2015), suggesting an active personalisation and transformation of technologies. People in the QS movement are typically young, affluent, male, Caucasian, heterosexual and technologically savvy (Nafus and Sherman 2014; Lupton 2016a) and self-track extensively and in detail, using data as a mirror to gain insights about the 'real' self. These 'data doubles' (Haggerty and Ericson 2003) can, in turn, be scrutinised and targeted for intervention, highlighting both the entanglement of bodies, technologies and selves (Lupton 2014) and how data comes to be invested with value and status (Lupton 2016b). This datapreneurial subject unfolds across many aspects of our lives, driven by an imperative to self-groom as a 'good consumer'—for example, in self-tracking consumer credit data towards adopting a 'creditworthy' identity (DuFault and Schouten 2020). Beyond the QS community, self-tracking also encompasses more mundane forms, where people pursuing everyday and limited goals engage in basic self-tracking to achieve temporary changes (Didžiokaitė, Saukko, and Greiffenhagen 2018). Here, self-tracking devices take on three roles that speak to device utility ('tool'), novelty and play ('toy') and an instructive capacity to guide users into the formation of routines ('tutor') (Lyall and Robards 2018). Yet whether consumed by enthusiasts or in mundane ways, research on self-tracking largely focusses on members of privileged social groups, with a lack of knowledge of how those who experience marginalisation or stigmatisation engage, resist or reinvent self-tracking (Lupton 2017).

Self-tracking one's bodily functions and activities is increasingly seen as a means of achieving one's personal goals (Ruckenstein 2014). Indeed, the metaphor of the 'digital doppelganger' describes self-tracking as a dynamic socio-technical arrangement that evokes a digital version of becoming a (better) self that is 'more you than you are yourself' (Bode and Kristensen 2016). Instrumental to this are technological features that motivate and provide feedback, reminders and support that in effect turn activities into play. Through making self-improvement a more pleasurable process, this gamification of everyday and private tasks promotes self-governance by tapping into aspirations of self-care and self-development (Whitson 2013). While this can foster feelings of pleasure and satisfaction, it can also be experienced as demoralising if the data generated is confronting or disappointing or as burdensome due to the intensive and time-consuming nature of self-tracking (Lupton 2019). For example, the extensive monitoring of temperatures and symptoms throughout the day for women self-tracking via fertility apps can be overwhelming and punctured with disappointments if pregnancy does not occur. This speaks to the 'teleoaffective shaping' of self-tracking, whereby associations of purpose and emotion come to shape tracked activities (Spotswood, Shankar, and Piwek 2020). Yet, the continuous self-surveillance of self-tracking technologies prioritises an 'algorithmic subjectivity' (Lupton 2015), whereby one comes to understand and experience their body through quantified data as opposed to embodied knowledge and sensations (Toner 2018). This, in turn, subjects bodies to rigid and normalised categories devoid of complexities, highlighting broader implications for how subjectivities, embodiment and gender relations are implicated through self-tracking.

Underpinning these emotional entanglements with self-tracking technologies and activities are cultural imperatives that emphasise self-responsibility and self-management towards improving one's life (Lupton 2016a). A large body of self-tracking research draws upon Foucauldian perspectives, conceiving self-tracking as a form of neoliberal governmentality that produces a subject engaged in endless self-improvement, undertaking responsible choices to manage and optimise the self as a healthy and productive biocitizen (Datta and Chakraborty 2018; Lupton 2016a). Indeed, self-tracking technologies are designed to reproduce ideals of the self as knowledgeable, aware, problem solving and in control (Lupton 2019) and make bodies more visible and amenable to regulation. Foucault's (1979) concept of biopower, namely the regulation of bodily activities and processes, is seen as central to this model of neoliberal governance of self-tracking cultures. For example, when fertility apps are connected to digital weight scales, calorie trackers and ovulation monitors to provide aggregated 'data-driven advice,' this fuels self-disciplinary mentalities and the responsibilisation of women to avoid health risks while trying to conceive (Lupton 2015). How systemic and structural conditions, such as those that reinforce gendered norms and ideals for men and women, come to intersect with notions of agency and personal responsibility is key here. For example, self-tracking of sexual activities through apps that focus on male performance (e.g., quantifying thrusts) and the ranking of sexual achievements (e.g., the number of sexual partners), reinforce gender stereotypes, promote competitive sexual prowess and frame limited sexualities (Lupton 2015).

Digital self-tracking fosters a culture of dataveillance, whereby people are watched through technologies (increasingly of a digitised form) that generate data about selves (van Dijck 2014). Self-tracking technologies collapse the boundaries between public and private surveillance, encouraging both self-surveillance and social surveillance through the tracking of personal data to optimise the self, the sharing of this information through social media platforms and the observation of other people's data (Lupton 2016b). This speaks to the increasingly liquid form of modern surveillance that spreads and seeps into many areas of modern life (Bauman and Lyon 2013). Charitsis, Yngfalk, and Skålén (2019) highlight how marketing further heightens this governance, whereby Nike+ consumers engage in the creation of an environment that appropriates value from their self-tracking activities as bound by corporate interests. These consumers both 'voluntary' put their lives under constant corporate surveillance and actively engage in surveillance themselves. As Hepworth (2019) evocatively describes, her experience of self-tracking is akin to a mini panopticon, where visualisations of her physiological data entertain and delight while obscuring systems of profit and surveillance. Indeed, the 'surveillance team' observing her activities includes herself, friends, Fitbit staff and those that Fitbit sells her data to, including advertisers, credit rating agencies and health insurance companies. This highlights how the data produced by self-tracking can be appropriated and mined for commercial purposes with ever expanding surveillance possibilities. As Bode and Kristensen (2016) observe, understanding self-tracking as a market phenomenon with exploitative possibilities is imperative. Additionally, such repositories of personal data house the potential for discrimination and stigmatisation, including social shaming, denial of insurance and excluded employment opportunities, if people are designated as failing to comply with 'responsible' norms of behaviour (Andrejevic 2013; Lupton 2017). In addition to inclusion and social justice concerns, the possibilities of technologically facilitated abuse and control, especially for women, are heightened by the collection of personal and intimate data that can be shared and hacked.

For scholars in marketing and consumer research, a feminist surveillance studies research agenda examining self-tracking through digital technologies offers rich and diverse opportunities. By problematising self-tracking technologies as neutral, examinations of how such devices promote gendered inequalities and the potential for resistance are enabled. First, acknowledging that digital self-tracking technologies are overwhelmingly designed by men and may reproduce a male evaluative gaze or male normativity (Sanders 2017), research should seek to understand the assumptions and norms that underscore how bodies and selves are incorporated into product design and marketing processes and whether problematic gender norms are reproduced as a result. Second, and relatedly, researchers should be attentive to whether and in what ways women engage with self-tracking that are disconnected from their bodily experiences and sensations, how they navigate this, their affective engagements with such technologies and the broader implications for gendered subjectivities. Third, given the potential for self-tracking devices to intensify self-surveillance and adherence to normative and narrow ideals of feminine and masculine embodiment, how self-tracking promotes compliance with bodily norms and reproduces oppressive body projects should be further examined. Finally, resistance to self-tracking that promotes adherence to gendered norms and inequities warrants further consideration. This may encompass alternative uses of self-tracking devices or data, challenging self-responsibilised practices of dataveillance that promote particular body norms or ways in which visibility is gained for those marginalised and neglected in self-tracking cultures.

Surveillance and technologically mediated relationships

Consumers' most personal relationships have been invaded by surveillance, as modern social technologies allow individuals to collect data on one another (Krasnova et al. 2009). Surveillance appears in everyday social relationships—tracking a partner's spending through a mobile banking portal (Kutin, Reid, and Russell 2019); monitoring a teenager's activities through GPS tracing (Simpson 2014); swiping potential matches in a dating app (Ward 2016); and more. Digital technologies alter the power dynamics within social relationships by using the surveillant gaze as an intermediary for interpersonal communication, emotional control and visibility (van der Meulen and Heynen 2016). What was once a one-to-one relationship between individuals becomes transformed into a three-pronged relationship, where digital technologies act as throughways. Families, romantic partners, friends, co-workers and even strangers mediate their interactions through digital technologies, which are expressly designed to demarcate the boundaries of social relationships and convey relational meaning (Marwick and boyd 2014). However, feminist surveillance studies scholars suggest social technologies themselves are gendered, in addition to being shaped by and within existing gender norms and inequalities.

In conceptualising critical studies of 'the gaze' and 'the body,' early feminist theorists recognised the acts of looking, watching and observing as intertwined with and informed by gender (Bartky 1990; Bordo 2004; Mulvey 1975). Digital technologies afford novel forms of visibility, wherein consumers have the potential to both watch and be watched in a network of social surveillance (Albrechtslund 2008; Marwick 2012; Tokunaga 2015)). As an extension of Mathiesen's (1997)) conceptualisation of the "viewer society"—where the many watch the few (e.g., television)—modern social media enables the many to watch the many in relational and functional ways (Cammaerts 2015; Manning et al. 2017). Prior research suggests an awareness of being actively surveilled leads people to alter their behaviours (Helten and Fischer 2004; Norris and Armstrong 1999), and in a digital era, consumers are acutely aware of being watched by an 'imagined audience' (Marwick and boyd 2010).

Social media have amplified the ability to watch and be watched. As such, consumers turn to digital technologies to prepare their bodies and behaviours for viewing. Self-surveillance through disciplinary gendered practices is not a new endeavour. Bartky (1988) theorises control and self-surveillance as feminine practices, whereby women discipline their bodies at all times—such as applying make-up touch-ups throughout the day or monitoring caloric intake—in preparation for potential surveillance. Self-representation in digital spaces mirrors these gendered practices, as consumers prepare their bodies for viewing. Elias and Gill (2018) argue these "self-monitoring practices constitute the 'nano surveillance' of visual appearance (one's own and that of other women) as a normative practice." They theorise the rise of a 'surveillant sisterhood,' whereby women police other women through digital technologies. Gendered ideals suggest women are burdened with heightened cultural expectations of beauty and appearance (Bartky 1988). In a consumer culture driven by visual media, these gendered beauty ideals seep into technologically mediated relationships.

Modern consumers display a preoccupation with watching others through digital technologies as well as internalising this surveillant gaze, resulting in one's own behaviour modification. This may include using digital beautification filters to edit images (Eshiet 2020); untagging images deemed 'ugly' (Delise 2014); or even altering one's physical body through plastic surgery (Oranges et al. 2016), colloquially dubbed "Snapchat dysmorphia" (Brucculieri 2018). The digital marketplace supports these practices through the rise of mobile applications and software programmes to virtually augment one's image to be viewed. Beauty apps like FaceTune and Adobe Photoshop Express digitally afford consumers the tools to perfect their appearance, using technological filters, creating a source of visual capital (Gill 2019; Rajanala, Maymone, and Vashi 2018). All of these aesthetic practices are gendered, shaped by the cultural standards of beauty. These forms of surveillance manifest across social media, as users both purposefully prepare their own bodies and behaviours for viewing while also engaging in voyeuristic surveillance of others—constituting a means of monitoring social relationships and self-presentation.

The cultural labour of such practices is harnessed for economic means in industries predicated on watching and being watched—such as online celebrities and social media influencers. Modern technologies allow consumers to develop parasocial relationships with online personalities (Chung and Cho 2017) or to become micro-celebrities themselves (Khamis, Ang, and Welling 2017). Similar to traditionally gendered forms of feminised labour (e.g., flight attendants), new forms of work in influencer culture are largely dominated by women who must navigate 'trans-mediated parasocial relationships' marked by lateral surveillance (Abidin 2015; Andrejevic 2004; Wellman 2020). Surveillance as a means of bodily presentation has collided with capitalism, giving rise to new forms of sexualised labour in the marketplace (Drenten, Gurrieri, and Tyler

2020) whereby the 'watched bodies' can be monetised on platforms like OnlyFans and Patreon. Such contexts have been positioned as entrepreneurial endeavours and analysed through the lens of labour and self-presentation (Törhönen et al. 2019); however, a feminist surveillance lens draws attention to the power relations and systemic forms of discrimination reproduced through such 'watching' enabled platforms (van Doorn 2017). Being 'watched' online results in the reproductions of objectification practices through new digital architectures (Adam 2005)—all under the guise of entrepreneurial femininity (Duffy and Hund 2015). Moreover, visible surveillance through social media can induce policing and hatred—particularly for women and gender non-conforming individuals (Duffy, Miltner, and Wahlstedt 2020).

Challenges in managing online scrutiny from a real or imagined audience are exacerbated by the varying relational actors (e.g., future employers, family, friends) within an ecosystem of multiple social media platforms (e.g., LinkedIn, TikTok, Twitter). Duffy and Chan (2019) contend the diversity in followers and platforms prompts consumers to devise self-presentation strategies bounded by 'imagined surveillance.' Using mechanisms like privacy settings and pseudonymous online accounts, people manage these many relationships, recognising the surveillant gaze may vary depending on its source. In some ways, this practice is akin to digital code-switching where social media users change how they interact through social media, depending on the audience. Women are more likely to code-switch in digital settings (Ikhwanurrosida 2020), which reflects existing gendered pressures to adapt their language to normative expectations of linguistic hegemony, particularly among women of colour (Nelson 1990). For example, women use milder, less vulgar language than men in social media spaces (Thelwall 2008), reflecting cultural expectations of feminine respectability and decorum (Coates 2015). In the digital space, these pressures are exacerbated as technology-mediated interactions—verbal or otherwise—act as 'relational capsules' and constitute relational rituals that enact and reaffirm intimacy (Su 2016).

Public communication provides relational reassurance and strengthens social bonds (Drenten 2012). However, behind the scenes, technologically mediated relationships require careful negotiation of boundaries and expectations within digital spaces, as they interact with offline lives. For example, a teenager may be required to text a parent upon arrival at a friend's house, and failure to do so results in punishment. A similar "text me when you get home" practice is a common safety precaution among female friends (Schaefer 2019), particularly when women live alone or are out late at night. The practice reflects lay strategies women develop to protect themselves and other women, such as getting a friend to help ward off unwanted advances while socially drinking (Graham et al. 2017). In the digital age, technologies facilitate this friend-to-friend protection. For example, mobile apps like Circle of 6 and bSafe send location updates and alerts to friends if a person feels unsafe. Surveillance technologies, such as GPS tracking, are marketed as safety-enhancing, but they may be fraught with harmful elements of gendered social control. The pressure to be in "perpetual contact" can challenge personal boundaries within relationships (Katz and Aakhus 2002). Su's (2016) study of young romantic partners suggests the need for constant connection through mobile phones acts as a form of bodily control, where even momentary silence can lead to conflict and impatience. Romantic partners challenge personal boundaries even further through the use of spy software, cyberstalking or other forms of interpersonal electronic surveillance (IES) (Calman 2005; Lukacs and Quan-Haase 2015). Surveillant digital media mediates, coordinates and regulates gendered domestic violence in the context of online misogyny (Dragiewicz et al. 2018). Women and girls are frequently digitally tethered to men, meaning they are less likely to have administrative privileges or jurisdiction over their own social media account settings and passwords, and they experience heightened emotional effects of digital dating abuse (Reed, Tolman, and Ward 2016; Stonard et al. 2015).

These tensions in relational control are evident within homes and among families. The modern home is a data factory, fortified with surveillant technologies—security systems (e.g., Ring), baby monitors (e.g., Owlet), entertainment systems (e.g., Netflix), cleaning products (e.g., Roomba) and voice-activated home management technologies (e.g., Google Home, Amazon Echo) (Maalsen and Sadowski 2019; Pridmore et al. 2019). All of these technologies promise simplified, streamlined, efficient management of domestic labour—much of which is rooted in gendered household expectations (Breen and Cooke 2005; Coskuner-Balli and Thompson 2013). Even home devices themselves—such as Apple's Siri and Amazon's Alexa—are gendered as feminine robots in what Strengers and Kennedy (2020) dub the 'smart wife': virtual helpers designed to replicate the 1950s housewife exemplar. They adopt feminine voices and mirror feminine tasks, reinforcing perceptions that a woman's place is in the home. These devices may even become proxies for social relationships. For example, anthropomorphic products mitigate social exclusion as consumers turn to 'smart products,' such as Roomba automated cleaning devices and iPhone-based Siri personal assistants (Mourey, Olson, and Yoon 2017).

Technologies are inserted into the rituals, identities and functioning of the modern family. The intersection of the home, family life and digital advances has given rise to the 'domestic panopticon' where digital nurturing and safety are enabled through surveillant technologies (Boesen, Rode, and Mancini 2010). However, this undermines trust—both in oneself and one another. For example, parents turn to technologies like a crib embedded with smart sensors and biometric devices for tracking their infants' heart rate and oxygen. These technologies have normalised intense 'intimate surveillance' with the promise peace of mind but at the cost of parents' trust in their own abilities (Leaver 2017). Further, trust between family members can be eroded as technologies allow family members to monitor the activities of one another. Parents can track what their children watch on YouTube or check a home security camera to verify a child's curfew. But surveilling family members in these seemingly protective ways has oppressive implications for power dynamics. For example, spouses may monitor their partners' online activity (Helsper and Whitty 2010), and the practice of downloading surveillance software on shared marital computers can constitute a modern form of spousal abuse (Calman 2005).

In approaching technologically mediated relationship through the lens of feminist surveillance studies, technologies should not be viewed as neutral. Instead scholars should explore consumers' practices of and resistance to social control within relationships—real or imagined. First, research is needed in the realm of self-presentation and the imagined audience. Feminist surveillance studies lends itself to questions of how the marketplace is used to prepare bodies and behaviours for viewing and how self-presentation is modified with an awareness of being watched. Feminist scholars should be particularly attentive to the gendered ideals that shape appearance and codify interactions as gender appropriate. Second, marketing scholars are equipped to examine how transactional relationships emerge and evolve based on lateral surveillance. That is, a fruitful pathway for future research lies in exploring the new economies driven by the surveillant gaze and implications of capitalism as it intersects with gendered buying and the selling of gendered bodies. Third, technologically mediated relationships are bounded by normative strategies, expectations, and tensions in social control, particularly within the home or within close relationships. Surveillant devices are designed to afford interactions among family members, often marketed on the premise of safety or intimacy, but what does this mean for power, oppression and privacy? A feminist lens highlights possibilities for abuse and control, specifically coercive forms of control that may facilitate abusive relationships.

Surveillance and the categorisation of consumers

The rise of surveillance capitalism is explicitly linked to the commodification of individuals' data for predicting consumption behaviours based on categorisation (Zuboff 2019). Categorising consumers is fundamental to marketing practice and its preoccupation with personalisation and market segmentation, or dividing a heterogeneous market into homogeneous groups of consumers (Foedermayr and Diamantopoulos 2008; Kotras 2020; Smith 1956). Market segmentation is presented as a necessary business strategy to better meet the needs of consumers, predict their future marketplace behaviours and effectively allocate marketing dollars (Yankelovich and Meer 2006). The principle driving market segmentation is that people may be treated differently based on their aggregate categorisation. But classifying consumers into sorted groups blurs the line between differentiated marketing and discriminatory marketing. Indeed, a marketplace in which consumers are under constant scrutiny reflects masculine, paternalistic and voyeuristic control logic. In contrast, a feminist surveillance studies perspective calls us to question how consumers come to be organised and valued through data-generated profiles.

Developments in digital technologies, the proliferation of Big Data and increased corporate tracking of consumers have amplified the categorisation of individuals into groups (Pridmore and Zwick 2011)—distilling their lives to bits of sortable code or 'data doubles' (Haggerty and Ericson 2003, p. 611). The emergent surveillant assemblage is marked by "the progressive 'disappearance of disappearance'" (Haggerty and Ericson 2003, p. 619)—wherein individual consumers are increasingly known and institutionally monitored, with little opportunity to escape large-scale surveillance (Fuchs 2011b). Marketers herald always-on surveillance as a form of consumer empowerment, by which consumers' choices are better because of highly sophisticated categorisation (Darmody and Zwick 2020). That is, consumers can make better choices—from movies on Netflix to household goods on Amazon—because online surveillance mechanisms "know precisely what consumers want and when they want it" (Darmody and Zwick 2020, p. 7). But this empowered form of personalised marketplace choices comes at the loss of anonymity. Anonymity provides freedom from surveillance and thereby freedom from judgement based on income, education, race, gender, religion, age and so on (Donath 1999). Panoptic methods are used to constantly and systematically surveil consumers' bodies, backgrounds and behaviours, thus placing value on consumer activity (Arvidsson 2003)—value that is imbued with cultural stereotypes, tropes and meanings. Indeed, the algorithms used to categorise individuals into market segments or to personalise marketplace offerings can reflect and reproduce biases. For example, in some languages Google Translate auto-corrects "she is a doctor" to "he is a doctor" (Douglas 2017), and Apple came under fire with allegations that the algorithm behind its credit card offered lower limits to women versus men of the same financial means (Knight 2019).

Lyon (2003) coins the term social sorting to describe the coding and classification of people into aggregate groups using raw data. He notes "surveillance today sorts people into categories, assigning worth or risk, in ways that have real effects on their lifechances. Deep discrimination occurs, thus making surveillance not merely a matter of personal privacy but of social justice" (Lyon 2003, p. 1). In the digital age, data doubles are merely representational amalgams of consumers' real-world embodiments, but this blurry line between real human and categorised data can overlook the "real, visceral, and devastating" effects of data science (Stark and Hoffmann 2019, p. 19). Categorising consumers through data flows influences and affects the choices and opportunities afforded to individual consumers (Lyon 2003). Danna and Gandy (2002) use the term "weblining" to describe the process by which consumers may be denied certain goods and services based on their categorical online profiles. It can lead to discrimination in credit or insurance offered, discriminatory dynamic pricing (e.g., airline tickets, rental cars), denial of bank loans and denial of health insurance. Weblining functions to target consumers in predatory ways. For example, research on the harmful use of Big Data finds invisible scoring mechanisms are employed to predict and suggest predatory services (e.g., payday loans, online for-profit universities) significantly impact on low-income consumers of colour (Yu et al. 2014).

The potential effect of categorisation schemes operates at a level of deterministic social control (Bentham 1995)—broadly categorising consumers as 'good' or 'bad' (Foss and Bond 2005). For example, in the United States economic system, credit scores are indicators of customer buying power and financial reliability. Credit scores inherently categorise consumers into 'good' or 'bad' classifications, based on their credit scores. While these scores are attributed to self-management, in line with the quantified self previously discussed, the categorisation schemes are culturally determined by credit bureaus and corporate surveillance—and reproduce gendered economic inequalities. Research suggests women spend less and have less debt, but on average, have lower credit scores relative to men (Henderson et al. 2015). Thus, women's access to the marketplace is limited by being categorised as 'bad' consumers with regard to credit. Such categorisation exploits non-normative, non-conforming consumers. This good-bad binary is further reflected in rating systems and personal profiles on digital platforms, which exacerbate the discriminatory ways in which consumers are organised and valued through surveillant technologies. For example, the rise of digital platform economy (Srnicek 2017) and gig-based mobile applications (Schor 2020) such as Airbnb, Uber and Postmates calls for often reciprocal rating of the service provider and the customer. Coupled with a user's profile, these ratings act as a form of categorisation to distinguish the 'good' actors from the 'bad.' Such categorisation mechanisms are meant to establish trust; however, surveillance technologies used to categorise bodies are rooted in a history of hyperpolicing and racist surveillance structures. For example, on the home rental platform Airbnb, non-Black hosts charge Black renters approximately 12% more than Black hosts (Edelman and Luca 2014) and Black consumers are less likely to be accepted for rentals (Edelman, Luca, and Svirsky 2017). These technologies are built on the premise of mutual service provider-consumer ratings, and lower ratings place an individual in a particular category of access. Wang (2020) dubs this 'algorithmic sociality,' that is, consumers are "measured and calculated based on algorithmically filtered information." Surveillant technologies amplify the sexist and racist tensions that are already threaded through the social contexts in which they operate (e.g., services industry).

Data mining can further divorce the extracted information from its original context (Moor 1990) and predictive models fed by surveillance data inherently reproduce past patterns (Conrad 2009). Categorisations of groups based on gender and other stereotypical features (e.g., class, race, ethnicity, age) function as a form of discrimination by assigning differential value to different target markets (Pager and Shepherd 2008). Marginalised populations continue to be unjustly denied equal access to services. For example, a 2019 study found evidence of significant racial bias in a health risk-prediction algorithm used on over 200 million people in the United States (Obermeyer et al. 2019). The algorithm falsely led hospitals and insurance providers to conclude chronically ill Black patients did not need high-risk care, when in fact they did. A caveat is that these surveillance-based categorisation schemes are not static. Relative to marketing databases of the past, modern digital technologies and categorisation algorithms reflexively shape the marketplace as users interact with them. Algorithms are dynamic processes designed and implemented by humans in conjunction with technical affordances and within broader political, social and cultural environments that are shaped by the continual interactions of strategies, structures and tactics (Willson 2017). Google, arguably the largest search engine in the world, works on the premise of keyword searches. These keywords fundamentally serve as shorthand categorisation schemes, devised through back-end algorithms and front-end user input. Google is constantly surveilling its users, learning and classifying results. Noble's (2018) work on the oppressive nature of Google algorithms demonstrates how search engines reproduce historical and cultural discrimination against women. For example, a search for 'black girls' results in hypersexualised and stereotypical content, while a search for 'college professor' results in archetypal images of older white men. That is, biases creep into the allegedly neutral search results—and feed those biases back to consumers. This manifests in the development of new technologies such as policing apps, facial recognition software and the use of AI in healthcare.

Through data sorting, data mining and new technology development, surveillance operates as a gendered mechanism to reproduce differences and the discriminatory biases associated with those differences. Highlighting the various ways in which categorisation filters into marketing strategy, a feminist surveillance studies perspective opens new pathways for research. First, scholars must problematise categorisation-driven marketing practices, such as market segmentation, personalisation, behavioural tracking. Long-held beliefs have championed such practices as empowering for consumers and effective for companies, but these beliefs overshadow the unethical and discriminatory ways that large-scale categorisation methods are harnessed to the detriment of access and inclusivity in the marketplace. Future research should question the masculine, paternalistic logic which serves as the foundation for market-based surveillance and explore how these practices of categorisation surveillance applied to virtual bodies in the digital space manifest in real-world ways. Second, methods of social sorting allow companies to categorise consumers as 'good' or 'bad.' However, a feminist view calls us to interrogate the social construction of moralised consumer categories. Future research must recognise any attempts made to categorise consumers on the premise of morality are inherently rooted in injustice and historically racist, heterosexist beliefs. Scholarship is needed to further understand the ways in which surveillance technologies and Big Data amplify existing biases in who the data represent. Third, interrogating how the biases get put back into the development of new technologies for categorisation could provide novel insights in understanding the reproduction of oppressive gendered discourses. A feminist perspective of surveillance suggests we examine how exclusion is generated through the development of new modes of categorisation. Similarly, consumer resistance towards and subversion of surveillant categorisation "epitomises the logic of the 'right to hide', a right to become non-existent and invisible to institutions" (Monahan 2015, p. 168)—including hiding from marketplace actors (e.g., companies, governments, other consumers). The strategies and technologies consumers use to elude surveillance are of interest.

Conclusion

This chapter has examined the elisions in consumer culture between digital technologies and surveillance and the importance of understanding the arising gendered implications. By drawing on the emerging field of feminist surveillance studies, an intersectional critical feminist perspective problematises a conception of technologies as 'neutral' and opens up examinations of how privilege and oppression come to operate through the use of surveillance practices and technologies that reproduce inequalities (Dubrofsky and Magnet 2015). We have identified three key conversations—surveillance and the tracking of selves through technology; surveillance and technologically mediated relationships; and surveillance and the categorisation of consumers—across which we have examined the gendered implications of digital technology consumption intensifying tracking and monitoring in our lives. Finally, we have proposed a feminist surveillance studies research agenda to further unpack the intersections of gender, surveillance and digital consumer culture. As digital technologies evolve, so do the capacities for surveillance that operate in highly gendered ways. We call upon scholars in marketing and consumer research to attend to this as a feminist priority with important consequences for our understanding of gender, technology and the marketplace.

References

Abidin, Crystal. 2015. "Communicative ♥ Intimacies: Influencers and Perceived Interconnectedness." *Ada: A Journal of Gender, New Media & Technology* November. https://adanewmedia.org/2015/11/issue8-abidin/.

Adam, Alison. 2005. "Internet Dating, Cyberstalking and Internet Pornography: Gender and the Gaze." In *Gender, Ethics and Information Technology*, edited by Alison Adam, 102–127. London: Palgrave Macmillan. https://doi.org/10.1057/9780230000520_6.

Albrechtslund, Anders. 2008. "Online Social Networking as Participatory Surveillance." *First Monday* 13 (March). https://doi.org/10.5210/fm.v13i3.2142.

Andrejevic, Mark. 2004. "The Work of Watching One Another: Lateral Surveillance, Risk, and Governance." *Surveillance & Society* 2 (4). https://doi.org/10.24908/ss.v2i4.3359.

———. 2013. *Infoglut: How Too Much Information Is Changing the Way We Think and Know*. Routledge. https://doi.org/10.4324/9780203075319.

Arvidsson, Adam. 2003. "On the 'Pre-History of The Panoptic Sort': Mobility in Market Research." *Surveillance & Society* 1 (4). https://doi.org/10.24908/ss.v1i4.3331.

Bartky, Sanda Lee. 1988. "Foucault, Femininity and the Modernization of Patriarchal Power." In *Feminism and Foucault: Reflections on Resistance*, edited by Irene Diamond and Lee Quinby, 94–111. Boston, MA: Northeastern University Press.

Bartky, Sandra Lee. 1990. *Femininity and Domination: Studies in the Phenomenology of Oppression*. New York: Psychology Press.

Bauman, Zygmunt, and David Lyon. 2013. *Liquid Surveillance: A Conversation*. Vol. 1. Aufl. Polity Conversations Series. Oxford: Polity Press.

Bentham, Jeremy. 1995. *The Panopticon Writings*. Edited by Miran Božovič. Second Edition. London: Verso.

Bode, Matthias, and Dorthe Brogaard Kristensen. 2016. "The Digital Doppelgänger within: A Study on Self-Tracking and the Quantified Self Movement." In *Assembling Consumption: Researching Actors, Networks and Markets*, edited by Robin Canniford and Domen Bajde, 119–35. New York: Routledge.

Boesen, Julie, Jennifer A. Rode, and Clara Mancini. 2010. "The Domestic Panopticon: Location Tracking in Families." In *Proceedings of the 12th ACM International Conference on Ubiquitous Computing*, 65–74. UbiComp '10. New York: Association for Computing Machinery. https://doi.org/10.1145/1864349.1864382.

Bordo, Susan. 2004. *Unbearable Weight: Feminism, Western Culture, and the Body*. Berkeley: University of California Press.

Boyd, Danah, and Alice E. Marwick. 2011. *Social Privacy in Networked Publics: Teens' Attitudes, Practices, and Strategies*. SSRN Scholarly Paper ID 1925128. Rochester, NY: Social Science Research Network. https://papers.ssrn.com/abstract=1925128.

Breen, Richard, and Lynn Prince Cooke. 2005. "The Persistence of the Gendered Division of Domestic Labour." *European Sociological Review* 21 (1): 43–57. https://doi.org/10.1093/esr/jci003.

Brucculieri, Julia. 2018. "'Snapchat Dysmorphia' Points to a Troubling New Trend in Plastic Surgery." *HuffPost*, February 22. https://www.huffpost.com/entry/snapchat-dysmorphia_n_5a8d8168e4b0273053a680f6.

Calman, Camille. 2005. "Spy vs. Spouse: Regulating Surveillance Software on Shared Marital Computers." *Columbia Law Review* 105: 2097.

Cammaerts, Bart. 2015. "Social Media and Activism." In *The International Encyclopedia of Digital Communication and Society*, 1–8. American Cancer Society. https://doi.org/10.1002/9781118767771.wbiedcs083.

Charitsis, Vassilis, Anna Fyrberg Yngfalk, and Per Skålén. 2019. "'Made to Run': Biopolitical Marketing and the Making of the Self-Quantified Runner:" *Marketing Theory*. https://doi.org/10.1177/1470593118799794.

Chung, Siyoung, and Hichang Cho. 2017. "Fostering Parasocial Relationships with Celebrities on Social Media: Implications for Celebrity Endorsement." *Psychology & Marketing* 34 (4): 481–495. https://doi.org/10.1002/mar.21001.

Coates, Jennifer. 2015. *Women, Men and Language: A Sociolinguistic Account of Gender Differences in Language*. London: Routledge.

Conrad, Kathryn. 2009. "Surveillance, Gender, and the Virtual Body in the Information Age." *Surveillance & Society* 6 (4): 380–387. https://doi.org/10.24908/ss.v6i4.3269.

Coskuner-Balli, Gokcen, and Craig J. Thompson. 2013. "The Status Costs of Subordinate Cultural Capital: At-Home Fathers' Collective Pursuit of Cultural Legitimacy through Capitalizing Consumption Practices." *Journal of Consumer Research* 40 (1): 19–41. https://doi.org/10.1086/668640.

Daniels, Jessie. 2009. "Rethinking Cyberfeminism(s): Race, Gender, and Embodiment." *Women's Studies Quarterly* 37 (1/2): 101–124.

Danna, Anthony, and Oscar H. Gandy. 2002. "All That Glitters Is Not Gold: Digging Beneath the Surface of Data Mining." *Journal of Business Ethics* 40 (4): 373–386. https://doi.org/10.1023/A:1020845814009.

Darmody, Aron, and Detlev Zwick. 2020. "Manipulate to Empower: Hyper-Relevance and the Contradictions of Marketing in the Age of Surveillance Capitalism." *Big Data & Society* 7 (1): 2053951720904112. https://doi.org/10.1177/2053951720904112.

Datta, Anisha, and Indranil Chakraborty. 2018. "Are You Neoliberal Fit? The Politics of Consumption under Neoliberalism." In *The Sage Handbook of Consumer Culture*, edited by Olga Kravets, Pauline Maclaran, Steven Miles and Alladi Venkatesh, 453–477. London: Sage.

Deleuze, Gilles. 1992. "Postscript on the Societies of Control." 59: 3–7.

Delise, Nathalie N. 2014. "How Do You Facebook? The Gendered Characteristics of Online Interaction." In *Illuminating How Identities, Stereotypes and Inequalities Matter through Gender Studies*, edited by D. Nicole Farris, Mary Ann Davis, and D'Lane R. Compton, 9–27. Dordrecht: Springer Netherlands. https://doi.org/10.1007/978-94-017-8718-5_2.

Didžiokaitė, Gabija, Paula Saukko, and Christian Greiffenhagen. 2018. "The Mundane Experience of Everyday Calorie Trackers: Beyond the Metaphor of Quantified Self." *New Media & Society* 20 (4): 1470–1487. https://doi.org/10.1177/1461444817698478.

Dijck, Jose van. 2014. "Datafication, Dataism and Dataveillance: Big Data between Scientific Paradigm and Ideology." *Surveillance & Society* 12 (2): 197–208. https://doi.org/10.24908/ss.v12i2.4776.

Donath, Judith. 1999. "Identity and Deception in the Virtual Community." In *Communities in Cyberspace*, edited by Peter Kollock and Marc A. Smith, 29–59. London: Routledge.

Doorn, Niels van. 2017. "Platform Labor: On the Gendered and Racialized Exploitation of Low-Income Service Work in the 'on-Demand' Economy." *Information, Communication & Society* 20 (6): 898–914. https://doi.org/10.1080/1369118X.2017.1294194.

Douglas, Laura. 2017. "AI Is Not Just Learning Our Biases; It Is Amplifying Them." *Medium*, December 10. https://medium.com/@laurahelendouglas/ai-is-not-just-learning-our-biases-it-is-amplifying-them-4d0dee75931d.

Dragiewicz, Molly, Jean Burgess, Ariadna Matamoros-Fernández, Michael Salter, Nicolas P. Suzor, Delanie Woodlock, and Bridget Harris. 2018. "Technology Facilitated Coercive Control: Domestic Violence and the Competing Roles of Digital Media Platforms." *Feminist Media Studies* 18 (4): 609–625. https://doi.org/10.1080/14680777.2018.1447341.

Drenten, Jenna. 2012. "Snapshots of the Self: Exploring the Role of Online Mobile Photo Sharing in Identity Development Among Adolescent Girls." In *Online Consumer Behavior: Theory and Research in Social Media, Advertising, and E-Tail*, edited by Angeline Close, 3–34. New York: Routledge.

Drenten, Jenna, Lauren Gurrieri, and Meagan Tyler. 2020. "Sexualized Labour in Digital Culture: Instagram Influencers, Porn Chic and the Monetization of Attention." *Gender, Work & Organization* 27 (1): 41–66. https://doi.org/10.1111/gwao.12354.

Dubrofsky, Rachel E., and Shoshana Amielle Magnet. 2015. *Feminist Surveillance Studies*. Durham, NC: Duke University Press. https://www.dukeupress.edu/feminist-surveillance-studies.

Dubrofsky, Rachel E., and Megan Wood. 2015. "Gender, Race, and Authenticity: Celebrity Women Tweeting for the Gaze." In *Feminist Surveillance Studies*, edited by Rachel E. Dubrofsky, and Megan Wood, 93–106. Durham, NC: Duke University Press.

DuFault, Beth Leavenworth, and John W. Schouten. 2020. "Self-Quantification and the Datapreneurial Consumer Identity." *Consumption Markets & Culture* 23 (3): 290–316. https://doi.org/10.1080/10253866.2018.1519489.

Duffy, Brooke Erin, and Ngai Keung Chan. 2019. "'You Never Really Know Who's Looking': Imagined Surveillance across Social Media Platforms." *New Media & Society* 21 (1): 119–138. https://doi.org/10.1177/1461444818791318.

Duffy, Brooke Erin, and Emily Hund. 2015. "'Having It All' on Social Media: Entrepreneurial Femininity and Self-Branding Among Fashion Bloggers." *Social Media + Society* 1 (2): 2056305115604337. https://doi.org/10.1177/2056305115604337.

Duffy, Brooke Erin, Kate Miltner, and Amanda Wahlstedt. 2020. "Policing 'Fake' Femininity: Anger and Accusation in Influencer 'Hateblog' Communities." In *AoIR Selected Papers of Internet Research*. https://doi.org/10.5210/spir.v2020i0.11204.

Edelman, Benjamin G., and Michael Luca. 2014. "Digital Discrimination: The Case of Airbnb. Com." *Harvard Business School Working Paper Summaries*, January. http://hbswk.hbs.edu/item/digital-discrimination-the-case-of-airbnb-com.

Edelman, Benjamin, Michael Luca, and Dan Svirsky. 2017. "Racial Discrimination in the Sharing Economy: Evidence from a Field Experiment." *American Economic Journal: Applied Economics* 9 (2): 1–22. https://doi.org/10.1257/app.20160213.

Elias, Ana Sofia, and Rosalind Gill. 2018. "Beauty Surveillance: The Digital Self-Monitoring Cultures of Neoliberalism." *European Journal of Cultural Studies* 21 (1): 59–77. https://doi.org/10.1177/1367549417705604.

Eshiet, Janella. 2020. "'Real Me Versus Social Media Me:' Filters Snapchat Dysmorphia, and Beauty Perceptions among Young Women." Thesis, California State University, San Bernadino. https://scholarworks.lib.csusb.edu/etd/1101.

Foedermayr, Eva K., and Adamantios Diamantopoulos. 2008. "Market Segmentation in Practice: Review of Empirical Studies, Methodological Assessment, and Agenda for Future Research." *Journal of Strategic Marketing* 16 (3): 223–265. https://doi.org/10.1080/09652540802117140.

Foss, Bryan, and Alison Bond. 2005. "Privacy, Risk and Good and Bad Consumers." *Journal of Database Marketing & Customer Strategy Management* 13 (1): 10–23. https://doi.org/10.1057/palgrave.dbm.3240275.

Foucault, Michel. 1979. *Discipline and Punish: The Birth of the Prison*. New York: Random House.

Fuchs, Christian. 2011a. "New Media, Web 2.0 and Surveillance." *Sociology Compass* 5 (2): 134–147. https://doi.org/10.1111/j.1751-9020.2010.00354.x.

———. 2011b. "Web 2.0, Prosumption, and Surveillance." *Surveillance & Society* 8 (3): 288–309. https://doi.org/10.24908/ss.v8i3.4165.

Galič, Maša, Tjerk Timan, and Bert-Jaap Koops. 2017. "Bentham, Deleuze and Beyond: An Overview of Surveillance Theories from the Panopticon to Participation." *Philosophy & Technology* 30 (1): 9–37. https://doi.org/10.1007/s13347-016-0219-1.

Gill, Rosalind. 2019. "Surveillance Is a Feminist Issue." In *The Routledge Handbook of Contemporary Feminism*, edited by Tasha Oren and Andrea Press, 1st ed., 148–161. Routledge. https://doi.org/10.4324/9781315728346-10.

Graham, Kathryn, Sharon Bernards, Antonia Abbey, Tara M. Dumas, and Samantha Wells. 2017. "When Women Do Not Want It: Young Female Bargoers' Experiences With and Responses to Sexual Harassment in Social Drinking Contexts." *Violence Against Women* 23 (12): 1419–1441. https://doi.org/10.1177/1077801216661037.

Haggerty, Kevin D., and Richard V. Ericson. 2000. "The Surveillant Assemblage." *The British Journal of Sociology* 51 (4): 605–622. https://doi.org/10.1080/00071310020015280.

———. 2003. "The Surveillant Assemblage." *The British Journal of Sociology* 51 (4): 605–622. https://doi.org/10.1080/00071310020015280.

Hansen, Mark. 2012. *Bodies in Code: Interfaces with Digital Media*. London: Taylor and Francis. https://doi.org/10.4324/9780203942390.

Haraway, Donna. 1985. "A Manifesto for Cyborgs: Science, Technology, and Socialist Feminism in the 1980s." *Socialist Review* 80: 65–108. https://doi.org/10.1080/08164649.1987.9961538.

Helsper, Ellen J., and Monica T. Whitty. 2010. "Netiquette within Married Couples: Agreement about Acceptable Online Behavior and Surveillance between Partners." *Computers in Human Behavior* 26 (5): 916–926. https://doi.org/10.1016/j.chb.2010.02.006.

Helten, Frank, and Bernd Fischer. 2004. "Reactive Attention: Video Surveillance in Berlin Shopping Malls." *Surveillance & Society* 2 (2/3). https://doi.org/10.24908/ss.v2i2/3.3381.

Henderson, Loren, Cedric Herring, Hayward Derrick Horton, and Melvin Thomas. 2015. "Credit Where Credit Is Due?: Race, Gender, and Discrimination in the Credit Scores of Business Startups." *The Review of Black Political Economy* 42 (4): 459–479. https://doi.org/10.1007/s12114-015-9215-4.

Hepworth, Katherine. 2019. "A Panopticon on My Wrist: The Biopower of Big Data Visualization for Wearables." *Design and Culture* 11 (3): 323–344. https://doi.org/10.1080/17547075.2019.1661723.

Ikhwanurrosida, Rahmatya. 2020. "Code-Switching and Code-Mixing by Male and Female Users of WhatsApp." Thesis, Universitas Negeri Malang. http://mulok.library.um.ac.id/index3.php/94304.html.

Katz, James E., and Mark Aakhus. 2002. *Perpetual Contact: Mobile Communication, Private Talk, Public Performance*. Cambridge: Cambridge University Press.

Khamis, Susie, Lawrence Ang, and Raymond Welling. 2017. "Self-Branding, 'Micro-Celebrity' and the Rise of Social Media Influencers." *Celebrity Studies* 8 (2): 191–208. https://doi.org/10.1080/19392397.2016.1218292.

Knight, Will. 2019. "Researchers Want Guardrails to Help Prevent Bias in AI." *Wired*, November 21, 2019. https://www.wired.com/story/researchers-guardrails-prevent-bias-ai/.

Kotras, Baptiste. 2020. "Mass Personalization: Predictive Marketing Algorithms and the Reshaping of Consumer Knowledge." *Big Data & Society* 7 (2): 2053951720951581. https://doi.org/10.1177/2053951720951581.

Krasnova, Hanna, Oliver Günther, Sarah Spiekermann, and Ksenia Koroleva. 2009. "Privacy Concerns and Identity in Online Social Networks." *Identity in the Information Society* 2 (1): 39–63. https://doi.org/10.1007/s12394-009-0019-1.

Kutin, Jozica Johanna, Mike Reid, and Roslyn Russell. 2019. "What Is This Thing Called Money? Economic Abuse in Young Adult Relationships." *Journal of Social Marketing* 9 (1): 111–28. https://doi.org/10.1108/JSOCM-03-2018-0028.

Leaver, Tama. 2017. "Intimate Surveillance: Normalizing Parental Monitoring and Mediation of Infants Online." *Social Media + Society* 3 (2): 2056305117707192. https://doi.org/10.1177/2056305117707192.

Lukacs, Veronika, and Anabel Quan-Haase. 2015. "Romantic Breakups on Facebook: New Scales for Studying Post-Breakup Behaviors, Digital Distress, and Surveillance." *Information, Communication & Society* 18 (5): 492–508. https://doi.org/10.1080/1369118X.2015.1008540.

Lupton, Deborah. 2014. *Digital Sociology*, 1st ed. Abingdon, Oxon: Routledge.

———. 2015. "Quantified Sex: A Critical Analysis of Sexual and Reproductive Self-Tracking Using Apps." *Culture, Health & Sexuality* 17 (4): 440–453. https://doi.org/10.1080/13691058.2014.920528.

———. 2016a. *The Quantified Self*. Cambridge, MA: Polity Press. https://www.wiley.com/en-au/The+Quantified+Self-p-9781509500598.

———. 2016b. "The Diverse Domains of Quantified Selves: Self-Tracking Modes and Dataveillance." *Economy and Society* 45 (1): 101–122. https://doi.org/10.1080/03085147.2016.1143726.

———. 2017. "Self-Tracking, Health and Medicine." *Health Sociology Review* 26 (1): 1–5. https://doi.org/10.1080/14461242.2016.1228149.

———. 2019. "'It's Made Me a Lot More Aware': A New Materialist Analysis of Health Self-Tracking." *Media International Australia* 171 (1): 66–79. https://doi.org/10.1177/1329878X19844042.

Lyall, Ben, and Brady Robards. 2018. "Tool, Toy and Tutor: Subjective Experiences of Digital Self-Tracking." *Journal of Sociology* 54 (1): 108–124. https://doi.org/10.1177/1440783317722854.

Lyon, David. 2001. *Surveillance Society: Monitoring Everyday Life*. London: Open University Press.

———. 2003. *Surveillance as Social Sorting: Privacy, Risk, and Digital Discrimination*. New York: Routledge.

Maalsen, Sophia, and Jathan Sadowski. 2019. "The Smart Home on FIRE: Amplifying and Accelerating Domestic Surveillance." *Surveillance & Society* 17 (1/2): 118–124. https://doi.org/10.24908/ss.v17i1/2.12925.

Manning, Nathan, Ruth Penfold-Mounce, Brian D. Loader, Ariadne Vromen, and Michael Xenos. 2017. "Politicians, Celebrities and Social Media: A Case of Informalisation?" *Journal of Youth Studies* 20 (2): 127–144. https://doi.org/10.1080/13676261.2016.1206867.

Marwick, Alice. 2012. "The Public Domain: Surveillance in Everyday Life." *Surveillance & Society* 9 (4): 378–393. https://doi.org/10.24908/ss.v9i4.4342.

Marwick, Alice E., and Danah Boyd. 2010. "I Tweet Honestly, I Tweet Passionately: Twitter Users, Context Collapse, and the Imagined Audience." *New Media & Society* 13 (1): 114–133. https://doi.org/10.1177/1461444810365313.

Marwick, Alice E, and Danah Boyd. 2014. "Networked Privacy: How Teenagers Negotiate Context in Social Media." *New Media & Society* 16 (7): 1051–1067. https://doi.org/10.1177/1461444814543995.

Mathiesen, Thomas. 1997. "The Viewer Society: Michel Foucault's `Panopticon' Revisited." *Theoretical Criminology* 1 (2): 215–34. https://doi.org/10.1177/1362480697001002003.

Meulen, Emily van der, and Robert Heynen. 2016. *Expanding the Gaze: Gender and the Politics of Surveillance*. Toronto: University of Toronto Press.

Monahan, Torin. 2015. "The Right to Hide? Anti-Surveillance Camouflage and the Aestheticization of Resistance." *Communication and Critical/Cultural Studies* 12 (2): 159–178. https://doi.org/10.1080/14791420.2015.1006646.

Moor, James H. 1990. "Ethics of Privacy Protection." *Library Trends* 39 (1 & 2): 69–82.

Mourey, James A., Jenny G. Olson, and Carolyn Yoon. 2017. "Products as Pals: Engaging with Anthropomorphic Products Mitigates the Effects of Social Exclusion." *Journal of Consumer Research* 44 (2): 414–431. https://doi.org/10.1093/jcr/ucx038.

Mulvey, Laura. 1975. "Visual Pleasure and Narrative Cinema." *Screen* 16 (3): 6–18. https://doi.org/10.1093/screen/16.3.6.

Nafus, Dawn, and Jamie Sherman. 2014. "Big Data, Big Questions|This One Does Not Go Up To 11: The Quantified Self Movement as an Alternative Big Data Practice." *International Journal of Communication* 8 (0): 11.

Nakamura, Lisa. 2002. *Cybertypes: Race, Ethnicity, and Identity on the Internet*. New York: Routledge.

———. 2015. "Afterword: Blaming, Shaming, and the Feminization of Social Media," May. https://doi.org/10.1215/9780822375463-013.

Nelson, Linda Williamson. 1990. "Code-Switching in the Oral Life Narratives of African-American Women: Challenges to Linguistic Hegemony." *Journal of Education* 172 (3): 142–155. https://doi.org/10.1177/002205749017200310.

Noble, Safiya Umoja. 2018. *Algorithms of Oppression: How Search Engines Reinforce Racism*. New York: NYU Press.

Norris, Clive, and Gary Armstrong. 1999. *The Maximum Surveillance Society: The Rise of CCTV*. London: Bloomsbury Publishing. https://www.bloomsbury.com/uk/the-maximum-surveillance-society-9781847881069/.

Nouraie-Simone, Fereshteh. 2005. *On Shifting Ground: Muslim Women in the Global Era*. New York: The Feminist Press.

Obermeyer, Ziad, Brian Powers, Christine Vogeli, and Sendhil Mullainathan. 2019. "Dissecting Racial Bias in an Algorithm Used to Manage the Health of Populations." *Science* 366 (6464): 447–453. https://doi.org/10.1126/science.aax2342.

Oranges, Carlo M., Kristin M. Schaefer, Andreas Gohritz, Martin Haug, and Dirk J. Schaefer. 2016. "The Mirror Effect on Social Media Self-Perceived Beauty and Its Implications for Cosmetic Surgery." *Plastic and Reconstructive Surgery Global Open* 4 (11). https://doi.org/10.1097/GOX.0000000000001088.

Pager, Devah, and Hana Shepherd. 2008. "The Sociology of Discrimination: Racial Discrimination in Employment, Housing, Credit, and Consumer Markets." *Annual Review of Sociology* 34 (1): 181–209. https://doi.org/10.1146/annurev.soc.33.040406.131740.

Pantzar, Mika, and Minna Ruckenstein. 2015. "The Heart of Everyday Analytics: Emotional, Material and Practical Extensions in Self-Tracking Market." *Consumption Markets & Culture* 18 (1): 92–109. https://doi.org/10.1080/10253866.2014.899213.

Pridmore, Jason, Michael Zimmer, Jessica Vitak, Anouk Mols, Daniel Trottier, Priya C. Kumar, and Yuting Liao. 2019. "Intelligent Personal Assistants and the Intercultural Negotiations of Dataveillance in Platformed Households." *Surveillance & Society* 17 (1/2): 125–131. https://doi.org/10.24908/ss.v17i1/2.12936.

Pridmore, Jason, and Detlev Zwick. 2011. "Editorial—Marketing and the Rise of Commercial Consumer Surveillance." *Surveillance & Society* 8 (3): 269–277. https://doi.org/10.24908/ss.v8i3.4163.

Rajanala, Susruthi, Mayra B. C. Maymone, and Neelam A. Vashi. 2018. "Selfies-Living in the Era of Filtered Photographs." *JAMA Facial Plastic Surgery* 20 (6): 443–444. https://doi.org/10.1001/jamafacial.2018.0486.

Reed, Lauren A., Richard M. Tolman, and L. Monique Ward. 2016. "Snooping and Sexting: Digital Media as a Context for Dating Aggression and Abuse Among College Students." *Violence Against Women* 22 (13): 1556–76. https://doi.org/10.1177/1077801216630143.

Ruckenstein, Minna. 2014. "Visualized and Interacted Life: Personal Analytics and Engagements with Data Doubles." *Societies* 4 (1): 68–84. https://doi.org/10.3390/soc4010068.

Ruckenstein, Minna, and Mika Pantzar. 2015. "Beyond the Quantified Self: Thematic Exploration of a Dataistic Paradigm:" *New Media & Society*. https://doi.org/10.1177/1461444815609081.

Sanders, Rachel. 2017. "Self-Tracking in the Digital Era: Biopower, Patriarchy, and the New Biometric Body Projects." *Body & Society*. https://doi.org/10.1177/1357034X16660366.

Schaefer, Kayleen. 2019. *Text Me When You Get Home: The Evolution and Triumph of Modern Female Friendship*. New York: Penguin.

Schor, Juliet B. 2020. *After the Gig: How the Sharing Economy Got Hijacked and How to Win It Back*. Oakland, CA: University of California Press. https://www.amazon.com/After-Gig-Sharing-Economy-Hijacked/dp/0520325052.

Simpson, Brian. 2014. "Tracking Children, Constructing Fear: GPS and the Manufacture of Family Safety." *Information & Communications Technology Law* 23 (3): 273–285. https://doi.org/10.1080/13600834.2014.970377.

Smith, Wendell R. 1956. "Product Differentiation and Market Segmentation as Alternative Marketing Strategies." *Journal of Marketing* 21 (1): 3–8. https://doi.org/10.2307/1247695.

Spotswood, Fiona, Avi Shankar, and Lukasz Piwek. 2020. "Changing Emotional Engagement with Running through Communal Self-Tracking: The Implications of 'Teleoaffective Shaping' for Public Health." *Sociology of Health & Illness* 42 (4): 772–788. https://doi.org/10.1111/1467-9566.13057.

Srnicek, Nick. 2017. *Platform Capitalism*, 1st ed. Cambridge, MA: Polity.

Stark, Luke, and Anna Lauren Hoffmann. 2019. "Data Is the New What? Popular Metaphors & amp; Professional Ethics in Emerging Data Culture." *Journal of Cultural Analytics* 1 (1): 11052. https://doi.org/10.22148/16.036.

Stonard, Karlie E., Erica Bowen, Kate Walker, and Shelley A. Price. 2015. "'They'll Always Find a Way to Get to You': Technology Use in Adolescent Romantic Relationships and Its Role in Dating Violence and Abuse:" *Journal of Interpersonal Violence*. https://doi.org/10.1177/0886260515590787.

Strengers, Yolande, and Jenny Kennedy. 2020. *The Smart Wife: Why Siri, Alexa, and Other Smart Home Devices Need a Feminist Reboot*. Cambridge: MIT Press. https://mitpress.mit.edu/books/smart-wife.

Su, Hua. 2016. "Constant Connection as the Media Condition of Love: Where Bonds Become Bondage." *Media, Culture & Society* 38 (2): 232–247. https://doi.org/10.1177/0163443715594037.

Thelwall, Mike. 2008. "Fk Yea I Swear: Cursing and Gender in MySpace." *Corpora* 3 (1): 83–107. https://doi.org/10.3366/E1749503208000087.

Tokunaga, Robert S. 2015. "Interpersonal Surveillance over Social Network Sites: Applying a Theory of Negative Relational Maintenance and the Investment Model." *Journal of Social and Personal Relationships*, February. https://doi.org/10.1177/0265407514568749.

Toner, John. 2018. "Exploring the Dark-Side of Fitness Trackers: Normalization, Objectification and the Anaesthetisation of Human Experience." *Performance Enhancement & Health* 6 (2): 75–81. https://doi.org/10.1016/j.peh.2018.06.001.

Törhönen, Maria, Max Sjöblom, Lobna Hassan, and Juho Hamari. 2019. "Fame and Fortune, or Just Fun? A Study on Why People Create Content on Video Platforms." *Internet Research* 30 (1): 165–190. https://doi.org/10.1108/INTR-06-2018-0270.

Turkle, Sherry. 1997. *Life on the Screen.* New York, NY: Simon and Schuster.

Wang, Shuaishuai. 2020. "Calculating Dating Goals: Data Gaming and Algorithmic Sociality on Blued, a Chinese Gay Dating App." *Information, Communication & Society* 23 (2): 181–197. https://doi.org/10.1080/1369118X.2018.1490796.

Ward, Janelle. 2016. "Swiping, Matching, Chatting: Self-Presentation and Self-Disclosure on Mobile Dating Apps." *Human IT: Journal for Information Technology Studies as a Human Science* 13 (2): 81–95.

Wellman, Mariah L. 2020. "Trans-Mediated Parasocial Relationships: Private Facebook Groups Foster Influencer–Follower Connection." *New Media & Society* 1461444820958719. https://doi.org/10.1177/1461444820958719.

Whitson, Jennifer R. 2013. "Gaming the Quantified Self." *Surveillance & Society* 11 (1/2): 163–176. https://doi.org/10.24908/ss.v11i1/2.4454.

Willson, Michele. 2017. "Algorithms (and the) Everyday." *Information, Communication & Society* 20 (1): 137–150. https://doi.org/10.1080/1369118X.2016.1200645.

Wolf, Gary. 2010. "The Data-Driven Life." *The New York Times*, April 28. https://www.nytimes.com/2010/05/02/magazine/02self-measurement-t.html.

Wood, David Murakami, and C. William R. Webster. 2009. "Living in Surveillance Societies: The Normalisation of Surveillance in Europe and the Threat of Britain's Bad Example." *Journal of Contemporary European Research* 5 (2): 259–273.

Yankelovich, Daniel, and David Meer. 2006. "Rediscovering Market Segmentation." *Harvard Business Review*, February 1. https://hbr.org/2006/02/rediscovering-market-segmentation.

Yu, Persis, Ed Mierzwinski, David Robinson, and Harlan Yu. 2014. "Weblining and Other Racial Justice Concerns in the Era of Big Data." Webinar presented at the Rebuilding Wealth and Economic Opportunity in Communities of Color, Racial Justice & Economic Opportunity Project, National Consumer Law Center, June 3. https://www.nclc.org/images/pdf/conferences_and_webinars/webinar_trainings/presentations/2013-2014/weblining_and_other_rj_concerns_in_the_era_of_big_data.pdf.

Zuboff, Shoshana. 2019. *The Age of Surveillance Capitalism: The Fight for a Human Future at the New Frontier of Power.* New York: PublicAffairs.

25 Seeking safety and solidarity through self-documentation

Debating the power of the self(ie) in contemporary feminist culture

Margaret Matich, Rachel Ashman and Elizabeth Parsons

This chapter explores how digital media is offering contemporary feminists opportunities for new modes of activism. A key facet of fourth-wave feminism is the way in which feminist visual culture has been shaped by new technological capabilities and considerations of how the body and representations/images of the body are translating into digital space. We identify the feminist selfie as one of the most poignant examples of these visual activist strategies in practice. Through their use of selfies, fourth-wave feminists are turning the camera on themselves to radically interrogate and deconstruct the way their bodies have been gendered, racialised and classed by, and within, society. This chapter re-examines the phenomenon of the selfie, opening with a survey of literature signalling the technological turn in contemporary feminism and extant work that debates the technical capabilities of digital corporeal feminist activism. In the latter half of the chapter, we draw on our notes from the field to explore how women, non-binary, trans and queer people are mobilising their bodies online through digital self-portraiture or 'selfies' to form a new mode of activism. We use these cases to explore the themes of self-documentation, visibility and solidarity. In closing, we reflect on the ways in which digital feminism represents a paradigm shift in feminist praxis and raise questions as to the efficacy of digital feminist activism and the politics of the feminist selfie.

Fourth-wave feminism's digital presence

The vibrancy of the recent resurgence in feminist discourse, culture and activism is undeniable. From Beyoncé standing in front of a giant sign reading 'feminist' on stage during her performance at the 2014 *VMAs*, to the meteoric rise in social media campaigns such as #MeToo, #SayHerName and #FreeTheNipple; the incorporation of feminist slogans on T-shirts in high street stores around the world; the explosion of feminist blogs, social media pages, websites, books and magazines and the emergence of new direct action groups such as *Sisters Uncut*, *The Pink Protest*, the *Women's March* and *Free Periods* – feminism is arguably more visible and pervasive than ever before.

Contemporary theorists and social commentators have signalled our arrival at 'fourth-wave feminism,' which has hitherto been characterised by its leveraging of digital media and networked communication, its mainstream visibility and intersection with consumer culture (Chamberlain, 2017; Munro, 2013; Wrye, 2009), and its focus on intersectionality, identity and inclusion (Cochrane, 2013; Maclaran, 2015).[1] One of the most heavily researched elements of fourth-wave feminism is the way it utilises digital technology and the internet. In two of the most wide-reaching excavations of fourth-wave feminism, both Chamberlain (2017) and Cochrane (2013) cite online feminist

DOI: 10.4324/9781003042587-30

activism as a defining characteristic of the movement. Chamberlain (2017) argues that networked communications have led to new forms of collective feminist feeling and strategising and that "the speed facilitated by online activism is central to considering this affective moment" (p.107). Further, online feminism has been used to signal our departure from the postfeminist era – where McRobbie (2009) characterised the neoliberal postfeminist period as the *undoing* of feminism, Baer (2016) has cast recent digital feminism as a project of *redoing* feminism.

Jackson (2018) has also demonstrated how young feminists are using digital spaces as precarious sites in which they can share knowledge, connect with other feminists and forge a feminist identity. This shift towards the digital is reflected in the sentiment of many key feminist groups, who have expressed their concern that up until now, there has been no "explicit, organized effort to repurpose technologies for progressive gender political ends" and that we must now "strategically deploy existing technologies to re-engineer the world" (Laboria Cuboniks, 2015, n.p.).

The technical capabilities of digital feminism: a new mode of activism?

The move towards a digital feminism has for many signalled a paradigm shift in feminist praxis. Digital feminism offers the potential to disseminate feminist concerns and ideas, share and distribute texts and resources, carve out new forms of discourse about sexism, connect vast and varying communities, and allow novel, creative modes of protest to emerge (Baer, 2016; Carstensen, 2014). Baer (2016) proposes that digital space facilitates the "interplay of individual stories and collective modalities" which works to "illustrate the crucial interrelationship between body politics experienced in a local context and feminist actions whose efficacy relies on their translocal and transnational articulation" (p.18). Thus, digital feminism is a site where specific personal stories are mapped onto global and transnational inequalities to make visible the global systemic operation of white supremacist hetero patriarchies.

Technofeminist scholars have gone a long way in demonstrating how "the materiality of technology affords or inhibits the doing of particular gender power relations" and the way in which "women's identities, needs and priorities are configured together with digital technologies" (Wajcman, 2010, p. 150). Further, and more widely, Darms (2013) has argued that the internet provides new opportunities for folks from marginalised backgrounds to create their own media. Schwartz (2016) has investigated how queer communities "politicise online space by using blogs as a tool to engage in identity production, community building and political theorising" (n.p.). By providing a space for different communities of feminists to congregate and communicate, digital feminism offers a vital opportunity for contemporary feminists to learn from others and to understand experiences and perspectives that are different to that of their own (Thelandersson, 2014). This, Thelandersson (2014) argues, has the potential to urge feminists to put their theoretical understanding of intersectionality into practice.

The overwhelming view appears to be that online spaces and platforms afford space for feminists to educate, organise and galvanise more easily than ever before, seeing a return to collective feminist activism (Baer, 2016). However, this optimism has been tainted by the rise of neoliberal social media projects, the curated self and the extreme rise of online misogyny, trolling and the alt-right. Further, the idea of emancipatory digital spaces and autonomy sits in direct opposition to the "emphasis of social media platforms on commodified self-representation and the widespread digital dissemination of images of the material body" that serves to "escalate the demands of hegemonic femininity" (Baer, 2016, p. 24). Cyberfeminist scholars such as Susan Luckman (1999) and Anna Munster (1999) have argued that these technologies themselves are embedded within systems and hierarchies of power, and the call for women to turn to technology avoided a conversation about the role technology assumed in society more widely. Thus, many urge caution around the internet as a tool for feminist activism (Elund, 2015).

The digital body and digital corporeal activism

The debate around the efficacy of digital feminism intensifies when considering corporeal bodily activism and the use of the body in online protest. Salime (2014) has argued that the rise of digital "bodies, body politics, and speech acts points to the new feminism's disillusionment with the state as a channel for gender justice" (p. 18). Further, Baer (2016) has argued that the interplay between digital activism and women's bodies "represents a provocative and risky space for an emergent feminist politics that moves away from an emphasis on equality and rights pursued through conventional legal and legislative channels" (p. 18). She characterises the body as a porous boundary between self and other, which "emerges at the conjunction of digital spaces and street protests as a symbolic and precarious site of control and resistance" (2016, p. 19). Thus, feminist body politics, representations of the body and their migration into digital space has been cast as a characteristic and radical element of contemporary feminist activism.

However, when one puts this proposed process of digital corporeal resistance into practice, corporeal digital activism has its limitations. In an online world, slippages often occur between how feminists wish for their images to be read, the way in which they attempt to write their own meanings; and how they are actually seen in the reception of digital feminist campaigns and movements. Intended meanings and attempts to shape those meanings are often lost in an online networked world where there is a significant disconnect of distance, intention and context between the viewer and the viewed (Khrebtan-Hörhager, 2015). Images of the defiant, radical body online or in the media are all too rapidly reconfigured to align with traditional patriarchal schemas and "normal sense-making devices" (Foust, 2010, p. 163).

Thus, the efficacy and import of corporeal activism in contemporary feminism is multifaceted and oftentimes contentious (Matich, Ashman & Parsons, 2019). Through their circulation and proliferation in the digital landscape, many corporeal feminist campaigns (such as #FreeTheNipple) are rapidly recuperated to align with traditional schemas of looking, thus sublimating and undermining their political efficacy (Matich, Ashman & Parsons, 2019). Corporeal activism is, as Khrebtan-Hörhager (2015) state, both "impossible to ignore and difficult to implement" (p. 246). Khrebtan-Hörhager recognise that although "corporeal reframing as a mode of resistance is a complex and at times controversial communicative strategy" (p. 246), it can oftentimes prove incredibly successful in gaining traction and attention due to its tangible, visual nature.

However, theorists and commentators alike have also critiqued corporeal digital activism from an intersectional standpoint. As O'Keefe (2014) states, "the body is very much a contextualised product of the relationship between capitalism, patriarchy, racism, colonialism and other systems of oppression" and as such, "it is important to decipher how bodies are located in movements that resist such structures" (p. 3). As such, whilst digital space, representation and image production is a great tool for contemporary activists, it is often embedded in thorny systems of looking and meaning production. As Elund (2015) argues, the digital world borrows codes from the physical world, and cyberbodies are subject to the same patriarchal schemas that physical bodies face. Potentially radical images of the body are often recuperated as fodder for the kyriarchal gaze. Further, the images that navigate their way to the fore tend to be that of white, slim, able, conventionally attractive bodies (Dean, 2016) or reinforce harmful stereotypes (Nagarajan, 2013). Thus, these images have the potential to be hijacked to align with conventional racist, sexist structures of bodily comportment.

Selfie culture

A key way in which women, non-binary, trans and queer people are mobilising their bodies online is through digital self-portraiture or 'selfies.' *Oxford English Dictionaries* declared 'selfie' their 2013 Word of the Year, defining it as a photograph one has taken of oneself, typically taken with a smartphone and uploaded to social media. Of course, selfie culture has emerged out of our ability to produce and share images instantly and prolifically. Online image-sharing platforms like *Instagram, Tumblr* and also text-based platforms like *Facebook* and *Twitter* are giving people new domains in which they can experiment with different ways of presenting, drawing and living the body.

The power to actively construct and produce our own images and aesthetics with new digital technology, rather than simply passively receive that of marketers and the media, provides fertile ground for marginalised communities to represent themselves on their own terms. Further, platforms like *Instagram, Pinterest* and *Facebook* give us access to subcultural communities, radical aesthetics and independent creatives, allowing us access to new visual languages and repertoires, which we can, in turn, use to feed back into our own personal aesthetic identities (Murray, 2015).

However, particularly in the press, selfies are often characterised as a negative byproduct of a neoliberal, capitalist, consumption-based fixation with superficial self-imaging and identity (Acocella, 2014). Similarly, Carr (2015) characterises them as an example of the self-obsessed, narcissistic nature of contemporary capitalism and consumption. Barnard (2016) argues that while selfies may *feel* empowering for those who take them, they conflate material and affective conceptions of empowerment, thus embodying a "(dis)empowerment paradox" as they often replicate and reproduce hegemonic norms, and so are limited in their capacity to affect social change. It is worth noting that most of the literature that we came across that lambasted women's participation in selfie culture was penned by men – suggesting that the power dynamic underlying their gaze and authority calls for caution and a fair degree of scepticism in a conversation surrounding women's self-representation and autonomy.

A great deal of feminist literature has challenged these contrarian discourses (e.g. Abidin, 2016; Rettberg, 2014), where selfies are characterised as an "engaged, self-affirmative and awareness raising pursuit," where the body "through critically self-aware self-care, emerges as agentic, sexual and distinctly female" (Tiidenberg & Gómez-Cruz, 2015, p. 77). Selfies have also been considered a key strategy by which women, non-binary people and other marginalised groups can take control over their representation and reclaim the gaze (e.g. Rocamora, 2011). In their study of bloggers who shared sex-positive and sexy selfies on *Tumblr*, Tiidenberg and Gómez-Cruz (2015) found that selfies were particularly empowering for women who had difficult relationships with their bodies, including those who had suffered with body dysmorphia and eating disorders, benefits which ought not be downplayed or trivialised. They also argue that selfie culture invites new, feminist and queer ways of looking at and understanding bodies, as well as fostering an engaging, inclusive and participatory visual space where people can interact with and support one another (2015).

Murray (2015) has argued that selfie culture may constitute "a radical colonization of the visual realm and an aggressive reclaiming of the female body" (p. 490). As Murray states, many of the women who engage in selfie culture characterise it as "a radical act of political empowerment" and "a means to resist the male-dominated media culture's obsession with and oppressive hold over their lives and bodies" (p. 490). In the wake of damning work that casts selfie culture as a consequence of neoliberal narcissistic consumption, Murray (2015) presents a productive counter-reading of selfies as an important, popular form of self-imaging and self-definition that "may offer the opportunity for political engagement, radical forms of community building – and most importantly, a forum to produce counter-images that resist erasure and misrepresentation" (p. 491).

Murray (2015) argues that the discourse on selfies that links women's subjectivity to narcissism, self-obsession and insatiable consumption are gendered tropes which belittle the agentic capacities of women. There is, of course, deep-seated processes of desire and self-reflection embedded in the taking and sharing of selfies, but Murray posits this as a "type of pleasure that is voraciously claimed: an oppositional desire and enjoyment in oneself as a response to a culture of devaluing and misrepresentation" (p. 512) which underlies the visual power of selfies as an "aesthetic form of resistance" (p. 490). Studying a group of young women who produce selfies in both personal and professional capacities, Murray (2015) concludes;

> In their *notes to self*, the young female photographers discussed in this essay, claim a representational agency that transcends the gender-specific slights and ideological trivializing of young women's efforts to define themselves; to make themselves visible, in a cultural climate that continues to negate, ridicule, malign, and sexualize them. Maybe the selfie is an instinct of self-preservation: a survivorship reflex – and perhaps it is in the young woman's representational contending with the most dehumanizing conditions of late capitalism, that they are able to envision themselves anew and to transcend the depreciatory vision that is so often imposed upon them.
> (p. 512)

These polarised and oppositional standpoints position selfie culture as either a reaffirmation of hegemonic patriarchally prescribed femininity and a process of self-objectification, or a radical act of self-love and empowerment. Arguably, both these analyses of women's engagement in selfie culture posit women as a homogenous group, neglecting a discussion of how women with differing, intersecting identities experience empowerment and objectification in vastly different ways (Gill, 2009, 2012).

Selfies and contemporary feminist culture: our notes from the field

Given the to and fro in the literature as to whether selfies and other forms of feminist self-documentation and representation online are of help or hinderance to the movement, we wanted to examine how selfies are being utilised, engaged with and positioned by feminists, and the extent to which they may be seen as a weapon in the contemporary feminist fight against the kyriarchy.

A key facet of fourth-wave feminism is the way in which feminist visual culture has been shaped by these new technological capabilities and considerations of how the body and representations/images of the body are translating into digital space. However, as we have seen, the ease and pace with which images circulate online brings benefits and drawbacks for feminists. On the one hand, it allows them to transmit their politics to a global audience and build digital communities; yet on the other hand, with a wider reach come new and often unwelcome gazes, as well as the opportunity for one's image to be misrepresented, misinterpreted, co-opted and recuperated. Not only do activists and marginalised bodies have to navigate multiple gazes offline, but they now also have to negotiate a variety of gazes online, where one often has less control over where their image travels, who it is shared with, or how it is manipulated.

As part of a wider ethnography examining fourth-wave feminist visual culture, we interviewed a range of contemporary feminist and intersectional activists. Many of the activists we spoke to discussed their experience of taking or engaging with selfies online. In the sections that follow, we present some of their reflections and the common themes that emerged throughout our conversations.

Selfies, seeking solace and networks of solidarity

Wary of the thorny 'systems of looking' in which images of themselves are embroiled, many activists are sharing information and images within closed, private social media discussion groups and forums on sites like Facebook and Reddit. We spoke to Kez (a young, queer, disabled, working class, Mixed Caribbean and African, non-binary activist and trainee solicitor from the North West of England who wished to remain anonymous under a pseudonym) who shared their experience in online discussion groups, and how this helped them in coming to terms with their own identity;

> I am in a transmasculine group which is the biggest one in the country which is mainly an advice and sharing of photos forum. I haven't really shared any photos, coz I don't really... I kind of use groups to tap into and get a bit more information and to feel a bit more a part of the community [...] I do find it quite comforting to be a part of those spaces. It's mainly for transitioning female to male, but as I kind of identify in the middle, I take what I need from that.
>
> I'm also in a queer makeup and beauty group, so that's like the sharing of photos, and they tend to have different days for people to post... it's quite regulated in that so like transfeminine people post on a Monday, people who identify as fat post on a Wednesday, People of Colour post on a Friday.
>
> (Kez)

These closed social media groups and forums are usually run by voluntary administrators who keep an eye on the happenings in the group during their spare time. Most groups will have house rules and guidelines which are designed to help group members get the most out of the group, and to ensure that groups are "safe spaces" where people can share and consume content without feeling judged, excluded or persecuted. As Kez demonstrates here, some groups dedicate certain days for people with certain identities –

a tool used to keep spaces as intersectional and inclusive as possible. For Kez, and for many others, these groups offer a vital space to connect with their community, to feel safe and comfortable to express oneself, and to see images and stories of people who look like them;

> I think it's... representation and seeing people who don't fit "the norm"... coz you're not gonna get these sort of images in the mainstream, and... knowing that it's a safe space to experiment with images and photos... try things.
>
> (Kez)

These safe and emancipatory spaces are sites of self-experimentation, expression and documentation. These sites are vital for marginalised individuals who are rarely addressed or represented elsewhere in society. This echoes Withers' (2015) elucidations around the ways in which "communities utilise resources such as texts, monuments, music, dance, images and so forth to construct identities and senses of cultural belonging" (p. 7), and as sites "struggle, contention and intervention" (p. 10).

Whilst many people might downplay the potential for social media activism to effect change, the positive impact these networks of solidarity have on the lives of individuals like Kez is undeniable. For people who are struggling with their sexuality, their gender identity or with their experiences of racism, sexism, ableism or classism, these groups allow marginalised voices to find and take solace in one another's presence. Our discussion with Kez illuminates the interrelationship and enmeshment between identity and contemporary uses of technology and social media, and how identities are being formed, shaped and shared online. It may seem like common sense to say that identity work is being carried out on social media, but this takes on a new dimension when considering marginalised, radical bodies and identities which have been historically silenced, oppressed and subjected to extreme and systemic violence. Kez's reflections may be seen as evidencing Baer's (2016) claim that digital space facilitates the "interplay of individual stories and collective modalities" which works to "illustrate the crucial interrelationship between body politics experienced in a local context and feminist actions whose efficacy relies on their translocal and transnational articulation" (p. 18).

There is a sense of safety and solace in finding ones community, and it appears this is happening both on and offline in contemporary feminist culture. Charlie Craggs (a young, white, working class, queer, transgender woman from West London) is an award-winning trans activist, author and founder of *Nail Transphobia*. Although Charlie's activism exists mostly offline, having accrued a large social media following through her activism and public appearances, she shared that social media is incredibly important for her because that is where she promotes her work, gets bookings and makes a living. Like Kez, Charlie shared her experience in finding her community online, and how this affected her transition;

> [Without social media] I don't even think if I would have had the courage to come out as trans so soon! I mean I would have eventually because times are slowly changing and people are becoming more accepting, but like, back then it really helped me to accept myself and *see* myself. Especially things like *Youtube* and stuff, or like reading peoples *Facebook* statuses and seeing their selfies. I dunno, you feel like... for me anyway, it helped me see myself for the first time and see that I would be okay if I transitioned.
>
> (Charlie Craggs)

Charlie and Kez's reflections echo Stryker's (as cited in Hester, 2018) comments about the digital transgender networks of solidarity in the mid-1990s, demonstrating that cyberspace continues to offer trans people vital enclaves of solidarity, affirmation and knowledge-exchange. As Hester (2018) states, still "today, trans people who cannot or do not wish to consult a medical professional are arguably far more likely to turn to *Google* or to a subreddit for answers" (p. 135). Charlie spoke at length about how mainstream media only ever depicts transgender people in negative, damaging ways and that social media provided a vital antidote to the toxic mainstream images that dominated when she was first coming to terms with being transgender. Now, in turn, she has also started using her platform to garner visibility that may help other young trans people in the way that social media helped her;

> When you're not normative, when your body is not the norm, [showing it] is activism in that people are not gonna like it… and you're choosing to post on social media and be proud… you're choosing to post it knowing that it will help other kids like you. So like trans girls, when they see me or maybe someone will look up to me… when I talk about when I'm having a shit day or when I talk about having to shave my face everyday, it's a way of sharing your experience and maybe helping other people understand theirs… it's like a solidarity thing, like a sisterhood.
>
> (Charlie Craggs)

Charlie and Kez, through their process of self-exploration and transition, came to see that there was a dearth of representation that reflected their experiences, mapping this onto the erasure and oppression of trans and non-binary identities. As such, they seek to find and create their own spaces and communities of representation, turning to social media as a vast and open space with the ability to bring together many people from around the world. Charlie discussed how her community congregate online, not only in solidarity, but also to organise and share information about their work and different projects they are working on.

For Charlie and Kez, selfies are not frivolous, self-indulgent practices, but they are powerful representative tools that are traded in intimate private networks which impact greatly on their own personal relationships with their body, their bodily practices and their transition process. These practices and forums allow individuals like Kez and Charlie to share information and to reflect on and take solace in their shared experiences. These spaces thus allow communities to discuss their shared experiences of systemic oppression and violence, but also to resist and offset the ways they are neglected and oppressed in society by creating their own sites for self-expression, celebration and knowledge-sharing. This goes some way in surfacing how bodywork online can impact on how one lives the body offline, drawing out the enmeshment of the two.

Selfies as radical self-documentation

However, having spoken to a host of diverse contemporary intersectional activists, the views expressed by our participants engendered a more positive appraisal of the selfie, more closely reflecting Murray's (2015) sentiment that selfie culture may constitute "a radical colonization of the visual realm and an aggressive reclaiming of the female body" (p. 490). On the whole, our participants position selfies as a key medium through which women and non-binary people are fighting for the visibility and representation which their bodies, identities and experiences have long been denied.

Flis Mitchell (a white, queer, middle-class, disabled, cisgender woman in her late 30s from the North West of England) explicitly linked this to our modern capability to author images of ourselves on our own terms;

> The thing I really like [about selfie culture] is it's women's unmediated visions of their own selves [...] we are always framed as... not just to be looked at, but as an *adjunct* to men... In the past, or when I was maybe 16 or 17, the only way to get sexy pictures was to have someone take sexy pictures of you, and now I can cut out the middle man, and I feel like there's a sense of ownership, and that's why there is such a pushback against selfie culture coz it's like women determining for themselves what is beautiful.
>
> (Flis Mitchell)

Ione Gamble (a young, white, chronically ill, queer, working class, cisgender woman from the South East of England) also reflected on this, further expressing the power of social media in facilitating the production, dissemination and proliferation of images taken by those whose image is seldom seen in mainstream visual culture;

> Anyone can take a picture of themselves now, that's an amazing thing because it means that people are not always looking at what they are told to see in magazines. Like I still find so many girls... fat people... amazing weirdos on *Instagram* that I would never ever find unless they did take that picture of themselves.
>
> (Ione Gamble)

Echoing Rocamora's (2011) understanding of selfies as a site where women, non-binary people and other marginalised groups can take control over their representation and reclaim the gaze, Flis elaborated on the politics of self-representation for individuals whose bodies, identities and subjectivities are abused, mistreated and misrepresented;

> People don't realise that if you have had... if your body, as most female bodies have been, a location of struggle, or abuse, or brutality, or hasn't felt like it belonged to you, or you have had to fight for ownership and authorship of yourself, that selfie is a radical act. That is important, that is so important because you are saying that you see yourself. And that is like, "oh my god"... you can't estimate the goodness in that [...] I think its really beautiful and to name yourself beautiful and to take pictures of your body.
>
> (Flis Mitchell)

Despite all of our participants speaking to the power of selfies, many of them also alluded to the limitations of selfie culture. As we have seen both in our participant's musings on and concerns about the body positivity movement online, and also in critiques of so-called 'selfie feminism,' others have argued that the images that are favoured online are still somewhat governed by patriarchal, white supremacist, ableist, classist, heteronormative paradigms of feminine respectability and palatability. In this way, their palatability not only reduces their radicality, but also, as Aria Dean (2016) argues, neglects the nuanced corporeal experiences of women and femmes of colour. Further, over and above its efficacy in a Western framework, as we have seen, selfie feminism neglects a discussion of different geo-cultural regimes of acceptance and (dis)taste (Patil, 2013), and has little to no relevance for women in the global South (Ortner, 2014).

Dean argues that selfie feminism derives its framework from "racist, classist, capitalist 'lean-in' equality-core predecessors" of the postfeminist movement, thus doing nothing to promote intersectional feminist progress (Dean, 2016). Dean emphasises that these sites and spaces were constructed and designed by those who enact our oppression – white, middle-class men like Mark Zuckerberg (founder of *Facebook*), Kevin Systrom and Mike Krieger (founders of *Instagram*). As O'Keefe (2014) states, "the body is very much a contextualised product of the relationship between capitalism, patriarchy, racism, colonialism and other systems of oppression" and as such, "it is important to decipher how bodies are located in movements that resist such structures" (p. 3). If those bodies that cause little damage to such systems are at the forefront of digital feminism, we may be upholding rather than subverting these forces.

Visibility, representation and resisting marginalisation

However, the overwhelming majority of our data stood in opposition to these impactful theoretical critiques of selfie feminism. In contrast to Dean's critique, it was appraised particularly positively by the women of colour, trans women and non-binary people who we spoke to. Rather than feeling excluded by selfie culture, many of them actively participated in it, feeling that their image was necessary, radical and important. They cited using selfies as a way to 'make visible' bodies, individuals and stories which have been historically marginalised and purposefully kept invisible as a means of resisting processes of othering and marginalisation.

As we have seen throughout the discussion of contemporary means of transmission, the central feminist project appears to be that of ensuring that hitherto marginalised, silenced and oppressed bodies and identities are seen and heard. The need for visibility and representation was reiterated time and time again throughout our discussions with feminists and intersectional activists. Rachel (a young, working class, Black British, lesbian, genderqueer artist from the South East of England who wished to remain anonymous under a pseudonym) reflected on her experience of sharing images of her body online, and the agency she feels this affords her;

> In a world where we have little to no free agency... I suppose it feels like there's some kind of control over who gets what of me... I just deserve it! I feel like I deserve to be wherever I want to be! [...] we have to surround ourselves with mirrors to see ourselves properly because we haven't had that before. So we need to surround ourselves with other people like us, women who we adore, so that we can see what we are like. And I think a lot of this movement has to do with that... there's a kind of solidarity in that. You adore the women around you... and then you learn to do that, to project that onto yourself as well.
>
> (Rachel)

For Rachel, seeing images of other women like her allows her to appreciate herself through an appreciation of, and love for, her community. It validates her existence in a world that is set up to erase her. This echoes Murray's (2015) reflections on image-based social media platforms such as *Instagram* and *Tumblr* as spaces that "enable like-minded folks to find each other and form communities: intellectual, sexual, political, and otherwise" (p. 479).

This poignant and political reflection on the diversification of contemporary visual culture diverges from intersectional critiques which argue that "even in efforts toward documenting one's life with the hope of subverting external expectations," it is inadvisable "for those of us whose subjectivities have not yet been recognized on a large scale to objectify ourselves further using the tools vetted by those who perpetuate our oppression to begin with" (Dean, 2016, n.p.). Our research suggests the contrary, signalling that social media sites represent claimable spaces which serve marginalised groups with feelings of safety and solidarity. Our respondents used these spaces to increase their visibility and representation and leveraged their potential to platform activist sentiments.

Conclusion

Twenty-first-century technological advances in digital media have profoundly shaped the fourth-wave feminist movement. Extant literature around contemporary feminism and intersectional activism goes a long way in hashing out how this technological-turn both helps and/or hinders the feminist agenda. While social media and other digital platforms give feminists new tools and spaces to connect, learn and make visible their bodies and their politics, scholars and activists alike have compellingly critiqued the neoliberal, passive, Western-centric use of digital media in the contemporary feminist movement. As we have seen, whilst digital space, representation and image production is a great tool for contemporary activists, it is embedded in thorny systems of looking and meaning-making, as well as systems of white supremacist heteropatriarchy and advanced capitalism.

As a key example of digital feminist visual culture, the selfie inevitably comes to be embroiled in these debates. The media often positions selfies as a negative byproduct of a neoliberal, capitalist, consumption-based fixation with superficial self-imaging and identity. However, recent work, including the findings presented here, position the selfie as a radical mode of self-representation with the power to forge culturally significant forms of self-representation, solidarity and visibility.

Considering these triumphs and trepidations, the picture looks complicated. In one sense, the production and publishing of these images provides a vital source of visibility and validation to marginalised identities and communities, and serves to complicate and undermine the oppressive stereotypes and narratives that surround them. However, zooming out from the positive impact these practices make on individuals, contemporary scholars argue that by broadening the range of imagery of marginalised bodies, we simply increase the ways in which these bodies and identities are objectified.

This back and forth in the debate around representation and visual culture poses important questions about when visibility is useful and when it is not, and how we might navigate and potentially circumvent those gazes and systems which aim to limit our agency and freedom of expression. In short, our findings suggest that we can neither reject or fully embrace selfie culture as either all good or all bad, rather as somewhere in between the two – a complex and shifting mode of representation that is inherently contradictory, complicated and context specific, and far more nuanced than the bulk of the literature would suggest.

Note

1 It is worth noting that in the work that follows, we use the term 'fourth-wave feminism' and appeal to the analogy of waves as a convenient and widely accepted metaphor for feminist

history. However, we also wish to acknowledge that scholars have long troubled the notion of feminist 'waves.' Gillis and Munford (2004) have argued that "the wave paradigm paralyses feminism, pitting generations against one another" (p. 165). More recently, Russell (2018) has argued that the wave model of feminist history fails to accurately reflect the posture of feminist activity, noting that feminist moments are mostly "retroactive in application – they gaze backwards, rather than reflecting the current moment or anticipating the near future" (n.p.). However, Russell (as cited in Bennetts, 2018, n.p.) also recognises the metaphor of the wave as a useful way to "clean up history" and present feminist histories in a linear and accessible manner. Further, heeding the well-established critiques of the wave narrative, Evans and Chamberlain (2015) advocate for a critical approach to the wave metaphor, one which leverages its "potential as a means by which to emphasise continuity, inclusivity and multiplicity within feminist identity, discourse and praxis" (p. 406).

References

Abidin, C. (2016). "Aren't These Just Young, Rich Women Doing Vain Things Online?": Influencer Selfies as Subversive Frivolity. *Social Media & Society*, 2(2), 2056305116641342.

Acocella, J. (2014, May 12). Selfie: How Big a Problem Is Narcissism. *The New Yorker*. Retrieved from http://www.newyorker.com/magazine/2014/05/12/selfie.

Baer, H. (2016). Redoing Feminism: Digital Activism, Body Politics, and Neoliberalism. *Feminist Media Studies*, 16(1), 17–34.

Barnard, S. R. (2016). Spectacles of Self(ie) Empowerment? Networked Individualism and the Logic of the (Post)Feminist Selfie. In L. Robinson, J. Schulz, S. R. Cotten, T. M. Hale, A. A. Williams and J. L. Hightower (Eds.) *Communication and Information Technologies Annual (Studies in Media and Communications, Volume 11)*. Bingley: Emerald Group Publishing Limited, pp. 63–88.

Bennetts, R. (2018, February 21). Glitch Feminism: An Interview with Legacy Russell. *Berfrois*. Retrieved from http://www.berfrois.com/2018/02/glitch-feminism-an-interview-with-legacy-russell/.

Carr, D. (2015, January 4). Selfies on a Stick, and the Social-Content Challenge for the Media. *New York Times*. Retrived from http://www.nytimes.com/2015/01/05/business/media/selfieson-a-stick-and-the-social-content-challenge-for-the-media.html.

Carstensen, T. (2014). Gender and Social Media: Sexism, Empowerment, or the Irrelevance of Gender? In C. Carter, L. Steiner and L. McLaughlin, (Eds.) *The Routledge Companion to Media and Gender*. New York: Routledge, pp. 483–502.

Chamberlain, P. (2017). *The Feminist Fourth Wave: Affective Temporality*. Cham: Palgrave Macmillan.

Cochrane, K. (2013). *All the Rebel Women: The Rise of the Fourth Wave of Feminism*. London: Guardian Books.

Darms, L. (2013). *The Riot Grrrl Collection*. New York: The Feminist Press.

Dean, A. (2016, March 1). Closing the Loop. *The New Inquiry*. Retrieved from http://thenewinquiry.com/essays/closing-the-loop/.

Elund, J. (2015). *Subversion, Sexuality and the Virtual Self*. Basingstoke: Palgrave Macmillan.

Evans, E. & Chamberlain, P. (2015). Critical Waves: Exploring Feminist Identity, Discourse and Praxis in Western Feminism. *Social Movement Studies*, 14(4), 396–409.

Foust, C. R. (2010). *Transgression as a Mode of Resistance: Rethinking Social Movement in an Era of Corporate Globalization*. Lanham, MD: Lexington Books.

Gill, R. (2009). Beyond the 'Sexualization of Culture' Thesis: An Intersectional Analysis of 'Sixpacks', 'Midriffs' and 'Hot Lesbians' in Advertising. *Sexualities*, 12(2), 137–160.

Gill, R. (2012). Media, Empowerment and the 'Sexualization of Culture' Debates. *Sex Roles*, 66(11–12), 736–745.

Gillis, S. & Munford, R. (2004). Genealogies and Generations: The Politics and Praxis of Third Wave Feminism. *Women's History Review*, 13(2), 165–182.

Hester, H. (2018). *Xenofeminism*. Cambridge, MA: Polity Press.

Jackson, S. (2018). Young Feminists, Feminism and Digital Media. *Feminism & Psychology*, 28(1), 32–49.

Khrebtan-Hörhager, J. (2015). Je Suis FEMEN! Traveling Meanings of Corporeal Resistance. *Women's Studies in Communication*, 38(4), 367–373.

Laboria Cuboniks. (2015). Xenofeminism: A Politics for Alienation. Retrieved from http://www.laboriacuboniks.net/qx8bq.txt.

Luckman, S. (1999). (En)gendering the Digital Body: Feminism and the Internet. *Hecate*, 25, 36–48.

McRobbie, A. (2009). *The Aftermath of Feminism: Gender, Culture and Social Change*. London: Sage.

Maclaran, P. (2015). Feminism's Fourth Wave: A Research Agenda for Marketing and Consumer Research. *Journal of Marketing Management*, 31(15), 1732–1738.

Matich, M., Ashman, R. & Parsons, E. (2019). #freethenipple – Digital Activism and Embodiment in the Contemporary Feminist Movement. *Consumption Markets & Culture*, 22(4), 337–362.

Munro, E. (2013, September 5). Feminism: A Fourth Wave? *Political Studies Association: Political Insight*. Retrieved from http://www.psa.ac.uk/insight-plus/feminism-fourth-wave.

Munster, A. (1999). Is There Postlife after Postfeminism? Tropes of Technics and Life in Cyberfeminism. *Australian Feminist Studies*, 14(29), 119–131.

Murray, D. C. (2015). Notes to Self: The Visual Culture of Selfies in the Age of Social Media. *Consumption Markets and Culture*, 18(6), 490–516.

Nagarajan, C. (2013). Femen's Obsession with Nudity Feeds a Racist Colonial Feminism. *The Guardian Online*. Retrieved from https://www.theguardian.com/commentisfree/2013/apr/11/femen-nudity-racist-colonial-feminism.

O'Keefe, T. (2014). My Body Is My Manifesto! SlutWalk, FEMEN and Femmenist protest. *Feminist Review*, 107(1), 1–19.

Ortner, S. B. (2014). Too Soon for Post-Feminism: The Ongoing Life of Patriarchy in Neoliberal America. *History and Anthropology*, 25(4), 530–549.

Patil, V. (2013). From Patriarchy to Intersectionality: A Transnational Feminist Assessment of How Far We've Really Come. *Signs*, 38(4), 847–867.

Rettberg, W. J. (2014). *Seeing Ourselves through Technology*. Basingstoke: Palgrave Macmillan.

Rocamora, A. (2011). Personal Fashion Blogs: Screens and Mirrors in Digital Self-Portraits. *Fashion Theory: The Journal of Dress, Body, & Culture*, 15(4), 407–424.

Russell, L (2018). Glitch Feminism. Retrieved from http://www.legacyrussell.com/GLITCHFEMINISM.

Salime, Z. (2014). New Feminism as Personal Revolutions: Microrebellious Bodies. *Signs*, 40(1), 14–20.

Schwartz, A. (2016). Critical Blogging: Constructing Femmescapes Online. *Ada: A Journal of Gender, New Media, and Technology*. Retrieved from https://adanewmedia.org/2016/05/issue9-schwartz/.

Thelandersson, F. (2014). A Less Toxic Feminism: Can the Internet Solve the Age Old Question of How to Put Intersectional Theory into Practice? *Feminist Media Studies*, 14(3), 527–530.

Tiidenberg, K. & Gómez-Cruz, E. (2015). Selfies, Image and the Re-making of the Body. *Body and Society*, 21(4), 77–102.

Wajcman, J. (2010). Feminist Theories of Technology. *Cambridge Journal of Economics*, 34(1), 143–152.

Withers, D. M. (2015). *Feminism, Digital Culture and the Politics of Transmission: Theory, Practice and Cultural Heritage*. Maryland, MD: Rowman & Littlefield International.

Wrye, H. K. (2009). The Fourth Wave of Feminism: Psychoanalytic Perspectives Introductory Remarks. *Studies in Gender and Sexuality*, 10(4), 185–189.

Section 6
Feminist futures
Problems, priorities, and predictions

26 How the economic sex/gender system excludes women from international markets

Linda Scott

When the executive director of the International Trade Center (ITC), Arancha González, announced ITC's 2015 resolution to bring a million women-owned businesses into global trade within five years, she cited a shocking statistic to make her case: 99% of international trade is controlled by men (*DXE* 283).[1]

To the policy community already working for women in the global economy, the 99% figure was not entirely a surprise, however. For 15 years, international policy programs, propelled by rigorous research, have been discovering the multiple, overlapping restrictions that bar women from full economic participation and trying various interventions to lift them. Over time, it has become clear that the numerous economic constraints on women extend well beyond unequal paid employment and constitute a total system that serves to hold females all over the world in a place of dependency and vulnerability (*DXE* 3–28). Barriers to capital control and networks, the burden of cheating and corruption, limited access to materials and labor, blocks against market information, and many other points of gender-based exclusion add up to a logical inference that women would be completely fenced out of international trade (*DXE* 267–287).

Importantly, the impact of this exclusion is not limited to wealthy women or large firms, but has a great impact on the poor (*DXE* 55–76). Impoverished women in agricultural economies have severely constrained access to larger markets and cannot earn a reliable living in small local markets for seasonal produce. Efforts made to link multiple smallholders have successfully aggregated volumes sufficient to appeal to large agricultural buyers, providing reliable income to female farmers, but also employment for other women in local services necessary to complete the transaction (*DXE* 267–270). Linking small manufacturers and handicraft artisans with large buyers has been less successful because the practical restraints require an even more expansive systemic adjustment (*DXE* 267–281). Because of the need for system-wide assistance, a few governments, such as Canada and Chile, have recently inserted gender-equality requirements into their trade agreements. These not only include reciprocal commitments to facilitate trade for women-owned businesses, but also promise to enforce equality laws in the partner countries. So, the potential for international trade to be an economic enabler for women, as well as an enforcement tool for existing legal protections, is significant (*DXE* 282–284).

Unfortunately, academic research contributes little to this potentially historic effort. On the one side, it is hampered by neoclassical economics, which axiomatically denies that inequality is built into the global system. On the other, it is bogged down by feminist theories that have been more concerned with a critique of capitalism than with defeat of the patriarchy.

I hope to fill this gap by asking feminist marketing academics to join the global effort to better understand the gendered nature of the marketplace. If a cadre of these feminists can build new theories based on their own expertise—just as the feminist economists of the 1990s did (beginning with Ferber and Nelson 1993)—rather than merely replicating feminist theories indebted to a single view of economics based on class instead of gender, a great deal can be done to free the world's women and reap substantial benefits for all of humanity (*DXE* 3–28, 289–292; Scott 2021).

Gender inequality is now known to be a significant drag on national prosperity, but also a structural *cause* of poverty (see Scott 2021 for a literature review). The direct path from women's oppression to major world scourges—like human trafficking, starvation, disease, and war—has been made starkly visible by research from multiple disciplines (Hudson et al. 2012, 2020). These findings solidly contradict any claim that the fight for women's freedom is narrow in impact and should be replaced by a political movement for "everyone." Evidence makes clear that a global movement on behalf of women—who are, after all, half the world's population—would indubitably benefit "everyone."

I further hope to shake a long-standing notion that holds practical activism to be a naïve, "neoliberal" betrayal of true feminism. I ask that feminist scholars in marketing reconsider whether furthering the freedom of women is best served by engaging with data and action or by chewing over theories that have become radically disengaged from the feminist political cause (Dietz 2003; "Feminist Political Philosophy" 2018), as well as from empirical data on the status of women.

My argument—and the actions undertaken within international policy—is underpinned by a plethora of statistical information gathered into international databases in the last 20 years, as well as the trove of historical evidence amassed since the 1980s by scholars retrieving the past that women have suffered (*DXE* 3–26). This comparatively recent evidence shows unequivocally that all countries have an economic gender problem perpetuated by a globally consistent set of mechanisms intended to keep women powerless by making them dependent on men even for basic necessities. These mechanisms have produced, over time, a specific pattern of inequality—unique to females but common to all—that can be discerned in every nation on the planet.

The explanation lies in the shared history of exclusion that women have faced over thousands of years, enforced by constraints that began before written history and that spread around the world with trade and conquest (*DXE* 55–120). Capitalism is merely the most recent version of the "sex/gender system" that has held women hostage in every known society (Eller 2001; Rubin 1975).

There have been brief moments in some places where women have had economic liberties, but all of these have been temporary. Women had substantial economic privileges in the Ottoman Empire; these liberties were wiped out, even after more than 100 years, by a swift regime change. Women's economic rights flourished over several hundred years during the Song Dynasty in China, but disappeared when the Yuan and Ming dynasties came into power (*DXE* 57). The countries of the West have had, within living memory, the same economic restrictions that plague women in Africa today, but the freedoms enjoyed by Western women should not be seen as some final point of progress. Given the rise of right-wing authoritarian groups in these countries over the past few years, it is easy to see that Western women could lose their rights as quickly as in *The Handmaid's Tale*. In the face of all this data, historical and macroeconomic, there is no longer any persuasive argument to be made that women in different cultures suffer *substantively* different experiences of oppression, at least when it comes to economics.

This new trove of data therefore produces an understanding of women's subordination that denies the disabling discussions over "essentialism" that brought feminist theory to an impasse in the 1990s and continue to this day in disputes over the legitimacy of an analytical "category of women" (Dietz 2003; "Feminist Political Philosophy" 2018). The new information also undercuts feminist theory's persistent conflation of patriarchy and capitalism, raising serious questions about the wisdom of subverting the needs of women to the agendas of men—no matter how marginalized the males may be—in the name of "inclusivity."

How data-blind theory blocks women's quest for freedom

Feminist activists from several institutions joined Arancha González in her WTO mission. Studies were undertaken, speeches were given, op-eds were written, and advocacy efforts organized. In late 2017, the team won an important opportunity: to formally request that the World Trade Organization (WTO) sign a *Declaration on Women and Trade*. The *Declaration* committed the WTO to the first steps of a plan to enable female entrepreneurs globally, whether small farmers or business owners, for better access to world trade. Though 122 of 164 member economies voted to support the *Declaration*, a stubborn cadre of 49 nations refused—including the United States, India, and all Muslim majority countries except Turkey and Pakistan.

Those who rejected the *Declaration* gave a predictable and purely ideological reason: economics-as-we-know-it insists that the world system is objective; therefore, it should not be turned toward the purpose of adjusting for inequality. As the Indian faction articulated, "trade," by definition, has nothing to do with gender (*DXE* 283–285).

The neoclassical economic thought that grounds this intransigent stance is built on a vision that excludes women. Its first principle is that the economy is built on the collective actions of rational, informed individuals who act independently to make free choices in their own interest. Such an economy is said to aggregate into the optimal outcomes for everyone—no matter how unequal things may look—as if guided by Adam Smith's famous "invisible hand."

More than 50% of the world's people struggle with conditions that falsify this philosophy. As a class, females have severely constrained choices, have important information actively withheld from them, and are punished for showing anything like self-interest. Indeed, when it comes to economic choices, women can seldom act independently; rather, they are often coerced into acting irrationally—that is, against their own best interests. Women contend with economic *exclusion*, not merely unequal economic outcomes, a concept that the prevailing conception of economics cannot even visualize. Yet women contribute significantly to the world economy: about 40% of GDP, for instance, and more than half the food supply (*DXE* 3–26). It's ironic that economics imagines itself to be a science when it can only maintain its central theory by studiously ignoring half the relevant population.

Feminist theory has not done much better. Since 1970, critics have consistently maintained a focus on capitalism—frequently to the extent of ignoring patriarchy and the institutions that perpetuate it ("Feminist Political Philosophy" 2018). Many leading feminists further assert that activism by the women's movement is naïve and "reformist" (or "neoliberal"). Such writers claim the only solution for women is to work through an alliance with working class men to bring about total revolution—willfully ignoring the conflict of interest between men and women that is easily observable even on factory floors and in farm fields. Under this rubric, a good feminist refuses to work with groups like the WTO, believing that she somehow *helps women* by burnishing her own ideological purity, regardless of any demonstrable benefits that changing the system—rather than burning it down—might have for the world's women.

Several streams of feminist theory emerging since the late 1990s use the term "essentialism" to question the legitimacy and need for a category of analysis called "women" (Dietz 2003). The arguments boil down to accusations against the elitism of white Western feminists, who are said to assume all women are like themselves and, as a consequence, are too exclusionary toward other women's experiences. No one seriously questions that this criticism of white Western feminism is valid. However, some leading theorists counter that the direction of this discourse displaces any attempt to take action in the real world: by denying the very existence of "women" as an identity group, the political mission of feminism itself disappears. On a discursive level, the end result of pushing a different group of oppressed people into the forefront is often to set aside the grievances of "the category of women" as if gender were not a legitimate concern at all. Ultimately, the constant attempts to "deconstruct" any effort to speak about the issues women have in common (and there are many) make it difficult to mount a program of change based on gender, especially at the global level.

The use of exceptionalist arguments has also been a problem. Anthropology has often focused on the ways that cultures are different from each other, especially as they differ from rich Western societies. Historians, apparently responding to a public demand that women must not be depicted as victims, have tended to focus on women who successfully defied the rules that kept the vast majority of other women subordinated (*DXE* 58–59, 100). These examples have been used to try to bring down documentable similarities among women, as if seeing one black swan falsifies the statement that most swans are white.

Given this contentious backdrop, it's predictable that the 2017 feminist effort that Arancha Gonzales led to change the consciousness of the WTO was *also* roundly condemned by women's organizations and civil society groups whose representatives argued that any effort involving cooperation with the WTO was evil. Equally unsurprising was that their objections lacked economic gender awareness; instead they treated women as an undifferentiated subset of "the poor" or "the peasants," just as feminist theory has tended to do for the past 50 years. It seems that in progressive politics, just as in conventional capitalism, economics has nothing to do with gender (*DXE* 286–287).

Any authentic attempt to free the world's females from economic exclusion must begin with recognition that "the category of women" suffers a common set of unacceptable economic constraints that must be eliminated with gender-specific interventions. As a result of these ubiquitous mechanisms, the women in *every subgroup on the globe* are economically disadvantaged compared to the men and thus have less autonomy as well as more vulnerability. Sublimating the gendered constraints in the name of a crusade to free "everyone"—which in practice means programs for males that refuse a gender perspective in the name of "gender neutrality"—merely replicates the system that advantages men over women, regardless of the subgroup involved.

To hide or ignore these facts necessarily cripples any effort to win equality. For example, if we cannot say that "the category of women" experiences unequal pay instead focusing on either the gap suffered by the poor or the (much larger) gap experienced by the most highly paid women, we ignore the simple fact that gender inequities are replicated within *every group*: poor women are paid less than poor men, minority women are paid less than minority men, high-flying women are paid less than high-flying men. So, any effort that attempts to equalize the poor, the black, or the rich without addressing the gender issues within each of those groups will merely perpetuate systemic inequalities they *all* share.

By focusing on class or race over gender, we further overlook the harm that gender inequality causes whole households. For instance, the gender pay gap costs British families, on average, £9,000 a year (*DXE* 197–198). In a country where average household income is only £33,000, unequal pay for females has a significant impact on family well-being, yet is treated as a standalone women's issue. Research has now shown the folly of ignoring women's economic disempowerment within programs that aim to improve family livelihoods—indeed studies have consistently shown that the best way to ensure family welfare is to get money into the hands of the women and to give them the freedom to spend it (*DXE* 14–15, 207–217). According to the evidence, the thought that class-based strategies should be favored over gender approaches when trying to help the poor is folly.

We can see more clearly why a gender-oriented practical agenda is needed by gaining a better understanding of the origins of women's economic exclusions and the way these were woven into a seamless barrier that separates women, as a class, from equality with men, as a class.

The origins and outlines of women's economic exclusion

The pattern and the mechanisms that produce gender inequality in the economy have been in place, all over the world, for thousands of years. A core text in feminist literature, Gayle Rubin's 1975 "The Traffic in Women," turns out to have been remarkably prescient. Building her theory of the "sex/gender system" up from anthropological accounts then existing, Rubin emphasized that women's oppression is universal among hunter-gatherer societies. That premise countered then-rising theories claiming gender oppression is unique to the modern industrial world.

> …to explain women's usefulness to capitalism is one thing. To argue that this usefulness explains the genesis of the oppression of women is quite another. It is precisely at this point that the analysis of capitalism ceases to explain very much about women and the oppression of women.
>
> Women are oppressed in societies which can by no stretch of the imagination be described as capitalist. … The ethnographic record is littered with practices whose effect is to keep women "in their place"—men's cults, secret initiations, arcane male knowledge, and so on. And precapitalist, feudal Europe was hardly a society in which there was no sexism. Capitalism has taken over and rewired notions of male and female which predate it by centuries.
>
> (Rubin 1975, 163)

"The Traffic in Women" was a foundational text for Radical Feminism, a leading theory of the Second Wave that has faded in importance during recent decades—but that should be pulled out and re-examined in light of the data we now have.

Radical Feminism posited that patriarchy was not a product of modern capitalism, but was instead ancient (Jaggar 1988). These theorists argued that the oppression of women was the original human inequality, and that *all* social systems and institutions have ever since codified, manifested, formalized, and enforced their subordination. Within a few years of Rubin's chapter, Gerda Lerner published the first account of women's oppression in the ancient world, *The Creation of Patriarchy* in 1987. Though Lerner asserts women were equal before writing was invented—something we now know is not true—her extensive documentation was important in drawing the trajectory of female oppression through from pre-literate to literate societies and eventually into the modern era. The institutional elaboration of gender inequality in ancient codes and practices set the template we still see today. Importantly, Radical Feminism insisted that male violence was both the origin of and the primary enforcement mechanism for the sex/gender system, an observation now being elaborated by institutions as unlikely as the World Bank. In sum, the new data to which I have been referring supports the Radical Feminist conception in a thorough and emphatic way, using sources and methods that range from history to econometrics.

A class of goods

From a markets perspective, the most important aspect of Rubin's work was her premise that the basis for women's subordination was that they had been *traded as goods* by all known hunter-gatherer societies, a profound observation since humans have spent 99% of their entire time on earth as hunter-gatherers. In the intervening decades, historians, anthropologists, archeologists, and evolutionary scientists have assembled an impressive body of evidence showing not only that Rubin was right, but that the trafficking of women was the everyday practice even of complex societies right up through the 20th century (*DXE* 55–128).

The trade in women has been applicable to all classes of females, including aristocrats. The history of this practice is long and wide: you can find it, for instance, in preliterate texts like the Norse Sagas and the Old Testament of the Bible. Most societies have understood marriage as a transaction between two men, in which the exclusive rights to a woman's body were sold, usually without her consent, in exchange for money or goods of value. The earliest written laws we have, stone tablets holding the Code of Ur-Nammu (2100 BCE), actually contain a kind of price list for different classes of women, the fines to be paid by any man who had sex with a woman owned by another. Even now, the 2017 International Labor Organization's *Global Estimates of Modern Slavery* report shows starkly that human slavery is bigger today than ever before and that 71% of the victims are female—about a third of them enslaved through forced marriage.

The historical foundation of widespread trafficking is important to the project of women's economic empowerment and should be central to any attempt among feminist marketing academics to theorize it. The "category of women" began as a class of goods, specifically one that afforded prestige to male owners (*DXE* 55–120). Even today in developing countries, it is common to hear that women *are* property and therefore cannot *own* property (*DXE* 33–40, 99–120). Since the exchange of property is central to concepts from consumption to macro-markets, feminist academics are in a unique position to develop both theory and data to support activists at the forefront of the battle against slavery.

Held captive

Since at least the emergence of complex societies, men have controlled the women they own by holding them captive. In part because they were a special class of valuable goods—one that was particularly vulnerable to having their value stolen through rape by men other than their owner—females have been closely guarded throughout history, often living their entire lives without interaction with the outside world (*DXE* 100-120). The Code of Hammurabi (1750 BCE) details practices of seclusion and veiling that can be traced as humans spread from Africa to Mesopotamia and through the Mediterranean north toward Europe, as well as east to the Indian subcontinent and south from there (*DXE* 99–120; see also Lerner 1987).

Since economic viability, whether at the personal or national level, depends mightily on having a network of connections with which one can exchange goods, get information, and so forth, women who were the property of one man (e.g. married) have been severely constrained by their incarceration. At the same time, women who *did not* have this kind of "protection," were, in the Code of Hammurabi, actually forbidden to veil, which announced their lack of protection whenever they went out to earn. This is how a woman alone and uncovered on the street became an invitation to rape—and how veiling and seclusion were refashioned as "respectability." Such practices, by making it *unsafe* for a woman to be without a man, further pushed women into a forced choice between bondage and economic autonomy.

The segregation and seclusion typical of *purdah*, still found in regions from North Africa and the Middle East to the Malaysian archipelago, are therefore actually vestiges of a cultural foundation we all share and *not* sovereign expressions of a unique community. Indeed, surveys now used in research on women's economic empowerment now frequently ask respondents whether they are allowed to leave home without their husband's permission—because male control over the whereabouts of women is a consistent proxy for gender inequality on a global scale. Today, analyses of entrepreneurship and market access for women-owned businesses consistently point to the limited networks women have, as well as their restricted opportunities to engage with other business owners, as central impediments to their viability (*DXE* 243–292).

Working women have been endangered on their commute for at least a thousand years. Today, women are attacked when they work late or in the workplace itself, in every country and every industry. Their safety is used as an excuse to restrict their occupations, working hours, and industry employment, usually without accompanying legal protections in the workplace (*DXE* 121–144).

Though less often recognized, safety in commercial movement is a significant restraint on women-owned businesses, which certainly acts to restrict their access to international trade. Hindrances for mobility further disadvantage even the smallest women-owned businesses (kiosks, roadside sellers, and the like). Being unable to move freely reduces women's access to market information, financial services, shipping and logistics, and a variety of resources from materials to labor. Limited access, in turn, means higher costs, which means women-owned businesses cannot prosper in the same way that a man's can.

Penniless laborers

Within the confines of marriage, women were not paid for their work—and they still are not paid today. This is true with regard to "reproductive work" like childcare and cooking, but it is also the case when women are engaged in home production or family agriculture. Because men consistently control—and are deemed to own—the means of production, even within a family, the fruits of women's labor are usually accorded to the male head of household.

A typical example is provided by a 2013 study of coffee production in Kenya (Johnstone-Louis 2013) which documents the answers given by local coffee farmers when asked whether men or women are responsible for the various stages in crop production. These reveal that the women do the work up until the coffee is taken to market and the cash collected. The community agreed, however, that the coffee belongs to the man and, presumably, so does the cash from its sale. And, indeed, the common practice around the developing world is for women to work unpaid, for the cash from crops to be pocketed by the men, then meted out for what they deem as "necessities," with the rest consumed, often by their personal indulgences (*DXE* 55–76, 84–89, 219–241).

Women in Africa and Asia have worked in their homes and farms for no compensation, as documented by Ester Boserup's landmark study in 1979, before any of these areas were substantially engaged with the modern economy and before European colonialism.

Chinese silk production provides a historical example (*DXE* 95–96). The opening of the ancient Asian trade routes made it possible for China to exchange with the Middle East. These routes were eventually known as the Silk Road because of the lucrative trade in Chinese silks, a development that made China wealthy. Women did the actual production of Chinese silk and they did it without pay. Quotas demanded of them required excruciating, even crippling, labor, eventually giving rise to the practice of foot-binding in order to hold female children at work spinning the silk (*DXE* 95–96).

Married women all over the world have historically been forbidden to work outside the home. Today, it seems logical to speculate that women worked at home to be near to children, but, given the long history of holding women captive, it makes much more sense to conclude females have worked at home because they were not allowed to leave. Women have been a free, private labor source to men for all of history. Even when women did leave the home to work (daughters in particular), they were required, often by law, to turn over any earnings to the male head of household. This was the law in the United States and Europe, for example, until the 20th century, and is still the law (or a strong customary expectation) in most of the developing world today (*DXE* 100–120).

From the perspective of women's subordination, it seems clear that keeping women cash poor was an effective way to enforce their captivity and dependency. From the perspective of trade, the inability to command the profit even from goods you made yourself would have made it impossible for women to have anything at all to trade. In any case, women would not have been able to travel along routes like the Silk Road without exposure to kidnapping and violence—and the same is true today.

Women's economic subordination thus is based, first, on being owned by men, and, then, on their owner's ability to command them to work for no pay and forbid them to go outside the home to earn money. These circumstances sum up to a shattering conclusion. If women have no money and must rely on the man who keeps them for basic necessities, if they are held captive by the person on whom they rely, if they must endure a lifetime of violent threats they cannot escape because they are without cash, and if they labor in that setting *without compensation*, they are living under conditions that define slavery in international policy.

It is common in public discourse, even among feminists, to assume that women's economic subordination is somehow less complete, less severe, less brutal, than that of poor men. In truth, the long history of women's labor abuse begins *in the home* and is created by an imbalance of power, enforced by brutality and total poverty. The interests of women, therefore, cannot be assumed to align with those of men, even within the working class, and are at least as deserving of our attention and advocacy.

Segregated spheres

Work has apparently been divided by sex since, literally, the Paleolithic Age and the categories haven't changed much: women have focused on textiles, food, and care, just as they do today. They have been paid nothing or paid less, whether the currency was coins or food, for millennia. The gender division of labor is somewhat malleable, however; whenever a certain type of work began to command a higher price, males have moved in and the job redefined as "men's work." Women are excluded from the higher-paid male-dominant industries mostly by the threat of violence. We can say definitively now that women clustering in certain low-paid industries happens *because they are women*, not because they are too stupid to choose higher-paying sectors.

Feminist writing about paid labor most often focuses on the abuses women suffer when they work in factories. However, this class-focused stance overlooks the bigger picture for the young, usually single, women who have populated factories since the beginning of industrialization (*DXE* 121–144). In rural villages, fathers have the right to "give" their daughters in marriage without their consent—this was true in the West and is still true in developing countries today. Daughters cannot refuse because of tradition and the threat of violence, but also because they have no means to escape. That's why, once the factories open in a country, masses of them migrate to the cities. By earning their own money, at a distance from their fathers, these young women (many of them mere girls) gain a self-determination that the village does not allow (*DXE* 121–144).

Within the factories, however, there remains a conflict of interest between the males and the females. Research shows that factory women are continually bullied by the men at work, are subject to sexual attack, and are blocked from advancement by their sabotage. At the same time, the jealousy of men at home, as well as the unequal burden of care and frequent pregnancies, keeps them from pursuing their own independence (*DXE* 121–144). In short, there is a clear conflict of interest between men and women within the factories, just as there is one at home. We are naïve to think that it would be any different among the working class than it is within professional or agricultural circles.

The segregation of women into industries like textiles, their restricted advancement, and the perpetual burden of "responsibilities" at home are replicated in enterprise. Women-owned businesses are disadvantaged because they are concentrated in "feminine" industries tagged as "slow growth," they lack business experience compared to men, and their time poverty makes it impossible for them to work as many hours as male business-owners do. All of this retards their abilities to attract capital and to grow when they own businesses.

Landless paupers

The distribution of real property is the most dramatic demonstration of women's structural exclusion. In Figure 26.1, the gender breakout of landholding in 106 countries is plotted. Overall, women own an average of 18.7% of the world's land. Men normally own large and better plots, so males currently own more than 80% of the land on the planet.

Notice how stark the pattern of landownership is; there is no way to argue that this dramatic divergence is a random occurrence. Because land has been the source of both wealth and power in world history, it is implausible to argue that women, all over the

412   Linda Scott

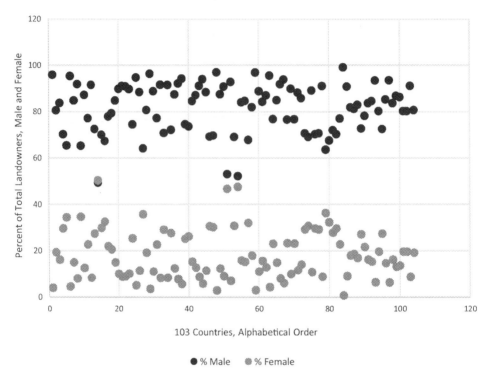

Figure 26.1. This scatterplot illustrates the vast gap between male and female ownership of land in a regionally balanced sample of about half the countries in the world. The black dots show that 70 to 90% of landholders in most countries, rich and poor, are men. Countries are shown alphabetically, starting with Algeria and ending with Zambia.
Source: Land and Gender Rights Database.

world, have made the irrational choice to reject land ownership, nor to say that all women, everywhere, just had "a taste" for landlessness. What we are looking at here is clearly the result of something massive, global, and, as it turns out, long-standing.

I call it "the Downton Abbey principle"—the rule that land can only pass from one male to another has been virtually universal in world history. (N.B.: Even in matrilineal societies, land normally just passes *through* women when it goes from one man to another.) These rules have proven to have very long legs. Even after decades of equal property rights, women in the wealthy nations are actually less likely to be landowners than in poor countries. In Britain, only 13.1% of landholders are female. Only 13.7% of Americans who hold land are women. In the Netherlands, it's only 6.1%, a figure comparable to the conservative countries of the Middle East.

There are, to be sure, outliers. Saudi Arabia is, unsurprisingly, the place where the fewest number of landholders are female (0.8%). Countries in Eastern Europe have the largest number of females who own land. If you look at the distribution in Figure 26.2, however, you can see that countries where women are less than 5% of landholders and

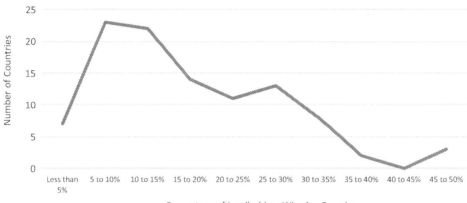

Figure 26.2 Here the same data that appeared as a scatterplot of an alphabetical list of countries in the previous figure has been re-graphed to show instead the distribution curve. We can thus see more easily that the handful of outliers fade in importance compared to the greater bulk of the distribution between 5 and 15%. The bigger picture that women have been excluded from land ownership should therefore not be subordinated by over-emphasizing the exceptions in analysis.
Source: Food and Agriculture Organization, Gender and Land Rights Database.

those where more than 40% are female, exist in opposite tails of a curve where the bulk of the distribution is countries where women are 5%–15% of the landholders.

When we see outliers in this data, we must also take care not to infer permanent achievements or restrictions. Saudi Arabia was once part of the Ottoman Empire, where women enjoyed property rights and other economic freedoms. In Eastern Europe, the distribution of land after the fall of the Soviet Union was sometimes equalized but since has been fraught with indecision and corruption. That advantage is already unstable and almost certainly will disappear, given the right-wing backlash against women's freedoms in those countries right now.

This image therefore teaches an important lesson: we must not use exceptions to undercut the overriding conditions that women around the world *have in common*.

Over time, the male monopoly on the world's main store of wealth has rolled up into a nearly exclusive control over capital. However, the foundation of the exclusion has not been class—even some of the world's poorest families have land—but gender. So the impact of capital exclusion among women is fundamentally different from those implied by class-based critiques.

Without resources

In agricultural economies, women and girls very often have less access to the most basic of economic resources, food. It goes back: women's unequal access to food can be discerned in the remains of pre-historic peoples and in the dental records of hunter-gatherer groups. Females are so consistently fed last and least that long-term effects can be discerned in their physical and cognitive development. Such practices lead to low birth weights and even birth defects in successive generations. There is even a move afoot to design a Gender Nutritional Index to measure the impact of unequal nutrition among women *at the species level*. Practices that result in feeding women less are not benign cultural habits but cruel violations of human rights (*DXE* 68–76).

In the first statutes, we can also see that women had no ownership of simple household goods, but could actually be killed, either by their husband or the state, for removing any object from the home. These restrictions point to an underlying condition: men have had total control over all assets, no matter how minor, and all income throughout human history. Men were in command of trade for all goods, including women, because they owned everything, Women's inability to access family wealth has effectively made them paupers even where they are members of a rich class. Contrary to what feminist theorists and critics sometimes claim, the impact of patriarchy on women's control over capital is evident across class lines, as well as racial and ethnic ones. When we see today that women have difficulty commanding even family resources in service to their own business growth, we should not be surprised (*DXE* 243–266).

Command over resources is a limitation that extends into business practice in the marketplace as well. Suppliers service women last, when materials are picked over, and fail to give women warnings about shortages and price increases that would impact their cost structures. They also charge higher prices and offer less favorable terms when women want to either purchase or sell materials. In much of the world, men still will not work for a woman, which translates to labor shortages for women-owned businesses at a systemic level. Even in remote agricultural areas, women are often unable to get men to help with harvests until the crop is at the end of its season, reducing their yields and the price they can command (*DXE* 61–63).

Information withheld

A continuing theme in women's economic oppression is the way that crucial information is withheld from them. Keeping information from women has been a patriarchal practice for a long time. Secret male societies have been common among hunter-gatherer groups; severe punishments, including death, were levied on women who gained any knowledge of them. Once complex societies with writing and mathematics emerged, females were barred from learning the new disciplines. Eventually, the exclusions grew into prohibitions against educating women at all.

Economists would have us believe that women simply chose not to go to school, preferring to stay home and execute their "responsibilities." The data at this point does not support that excuse. Much more explanatory is the array of practices, including bars to education, that have kept women captive, dependent, and servile by enforcing ignorance, holding back information, and controlling communication.

Men's secrecy over pay is a key factor in perpetuating the gender pay gap, as is their restricted discussion of promotion opportunities at work. Control over information is used to hamper women's progress in business, whether the question is contracts, procedures, prices, or resource availability. In addition, sexual hostility and the threat of assault are used to intimidate women, especially in industries that are most male-dominated (*DXE* 223–236).

A particularly pernicious example of women's blocks to information is the digital gender divide. Though access to the technology as consumers is equalizing, there has been a large gap between the sexes, particularly in the developing world, over the past 15 years. This is the result of long-standing practices that allow men to filter the information that women have and to block their ability to inform themselves by shutting them away from the outside world. The hostility that the tech industry continues to have toward women is another example; evidence shows that women are avoiding tech not because they aren't smart enough to do the work, as the industry sometimes claims, but because the environments are toxic to females and the level of sexual aggression is high (*DXE* 171–187).

Shut out of finance

The financial sector may be the most gender-unfriendly of all and it has a particularly negative impact on women's economic participation, with barriers ranging from personal checking accounts to venture capital.

Illiteracy and innumeracy would have effectively excluded women from the money system from its beginning. Being denied access to the financial system meant women had no way to store any money they managed to accumulate (often by holding back their pay in pennies at a time), which not only kept them from building enterprises, but further impaired their ability to escape. In financial inclusion programs around the world today, research finds that a major benefit to banking women is that, because even those who work or have businesses often cannot keep their incomes, they can now control their income. Women consistently spend their money in a way different from men, usually for poverty-fighting expenditures such as good nutrition and child education. However, another frequently observed phenomenon is that when women accumulate enough money, they use it to take their children and leave an abusive husband.

Because women did not have access to bank accounts until the mid-20th century in the West, and still do not in many places today—they are often forced to hide money at home. These funds are easily discovered by male partners and usually taken away from them. Consequently, accumulation of savings by women is very difficult. Bank accounts allow women to maintain control over money by giving them privacy, which, in turn, enables them to save, especially as a defense against emergencies, disasters, and abandonment (*DXE* 223–236).

Females have been denied credit for many hundreds of years, often devising their own parallel money system, in order to make loans available among themselves. The pervasive cash poverty among women, however, has meant that the women's system could never produce the kind of loans and investment that compounded into wealth the way men's did (*DXE* 205–226).

The near-total male control of both the financial sector and the capital under its management has meant severe limits on what women-owned businesses can attract as investments. In some areas, such as venture capital, the research shows a very clear prima facie gender bias, while in other areas, such as conventional business credit, the bias is built into the "objective" lending criteria (DXE 227–233, 256–266). The upshot is a strong skew against investment in women-owned businesses.

International market access

Feminists have long asserted that markets are inimical to women, an ironic proposition, given that females have been excluded from large markets, to their considerable detriment. For all the reasons I have discussed, women have been excluded from large contracts and markets, with international trade no exception. Typically, given their limited capital, resources, and mobility, women's only option has been taking whatever goods they made or grew to sell through petty trade, effected close to home. Even then, they were only sometimes "allowed" to keep their proceeds by the men who owned them.

Women have been excluded from guilds or trade associations since at least medieval times. They have virtually never participated in international trade, though that activity is itself as old as humanity. Women's unique vulnerability in trade situations included gender-based violence, but also the risk of being kidnapped for sale—because they were goods, just as were the beads, spices, and silks.

Danger still plagues women engaged in international trade. It is well documented, for instance, that government corruption falls more heavily on females, which has implications for enterprise, all the way from business registration to import/export. Customs agents and tax inspectors extort bribes, including sexual favors, from females in a way they do not do with men (*DXE* 258–259).

Women have been unable to access large, lucrative markets because of their immobility, sexual vulnerability, limited information, and lack of access to capital.

By various means, critical economic information is withheld from women. The restricted mobility of female smallholder farmers keeps them from knowing what current prices are, thereby reducing the gain they can get from selling their produce. In agricultural economies everywhere, specialists in farming technology go out from the cities to inform farming communities about the latest innovations to improve the quality and quantity of their crops. Females are often excluded from the meetings where such information is shared because they aren't given permission to leave home or they have household work that interferes—or because local men's groups simply do not allow women in their meetings. Agriculture technology agents assume that whatever they have communicated will "trickle down" to the women.

A trans-national reform of the circumstances that keep women out of international trade will require a concerted effort among governments and large buyers: only large multilateral organizations like the WTO are in a position to make that happen across global trade. That is to say, if women are to have equal economic access, not just in employment, but in all aspects of the world economy, then actions such as those taken by Arancha González and her activist team are not neoliberal or superficial, nor taken without regard to the welfare of the poor, but essential steps toward systemic change.

What the world community is doing

The word "neoliberal" has been used with such promiscuity that it is hard to find an authoritative definition. Sometimes, "neoliberal" appears to denote laissez-faire capitalism, but the term is also used by feminists to deride and discredit efforts to reform world institutions, such as Arancha González and her colleagues' efforts to redirect the WTO in a more gender-friendly path. The word usually aligns with claims that the reforms do not engage in systemic change, but instead put the burden of change on individuals. The recommended alternative is usually total, presumably violent, destruction of the current system, whether this is explicitly stated or merely heavily implied.

Yet international programs designed to give women economic autonomy and the freedoms that come with it have been proliferating around the world for about 15 years, gaining steam as the negative world-scale impact of gender inequality becomes ever clearer. The organizations involved include international agencies, global charities, foundations, and multinational corporations, but, to date, universities have shown little appetite for engagement. More academic participation is badly needed, *especially* from business schools since so many of the problems are business issues.

The programs that have been undertaken, as well as those in progress now, are *all* meant to be scaled into systemic change. Indeed, all grants and other remits stipulate a requirement that any funded program demonstrate the possibility for scale. Since the nature of the problem itself has only recently become clear and because the risks to women (especially retaliatory violence) are considerable, the "interventions" are always tested on a small scale first. That fact sometimes results in uninformed critics disparaging the movement, in general, as individualistic and uninterested in system change. I cannot overstate how wrong this impression is. The interventions that have been tested or are being tested now include financial inclusion programs ranging from helping women open bank accounts to creating large shared-risk funds to encourage banks to lend to women. There are also special programs (some under the ITC) that connect large buyers with women-owned businesses. There are organizations that focus on getting women land rights and others that do business training. Emerging alongside the purely business efforts are mechanisms to reduce and guard against gender-based violence.

Taken as a whole, the effort now underway covers 360° of the world economy and reaches around the globe. And, in part because this is a relatively new initiative, the need to monitor and evaluate through research, as well as to generate new ideas from fieldwork, is well recognized. There is a serious need for more academic engagement, specifically with a gendered lens.

Future research

The possibilities for research engagement are too numerous to list all of them here, so I will itemize just a few of the more salient needs.

An overriding demand right now is for a way to measure "women's empowerment" that can be used across cultures and for all types of intervention. The lessons learned so far include the understanding that we cannot infer empowerment from proxies like increased sales in a business or more access to credit. Though those are good outcomes, they tell us nothing about whether the women involved have more freedom and dignity as a result of the intervention. Since, ultimately, the women's economic empowerment movement intends to encourage autonomy and agency, as well as ensure safety, it is critical that such measures be developed and tested widely.

As interventions are designed and tested, new barriers are discovered that require new designs and fresh tests. Academics are in a good position to join with other organizations—profit and nonprofit—to implement and assess the effectiveness, as well as draw key drivers and barriers out of the data that can guide the next steps for action.

Some areas of women's economic empowerment are well-tested and fully documented, such as the impact of business training on female entrepreneurial success. However, there are other areas where some research has been done but more is needed, such as corruption, male hostility in markets, supplier and customer behavior toward women, the impact of female owners on their employees. There are gaps in the system that need elaboration, such as transportation links that seem less open to women than to men. There have been a few institutional studies, but these have limited credibility because they are nearly always self-funded (by NGOs or corporations). Yet most of the institutions involved in these efforts are new to the entire area of women's economics (arguably, everyone in the world is new to the topic) and engage on the basis of hunches and good faith. Comparative studies of their efforts would be extremely useful.

The field has need for both quantitative and qualitative research. Prior to significant investment, there is usually a demand for randomized, controlled trials. However, prior to the RCT, there is usually a need for depth interviews, participant observation, and other more ethnographic studies, since it is important that interventions be designed that maximize effectiveness, but do not hit the ground negatively. Further, even the RCTs are often multimethod, since qualitative data is often needed to explain the quantitative outcomes.

In sum, this is an important worldwide effort on behalf of women's freedoms everywhere. It is worthy of academic attention and in need of it. The entire effort needs a gender lens—that is, a feminist perspective—and the institutions involved *already know that*. There are grants available; academic publishing is welcomed because the international community sees that as a warranty of research quality. This is an opportunity for feminist researchers in marketing to make a substantial contribution to the world, while also doing interesting, satisfying work. I hope I have convinced readers to investigate further.

Note

1 In my recent book, *The Double X Economy* (2020), I have synthesized the research on women's disempowerment in the global economy and added historical context. In this chapter, I am usually summarizing that material and, because it is impractical to list all the sources I used, I will instead give page numbers from the book, so that readers can easily consult the footnotes in it for further documentation on any one point. I am going to format these references as *DXE*, followed by the page numbers.

References

Dietz, Mary G. (2003), "Current Controversies in Feminist Theory," *Annual Review of Political Science*, 6: 399–431.

Eller, Cynthia (2001), *The Myth of Matriarchal Prehistory: Why an Invented Past Won't Give Women a Future*, New York: Beacon.

Ferber, Marianne A. and Julie A. Nelson (1993), *Beyond Economic Man*, Chicago: University of Chicago Press.

"Feminist Political Philosophy" (2018), Stanford Encyclopedia of Philosophy, https://plato.stanford.edu/entries/feminism-political/.

Hudson, Valerie M., Donna Lee Brown, and Perpetua Lynne Nielsen (2020), *The First Political Order: How Sex Shapes Governance and National Security Worldwide*, New York: Columbia University Press.

Hudson, Valerie M. Bonnie Ballif-Spanvill, Mary Caprioli, Chad F. Everett (2012), *Sex and World Peace*, New York: Columbia University Press.

International Labor Organization and Walk Free Foundation (2017), *Global Estimates of Modern Slavery*, Geneva: International Labor Office.

Jaggar, Alison (1988), *Feminist Politics and Human Nature*, Maryland, MD: Rowman and Littlefield.

Johnstone-Louis, Mary (2013), Case Study: International Women's Coffee Alliance, Power Shift: The Oxford Forum for Women in the World Economy. https://powershift-test.eyedivision.com/wp-content/uploads/2018/11/Power-Shift-IWCA-Case.pdf.

Lerner, Gerda (1987), *The Creation of Patriarchy*, Oxford: Oxford University Press.
Rubin, Gayle (1975), "The Traffic in Women," *Toward an Anthropology of Women*, ed. Rayna Reiter, London: Monthly Review Press, 157–210.
Scott, Linda (2020), *The Double X Economy: The Epic Potential of Women's Empowerment*, London: Faber & Faber.
Scott, Linda (2021), "Gender Inequality Causes Poverty," *USAID*, https://banyanglobal.com/wp-content/uploads/2021/03/Gender-Inequality-Causes-Poverty-Briefer.pdf.

27 The politics of epistemic marginality

Testimonies-in-opposition

Benedetta Cappellini and Martina Hutton

In this chapter we propose a reflection on the *politics of epistemic marginality* which we conceptualise as the relationships between the 'subjects/objects' of enquiry, the 'knowers' and their experiences of theorising and disseminating within their disciplinary boundaries. We examine these relationships via the intertwined testimonies of marketing scholars who self-identify as feminist-oriented academics doing research at the margins and/or have experienced first-hand marginality in our field. Inspired by these testimonies, we explore how *multiple marginalities* emerged from various revealing moments of oppositional and split consciousness: definitions of marginal subjectivities, the process of doing research and the challenges of making spaces in the marketing field. In analysing such moments, we argue that being at the margins can be a form of epistemic privilege, providing critical resources to dislodge structural disciplinary hierarchies and anchors in knowledge (re)production.

Edgeworker
Social kerb crawling
Slipping in marginal spaces,
Places, where poetic pulses
Beat uniformly, yet invisibly
Against institutionally trained
Tête-à-tête; clashing, smashing
Up habitual homily. Dislocating
Discourse, advancing othering,
Ogling beneath the panoptic gaze
A daring dalliance of fit and
Tight-lipped shit, mark out
Valued and valueless

Closed cabinets displaying worth,
Hold no space for other diction.
Sardined stalwarts, squeezing out
Rebellious, loose-lipped avowals
No room to spin, to turn a phrase
Of humanity. Only one chapbook
Slipping through. One enough
To witness disparities, locally

Edgeworkers tenderly temper
Down bouncing boundaries,

Eclectic, inclusive, exclusive,
Interdisciplinary jigsaw of work
No missing piece, where is the fit?
Rubbing down edges, I get to sit
Mouthing mainstream mutterings

(Hilary Downey)

Introduction

This chapter provides a reflection on the politics of epistemic marginality in marketing. By politics of marginality, we mean the relationships between the 'subjects/objects' of enquiry, the 'knowers' and their experiences of theorising and disseminating within their disciplinary boundaries. While feminist scholars have debated on epistemic marginality, often talking in single terms about *an* object/subject and *a* knower (see, for example, Code 1993), we think that using plurals reflects more accurately the experiences and politics of doing research in a *here and now* in which researchers are rarely alone in their epistemological journeys. Using plurals also allows us to discuss a less theorised aspect of epistemic marginality, such as the relationships between knowers who work on/for/by/with marginality and their (often) marginalised subjectivities in their disciplinary fields. We think that this is a very crucial point about epistemology and marginality which can be openly addressed in a book on feminism and critical marketing studies.

To discuss the politics of marginality, we provide the intertwined testimonies of colleagues who have experienced marginality in their epistemological journeys, often as a consequence of their research interest and/or their identities. With this chapter, we do not aim to 'holiday on other people's misery', as McRobbie's would say (1982: 55), but to present the experiences of colleagues who have been and are marginalised and Othered and to reveal how this is/has been done. It also an occasion to reflect on the epistemic violence that colleagues might suffer in our own field but also their resilience and creativity in seeking to dismantle the masters and mistresses' villas, to paraphrase Audre Lorde (1984). It is noteworthy to point out that we collected testimonies from a diverse group of marketing academics, including well-established professors, senior colleagues, retrained colleagues, junior colleagues and doctoral students. As such, what we propose here are testimonies of the politics of epistemic marginality from colleagues at various stages of their careers, which in some cases have been very successful careers in terms of peer recognition, publications and job security. Why does it matter to discuss the politics of marginality in 2020, in the middle of a pandemic? It does matter because the pandemic has shown to all of us the need to have better knowledges and understandings of how and why (and we really mean why) coronavirus is hitting minorities harder and why public policy interventions repeatedly failed to address the structural inequalities making marginalised groups more at risk of infection. The absence of current understandings of these issues poses questions about the limited marketing interest in and knowledge of such matters.

To render this absence more visible, we merge our participants' voices with our own to provide a textual staging of knowledge *writing back* to the marketing discipline, displacing the boundaries between the personal and the academic. We are fully aware that this chapter is an act of preaching to the choir, thus our readers do not need much convincing about the necessity of understanding the politics of marginality and its current relevance. To provide a provocative reading that might question also our own behaviour as writers, readers and reviewers, we have engaged with literature that is outside the boundaries of the marketing discipline. This is not to ignore the work of marketing colleagues who have guided and inspired our research. It is an attempt to move away from a predictable and self-indulgent position and sing to the choir something very familiar, but with a different tempo.

Epistemic marginality

Epistemological journeys assume particular assumptions about the world: how and what is worth knowing and indeed who are the 'legitimate' knowers, their aims and their audiences. All these aspects of epistemological enquiries have been debated by feminist philosophers and social scientists, who have been fighting battles within their disciplines and institutions with the attempt to defend different ways of knowing and doing research (see for example, Hawkesworth 1989; Code 1993). Opening intra-disciplinary debates around what can be studied, how and by whom and for whom constitutes battles for legitimacy, recognition and authority in which links between knowledge, power, ethics and politics become evident. Feminist philosophers and social scientists have denounced that epistemology is always political (Alcoff 1993) and that research, its legitimisation and dissemination are not 'value free' but always the results of political investments and battles between who has the power of legitimising knowledge and who aspires to acquire it. They have pointed out the harms that epistemology can do to research and academic enquiries and have been vocal in talking about epistemic injustice (Fricker 2007) and epistemic scandal (Chow 2006). Feminist critiques have also produced new forms of knowledges and understandings aiming at shaking the normative power of certain ontologies and epistemologies (Olesen 2011).

These criticisms have been welcomed by marketing feminist scholars, but they have rarely become 'mainstream' in the discipline. If epistemological concerns about 'what is worth knowing' have been embraced by critical marketing studies and absorbed into an apolitical celebration of qualitative methods, other concerns remained marginalised, unresolved and often unseen. In particular the role that difference plays in the communication of knowledge and how epistemic authority is structured in ways that award credibility and knowledge to some but not others (Intemann et al., 2010). Recognising the knower to be situated in real-world conditions, we align with Bergin's (2002) central concern that human access to knowledge and knowledge-production is not equally distributed, with some knowers listened to, heard and taken seriously, some not; some are in positions that privilege them as knowledge gainers and producers, some are not so positioned. Structurally anchored prejudice therefore creates epistemic othering in the academy, these "otherings" are legitimised by knowledge and this rendered, for the most part, invisible to the academy itself (Keet 2014: 24).

If the knower is not taken seriously, how can their research gain recognition and value? As many of our testimonies will reveal, being a marginal knower and studying marginality are often interrelated. Defending the importance of studying marginality, here understood as studying phenomena that are not based in the US or Europe and for participants who are at the margins or simply unknown to academics in management, might be a hard task for getting funding and space in journals (Boussebaa and Tienari 2019). There are certain marginalities that are more 'interesting' to investigate, simply because they are somehow closer to the 'centre'. Redirecting the interest towards phenomena that are further removed from the centre can and has been done in marketing but there is always the risk of reproducing exoticism. In interpreting data using Western authors and perspectives to non-Western contexts (a common trend in marketing journals, often pushed by reviewers) inevitably induces in theorising the context as 'Other', as different, deviant and indeed exceptional. Feminist theorists have been vocal in noticing that marginality is often theoretically framed with theoretical concepts which do not belong to marginal contexts (Code 2014). If we agree with the feminist assumption that knowledge is and context related, the tools for theorising those should be situated (Olesen 2011). Ignoring this might risk perpetuating epistemic privilege and reproducing a way of speaking in an authoritative and colonial way. This is a contentious point, and as many have pointed out is linked to the politics of publishing and of reproducing intellectual hierarchies in which the US and the UK are the main centres (Grey 2010; Tourish and Willmott 2015). In other words, theorising is a work of translation in which non-Anglo-Saxon contexts and phenomena need to be tamed and aligned to the normalised epistemologies and ontologies of the centre (Boussebaa and Tienari, 2019). How to move from this impasse in a discipline in which monographs are devalued, journal articles are highly regarded, and US/UK-based journals are considered the only path to an academic career? We provide here some testimonies of colleagues that have reflected on these issues and taken a different path, which in some cases has proven to be a challenging but also a rewarding one.

Testimonies

Testimonies have been used to elucidate forms of repression, violence, marginalisation and isolation experienced by marginalised groups (Code 2014). Often dismissed as 'too subjective', studies based on testimonies offer a space for giving legitimacy to other ways of knowing and understanding and also a space in which marginality is discussed and celebrated. Unfortunately, these works are appreciated only among a supportive but limited audience and only rarely become central in discipline-specific debates. There are notable exceptions (see, for example, bell hooks' work), which should provide some encouragement to all of us who want to move away from the punitive mechanisms of knowledge production. Feminist studies have used testimonies to unveil, analyse and challenge gender discrimination and oppression in specific sectors of society including schools, workplace and society at large (see, for example, Beverly 2005). Testimonies have been used also to show counter stories, and indeed stories of resistance, solidarity, dignity and pride in the daily struggling (Cervantes-Soon 2012). In the context of higher education, marginalised academics have used testimonies to unveil hegemony, patriarchy, racism and elitism in academia (Faifua 2010; hooks 2010; Prieto and Villenas 2012). An inspiring piece which informed our current work is the recent article by Orelus (2018) in which testimonies are used to provide examples of how systemic marginalisation related to gender, sexuality, race and language is at play in US institutions and creates *subaltern* academics.

In writing our piece we asked colleagues to share with us their testimonies. Instead of the view that knowers are essentially the same and that knowledge is perspective-less, we argue that knowledge is what we are able to gain – through testimony (Welbourne 1986; Bergin 2002). Thus, situated and or subjective understandings of knowledge are more accurate: differing social situations (economic, sexual, cultural, etc.) produce differing understandings of the world, differing knowledges of reality (Bergin 2002). The main question that we asked was 'what is your experience of studying marginalities and producing accounts of marginalities in/for marketing studies?' Colleagues were encouraged to select their own ways of communicating their experiences via drawings, photos, short essays or poetries. We received a poem and ten essays, which were collected from July to September 2020. We added also our own testimonies. Our invite was sent to colleagues who have published on marginalities, or/and have mentioned their experiences of subalternity in their own institutions or our discipline. As previously mentioned, we invited colleagues at various stages of their careers: from PhD students to retired academics, from full professors to junior colleagues under probation. Colleagues from various countries, genders, ethnicities, religions, ages and sexual orientations responded to our invite. Our initial aim was to reproduce each testimony as it was provided to us without any editing. The poetic testimony has been reproduced entirely at the beginning of the chapter, but we could not do the same for the others due to the length of many testimonies. Also, some colleagues wanted to remain anonymous and asked us to edit their testimonies. Considering these constraints, we provide a 'loose' thematic analysis in which major patterns across testimonies were identified. However, the challenge of feminist work is to operate within contemporary regimes of truth telling in ways that are acceptable within dominant disciplines. As Adrienne Rich (1975) reminds us "this is the oppressor's language, yet I need it to talk to you". Therefore, in an act of methodological disobedience, we break with the continuity of what is expected, to provide a series of intertwined testimonies, fracturing the linearity and dominance of conventional "data analysis" and representational practices. Our intertwined testimonies are multi-vocal, evocative accounts which recognise the simultaneity of difference and solidarity across participants. We experiment with textual form, voices and content to situate us all as living, experiencing subjects and to deny the "comfort text" (Lather and Smithies 1997) that maps easily onto the usual ways of marketing sense-making. Our aim is to create consciousness-in-opposition through testimony (Sandoval 2000), stepping outside of convention to produce a series of unified, yet uncooperative testimonies. The initial draft of the chapter was shared with colleagues who sent us their testimonies and their comments were addressed in the final draft. We are very grateful for their openness and generosity and hope to have done justice (and we really mean justice) to their testimonies.

Testimonies of multiple marginalities

Multiple marginalities is an expression coined by Code (2014: 15) in describing how epistemic marginality is in reality an intersection of various marginalities, including

> being left out as known or knowable and being left out, side-lined, as putative knower, being diminished or damaged by/in bodies of knowledge; being denied credibility in testimonial and other epistemic processes and practices; being discredited within a certain hegemonic formula of set of directives for what counts as *bona fide* knowledge.

In the following sections we provide a vivid account of such intersections via three intertwined testimonies around definitions of marginal subjectivities, the process of doing research and the challenges of making spaces in the marketing field.

Testimony of marginal and resistant subjectivities

When I started studying gender for my PhD, more than 15 years ago, I often got a sad look from senior academics… oh, gender, well, good luck with that! They told me to not become defined by that label – Gender Scholar – as if doing so would segment me into a group of radical scholars whose work was not taken seriously. I am not sure if you take a certain path in your research (being a topic to study, a method to select, a journal to read and to publish in) because you are somehow marginal, or if you become marginal because of your research.

I feel that my experience of thinking-with-feminism is situated at the margins. By allowing my thinking to be feminist I am at the margins of the marketing mainstream, in which 'gender' remains a discrete area of research rather than a thinking-rhetorical device through with to research. Marginalisation encompasses the topics I have sought out, the methods I have engaged with – until the central university adopted a social justice focus; then I became flavour of the month and a means to "rescue" the department's tarnished reputation as if everyone had been involved and supportive. An ironic impact of ideas – sometimes I ask myself whether I should just reorient my research focus.

Being a feminist academic is a dirty business, a paradoxical position of marginalised-privilege (or privileged-marginalisation). It is a dynamic dis/comfort. So where does that leave people like us who might identify as marginal scholars, working with marginal people or using marginal (non-dominant) modes of critical enquiry? Excellence in academia is often built on the backs of the excluded. Being a feminist in a discipline such as marketing is not easy but being…

…An African American male academic…
…A Woman from a modest background, growing up poor in a rich part of my country
…A Queer, Muslim QTIPOC Feminist
…A Feminist-Thinking CIS Gender Male
…An Intersectionality Scholar
…A Malay Hijab-wearing Woman
…A Thai Female Academic in Europe

…is even harder and for some of us, borderline impossible. "I" am/"We" are, what Maldonado-Torres calls the "Damné"; either totally invisible or excessively visible because of this positionality.

I do not want to be the token academic in my department and beyond to be called upon to fill diversity quotas – both in terms of representation and diversity of research. I'm left to ponder why it is, once again, my (our) responsibility to help our White colleagues, with fucking PhDs mind you, understand the centuries of injustice we've had to endure or the trauma of a faculty meeting where the Diversity, Equity, and Inclusion Task Force is unveiling its official statement on behalf of the School of Business, only to have some question, why the statement reads, People of Color, and not people of all races…did you really just say, 'All Lives Matter?!' Furthermore, if Islam encourages woman scholars. Are we not supposed to be studying marketing? Because Islam encourages communications and entrepreneurship. Is having and practising a faith medieval? We are all asked to declare our ontology and epistemology in our thesis. Yet, mine is silenced because they are Islamic…?

The outsider within, and an observer with ideas about which I am passionate, I work to find ways around the discomfort, avoid the silencing, evade the interruptions and engage instead with oppositional consciousness, seeking out others of a like mind. It is exhausting at times, lonely at other times but where else can I go that is different? Because…

Feminism offers a space to develop theories and positions of refusal and resistance. Marginalization allows you to stand out as that rare expert. There is no reason why feminist thinking should be exclusive to feminine embodiments – indeed, feminist thinking is most successful when it sways minds and hearts of all genders. Yes, we are marginalised, but we are not compromised. We have a responsibility to stick to principles, such as not stripping the politics out of our research. Yes, we need to maintain a position where we can exist, but existence is enough… once we can do this, keep on keeping on, and eventually, if we continue working together, I'm hoping we can live to change our academy and the institutions built around it.

Non-feminist characterisations of feminist epistemology are misleading particularly in how it is viewed as an epistemology of "women's ways of knowing". This has not only consigned it to the margins but has also revealed the particular ways dominant epistemological views are distinctly un-feminist in their wilful avoidance of historical, reflexive and political issues. As the above testimony illustrates, when people are cut out and excluded from participating in conversations, they are not allowed to have any say about how they are treated (Schulman 2009). Our testimony speaks back to this marginality by highlighting participants' "continuities of exclusion" (Schulman 2009). As figures of interruption, out of place and out of bounds; women, queer, non-Western, non-white and radicalised voices don't just happen to get interrupted; some voices are understood to be interruptible in a way that others are not, suppressed because they are deemed of less value or even threatening (Gedalof 2012). Although our *"Damné"* vividly describe their marginal experiences – no matter how else we identify ourselves, we are also academics, part of Western academic culture, albeit on the margins. Dialectically speaking this completes the oppressor–oppressed relationship; our very presence at the margins defines and normalises the dominant centre, even as we struggle against that centre (Kress 2011). Feminists speak of the politics of location as a location in contradiction (Brah 2012). A form of split-consciousness and positions of oddity threatens the centrality, legitimacy and privilege of the norm (Harding 2015). We and our participants speak of the constraining and enabling nature of marginality, the in and out, the privilege and the exclusion, being loud and being silenced. We must therefore ask how can marginal subjectivities and experiences be a productive force as well as a destabilising one? How do we unbalance the hegemony and open up a set of new possibilities (Baraitser 2009) by interrupting dominant way of knowing to critically cultivate community and resistance?

Testimony of researcher as othered – defiant – progressive

I'm left to ponder why research highlighting OUR experiences is never worthy of publication in the top outlets if we're the authors – only when conducted by White authors? Why are our experiences never generalizable, yet those of Greenlanders are? But we know the reason for this…it gives you a reason to say we're not worthy. We haven't hit the Holy Grail journals, so we're not fit to enter your hallowed halls. And there's that word "fit" everyone loves to throw around when talking about hiring us…let's get real, you hate most of your colleagues, yet somehow, WE won't/don't fit. None of my British participants anticipate an Asian woman while signing up for the call for research participation. Although being from an under-represented background, I don't study marginal topics. I took it as my political standing to study general topics that can contribute to a broad scheme of things. To write an article that explores racial or gender differences just does not have sufficient merit for the top journals. No A+ publications for me. So, I have cobbled together numerous A-level journals, pushing myself at a relentless pace to get my work into special issues. At least here my work is not rejected solely on the basis of what is being studied. This is when problems start, I guess. I have been told many times that successful academic writing is a work of translation, but it is also a work of taming, of polishing, of removing, of ordering. I have also been lectured on joining 'the' conversation... whatever this means. It is hard because how marginalised feminist research is in the management school – and particularly in the marketing discipline. It is hard because of the strains put on our jobs by the journal metrics and rankings, and the overall lack of outlets for feminist research in marketing. It is also hard because of the lack of representation of people like me within the academic feminist community in marketing.

Most of the people I meet in my fieldwork, are people 'out of place' to cite Mary Douglas, people who do not fit in. The irony is that in publishing for marketing journals, regardless of their level of criticality, you tame their existences so much...so, struggling existences are described as caring consumers, reflexive consumers, or low literate consumers. I see the moving of marginal existences back into 'the place' (i.e. calling them consumers) as an act of epistemic violence. We do not give voice to anyone in calling participants 'consumers', in fact we mute them, patronise them and re-insert them into an ideology which destroys their existences. Yet, I have had the honour to work alongside women and men who experience extreme restriction and deprivation in their marketplaces. That white and male privilege exists around the world is without question, and recent events associated with the US president have brought to light systemic ways in which racism and sexism are still embedded in developed nations. Yet recognizing these issues is a far cry from doing something about them. Participants and communities want researchers to present an honest account of their reality, yet this doesn't always fit with our theories and constructs and can shatter our preconceived ideas prior to entering the field. Yet we should persist in getting dirty to uncover incongruities and misrepresentations. Sometimes this means not providing a happy ending, a solution, or an account of participants "making good". I refuse to make it nice! You cannot fully understand and study marginality if you have not acquired a certain sensibility and respect for what you study. I have worked with ex-offenders, women's groups, the travelling community, those experiencing homelessness, disability, drug abuse, prostitution and "hidden women" – living in households with very little power in their lives. As a consequence, I aim to increase awareness of and challenge the contradictory and distorted views of such people who experience life at the margins. I do not pretend to 'give my participants a voice'. They do have 'a voice' and many have been shouting for so long that they are hoarse. In my work I have a more modest aim than speaking for others: I hope to be truthful to what I have seen and heard in my fieldwork.

For me it is important to frame feminist thinking in far broader terms: it is an array of approaches to research that can be applied to any topic by any embodiment. In research, marginalities allow questions to arise, marginalities provide novel (and publishable) points of view with the potential to shift marketing activities or the perspectives of academics. It is surprising how often and how easily a challenging point of view can be introduced into teaching, supervising and research. Although being marginal or working on marginal issues has its disadvantages, the "margins" is also a place from which to widen the lens so we can see and know the world differently. It adds intensity and creativity to the questions we pose, because we are unencumbered by apolitical value systems and conventionality. So, I pursue work that communities and participants care about and hopefully work, which other scholars might be interested in reading and supportive editors/journals want to publish. Yet, the key (for me) is not to further fragment with an ever-increasing list of specialist labels, but rather to find solidarity across these differences. That is to say, one needs to engage in a disruptive doublethink of recognising and celebrating differences without reifying or commodifying them. (Post-)identity politics can be a powerful force, but it runs the risk of too much strategic essentialisation and fragmentation. This allows capitalism to divide and conquer – or segment and profit – by dissolving solidarity-across-differences into consumer-identity-delimited-by-difference. The symbiotic sensibility that 'we' (in the broadest sense) are all in this together is what I see across *feminism, queer theory, post-colonialism, posthumanism, and more. As my career has unfolded it has become clear to me that scholars must do more than study underserved people; we must be compelled to make a difference. One way is to tell the story of such individuals in ways that represent their lived experiences and enlighten others to their situations. But we must go beyond our ivory tower and use our forum to help them, even if it is only a few individuals at a time.*

Historically the Western academy has been a white male-dominated institution. Specifically, since its inception, scholarship and research in universities have been dominated by the values of white males, who tend to be Christian, abled-bodied and presumably heterosexual (Tillman 2001; Turner 2002, 2003; Ahmed 2012; Orelus 2018). Against this backdrop radical voices are rendered marginal, often criticised by the academy for being too political and the research so produced, criticised for not being serious research (Byrne and Lentin, 2000). In this way, those who study marginality occupy contradictory locations within the discipline; the *feminist-thinker* committed to political change and the *researcher* committed to producing social research that is ethical, credible and authentic (Friedman 1999). Identifying resistance to intellectual fluidity and boundary-pushing scholarship, participants recognise how prestige is assigned to those who "accept the limits assigned by the institution" (Bourdieu 1988: 95). Subtle forms of constraint operate for academics, although they are rarely named as such; to be published, for example, requires a high degree of conformity to disciplinary rules – all too frequently the line of least innovation is the line of ascent (Lynch 2000). Success therefore is bestowed more readily upon those who conform, remain silent (apolitical) and comply with the disciplinary orthodoxy. What is clear from this testimony is how researchers in marginal spaces make concerted efforts to privilege the marginal in their work, as those who know from everyday reality have access to distinctive and unique forms of knowledge. Moving forward it is essential this work continues, as the hermeneutical gaps that emerge from structures of oppression and identity prejudices create bodies of active ignorance for those subjects whose privileged positions are protected by the hermeneutical blind-spots and insensitivities to marginal issues in question (Medina 2012: 212). In short, the marketing discipline should be reconstituted in its structural relations with marginality, if progress is to be achieved for academics to set out the terms of epistemic marginalities and Other knowledges as recognised and valued.

Testimony of making spaces – being silenced – interrupting

For some time now, and after exchanging with colleagues, I have come to realise that there's a massive problem with marketing. What is it about marketing that it cannot recognise feminist, gender or intersectional perspectives and the "value" they present? Even when I say "value" it shows how this is the only way to potentially "package" feminism in this, our, community. Isn't it odd? How can organisation studies, management, HRM and even economics and finance and accounting have quite influential and recognised research on feminism, gender and all its intersections – and in marketing a) either feminism does not exist or b) it is apolitical. And honestly, I don't know what's worse… either ignoring feminism, or not politicising it. When the hard truth is: marketing is political! And the topics we study are too. Ideas that care for people and planet are far more important, invigorating and inspiring. And beyond my workplace I found others that engaged with the ideas I found so precious. The paradox of ideas sustained me. For me it is essential for navigating academia which is contaminated by exclusion and hierarchy, cloaked in the rhetoric of values and diversity as if we can't see through to the murky underbelly of rampant academic capitalism and the tyranny of new managerialism. Not wanting visibility in today's academia clashes with various modes of valuations of marketized higher education. HE metrics would want me to generate a specific form of 'IMPACT' – the type that can be measured easily, and which quantification fits within predetermined sets of criteria. I don't engage in this work to follow the rules set by Them.

The word feminist was condemned. And gender was not welcomed at most. To make a marginalized group relevant required hard work of organizing tracks and pushing senior scholars to allow the tracks to happen. Another terrain of struggle is academic conferences and networks, where the majority of feminist researchers in marketing are... hmmm... very... white! as well as predominantly western-centric, cis-gendered, and able-bodied. I often feel that I don't belong, which has been an ongoing narrative in other spheres of my life. The marketing feminist arena feels like another school courtyard at times, unfortunately. As for community: it is extremely difficult to find allies and like-minded friends to work with on these topics. As for senior professors: even if they call themselves 'feminists', some are too often absorbed in and reproduce the very neoliberal structures they have developed a career on critiquing. Yet, I feel the inability to 'fit in' in conversations and conferences. I've been made to feel as though I have no right to engage in 'reverse anthropology' by studying European consumers and their habits. At the time I felt really disappointed – my hopes were dashed – I wanted more 'engagement'. I also thought that the issues I tried to communicate were important. I felt passed over and un-recognised (not sure this is a word – but I don't mean mis-recognised just not recognised at all)... Should I communicate differently? Do I come across as defensive – and not open enough to the objectives of the event? Am I just overthinking all of this? Perhaps, then, I am self-marginalising.

When I speak about something, I either easily impress some people because they might have a very low expectation of me OR that I don't impress them because they wouldn't want to listen to what I was saying anyway, because they can see me. It is tiring because I am left to figure out what these comments actually meant and what value do they bring to my work? I often only realise much later in the day how the room might have put me on mute too. What is so wrong with heterogeneity? It seems easier for some of my peers who look like each other, speak with a British accent and add the word "nuance" in every other sentence. This impact how many academics evaluate me. I cannot count the number of times I have been turned away or cut off from introducing my research because I am different. Silencing was often self-imposed. The overwhelming pointlessness of speaking out was made abundantly clear. The taken for granted assumptions around the inherent value of the minutiae of marketing the bedrock of the dominant clique. Questioning this was simply ignored or met with astonishment or viewed as not being part of "the team". When I did speak out, more often than not I would be cut off, or reprimanded, or ridiculed. Despite the odds, I've made it this far, and have been able to make academic friends. Still, I think that by building community, even if we diverge in some ways, we can make a difference and eventually make our voices heard. I won't be silenced, I won't be interrupted, and I won't make it perfect – to my feminist colleagues I urge you to embrace the disobedience and continue to get dirty! Is the reckoning finally here? Is this when our academic lives will matter? I'm left to ponder...YET WE PERSIST!

In identifying new developments of feminist research Olesen (2011) highlights how knowledge production can be a dynamic battlefield in which spaces for hosting new theoretical frames can be found. 'Rage is not enough' for making space, as she highlighted more than 40 years ago (Olesen 1975), but passion can be productive in regalvanising the margins with innovative questions and new agendas. Passion can also increase solidarity among the marginalised. As some of our colleagues have pointed out, collaborations are often the result of common experiences of being silenced, self-marginalisation and failing attempts of making an interruption. Margins can be productive and creative but their efficacy in making space is also a consequence of their relationship with the centre. Code (1993, 2014) reminds us that not all centres are equally privileged and equally unjust, thus there are some centres in which some space can be found. While some marketing circles are by definition more open in valuing differences within the discipline, we cannot deny that some colleagues have experienced marginalisation in attending these circles. Marginalisation has become so pervasive that some have given up speaking and interrupting.

According to some, making spaces from the margins is strategy that requires an in-depth knowledge of the field: it structures, logics and norms which are dynamics and in transformation. More than 40 years ago Bar On B.A. (1973), for example, affirms that being at the margins implies being epistemically privileged over the ones located at the centre. As she argues, being able to survive away from the centre implies knowing the structures and implications of the centre more accurately than those who are located at the centre. If those at the centre can afford to ignore the lives and experiences of the marginalised, the ones at the margins cannot ignore the centre and such they have a more comprehensive understanding of their field. The perspective of those at the margins are revealing and should be considered by everyone who is genuinely interested in making space for feminist and critical research in marketing. Take for example the critique on the apolitical nature of some gendered studies, the absence of a feminist debate in certain journals and the lack of collective solidarity against the corrosive nature of the neoliberal ideology in academia. These are absences that are perhaps less visible to colleagues who are not at the margins.

Concluding comments

Our testimonies-in-opposition have revealed how epistemological concerns are linked to the functions of culturally hegemonic domination in knowledge production and reproduction. If we suggest that the centre functions to perpetuate its existence and dominance by absorbing some elements of the margins that are less contentious, then we ask what is the function of the margins? Provocatively, we might argue, that the privileged epistemological position of being at the margins can be used to make the centre more inclusive and dynamic. If the centre needs an audience positioned at the margins, the audience can be disobedient and persist in interrupting, talking back or turning their backs. For some of us who are not based in US institutions, publishing in outlets more sympathetic to feminist perspectives is a valuable option. Interdisciplinary research is also an option and a way of finding a different set of literature and research questions. Does this mean leaving the field? No, it means persisting by interrupting, contesting, retheorising and reshaping the field with different ideas and critique.

Current disciplinary assumptions about what feminist-oriented work ought to involve or how feminist theory should be applied, disciplined and codified has led us to a point in marketing where we know what it is like to be "known" and it is not pleasant (Longino 2010). By highlighting the politics of epistemic marginality, we have examined the relationships between the 'subjects/objects' of enquiry, the 'knowers' and experiences of theorising and disseminating within our disciplinary boundaries. Drawing on feminist work on testimony, we have emphasised different situated knowers and the power relations endemic to knowledge production. Our testimonies-in-opposition have revealed the dangers of uniformity and warped attempts to control knowers, as

Fine (2018) cautions, "conformity and elitism produce distorted thinking, dangerous to Others" (117).

The need to interrogate and learn from the ways in which neo-conservatism and neo-liberalism impact upon academics' lives, both inside and outside the discipline is a critical issue of concern (Spongberg 2008). Knowing how our own academic lives relate to the condition of knowledge making in our discipline is a fundamental part of consciousness raising. It has been our aim with this chapter to provide intertwined and collective testimonies as a way to contest the exclusion of marginal topics, methods and wrongly demarcated Othered academics from being expelled from the categories of valuable "knowers". In an era of accountability, efficiency and productivity, we have sought to arrive at these marginal truths by daring to speak about our experiences and through a refusal to do what is expected of us. Consciousness-raising is neither an end in itself nor a stage, a means to a different end, but a significant part of a very inclusive commitment to arriving at a change (Sarachild 1968). Action and transformation are therefore defining characteristics of feminist-inspired work, in short, feminist scholarship is *lived* research (Fonow and Cook 1991). As an outsider perspective, feminism offers a critical edge that challenges and despite its resistance from the mainstream, can move and improve our discipline, bringing specialised theory and empirical knowledge *into* marketing. It is with this in mind that we leave you with a testimonial excerpt from a world-renowned scholar who has researched marginalities throughout the entirety of their career and continues to provide marketing scholars with inspiration to pursue work at the margins:

> We need to realize that people (not consumers) often go without adequate food, shelter, healthcare, clothing, and education or job opportunities, and our skills can be used to advocate for them. Anything less is an abrogation of our larger responsibilities to humankind.

As we have noted, feminist contributions to marketing position it as *something other* than mainstream. As feminist-oriented scholars this other-than marginality allows us to build fugitive spaces (Kelley 2017) and interrupt the social anaesthesia (Fine 2018) and disciplinary paralysis which has emerged from complacency, consensus and the collective reassurance that dominant knowers – know best. We hope our collective and intertwined testimonies and thoughts strike a chord with those dissatisfied with the status quo, as we firmly believe marginal spaces are now more important than ever.

Acknowledgements

Our heartfelt thanks to our marketing colleagues, friends and fellow travellers on the margins who took the time to provide deeply personal accounts of their experiences and views on this subject.

References

Ahmed, S. (2012). *On Being Included: Racism and Diversity in Institutional Life*, Duke University Press Books, Durham, NC.

Alcoff, L. (1993). "How is epistemology political?" in Gottlied, R. (Ed) *Radical Philosophy: Tradition, Counter-Tradition, Politics*, Temple University Press, Philadelphia, PA, pp. 65–85.

Bar On B.A. (1973). "Marginality and epistemic privilege", in Alcoff, L. and Potter, E. (Eds) *Feminist Epistemologies*, Routledge, New York, pp. 983–1000.

Baraitser, L. (2009). *Maternal Encounters: The Ethics of Interruption*, New York and London: Routledge.

Bergin, L.A. (2002). "Testimony, epistemic difference and privilege: How feminist epistemology can improve our understanding of the communication of knowledge", *Social Epistemology*, 16(3), 197–213.

Beverly, J. (2005). "Testimonio, subalternity, and narrative authority", in Denzin, N.K. and Lincoln, Y.S. (Eds) *Handbook of Qualitative Research*, Sage, Thousand Oaks, CA, pp. 555–565.

Bourdieu, P. (1988). *Homo Academicus*, Stanford University Press, Stanford, CA.

Boussebaa, M. and Tienari, J. (2019). "Englishization and the politics of knowledge production in management studies", *Journal of Management Enquiry*, 30 (1), 59-67.

Brah, A. (2012). "Some fragments by way of an afterword", *Feminist Review*, 100, 172–180.

Byrne, A. and Lentin, R. (2000). "Feminist research methodologies in the social sciences", in Byrne, A. and Lentin, R. (Eds) *(Re)searching Women: Feminist Research Methodologies in the Social Sciences in Ireland*, IPA, Dublin, pp. 1–59.

Cervantes-Soon, C. (2012). "Testimonios of life and learning in the borderlands: Subaltern Juarez girls speak", *Equity & Excellence in Education*, 45(3), 373–391.

Chow, R. (2006). *The Age of the World Target: Self Referentiality in War, Theory and Comparative Work*, Duke University Press, Durham, NC.

Code, L. (1993). 'Taking subjectivity into account', in Alcoff, L. and Potter, E. (Eds) *Feminist Epistemologies*, Routledge, New York, pp. 15–148.

Code, L. (2014). "Feminist epistemology and the politics of knowledge: Questions of marginality", in Madhok, S. and Evans, M. (Eds) *The Sage Handbook of Feminist Theory*, Sage, London, pp. 9–25.

Faifua, D. (2010). "Reclaiming the outsider-within space: An auto-ethnography", *Tamara Journal for Critical Organisation Inquiry*, 8(3), 119–132.

Fine, M. (2018). *Just Research in Contentious Times: Widening the Methodological Imagination*, Columbia University; Teachers College Press, New York.

Fonow, M.M. and Cook, J.A. (1991). "Back to the future: A look at the second wave of feminist epistemology and methodology", in, Fonow, M.M. and Cook, J.A. (Eds) *Beyond Methodology: Feminist Scholarship as Lived Research*, Indiana University Press, Indiana, pp. 12–27.

Fricker, M. (2007). *Epistemic Injustice: Power and the Ethics of Knowing*, Oxford University Press, Oxford.

Friedman, A. (1999). "On Israeli women's feminism, femininity and power", in Izraeli, D. et al. (Eds) *Sex Gender Politics*, Hakibbutz Hameuchad, Tel Aviv, 400, pp. 167–215.

Gedalof, I. (2012). "Interruption, reproduction and genealogies of 'staying put' in diaspora space", *Feminist Review*, 100, 72–87.

Grey, C. (2010). "Organizing studies: Publications, politics and polemic", *Organization Studies*, 31, 677–694.

Harding, S. (2015). *Objectivity & Diversity: Another Logic of Scientific Research*, University of Chicago Press, Chicago, IL.

Hawkesworth, M. (1989). "Knowers, knowing, known: Feminist theory and claims of thurth", *Signs: Journal of Women in Culture and Society*, 14(3), 533–557.

hooks, b. (2010). *Teaching Critical Thinking: Practical Wisdom*, New York, Taylor & Francis.

Intemann, K., Lee, S.A., McCartney, K., Roshanravan, S. and Schriempf, A. (2010). "What lies ahead: Envisioning new futures for feminist philosophy", *Hypatia*, 25(4), 927–934.

Keet, A. (2014). "Epistemic 'othering' and the decolonisation of knowledge", *Africa Insight*, 44(1), 23–37.

Kelley, R.D.G. (2017). *Black Study, Black Struggle*. Retrieved from boston-review.net/forum/robin-d-g-kelley-black-study-black-struggle.

Kress, T.A. (2011). "Stepping out of the academic brew: Using critical research to break down hierarchies of knowledge production", *International Journal of Qualitative Studies in Education*, 24(3), 267–283.

Lather, P. and Smithies, C. (1997). *Troubling the Angels: Women Living with HIV/AIDS*. Westview/Harper Collins, Boulder, CO.

Longino, H. (2010). "Feminist epistemology at Hypatia's 25th Anniversary", *Hypatia*, 25(4), 733–741.

Lorde, A. (1984). "The master's tools will never dismantle the master's house", in A. Lorde (Ed.) *Sister Outsider*, The Crossing Press, Tramansburg, NY, pp. 110–113.

Lynch, K. (2000). "Emancipatory research in the academy", in Byrne, A. and Lentin, R. (Eds.) *(Re)searching Women: Feminist Research Methodologies in the Social Sciences in Ireland*, IPA, Dublin, pp. 73–99.

McRobbie, A. (1982). "The politics of feminist research: Between talk, text and action", *Feminist Review*, 12, 46–57.

Medina, J. (2012). "Hermeneutical injustice and polyphonic contextualism: Social silences and shared hermeneutical responsibilities", *Social Epistemology*, 26(2), 201–220.

Olesen, V.L. (1975). "Rage is not enough: Scholarly feminist and research in women's health", in Olesen, V.L. (Ed) *Women and Their Health: Research Implications for a New Era'*, Department of Education and Welfare, Public Health Service, Washington, DC, pp. 1–2.

Olesen, V.L. (2011). "Feminist qualitative research in the millennium's first decade: Developments, challenges, prospects", in Denzin, N.K. and Lincoln, Y.S. (Eds) *The Sage Handbook of Qualitative Research*, Sage, London, pp. 129–146.

Orelus, P.W. (2018). "Can subaltern professors speak?: Examining micro-aggressions and lack of inclusion in the academy", *Qualitative Research Journal*, 2, 169–179.

Prieto, L. and Villenas, S. (2012). "Pedagogies from Nepantla: Testimonio, Chicana/Latina feminisms and teacher classrooms", *Equity & Excellence in Education*, 45(3), 411–429.

Rich, A. (1975). *The Burning of Paper Instead of Children. Poems: Selected and New, 1950–1974*, W.W. Norton, New York.

Sandoval, C. (2000). "U.S. Third World Feminism: Differential Social Movement", in Sandoval, C. (Ed) *Methodology of the Oppressed*, University of Minnesota Press, Minneapolis, pp. 40–78.

Sarachild, K. (1968). "Program for feminist consciousness-raising," in Crown, B. (Ed), *Notes from the Second Year: Women's Liberation*, Shulamith Firestone, New York, pp. 273–276.

Schulman, S. (2009). *Ties That Bind: Familial Homophobia and Its Consequences*, The New Press, New York.

Spongberg, M. (2008). "Australian women's history in Australian feminist periodicals 1971–1988", *History Australia*, 5(3), 1–73.

Tillman, L.C. (2001). "Mentoring African American faculty in predominantly white institutions", *Research in Higher Education*, 42, 295–325.

Tourish, D. and Willmott, H. (2015). "In defiance of folly: Journal rankings, mindless measures and the ABS guide", *Critical Perspectives on Accounting*, 26, 37–46.

Turner, C. (2002). "Women of color in academe", *Journal of Higher Education*, 73, 74–93.

Turner, C. (2003). "Incorporation and marginalization in the academy: From border toward center for faculty of color?", *Journal of Black Studies*, 34, 112–125.

Welbourne, M. (1986). *The Community of Knowledge*, Aberdeen University Press, Aberdeen.

28 Women who work
The limits of the neoliberal feminist paradigm

Catherine Rottenberg

Introduction

When Ivanka Trump's how-to-succeed guide *Women Who Work* was released in May 2017, it generated a flurry of negative reviews in the mainstream media (i.e. Brooks 2017). Many commentators excoriated the book, claiming that this newest 'having it all' manifesto is composed of jargon, which could just as easily have been found by Googling 'inspirational quotes' (Tolentino 2017). Summing up the general reaction, Megan Garber (2017) explains that Trump's book has been dismissed in large part because it relies on upbeat platitudes to convey a message of female empowerment while offering a vision of feminism that is not very feminist at all. Yet, notwithstanding this widespread criticism, *Women Who Work* quickly became a *New York Times* bestseller.

While it is true that *Women Who Work* is littered with clichés and unabashedly endorses the Ivanka lifestyle brand, I suggest that Trump's manifesto warrants serious analysis. Her main message—and the one that serves as her repetitive mantra—is that women should work on all facets of their life, namely, their 'career, relationship, family, friendships, hobbies, and passions' (2017, p. 133). The address is directed, not surprisingly, toward so-called aspirational women (see McRobbie, 2009; Allen, 2014), who are incessantly incited to achieve their 'best self', both professionally and personally. Success is defined as facing obstacles with resilience, initiative, and creativity, while one's ability to thrive is described as 'limited only by one's own hunger, drive, passion, and execution' (Trump, 2017, p. 91). According to Trump, then, empowerment and achievement involve individual women consciously choosing to create the life they desire and proactively crafting such a life through continuous labor and perseverance.

It is in this way that *Women Who Work* captures and reproduces a key contemporary and neoliberal expectation that individuals—and particularly women—should never cease working on themselves in order to enhance their value. The book deserves serious attention precisely for the way that it lays bare the intensive labor—affective and physical—that women are expected to invest in themselves in order to approximate the contemporary norm of female—and as I will argue *feminist*—accomplishment (see also Gill and Orgad 2015, 2017; McRobbie, 2015; Elias, Gill, and Scharff, 2017; Scharff, 2017). Furthermore, a close examination of *Women Who Work* reveals that the ideal female subject is not only conceived of (and incited to conceive herself) as human capital but the self is produced as well as produces itself as 'an individual firm' or business enterprise, where all activities and practices are understood as investments that aim to appreciate the value of the self-as-firm. Trump's text, in other words, encourages women to consider themselves as a form of 'stock', where their normative role is to augment their

DOI: 10.4324/9781003042587-34

market value. This entails incessant labor, particularly the modification of behavior, aspirations, and affective orientation—much like a corporation that alters its practices in an attempt to increase its stocks' value by becoming more 'efficient' (see Feher, 2009). The woman-as-stock framework, I argue, conjures the newest permutation of the neoliberal feminist subject, since she is completely shorn of any and all liberal trappings.

In order to make the argument that Trump's manifesto can and should be read as registering and helping constitute the newest permutation of the neoliberal feminist subject, I first provide an overview of my theoretical arguments with respect to the rise of neoliberal feminism and the engendering of the neoliberal feminist subject (Rottenberg, 2014b, 2018). I simultaneously underscore that the book should not be considered an outlier but, rather, as part and parcel of the wider cultural landscape in which neoliberal feminism has become part of mainstream common sense. I then turn to analyze *Women Who Work* in some detail, showing how neoliberal feminism has been erasing long-standing divisions and political differences. This erasure pivots on neoliberal rationality's colonization of more domains of our lives, refiguring these domains in market metrics while undoing conceptual and political boundaries constitutive of liberalism and liberal thought. Not only does the private–public divide collapse, but so, too, does the distinction between one's 'private' self and one's 'public' enterprise as the self itself becomes an enterprise. This dual process of collapse and reconfiguration shapes the ideal neoliberal feminist subject, the main protagonist of Trump's *Women Who Work*.

The rise of neoliberal feminism

As I have argued elsewhere (2014a, 2014b, 2017, 2018), in the past decade we have witnessed the publication of a flurry of feminist manifestos that have garnered intense media attention and reenergized feminist debates in the US, most trenchantly around the question of why well-educated middle-class women are still struggling to cultivate careers and raise children at the same time. Two of these, former Princeton University professor Anne-Marie Slaughter's 'Why Women Still Can't Have It All' (2012) and Facebook's chief operating officer Sheryl Sandberg's best-selling *Lean In: Women, Work and The Will to Lead* (2013) might well be said to have initiated a trend of high-power women publicly identifying as feminists. Concurrently, there has been a veritable explosion of feminist discourse in popular and mainstream venues in both the US and the UK. This is what Sarah Banet-Weiser (2017) has aptly termed popular feminism. Yet, feminist themes have not merely been popularized and 'mainstreamed', but, as scholars such as Lynne Segal (2017a, 2017b), Nancy Fraser (2013), and Angela McRobbie (2013, 2015) have argued in different contexts, they have also become increasingly compatible with neoliberal political and economic agendas (see also Eisenstein, 2009; Prügl, 2015; Farris, 2017; Wilson, 2015).

Building on the growing scholarship that attempts to account for the mutual entanglement of feminism and neoliberalism, I have argued that we have been witnessing the emergence of a new variant of feminism, one that revolves centrally around the notion of happy work-family balance. Balance has not only been incorporated into the social imagination as a cultural good but has helped to engender a new model of emancipated womanhood: a professional woman able to balance a successful career with a satisfying family life. A 'happy work-family balance', in other words, is currently being (re)presented not merely as a normative ideal for women but as a progressive *feminist* ideal, particularly in the Anglo-American world (Rottenberg, 2014a; Orgad, 2017, 2018; see also Adamson, 2017; Armstrong, 2017). This new feminist ideal not only helps to shape women's desires, aspirations, and behavior, but also to produce a feminist subject informed through and through by a market metrics. I call this new variant of feminism neoliberal feminism and show how it has been unsettlingly unmoored from key liberal political goals such as equality, justice and emancipation. Disavowing the socio-economic and cultural structures shaping our lives, this feminism spawns a feminist subject who accepts full responsibility for her own well-being and self-care that are predicated on crafting a felicitous work-family balance, which is itself based on a cost-benefit—namely, a market—calculus.

It is important to underscore that I do not understand neoliberalism merely as an economic system or a set of policies that facilitate intensified privatization and deregulation, but rather, following political theorists Michel Feher (2009) and Wendy Brown (2015, 2016), as a dominant political rationality or a normative form of reason that moves to and from the management of the state to the inner workings of the subject. In his germinal article 'Self-Appreciation; or The Aspirations of Human Capital' Feher (2009) has described the historic shift in governance that has occurred under neoliberalism's hegemony, arguing that neoliberalism is creating new forms of subjectivation, which produce human beings as human capital. Human beings consequently become investors in themselves as capital, wishing to enhance their own value over time. Feher further claims that neoliberalism's 'subjective apparatus'—the apparatus through which subjects are constituted and gain intelligibility—is radically different from the one operating under liberalism. If under liberalism human beings are conceived of as free laborers with labor power to sell, under neoliberalism human beings are engendered as subjects who cultivate a *speculative* relationship to the human capital that they have become. The focus accordingly shifts from selling labor or even human capital in the marketplace to increasing one's value everywhere—and all the time—by altering and diversifying assets or modifying behaviors and social interactions. Every alteration or lack thereof is considered either to appreciate or depreciate the value of the self-as-human-capital.

Brown (2016, p. 3) has more recently claimed that neoliberalism economizes political and social life in distinctive ways, producing subjects for which consumption, education, training, and mate-selection are all configured as practices of self-investment, where the self is perceived not only as an entrepreneur, as scholars such as Nikolas Rose (1992) have already argued, but also as an individual firm or business enterprise. Moreover, through processes of devolution and responsibilization, neoliberal governance constructs and manages subjects who are configured as agents wholly responsible and blameable for their own individual lives.[1] The conversion of subjects—and, I argue, particularly female subjects—into self-investing capital consequently undoes traditional forms of social ties and relations. Furthermore, given that neoliberalism is remolding all spheres of life into the model of the market—where competition and capital appreciation override all else—the world is, according to Cruz and Brown (2016), increasingly becoming a place in which there are only winners and losers, capital enhancing subjects and those deemed 'disposable' because they are 'unbankable'.

And, yet, even as neoliberal rationality colonizes more and more domains of our lives, recasting them in market terms, I suggest that neoliberalism has actually 'needed' feminism to resolve—at least temporarily—one of its internal tensions in relation to gender.

As an economic order, neoliberalism relies on reproduction and care work in order to reproduce and maintain human capital. However, as a political rationality—and in stark contrast to liberalism—neoliberalism has no lexicon that can recognize let alone value reproduction and care work. Everything is reduced to a market metrics—even our political imagination. The disappearance of a distinctive political lexicon is not only due to human subjects being increasingly converted into generic human capital, where gender is disavowed, but also because the division of the public-private spheres—informing liberal thought and the traditional sexual division of labor—is being eroded through the conversion of everything into capital and the infiltration of a market rationality into all spheres of life, including the most private ones. Different registers—political, economic, social, and affective—collapse under neoliberalism, and all forms of valuation transpire through a cost-benefit metrics.

Neoliberal feminism has, in other words, operated as a kind of pushback to the total conversion of educated and upwardly mobile women into generic human capital. By paradoxically and counterintuitively maintaining reproduction as part of middle-class or so-called aspirational women's normative trajectory and positing *balance* as its normative frame and ultimate ideal, neoliberal *feminism* helps to both maintain a discourse of reproduction care-work while ensuring that all responsibility for these forms of labor—but not necessarily all of the labor itself—falls squarely on the shoulder of aspirational women. In this way it solves its own constitutive tension—the quandary of reproduction and care-work—at least temporarily. Indeed, neoliberal *feminism* produces and maintains a distinctive and affective lexiconic register of reproductive and care work within neoliberalism, even as neoliberal rationality collapses the private-public divide.

Women Who Work

An analysis of *Women Who Work* reveals that the book not only assumes the neoliberal feminist subject I have outlined above but also conjures a subject that further propels or accelerates the conversion of so-called aspirational women into generic rather than gendered human capital. This is best exemplified in the reworking of motherhood in increasingly managerial terms. However, this conversion process still remains incomplete, since the ideal of a happy work-family balance continues to serve as a pushback to the complete erasure of traditional notions of sexual difference. Indeed, if reproduction and balance were not retained as part of the discussion, then the transformation of aspirational women into generic human capital would be 'complete' and neoliberal feminist discourse would disappear. It is precisely through maintaining balance as part of its ideal on the one hand, while furthering the conversion of women into specks of human capital through construing motherhood in managerial terms on the other, that neoliberal feminism appears to move closer toward its logical limit.

Like many of the bestselling neoliberal feminist manifestos that have been published in the last few years, such as Sheryl Sandberg's *Lean In* (2013) and Megyn Kelly's *Settle For More* (2016), Trump clearly states her conviction that working toward greater gender equality is of paramount importance, explicitly acknowledging that gender parity has yet to be reached in the US. In her introductory chapter, Trump (2017, p. 4) declares that despite the progress and the many advances women have made since her mother's generation, 'we've still got a long way to go'. Moreover, she advocates for certain structural changes, such as paid maternity leave. These avowals of continued gender inequality, which can be understood as one of the signs marking the shift from a postfeminist moment to a feminist one, are, however, overlaid by a much more profound and general disavowal. Trump spends approximately one page of her 212-page book expounding on structural obstacles. The overwhelming majority of the advice and instruction given by Trump to less famous and wealthy women revolves around the labor individual women are required to invest in themselves in order to achieve success. Indeed, Trump (2017, pp. 47, 176) insists that women must 'plot a plan for success' and if they are passionate, work hard and are committed to excellence, they will inevitably succeed. The underlying assumption, then, is that individual women are ultimately responsible for both their successes and their failures.

Women Who Work can therefore be read as exposing the processes through which aspirational women are interpellated as (potentially) capital-enhancing subjects. Through her constant exhortation that women invest in and labor on all domains of their lives, Trump reveals, performs, and helps to (re)produce the conversion of women from ostensible autonomous rights bearing liberal subjects who need to fight discrimination in order to gain access to the marketplace to sell their labor into subjects who must work tirelessly on themselves in order to produce and cultivate their selves *as* human capital. This human capital, she intimates, must be cultivated continuously. Every aspect of the self becomes a site of speculation, intense scrutiny and affective investment—a process whose objective is to increase and diversify the self's assets, to facilitate its appreciation, but just as importantly, to prevent its depreciation.

This 'totalizing' approach to the self as human capital serves to facilitate the transmutation of the self into a business enterprise, while simultaneously helping to further unravel the private-public divide. The neoliberal subject herself—recast as an individual firm—is compelled and encouraged to perceive all aspects of her life and self—including reproduction and care work—as requiring continuous capital investment, rendering the separation of public-private increasingly unintelligible. In other words, as neoliberal rationality transforms more and more elements of society into enterprises informed by a business model with financialization at its heart, not only do all remaining private-public distinctions collapse but the self (itself) becomes increasingly indistinguishable from any other kind of business enterprise, which ultimately undermines the very logic upholding the separation between the spheres.

Trump's manifesto reveals as well as enacts the two-fold and concurrent collapsing of these traditionally distinct realms: the public versus the private as well as one's enterprise versus one's self. Following her prolonged introduction, Trump (2017, pp. 28, 47) urges women to draft a personal mission statement, which, she claims, will pay certain 'dividends' in the future by helping them to identify their passions and 'true north'. This exercise will help them maximize their influence later on. After identifying what their passions are—preferably in their twenties—women are subsequently encouraged to enter the business or professional world and to cultivate a wide array of capabilities, such as networking and negotiating deals 'thoughtfully and effectively'. These capabilities are depicted as part of the self's overall 'portfolio of conducts' (Feher, 2009, p. 30) which are considered key for increasing the probabilities of creating a successful enterprise and 'making one's mark' (Trump, 2017, p. 14).

Yet this is precisely the moment when the boundary between self and business becomes blurred, since the advice to foster these abilities—networking, negotiating skills—is meant to enhance not only the business one works for (or runs) but also—and perhaps most crucially—the self itself. This helps explain why *Women Who Work* repeatedly insists that it is important for women who have begun to make their mark professionally to create to-do charts to 'prioritize [their] time so that [they] are always adding value' (2017, p. 121). Planning well, which includes making endless lists about what women want to accomplish—from mission statements to everyday color-coded to-do lists—is central to ensuring that hard work will enhance value and yield the proper results. The self becomes, in the words of feminist theorist Angela McRobbie (2015, p. 10), a kind of 'neoliberal spreadsheet' indistinguishable from a business, where one calculates one's assets, one's losses, and what is more or less valuable in order to decide where more capital investment—in the form of developing entrepreneurial skills, resources, or capacities—is necessary. In *Women Who Work*, the self has indeed been unashamedly transformed into an enterprise, and, as such, there is no longer any need to presuppose the separation of the private and public spheres.

The reconfiguration and collapse of the private-public divide is perhaps most evident as Trump (2017, p. 128) includes domains traditionally and historically excluded from notions of 'boosting one's productivity' and 'maximizing one's efficiency' in neoliberalism's calculative schema. Hobbies, friendships, and other intimate relationships that under liberalism were separate—at least conceptually—from a calculative matrix are now carefully remade into forms of investment and value management. As Joan Scott (2017, p. 13) has highlighted, the public and private dichotomy historically separated, conceptually, the 'market and politics' from 'home and family' as well as 'affective relationality'. While *Women Who Work* merely intimates that decisions about who one dates and marries should also be part of this calculus, it explicitly encourages women to foster friendships and hobbies—namely, 'affective relationalities'—not as ends in and of themselves but instead as part of the self-as-business's capital enhancing process. When discussing the importance of networking for women just starting out on their career, Trump urges these women to make one new strong bond each time they meet people at a party or conference. Although there is some attempt to play down the instrumentalization of other people, the emphasis is nonetheless on the new contact or friend as beneficial for business as well as for enhancing one's own value. Indeed, both the cultivation of intimacies as well as self-care and leisure activities are transposed into business-like strategies, which also illustrates how neoliberal rationality dissolves traditional forms of social ties and relations, even toward one's self.

What we witness, then, is the economization of domains once closely associated with the non-market interests of the private sphere. Particularly striking is how affect—again, once inextricably linked to the domestic realm—has been transformed into its own form of asset or capital, which now requires smart investment so as to increase the probability of 'dividends' in the future (see also Brown, 2015, Rottenberg, 2017). One's affective attachments are perceived as forms of capital to be cultivated and invested in order to enhance the value of the self's overall portfolio. Savvy self-investment and entrepreneurial strategies of self-care have become paramount. In this way, Trump's how-to-succeed book provides readers with a clear vision of a world in which all spheres of human life have become completely saturated not only by a calculative reason but also reconfigured by neoliberalism's moral imperative to appreciate—or at least maintain—one's own market value as the ultimate aim in life.

Consequently, *Women Who Work* clearly exposes many of the processes by and through which subjects are required to remake themselves into various credit seeking assets, endlessly working on themselves in order to increase their worth. Trump lays out in some detail the various kinds of temporal, physical, aesthetic and affective investments that women must make in order to ensure that they can manage themselves successfully as capital-enhancing subjects. Taking care of ourselves and professional development are, Trump (2017, p. 104) insists, things that 'we must prioritize so that we may become the best version of ourselves and achieve our goals'. These activities are meant to maximize women's value. The text can therefore be read as encouraging and *further* enacting the conversion of aspirational women into generic rather than gendered human capital, and this process is, I suggest, most strikingly and best exemplified in the refiguring of motherhood in managerial terms.

Although Trump does pay tribute to norms of intensive and hands-on motherhood, she simultaneously provides a range of directives about how to better *manage* the care-giving role. She tells us that she writes lists for 'connecting with each of [her] kids' putting real thought into ideas for producing 'memorable moments' she can create with them (2017, p. 117). Her approach to care work is calculative and thus reads more like ticking off the right boxes in order to demonstrate 'correct investment' for eventual returns in the form of future memories. She also informs her readers that she makes sure to have concrete family goals, which then enable her to pencil in time with her family. These goals include official date nights with her husband, dates that are scheduled into the general family list well in advance. In *Women Who Work* the realm of reproduction and care is transmogrified into regulated, calculative and carefully planned affective investment. The way in which reproductive and care work is presented here, namely, in more managerial terms—thus undermining discourses of 'natural' female nurturing instincts—gestures to the further saturation of a market metrics into domains that have traditionally upheld the gendered division of labor, attenuating in interesting ways the link between women—or, to be more precise—a certain strata of women—and care work. As a result, the ideal female self who Trump presents potentially undermines traditional notions of sexual difference.

Yet, on the other hand—and crucially—the conversion of 'aspirational' women into generic human capital remains incomplete, and not merely because women are the ones deemed responsible for managing the to-do lists. Rather, Trump's normative trajectory still includes reproduction, while her ideal of female success remains a happy work-family balance, which is precisely why *Women Who Work* should be considered a neoliberal feminist manifesto par excellence. Interestingly, Trump (2017, p. 147) ostensibly eschews the notion of work-family balance, claiming that such balance is often impossible on a day-to-day basis, opting, instead, for the term work/life rhythm. However, rhythm turns out to be interchangeable with equilibrium, and the term balance nevertheless reinserts itself into Trump's happiness script when she posits that her overall objective is to 'attain balance over her lifetime' (pp. 144, 147) by which she means an equilibrium between being an involved parent and a successful businesswoman. Hence, the work/life rhythm might need to be recalibrated occasionally—or even quite often—in order to ensure happiness, but a happy equilibrium between work and family over time remains the ultimate end game. In this way, reproduction and care work continue to function as a pushback to neoliberalism's conversion of aspirational women into generic subjects.

As a result of its adherence to the how-to-succeed genre, offering step-by-step advice, *Women Who Work* exposes in great and disturbing detail neoliberalism's moral imperative. Through constantly inciting each individual woman to pursue 'savvy self-investment and entrepreneurial strategies of self-care' (Brown, 2016, p. 9). Trump's manifesto helps demonstrate how individual women are being construed as specks of human capital. Indeed, she encourages women to labor ceaselessly on themselves in order to produce, maintain, and appreciate themselves *as* human capital albeit without forfeiting reproductive and care work responsibilities. In a sense, then, *Women Who Work* thematizes with disturbing clarity how neoliberal feminist discourses around benchmarks, competition, and success are eclipsing demands for equal rights, as well as how notions of the self-as-stock are replacing discussions of autonomy and emancipation, leaving few if any traces of the liberal feminist subject in their wake.

Conclusion

In *Undoing the Demos*, Wendy Brown (2015, p. 36) provocatively suggests that neoliberalism's revolution is one that transpires by stealth, termite-like, boring 'in capillary fashion into the trunks and branches of workplaces, schools, public agencies, social and political discourse, and above all, the subject'. Thus, as neoliberal rationality permeates ever more domains of our lives, the conceptual and political boundaries constitutive of liberalism and liberal thought are being undone, while more and more domains are being retooled through market metrics. This dual process of collapse and reconfiguration helps produce the neoliberal feminist subject who stars in Ivanka Trump's *Women Who Work*. Neoliberalism as a political rationality, in other words, not only undoes conceptual boundaries but also—and crucially—brings into being 'new subjects, conduct, relations, and worlds' (Brown, 2015, p. 36).

By way of conclusion, it is important to underscore that *Women Who Work* ultimately fails to address the challenges and difficulties of the vast majority of women who work. Trump's 'how-to-succeed' guide effectively erases from view most of the women (with or without children) who participate in the labor force, many of whom work in precarious conditions in the so-called 'gig economy', enduring double shifts, night shifts, or taking on two to three jobs just in order to make ends meet.[2] As such, Trump's text resonates and dovetails with Sandberg's (2013) and Slaughter's (2015) well-known neoliberal feminist manifestos, which are unabashedly exclusionary, encompassing as they do only so-called aspirational women in their interpellative address. In this way, neoliberalism feminism also helps to reify white and class privilege as well as heteronormativity.

Given the reality that, most often, women of color, poor, and immigrant women serve as the unacknowledged care workers who enable professional women to strive toward 'balance' in their lives, neoliberal feminism helps to (re)produce and legitimize the exploitation of these 'other' female subjects while simultaneously disarticulating the very vocabulary with which to address the glaring inequalities that these women experience in their daily lives. In one sense, neoliberal feminism enables wages for housework and childrearing by outsourcing these tasks to 'non-aspirational' women. But rather than serving as a path to liberation, wages for housework and care work serve to further expand and entrench a market rationality while concurrently creating new and reinforcing old class-based and racialized gender stratification (see Glenn, 2010; Briggs, 2017). Indeed, the outsourcing of reproduction and care work further splits female subjecthood, deepening the bifurcation between the worthy capital enhancing feminist few and the disavowed female rest. What neoliberal feminism ultimately facilitates is the production of a small class of so-called aspirational subjects who self-invest wisely and augment their capital value, alongside a large class of women who are rendered expendable, exploitable, and disposable. This feminism, in sum, forsakes most women, helping to create new and intensified forms of racialized and class-stratified gender exploitation, which increasingly constitutes the invisible yet necessary infrastructure of our new neoliberal order.

Additionally, due to the way in which it serves to bolster neoliberal hegemony, and as part of what Sara Farris and I have called the 'righting of feminism' (Farris and Rottenberg, 2017), neoliberal feminism in no way constitutes a threat to the powers that be. It effectively defangs feminism of its oppositional force by individualizing and responsibilizing women and by helping neoliberal rationality resolve one of its constitutive tensions by maintaining a distinctive lexicon of reproduction and care work. Simultaneously, the notion of a happy work-family balance helps render this variant of feminism palatable and legitimate, enabling neoliberal feminism's widespread embrace and circulation within the Anglo-American mainstream cultural landscape. Over the past few years, we have encountered it in multiple sites: from best-selling books through mainstream magazine articles and popular television series to well-trafficked mommy blogs.

Precisely because neoliberal feminism incites individual women to 'internalize the revolution' (Sandberg, 2013, p. 11) and focus on themselves and their own aspirations, thus buttressing neoliberalism's hegemony, it can more easily be popularized, sold, and capitalized upon in the market place. As the 'f-word' has literally inundated mainstream and social media, identifying as feminist has increasingly become a source of pride, serving as cultural capital for celebrities and high-profile women alike (see McRobbie, 2013, 2015; Banet-Weiser, 2017; Sarah Banet-Weiser and Portwood-Stacer, 2018; Farris and Rottenberg, 2017; Gill and Orgad, 2017; Hemmings 2018). The rise of neoliberal feminism has, in other words, helped to render feminism popular in ways few scholars could have predicted just a few years ago. And, yet, this process of popularization may constitute a double edge sword, since as Susan Buck Morss (2003) has convincingly argued, power always produces its own vulnerability.

By facilitating feminism's widespread embrace, neoliberal feminism has also—and paradoxically—helped to pave the way for more militant and mass feminist movements, such as #MeToo, the Woman's March and the International Women's Strike.[3] Clearly some of the infrastructure for the recent oppositional feminist groundswell was already in place. It is crucial to remember that the MeToo campaign initially emerged over a decade ago as part of a grassroots movement spearheaded by the African American activist Tarana Burke, and that it comes on the heels of other mobilizations, such as SlutWalk, the transnational movement that organized protests across the globe against rape culture and its attendant victim-blaming. But I suggest that in addition to (father) Trump's election and the reappearance of a shameless sexism in the public sphere, which has had its own galvanizing effect, #MeToo was able to gain such widespread traction at this particular moment in history, at least in part, because feminism had already been embraced and rendered desirable by high-power corporate women like Sheryl Sandberg, Hollywood stars like Emma Watson as well as music celebrities like Beyoncé (Agostinho, 2016)—to name just a few.

Finally, while more visible movements such as #MeToo are currently carrying out important cultural work—(at best) exposing just how thoroughly male entitlement saturates our culture—other feminist movements, such as Feminism for the 99%, which helped organize the Global Women's Strike—have been mobilizing on the ground, widening their reach, and significantly expanding the single analytic frame of gender, articulating and protesting a dizzying array of inequalities facing women, minorities, and precarious populations more generally. These feminist movements, like their more radical predecessors (Segal 2017a, 2017b), are demanding dramatic economic, social, and cultural transformations, thereby challenging the neoliberal consensus while creating alternative visions that cultivate hope for the future. Given just how bleak the future currently looks for an ever-increasing number of people across the globe—and particularly in the post-COVID era—this is exactly the kind of threatening feminism that we need. The urgent question, then, is how we can sustain and broaden this feminist renaissance *as counter-hegemonic*, while rejecting the neoliberal feminist logic informing Ivanka Trump's *Women Who Work*.

Notes

1 Brown also underscores, this 'devolution' of responsibility is occurring precisely at a time when social safety nets are being further dismantled.
2 See the National Women's Law Center website: https://nwlc.org/issue/poverty-economic-security.
3 Of course, father Trump's election and policies are also part of this larger picture. One of the great ironies here is that even as Ivanka Trump has written a neoliberal feminist manifesto par excellence, her father's unabashed sexist administration has galvanized the feminist resistance.

References

Adamson, M. (2017) Postfeminism, neoliberalism and a 'successfully' balanced femininity in celebrity CEO autobiographies. *Gender, Work and Organization*, 24, 3, 314–327.
Agostinho, D. (2016) Ghosting and ghostbusting feminism. *Diffractions*, 6, 1–16.
Allen, K. (2014) 'Blair's children': young women as 'aspirational subjects' in the psychic landscape of class. *The Sociological Review*, 62, 4, 760–779.
Armstrong, J. (2017) Higher stakes: generational differences in mother and daughters feelings about combining motherhood with a career, *Studies in the Maternal*, 9, 1, 1–25.
Banet-Weiser, S. (2018) *Empowered: Popular Feminism and Popular Misogyny*. Durham, NC: Duke University Press.
Banet-Weiser, S., and Portwood-Stacer, L. (2017). The traffic in feminism: an introduction to the commentary and criticism on popular feminism. *Feminist Media Studies*, 17, 5, 884–888.
Briggs, L. (2017) *How All Politics Became Reproductive Politics: From Welfare Reform to Foreclosure to Trump*. Berkeley: University of California Press.
Brooks, K. (2017) Ivanka Trump's 'vapid' new book earns a series of savage reviews. *Huff-Post*, May 3. https://www.huffingtonpost.co.uk/entry/ivanka-trump-women-who-work-reviews_us_5907a3f8e4b05c3976819069 (accessed May 14, 2018).
Brown, W. (2015) *Undoing the Demos: Neoliberalism's Stealth Revolution*. Cambridge: MIT Press.
Brown, W. (2016) Sacrificial citizenship: neoliberalism, human capital, and austerity politics, *Constellations* 23, 1, 3–14.
Buck-Morss, S. (2003) *Thinking Past Terror: Islamism and Critical Theory on the Left*. London: Verso.
Cruz, K., and Brown, W. (2016) Feminism, law, and neoliberalism: an interview and discussion with Wendy Brown. *Feminist Legal Studies*, 24, 1, 69–89.
Eisenstein, H. (2009) *Feminism Seduced: How Global Elites use Women's Labor and Ideas to Exploit the World*. Boulder, CO: Paradigm.
Elias, A., Gill, R., and Scharff, C. (2017) Aesthetic labour: beauty politics in neoliberalism. In Elias, A., Gill, R., and Scharff, C. (eds) *Aesthetic Labour: Rethinking Beauty Politics in Neoliberalism*, pp. 3–49. London: Springer

Farris, S. (2017) *In the Name of Women's Rights: The Rise of Femonationalism*. Durham, NC: Duke University Press.

Farris, S., and Rottenberg, C. (2017) Introduction: righting feminism. *New Formations: A Journal of Culture/Theory/Politics*, 91, 5–15.

Feher, M. (2009) Self-appreciation; or, the aspirations of human capital. *Public Culture*, 21, 1, 21–41.

Fraser, N. (2013) *Fortunes of Feminism: From State-Managed Capitalism to Neoliberal Crisis*. London: Verso Books.

Garber, M. (2017) The borrowed words of Ivanka Trump *The Atlantic*, May 5, online: https://www.theatlantic.com/entertainment/archive/2017/05/the-borrowed-words-of-ivanka-trump/525621/ (accessed May 14, 2018).

Gill, R., and Orgad, S. (2015) The confidence cult (ure). *Australian Feminist Studies*, 30, 86, 324–344.

Gill, R., and Orgad, S. (2017) Confidence culture and the remaking of feminism. *New Formations*, 91, 16–34.

Glenn. E. (2010). *Forced to Care: Coercion and Caregiving in American*. Cambridge, MA: Harvard University Press.

Hemmings, C. (2018) Resisting popular feminisms: gender, sexuality and the lure of the modern. *Gender, Place & Culture*, 1–15. https://doi.org/10.1080/0966369X.2018.1433639.

McRobbie, A. (2009) *The Aftermath of Feminism: Gender, Culture and Social Change*. London: Sage.

McRobbie, A. (2013) Feminism, the family and the new 'mediated' maternalism. *New Formations*, 80, 4, 119–137.

McRobbie, A. (2015) Notes on the perfect: competitive femininity in neoliberal times. *Australian Feminist Studies*, 30, 83, 3–20.

Orgad, S. (2017) The cruel optimism of the good wife: the fantastic working mother on the fantastical treadmill. *Television & New Media*, 18, 2, 165–183.

Orgad, S. (2018) *Heading Home: Work and the Failed Promise of Equality*. New York: Columbia University Press.

Prügl, E. (2015). Neoliberalising feminism. *New Political Economy*, 20, 4, 614–631.

Rose, N. (1992) Governing the enterprising self. In Hellas, P., and Morris, P. (eds) *The Values of the Enterprise Culture: The Moral Debate*, pp. 141–164. London: Routledge.

Rottenberg, C. (2014a) Happiness and the liberal imagination: How superwoman became balanced. *Feminist Studies*, 40, 1, 144–168.

Rottenberg, C. (2014b) The rise of neoliberal feminism. *Cultural Studies*, 28, 3, 418–437.

Rottenberg, C. (2017) Neoliberal feminism and the future of human capital. *Signs: Journal of Women in Culture and Society*, 42, 2, 329–348.

Rottenberg, C. (2018) *The Rise of Neoliberal Feminism*. New York: Oxford University Press.

Sandberg, S. (2013) *Lean in: Women, Work, and the Will to Lead*. New York: Alfred A. Knopf.

Scharff, C. (2017) *Gender, Subjectivity, and Cultural Work: The Classical Music Profession*. London: Routledge.

Scott, J. W. (2017) *Sex and Secularism*. Princeton, NJ: Princeton University Press.

Segal, L. (2017a) *Making Trouble: Life and Politics*. London: Verso.

Segal, L. (2017b) *Radical Happiness: Moments of Collective Joy*. London: Verso.

Slaughter, A. (2012) Why women still can't have it all. *The Atlantic*, July/August.

Slaughter, A (2015) *Unfinished business: Women men work family*. New York: Simon and Schuster.

Tolentino, J. (2017) Ivanka Trump wrote a painfully oblivious book for basically no one. *The New Yorker*, May 5: https://www.newyorker.com/books/page-turner/ivanka-trump-wrote-a-painfully-oblivious-book-for-basically-no-one (accessed May 14, 2018).

Trump, I. (2017) *Women Who Work: Rewriting the Rules for Success*. New York: Penguin.

Wilson, K. (2015). Towards a radical re-appropriation: Gender, development and neoliberal feminism. *Development and Change*, 46, 4, 803–832.

29 Putting pornography on the marketing agenda

A radical feminist centring of harm for women's marketplace inequality

Laura McVey, Meagan Tyler and Lauren Gurrieri

Introduction

Feminist marketers have begun to develop an agenda that addresses the commodification and trading of women (Scott 2017). There is also a growing recognition that the sex trade contributes to women's economic and social injustice (Hein et al. 2016). However, discussions on pornography – as a prominent sector of the sex industry – have largely been absent from the discipline (Bettany et al. 2010). Indeed, while the connections between women's inequality and pornography were highlighted in the early scholarship of feminist marketers (Hirschman 1991; Stern 1991), not only have analyses on pornography been relatively neglected since their groundbreaking works, but in this time, the pornography market has also undergone a considerable expansion in its cultural normalisation, its scale and business model, and its levels of violence against women. While the normalising of pornographic imagery and signifiers has become a growing point of interest for feminist marketers (Drenten, Gurrieri, and Tyler 2020; Maclaran 2015; Rome herein, Schroeder and McDonagh 2005), both within and outside the discipline, pornography – *as a market* – rarely receives the same scrutiny applied to critical analyses of advertising, film, television and social media (Bettany et al. 2010; Jensen 2020). Therefore, with this chapter we suggest that the pornography market, as a marketplace that fosters practices and conditions that (re)produce women's inequality, should be analysed within a similar, critical lens.

To do this, we turn to the branch of feminist theory that has been foundational and enduring in critiquing pornography as a capitalist market. Radical feminist analyses of pornography, as a market, were significant because they offered a departure from the dominant view of pornography as a disembodied text or a form of men's consumption. One of the most notable ways radical feminists have done this is by drawing attention to the ways in which women are literally harmed through the pornography market's production processes. Pornography for radical feminists is not just a representation, it is a documentation of what is done to someone (Boyle 2010). So, in understanding pornography as something other than just representation, or a harmless fantasy, radical feminist analyses have been exceptional in highlighting that this is a market with very real practices of racism and violence against women (Dworkin 1993; Jeffreys 2008). These market practices of racism and sexism are not coded or subtle but explicit, violent and based on highly sexualised and racist stereotypes (Collins 2002; MacKinnon 1991). As an example, acts that *frequently* appear in pornography include African American women being bound, sometimes in scenes involving or referencing slavery, and with more than one white man (Collins 2002). Pornography titles such as *Coco gets Interracial*

Facial (DeKeseredy 2018c) and *Black Poles in White Holes* (Dines 2006) are standard in the mainstream market; as are scenes featuring painful anal penetration, brutal gang rapes, and men slapping or choking women or pulling their hair as they penetrate them orally, vaginally and anally (DeKeseredy 2018c). Websites such as *Anal Suffering* openly promote that, 'Every week, we'll bring you a new Suffering Slut. Weak, Destroyed, Agonizing in Anal Pain …' (Dines 2010). While these examples may seem extreme, it is critical to note that these are not niche categories, these are the most popular and profitable acts of the mainstream market (DeKeseredy 2018a; Dines 2010).

As a means of analysing this capitalist market of white supremacist patriarchy, as something other than a form of art, representation or sexual expression, radical feminists have sought to centre issues of harm. Harm is especially useful for understanding marketplace inequality and violence against women because it was built from women's experiences of pornography, so it facilitates examinations on both the material harm women experience in markets, as well as the more macro-cultural inequalities women suffer from marketplace practices. This, in turn, meets the discipline's calls for more 'materialist' (Catterall, Maclaran, and Stevens 2005), 'radical' (Dholakia and Fırat 2018) and 'macro' (Rome, O'Donohoe, and Dunnett 2019) approaches. Although there is an emergent stream of work looking to 'unpick' the mechanisms and structures of marketplace gender inequality (Kravets, Preece, and Maclaran 2020), there is still much to be done in revealing the marketing of inequality, including how inequality can be rendered invisible, innocuous, acceptable, and even laudatory (Dholakia and Firat 2016). As others recognise, to interrogate women's inequality requires more thorough investigations that account for both material and cultural dimensions, and how these processes intersect to create and sustain patterns of inequality (Ridgeway 2014). It is through the radical feminist focus on harm that we extend upon the work of feminist marketers concerned with both material and discursive approaches to making visible women's inequalities (Steinfield 2019). Thus, harm – as a way of centring violence against women in the marketplace – offers feminist marketing scholars another way to keep research grounded in material reality, while also addressing the socio-cultural forces that shape human consciousness and experience (Maclaran and Stevens 2008).

Our chapter is set out as follows. We begin by highlighting some of the features of the contemporary pornography market, specifically drawing attention to how this market has been normalised while also growing in its scale, its business model, and its violent content. Then, as a practical analysis that prioritises the status and well-being of women, we map the radical feminist analysis of pornography that centres harm. Through applying harm to some of the newer practices of the pornography market, we expand upon the discipline's discussions on the material manifestations and cultural conditions of women's marketplace inequality. This, in turn, allows us to locate pornography as commercialising the production and reproduction of sexualised and racialised inequality and violence against women. Finally, we finish by highlighting some key research avenues for future scholarship and thus, we position pornography as a priority for a feminist marketing agenda.

The contemporary pornography market

There are four key points critical to understanding the shape of the contemporary pornography market. They are: its (i) embeddedness in mainstream culture, (ii) escalating scale (iii) changing business model, and (iv) increasing and severe levels of violence against women. We start by tracing pornography's normalisation in society.

The cultural normalisation of pornography has resulted in the mainstreaming of sexual content, whereby the boundary between popular media culture and pornography is increasingly blurred (Attwood 2002; Boyle 2010; McNair 2002). Referred to as pornographication, pornification and porn(o)-chic, it is a phenomenon that has been conceptualised across multiple disciplines (Tyler and Quek 2016). This mainstreaming has been noted as manifesting in various practices and products in popular culture, including trends in technology, music, fashion, beauty, and even children's merchandise (c.f. Jeffreys 2014; Rome herein, Tyler and Quek 2016). While early scholarship in the area extensively documented, and largely celebrated, the abundance of sexual representations appearing in the mainstream, there was very little critical analysis of the harms of pornographication until radical feminists positioned the pornification of society as a *commercial* function of white supremacist, capitalist patriarchy (Boyle 2018; hooks 2000; Jeffreys 2014).

From this perspective, pornographication does not solely mainstream sex, it mainstreams the commercialisation of a particular kind of sex that eroticises women's inequality (Tyler and Quek 2016). Feminist marketers have noted the potential harms to women from a 'logic of pornography' (Schroeder and McDonagh 2005), a porn-chic aesthetic (Drenten, Gurrieri, and Tyler 2020), and the pornification of culture (Maclaran 2015, Rome herein). However, as radical feminists maintain, to understand how pornographication threatens the equality of women and girls, the pornification of society needs to be considered within critical analyses of pornography *as a market* (Dines 2010). It is not only that pornographication can be seen as normalising or even eroticising sexualised violence against women but, also, that this is a circular process of the market system, because pornography's creation of women as commodities feeds back into normalising the market's harmful practices (Russo 1998). Although a pornified culture can and often does inform women's individual consumption choices, it also harms women culturally, as a sex-class, through making the sex industry and its practices of violence against women appear 'chic' (Jeffreys 2014). So, the significance of pornographication for radical feminists is that once the pornography market is normalised it becomes much more difficult to conceive its harms (Langton 2008).

Alongside the trend of normalisation, shifts in technology have significantly impacted the pornography market. The emergence and spread of high-speed internet, and mobile devices, have facilitated a considerable expansion in the scale of the pornography market. While videos and DVDs drove the growth of the market from the mid-1970s until the mid-1990s (Dines 2010), the shift to being primarily online has significantly escalated pornography's scale. In 2001, figures from the US estimated pornography to be worth US$4 billion a year (Jeffreys 2014). Despite digital technologies enabling access to a proliferation of free and pirated pornography, the US market has grown to be worth more than US$15 billion a year (Anciaux 2020); sizeable when compared to Hollywood's annual revenue of US$10 billion (Tangmanee 2019). While pornography's evolution into online spaces has only compounded existing uncertainty and clandestine revenue reporting, various sources agree the global earnings of the pornography market are now in excess of US$100 billion per year (Anciaux 2020; DeKeseredy 2018b; Tangmanee 2019). In addition, pornography's expansive scale is also well-evidenced in its levels and patterns of consumption.

Pornography consumption is at an all-time high; it is primarily consumed online, by men (DeKeseredy 2018a, 2018b). In 2018, one of the most comprehensive studies on pornography consumption found an average of 91.5% of men had consumed pornography within the last month; and when studied across time, men's consumption rates were consistently found to be between 91% and 99% (Solano et al. 2020). While this study was significant in capturing a wider age range (18–73 years) than previous studies, it is also widely accepted that more than 90% of young people (aged 9–24 years) have consumed online pornography at some point (de Heer, Prior, and Fejervary 2020). These figures are in keeping with other reports that three of the top ten most visited websites on the internet are pornography sites (Bridges 2019), and that online pornography reportedly attracts over 30,000 users every second (DeKeseredy 2018b). In the first half of 2018, one website, xvideos.com, recorded the sixth highest levels of web traffic in the US (only after Google, Facebook, YouTube, Amazon and Yahoo), with an estimated 3.07 billion visits (Bridges 2019). Also facilitating these levels of consumption has been the widespread adoption of mobile devices. In 2008, one of the world's largest pornography websites reported 1% of their traffic coming from mobile devices (Tangmanee 2019), by 2019 that figure had grown to 80% (Pornhub 2019). Indeed, the way in which online pornography is now consumed is fundamental to understanding the market's evolving business model.

In addition to digital and mobile technologies, one of the most significant shifts in the changing business model of this market has been the rise of 'tube sites'. Based on a YouTube like format, tube sites combine free-to-view clips and trailers, user-generated content, pirated and commercial pornography (Arroyo 2016). These sites do not just facilitate the consumption of content, they also enable (and encourage) users to upload their own pornographic material (Forrester 2016). Not only are tube sites now the dominant place for the consumption of pornography online (Arroyo 2016), but today the most important tube sites all fall under the same conglomerate: MindGeek (Forrester 2016). With a significant monopoly on the market, MindGeek owns and manages over 150 pornography websites, including the highest trafficked tube sites of PornHub, RedTube and YouPorn, as well as owning many of the market's production and distribution companies (Bridges 2019). MindGeek has a bandwidth that exceeds that of Amazon and Facebook (Forrester 2016), and Pornhub, *as just one* of MindGeek's subsidiaries, reported over 115 million daily visitors in 2019: the '…equivalent [to] the populations of Canada, Australia, Poland and the Netherlands all visiting in one day' (Pornhub 2019). Pornhub also records uploading highs from users every year, reporting over 6.83 million new videos uploaded in 2019 – a figure amounting to 169 years of continuous viewing content uploaded in that one year (Pornhub 2019). However, it is widely acknowledged that technology has not only facilitated the rise of tube sites, it has also been directly linked to the changing content of the market.

In the shift to being an online market, pornography has also become much more extreme in its levels of violence against women (Brodesco 2016; Dines 2010). One well-cited study examining the most popular pornography videos in the market found that 88% of scenes involved sex acts with physical aggression – acts such as slapping, choking and bondage – predominantly enacted by men, against women (Bridges et al. 2010). While another study focussing on pornography videos taken from the tube sites of Pornhub, RedTube, YouPorn and xHamster found higher levels of objectification, power and violence than in traditional professional productions (Klaassen and Peter 2015). The market's levels of violence against women are most often noted as a feature of the category known as 'gonzo' pornography (Brodesco 2016; Dines 2010). Although the name may imply a niche category, gonzo is the most dominant type of pornography now available (DeKeseredy 2018a;Dines 2010), and the most profitable (DeKeseredy 2018c). Some of the standard practices in gonzo, and hence the contemporary market broadly, involve: (i) a woman being penetrated vaginally, anally and orally by two, three or more men at the same time; (ii) gagging, in which a woman has a penis thrust so far down her throat she gags or vomits; (iii) ass-to-mouth, in which a penis goes from a woman's anus to her mouth without washing and (iv) bukkake, in which any number of men ejaculate, often at the same time, onto a woman's body, face, hair, eyes, ears or mouth (Dines 2010; Sun 2014). This new mainstream form of pornography makes no attempt at a story line like more traditional forms of film-based pornography, it is, as other describe, 'scene after scene of violent penetration, in which the woman's body is literally stretched to its limit': with hair being pulled, throats in a vicelike grip, nostrils being pinched so the woman cannot breathe as a penis fill her mouth, mouths that are distended by either hands or penises pulling them apart (Dines 2006, 286, 2010).

Another key element of these market acts of sexual violence against women are practices of frequent and overt racism. As we raised earlier, pornography has traditionally been based on the intersection of women's racialised and sexualised inequality, a trend which is equally foundational to the contemporary market. Pornhub features over 50,000 videos under the category of 'interracial' including series' such as '*Oh No! There's a Negro in My Wife*' (Dines and West 2020), using racist language and playing on racist tropes about black male sexuality as well as promoting objectification and violence against women (Dines 2006). The contemporary market also relies on reproducing historic and racist stereotypes of women, positioning Asian women as passive, servile and childlike possessions for white colonial consumption, whereas Latina women are 'all-ass' and always ready for public penetration, and Black women are deviant, hypersexual and animal-like (Donevan 2015). Crucially, Black women are not an afterthought in pornography – they are the key pillar on which contemporary pornography rests – because the treatment of all women in pornography is connected to the portrayal of Black women as animals (Collins 2002). So, although there is always an element of dehumanisation, this can manifest differently; while white women may be positioned as objects in pornography, Black women are constructed as animalistic; and the economics of these constructions is key to the pornography market because, as Walker (1981) argues, animals can be economically exploited, sold, killed and consumed. As a means of centring these racialised and sexualised harms to women, we now turn to an area of feminism that offers great depth on theorising inequality and violence against women – radical feminism (DeKeseredy 2020).

The radical feminist centring of harm

Radical feminism is a branch of feminist theory that has rarely been applied in marketing. However, feminist marketing scholars have consistently acknowledged the groundwork of radical feminists in critiquing the market practices that impact women (Catterall, Maclaran, and Stevens 2005; Maclaran 2018; Parsons, Maclaran, and Chatzidakis 2017; Scott 2017). For Scott (2017, 112):

> The radical feminists of the Second Wave, it turns out, were right on several issues… Violence is used as a "disciplinary" measure [and]… [e]very institutional structure… seems to have some provision or practice that keeps women subordinate…

While radical feminism has been foundational and enduring in locating pornography as one such institution of women's subordination, a principal way in which the connections between women's inequality and pornography are discussed, is through a centring of harm.

Harm has been important for radical feminists because it offers a departure from offense (Dines, Jensen, and Russo 1998). A claim of offense has traditionally been more reflective of conservative oppositions that (rarely foreground women, and instead) object to pornography on the grounds of lewdness, obscenity or sin (Eaton 2007). Harm, as radical feminists conceive, is distinct from offense because it is an objective condition, not a way of feeling; and thus, it can occur with or without one's consent or with or without one's knowing about it (Whisnant 2004). Consequently, notions of choice and agency for radical feminists are not always key indicators of whether harm has, or has not, occurred (Quek 2018). Therefore, through focussing on women's experiences of pornography, radical feminists sought to prioritise harm in analyses, which, in turn, offers a practical approach that prioritises women, their status and well-being.

A further utility of harm is that it offers two (interconnected) ways to understand pornography's violations of women. Through drawing attention to the harms of live-actor pornography, radical feminists have argued that the material, embodied harm women experience in the process of production can be seen as connected to the conditions this fosters for women generally (Spector 2006). We suggest that to centre harm against women in this way may be especially useful for feminist marketing scholars because, as others have emphasised, market-level gender inequality research needs to address both the production of positional inequalities and the dynamic intersections of this with the perpetuation of cultural stereotypes (Fischer 2015).

Finally, an additionally valuable aspect of harm is that it was built from understanding *women's* experiences of pornography (MacKinnon and Dworkin 1997). As we previously raised, this offered a significant counter to the dominant approach that analysed pornography as a form of men's leisure or consumption. As an analytical and practical approach, a focus on harm has continued to be key to opposing the prevailing liberal and postmodern positions that view pornography as a form of art or harmless 'fantasy', and centrally focus on the experience for male consumers (Dworkin 1993; Jeffreys 2008). This echoes the concerns of feminist marketers who note that a dominant attention to consumption often comes at the expense of more critical analyses on the interrelationship between production, reproduction and consumption – and crucially, the implications this can have for women (Catterall, Maclaran, and Stevens 2005).

Producing material harm and embodied violence against women

Women's material realities and embodied experiences have been a continued point of interest for feminist marketers (Catterall, Maclaran, and Stevens 2005; Maclaran and Stevens 2008), including how these intersect with inequality (Steinfield et al. 2019). An attention to the reality of production processes is not only central to understanding the violence of markets for critical scholars (Eckhardt, Varman, and Dholakia 2018; Tadajewski 2016; Zwick and Cayla 2011), but it is also important for feminist marketers because marketplace analyses often fail to account for the many women who suffer as a part of the market's production processes (Catterall, Maclaran, and Stevens 2005). With the harms of production a central concern for radical feminists and (feminist) marketing scholars alike, we begin this section by mapping the ways in which radical feminists have traditionally theorised women's material, embodied harms in pornography. Then we apply this focus on harm to understanding some of the evolving ways women's inequality is being produced by the online pornography market.

Material inequality for radical feminists can include direct forms of violence against women as well as other embodied and coercive variants of harm. The coercive harm of the market system has been observed with agencies increasingly known to only represent female actors who have purged their 'no list' – meaning these women are expected to perform any act, regardless of their comfort or preference (Whisnant 2016a). While personal accounts from pornography performers provide insight into the rape, trafficking and coercion women experience in the more traditional production models of mainstream pornography (Dworkin 1985; Russell 1993; Whisnant 2004), it is not only performers who attest to the violence against women in production. Pornography producers openly admit violent sex is a part of the status quo of the market (DeKeseredy 2018c; Dines 2010), including that the acts of spitting, choking, 'ass busting', 'gangbanging' and pushing women's bodies 'to their limit' are not a mere fantasy or representation but a routine reality in the production process (Whisnant 2004). Some of the health risks from these common market practices include tearing in the vagina, throat and anus, prolapses, HIV, hepatitis, rectal chlamydia and gonorrhoea of the throat (Sun 2014). Accordingly, in radical feminist analyses, the embodied violation of women in pornography also takes account of their high exposure to sexually transmitted diseases, drug and alcohol dependencies, and psychological harm (Bridges and Jensen 2011; Dines 2016, 2010; Tyler 2015). However, with pornography's shift into online spaces, the harms against women being produced by newer (often user-generated) production models are only beginning to become apparent.

Just as marketing scholars are bringing attention to the harms of labour production in the sharing economy (Belk, Eckhardt, and Bardhi 2019), the digitisation of pornography is also being highlighted as producing an exploitative business model that mirrors much of that of providers such as Uber and TaskRabbit (Dines and Levy 2018). With online pornography controlled by the monopolistic structure of MindGeek and driving a low-cost production model that profits from decentralised, unregulated and user-generated productions (Forrester 2016), women are now being considered a part of a market system of 'porn sweatshops' (Dines and Levy 2018). Within this market system, women are not only afforded fewer labour rights than ever before, but they are also being forced to perform more extreme physical acts – acts that often mean women average a 'career' span of four to six months (Forrester 2016). Further, the racism of this evolving labour market is not only prevalent at the level of content, as discussed, but performers of colour also report being paid less than white performers (Dines and West 2020). While it is not our position that improving women's labour conditions in pornography necessarily removes the (embodied or socio-cultural) harm done to them, it is an important part of demonstrating the materiality of inequality and violation in this evolving market. It is because some specific harms can become more apparent as women become more active in the labour market (Maclaran 2018) that affirms our concern on women's inequality as manifest materially in this new market.

(Re)producing cultural harm and the construction of women's sexuality

In addition to centring the material harms of pornography, radical feminists have also focussed on the connections to the broader harm that pornography has with regard to women's social status. Through this, radical feminists have argued pornography is not solely a documentation of the harms against women (in the process of production), it can also be conceived as a form of harm in its very existence (Langton 2008). To understand the way pornography is harmful to women, not just individual women – but to all women, as a class – we first need to understand the messages pornography creates (and circulates) about women.

For radical feminists, pornography is a socialising force that creates and maintains women's second-class status (MacKinnon 1987). In addition to producing and circulating unrealistic, racist and infantilised images of women (Collins 2002; Sarikakis and Shaukat 2007), one of the central ways it does this is through its construction of women's (hetero)sexuality. Women's (hetero)sexuality in pornography is centrally marketed by defining women as masochistic because masochism is intrinsically both provocation and submission (Dworkin 1981). It is this construction of women's sexuality in pornography that, for feminists like Dworkin (1993), is the first principle of all pornography: that women want violence and degradation enacted upon them – that they enjoy these things. By showing sexual inequality (ranging from passivity, to coercion and even force) as what women desire – a basis of their sexuality – pornography can be seen to legitimise discrimination, degradation and abuse against women (Eaton 2007; Russo 1998). The pornography market's proliferation of images of women accepting or welcoming abuse is not only harmful to the women depicted but for all women because pornography, for radical feminists, works like propaganda: it uses individuals as stand-ins for entire groups (Jensen 2014; Whisnant 2016b). So, in the cycle of producing and reproducing a cultural construction of women's (hetero)sexuality, pornography can be seen as both a symptom and a cause of women's inequality (Dworkin and MacKinnon 1993). With 'gonzo' pornography now the dominant form of pornography being consumed and circulated, en-masse, renewed critical analyses of the pornography market's commercialisation and distribution of women's heterosexuality are, arguably, overdue.

As previously discussed, feminist marketing scholars are increasingly attending to the potential cultural harms to women from pornography's normalisation in society (Drenten, Gurrieri, and Tyler 2020; Maclaran 2015). This has even begun to include the 'perils' of pornified culture in conceptualisations of women's sexuality (Rome herein). With mainstream media and advertising beginning to reflect not just 'softcore' but also the 'hardcore' pornography typical of the contemporary market (Jeffreys 2014), we raise concern over the online market's mass distribution and mainstreaming of *overtly* violent and racist constructions of women's heterosexuality. Racist and sexist stereotypes that fetishise, eroticise and sexualise women are being noted as a key feature in contributing to a rape culture that normalises racist sexual violence (Kuo 2017). However, the role of *the market* in creating and legitimising a racist and sexist pornified culture is only beginning to be noted (Jensen 2020; Tyler and Quek 2016). Coupled with the expansive presence of online pornography that is enabled by digital technologies, and men's high consumption rates, affirms the need to attend to the online pornography market's explicit, violent and racist pornification of society, and the impact this has for women's status and sexuality. Next, we develop this and other sites for future work, and thereby secure the pornography market as an urgent priority within a more *radical* feminist marketing agenda.

Prioritising pornography: a radical feminist marketing agenda

With this chapter, we have provided a structure for thinking about women's marketplace inequality through the radical feminist centring of harm and its applications to pornography. It is through engaging with specific contexts that we can develop the kind of nuanced understanding required to address inequalities (Amis et al. 2018). In raising pornography as a priority for feminist marketers and tracing some of the connected harms women experience materially and culturally, we have revealed a site and particular analysis through which to understand the marketplace (re)production of gender inequality and violence against women. The ways in which harm facilitates both a material and cultural approach to understanding women's intersecting marketplace violation and inequality is especially useful because it is not enough to identify women's subordination, we need to uncover why gender inequality has remained so resilient (Fischer 2015). However, there is still much work to be done in this field.

As we write this in the global pandemic of COVID-19, the impact of this public health crisis on exacerbating existing gender inequalities is being observed across the globe (Hunnicutt 2020). This pandemic has also been explicitly linked to boosting rates of pornography consumption[1] (Attwood, Smith, and Mercer 2020; Kannan 2020). At the same time, the uploading of self-made pornographic content is also increasing (Jones 2020; Pornhub 2020). Pornhub recently reported record numbers of 'amateur' models joining their site as content producers (Pornhub 2019), with daily uploads from these models also increasing by more than 30% (Pornhub 2020). As this collection highlights, technological advancements are a pressing concern for feminist marketers. Not least because new technologies have historically done little to advance women's equality, instead, often reproducing existing ideologies of gender and increasing women's labour by blurring the boundaries of consumption and production (Maclaran 2018). We therefore raise several points for investigation into how this evolving market is (re)producing women's material and cultural harm.

First, as noted, there is an absence of work exploring how the mass circulation of explicitly violent and racist pornography impacts women and their sexuality at a cultural level. This is especially pressing today when the pornography market's creation and distribution of women as commodities is notably racist, violent, and widespread. With the traditional pornography market originally considered a major medium for the sexualisation of racial hatred (Collins 2002; MacKinnon 1987), and it still being noted as one of the most openly racist mass-media genres in contemporary society (Dines and West 2020; Jensen 2014), we suggest pornography requires urgent examination by feminist marketers interested in the historical roots and contemporary manifestations of women's racialised and sexualised inequality (Collins 2002; Crenshaw 2010). The emerging work from feminist marketers on the role of pornographication in women's sexual narratives and self-commodification (Drenten, Gurrieri, and Tyler 2020; Rome herein, Rome and Lambert 2020) offers a fitting and timely foundation for future investigations into how contemporary pornography – as a distinctly 'hardcore' market – constructs a view of women's heterosexuality, and how this intersects with women's status and well-being on a macro-cultural level. Marketplaces do not solely perpetuate norms and stereotypes that have a very real impact on people's lives, they also position us hierarchically in a social order (Parsons, Maclaran, and Chatzidakis 2017). We therefore hope to see future examinations into the pornification of culture expanded to include the role of pornography *as a market*, its normalising and commercialising of extreme racism and violence against women, and the intersections of this with a racist rape culture.

Second, we also urge for further work on the evolving ways the pornography market is harming women in production processes. This could include the ways in which women's sexualised labour collides with the exploitation of labour production in the highly decentralised, technologised markets of the sharing economy (Drenten, Gurrieri, and Tyler 2020; Eckhardt, Varman, and Dholakia 2018). Although women's participation in the global economy may become better recognised, it has not removed their socio-cultural or economic inequalities (Hein et al. 2016). Whether it is women's participation in the labour market (Fischer 2015), their exploitation in farming practices (Steinfield and Holt 2020), in sweatshops and as low paid service workers (Catterall, Maclaran, and Stevens 2005), or their forced enslavement into the sex trade and domestic services (Hein et al. 2016; Scott 2017), the market's production processes are widely implicated in the creation and maintenance of women's inequality. Even in the early years of pornography's digitalisation, scholars noted that women in pornography were the most flexible, replaceable and unprotected workforce (Sarikakis and Shaukat 2007). Given that relatively little is known about women's conditions in this new market (one fuelled by user-generated and pirated content) (Forrester 2016), we argue this should be a key site for future feminist market research.

Also intersecting with women's harm in online production systems is the growing trend towards women's self-made and 'amateur' pornographic content. Women's production of user-generated and 'selfie' content is a growing point of interest in the discipline (Gurrieri and Drenten 2019; Maclaran 2018). These discussions provide an apt opportunity to extend concern to women's production of explicitly pornographic self-made content, especially how websites market women to create and upload such user-generated and 'amateur' content. Recent theorising from radical feminists has begun to highlight the harm of humiliation, particularly for women who are active participants in their own violation (Whisnant 2016b). As marketing scholars acknowledge, some of the strongest successes in the 'marketing of ideas' has been in the ideas that are injurious to those adopting them (Dholakia and Firat 2016). Enquiries into women's self-made pornography may thus begin to address how subordinated groups contribute to the reproduction of systems of domination, and how this is engineered by markets and marketing (Martí and Fernández 2013). Or as radical feminists have highlighted, pornography has so entrenched the practice, promotion and enforcement of sexualised inequality that it should be no surprise that women participate in recreating their subordination: the surprise is that more women do not (MacKinnon 1987; Spector 2006).

Finally, while we have assembled these sites for future research to secure pornography within a feminist marketing agenda, we also encourage a harm-based lens be applied to 'demystifying' the many forms of market inequality currently being (re)produced (Dholakia 2016). Just as radical feminists have argued that to consider pornography as a political economy foregrounds the varied forms of structural harm and inequality pornography produces (Dines 1998), so too marketers are pushing for a political economy of marketing (Eckhardt, Varman, and Dholakia 2018; Zwick and Cayla 2011), one which emphasises the production of labour in industry and the production of ideas in culture. Such an approach requires scholars to look at how the market system operates inside as well as outside (Zwick and Cayla 2011). We offer a focus on harm as a way to address the sexist, racist, colonial and other discourses that shape the dark side of the market (Tadajewski 2016). A centring of harm in analyses is fitting for broader critiques of the market because it is through revealing inequality under sexism that we can begin to locate other branches of (patriarchal) injustice, such as racism, classism, ageism, as well as ecological and economic exploitation (Rowland and Klein 1996; Steinfield and Holt 2020).

As we have traced in this chapter, for feminist marketing scholars 'there is no denying that marketing is implicated in the perpetuation of gender inequality' (Bettany et al. 2010, 6); however, approaches that address the complex, systemic, glocalised, institutionalised and embodied nature of gender injustice are still an emergent field of enquiry (Hein et al. 2016). We suggest one way that we can begin to address the multilevel nature of inequality and injustice is by making room for a view that is both more complex and more practical (Spector 2006), and a radical feminist demand to focus on harm to women offers feminist marketers one such view.

Note

1 Noted as a cumulative consequence of the online pornography market offering free premium subscriptions during this time, along with restriction rules curtailing parts of the global prostitution market.

References

Amis, John M., Kamal A. Munir, Thomas B. Lawrence, Paul Hirsch, and Anita McGahan. 2018. "Inequality, institutions and organizations." *Organization Studies* 39 (9):1131–1152. doi: 10.1177/0170840618792596.

Anciaux, Arnaud 2020. "A Digital Redefinition of the Pornography Industries." In *Digitalization of Society and Socio-Political Issues 1: Digital, Communication, and Culture*, edited by Éric George, 126–133. Newark, NJ: John Wiley & Sons, Incorporated.

Arroyo, Brandon. 2016. "From flow to float: Moving through porn tube sites." *Porn Studies* 3 (3):308–310. doi: 10.1080/23268743.2016.1148328.

Attwood, Feona. 2002. "Reading porn: The paradigm shift in pornography research." *Sexualities* 5 (1):91–105. doi: 10.1177/1363460702005001005.

Attwood, Feona, Clarissa Smith, and John Mercer. 2020. "Editorial." *Porn Studies* 7 (2):139–142. doi: 10.1080/23268743.2020.1761107.

Belk, Russell W., Giana M. Eckhardt, and Fleura Bardhi. 2019. *Introduction to the Handbook of the Sharing Economy: The Paradox of the Sharing Economy, Handbook of the Sharing Economy*. Cheltenham: Edward Elgar Publishing.

Bettany, Shona, Susan Dobscha, Lisa O'Malley, and Andrea Prothero. 2010. "Moving beyond binary opposition: Exploring the tapestry of gender in consumer research and marketing." *Marketing Theory* 10 (1):3–28. doi: 10.1177/1470593109355244.

Boyle, Karen (Ed.). 2010. *Everyday Pornography*. London: Routledge.

Boyle, Karen. 2018. "The implications of pornification: Pornography, the mainstream and false equivalences." In *The Routledge Handbook of Gender and Violence*, edited by Nancy Lombard, 85–96. Abingdon: ProQuest Ebook Central; Routledge.

Bridges, Ana J. 2019. "Pornography and sexual assault." In *Handbook of Sexual Assault and Sexual Assault Prevention*, edited by W. T. O'Donohue and P. A. Schewe, 129–149. Cham: Springer.

Bridges, Ana J., and Robert Jensen. 2011. "Pornography." In *Sourcebook on Violence against Women*, edited by Claire M. Renzetti, Jeffrey L. Edleson, and Raquel Kennedy Bergen, 133–150. Thousand Oaks, CA: Sage.

Bridges, Ana J, Robert Wosnitzer, Erica Scharrer, Chyng Sun, and Rachael Liberman. 2010. "Aggression and sexual behavior in best-selling pornography videos: A content analysis update." *Violence against Women* 16 (10):1065–1085. doi: 10.1177/1077801210382866.

Brodesco, Alberto. 2016. "POV to the people: Online discourses about gonzo pornography." *Porn Studies* 3 (4):362–372. doi: 10.1080/23268743.2016.1241158.

Catterall, Miriam, Pauline Maclaran, and Lorna Stevens. 2005. "Postmodern paralysis: the critical impasse in feminist perspectives on consumers." *Journal of Marketing Management* 21 (5–6):489–504. doi: 10.1362/0267257054307444.

Collins, Patricia Hill. 2002. *Black Feminist Thought: Knowledge, Consciousness, and the Politics of Empowerment*. New York: Routledge.

Crenshaw, Kimberlé W. 2010. "Close encounters of three kinds: On teaching dominance feminism and intersectionality." *Tulsa Law Review* 46:151. https://digitalcommons.law.utulsa.edu/tlr/vol46/iss1/13.

de Heer, Brooke, Sarah Prior, and Jenna Fejervary. 2020. "Women's Pornography Consumption, Alcohol Use, and Sexual Victimization." *Violence against Women* :1–18. doi: 10.1177/1077801220945035.

DeKeseredy, Walter S. 2018a. "Adult pornography and violence against women." In *The Routledge International Handbook of Violence Studies*, edited by Walter S. DeKeseredy, Callie Marie Rennison and Amanda K. Hall-Sanchez, 224–234. Milton: Routledge.

DeKeseredy, Walter S. 2018b. "Confronting adult pornography." In *Routledge Handbook of Critical Criminology*, edited by Walter S. DeKeseredy and Molly Dragiewicz, 455–464. Milton: Routledge.

DeKeseredy, Walter S. 2020. "Bringing Feminist Sociological Analyses of Patriarchy Back to the Forefront of the Study of Woman Abuse." *Violence against Women* :1–18. doi: 10.1177/1077801220958485.

DeKeseredy, Walter S., and Amanda Hall-Sanchez. 2018c. "Thinking critically about contemporary adult pornography and woman abuse." In *Routledge Handbook of Critical Criminology*, edited by Walter S. DeKeseredy and Molly Dragiewicz, 280–294. Milton: Routledge.

Dholakia, Nikhilesh. 2016. "Marketing as mystification." *Marketing Theory* 16 (3):401–426. doi: 10.1177/1470593115619971.

Dholakia, Nikhilesh, and A. Fuat Firat. 2016. "Mystifying class: Marketing of inequality and the rise of delusive consciousness." *Marketing Theory* 16 (3):406–410. doi: 10.1177/1470593115619971.

Dholakia, Nikhilesh, and Fuat A. Fırat. 2018. "Postmodernism and critical marketing " In *The Routledge Companion to Critical Marketing*, edited by Mark Tadajewski, Matthew Higgins, Janice Denegri-Knott and Rohit Varman, 482–499. London: Routledge.

Dines, Gail. 1998. "Dirty business: Playboy magazine and the mainstreaming of pornography." In *Pornography: The Production and Consumption of Inequality*, edited by Gail Dines, Bob Jensen and Ann Russo, 37–64. New York: Routledge.

Dines, Gail. 2006. "The white man's burden: Gonzo pornography and the construction of black masculinity." *Yale JL & Feminism* 18:283. https://heinonline.org/HOL/P?h=hein.journals/yjfem18&i=287.

Dines, Gail. 2010. *Pornland: How Porn has Hijacked our Sexuality*. Boston, MA: Beacon Press.

Dines, Gail. 2016. ""There is no such thing as IT": Toward a critical understanding of the porn industry." In *The Sexualised Body and the Medical Authority of Pornography*, edited by Heather Brunskell-Evans, 21–39. Newcastle Upon Tyne: Cambridge Scholars Publishing.

Dines, Gail, Bob Jensen, and Ann Russo. 1998. *Pornography: The Production and Consumption of Inequality*. New York: Routledge.

Dines, Gail, and David L. Levy. 2018. "Porn 'disruption' makes Stormy Daniels a rare success in increasingly abusive industry." *The Conversation*, Last Modified April 2, 2019 accessed 24 March. https://theconversation.com/porn-disruption-makes-stormy-daniels-a-rare-success-in-increasingly-abusive-industry-94534.

Dines, Gail, and Carolyn West, M. 2020. ""White girl moans black lives matter": Pornhub's #BLM genre and the industry's brash racism." *Slate*, accessed 4 August 2020. https://slate.com/human-interest/2020/07/pornhub-black-lives-matter-genre-racism.html.

Donevan, Meghan. 2015. "If pornography is sex education, what does it teach?" In *Freedom Fallacy: The Limits of Liberal Feminism*, edited by Mirander Kiraly and Meagan Tyler, 43–54. Ballarat: Connor Court Publishing.

Drenten, Jenna, Lauren Gurrieri, and Meagan Tyler. 2020. "Sexualized labour in digital culture: Instagram influencers, porn chic and the monetization of attention." *Gender, Work & Organization* 27:41–66. doi: 10.1111/gwao.12354.

Dworkin, Andrea. 1981. *Pornography: Men Possessing Women*. New York: Perigee.
Dworkin, Andrea. 1985. "Against the male flood: Censorship, pornography, and equality." *Harvard Women's Law Journal* 8:1. https://heinonline.org/HOL/P?h=hein.journals/hwljl8&i=9.
Dworkin, Andrea. 1993. *Letters from a War Zone*. Brooklyn, NY: Lawrence Hill Books.
Dworkin, Andrea, and Catharine MacKinnon. 1993. "Questions and anwers." In *Making Violence Sexy: Feminist Views on Pornography*, edited by Diana E.H. Russell, 302 pp. New York: Teachers College Press.
Eaton, Anne W. 2007. "A sensible antiporn feminism." *Ethics* 117 (4):674–715. doi: 10.1086/519226.
Eckhardt, Giana, Rohit Varman, and Nikhilesh Dholakia. 2018. "Ideology and critical marketing studies." *Routledge Companion to Critical Marketing Studies* :306–318. doi: 10.4324/9781315630526.
Fischer, Eileen. 2015. "Towards more marketing research on gender inequality." *Journal of Marketing Management* 31 (15–16):1718–1722. doi: 10.1080/0267257X.2015.1078397.
Forrester, Katrina. 2016. "Making Sense of Modern Pornography." *The New Yorker*. September 19, https://www.newyorker.com/magazine/2016/09/26/making-sense-of-modern-pornography
Gurrieri, Lauren, and Jenna Drenten. 2019. "The hashtaggable body: Negotiating gender performance in social media." In *Handbook of Research on Gender and Marketing*. edited by Susan Dobscha, 101–116. Cheltenham, UK: Edward Elgar Publishing.
Hein, Wendy, Laurel Steinfield, Nacima Ourahmoune, Catherine A. Coleman, Linda Tuncay Zayer, and Jon Littlefield. 2016. "Gender justice and the market: A transformative consumer research perspective." *Journal of Public Policy & Marketing* 35 (2):223–236. doi: 10.1509/jppm.15.146.
Hirschman, Elizabeth C. 1991. "Exploring the dark side of consumer behavior: Methaphor and ideology in prostitution and pornography." In *GCB – Gender and Consumer Behavior*. Salt Lake City, UT. http://www.acrwebsite.org/volumes/15533/gender/v01/GCB-01.
hooks, bell. 2000. *Feminist Theory: From Margin to Center*. London: Pluto Press.
Hunnicutt, Gwen. 2020. "Commentary on the special issue: New ways of thinking theoretically about violence against women and other forms of gender-based violence." *Violence against Women*. doi: 10.1177/1077801220958484.
Jeffreys, Sheila. 2008. *The Industrial Vagina: The Political Economy of the Global Sex Trade*. Oxon: Routledge.
Jeffreys, Sheila. 2014. *Beauty and Misogyny: Harmful Cultural Practices in the West*. New York: Routledge.
Jensen, Robert. 2014. "Stories of a rape culture: Pornography as propaganda". In *Big Porn Inc: Exposing the Harms of the Global Pornography Industry*, edited by Abigail Bray and Melinda Tankard Reist, 150–159. North Melbourne: Spinifex Press.
Jensen, Robert. 2020. "What is really radical in sex/gender politics?". *Culturico*, accessed 6 August 2020. https://culturico.com/2020/07/26/what-is-really-radical-in-sex-gender-politics/?fbclid=IwAR3CQ8QwZnckaTDn3yhvbnWqS_fjekmGl78GZiGqQ1f6iAlxPlqwiRRIp-o.
Jones, Lora. 2020. "OnlyFans: 'I started selling sexy photos online after losing my job'." *BBC News*, 15 July 2020. https://www.bbc.com/news/business-53338019?fbclid=IwAR1_J5KHsgy5cm6L0fT-h8zle0Oy1AmcPkhfCqKo9vBmpHXLLGy3H6QvAao.
Kannan, Saikiran 2020. "Pornography gets a pandemic boost, India reports 95 per cent rise in viewing." India Today, accessed 5 August 2020. https://www.indiatoday.in/news-analysis/story/pornography-gets-a-pandemic-boost-india-reports-95-per-cent-rise-in-viewing-1665940-2020-04-11.
Klaassen, Marleen J.E., and Jochen Peter. 2015. "Gender (in)equality in Internet pornography: A content analysis of popular pornographic Internet videos." *The Journal of Sex Research* 52 (7):721–735. doi: 10.1080/00224499.2014.976781.
Kravets, Olga, Chloe Preece, and Pauline Maclaran. 2020. "The uniform entrepreneur: Making gender visible in social enterprise." *Journal of Macromarketing* 40 (4):445–458. doi: 10.1177/0276146720930331.

Kuo, Rachel. 2017. "How rape culture and racism combine to hurt Asian women." *HuffPost*, accessed 24 October 2020. https://www.huffpost.com/entry/how-rape-culture-and-racism-combine-to-hurt-asian-women_b_592a15ade4b0a7b7b469cb22.

Langton, Rae. 2008. "Comments on AW Eaton's 'a sensible antiporn feminism'." *Symposia on Gender, Race and Philosophy* 4 (2):1–5.

MacKinnon, Catharine A. 1987. *Feminism Unmodified: Discourses on Life and Law*. Cambridge, MA: Harvard University Press.

MacKinnon, Catharine A, and Andrea Dworkin. 1997. *In Harm's Way: The Pornography Civil Rights Hearings*. Cambridge, MA: Harvard University Press.

MacKinnon, Catharine A. 1991. "From practice to theory, or what is a white woman anyway." *Yale Journal of Law and Feminism* 4 (1):13–22. https://heinonline.org/HOL/P?h=hein.journals/yjfem4&i=19.

Maclaran, Pauline. 2015. "Feminism's fourth wave: A research agenda for marketing and consumer research." *Journal of Marketing Management* 31 (15–16):1732–1738. doi: 10.1080/0267257X.2015.1076497.

Maclaran, Pauline, and Olga Kravets. 2018. "Feminist perspectives in marketing: Past, present, and future." In *The Routledge Companion to Critical Marketing*, edited by Mark Tadajewski, Matthew Higgins, Janice Denegri-Knott and Rohit Varman, 64–82. Milton: Taylor & Francis Group.

Maclaran, Pauline, and Lorna Stevens. 2008. "Thinking through theory: Materialising the oppositional imagination." In *Critical Marketing: Issues in Contemporary Marketing*, edited by Mark Tadajewski and Douglas T. Brownlie, 345-361. London: Routledge.

Martí, Ignasi, and Pablo Fernández. 2013. "The institutional work of oppression and resistance: Learning from the Holocaust." *Organization Studies* 34 (8):1195–1223. doi: 10.1177/0170840613492078.

McNair, Brian. 2002. *Striptease Culture: Sex, Media and the Democratisation of Desire*. London: Routledge.

Parsons, Elizabeth, Pauline Maclaran, and Andreas Chatzidakis. 2017. *Gender, Feminism and Consumer Behaviour, Contemporary Issues in Marketing and Consumer Behaviour*. London: Routledge.

Pornhub. 2019. "2019 Year in review." Accessed 10 March 2020. https://www.pornhub.com/insights/2019-year-in-review.

Pornhub. 2020. "New video uploads from verified models." Accessed 5 August 2020. https://www.pornhub.com/insights/verified-model-uploads.

Quek, Kaye. 2018. *Marriage Trafficking: Women in Forced Wedlock*. New York: Routledge.

Ridgeway, Cecilia L. 2014. "Why status matters for inequality." *American Sociological Review* 79 (1):1–16. doi: 10.1177/0003122413515997.

Rome, Alexandra S., and Aliette Lambert. 2020. "(Wo)men on top? Postfeminist contradictions in young women's sexual narratives." *Marketing Theory* 20 (4): 501-525. doi: 10.1177/1470593120926240.

Rome, Alexandra S., Stephanie O'Donohoe, and Susan Dunnett. 2019. "Rethinking feminist waves." In *Handbook of Research on Gender and Marketing*, edited by Susan Dobscha, 252–272. Cheltenham: Edward Elgar Publishing Limited.

Rowland, Robyn, and Renate Klein. 1996. "Radical feminism: History, politics, action." In *Radically Speaking: Feminism Reclaimed*, edited by Diane Bell and Renate Klein, 9–36. North Melbourne: Spinifex Press.

Russell, Diana E.H. 1993. *Making Violence Sexy: Feminist Views on Pornography*. New York: Teachers College Press.

Russo, A. 1998. "Feminists confront pornography's subordinating practices: Politics and strategies for change." In *Pornography: The Production and Consumption of Inequality*, edited by Gail Dines, Bob Jensen and Ann Russo, 9–35. New York: Routledge.

Sarikakis, Katharine, and Zeenia Shaukat. 2007. "The global structures and cultures of pornography: The global brothel." In *Feminist Interventions in International Communication: Minding the Gap*, edited by Katharine Sarikakis and Leslie Regan Shade, 106–128. Maryland, MD: Rowman & Littlefield Publishers.

Schroeder, Jonathan E, and Pierre McDonagh. 2005. "The logic of pornography in digital camera promotion." In *Sex in Consumer Culture: The Erotic Content of Media and Marketing*, edited by Tom Reichert and Jacqueline Lambiase, 219–242. New York: Routledge.

Scott, Linda. 2017. "Consumption on the feminist agenda." In *Contemporary Consumer Culture Theory*, edited by John F. Sherry and Eileen M. Fischer, 107–129. New York: Routledge.

Solano, Ingrid, Nicholas R. Eaton, and K. Daniel O'Leary. 2020. "Pornography consumption, modality and function in a large internet sample." *The Journal of Sex Research* 57 (1):92–103. doi: 10.1080/00224499.2018.1532488.

Spector, Jessica. 2006. *Prostitution and Pornography: Philosophical Debate about the Sex Industry*. Stanford, CA: Stanford University Press.

Steinfield, Laurel A. 2019. "1, 2, 3, 4. I declare…empowerment? A material-discursive analysis of the marketisation, measurement and marketing of women's economic empowerment." *Journal of Marketing Management* :1–37. doi: 10.1080/0267257X.2019.1699850.

Steinfield, Laurel A., Catherine A. Coleman, Linda Tuncay Zayer, Nacima Ourahmoune, and Wendy Hein. 2019. "Power logics of consumers' gendered (in)justices: Reading reproductive health interventions through the transformative gender justice framework." *Consumption Markets & Culture* 22 (4):406–429. doi: 10.1080/10253866.2018.1512250.

Steinfield, Laurel, and Diane Holt. 2020. "Structures, systems and differences that matter: Casting an ecological-intersectionality perspective on female subsistence farmers' experiences of the climate crisis." *Journal of Macromarketing* 40 (4):563–582. doi: 10.1177/0276146720951238.

Stern, Barbara. 1991. "Two pornographies: A feminist view of sex in advertising." In *Advances in Consumer Research*, edited by Rebecca H. Holman and Michael R. Solomon, 384–391. Provo, UT: Association for Consumer Research.

Sun, Chyng. 2014. "Investigating Pornography: The Journey of a Filmmaker and Researcher." In *Big Porn Inc: Exposing the Harms of the Global Pornography Industry*, edited by Abigail Bray and Melinda Tankard Reist, 171-178. North Melbourne: Spinifex Press.

Tadajewski, Mark. 2016. "Relevance, responsibility, critical performativity, testimony and positive marketing: contributing to marketing theory, thought and practice." *Journal of Marketing Management* 32 (17–18):1513–1536. doi: 10.1080/0267257X.2016.1244974.

Tangmanee, Chatpong. 2019. "An empirical analysis of the pageview and visit duration of pornography websites." *International Journal of Research in Business and Social Science* 8 (3):72–82. doi: 10.20525/ijrbs.v8i3.250.

Tyler, Meagan. 2015. "Harms of production: Theorising pornography as a form of prostitution." *Women's Studies International Forum* 48:114–123. doi: 10.1016/j.wsif.2014.11.014.

Tyler, Meagan, and Kaye Quek. 2016. "Conceptualizing pornographication: A lack of clarity and problems for feminist analysis." *Sexualization, Media, & Society* 2 (2):1–14. doi: 10.1177/2374623816643281.

Walker, Alice. 1981. "Coming Apart." In *You Can't Keep a Good Woman Down*, edited by Alice Walker, 41–53. New York: Harcourt Brace Jovanovich.

Whisnant, Rebecca. 2004. "Confronting pornography: Some conceptual basics." In *Not for sale: Feminists resisting prostitution and pornography*, edited by Christine Stark and Rebecca Whisnant, 15–27. Dayton, OH: University of Dayton, Philosophy Faculty Publications.

Whisnant, Rebecca. 2016a. "'But what about feminist porn?' Examining the work of Tristan Taormino." *Sexualization, Media, & Society* 2 (2):1–12. doi: 10.1177/2374623816631727.

Whisnant, Rebecca. 2016b. "Pornography, humiliation, and consent." *Sexualization, Media, & Society* 2 (3):1–7. doi: 10.1177/2374623816662876.

Zwick, Detlev, and Julien Cayla (Eds.). 2011. *Inside Marketing: Practices, Ideologies, Devices*. Oxford: Oxford University Press.

30 Manifesting feminist marketing futures

Undertaking a 'visionary' inventory

Feminist Collective

Elizabeth Parsons, Daniela Pirani, Rachel Ashman, Athanasia Daskalopoulou, Katy Kerrane and Cathy McGouran[*]

With each passing year, feminist scholarship in marketing is steadily growing. At present we see a new generation of scholars taking up the baton and so in this chapter we explore the tenor and direction of this work. Obviously, we cannot cover everything here, so we have followed Pauline Maclaran's cue in her 2015 commentary in the *Journal of Marketing Management* where she identified three areas of particular lacunae: intersectionality and identity, the pornification of culture, and austerity and the feminisation of poverty. Five years on we revisit these areas and document how they have developed, reviewing studies published from 2015 to the present. In closing we provide a critique and propose a feminist marketing research agenda for the coming five years.

We write this chapter in both harrowing but also hopeful times for feminist and critical race scholars and activists. The killing of George Floyd in May 2020 at the hands of police in Minneapolis and resultant multiracial 'Black Lives Matter' protests have reignited debate on structural racial inequality and oppression. As we write deaths from the Covid-19 pandemic have exceeded one and a half million globally. Both of these crises are triggering reflection around our roles and futures in a range of spheres. Importantly for the present chapter, digital and social media which have long been the vehicle of organising and activism for fourth-wave feminists, have taken on a renewed significance. We 'log on' to make sense of our fast-changing world and connect emotionally with others in isolating and bewildering times. The current pandemic has also rendered the work of care both at home and in institutional settings highly visible. This visibility may be seen as a good thing; however, we see that women continue to take on the increased weight of unpaid domestic care therefore retrenching old patriarchal norms. It seems women are now 'back in the home, up to their ears in dishes, dinners and nappies, watching their careers evaporate as the pay gap widens' (Scott, 2020a). We also find that Covid-19 has hit marginal communities the hardest including those on low incomes, Black, Asian and Minority Ethnic (BAME) individuals, disabled people, women and older people.

The above events occur at a time when a series of feminisms have been experiencing a 'comeback' in Western cultures (Maclaran, 2015; Maclaran and Kravets, 2018). From the highly visible popular cultural corporate manifestations such as the $710 Dior T-shirt proclaiming that "We Should All Be Feminists", to the sub-cultural grassroots

---

[*] The convention of 'author ordering' sits unhappily with our collective ethos, therefore this author order is random and reflects the fact that all authors made their own different and important contributions over the life of the project.

DOI: 10.4324/9781003042587-36

feminist organising such as the #FreeTheNipple campaign that addresses the sexualisation and censorship of women's breasts (Matich et al., 2019) to participation in 'Black digital spaces' in self-exploratory, self-educating, resistant and collective ways (Sobande, 2017). Equally, many feminist scholars have raised concerns about the role of marketing in co-opting feminist organising and erasing intersectional, feminist and Black social justice issues through woke-washing (Sobande, 2019).

The six female authors of this chapter, who at the time of writing all work at the University of Liverpool Management School, comprise our feminist collective. Formed in 2018, our group regularly meets to read contemporary feminist scholarship. As a group we discuss our experiences of navigating academic structures as women and conspire to produce influential research. Reflexivity is at the heart of feminist scholarship and it is important to note that as white, European, able-bodied academics we write from a position of privilege. More importantly we acknowledge that with privilege comes power, and with power comes responsibility, so our aim here is not only to reflect on our privilege but to put it to use in undoing the structures and economic logics that perpetuate intersectional and racial inequality. It is in this spirit that we approach this chapter.

Intersectionality and identity

To embrace intersectionality is to perceive and engage with issues that run counter to the grain of entrenched theory and long-established practices that potentially oppress. Defining intersectionality is complex, but fundamentally it encourages users to consider varying categories of disadvantage such as disability, race, class, sexuality and gender when viewing and studying the world. Developed by black feminist thinkers, intersectionality is considered a revolutionary concept by some, cited as radically defining theoretical and methodological approaches, and by others accused of being descriptive, problematising identity politics and focussing too heavily on a small subset of structural constraints (Méndoz, 2018). Some marketing journals are embracing intersectionality, with a recent special issue on transformative consumer research in the *Journal of Business Research* including two intersectional studies developing an agenda for marketing academics and practitioners (Demangeot et al., 2019; Steinfield et al, 2019b), although not specifically feminist/gender focussed in orientation, this is a step in the right direction.

Considering the world of marketing and consumption through an intersectional lens is illuminating. Why, for instance, do cosmetic companies predominantly "hire white consultants, stores carry products developed for white consumers, and ads carry pictures of smiling white faces" Weston (2011, p. 31)? Judy Foster Davis (2018) demonstrates that 'selling whiteness' has occurred for hundreds of years, through the large-scale amplification of racist norms and ideals transmitted via marketing media. And when considering the field of marketing and consumer research, we encounter similar glaring issues of inequality and one-sidedness such as the prevalence of white Western scholars whose prominence obscures and overshadows that of others. In this section of the chapter, we investigate feminist marketing research's spectrum of visibility, identifying frontiers of opportunity in intersectional research. Given constraints on word limit, we do not claim to be reviewing all the work in this expansive area but instead highlight places whereby we believe feminist scholarship needs to be more visible. Thus, from our standpoint, we (inter)section our chapter into three areas within the feminist marketing literature: research focussing on racial and gender intersections, research focussing on gendered and sexual subjectivities, research focussing on ableness and intersectionality, before adding some concluding thoughts.

Visible: research focussing on racial and gender intersections

Intersectionality is significant to feminism. It is being heralded as creating a 'waveless' feminism, re-defining the movement as 'intersectional feminism' with gender scholar April Sizemore-Barber commenting that "we are in a place of multiple feminisms", meaning that as feminists we must not only consider the oppression of women, but the oppression of all (Grady, 2018). This shifting perspective creates unexplored territories for feminist researchers.

When reviewing intersectional literature in marketing, racial inequality is an area considerably more populated than others (Olivotti, 2016; Ndichu and Upadhyaya, 2019; Schaap and Berkers, 2019). This is due to the historical tradition of black feminist, critical race and women of colour scholars and activists using intersectional lenses to render visible assumptions of whiteness embedded in ideas about womanhood and feminism (May, 2015; Hancock, 2016). Specifically, in marketing, as well as those cited above, key scholars innovating within this arena include Francesca Sobande, who has conducted research around the intersections of gender and race (Sobande, 2017; Hill and Sobande, 2018). She has also considered how black women use technology to resist media marginalisation (Sobande et al., 2019) and examined the production and use of intersectionality in advertising (Sobande, 2019, see also Gopaldas and Siebert, 2018). In addition, there are a number of emergent scholars employing intersectional ontologies to study highly marginalised groups (Morris, 2017; Matich, 2019). Matich's (2019) thesis uncovers the technologically influenced and trans-generational 'means of transmission' fourth-wave feminists use to disturb dominant and oppressive hegemonic 'other'. In doing this, her study explores the intersections of race, sexuality and gender within the context of 'Galdem' zine culture. Consequently, research focussing on racial and gender intersections is fruitful and visible, although mostly tends to focus on black women.

Barely visible: research focussing on gendered and sexual subjectivities

Within her commentary, Maclaran (2015) called for research into the experiences of gay, lesbian, bisexual and transgender identities. This area has received some attention, but it remains sparsely populated, and the experiences of these groups are therefore barely visible in the marketing literature (Bettany, 2016). One of the main disadvantages within consumer research is that studies focus on middle-class, cis-gendered gay men, living in urban and Western contexts, largely ignoring the broad array of other sexual subjectivities and cultures around the globe (Coffin et al., 2019). Most studies in marketing focus on the portrayal and effects of including such LGBT identities within advertising (Han and Tsai, 2016; Pounders and Mabry-Flynn, 2016; Åkestam et al., 2017; Descubes et al., 2018). Consequently, there is a paucity of specifically feminist intersectional work. Coffin et al. (2016) focusses on how LGBT consumers experience Manchester's gay village and how they interpret it in relation to other places in the city. They uncovered how consumers' perceptions of the 'gay village' changed dependent on individual sexual orientations. For example, while some gay men found the village to be over themed and overpriced, transgender respondents praised the village for providing a 'safe haven' away from the other discriminatory and more mainstream social spaces. Nölke (2018) also performed an intersectional analysis of LGBT portrayals in advertising between 2009 and 2015. She found that LGBT characters in advertisements are often Caucasian, middle aged, middle-class gay men with Hispanic, mature, working class, FtM trans persons and bisexuals the least represented. Additionally, Bettany and Rowe (2016) explore the lived experiences of bisexual consumers uncovering that they often feel vilified and othered by not 'fitting into' the binary category of gay or straight. In their results, these studies communicate the complex nature of what Maclaran (2015) terms 'multiple femininities and masculinities' and assert the need for better granular yet intersectional understanding of LGBT (or as today named LGBTQIA+) within marketing scholarship.

Invisible: research focussing on ableness and intersectionality

From our review of the intersectional marketing literature, an area with great scope for future research is focussing on ableness. Very few studies in the last five years have explored this interface. Kearney et al. (2019) theorise the role of ableism in (mis)representational mythology of disability in the marketplace, demonstrating "how adopting an ableism lens enables an intersectional conceptualization of the various 'isms' and their resultant forms of inclusion and exclusion meanings in the marketplace" (p. 562). Similarly, Nejad and O'Connor (2016) take an intersectional approach to evaluating consumer financial literacy, finding that Generation Y females who are members of ethnic minorities are at the greatest risk of being financially vulnerable. In this case, using an intersectional analytical tool helped to mine the data and generate highly granular and nuanced results. Clearly, intersectionality has potential as both an analytical tool and theoretical driver of a study, but this must be applied more to the area of ableness and education. Ableness is invisible not only in feminist marketing research, but many other walks of society too.

The pornification of culture

Maclaran (2015) identifies 'the pornification of culture' as a key area for further theorising in marketing and consumer research. Maclaran (2015) situates this research stream within fourth-wave feminism and argues that fourth-wavers have brought sex and sex representations into the forefront of popular culture. For example, terms such as 'pornographication', 'pornified' and 'porno-chic' (Paul, 2005; McNair, 2013) are often used in the literature to illustrate how sex has become more visible and liberalised in Western cultures. The normalisation of sex and sexual displays has been largely fuelled by the use of social media and celebrity culture (Veer and Golf-Papez, 2018) and marketers have had a role in promoting 'raunch' culture (Rogan et al., 2016).

Since Maclaran's (2015, p. 1736) call for more research into this "new sexism [that] seems to be stalking us", a number of marketing and consumer research studies have looked into the ways in which cultural sexualised texts intersect with individuals' sexualities. Research in our discipline has also provided important insights into the embodied nature of feminism (Maclaran and Stevens, 2019) and has contributed to the debate of 'empowered eroticism' (Glick, 2000; Evans et al., 2010). The review of scholarship on the pornification of culture highlights a limited engagement with the subject and a lack of feminist conceptualisations in the past five years. Although there are various feminist, non-feminist or post-feminist ways of conceptualising gender and sexuality (Hearn and Hein, 2015), the majority of studies in this research stream did not adhere to specific gender and feminist traditions (Bristor and Fischer, 1993; Maclaran and Stevens, 2019).

More specifically, our analysis highlighted five themes related to the 'pornification of culture': gender and sexual displays online, objectification and the male gaze, desire and taboo, empowered eroticism, and the body beyond eroticism.

Gender and sexual displays online

Scholars are increasingly arguing that the display of sexual and gender performances in online spaces, both reproduces and resists gender stereotypes. Selfies enable physical appearance to become a communicative focus, where self-esteem is both the motivation and the intended output of such communication (Pounders et al., 2016). Postfeminist sensibility helps explain the dynamics of fashion blogging for plus-sized consumers, who seek legitimisation while practising constant self-control (Harju and Huovinen, 2015). Likewise, the athletic 'ideal' body is pursued through an ambiguous body positive rhetoric and is in constant comparison with influencers' images (Ferguson et al., 2020). Yet, fashion blogs allow subversive identity work for consumers who do not embody normative standards of femininity and wish to establish themselves as fashionable subjects (Harju and Houvinen, 2015; Zanette and Brito, 2019). The same tension is witnessed in the use of body-related hashtags that reinforce cultural stereotypes over sexualised and gendered bodies, but also offer a platform to build group identity and to engage with digital protests (Gurrieri and Drenten, 2019b). As such, recent consumer research shows that digital activism that harnesses online bodywork can potentially question hegemonic imagery of female bodies, although the politics of the patriarchal gaze endure (Matich et al., 2019), nonetheless, in some instances, the online expression of a sexualised self can be empowering (Veer and Golf-Papez, 2018).

Objectification and the male gaze

Feminist marketing scholars have dealt extensively with the representation of female bodies in the marketplace and the objectification of women. However, objectification has been theorised differently depending on which feminist perspective is adopted (Bristor and Fischer, 1993). Hongsmark Knudsen (2019) provides a detailed review of such perspectives and argues that objectification differs under material and rhetorical feminist perspectives. Material feminism highlights that individuals are bound by patriarchal structures, with little room for change, thus objectification is driven by the male gaze, which elides the physical materiality of bodies being scrutinised (Brace-Govan and Ferguson, 2019). While rhetorical feminism acknowledges that there can be multiple readings of the body, thus a rhetorical analysis of objectification recognises that women might adopt a variety of subject positions. For example, recent material feminist marketing research claims that advertising contributes to objectifying women and encourages rape culture by representing women as 'sexualised, zoomorphic and subjugated beings' (Gurrieri et al., 2016, p. 1457). However, recent work has criticised conceptualisations of the female consumer as uncritical and unable to reflect on objectifying and stereotypical advertising images and other media representations (Hongsmark Knudsen, 2019). Finally, the 'pornification of culture' paradigm includes work on the objectification of female bodies in other social strata. In political marketing, for example, Sanghvi and Hodges (2015) find that the objectification of female politicians based on their appearance undermines them politically. Gender representation in food practices is affected and limited by normative gazes (Pirani et al., 2018), while women's bodies are literally shaped by such gazes, as illustrated by the history of shapewear (Zanette and Scaraboto, 2019; Scaraboto and Zanette, 2020).

Desire and taboo

According to Larsen et al. (2018, p. 1067) taboos influence consumption and markets because they "regulate the ability of markets to provide access to consumption objects and activities, the nature of our contact with those objects and activities, and the manner in which we put them to use". In essence, although consumers engage with a wide range of taboo behaviours and products, for example, sex toys (Walther and Schouten, 2016; Wilner and Dinnin Huff, 2017; Piha et al., 2018), pornography (Daskalopoulou and Zanette, 2020; Zanette and Daskalopoulou, 2020) or seemingly non-sexual offerings (Lanier Jr. and Rader, 2019), taboos also impose limits or prohibit consumers' behaviour (Larsen and Patterson, 2018). Recent papers outline consumer's perceptions of taboo advertisements. For example, Theodorakis and Painesis (2018) discuss the role of psychological distance in consumers' attitudinal and behavioural reactions to taboo ads, while Sabri (2017) looks at the communication context itself to understand consumers' perceptions of taboo ads. Focussing on the intersection between taboo and desire, Veer and Golf-Papez (2018) explain how consumers attempt to break taboos online by displaying freely their sexual self, Hongsmark Knudsen (2019) explains how women reading Fifty Shades of Grey in public address and negotiate taboos about female sexuality, while Piha et al. (2018) argue that some consumers are willingly constructing taboos about buying sex toys because the controlled violation of taboo is sexually exciting. Finally, recent studies focussing on the intersection of gender, religion and taboo show that despite the disciplinary role of religion and religious ideology (Rauf et al., 2019), consumption practices can also offer respite from sociocultural taboos as exemplified in the context of Turkish soap operas (Yalkin and Veer, 2018).

Empowered eroticism

Marketing has helped to position a plethora of new markets as empowering for women, such as pole-dancing and sex toy shopping (Maclaran, 2015). Recent consumer research on empowerment has largely focussed on the individual empowered woman. For example, Walther and Schouten (2016) illustrate that lingerie and sex toys help some women to discover a 'newfound empowerment', Walther (2019, p. 155) argues that self-satisfaction is empowering because it allows women to become "authors and protagonists of their own orgasms", and Matich et al. (2019) show that some women feel empowered when they participate in online campaigns such as #FreeTheNipple. However, the controversial and gendered history of certain consumption practices and products illustrates the ambivalent relationship between consumer choice, agency and empowerment. For example, high heels can be both women's 'power tool' and instruments of torture (Parmentier, 2016), while lipstick's cultural meanings have varied historically from a sign of Satan, a playful and deliberate choice, to an emblem of idealised feminine beauty (Gurrieri and Drenten, 2019a). In the current context, consumption and marketing practices accommodate a commodified and pornified version of consumer empowerment. As such, even though consumers might feel empowered on some level, their consumption practices do not necessarily challenge gender hierarchies and patriarchal structures (Glick, 2000; Evans et al., 2010).

The body beyond eroticism

Reclaiming the body has started to receive more attention in recent consumer research. This is a welcome addition that moves beyond eroticism and the 'pornification of culture' paradigm. Bodies are reclaimed from disciplining and governing market strategies, as shown in the complicit resistance of plus-sized consumers (Zanette and Brito, 2019). Another example is women's experience of menstruation, a natural rhythm that contrasts with the disembodied marketing of feminine hygiene products devising menstruation as something women need to be protected from (de Waal Malefyt and McCabe, 2016). Other disciplining strategies that reinforce marginalisation in the marketplace have been challenged recently such as in the case of single consumers, whose status reflects the hegemony of heterosexual coupledom and family in the marketplace (Lai et al., 2015).

Austerity and the feminisation of poverty

The third topic highlighted by Maclaran (2015) 'austerity and the feminisation of poverty' is concerned with the operation of inclusion and exclusion, empowerment and disempowerment for women via the market. Recent work falls into three thematic areas each drawing on different sets of feminist theory to explore injustice and inequality. Drawing largely on material-discursive feminist theory the first set of studies 'women's economic empowerment' explore the positive potential of the market to empower women and lift them out of poverty. This work is global in view and takes a pragmatic approach driven by the need to respond immediately and practically to injustices to women, as such it is activist in form. A second set of studies 'coping and caring in poverty' might be viewed in the materialist feminist tradition. This work focusses on class in exploring the relations between productive and reproductive labour. Focussing on the domestic sphere, it reveals alternative understandings of value not necessarily grounded in capital accumulation. Broadly speaking these studies see the economy as a gendered (androcentric) construct and propose a shift towards an alternative economy of care. The third set of studies 'performativity, precarity, and sexual violence' draws on poststructural feminism (Butler) to explore how the perpetuation of poverty and norms of sexual violence towards women in India are grounded in iterative acts of consumption.

Women's economic empowerment?

Inequalities are most often perpetuated by the economy. Linda Scott's recent book *The Double X Economy* (2020) uses a plethora of often quite disturbing data to reveal the stark gender inequalities built into the global economic system. Scott (2020b) is a long term and committed proponent of women's economic empowerment seeing it as one of the keys to significantly improving financial, social and environmental conditions for women (and in fact everyone) particularly in developing countries. She argues that legislation can only go so far and that corporations are often particularly well placed to contribute to the much-needed improvement of women's position in the economy. At the localised level, Godefroit-Winkel and Peñaloza's (2020) study of women in Moroccan supermarkets finds that they develop competencies in these spaces which empower them in what can be controlling relations with husbands and other women.

Recent research has examined how women's economic empowerment schemes have become increasingly marketised (Steinfield, 2019). Such schemes are developed by private-sector companies to help enable women gain access to resources, training and sources of income to improve their (and their families') lives. Steinfield (2019) adopts a material-discursive feminist approach to examine how human and non-human elements interact within women's economic empowerment schemes, to better understand how power operates within these 'entanglements'. She finds that in attempting to demonstrate impact, private sector companies are introducing performance metrics which then serve to reinforce the exploitative dynamics inherent within capitalism. Referring to Laclau and Mouffe's theory of discourse, Hopkinson and Aman (2017) explore how discursive construction of entrepreneurs and empowered mothers within Unilever's scheme for women serves to obscure and gloss over the economics of the arrangement and as such traditional hierarchies remain in place. They cast doubt on whether such schemes do empower women, instead creating 'one way dependent relationships', giving women little freedom for defining their 'subject position' as 'new rural Indian women' (2017, p. 316). Kravets, Preece and Maclaran (2020) similarly reveal the way in which social enterprise initiatives can gloss over difference. In applying feminist critical discourse analysis to media reports of the Uniform Project (a social enterprise project undertaken by an individual) they expose gender ideologies that serve to reproduce dominant patriarchal narratives. However, Steinfield (2019) also argues that embracing a viewpoint that goes beyond solely discourse and includes both human and non-human elements renders entanglements of intra-activity visible which may be empowering as well as oppressive for women.

Recognising the complex and multi-faceted nature of gender injustice a group of feminist scholars within the Transformative Consumer Research (TCR) school have developed the ambitious 'transformative gender justice framework' (Hein et al., 2016; Steinfield et al., 2019a). The framework draws on three sets of theory for its grounding: 'social and distributive justice theory, which predominantly identifies inequalities at the structural socioeconomic level; capabilities approach, which highlights barriers individuals face in realizing their desired potential; and recognition theory, which locates disenfranchisement in sociocultural, symbolic, and discursive dynamics' (Hein et al., 2016, p. 224). As such the framework is intended as an analytical device to 'assess the interactions between structural, agentic, and sociocultural forces that underlie gender injustices' with a view to creating practical policy-based solutions (Hein et al., 2016, p. 223).

Coping and caring in poverty

There is a growing body of literature that examines how women cope both physically and emotionally with poverty and the additional work women perform to budget, provide food and manage the household (Cappellini, Marilli and Parsons, 2014; Hutton, 2015, 2016; Cappellini et al., 2019). Research into food well-being in very low-income families in rural India (Voola et al., 2018) finds that food practices reveal entrenched inequalities between men and women, particularly through the relational production of masculinities and femininities. Building on the idea that much work of food provision is about enacting care for others, Parsons, Harman and Cappellini (forthcoming) develop the concept of foodcare arguing that it potentially offers low-income mothers in the UK an alternative to the logic of capital for their demonstration of worth. More recently, Hutton (2019) adopts 'pro-care' feminist theory to understand 'affective inequality' and complex power relations that are involved in care relations as part of poverty-induced marketplace exclusion.

Some of the work on care and coping builds on Beverley Skeggs' (1997) work on respectability and working-class femininity. For example, Banister et al. (2016) offer insight into how low-income young mothers in the UK encounter the challenges of becoming 'respectable' young mothers via their consumption. Similarly, Parsons et al explore how working-class mothers attempt to gain access to structures of value through their food provision practices (Parsons, Harman and Cappellini, forthcoming). All of these studies find middle-class understandings and practices of mothering as constituting norms of 'good mothering' against which other groups evaluate themselves (Parsons and Cappellini, 2020).

Consumer researchers are also producing insightful interdisciplinary thinking about care, making a strong argument for its unyoking from gender and forms of femininity. The Care Collective's (2020) *Care Manifesto* explores our world through the lens of care at all levels. They propose a model of 'universal care' which would underpin a caring economy, saturating kinship groups, community, state and planet. Here care is 'distributed in an egalitarian way – neither assumed to be unproductive and primarily women's work by nature, nor, when paid, carried out by women who are poor, immigrant or of colour' (2020, p. 19). As such their manifesto is a feminist, queer, anti-racist and eco-socialist project, one which involves a rejection of capitalist market logics seeing them as completely irreconcilable with logics of care.

Performativity, precarity and sexual violence

Emergent literature looking at links between consumption, sexual violence, class and caste in India, similarly finds 'respectability' to be a significant proxy for how a woman is valued. Joy et al. draw on the work of Butler to show how in India, despite structural changes, including women's increasing involvement in education and employment, patriarchal gender norms continue to dominate notions of respectability, and the country has 'a shockingly high incidence of sexual assault' (2015, p. 1740). The chapter notes that while lower-class and -caste women are at greater risk of sexual violence, women of all statuses occupy vulnerable/precarious positions.

Varman et al. (2018) examine how interconnected circuits of patriarchy (capitalist patriarchy and a local circuit of izzat, i.e. respect/honour) normalise both what constitutes respectable behaviour for women, and sexual violence against women. Specifically, they examine how 'different aspects of consumption, such as clothes, cosmetics, alcohol, cigarettes and spaces are brought together in discourse of izzat to create a divide between respectable and unrespectable' (2018, p. 933). As such they reveal how women are blamed for the violence they face because of the consumption practices they engage in. They explore how class and caste intersect with notions of honour; izzat permeates much more than just women's experience – it affects her family as well.

Varman et al. (2021) further examine the encoding of violence within consumption norms in a study of female domestic service workers in India. They find that these women face regular caste-based segregation, physical and sexual violence at the hands of their employers. Drawing on the work of Butler they observe of norms that they 'create a grid of intelligibility and those who become unintelligible are susceptible to violence' (2021, p649). They find that in this context at least, norms not only reinforce hierarchies and distinctions but also 'delimit and seemingly elevate livable lives' and render others unintelligible or, using Butlers' (2004) term, 'ungrievable'. Existing beyond dominant norms then the ungrievable lives of these women can seemingly be exploited at will.

Conclusion: we have made progress but we are still 'missing feminisms'

Back in 2015 Hearn and Hein lamented that work on 'queer theory; critical race, intersectional and transnational feminisms; material discursive feminism; and critical studies on men and masculinities' was missing from the cannon of marketing research. As our review highlights there have been some pockets of progress, however we have also identified some enduring absences. In particular there is a dearth of work which takes an intersectional approach to exploring how structural inequalities are perpetuated by the current dominant economic system of neoliberal capitalism. Despite calls for more intersectional research within marketing (Gopaldas and DeRoy, 2015; Maclaran, 2015; Maclaran and Kravets, 2018; Maclaran and Stevens, 2019), empirical studies remain scarce.

As we explore above, in the section on pornification of culture, there has been significant growth in work which parallels the societal shift towards digital and social media. This has been a rich seam for marketers and consumer researchers. Confirming Maclaran's prediction (2015) fourth-wave feminism has contributed to highlight the tension between the display of gender and sexual performances in digital settings and the agency of the subject over such displays. Promising areas for future research are in the commodification of consumers' empowerment, and in the return of material feminism to study the objectification of female bodies and desires (see Brace-Govan and Ferguson, 2019).

Work on austerity and the feminisation of poverty underlines the need for renewed focus on the material circumstances of women. There is still much to do to explore the way in which individuals live in very different relations to capital. Recent work underscores that these relations do not only structure their access to resources (money, time, skills) but also to different possibilities for both self-presentation and the accrual of value and respectability (Joy et al., 2015; Parsons and Cappellini, 2020). Further work is also needed on the transformation of relationships between production and social reproduction, this will become increasingly pressing in the new post Covid-19 world of work where paid labour moves increasingly into the home sphere.

The present moment

Feminist ideas and theorising emerge through the historical conditions of their production and we are indeed living in interesting times. The present moment is characterised by upheaval, uncertainty and unrest, with global events such as the Covid-19 pandemic exacerbating gender, class and racial inequalities around the world (Qasim, 2020). Ongoing racial tensions, violence and protests highlight how deeply ingrained racism and inequality continue to manifest within society. There is growing evidence of the disparities in risk and outcomes of Covid-19 for BAME communities, alongside political discourses that appear to scapegoat or apportion blame to minority communities, particularly multi-generational and large households. Alongside racial inequalities, these global events also reveal and aggravate gender and class inequalities, with growing gender pay gaps as women shoulder much of the burden for childcare and domestic responsibilities, preventing them from working or rendering them at risk of illness or precarious contracts or redundancy (Scott, 2020a).

We view the present conditions as a precipice or crossroads, a moment which reveals and potentially retrenches longstanding patriarchal structures and inequalities, yet such circumstances may nevertheless serve as a catalyst for hope and positive change. Within marketing scholarship, we seem to be on the edge of an exciting shift, albeit incremental, in new work. As we write there are four special issues of marketing and consumer research journals in the making which bring gender issues to the fore. In the *Journal for the Association of Consumer Research*, Coleman, Fischer and Zayer focus on gender, markets and consumers and in particular gender equality, justice and welfare. Dobscha and Ostberg, in their *Journal of Marketing Management* special issue, seek to address some of the 'missing feminisms', missing contexts and missing LGBTQI perspectives. Gurrieri, Previte and Prothero's (2020) special issue seeks to highlight gender dynamics and inequalities within the *Journal of Macromarketing*. Finally, Prothero and Tadajewski's *Journal of Marketing Management* special issue, inspired by the #MeToo movement, examines gender inequalities within marketing practice and academia. The task we are charged with as feminist marketing scholars going forward is to ensure that, both within and despite the challenging circumstances we are currently facing, we continue to build upon this research. Our aim is to better understand the present conditions, render visible more of the missing feminisms within our field and contribute to more polyvocal feminist research within marketing academia.

The future

Clearly there is a pressing need to return to structures of knowledge production within the marketing academy. One of the glaring challenges is, to use Kravets and Varman's (2020) term, the 'institutional publishing apparatus' that at present serves to entrench existing privileges and norms. In this respect, McDonagh and Prothero (2018) reveal the relative absence of female voices in marketing and consumer research journals, finding 18.5% of Editors in Chief, 28% of Associate Editors and 28.3% of Editorial Review Board members are female. Were we to include multiple axes of protected characteristics (and we now should) these figures would look much worse. While there remains an imbalance in the constitution of the publishing gatekeepers in marketing academia, there is also a missed potential for feminist theorising to have much deeper influence on structures of knowledge production within our field (Kravets and Varman, 2020; Cappellini and Hutton this volume). As feminists seeking to dislodge oppressive logic, we need to entirely unpick and rethink how we approach our work. Hancock (2016) underscores this point in her fascinating study of the intellectual roots of intersectionality. She opens her book by wondering why her colleague chose to frame her discussion of power relations using a framework offered by Foucault, a white male philosopher, rather than the work of the black feminist theorist, Patricia Hill Collins. The same criticism could easily be applied to much work within marketing and consumer research. The issue then embraces both missing theories but also missing subjectivities as feminist, queer and subalternised 'ways of knowing' are consistently marginalised. The time therefore is ripe for an overhaul, an excavation of the histories, geographies and institutional arrangements that produced current valued ways of knowing in marketing academia.

As cogs working in an entrenched academic system, we are no doubt caught within the apparatus. Nevertheless, in the last five years, but particularly throughout 2020, the curtain has dropped to reveal certain structural inequalities in society. Certainly, from our standpoints and with our resources, there are things we can do to forge ahead and progress towards being inclusive. One of the most powerful things we can do is to have a strong collective commitment to both intellectual advancement and participative action (David, 2018). Without the strength and support of a community of engaged scholars, it is difficult to break free of ingrained working patterns. This is vital. Second, within these communities, we need to be having honest discussions about what is right for the field, welcoming difficult debates and varying perspectives about how we can tackle entrenched issues of inequality without fear of judgement and recrimination. Academia needs to become (or return to being) a safer, protected space, with less doublespeak. Finally, we must appreciate that through our individual and collective actions, those working within the academy can either exacerbate existing tensions or support successful intersectional engagement.

References

Åkestam, Nina. Rosengren, Sara and Dahlen, Micael. (2017) Think about it – can portrayals of homosexuality in advertising prime consumer-perceived social connectedness and empathy? *European Journal of Marketing*, 51 (1), pp. 82–98.

Banister, Emma, Hogg, Margaret, Budds, Kirsty and Dixon, Mandy. (2016) Becoming respectable: low-income young mothers, consumption and the pursuit of value. *Journal of Marketing Management*, 32 (7–8), pp. 652–672.

Bettany, Shona M. (2016) Vive la sexual revolution! Liberté, Égalité (and beyond) Fraternité in CCT sexuality research. In *Consumer Culture Theory Conference*, Lille, France.

Bettany, Shona M. and Rowe, David. (2016) The politics of in/appropriate/d others: moving beyond the vulnerable consumer in the LGBT market/movement. In *Consumer Culture Theory Conference*, Lille, France.

Brace-Govan, Jan and Ferguson, Shelagh. (2019) Gender and sexed bodies: embodiment, Corporeality, Physical Mastery and the Gaze. In Dobscha, S. (ed). *Handbook of Research on Gender and Marketing*. Cheltenham and Northampton, MA: Edward Elgar Publishing, pp. 63–100.

Bristor, Julia M. and Fischer, Eileen. (1993) Feminist thought: implications for consumer research. *Journal of Consumer Research*, 19(4), pp. 518–536.

Butler, Judith. (2004) *Precarious Life: The Powers of Mourning and Violence*. London: Verso.

Cappellini, Benedetta, Harman, Vicki, Marilli, Alessandra and Parsons, Elizabeth. (2019) Intensive mothering in hard times: Foucauldian ethical self-formation and cruel optimism. *Journal of Consumer Culture*, 19 (4), pp. 469–492.

Cappellini, Benedetta, Marilli, Alessandra and Parsons, Elizabeth. (2014). The hidden work of coping: gender and the micro-politics of household consumption in times of austerity. *Journal of Marketing Management*, 30 (15–16), pp.1597–1624.

Coffin, Jack, Banister, Emma and Goatman, Anna. (2016) Revisiting the Ghetto: how the meanings of gay districts are shaped by the meanings of the city. *ACR North American Advances*, 14, pp. 290–295.

Coffin, Jack, Eichert, Christian A. and Nolke, Ana-Isabel. (2019) Towards (and beyond) LGBTQ+ studies in marketing and consumer research. In Dobscha Susan. (ed), *Handbook of Research on Gender and Marketing*. Cheltenham and Northampton: Edward Elgar Publishing, pp. 273–293.

Daskalopoulou, Athanasia and Zanette, Maria Carolina. (2020) Women's consumption of pornography: pleasure, contestation, and empowerment. *Sociology*, 54 (5), pp. 969–986.

David, Miriam. (2018) Femifesta? A feminist manifesto for the 21st century. *Social Sciences*, 7, 91. doi: 10.3390/socsci7060091.

De Waal Malefyt, Timothy and McCabe, Maryann. (2016) Women's bodies, menstruation and marketing "protection:" interpreting a paradox of gendered discourses in consumer practices and advertising campaigns. *Consumption Markets & Culture*, 19 (6), pp. 555–575.

Demangeot, Catherine, Kipnis, Eva, Pullig, Chris, Cross, Samantha N., Emontspool, Julie, Galalae, Cristina, Grier, Sonya A., Rosenbaum, Mark S. and Best, Susy F. (2019) Constructing a bridge to multicultural marketplace well-being: a consumer-centered framework for marketer action. *Journal of Business Research*, 100, pp. 339–353.

Descubes, Irena, McNamara, Tom and Bryson, Douglas. (2018) Lesbians' assessments of gay advertising in France: not necessarily a case of 'La Vie en Rose?'. *Journal of Marketing Management*, 34 (7–8), pp. 639–663.

Evans, Adrienne, Riley, Sarah and Avi, Shankar. (2010) Technologies of sexiness: theorizing women's engagement in the sexualization of culture. *Feminism & Psychology*, 20(1), 114–131.

Ferguson, Shelagh, Brace-Govan, Jan and Welsh, Briget. (2020) Complex contradictions in a contemporary idealised feminine body project. *Journal of Marketing Management*. doi: 10.1080/0267257X.2020.1721553.

Foster Davis, Judy. (2018) Selling whiteness? – a critical review of the literature on marketing and racism. *Journal of Marketing Management*, 34 (1–2), pp. 134–177.

Glick, Elisa. (2000) Sex positive: feminism, queer theory, and the politics of transgression. *Feminist Review*, 64 (1), pp. 19–45.

Godefroit-Winkel, Delphine and Peñaloza, Lisa. (2020) Women's empowerment at the Moroccan supermarket: an ethnographic account of achieved capabilities and altered social relations in an emerging retail servicescape. *Journal of Macromarketing*, 40 (4), pp. 492–509.

Gopaldas, Ahir and DeRoy, Glenna. (2015) An intersectional approach to diversity research. *Consumption Markets & Culture*, 18 (4), pp. 333–364.

Gopaldas, Ahir and Siebert, Anton. (2018) Women over 40, foreigners of color, and other missing persons in globalizing mediascapes: understanding marketing images as mirrors of intersectionality. *Consumption, Markets, and Culture*, 21 (4), pp. 323–346.

Grady, Constance. (2018) The waves of feminism, and why people keep fighting over them, explained. Available at: https://www.vox.com/2018/3/20/16955588/feminism-waves-explained-first-second-third-fourth.

Gurrieri, Lauren, Brace-Govan, Jan and Cherrier, Helene. (2016) Controversial advertising: transgressing the taboo of gender-based violence. *European Journal of Marketing*, 50 (7), pp. 1448–1469.

Gurrieri, Lauren and Drenten, Jenna. (2019a) The feminist politics of choice: lipstick as a marketplace icon. *Consumption Markets & Culture*. doi: 10.1080/10253866.2019.1670649.

Gurrieri, Lauren and Drenten, Jenna. (2019b) The hashtaggable body: negotiating gender performance in social media. In Dobscha, S. (ed). *Handbook of Research on Gender and Marketing*. Cheltenham and Northampton, MA: Edward Elgar Publishing, 342 pp.

Gurrieri, Lauren, Previte, Josephine and Prothero, Andrea. (2020) Hidden in plain sight: building visibility for critical gender perspectives exploring markets, marketing and society. *Journal of Macromarketing*, 40 (4), pp. 437–444.

Han, Xiaoqi and Tsai, Sunny W. (2016) Beyond targeted advertising: representing disenfranchised minorities in 'inclusive' advertising. *Journal of Cultural Marketing Strategy*, 1 (2), pp. 154–169.

Hancock, Ange-Marie. (2016) *Intersectionality: An Intellectual History*. Oxford: Oxford University Press.
Harju, Anu A. and Huovinen, Annamari. (2015) Fashionably voluptuous: normative femininity and resistant performative tactics in fatshion blogs. *Journal of Marketing Management*, 31 (15–16), pp. 1602–1625.
Hearn, Jeff and Hein, Wendy. (2015) Reframing gender and feminist knowledge construction in marketing and consumer research: missing feminisms and the case of men and masculinities. *Journal of Marketing Management*, 31 (15–16), pp. 1626–1651.
Hein, Wendy, Steinfield, Laurel, Ourahmoune, Nacima, Coleman, Catherine A., Zayer, Linda T. and Littlefield, Jon. (2016) Gender justice and the market: a transformative consumer research perspective. *Journal of Public Policy & Marketing*, 35 (2), pp. 223–236.
Hill, Layla Roxanne and Sobande, Francesca. (2018) In our own words: organising and experiencing exhibitions as black women and women of colour in Scotland. In Fink, R., Sharp, B. and Sweeney, M. (eds). *Accessibility, Inclusion, and Diversity in Critical Event Studies*. London: Routledge, pp. 107–121.
Hongsmark Knudsen, G. (2019) Critical consumers: discourses of women, sexuality, and objectification. In Dobscha, S. (ed) *Handbook of Research on Gender and Marketing*. Cheltenham and Northampton, MA: Edward Elgar Publishing, pp. 168–185.
Hopkinson, Gillian and Aman, Asad. (2017) Women entrepreneurs: how power operates in bottom of the pyramid-marketing discourse. *Marketing Theory*, 17(3), pp. 305–321.
Hutton, Martina. (2015) Consuming stress: exploring hidden dimensions of consumption-related strain at the intersection of gender and poverty. *Journal of Marketing Management*, 31, pp. 1695–1717.
Hutton, Martina. (2016) Neither passive nor powerless: reframing economic vulnerability via resilient pathways. *Journal of Marketing Management*, 32 (3–4), pp. 252–274.
Hutton, Martina. (2019) The care-less marketplace: exclusion as affective inequality. *Consumption Markets & Culture*, 22 (5–6), pp. 528–544.
Joy, Annamma, Belk, Russell and Bhardwaj, Rishi. (2015) Judith Butler on performativity and precarity: exploratory thoughts on gender and violence in India. *Journal of Marketing Management*, 31(15–16), 1739–1745.
Kearney, Shauna, Brittain, Ian, and Kipnis, Eva. (2019) "Superdisabilities" vs "disabilities"? Theorizing the role of ableism in (mis)representation mythology of disability in the marketplace. *Consumption, Markets & Culture*, 22 (5–6), pp. 545–567.
Kravets, Olga, Preece, Chloe and Maclaran, Pauline. (2020). The uniform entrepreneur: making gender visible in social enterprise. *Journal of Macromarketing*, early view. https://journals.sagepub.com/doi/10.1177/0276146720930331.
Kravets, Olga and Varman, Rohit (2020) Hierarchies of knowledge in marketing theory. Special issue call for papers, *Marketing Theory*. https://journals.sagepub.com/pb-assets/cmscontent/MTQ/CFP_Hierarchies_of_Knowledge.pdf.
Lai, Ai Ling, Lim, Ming and Higgins, Matthew. (2015) The abject single: exploring the gendered experience of singleness in Britain. *Journal of Marketing Management*, 31 (15–16), pp. 1559–1582.
Lanier Jr, Clinton D. and Rader, Scott. (2019) The irrepressible and uncontrollable urge: sex, experience, and consumption. *Consumption Markets & Culture*, 22 (1), pp. 17–43.
Larsen, Gretchen. and Patterson, Maurice. (2018) Consumption, marketing and taboo. *Journal of Marketing Management*, 34 (13–14), pp. 1063–1066.
Larsen, Gretchen, Patterson, Maurice, Sabri, Ouidade and Walther, Luciana. (2018) A commentary on the treatment of taboo in consumption and marketing. *Journal of Marketing Management*, 34 (13–14), pp. 1067–1077.
McDonagh, Pierre and Prothero, Andrea. (2018) An assessment of the gender discourse and gender representation in marketing's journals: 1993–2016. In *14th ACR Gender, Marketing and Consumer Behavior Conference*, Dallas, TX.

Maclaran, Pauline. (2015) Feminism's fourth wave: a research agenda for marketing and consumer research, *Journal of Marketing Management*, 31(15–16), pp. 1732–1738.

Maclaran, Pauline. (2017) Judith Butler: gender performativity and heteronormative hegemony. In Ostergaard, S. and Heilbrunn, B. (eds.). *The Routledge Companion to Canonical Authors in Social Theory on Consumption*. London: Routledge, pp. 227–234.

Maclaran, Pauline and Kravets, Olga. (2018) Feminist perspectives in marketing: past, present and future, In Tadajewski, M., Higgins, M., Denegri-Knott, J. and Varman, R. (eds). *The Routledge Companion to Critical Marketing*. London: Routledge, pp. 64–82.

Maclaran, Pauline and Stevens, Lorna. (2019) Thinking through feminist theorising: poststructuralist feminism, ecofeminism and intersectionality. In Dobscha, S. (ed). *Handbook of Research on Gender and Marketing*. Cheltenham and Northampton, MA: Edward Elgar Publishing, pp. 229–251.

Matich, Margaret. (2019) Rethinking contemporary feminist activism: zines, social media and body politics in the fourth-wave. PhD thesis, University of Liverpool.

Matich, Margaret, Ashman, Rachel and Parsons, Elizabeth. (2019) #freethenipple Digital activism and embodiment in the contemporary feminist movement. *Consumption Markets & Culture*, 22 (4), pp. 337–362.

May, Vivian M. (2015) *Pursuing Intersectionality, Unsettling Dominant Imaginaries*. London: Routledge.

McNair, Brian. (2013) *Porno? Chic!* London: Routledge.

Morris, Angelica Noelle. (2017) Fashion, social media, and identity expression: an intersectional approach to understanding the fashion consumption patterns of black middle-class women. Doctoral thesis, The University of Texas.

Méndez, Maria José. (2018). "The river told me": rethinking intersectionality from the world of Berta Cáceres. *Capitalism Nature Socialism*, 29 (1), pp. 7–24.

Ndichu, Edna G. and Upadhyaya, Shika. (2019) "Going natural": black women's identity project shifts in hair care practices. *Consumption Markets & Culture*, 22 (1), pp. 44–67.

Nejad, Mohammad G. and O'Connor, Genevieve. (2016) An intersectional approach to evaluating consumer financial literacy. *Journal of Financial Services Marketing*, 21 (4), pp. 308–324.

Nölke, Ana-Isabel. (2018) Making diversity conform? An intersectional, longitudinal analysis of LGBT-specific mainstream media advertisements. *Journal of Homosexuality*, 65 (2), pp. 224–255.

Olivotti, Francesca. (2016) The paradox of exclusion and multiculturalism in postcolonial identity. *Consumption Markets & Culture*, 19 (5), pp. 475–496.

Parmentier, Marie-Agnés. (2016) High heels. *Consumption Markets & Culture*, 19 (6), pp. 511–519.

Parsons, Elizabeth and Cappellini, Benedetta. (2020) Class, selfhood and the "subject of value" under conditions of liquidity, essay in the collection by Caldwell, M.L. and Henry, P. 'The Continuing Significance of Social Structure in Liquid Modernity'. *Marketing Theory*, 20 (4), pp. 547–572.

Parsons, Elizabeth, Harman, Vicki and Capppellini, Benedetta. (forthcoming) Foodwork and foodcare in hard times: mothering, value and values. *Gender Work and Organisation* special section on Foodwork: Racialised, Gendered and Classed Labours. https://onlinelibrary.wiley.com/doi/10.1111/gwao.12630

Paul, Pamela. (2005) *Pornified: How Pornography Is Transforming Our Lives, Our Relationships and Our Families*. New York: Times Books.

Piha, Samuel, Hurmerinta, Leila, Sandberg, Birgitta and Järvinen, Elina. (2018) From filthy to healthy and beyond: finding the boundaries of taboo destruction in sex toy buying. *Journal of Marketing Management*, 34 (13–14), pp. 1078–1104.

Pirani, Daniela, Cappellini, Benedetta and Harman, Vicki. (2018) The Italian breakfast: Mulino Bianco and the advent of a family practice (1971–1995). *European Journal of Marketing*, 52 (12), pp. 2478–2498.

Pounders, Kathrynn, Kowalczyk, Christine M. and Stowers, Kirsten. (2016) Insight into the motivation of selfie postings: impression management and self-esteem. *European Journal of Marketing*, 50 (9/10), pp. 1879–1892.

Pounders, Kathrynn and Mabry-Flynn, Amanda. (2016) Consumer response to gay and lesbian imagery. *Journal of Advertising Research*, 56 (4), pp. 426–440.

Qasim, Salaado. (2020) How racism spread around the world alongside COVID-19. *World Economic Forum website*. https://www.weforum.org/agenda/2020/06/just-like-covid-19-racism-is-spreading-around-the-world/ (accessed 28th September 2020).

Rauf, Ateeq Abdul, Prasad, Ajnesh and Ahmed, Abdullah. (2019) How does religion discipline the consumer subject? Negotiating the paradoxical tension between consumer desire and the social order. *Journal of Marketing Management*, 35 (5–6), pp. 491–513.

Rogan, Frances, Piacentini, Maria and Szmigin, Isabelle. (2016) Marketing "raunch culture": sexualisation and constructions of femininity within the night-time economy. In Moreau, P. and Puntoni, S. (eds). *NA – Advances in Consumer Research*. Duluth, MN: Association for Consumer Research, Volume 44, pp. 603–604.

Sabri, Ouidade. (2017) Does viral communication context increase the harmfulness of controversial taboo advertising? *Journal of Business Ethics*, 141 (2), pp. 235–247.

Sanghvi, Minita and Hodges, Nancy. (2015) Marketing the female politician: an exploration of gender and appearance, *Journal of Marketing Management*, 31 (15–16), pp. 1676–1694.

Scaraboto, Daiane and Zanette, Maria Carolina. (2020) 'Shapewear or nothing to wear'. The ambiguity of shapewear in the plus-size fashion market. In de Waal Malefyt, T. and McCabe, M. (eds). *Women, Consumption and Paradox*. Oxton and New York: Routledge, pp. 168–172.

Schaap, Julian and Berkers, Pauwke. (2019) "Maybe it's… skin colour?" How race-ethnicity and gender function in consumers' formation of classification styles of cultural content. *Consumption Markets & Culture*, 23 (6), pp. 1–17.

Scott, Linda (2020a) How coronavirus is widening the UK gender pay gap. *The Guardian*, 7 July 2020. https://www.theguardian.com/world/2020/jul/07/how-coronavirus-is-widening-the-uk-gender-pay-gap.

Scott, Linda. (2020b). *The Double X Economy: The Epic Potential of Women's Empowerment*. New York: Farrar, Straus and Giroux.

Skeggs, Beverly. (1997) *Formations of Class & Gender: Becoming Respectable*. London: Sage.

Sobande, Francesca. (2017) Watching me watching you: black women in Britain on YouTube. *European Journal of Cultural Studies*, 20 (6), pp. 655–671.

Sobande, Francesca. (2019) Woke-washing: "Intersectional" femvertising and branding "woke" bravery. *European Journal of Marketing*, 54 (11), pp. 2723–2745.

Sobande, Francesca, Fearfull, Anne and Brownlie, Douglas. (2019). Resisting media marginalisation: black women's digital content and collectivity. *Consumption Markets & Culture*, 23 (5), pp. 413–428.

Steinfield, Laurel A. (2019). 1, 2, 3, 4. I declare… empowerment? A material-discursive analysis of the marketisation, measurement and marketing of women's economic empowerment. *Journal of Marketing Management*,37(3–4), pp. 320–356. .

Steinfield, Laurel, Littlefield, Jon, Hein, Wendy, Coleman, Catherine and Zayer, Linda Tuncay. (2019a) The TCR perspective of gender: moving from critical theory to an activism-praxis orientation. In Dobscha, S. (ed) *Handbook of Research in Gender and Marketing*. Cheltenham: Elgar Publishing, pp. 186–210.

Steinfield, Laurel, Sanghvi, Minita, Zayer, Linda Tuncay, Coleman, Catherine A., Ourahmoune, Nacima, Harrison, Robert L., Hein, Wendy and Brace-Govan, Jan. (2019b). Transformative intersectionality: moving business towards a critical praxis. *Journal of Business Research*, 100, pp. 366–375.

The Care Collective (2020) *The Care Manifesto: The Politics of Interdependence*. London: Verso.

Theodorakis, Ioaniss and Grigorios Painesis. (2018) The impact of psychological distance and construal level on consumers' responses to taboos in advertising. *Journal of Advertising*, 47 (2), pp. 161–181.

Varman, Rohit, Goswami, Paromita and Vijay, Devi. (2018) The precarity of respectable consumption: normalising sexual violence against women. *Journal of Marketing Management*, 34 (11–12), pp. 932–964.

Varman, Rohit, Skålén, Per, Belk, Russell W. and Chaudhuri, Himadri Roy. (2021) Normative violence in domestic service: a study of exploitation, status, and grievability. *Journal of Business Ethics*,171, pp. 645–665.

Veer, Ekant. and Golf-Papez, Maja. (2018) Physically freeing: breaking taboos through online displays of the sexual self. *Journal of Marketing Management*, 34 (13–14), pp. 1105–1125.

Voola, Archana P., Voola, Ranjit, Wyllie, Jessica, Carlson, Jamie, and Sridharan, Srinivas. (2018). Families and food: exploring food well-being in poverty. *European Journal of Marketing*, 52 (12), pp. 2423–2448.

Walther, Luciana. (2019) Patriarchal myths debunked: applying a dialectic of extremes to women's erotic consumption. In Dobscha, S. (ed). *Handbook of Research on Gender and Marketing*. Cheltenham and Northampton, MA: Edward Elgar Publishing.pp. 117–167.

Walther, Luciana and Schouten, John W. (2016) Next stop, pleasure town: identity transformation and women's erotic consumption, *Journal of Business Research*, 69 (1), pp. 273–283.

Weston, Kath. (2011). Me, myself and I. In Taylor, Y., Hines, S., and Casey, M. (eds). *Theorizing Intersectionality and Sexuality*. Basingstoke: Palgrave Macmillan, pp. 15–36.

Wilner, Sarah J.S. and Dinnin Huff, Aimee. (2017) Objects of desire: the role of product design in revising contested cultural meanings. *Journal of Marketing Management*, 33 (3–4), pp. 244–271.

Yalkin, Cagri and Veer, Ekant. (2018) Taboo on TV: gender, religion, and sexual taboos in transnationally marketed Turkish soap operas. *Journal of Marketing Management*, 34 (13–14), pp. 1149–1171.

Zanette, Maria Carolina and Brito, Eliane Pereira Zamith. (2019) Fashionable subjects and complicity resistance: power, subjectification, and bounded resistance in the context of plus-size consumers, *Consumption Markets & Culture*, 22 (4), pp. 363–382.

Zanette, Maria Carolina and Daskalopoulou, Athanasia. (2020) Women who watch porn: market-mediated gendered discourses and consumption of pornography. In Argo, J., Lowrey, T.M., and Schau, H.J. (eds). *NA – Advances in Consumer Research*. Paris: Association for Consumer Research, Volume 48, pp. 168–172.

Zanette, Maria Carolina and Scaraboto, Daiane. (2019) From the corset to Spanx: shapewear as a marketplace icon. *Consumption Markets & Culture*, 22 (2), pp. 183–199.

Index

Note: **Bold** page numbers refer to tables; *italic* page numbers refer to figures and page numbers followed by "n" denote endnotes.

academic activism 171
account executive 67
ACR *see* Association for Consumer Research (ACR)
Actor-Network Theory 167
Addams, Jane 17, 22
Adland News 64, 66
Adriaanse, J. 180
advertising 1, 4–6, 19, 23–27, 31–38, 40, 42, 78–80, 94, 105–108, 113, 123–125, 127, 132–134, 147, 160, 191, 227, 228, 232, 296, 298, 302, 315, 326, 341, 345–347, 368, 445, 452, 462, 464; Black women leaders in 45–55; rhetorical work of women's clubs 59–69
Advertising Age 49, 51
Advertising Beckons Woman 63
Advertising Careers for Women (Clair) 60, 63
Advertising Federation of America (AFA) 69n2
Advertising Women of New York 51, 59
AFA *see* Advertising Federation of America (AFA)
"African-American Women: Our Science, Her Magic" (Nielsen) 341, 346
ageism 309–310
agency: role in digital (anti-)feminist activism 356–358
agential realism 275, 279–282; agency & discourse 280; binaries of Euro-Western academic thought, dismantling 271–275; diffractive methods 281–282; intra-activities 279–280; time and space 280–281
aging bodies 323–335; demographics of 325–326; Family Life Cycle 327; family life cycle 327; future trends and directions 333–335; generational and cohort analysis 326; history of 324–325; institutions 329–332, *330*; mind and 327–329; subjectivities 329
aging successfully 311–312
aging women 310
Ahmed, S. 242–243
Ain't I a Woman? Black Women and Feminism (hooks) 9, 248
Airbnb 378
Alaimo, Stacy: *Material Feminisms* 161–162
Alderson, W. 39
Alexa 376
Algeria 262, 263
alignment *vs.* extension **276–278**
Alvesson, M. 180
Always' #LikeAGirl campaign 6, 102, *103*, 106–108, 112–114
Aman, A. 467
Amazon 376
American Association of Advertising Agencies 49
American Association of Retired Persons (AARP) 332
American Civil Liberties Union 330
American Family Insurance 50
American Home Economics Association 17, 18
American Marketing Association 91
Anal Suffering 446
ANA *see* Association of National Advertisers (ANA)
Anthias, F. 270
anti-racist activism 249
Antler, J. 61–63
Anzaldúa, G. 269, 273, 274, 280, 290n2; *Borderlands* 248
Apple 376
Arab feminisms 260–262

Index

Arab Spring 257, 262–264
Ardern, J. 171
Arnold, P. 31
Arnould, E. J. 190
Arrhenius, S. 90
Associated Advertising Clubs of America 69n1
Association for Consumer Research (ACR) 334
Association for Consumer Research Conference 189–191
Association of National Advertisers (ANA) 48
Atwood, M.: *The Handmaid's Tale* 334
Aurat March, Pakistan 1
Away from Her (Polley) 331
Awes, R. 81
axes of domination 250–251
Ayer, H. H. 332

Baer, H. 389, 390, 394
Baker, S. M. 298
Ballard, M. S. 94
Bane, L. 24, 26
Banet-Weiser, S. 435
Barad, K. 270, 271, 274, 275, 279, 282–284, 291n6
Barnard, S. R. 391
Bar On B.A. 430
Barr, R. 210
Barrows, A. 21
Bartky, S. L. 374
BBD&O 50, 51
Bear, L. L. 271
de Beauvoir, S. 241
Belk, R. 258
de la Bellacasa, M. P. 163, 165
Bellamy, E.: *Looking Backward* 35
Bentsen, D. 331
Bergin, L. A. 422
Bettany, S. M. 222, 463
Bevier, I. 21
Bhardwaj, R. 258
Biden, J. 308, 313
Big Data 377, 380
biographical notes 138–140
biological determinism 272
biopower 372
Bissett, E. 128
Black feminism 45–47
#BlackLivesMatter (BLM) movement 48, 149, 342, 346–348, 460
Black Poles in White Holes 446
Black Pound Day 345–346

Black Twitter UK 345
Black women: advertising business 47–49; digital media experiences of (*see* digital media experiences, of Black women)
BLM *see* #Black Lives Matter (BLM) movement
#BloodNormal movement 102
Boatwright, B. 176
Bode, M. 372
bodies: aging 323–335; caring for food waste 165–166; feminist new materialist approach to 161–166; materializing 159–167; previous feminist consumer research on 159–161; sleeping 163–165
bodily entanglements 251
Boecklen, E. J. 131
Bolin, B. 90
Borderlands (Anzaldúa) 248
Bordo, Susan 78
Borgerson, J. L. 302
Boston Consulting Group 258
Bourdieu, P. 352, 354, 355
Bowie, D. 139
Brickell, C. 299
Bridesmaids 210
Brown, W. 436; *Undoing the Demos* 441
Bruce, K. 344
Brzuzy, S. 301
bSafe 375
Bumble: #MyLoveIsBlackLove 346–347
Bureau of Home Economics 19
Burke, M. 173–174
Burke, T. 46, 181, 353
Burnett, L. 53
Butler, J. 147, 171, 272, 274, 281, 297, 299
Butler, R. 309

Cajete, G. 271
Calkins, E. E. 62
Call me (Withers) 335
Callon, M. 273
Calvin Klein 227
capital: cultural **355**; economic **355**; social **355**; symbolic **355**
carbon neutrality 281
Care Manifesto (Care Collective) 468
Caroline Jones Advertising/Caroline Jones, Inc. 50
Carr, D. 391
Carsky, M. 4
Catholicism 197
Catt, C. C. 17

Catterall, M. 47, 78; *Marketing and Feminism: Current Issues and Research* 2, 343
Caudwell, J. 173
CCT *see* Consumer Culture Theory (CCT)
Cederstrom, C. 180–181
Center for Talent Innovation (CTI) 48
Chamberlain, K. 63
Chamberlain, P. 388, 389, 399n1
Chan, N. K. 375
Charitsis, V. 372
Charles Morris Price School of Advertising and Journalism 60
Chicago's Cosmopolitan Chamber of Commerce 50
Chidgey, R. 82
Chipko movement, India 96
Cho, M. 107
Cieslak, J. 252
Circle of 6 375
Civil Rights Act of 1964 48
civil rights legislation 48
Clair, B.: *Advertising Careers for Women* 60, 63
climate crisis 90–91; ecofeminism and 95
climate emergency 90
Clinton, H. 308, 315, 316, 317, 330
Cochrane, K. 388
Coco gets Interracial Facial 445–446
Code of Hammurabi 409
Code of Ur-Nammu 408
Coffin, J. 462
Cohan, S. 150n2
Cohen, M. 82
cohort analysis 326
Cole, J. 262
Cole, S. 262
Coleman, C. 3
College of Human Ecology 17
Collins, P. H. 45, 269, 470
Combs, G. 49
commodification of feminism 344–345
Connell, C. 297–298
consumer: conceptualising 34–35; critical, creating 31–43
consumer culture theory 2
Consumer Culture Theory (CCT) 190, 194
consumer decision-making: Kyrk on 40–42
The Consumers' Guide 37
Consumers' Union 37
consuming (trans)gender 297–299
consumption 22, 25, 32, 35, 37–43, 91, 94, 98, 123, 130, 140, 141, 145–148,. 159–161, 166, 208, 216–218, 245, 309, 323, 324, 326–330, 332, 345, 364, 368, 370, 377, 380, 391, 392, 398, 408, 436, 445, 447–450, 452, 453, 461, 465, 466, 468; -based self-objectification 222–235; behavior 4, 19, 31; beyond the binary 296–304; economics 38; erotic 8, 189–198; informed 18; libidinal 125
Contexto Internacional 304
Cornell Home Economics 22
Cornell University 19–21, 25–28
Cortese, A. 47
Cortez, A. O. 317, 318n1
Corus, C. 270, 272
Cottom, M. 344
Cowie, M. 140
Craggs, Charlie 394
The Creation of Patriarchy (Lerner) 408
Creative Department 52
Crenshaw, K. 45, 46, 269
critical consumer, creating 31–43; conditions of possibility 32; consumer, conceptualising 34–35; consumer decision-making 40–42
Critical Studies on Men and Masculinities (CSMM) 141–143
Critical Theory of the Family (Poster) 333
Crosby, E. 298, 304
Cruz, K. 436
CSMM *see* Critical Studies on Men and Masculinities (CSMM)
CTI *see* Center for Talent Innovation (CTI)
cultural capital **355**
cultural harm, (re)producing 451–452
Cyrus, M. 82

d'Alessio, K. 127
Dalí, S. 130
Dallyn, S. 180–181
Daly, K. 127
Danna, A. 378
Darms, L. 389
data-blind theory: and women's quest for freedom 405–407
Daub, D. R. 66
Davis, B. 323
Davis, J. F. 461; *Pioneering African-American Women in the Advertising Business: Biographies of MAD Black Women* 347
Dean, A. 396, 397
d'Eaubonne, F. 93
Declaration on Women and Trade (WTO) 405
decolonial feminism 259–260
Deep Throat 206
De Line, S. 273, 275, 280, 290n3

480 Index

Delineator 17, 24–28
Designer 26
Desmond, J. 133
Desperate Housewives 215
#DestroyingTheJoint (DtJ) 181
Dewey, M. 18
Dichter's Institute for Motivational Research 125
Diderot effect 37
digital body 390–391
digital corporeal activism 390–391
digital feminism, technical capabilities of 389–390
digital (anti-)feminist activism, symbolic violence of 351–365; agency, role of 356–358; context and methodological framework 353–356, **355**; desire for/desire to escape 'tradition' 360–362; embodied habitus 358–360; fourth wave feminism 352–353
digital media experiences, of Black women 341–348; antiblackness, combating 346–347; Black influencers 345–346; Black Pound Day 345–346; commodification of feminism 344–345; corporate co-optation **348**; critical studies 341–344; male gaze 347; matrix of oppression and intersectionality 343; oppressions, intersecting 346–347; racial capitalism 344–345; visibility 346–347
digital-trendsetters 341
Dignam, D. 68; "Ideas and Copy," 64; "Women Know Women," 61
Disclosure (Netflix) 303
Dobscha, S. 3, 85, 94, 95
Dolce & Gabbana 232
Donohue, T. 323
The Double X Economy (Scott) 418n1, 466
Douglas, S. 332
Dove: "Campaign for Real Beauty" (2004) 106
Dowd, Maureen 316
doxa **355**
Doyle, Jude 313, 315
The Drum 346
DtJ see #DestroyingTheJoint (DtJ)
Duffy, B. E. 375
Dunham, L. 82, 209
Dvorak, Petula 316
Dworkin, A. 452`
Dylan, B. 138

Eastern Europe 145
ecofeminism 93–95; *Extinction Rebellion* 95–97; messaging dialogue 97–98; war metaphors and climate crisis 95; *WorldWarZero* 95–97

economic capital **355**
EDI (equality, diversity, and inclusion) 347, 348
EEOC see Equal Employment Opportunity Commission (EEOC)
Egypt 262
Ekpo, A. E. 244
Elliott, M. 21
Elliott, R. 227
Ellsworth, E. 66–68
Elund, J. 391
embodied violence against women 450–451
embodiment 75, 105, 143, 159–161, 166, 171, 173, 179, 352, 358, 360, 364, 371–373, 378
emotional outsourcing 212–214
employment discrimination 48
empowered eroticism 465
Endless Wardrobe 304
#EndPeriodPoverty 113–115
epistemic marginality, politics of 420–431
Equal Employment Opportunity Commission (EEOC) 48, 49
Eriksson, E. 90
erotic capital 229, 234
ER see Extinction Rebellion (ER)
essentialism 406
ethico-onto-epistem-ology 282–284
ethnographic moment 143–146
ethos 68
Evans, E. 399n1
Eve, F. 247
#EverydaySexism 181
Extinction Rebellion (ER) 91; ecofeminism and 95–97

Family Life Cycle (FLC) 327
fatphobia 250
Feher, M. 436
Feinstein, Dianne 316, 317
female consumers nationwide, educating 24–27
female gaze 120–134; in historical record 122–124
feminism: Arab 260–262; Black 45–47; commodification of 344–345; decolonial 259–260; fourth-wave 352–353, 388–389; liberal 35; Marxist 35; material 164; postcolonial 242; poststructuralist 195, 196; Radical Feminism 407–408; righting of 441; third-wave 171; and trans consumers 301–303; in transgender lives 296–304; Woodward on 33–34
feminist activism, in women's sport 171–174; activist interviews and method 174–179, **175**; disadvantaged women into work 177;

distilling ideas and points of connection for transformations 178–179; future research 182–184, **183**; lawyer and unconscious bias training 176; list giving support 176–177; mentoring to women federal politicians 176–177; president of peak trade union body 177–178; sport leadership and academic activism 179–182; state politician and local community organising 175–176
feminist branded movements 82–83
feminist brands 75–85; academic research, directions for 83–84; categories of 80–83; contemporary strands of feminist thought 76–77; definition of 79; future research 83–85; marketing scholarship on 78–79; practitioner-oriented research, directions for 84–85
Feminist Collective': *Our Bodies, Ourselves* 329
feminist marketing futures, manifesting 460–471; ableness 463; body beyond eroticism 466; coping and caring in poverty 467–468; desire and taboo 465; economic empowerment 466–467; empowered eroticism 465; future 470–471; gender and sexual displays online 464; gendered and sexual subjectivities 462–463; identity 461–463; intersectionality 461–463; objectification and male gaze 464; performativity 468–469; pornification of culture 463–466; precarity 468–469; present moment 469–470; racial and gender intersections 462; sexual violence 468–469
feminist new materialism **276–278**
feminist new materialist approach to body 161–166
feminist person brands 81–82
feminist product brands 80–81
feminist surveillance studies 368–370; and digital consumer culture 370–380; surveillance and categorisation of consumers 377–380; surveillance and technologically mediated relationships 373–377; surveillance and tracking selves through technology 370–373
Femmes, D.: *Notre Corps, Nous-Mêmes* 329
femvertising 105–107
Fennell, D. 94
Fifty Shades 191, 192
Fillius, M. 127
Fine, M. 431
Fischer, E. 3, 181, 332, 334
Fisher, K. 24, 26
flâneuse 130

FLC *see* Family Life Cycle (FLC)
Fleabag 210
Fleischer, R. 334
Fonda, J. 3, 331, 332
Foucault, M. 372
fourth age 328–329
fourth-wave feminism 352–353; digital presence 388–389
Frankenhauser, H. 229
Frankfurters as You Like Them (Frederick) 26
Fraser, N. 435
Frederick, Christine 24–26, 31, 64–65; *Frankfurters as You Like Them* 26; *Selling Mrs. Consumer* 19
Fredrickson, B. L. 224, 225, 229
#FreeTheNipple 388, 390, 461, 465
#freethenipple campaign 161
Friedan, B. 1

Gamble, I. 396
Gandy, O. H. 378
Garbo, G. 332
Gaviria, P. 329
gender inequality 404, 455
Gender Recognition Act (2004) 302
General Federation of Women's Clubs 37
generational analysis 326
GENMAC 324
Gentry, J. W. 298
Ger, G. 104, 163
Gergen, K. 328
Gergen, M. M. 328
German Historical School 39
Geronimus, A. T. 310
Gilbreth, L. 26, 31
Gilchrist, M. 66, 67
Gill, R. 223, 228–229, 232
Gillard, J. 171, 308
Gillis, S. 399n1
Gilmore, R. W. 342, 344
Ginsburg, R. B. 75, 81–82
Girls (HBO) 209
Glaser, N. 210
Glasshouse Effect 47
Glitch 348
Global Estimates of Modern Slavery (ILO) 408
Global Gender Report 149
Global South 257, 258
global warming 90
Godefroit-Winkel, D. 329, 466
Goffman, E. 103, 150n2
Gokariksel, B. 242
Goldman, R. 80, 235

Goldman Sachs 79
Golf-Papez, M. 465
Gómez-Cruz, E. 391
González, A. 403, 406
'gonzo' pornography 449
Goodfellowship Corset Club 133
Good Girls 215
Goodin, S. M. 229
Google 379
Gopaldas, A. 272
Gordon, L. D. 61
Gore, Al 91
Gould, S. 189, 190–191, 197
Grace and Frankie (Tomlin) 331, 332
Graves, V. 51–53, 55
Great Masculine Renunciation 226
Gregory, T. 208
Grier, S. A. 341
Gross Domestic Product 39
Grosz, E. 162, 164
Grove, M. 131
Guinn, L. 331
Gurrieri, L. 147

habitus **355**; embodied 358–360
Hakim, C. 229
Hampton Advertising Agency 34
Handelman, J. 181
The Handmaid's Tale (Atwood) 330, 334, 404
Haraway, D. 163, 274, 291n4
Harbor, B. 50
Harju, A. A. 161
Hark, I. R. 150n2
Harris, K. 308
hashtags 107–108
Hausman, B. L. 300
HBO: *Girls* 209; *Sex and the City* (*SATC*) 209
Hearn, J. 223
Heath, D. 80
hegemonic masculinity 225
Hein, W. 223, 273, 331
Hekman, S.: *Material Feminisms* 161–162
Hennock, F. B. 140
Henwood, K. 223, 232
Hester, H. 395
Hidden Figures 45
The Hidden Persuaders (Packard) 124–125
Hilkey, J. A. 61
Hirschman, E. C. 94, 160
Hodges, N. 464
holistic agential praxis: analysis and findings 287–290; data collection 286–287; intervention 285–286; research questions 286

home economics 4, 17–23
home economists 18–19
Homemakers' Conference 21, 27
Home Service Institute 27
hooks, b.: *Ain't I a Woman? Black Women and Feminism* 9, 248; *Talking Back* 247–248
Hopkin, C. 62
Hopkinson, G. 165
Hoyt, E. 19
Huff, A. D. 192
Hulko, W. 280
Huovinen, A. 161
Hutton, M. 468
Hyatt, E. M. 300

ICTs *see* information and communication technologies (ICTs)
"Ideas and Copy" (Dignam) 64
IES *see* interpersonal electronic surveillance (IES)
An Inconvenient Truth 91
information and communication technologies (ICTs) 139, 145
Insecure 210
Instagram 107–108, **110–111**; #ShareBlackStories 346
Intergovernmental Panel on Climate Change (IPCC) 91
Internal Revenue Service 81
International Day for the Elimination of Violence Against Women 1
International Labor Organization: *Global Estimates of Modern Slavery* 408
International Trade Center (ITC) 403
International Women's Strike/Global Women's Strike 442
International Working Group (IWG) 179
interpersonal electronic surveillance (IES) 375
intersectionality 45–47
intersectionality theory 268–271, **276–278**
intimate surveillance 376
invisible labour 3
IPCC *see* Intergovernmental Panel on Climate Change (IPCC)
ITC *see* International Trade Center (ITC)
iterative citationality 281
It's Complicated (Streep) 331
IWG *see* International Working Group (IWG)
#IWillGoOut campaign 2

Jackson, S. 389
J. A. Hill Company 34
Jemima, A. 55
Jewel Food Stores 50

Johnson, L. 149
Jones, C. R. 31, 50–51, 54
Jorgensen, C. 302
Journal for the Association of Consumer Research 469
Journal of Consumer Research 191
Journal of Macromarketing 2–3, 470
Journal of Marketing Management 3, 460, 470
Journal of Public Policy and Marketing 148
Journal of the Association for Consumer Research 3
Joy, A. 78, 160, 258, 468
J.P. Martin and Associates 51

Kamen, N. 227
Kandiyoti, D. 261
Kane, K. 105
Karababa, E. 258
Karreman, D. 180
Kay, M. 332
Kearney, M. 94
Kearney, S. 463
Keaton, D.: *Something's Gotta Give* 331
Keeling Curve 91
Keller, J. 107
Kelly, M. 313; *Settle For More* 437
Kennedy, J. 376
Khrebtan-Hörhager, J. 390
King, M. L., Jr. 51
Kirkbride, A. 224
knitting: black people 246–247; story 245–246
Knitting 247
Knudsen, H. 464
Koller, V. 92, 93
Kozak, M. 229
Kraft Foods 50
Kraidy, M.: *The Naked Blogger of Cairo* 264
Kravets, O. 344, 467, 470
Kravetz, O. 102
Kristensen, D. B. 372
Kuokkanen, R. 290n1
Kuruoğlu, A. 163
Kyrk, H. 19, 32, 33, 38; on consumer decision-making 40–42; on socialism and power relations 38–39; *A Theory of Consumption* 42–43

Ladies Home Journal 123
Laird, P. W. 69n3
Lally, E. H. 67; "The Advertising Manager's Job" 65
Lambert, A. 189, 192, 195, 206
Larsen, G. 465
Lathrop, J. 22
Latour, B. 273

Lauder, E. 332
Law, J. 273
Lawrence, J. 82
League for Industrial Democracy 38–39
League of New York Women 60
League of Women Shoppers (LWS) 34, 41
Lean In: Women, Work and The Will to Lead (Sandberg) 435, 437
Leave it to Beaver (Cleaver) 326
Lebanon 263
Legends in Marketing 4
Lennon, M. 113
Lerner, G. 325; *The Creation of Patriarchy* 408
liberal feminism 35
Liebes, D. 31
Life 125
#likeaboy 102
Littlefield, J. 94
Looking Backward (Bellamy) 35
Lorange, A. 208
Lorde, A. 243–244, 248–249, 252, 421
Lovely Day (Withers) 335
Lowrey, L. S.: *Mrs. Lowrey and son* 327
Luckman, S. 390
Lugones, M. 259–260
Lund, R. 182
LWS *see* League of Women Shoppers (LWS)
Lyon, D. 378

Maciel, A. F. 244–245
MacKinnon, C. A. 171, 270
Maclaran, P. 47, 78, 93, 94, 102, 461–463, 467, 469
Maidenform archive 120–134; querying 126–133, *127–129, 132, 133*
Maidenform Dreams, as psychoanalytic trips 124–126
Maidenform Mirror 121, 124, 126, 130, 131
Maiden-forum 126, *127,* 130, *132, 133*
Makdisi, J. S. 260
Malefyt, Timothy de Waal 105, 115
male gaze 120, 347, 464
Mandziuk, R. M. 105
Man Repeller 82
#March4Women 83
marginalization 9, 11, 300, 304, 371, 397–398, 423, 425, 430, 462, 466
marginalities 250–251
Marinetto, M. 180–181
marketing 18–19, 257–264, 296; education 59–69; hidden figures 45–55; masculinities and transpatriarchies matter in 147; menstruation in 102–116; scholarship on feminism, brands, and branding 78–79

marketing and consumer research (MCR) 138, 143, 145–150; men, masculinities and gender representations in 140–141; momentum on men, masculinities and transpatriarchies, maintaining 147–149
Marketing and Feminism: Current Issues and Research (Catterall) 2, 343
markets 1, 3, 12, 20, 92, 140, 144, 147, 149, 258, 285, 311, 327, 346, 379, 446, 450, 454, 465, 470; economic sex/gender system, exclusion of women from 403–418; LGBT+ 298; privatising 139; segmentation 377
Marques, A. C. 296
Martin, E. 171
Martin, J. P. 51, 53, 54
Martins, Y. 224
Marxist feminism 35
Mary Tyler Moore (Cleaver) 326
Marzouki, N. 262
masculinity 142–143; critical study of 141–142; and gray sweatpants 226–227; hegemonic 225
Mason, R. S. 43
Massey, D. 243
material feminism 164
Material Feminisms (Alaimo and Hekman) 161–162
material harm 450–451
Mathiesen, T. 374
Matich, M. 161, 462, 465
Matrix of Domination 46, 47, 49
Matthews, G. 26
McCabe, M. 105, 115
McCall, L. 273
McDonagh, P. 470
McGeehan, J. 331
McGovern, C. 28n1
McKeage, K. 298, 304
McLachlan, F. 172–173
McLean, C. 223, 232
McRobbie, A. 173, 389, 421, 435
MCR *see* marketing and consumer research (MCR)
Meloney, M. M. 24, 25, 27
men: critical study of 141–142; gender hegemony of 142–143
menstruation, in marketing 102–116; femvertising 105–107; method of analysis 108–109; sites of analysis 107–108; stigma 102–105
mestiza consciousness 269, 274
Meta, M. H. 140

#MeToo movement 1, 46, 102, 107, 149, 171, 174, 181, 214, 216, 234, 263, 351, 352, 388, 442
midriff advertising 228
Miles, R. 324–325; *Who Cooked the Last Supper* 324
mind, and body 327–329
MindGeek 448
Mingo, F. 54
Mingo-Jones Advertising 50
Mirabito, A. M. 303
Mirren, H. 331
Mitchell, F. 396
Modern Family 326
Moghissi, H. 261
Mol, A. M. 165
Moorman, S. 331
Moreton-Robinson, A. 259
Mort, F. 227
Moscovici, S. 302
Mrs. Lowrey and son (Lowrey) 327
multiepistemic literacy 290n1
multiple marginalities, testimonies of 424
Mulvey, L. 122, 150n2, 224
Munford, R. 399n1
Murnen, S. K. 229
Murray, D. C. 392, 395, 397
Myers, T. A. 229
#MyLoveIsBlackLove 346–347
#MyRoots 347
MySpace campaign 353

Nagoshi, J. L. 301
Nail Transphobia 394
Nakamura, L. 249
The Naked Blogger of Cairo (Kraidy) 264
The Nation 35
National Bureau of Standards 28n1
National League of Women Voters 4, 17
Neale, S. 150n2
neoliberal feminism 2; limits of 434–443; rise of 435–437
Netflix: *Disclosure* 303
New Sexual Agendas 222
New York Club 60
New York League of Advertising Women (NYLAW) 59, 64, 69
New York State Home Bureaus 17
Nielsen: "African-American Women: Our Science, Her Magic" 341, 346
Nike 173
Nike+ 372

1984 (Orwell) 335
Noble, S. U. 272–273, 379
Nochlin, L. 131
Nölke, A.-I. 462
Northrup, M. 64
Notre Corps, Nous-Mêmes (Femmes) 329
NYLAW *see* New York League of Advertising Women (NYLAW)

The Office Economist 63
'*Oh No! There's a Negro in My Wife*' 449
O'Keefe, T. 390, 397
Oldenburg, H. 131
Olesen, V. L. 429
online/digital intersectionality 244–245
OnlyFans 375
oppression 269, 302, 343, 346–347, 404
Orange Is the New Black 303
Orwell, G.: *1984* 335
Ostberg, J. 3
Our Bodies, Ourselves (Feminist Collective) 329
"Our Lecture Course Committee" 63

Packard, V.: *The Hidden Persuaders* 124–125
Paddock, J. R. 94
Painesis, G. 465
Parmentier, M. 315
Patreon 375
patriarchal acculturation 59–69
patriarchy 3, 6–9, 12, 84, 93, 94, 139–141, 145, 147, 150, 196, 223, 234, 259, 263, 273, 290, 308, 309, 317, 357, 404, 405, 407, 414, 423; capitalist 343, 348, 447, 468; disaster 148; neoliberal 142–143; supremacist 446
Patterson, M. 161, 227
PCAW *see* Philadelphia Club of Advertising Women (PCAW)
pedagogy, appropriation of 247–250
Pelosi, N. 308, 309, 312–317
Peñaloza, L. 466
performative allyship 249
performativity 468–469
Period Products (Free Provision) (Scotland) Bill 113
person branding 81
Petty, K. 172
phenomenology 241
Philadelphia Club of Advertising Women (PCAW) 59, 60, 63–69
Philippines 145
Piggott, L. V. 180
Piha, S. 192, 465

Pike, E. C. J. 180
Pink Protest 388
Pioneering African-American Women in the Advertising Business: Biographies of MAD Black Women (Davis) 347
Place-Thought 279
Playboy 206
Polley, S.: *Away from Her* 331
Ponty, M. 241
Poole, S. M. 341
Pope, S. 172
Pornhub 448, 449, 453
pornification 207–208; of culture 463–466; perils of 218
pornography 445–455; contemporary market 446–449; cultural harm, (re)producing 451–452; embodied violence against women 450–451; 'gonzo' 449; material harm 450–451; radical feminist centring of harm 449–452; radical feminist marketing agenda 452–455; women's sexuality, construction of 451–452
Portwood-Stacer, L. 435
Pose 303
postcolonial feminism 242
Poster, M.: *Critical Theory of the Family* 333
postfeminism 351–353
postfeminist climate, digital activism in 352–353
post-humanism 290–291n4
poststructuralist feminism 195, 196
power matrix 47–49
power relations, Kyrk on 38–39
Pozner, J. 312
pragmatic feminists 50–55; activism 54–55; empowerment 54–55; navigation of oppressions in advertising organizations 52–54; resistance 54–55
Preece, C. 467
Price, L. 331
Prine, J. 138, 323
Procter & Gamble 106
Proctor, B. G. 31, 50, 54
prosumption 190
Prothero, A. 3, 85, 95, 470
public stigma 104, 109, 111
"Pussy Hat Project" 242
Puwar, N. 243

Quantified Self (QS) 371
Queer Phenomenology 243
queer theory 300

racial capitalism 344–345
radical feminism 407–408, 449–450
radical feminist centring of harm 449–452
Raitt, B. 323
'The Rapist Is You' 1
Raymond, J.: *The Transsexual Empire* 302
Reagan, R. 50
Reclaim the Night movement 2
Reclaim These Streets campaign 2
Redgrave, V. 327
RedTube 448
Rehm, D. 331
Rent the Runway 304
Resor-Stanley, H. 69n4
Revelle, R. 90
Review of Reviews 34
Rich, A. 249, 252, 424
Richards, E. 21
Riddle, D. 22
Ries, A. 92
Rigney, S. 140
Rinallo, D. 226
Rindfleisch, A. 92
Rittenburg, T. L. 298
Roberts, T. A. 229
Rocamora, A. 396
Roche Sisters 138
Rome, A. S. 189, 192, 195, 206
Roosevelt, E. 22, 41, 140
Roosevelt, F. D. 22
Rose, F. 17, 18, 20
Rose, N. 436
Rose, O. 247
Rosenthal, I. 129
Rosenthal, W. 129
Rotaro 304
Rowe, D. 463
Rubin, G.: "The Traffic in Women" 407
rural consumers, educating 20–24
Russell, L. 399n1

Saatcioglu, B. 272
Sabri, O. 465
Sacks, O. 331
Sagas, N. 408
Sandberg, S.: *Lean In* 437; *Lean In: Women, Work and The Will to Lead* 435
Sanders, B. 308, 313
Sandikci, O. 104
Sanghvi, M. 310, 464

Sarpila, O. 229
SATC see Sex and the City (SATC)
#SayHerName 388
Scanlon, J. 69n4
Scaraboto, D. 332
Schep, D. 299
Schilling, P. 139
Schoen, D. 64
Schools of Agriculture 20, 21
Schouten, J. W. 465
Schroeder, J. E. 161, 228, 302
Schumer, A. 210
Schwartz, A. 389
Scott, J. 439
Scott, L. M. 2, 332, 449; *The Double X Economy* 418n1, 466
Sears 50
Second World War 138
Segal, L. 435
self-branding 82
self-documentation 388–399
selfies: and contemporary feminist culture 392–396; culture 391–392; as radical self-documentation 395–397; representation 397–398; resisting marginalisation 397–398; seeking solace and networks of solidarity 393–395; visibility 397–398
self-objectification 222–235; method 229–231; preliminary results 231–233
self-sexualization: definition of 224
self-stigma 104, 109, 111
self-surveillance 372, 374
self-tracking 370–373
Settle For More (Kelly) 437
Sex and the City (SATC) 209
sexual abjectification 209–216; emotional outsourcing 212–214; sexual (dis) empowerment, reconciling 214–216; unruly body, managing 210–212
sexism 77, 210, 217, 244, 270, 308–318, 343, 346, 348, 353, 389, 394, 442, 445, 454, 463; patriarchal 197; systemic 181
sexual (dis)empowerment, reconciling 214–216
sexuality 296
sexual subject 228–229
sexual subjectification 208–209
sexual violence 468–469
sexy man, becoming 225–226
#ShareBlackStories 346
SheKnows 106

SheKnowsMedia 78
SHE Media 106
Sherman, C. 332
Siebert, A. 272
Siebler, K. 303
Siri 376
Sisters Uncut 388
sites of analysis 107–108
60 Minutes 50
Sizemore-Barber, A. 462
Sjöden, G. 80–81
Skålen, P. 372
Skeggs, B. 468
Slate, J. 210
Slaughter, A.-M.: 'Why Women Still Can't Have It All' 435
sleeping bodies 163–165
SlutWalks 82–83
Smith, A. S. 66
Smith, S. 242
Smith, S. L. 80
Smith D. E. 182
Smithsonian's National Museum of American History's Archives Center 126
Smolak, L. 229
Sobande, F. 244, 251
social capital **355**
socialism: Kyrk on 38–39; Woodward on 33–34
social surveillance 372
Something's Gotta Give (Keaton) 331
Soujourner Truth 243
Soylent Green 334
Spicer, A. 180
Splint, S. 24
Stanley, L. 19
Steinfield, L. 270, 273, 467
Stevens, L. 47, 78, 93, 94
stigma: by association 104; management 104–105; and menstruation 103–104; public 104, 109, 111; reappropriate stigmatized bodies 111–112; self-stigma 104, 109, 111; structural 104, 112; theory 103
Streep, M.: *It's Complicated* 331
Strengers, Y. 376
Strom, S. H. 61, 62
Strong, F. D. 132
structural stigma 104, 112
Stryker, S. 304
subjectivities 329
Suess, H. E. 90

Sunday Times 173
Sundberg, J. 271, 273
surveillance capitalism 368
sustainability 94–95
Sustainable Development Goal 179
Swanson, G. 332
Swift, T. 82
symbolic capital **355**
symbolic power: definition of **355**; theory of 352, 354
symbolic violence: definition of **355**; of digital (anti-)feminist activism 351–365
Systrom, K. 397

taboo 465
Tadajewski, M. 3, 59, 93
Tahuwai-Smith, L. 259
Talbot, M. 21
Talking Back (hooks) 247–248
Taos Institute 328
TaskRabbit 451
TCR *see* Transformative Consumer Research (TCR)
testimonies 423–424; of making spaces 428–430; of marginal and resistant subjectivities 425–426; of multiple marginalities 424; of researcher as othered 426–428
Thatcher, M. 308
Thelandersson, F. 389
Theodorakis, I. 465
A Theory of Consumption (Kyrk) 42–43
third age 328
third-wave feminism 171
Thomas, M. C. 17
Thompson, C. J. 160, 190, 299
Thompson, Governor 50
Tienari, J. 182
Tiggemann, M 224
Tiidenberg, K. 391
TikTok: #MyRoots 347
#TimesUp campaign 1, 351
Time to Care (Oxfam) 144
Toffler, A. 190
Tomlin, L.: *Grace and Frankie* 331, 332
"The Traffic in Women" (Rubin) 407
trans consumers, feminism and 301–303
transcorporeality 162
Transformative Consumer Research (TCR) 467
transnational capitalist class 143

trans(national)patriarchies 143–146
transpatriarchies, critical study of 141
The Transsexual Empire (Raymond) 302
trans theory 300–301
von Trapp, M. 130
trickle-down theory 40
Trout, J. 92
Trump, D. 149, 209, 242, 308, 313, 351, 443n3
Trump, I.: *Women Who Work* 434, 435, 437–443
Tumblr: *Who Needs Feminism?* (WNF?) 352, 354–364; *Women Against Feminism* (WAF) 352–354, 356, 360–364
Tuncay, L. 226
Tuncay-Zayer, L. 3
Tyndall, J. 90

Uber 451
Undoing the Demos (Brown) 441
United Nations 171
University of Liverpool Management School 461
US Aid 143
US Census 325–326
US Congress 308
user-generated content (UGC) 112–114
Ustuner, T. 299

Vanity Fair (CBS) 130
Van Rensselaer, M. 4, 17–28
Vanwesenbeeck, I. 222
Varman, R. 147, 468–470
Venkatesh, A. 78, 160
Veresiu, E. 315
Victorian Women's Trust 175
Vincent, B. W. 296–297, 301
Visconti, L. M. 299
Vogue 303
Vogue Knitting 253n5
Vox 247

Wacquant, L. J. 355
WAF *see* Women Against Feminism (WAF)
Walker, A. 31
Walker, Madam C. J. 31
Wallendorf, M. 244–245
Wall Street Journal 51
Walther, L. 465
Wang, S. 378–379
war metaphor 91–93; ecofeminism and 95
Warner, K. 346
Waters, M. 316, 317

Watson, E. 82
Watts, V. 271, 279–280
Ways of Seeing 122–123
Wearing, B. 173
WEF *see* World Economic Forum (WEF)
Wells, I. 64
West, C. 297
Who Cooked the Last Supper (Miles) 324
Who Needs Feminism? (WNF?) 352, 354–365
'Why Women Still Can't Have It All' (Slayghter) 435
Williams, C. H. 52–54
Williams, S. 173
Williams-Johnson, D. 246
Williamson, J. 80, 150n2
Wilner, S. J. S. 192
Wirka, E. 131
Withers, B.: *Call me* 335; *Lovely Day* 335
Witkowski, T. H. 59
Wolfe, T. 335
Woman's Home Companion 34
Woman's March 442
Women Against Feminism (WAF) 352–354, 356, 360–364
"Women Know Women" (Dignam) 61
Women's Advertising League of New York 59
women's economic exclusion 407–417; class of goods 408; held captive 409–410; information withheld 414–415; international market access 415–416; landless paupers 411–413, *412, 413*; penniless laborers 410–411; segregated spheres 441; shout out of finance 415; without resources 413–414; world community 416–417
Women's March 75, 242, 353, 388
women's sexuality 189–198; analysis of 194–197; construction of 451–452; epistemological blind spot 190–194, **193–194**
Women's Soccer World Cup 172
Women's Trade Union League 35
Women Who Work (Trump) 434, 435, 437–443
Wong, A. 210
Woodward, H. 31–32, 43, 62; on feminism and socialism 33–34
Woolman, M. S. 21
Working Moms 215
World Bank 408
World Economic Forum (WEF) 149

World Trade Organization (WTO) 406; *Declaration on Women and Trade* 405
World War One 17
World War Zero 90; ecofeminism and 95–97

xHamster 448
Xiong, Y. 107

Yngfalk, A. F. 372
Young, I. M. 171, 241
Young, N. 138
YouPorn 448
Yudina, O. 94

Zayer, L. T. 331
Zebra Associates 50
Zheng, R. 212
Zimmerman, D. H. 297
Zuckerberg, M. 397
Zuckerman, M. E. 4
Zwick, D. 228

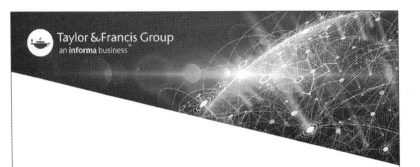

Taylor & Francis eBooks

www.taylorfrancis.com

A single destination for eBooks from Taylor & Francis with increased functionality and an improved user experience to meet the needs of our customers.

90,000+ eBooks of award-winning academic content in Humanities, Social Science, Science, Technology, Engineering, and Medical written by a global network of editors and authors.

TAYLOR & FRANCIS EBOOKS OFFERS:

- A streamlined experience for our library customers
- A single point of discovery for all of our eBook content
- Improved search and discovery of content at both book and chapter level

REQUEST A FREE TRIAL
support@taylorfrancis.com

 Routledge
Taylor & Francis Group

 CRC Press
Taylor & Francis Group

Printed in the United States
by Baker & Taylor Publisher Services